THE
GENDERED
SOCIETY
READER

THE
GENDERED
SOCIETY
READER

Second Edition

edited by

MICHAEL S. KIMMEL

State University of New York at Stony Brook

with Amy Aronson

New York   Oxford
OXFORD UNIVERSITY PRESS
2004

Oxford University Press

Oxford   New York
Auckland   Bangkok   Buenos Aires   Cape Town   Chennai
Dar es Salaam   Delhi   Hong Kong   Istanbul   Karachi   Kolkata
Kuala Lumpur   Madrid   Melbourne   Mexico City   Mumbai
Nairobi   São Paulo   Shanghai   Taipei   Tokyo   Toronto

Published by Oxford University Press, Inc.
198 Madison Avenue, New York, New York, 10016
http://www.oup-usa.org

Oxford is a registered trademark of Oxford University Press

Library of Congress Cataloging-in-Publication Data

The gendered society reader / edited by Michael S. Kimmel with Amy Aronson.—2nd ed.
    p.   cm.
  Complements the text: The gendered society.
  Includes bibliographical references and index.
  ISBN 0-19-514976-9 (pbk. : alk. paper)
  1. Sex role. 2. Sex differences (Psychology) 3. Gender identity. 4. Sex discrimination.
  5. Equality. I. Kimmel, Michael S. II. Aronson, Amy. III. Kimmel, Michael S. Gendered
  society.
HQ1075 .G4672 2003
305.3—dc21   2003034560

Printing number: 9 8 7 6 5 4 3 2 1

Printed in the United States of America
on acid-free paper

For
Zachary Aaron Kimmel
Kate Morris
Kadeem Nelson
H. Perry Tunick-Hatchfield

and the transformation of gender relations
of which they will be a part

CONTENTS

~

Contents

THE
GENDERED
SOCIETY
READER

INTRODUCTION

~

Michael S. Kimmel

Every day there's another story about how women and men are different. They say we come from different planets—women from Venus, men from Mars. They say we have different brain chemistries, different brain organization, different hormones. Different bodies, different selves. They say we have different ways of knowing, listen to different moral voices, have different ways of speaking and hearing each other.

You'd think we were different species. In his best-selling book, the pop psychologist John Gray informs us that not only do women and men communicate differently, "but they think, feel, perceive, react, respond, love, need, and appreciate differently" (Gray 1995, 5). It's a miracle of cosmic proportions that we ever understand one another!

Yet here we all are, together, in the same classes, eating in the same dining halls, walking on the same campus, reading the same books, being subject to the same criteria for grading. We live in the same houses, eat the same meals, read the same newspapers, and watch the same TV shows. What gives?

One thing that seems to be happening is that we are increasingly aware of the centrality of gender in our lives. In the past three decades, the pioneering work of feminist scholars, both in traditional disciplines and in women's studies, has made us increasingly aware of the centrality of gender in shaping social life. We now know that gender is one of the central organizing principles around which social life revolves.

This wasn't always the case. Three decades ago, social scientists would have only listed social class and race as the master statuses that defined and proscribed social life. If you wanted to study gender in the 1960s in social science, for example, you would have found one course to meet your needs—"Marriage and the Family"—which was sort of the "Ladies Auxiliary" of the Social Sciences. There were no courses on gender. But today, gender has joined race and class in our understanding of the foundations of an individual's identity. Gender, we now know, is one of the axes around which social life is organized, and through which we understand our own experiences.

While much of our cultural preoccupation seems to be about the differences between women and men, there are two near-universal phenomena that define the experiences of women and men in virtually every culture we have ever known. First: *Why is it that virtually every single society differentiates people on the ba-*

sis of gender? Why are women and men perceived as different in every known society? What are the differences that are perceived? Why is gender at least one—if not the central—basis for the division of labor? And, second: *Why is it that virtually every known society is also based on male domination?* Why does virtually every society divide social, political, and economic resources unequally between the genders? Why is a gendered division of labor also an unequal division of labor? Why are women's tasks and men's tasks valued differently?

Of course, there are dramatic differences among societies regarding the type of gender differences, the levels of gender inequality, and the amount of violence (implied or real) that is necessary to maintain both systems of difference and domination. But the basic facts remain: *virtually every society known to us is founded upon assumptions of gender difference and the politics of gender inequality.*

Most of the arguments about gender difference begin, as will this book, with biology. Women and men *are* biologically different, after all. Our reproductive anatomies are different, as are our reproductive destinies. Our brain structures differ, our brain chemistries differ. Our musculature is different. We have different levels of different hormones circulating through our different bodies. Surely, these add up to fundamental, intractable, and universal differences, and these differences provide the foundation for male domination, don't they?

In these models, biological "sex"—by which we mean the chromosomal, chemical, anatomical apparatuses that make us either male or female—leads inevitably to "gender," by which we mean the cultural and social meanings, experiences, and institutional structures that are defined as appropriate for those males and females. "Sex" is male and female; "gender" refers to cultural definitions of masculinity and femininity—the meanings of maleness or femaleness.

Biological models of sex difference occupy the "nature" side of the age-old question about whether it is nature or nurture that determines our personalities. Of course, most sensible people recognize that both nature *and* nurture are necessary for gender development. Our biological sex provides the raw material for our development—and all that evolution, different chromosomes, and hormones have to have some effect on who we are and who we become.

But biological sex varies very little, and yet the cultural definitions of gender vary enormously. And it has been the task of the social and behavioral sciences to explore the variations in definitions of gender. Launched originally as critiques of biological universalism, the social and behavioral sciences—anthropology, history, psychology, sociology—have all had an important role to play in our understanding of gender.

What they suggest is that what it means to be a man or a woman will vary in four significant ways. First, the meanings of gender vary from one society to another. What it means to be a man or a woman among aboriginal peoples in the Australian outback or in the Yukon territories is probably very different from what it means to be a man or a woman in Norway or Ireland. It has been the task of anthropologists to specify some of those differences, to explore the different meanings that gender has in different cultures. Some cultures, like our own, encourage men to be stoic and to prove their masculinity, and men in other cultures seem even more preoccupied with demonstrating sexual prowess than American men seem to be. Other cultures prescribe a more relaxed definition of masculinity, based on civic participation, emotional responsiveness, and the collective provision for the community's needs. Some cultures encourage women to be decisive and competitive; others insist that women are naturally passive, helpless, and dependent.

Second, the meanings of masculinity and femininity vary within any one culture over time. What it meant to be a man or a woman in seventeenth-century France is probably very different from what it might mean today. My own research has suggested that the meanings of manhood have changed dramatically from the founding of America in 1776 to the present (see Kimmel 1996). (Although for reasons of space I do not include any historical material in this volume, inquiries into the changing definitions of gender have become an area of increasing visibility.)

Third, the meaning of masculinity and femininity will change as any individual person grows. Following Freudian ideas that individuals face different developmental tasks as they grow and develop, psychologists have examined the ways in which the meanings of masculinity and femininity change over the course of a person's life. The issues confronting a man about proving himself, feeling successful, and the social institutions in which he will attempt to enact those experiences will change, as will the meanings of femininity for prepubescent women, women in child-bearing years, and post-menopausal women, or for women entering the labor market or those retiring from it.

Finally, the meanings of gender will vary *among* different groups of women and men within any particular culture at any particular time. Simply put, not all American men and women are the same. Our experiences are also structured by class, race, ethnicity, age, sexuality, region of the country. Each of these axes modifies the others. Just because we make gender visible doesn't mean that we make these other organizing principles of social life invisible. Imagine, for example, an older, black, gay man in Chicago and a young, white, heterosexual farm boy in Iowa. Wouldn't they have different definitions of masculinity? Or imagine a twenty-two-year-old heterosexual poor Asian American woman in San Francisco and a wealthy white Irish Catholic lesbian in Boston. Wouldn't their ideas about what it means to be a woman be somewhat different? The interplanetary theory of gender differences collapses all such differences, and focuses *only* on gender. One of the important elements of a sociological approach is to explore the differences *among* men and *among* women, since, as it turns out, these are often more decisive than the differences between women and men.

If gender varies across cultures, over historical time, among men and women within any one culture, and over the life course, that means we really cannot speak of masculinity or femininity as though they were constant, universal essences, common to all women and to all men. Rather, gender is an ever-changing fluid assemblage of meanings and behaviors. In that sense, we must speak of *masculinities* and *femininities,* in recognition of the different definitions of masculinity and femininity that we construct. By pluralizing the terms, we acknowledge that masculinity and femininity mean different things to different groups of people at different times.

At the same time, we can't forget that all masculinities and femininities are not created equal. American men and women must also contend with a dominant definition, a culturally preferred version that is held up as the model against which we are expected to measure ourselves. We thus come to know what it means to be a man or a woman in our culture by setting our definitions in opposition to a set of "others"—racial minorities, sexual minorities. For men, the classic "other" is of course, women. If often feels imperative that men make it clear—eternally, compulsively, decidedly—that they are not "like" women.

For both women and men, this is the "hegemonic" definition—the one that is held up as the model for all of us. The hegemonic definition of masculinity is "constructed in relation to various subordinated masculinities as well as in relation to women," writes sociologist R. W. Connell (1987, 183). The sociologist Erving Goffman once described this hegemonic definition of masculinity like this:

> In an important sense there is only one complete unblushing male in America: a young, married, white, urban, northern, heterosexual, Protestant, father, of college education, fully employed, of good complexion, weight, and height, and a recent record in sports. . . . Any male who fails to qualify in any one of these ways is likely to view himself—during moments at least—as unworthy, incomplete, and inferior. (Goffman 1963, 128)

Women also must contend with such an exaggerated ideal of femininity. Connell calls it "emphasized femininity." Emphasized femininity is organized around compliance with gender inequality, and is "oriented to accommodating the interests and desires of men." One sees emphasized femininity in "the display of sociability rather than technical competence, fragility in mating scenes, compliance with men's desire for titillation and ego-stroking in office relationships, acceptance of marriage and child care as a response to labor-market discrimination against women" (Connell 1987, 183, 188, 187). Emphasized femininity exaggerates gender difference as a strategy of "adaptation to men's power" stressing empathy and nurturance; "real" womanhood is described as "fascinating" and women are advised that they can wrap men around their fingers by knowing and playing by "the rules."

The articles in the first four sections of this book recapitulate these disciplinary concerns and also presents the development of the sociological argument chronologically. Following Darwin and others, biological evidence was employed in the nineteenth century to assert the primacy of sex differences, and the section on biological differences presents some evidence of distinct and categorical biological differences, and a couple of critiques of that research from a neurobiologist and a psychologist respectively. Cross-cultural research by anthropologists, among them Margaret Mead, perhaps the nation's most historically celebrated cultural anthropologist, offered a way to critique the claims of biological inevitability and universality lodged in those biological arguments. The selections in this section demonstrate how anthropologists have observed those cross-cultural differences and have used such specific cultural rituals as initiation ceremonies or the prevalence of rape in a culture to assess different definitions of gender.

Psychological research also challenged biological inevitability, locating the process of *acquiring* gender within the tasks of the child in his or her family. Achieving successful gender identity was a perilous process, fraught with danger of gender "inversion" (homosexuality) as the early and renowned social psychologist Lewis Terman saw it in his treatise on *Sex and Personality* in 1936. Subsequent psychological research has refined our understanding of how individuals acquire the "sex roles" that society has mapped out for them.

And it falls to the sociologist to explore the variations *among* different groups of women and men, and also to specify the ways in which some versions of masculinity or femininity are held up as the hegemonic models against which all others are arrayed and measured. Sociologists are concerned less with the specification of sex roles, and more with the understanding of *gender relations*—the social and political dynamics that shape our conceptions of "appropriate" sex roles. Thus, sociologists are interested not only in gendered individuals—the ways in which we acquire our gendered identities—but also in gendered institutions—the ways in which those gendered individuals interact with one another in the institutions of our lives that shape, reproduce, and reconstitute gender.

In that sense, sociologists return us to the original framing questions—the near-universality of assumptions about gender difference and the near-universality of male domination over women. Sociologists argue that male domination is reproduced not only by socializing women and men differently, but also by placing them in organizations and institutions in which specifically gendered norms and values predominate and by which both women and men are then evaluated and judged. Gendered individuals do not inhabit gender-neutral social situations; both individual and institution bear the mark of gender.

The three central, institutional sections of this book explore how the fundamental institutions of family, education, and the workplace express and normalize gender difference, and, in so doing, reproduce relations of inequality between women and men. In each of these arenas, the debates about gender difference and inequality have been intense—from the questions about the division of household labor, divorce, day care, coeducation or single-sex schooling, comparable worth, sexual harassment, workplace discrimination, and a variety of other critical policy debates. The articles in these sections will enable the reader to make better sense of these debates and understand the ways in which gender is performed and elaborated within social institutions.

Finally, we turn to our intimate lives, our bodies, and our experiences of friendship, love, and sex. Here differences between women and men do emerge. Men and women have different ways of loving, of caring, and of having sex. And it turns out that this is true whether the women and men are heterosexual or homosexual—that is, gay men and heterosexual men are more similar to each other than they are different; and, equally, lesbians and heterosexual women have more in common than either does with men. On the other hand, the differences between women and men seem to have as much to do with the shifting definitions of love and intimacy, and the social arenas in which we express (or suppress) our emotions, as they do with the differences in our personalities. And there is significant evidence that the gender gap in love and sex and friendship is shrinking as women claim greater degrees of sexual agency and men find their emotional lives (with lovers, children, and friends) impoverished by adherence to hegemonic definitions of masculinity. Men and women do express some differences in our intimate lives, but these differences are hardly of interplanetary cosmic significance. It appears that women and men are not from different planets—not opposite sexes, but neighboring sexes. And we are moving closer and closer to each other.

This may be the most startling finding that runs through many of these articles. What we find consistently is that the differences between women and men do not account for very much of the different experiences that men and women have. Differences *between* women and men are not nearly as great as the differences *among* women or *among* men—differences based on class, race, ethnicity, sexuality, age, and other variables. Women and men enter the workplace for similar reasons, though what they find there often reproduces the differences that "predicted" they would have different motivations. Boys and girls are far more similar to each other in the classroom, from elementary school through college, although everything in the school—from their textbooks, their teachers, their experiences in the playground, the social expectations of their aptitudes and abilities—pushes them to move farther and farther apart.

The most startling conclusion that one reaches from examining the evidence on gender difference is that women and men are not from different planets at all. In the end, we're all Earthlings!

References

Connell, R. W. *Gender and Power*. Stanford: Stanford University Press, 1987.

Goffman, Erving. *Stigma*. Englewood Cliffs, NJ: Prentice-Hall, 1963.

Gray, John. *Men Are from Mars, Women Are from Venus*. New York: Harper Collins 1995.

Kimmel, Michael. *Manhood in America: A Cultural History*. New York: The Free Press, 1996.

PART 1 ANATOMY AND DESTINY

Biological Arguments About Gender Difference

Anatomy, many of us believe, is destiny; our constitution of our bodies determines our social and psychological disposition. Biological sex decides our gendered experiences. Sex is temperament. Biological explanations offer perhaps the tidiest and most coherent explanations for both gender difference and gender inequality. The observable differences between males and females derive from different anatomical organization, which make us different as men and women, and those anatomical differences are the origin of gender inequality. These differences, as one biologist put it, are "innate, biologically determined, and relatively resistant to change through the influences of culture."

Biologists rely on three different sets of evidence. Evolutionists, such as sociobiologists and evolutionary psychologists, argue that sex differences derive from the differences in our reproductive anatomies—which compel different reproductive "strategies." Because females must invest much energy and time in ensuring the survival of one baby, their "natural" evolutionary instinct is toward high sexual selectivity and monogamy; females are naturally modest and monogamous. Males, by contrast, are naturally promiscuous, since their reproductive success depends upon fertilizing as many eggs as possible without emotional constraint. Males who are reproductively unsuccessful by seduction, biologists tell us, may resort to rape as a way to ensure their reproductive material is successfully transmitted to their offspring.

A second source of evidence of biological difference comes from some differences in brain function and brain chemistry. In the late nineteenth century, studies showed definitively that men's brains were heavier or more complex than women's, and thus that women ought not to seek higher education or vote. (Similar studies also "proved" that the brains of white people were heavier and more complex than those of black people.) Today, such studies are largely discredited, but we still may read about how males and females use different halves of their brains, or that they use them differently, or that the two halves are differently connected.

Finally, some biologists rely on the ways in which the hormonal differences that produce secondary sex characteristics determine the dramatically divergent paths that males and females take from puberty onwards. Testosterone causes aggression, and since males have far more testosterone than females, male aggression—and social, political, and economic dominance—is explained.

To the social scientist, though, this evidence obscures as much as it reveals, telling us more about our own cultural needs to find these differences than the differences themselves. Biological explanations collapse all other sources of difference—race, ethnicity, age—into one single dichotomous variable that exaggerates the differences between women and men, and also minimizes the similarities between them. "Believing is seeing," notes sociologist Judith Lorber in the title of her selection here, and seeing these differences as decisive is often used as a justification for gender inequality.

The readings in this section offer a cross-section of those biological arguments. David Buss summarizes the evidence from evolutionary psychology that different reproductive strategies determine different psychological dispositions. Neurobiologist Robert Sapolsky suggests that the research on hormonal differences do not make a convincing case, while Judith Lorber takes on the assumptions of biological research, arguing that biology's inherent conservatism—justifying existing inequalities by reference to observed differences and ignoring observed similarities—is more than bad politics: it's also bad science.

DAVID M. BUSS

Psychological Sex Differences: Origins Through Sexual Selection

Evolutionary psychology predicts that males and females will be the same or similar in all those domains in which the sexes have faced the same or similar adaptive problems. Both sexes have sweat glands because both sexes have faced the adaptive problem of thermal regulation. Both sexes have similar (although not identical) taste preferences for fat, sugar, salt, and particular amino acids because both sexes have faced similar (although not identical) food consumption problems. Both sexes grow callouses when they experience repeated rubbing on their skin because both sexes have faced the adaptive problem of physical damage from environmental friction.

In other domains, men and women have faced substantially different adaptive problems throughout human evolutionary history. In the physical realm, for example, women have faced the problem of childbirth; men have not. Women, therefore, have evolved particular adaptations that are absent in men, such as a cervix that dilates to 10 centimeters just prior to giving birth, mechanisms for producing labor contractions, and the release of oxytocin in the blood-stream during childbirth.

Men and women have also faced different information-processing problems in some adaptive domains. Because fertilization occurs internally within the wo-

Reprinted by permission of David M. Buss, Dept. of Psychology, University of Michigan, Ann Arbor, MI 48109-1109. References have been edited.

man, for example, men have faced the adaptive problem of uncertainty of paternity in putative offspring. Men who failed to solve this problem risked investing resources in children who were not their own. All people descend from a long line of ancestral men whose adaptations (i.e., psychological mechanisms) led them to behave in ways that increased their likelihood of paternity and decreased the odds of investing in children who were putatively theirs but whose genetic fathers were other men. This does not imply, of course, that men were or are consciously aware of the adaptive problem of compromised paternity.

Women faced the problem of securing a reliable or replenishable supply of resources to carry them through pregnancy and lactation, especially when food resources were scarce (e.g., during droughts or harsh winters). All people are descendants of a long and unbroken line of women who successfully solved this adaptive challenge—for example, by preferring mates who showed the ability to accrue resources and the willingness to provide them for particular women. Those women who failed to solve this problem failed to survive, imperiled the survival chances of their children, and hence failed to continue their lineage.

Evolutionary psychologists predict that the sexes will differ in precisely those domains in which women and men have faced different sorts of adaptive problems. To an evolutionary psychologist, the likelihood that the sexes are psychologically identical in domains in which they have recurrently confronted different adaptive problems over the long expanse of human evolutionary history is essentially zero. The key question, therefore, is not whether men and women differ psychologically. Rather, the key questions about sex differences, from an evolutionary psychological perspective, are (a) In what domains have women and men faced different adaptive problems? (b) What are the sex-differentiated psychological mechanisms of women and men that have evolved in response to these sex-differentiated adaptive problems? (c) Which social, cultural, and contextual inputs moderate the magnitude of expressed sex differences?

SEXUAL SELECTION DEFINES THE PRIMARY DOMAINS IN WHICH THE SEXES HAVE FACED DIFFERENT ADAPTIVE CHALLENGES

Although many who are not biologists equate evolution with natural selection or survival selection, Darwin (1871) sculpted what he believed to be a second theory of evolution—the theory of sexual selection. Sexual selection is the causal process of the evolution of characteristics on the basis of reproductive advantage, as opposed to survival advantage. Sexual selection occurs in two forms. First, members of one sex can successfully outcompete members of their own sex in a process of intrasexual competition. Whatever characteristics lead to success in these same-sex competitions—be they greater size, strength, cunning, or social skills—can evolve or increase in frequency by virtue of the reproductive advantage accrued by the winners through increased access to more numerous or more desirable mates.

Second, members of one sex can evolve preferences for desirable qualities in potential mates through the process of intersexual selection. If members of one sex exhibit some consensus about which qualities are desirable in the other sex, then members of the other sex who possess the desirable qualities will gain a preferential mating advantage. Hence, the desirable qualities—be they morphological features such as antlers or plumage or psychological features such as a lower threshold for risk taking to acquire resources—can evolve by virtue of the reproductive advantage attained by those who are preferentially chosen for possessing the desirable qualities. Among humans, both causal processes—preferential mate choice and same-sex competition for access to mates—are prevalent among both sexes, and probably have been throughout human evolutionary history.

HYPOTHESES ABOUT PSYCHOLOGICAL SEX DIFFERENCES FOLLOW FROM SEXUAL ASYMMETRIES IN MATE SELECTION AND INTRASEXUAL COMPETITION

Although a detailed analysis of psychological sex differences is well beyond the scope of this article, a few of the most obvious differences in adaptive problems include the following.

Paternity Uncertainty

Because fertilization occurs internally within women, men are always less than 100% certain (again, no conscious awareness implied) that their putative children are genetically their own. Some cultures have phrases to describe this, such as "Mama's baby, papa's maybe." Women are always 100% certain that the children they bear are their own.

Identifying Reproductively Valuable Women

Because women's ovulation is concealed and there is no evidence that men can detect when women ovulate, ancestral men had the difficult adaptive challenge of identifying which women were more fertile. Although ancestral women would also have faced the problem of identifying fertile men, the problem is considerably less severe (a) because most men remain fertile throughout their life span, whereas fertility is steeply age graded among women, and (b) because women invest more heavily in offspring, making them the more "valuable" sex, competed for more intensely by men seeking sexual access. Thus, there is rarely a shortage of men willing to contribute the sperm necessary for fertilization, whereas from a man's perspective, there is a pervasive shortage of fertile women.

Gaining Sexual Access to Women

Because of the large asymmetry between men and women in their minimum obligatory parental investment—nine months gestation for women versus an act of sex for men—the direct reproductive benefits of gaining sexual access to a variety of mates would have been much higher for men than for women throughout human evolutionary history. Therefore, in social contexts in which some short-term mating or polygynous mating were possible, men who succeeded in gaining sexual access to a variety of women, other things being equal, would have experienced greater reproductive success than men who failed to gain such access.

Identifying Men Who Are Able to Invest

Because of the tremendous burdens of a nine-month pregnancy and subsequent lactation, women who selected men who were able to invest resources in them and their offspring would have been at a tremendous advantage in survival and reproductive currencies compared with women who were indifferent to the investment capabilities of the men with whom they chose to mate.

Identifying Men Who Are Willing to Invest

Having resources is not enough. Copulating with a man who had resources but who displayed a hasty postcopulatory departure would have been detrimental to the woman, particularly if she became pregnant and faced raising a child without the aid and protection of an investing father. A man with excellent resource-accruing capacities might channel resources to another woman or pursue short-term sexual opportunities with a variety of women. A woman who had the ability to detect a man's willingness to invest in her and her children would have an adaptive advantage compared with women who were oblivious to a man's willingness or unwillingness to invest.

These are just a few of the adaptive problems that women and men have confronted differently or to differing degrees. Other examples of sex-linked adaptive problems include those of coalitional warfare, coalitional defense, hunting, gathering, combating sex-linked forms of reputational damage, embodying sex-linked prestige criteria, and attracting mates by fulfilling the differing desires of the other sex—domains that all have consequences for mating but are sufficiently wide-ranging to span a great deal of social psychology. It is in these domains that evolutionary psychologists anticipate the most pronounced sex differences—differences in solutions to sex-linked adaptive problems in the form of evolved psychological mechanisms.

PSYCHOLOGICAL SEX DIFFERENCES ARE WELL DOCUMENTED EMPIRICALLY IN THE DOMAINS PREDICTED BY THEORIES ANCHORED IN SEXUAL SELECTION

When Maccoby and Jacklin (1974) published their classic book on the psychology of sex differences, knowledge was spotty and methods for summarizing the literature were largely subjective and interpretive. Since that time, there has been a veritable explosion of empirical findings, along with quantitative meta-analytic procedures for evaluating them. Although new domains of sex differences continue to surface, such as the recently documented female advantage in spatial location memory, the outlines of where researchers find large, medium, small, and no sex differences are starting to emerge more clearly.

A few selected findings illustrate the heuristic power of evolutionary psychology. Cohen (1977) used the widely adopted d statistic as the index of magnitude of effect to propose a rule of thumb for evaluating effect sizes: 0.20 = "small," 0.50 = "medium," and 0.80 = "large." As Hyde has pointed out in a chapter titled "Where Are the Gender Differences? Where Are the Gender Similarities?," sex differences in the intellectual and cognitive ability domains tend to be small. Women's verbal skills tend to be slightly higher than men's ($d = -0.11$). Sex differences in math also tend to be small ($d = 0.15$). Most tests of general cognitive ability, in short, reveal small sex differences.

The primary exception to the general trend of small sex differences in the cognitive abilities domain occurs with spatial rotation. This ability is essential for successful hunting, in which the trajectory and velocity of a spear must anticipate correctly the trajectory of an animal as each moves with different speeds through space and time. For spatial rotation ability, $d = 0.73$. Other sorts of skills involved in hunting also show large magnitudes of sex differences, such as throwing velocity ($d = 2.18$), throwing distance ($d = 1.98$), and throwing accuracy ($d = 0.96$; Ashmore, 1990). Skilled hunters, as good providers, are known to be sexually attractive to women in current and traditional tribal societies.

Large sex differences appear reliably for precisely the aspects of sexuality and mating predicted by evolutionary theories of sexual strategies. Oliver and Hyde (1993), for example, documented a large sex difference in attitudes toward casual sex ($d = 0.81$). Similar sex differences have been found with other measures of men's desire for casual sex partners, a psychological solution to the problem of seeking sexual access to a variety of partners. For example, men state that they would ideally like to have more than 18 sex partners in their lifetimes, whereas women state that they would desire only 4 or 5. In another study that has been replicated twice, 75% of the men but 0% of the women approached by an attractive stranger of the opposite sex consented to a request for sex.

Women tend to be more exacting than men, as predicted, in their standards for a short-term mate ($d = 0.79$). Women tend to place greater value on good financial prospects in a mate—a finding confirmed in a study of 10,047 individuals residing in 37 cultures located on six continents and five islands from around the world (Buss, 1989). More so than men, women especially disdain qualities in a potential mate that signal inability to accrue resources, such as lack of ambition ($d = 1.38$) and lack of education ($d = 1.06$). Women desire physical protection abilities more than men, both in short-term mating ($d = 0.94$) and in long-term mating ($d = 0.66$).

Men and women also differ in the weighting given to cues that trigger sexual jealousy. Buss, Larsen, Westen, and Semmelroth (1992) presented men and women with the following dilemma: "What would upset or distress you more: (a) imagining your partner forming a deep emotional attachment to someone else or (b) imagining your partner enjoying passionate sexual intercourse with that other person" (p. 252). Men expressed greater distress about sexual than emotional infidelity, whereas women showed the opposite pattern. The difference between the sexes in which scenario was more distressing was 43% ($d = 0.98$). These sex differences have been replicated by different investigators with physiological recording devices and have been replicated in other cultures.

These sex differences are precisely those predicted by evolutionary psychological theories based on sexual selection. They represent only a sampling from a larger body of supporting evidence. The sexes also differ substantially in a wide variety of other ways that are predicted by sexual selection theory, such as in thresholds for physical risk taking, in frequency of perpetrating homicides, in thresholds for inferring sexual intent in others, in perceptions of the magnitude of upset people experience as the victims of sexual aggression, and in the frequency of committing violent crimes of all sorts. As noted by Donald Brown (1991), "it will be irresponsible to continue shunting these [findings] aside, fraud to deny that they exist" (p. 156). Evolutionary psychology sheds light on why these differences exist.

CONCLUSIONS

Strong sex differences occur reliably in domains closely linked with sex and mating, precisely as predicted by psychological theories based on sexual selection. Within these domains, the psychological sex differences are patterned in a manner that maps precisely onto the adaptive problems men and women have faced over human evolutionary history. Indeed, in most cases, the evolutionary hypotheses about sex differences were generated a decade or more before the empirical tests of them were conducted and the sex differences discovered. These models thus have heuristic and predictive power.

The evolutionary psychology perspective also offers several insights into the broader discourse on sex differences. First, neither women nor men can be considered "superior" or "inferior" to the other, any more than a bird's wings can be considered superior or inferior to a fish's fins or a kangaroo's legs. Each sex possesses mechanisms designed to deal with its own adaptive challenges—some similar and some different—and so notions of superiority or inferiority are logically incoherent from the vantage point of evolutionary psychology. The metatheory of evolutionary psychology is descriptive, not prescriptive—it carries no values in its teeth.

Second, contrary to common misconceptions about evolutionary psychology, finding that sex differences originated through a causal process of sexual selection does not imply that the differences are unchangeable or intractable. On the contrary, understanding their origins provides a powerful heuristic to the contexts in which the sex differences are most likely to be manifested (e.g., in the context of mate competition) and hence provides a guide to effective loci for intervention if change is judged to be desirable.

Third, although some worry that inquiries into the existence and evolutionary origins of sex differences will lead to justification for the status quo, it is hard to believe that attempts to change the status quo can be very effective if they are undertaken in ignorance of sex differences that actually exist. Knowledge is power, and attempts to intervene in the absence of knowledge may resemble a surgeon operating blindfolded—there may be more bloodshed than healing.

The perspective of evolutionary psychology jettisons the outmoded dualistic thinking inherent in much current discourse by getting rid of the false dichotomy between biological and social. It offers a truly interactionist position that specifies the particular features of social context that are especially critical for processing by our evolved psychological mechanisms. No other theory of sex differences has been capable of predicting and explaining the large number of precise, detailed, patterned sex differences discovered by research guided by evolutionary psychology. Evolutionary psychology possesses the heuristic power to guide investigators to the particular domains in which the most pronounced sex differences, as well as similarities, will be found. People grappling with the existence and implications of psychological sex differences cannot afford to ignore their most likely evolutionary origins through sexual selection.

References

Brown, D. (1991). *Human universals.* Philadelphia: Temple University Press.

Buss, D. M. (1989). Sex differences in human mate preferences: Evolutionary hypotheses tested in 37 cultures. *Behavioral and Brain Sciences, 12,* 1–49.

———. Larsen, R., Westen, D., & Semmelroth, J. (1992). Sex differences in jealousy: Evolution, physiology, and psychology. *Psychological Science, 3,* 251–255.

Cohen, J. (1977). Statistical power analysis for the behavioral sciences. San Diego, CA: Academic Press.

Darwin, C. (1871). *The descent of man and selection in relation to sex.* London: Murray.

Hyde, J. S. (1996). Where are the gender differences? Where are the gender similarities? In D. M. Buss & N. Malamuth (Eds.), *Sex, power, conflict: Feminist and evolutionary perspectives.* New York: Oxford University Press.

Maccoby, E. E., & Jacklin, C. N. (1974). *The psychology of sex differences.* Stanford, CA: Stanford University Press.

Oliver, M. B. & Hyde, J. S. (1993). Gender differences in sexuality: A meta-analysis. *Psychological Bulletin, 114,* 29–51.

JUDITH LORBER

Believing Is Seeing: Biology as Ideology

Until the eighteenth century, Western philosophers and scientists thought that there was one sex and that women's internal genitalia were the inverse of men's external genitalia: the womb and vagina were the penis and scrotum turned inside out (Laqueur 1990). Current Western thinking sees women and men as so different

Judith Lorber, *Gender & Society,* Vol. 7, No. 6, pp. 568–81, copyright © 1993 by Sage Publications, Inc. Reprinted by permission of Sage Publications, Inc.

physically as to sometimes seem two species. The bodies, which have been mapped inside and out for hundreds of years, have not changed. What has changed are the justifications for gender inequality. When the social position of all human beings was believed to be set by natural law or was considered God-given, biology was irrelevant; women and men of different classes all had their assigned places. When scientists began to question the divine basis of social order and replaced faith with empirical knowledge, what they saw was that women were very different from men in that they had wombs and menstruated. Such anatomical differences destined them for an entirely different social life from men.

In actuality, the basic bodily material is the same for females and males, and except for procreative hormones and organs, female and male human beings have similar bodies (Naftolin and Butz 1981). Furthermore, as has been known since the middle of the nineteenth century, male and female genitalia develop from the same fetal tissue, and so infants can be born with ambiguous genitalia (Money and Ehrhardt 1972). When they are, biology is used quite arbitrarily in sex assignment. Suzanne Kessler (1990) interviewed six medical specialists in pediatric intersexuality and found that whether an infant with XY chromosomes and anomalous genitalia was categorized as a boy or a girl depended on the size of the penis—if a penis was very small, the child was categorized as a girl, and sex-change surgery was used to make an artificial vagina. In the late nineteenth century, the presence or absence of ovaries was the determining criterion of gender assignment for hermaphrodites because a woman who could not procreate was not a complete woman (Kessler 1990, 20).

Yet in Western societies, we see two discrete sexes and two distinguishable genders because our society is built on two classes of people, "women" and "men." Once the gender category is given, the attributes of the person are also gendered: Whatever a "woman" is has to be "female"; whatever a "man" is has to be "male." Analyzing the social processes that construct the categories we call "female and male," "women and men," and "homosexual and heterosexual" uncovers the ideology and power differentials congealed in these categories (Foucault 1978). This article will use two familiar areas of social life—sports and technological competence—to show how myriad physiological differences are transformed into similar-appearing, gendered social bodies. My perspective goes beyond accepted feminist views that gender is a cultural overlay that modifies physiological sex differences. That perspective assumes either that there are two fairly similar sexes distorted by social practices into two genders with purposefully different characteristics or that there are two sexes whose essential differences are rendered unequal by social practices. I am arguing that bodies differ in many ways physiologically, but they are completely transformed by social practices to fit into the salient categories of a society, the most pervasive of which are "female" and "male" and "women" and "men."

Neither sex nor gender are pure categories. Combinations of incongruous genes, genitalia, and hormonal input are ignored in sex categorization, just as combinations of incongruous physiology, identity, sexuality, appearance, and behavior are ignored in the social construction of gender statuses. Menstruation, lactation, and gestation do not demarcate women from men. Only some women are pregnant and then only some of the time; some women do not have a uterus or ovaries. Some women have stopped menstruating temporarily, others have reached menopause, and some have had hysterectomies. Some women breast-feed some of the time, but some men lactate (Jaggar 1983, 165 fn). Menstruation, lactation, and gestation are individual experiences of womanhood (Levesque-Lopman 1988), but not determinants of the social category "woman," or even "female." Similarly, "men are not always sperm-producers, and in fact, not all sperm producers are men. A male-to-female transsexual, prior to surgery, can be socially a woman, though still potentially (or actually) capable of spermatogenesis" (Kessler and McKenna [1978] 1985, 2).

When gender assignment is contested in sports, where the categories of competitors are rigidly divided into women and men, chromosomes are now used to determine in which category the athlete is to compete. However, an anomaly common enough to be found in several women at every major international sports competition are XY chromosomes that have not produced male anatomy or physiology because of a genetic defect. Because these women are women in every way significant for sports competition, the prestigious International Amateur Athletic Federation has urged that sex be determined by simple genital inspection (Kolata 1992). Transsexuals would pass this test, but it took a lawsuit for Renée Richards, a male-to-female transsexual, to be able to play tournament tennis as a woman, despite his male sex chromosomes (Richards 1983). Oddly, neither basis for gender categorization—chromosomes nor genitalia—has anything to do with sports prowess (Birrell and Cole 1990).

In the Olympics, in cases of chromosomal ambiguity, women must undergo "a battery of gynecological and physical exams to see if she is 'female enough' to compete. Men are not tested" (Carlson 1991, 26). The purpose is not to categorize women and men accurately, but to make sure men don't enter women's competitions, where, it is felt, they will have the advantage of size and strength. This practice sounds fair only because it is assumed that all men are similar in size and strength and different from all women. Yet in Olympics boxing and wrestling matches, men are matched within weight classes. Some women might similarly successfully compete with some men in many sports. Women did not run in marathons until about twenty years ago. In twenty years of marathon competition, women have reduced their finish times by more than one-and-one-half hours; they are expected to run as fast as men in that race by 1998 and might catch up with men's running times in races of other lengths within the next 50 years because they are increasing their fastest speeds more rapidly than are men (Fausto-Sterling 1985, 213–18).

The reliance on only two sex and gender categories in the biological and social sciences is as epistemologically spurious as the reliance on chromosomal or genital tests to group athletes. Most research designs do not investigate whether physical skills or physical abilities are really more or less common in women and men (Epstein 1988). They start out with two social categories ("women," "men"), assume they are biologically different ("female," "male"), look for similarities among them and differences between them, and attribute what they have found for the social categories to sex differences (Gelman, Collman, and Maccoby 1986).

These designs rarely question the categorization of their subjects into two and only two groups, even though they often find more significant within-group differences than between-group differences (Hyde 1990). The social construction perspective on sex and gender suggests that instead of starting with the two presumed dichotomies in each category—female, male; woman, man—it might be more useful in gender studies to group patterns of behavior and only then look for identifying markers of the people likely to enact such behaviors.

WHAT SPORTS ILLUSTRATE

Competitive sports have become, for boys and men, as players and as spectators, a way of constructing a masculine identity, a legitimated outlet for violence and aggression, and an avenue for upward mobility (Dunning 1986; Kemper 1990, 167–206; Messner 1992). For men in Western societies, physical competence is an important marker of masculinity (Fine 1987; Glassner 1992; Majors 1990). In professional and collegiate sports, physiological differences are invoked to justify women's secondary status, despite the clear evidence that gender status overrides physiological capabilities. Assumptions about women's physiology have influenced rules of competition; subsequent sports performances then validate how women and men are treated in sports competitions.

Gymnastic equipment is geared to slim, wiry, prepubescent girls and not to mature women; conversely, men's gymnastic equipment is tailored for muscular, mature men, not slim, wiry, prepubescent boys. Boys could compete with girls, but are not allowed to; women gymnasts are left out entirely. Girl gymnasts are just that—little girls who will be disqualified as soon as they grow up (Vecsey 1990). Men gymnasts have men's status. In women's basketball, the size of the ball and rules for handling the ball change the style of play to "a slower, less intense, and less exciting modification of the 'regular' or men's game" (Watson 1987, 441). In the 1992 Winter Olympics, men figure skaters were required to complete three triple jumps in their required program; women figure skaters were forbidden to do more than one. These rules penalized artistic men skaters and athletic women skaters (Janofsky 1992). For the most part, Western sports are built on physically trained men's bodies:

> Speed, size, and strength seem to be the essence of sports. Women *are* naturally inferior at "sports" so conceived.
>
> But if women had been the historically dominant sex, our concept of sport would no doubt have evolved differently. Competitions emphasizing flexibility, balance, strength, timing, and small size might dominate Sunday afternoon television and offer salaries in six figures (English 1982, 266, emphasis in original).

Organized sports are big businesses and, thus, who has access and at what level is a distributive or equity issue. The overall status of women and men athletes is an economic, political, and ideological issue that has less to do with individual physiological capabilities than with their cultural and social meaning and who defines and profits from them (Messner and Sabo 1990; Slatton and Birrell 1984). Twenty years after the passage of Title IX of the U.S. Civil Rights Act, which forbade gender inequality in any school receiving federal funds, the goal for collegiate sports in the next five years is 60 percent men, 40 percent women in sports participation, scholarships, and funding (Moran 1992).

How access and distribution of rewards (prestigious and financial) are justified is an ideological, even moral, issue (Birrell 1988, 473–76, Hargreaves 1982). One way is that men athletes are glorified and women athletes ignored in the mass media. Messner and his colleagues found that in 1989, in TV sports news in the United States, men's sports got 92 percent of the coverage and women's sports 5 percent, with the rest mixed or gender-neutral (Messner, Duncan, and Jensen 1993). In 1990, in four of the top-selling newspapers in the United States, stories on men's sports outnumbered those on women's sports 23 to 1. Messner and his colleagues also found an implicit hierarchy in naming, with women athletes most likely to be called by first names, followed by black men athletes, and only white men athletes routinely referred to by their last names. Similarly, women's collegiate sports teams are named or marked in ways that symbolically feminize and trivialize them—the men's team is called Tigers, the women's Kittens (Eitzen and Baca Zinn 1989).

Assumptions about men's and women's bodies and their capacities are crafted in ways that make unequal access and distribution of rewards acceptable (Hudson 1978; Messner 1988). Media images of modern men athletes glorify their strength and power, even their violence (Hargreaves 1986). Media images of modern women athletes tend to focus on feminine beauty and grace (so they are not really athletes) or on their thin, small, wiry, androgenous bodies (so they are not really women). In coverage of the Olympics,

> loving and detailed attention is paid to pixie-like gymnasts; special and extended coverage is given to graceful and dazzling figure skaters; the camera painstakingly records the fluid movements of swimmers and divers. And then, in a blinding flash of fragmented images, viewers see a few minutes of volleyball, basketball, speed skating, track and field, and alpine skiing, as television gives its nod to the mere existence of these events (Boutilier and SanGiovanni 1983, 190).

Extraordinary feats by women athletes who were presented as mature adults might force sports organizers and audiences to rethink their stereotypes of women's capabilities, the way elves, mermaids, and ice queens do not. Sports, therefore, construct men's bodies to be powerful: women's bodies to be sexual. As Connell (1987, 85) says,

> The meanings in the bodily sense of masculinity concern, above all else, the superiority of men to women, and the exaltation of hegemonic masculinity over other groups of men which is essential for the domination of women.

In the late 1970s, as women entered more and more athletic competitions, supposedly good scientific studies showed that women who exercised intensely would cease menstruating because they would not have enough body fat to sustain ovulation (Brozan 1978). When one set of researchers did a yearlong study that compared 66 women—21 who were training for a marathon, 22 who ran more than an hour a week, and 23 who did less than an hour of aerobic exercise a week—they discovered that only 20 percent of the women in any of these groups had "normal" menstrual cycles every month (Prior et al. 1990). The dangers of intensive training for women's fertility therefore were exaggerated as women began to compete successfully in arenas formerly closed to them.

Given the association of sports with masculinity in the United States, women athletes have to manage a contradictory status. One study of women college basketball players found that although they "did athlete" on the court, "pushing, shoving, fouling, hard running, fast breaks, defense, obscenities and sweat" (Watson 1987, 441), they "did woman" off the court, using the locker room as their staging area:

> While it typically took fifteen minutes to prepare for the game, it took approximately fifteen minutes after the game to shower and remove the sweat of an athlete, and it took another thirty minutes to dress, apply make-up and style hair. It did not seem to matter whether the players were going out into the public or getting on a van for a long ride home. Average dressing time and rituals did not change (Watson 1987, 443).

Another way women manage these status dilemmas is to redefine the activity or its result as feminine or womanly (Mangan and Park 1987). Thus women body-builders claim that "flex appeal is sex appeal" (Duff and Hong 1984, 378).

Such a redefinition of women's physicality affirms the ideological subtext of sports that physical strength is men's prerogative and justifies men's physical and sexual domination of women (Hargreaves 1986, Messner 1992, 164–72; Olson 1990; Theberge 1987; Willis 1982). When women demonstrate physical strength, they are labeled unfeminine:

> It's threatening to one's takeability, one's repeability, one's femininity, to be strong and physically self-possessed. To be able to resist rape, not to communicate rapeability with one's body, to hold one's body for uses and meanings other than that can transform what *being a woman means* (MacKinnon 1987, 122, emphasis in original).

Resistance to that transformation, ironically, was evident in the policies of American women physical education professionals throughout most of the twentieth century. They minimized exertion, maximized a feminine appearance and manner, and left organized sports competition to men (Birrell 1988, 461–62; Mangan and Park 1987).

DIRTY LITTLE SECRETS

As sports construct gendered bodies, technology constructs gendered skills. Meta-analyses of studies of gender differences in spatial and mathematical ability have found that men have a large advantage in ability to mentally rotate an image, a moderate advantage in a visual perception of horizontality and verticality and in mathematical performance, and a small advantage in ability to pick a figure out of a field (Hyde 1990). It could be argued that these advantages explain why, within the short space of time that computers have become ubiquitous in offices, schools, and homes, work on them and with them has become gendered: Men create, program, and market computers, make war and produce science and art with them; women microwire them in computer factories and enter data in computerized offices; boys play games, socialize, and commit crimes with computers; girls are rarely seen in computer clubs, camps, and classrooms. But women were hired as computer programmers in the 1940s because

> the work seemed to resemble simple clerical tasks. In fact, however, programming demanded complex skills in abstract logic, mathematics, electrical circuitry, and machinery, all of which . . . women used to perform in their work. Once programming was recognized as "intellectually demanding," it became attractive to men (Donato 1990, 170).

A woman mathematician and pioneer in data processing, Grace M. Hopper, was famous for her work on programming language (Perry and Greber 1990, 86). By the 1960s, programming was split into more and less skilled specialties, and the entry of women into the computer field in the 1970s and 1980s was confined to the lower-paid specialties. At each stage, employers invoked women's and men's purportedly natural capabilities for the jobs for which they were hired (Cockburn 1983, 1985; Donato 1990; Hartmann 1987; Hartmann, Kraut, and Tilly 1986; Kramer and Lehman 1990; Wright et al. 1987; Zimmerman 1983).

It is the taken-for-grantedness of such everyday gendered behavior that gives credence to the belief that the widespread differences in what women and men do must come from biology. To take one ordinarily unremarked scenario: In modern societies, if a man and woman who are a couple are in a car together, he is much more likely to take the wheel than she is, even if she is the more competent driver. Molly Haskell calls this taken-for-granted phenomenon "the dirty little secret of marriage: the husband-lousy-driver syndrome" (1989, 26). Men drive cars whether they are good drivers or not because men and machines are a "natural" combination (Scharff 1991). But the ability to drive gives one mobility; it is a form of social power.

In the early days of the automobile, feminists co-opted the symbolism of mobility as emancipation: "Donning goggles and dusters, wielding tire irons and tool kits, taking the wheel, they announced their intention to move beyond the bounds of women's place" (Scharff 1991, 68). Driving enabled them to campaign for women's suffrage in parts of the United States not served by public transportation, and they effectively used motorcades and speaking from cars as campaign tactics (Scharff 1991, 67–88). Sandra Gilbert also notes that during World War I, women's ability to drive was physically, mentally, and even sensually liberating:

> For nurses and ambulance drivers, women doctors and women messengers, the phenomenon of modern battle was very different from that experienced by

entrenched combatants. Finally given a chance to take the wheel, these post-Victorian girls raced motorcars along foreign roads like adventurers exploring new lands, while their brothers dug deeper into the mud of France. . . . Retrieving the wounded and the dead from deadly positions, these once-decorous daughters had at last been allowed to prove their valor, and they swooped over the wastelands of the war with the energetic love of Wagnerian Valkyries, their mobility alone transporting countless immobilized heroes to safe havens (1983, 438–39).

Not incidentally, women in the United States and England got the vote for their war efforts in World War I.

SOCIAL BODIES AND THE BATHROOM PROBLEM

People of the same racial ethnic group and social class are roughly the same size and shape—but there are many varieties of bodies. People have different genitalia, different secondary sex characteristics, different contributions to procreation, different orgasmic experiences, different patterns of illness and aging. Each of us experiences our bodies differently, and these experiences change as we grow, age, sicken, and die. The bodies of pregnant and non-pregnant women, short and tall people, those with intact and functioning limbs and those whose bodies are physically challenged are all different. But the salient categories of a society group these attributes in ways that ride roughshod over individual experiences and more meaningful clusters of people.

I am not saying that physical differences between male and female bodies don't exist, but that these differences are socially meaningless until social practices transform them into social facts. West Point Military Academy's curriculum is designed to produce leaders, and physical competence is used as a significant measure of leadership ability (Yoder 1989). When women were accepted as West Point cadets, it became clear that the tests of physical competence, such as rapidly scaling an eight-foot wall, had been constructed for male physiques—pulling oneself up and over using upper-body strength. Rather than devise tests of physical competence for women, West Point provided boosters that mostly women used—but that lost them test points—in the case of the wall, a platform. Finally, the women themselves figured out how to use their bodies successfully. Janice Yoder describes this situation:

> I was observing this obstacle one day, when a woman approached the wall in the old prescribed way, got her fingertips grip, and did an unusual thing: she walked her dangling legs up the wall until she was in a position where both her hands and feet were atop the wall. She then simply pulled up her sagging bottom and went over. She solved the problem by capitalizing on one of women's physical assets: lower-body strength (1989, 530).

In short, if West Point is going to measure leadership capability by physical strength, women's pelvises will do just as well as men's shoulders.

The social transformation of female and male physiology into a condition of inequality is well illustrated by the bathroom problem. Most buildings that have gender-segregated bathrooms have an equal number for women and for men. Where there are crowds, there are always long lines in front of women's bathrooms but rarely in front of men's bathrooms. The cultural, physiological, and demographic combinations of clothing, frequency of urination, menstruation, and child care add up to generally greater bathroom use by women than men. Thus, although an equal number of bathrooms seems fair, equity would mean more women's bathrooms or allowing women to use men's bathrooms for a certain amount of time (Molotch 1988).

The bathroom problem is the outcome of the way gendered bodies are differentially evaluated in Western cultures: Men's social bodies are the measure of what is "human." Gray's *Anatomy*, in use for 100 years, well into the twentieth century, presented the human body as male. The female body was shown only where it differed from the male (Laqueur 1990, 166–67). Denise Riley says that if we envisage women's bodies, men's bodies, and human bodies "as a triangle of identifications, then it is rarely an equilateral triangle in which both sexes are pitched at matching distances from the apex of the human" (1988, 197). Catharine MacKinnon also contends that in Western society, universal "humanness" is male because

> virtually every quality that distinguishes men from women is already affirmatively compensated in this society. Men's physiology defines most sports, their needs define auto and health insurance coverage, their socially defined biographies define workplace expectations and successful career patterns, their perspectives and concerns define quality in scholarship, their experiences and obsessions define merit, their objectification of life defines art, their military service defines citizenship, their presence defines family, their inability to get along with each other—their wars and rulerships—define history, their image defines god, and their genitals define sex. For each of their differences from women, what amounts to an affirmative action plan is in effect, otherwise known as the structure and values of American society (1987, 36).

THE PARADOX OF HUMAN NATURE

Gendered people do not emerge from physiology or hormones but from the exigencies of the social order, mostly, from the need for a reliable division of the work of food production and the social (not physical) reproduction of new members. The moral imperatives of religion and cultural representations reinforce the boundary lines among genders and ensure that what is demanded, what is permitted, and what is tabooed for the people in each gender is well-known and followed by most. Political power, control of scarce resources, and, if necessary, violence uphold the gendered social order in the face of resistance and rebellion. Most people, however, voluntarily go along with their society's prescriptions for those of their gender status because the norms and expectations get built into their sense of worth and identity as a certain kind of human being and because they believe their society's way is the natural way. These beliefs emerge from the imagery that pervades the way we think, the way we see and hear and speak, the way we fantasize, and the way we feel. There is no core or bedrock human nature below these endlessly looping processes of the social production of sex and gender, self and other, identity and psyche, each of which is a "complex cultural construction" (Butler 1990, 36). The paradox of "human nature" is that it is always a manifestation of cultural meanings, social relationships, and power politics—"not biology, but culture, becomes destiny" (Butler 1990, 8).

Feminist inquiry has long questioned the conventional categories of social science, but much of the current work in feminist sociology has not gone beyond adding the universal category "women" to the universal category "men." Our current debates over the global assumptions of only two categories and the insistence that they must be nuanced to include race and class are steps in the direction I would like to see feminist research go, but race and class are also global categories (Collins 1990; Spelman 1988). Deconstructing sex, sexuality, and gender reveals many possible categories embedded in the social experiences and social practices of what Dorothy Smith calls the "everyday/everynight world" (1990, 31–57). These emergent categories group some people together for comparison with other people without prior assumptions about who is like whom. Categories can be broken up and people regrouped differently into new categories for comparison. This process of discovering categories from similarities and differences in people's behavior or responses can be more meaningful for feminist research than discovering similarities and differences between "females" and "males" or "women" and "men" because the social construction of the conventional sex and gender categories already assumes differences between them and similarities among them. When we rely only on the conventional categories of sex and gender, we end up finding what we looked for—we see what we believe, whether it is that "females" and "males" are essentially different or that "women" and "men" are essentially the same.

References

Birrell, Susan J. 1988. Discourses on the gender/sport relationship: From women in sport to gender relations. In *Exercise and Sport Science Reviews,* Vol. 16, edited by Kent Pandolf. New York: Macmillan.

———, and Sheryl L. Cole. 1990. Double fault: Renee Richards and the construction and naturalization of difference. *Sociology of Sport Journal* 7:1–21.

Boutilier, Mary A., and Lucinda SanGiovanni. 1983. *The Sporting Woman.* Champaign, IL: Human Kinetics.

Brozan, Nadine. 1978. Training linked to disruption of female reproductive cycle. *New York Times,* 17 April.

Butler, Judith. 1990. *Gender Trouble: Feminism and the Subversion of Identity.* New York and London: Routledge & Kegan Paul.

Carlson, Alison. 1991. When is a woman not a woman? *Women's Sport and Fitness* March, 24–29.

Cockburn, Cynthia. 1983. *Brothers: Male Dominance and Technological Change.* London: Pluto.

———. 1985. *Machinery of Dominance: Women, Men, and Technical Know-How.* London: Pluto.

Collins, Patricia Hill. 1990. *Black Feminist Thought: Knowledge, Consciousness, and the Politics of Empowerment.* Boston: Unwin Hyman.

Connell, R. W. 1987. *Gender and Power.* Stanford, CA: Stanford University Press.

Donato, Katharine M. 1990. Programming for change? The growing demand for women systems analysts. In *Job Queues, Gender Queues: Explaining Women's Inroads into Male Occupations,* edited by Barbara F. Reskin and Patricia A. Roos. Philadelphia: Temple University Press.

Duff, Robert W., and Lawrence K. Hong. 1984. Self-images of women bodybuilders. *Sociology of Sport Journal* 2:374–80.

Dunning, Eric. 1986. Sport as a male preserve: Notes on the social sources of masculine identity and its transformations. *Theory, Culture, and Society* 3:79–90.

Eitzen, D. Stanley, and Maxine Baca Zinn. 1989. The deathleticization of women: The naming and gender marking of collegiate sport teams. *Sociology of Sport Journal* 6:362–70.

English, Jane. 1982. Sex equality in sports. In *Femininity, Masculinity, and Androgyny,* edited by Mary Vetterling-Braggin. Boston: Littlefield, Adams.

Epstein, Cynthia Fuchs. 1988. *Deceptive Distinctions: Sex, Gender, and the Social Order.* New Haven, CT: Yale University Press.

Fausto-Sterling, Anne. 1985. *Myths of Gender: Biological Theories about Women and Men.* New York: Basic Books.

Fine, Gary Alan. 1987. *With the Boys: Little League Baseball and Preadolescent Culture.* Chicago: University of Chicago Press.

Foucault, Michel. 1978. *The History of Sexuality: An Introduction.* Translated by Robert Hurley. New York: Pantheon.

Gelman, Susan A., Pamela Collman, and Eleanor E. Maccoby. 1986. Inferring properties from categories versus inferring categories from properties: The case of gender. *Child Development* 57:396–404.

Gilbert, Sandra M. 1983. Soldier's heart: Literary men, literary women, and the Great War. *Signs: Journal of Women in Culture and Society* 8:422–50.

Glassner, Barry. 1992. Men and muscles. In *Men's Lives,* edited by Michael S. Kimmel and Michael A. Messner. New York: Macmillan.

Hargreaves, Jennifer A., ed. 1982. *Sport, Culture, and Ideology.* London: Routledge & Kegan Paul.

———. 1986. Where's the virtue? Where's the grace? A discussion of the social production of gender relations in and through sport. *Theory, Culture, and Society* 3:109–21.

———, ed. 1987. *Computer Chips and Paper Clips: Technology and Women's Employment.* Vol. 2. Washington, DC: National Academy Press.

———, Robert E. Kraut, and Louise A. Tilly, eds. 1986. *Computer Chips and Paper Clips: Technology and Women's Employment.* Vol. 1. Washington, DC: National Academy Press.

Haskell, Molly. 1989. Hers: He drives me crazy. *New York Times Magazine,* 24 September, 26, 28.

Hudson, Jackie. 1978. Physical parameters used for female exclusion from law enforcement and athletics. In *Women and Sport: From Myth to Reality,* edited by Carole A Oglesby. Philadelphia: Lea and Febiger.

Hyde, Janet Shibley. 1990. Meta-analysis and the psychology of gender differences. *Signs: Journal of Women in Culture and Society* 16:55–73.

Jaggar, Alison M. 1983. *Feminist Politics and Human Nature.* Totowa, NJ: Rowman & Allan-held.

Janofsky, Michael. 1992. Yamaguchi has the delicate and golden touch. *New York Times,* 22 February.

Kemper, Theodore D. 1990. *Social Structure and Testosterone: Explorations of the Sociobiosocial Chain.* New Brunswick, NJ: Rutgers University Press.

Kessler, Suzanne J. 1990. The medical construction of gender: Case management of inter-sexed infants. *Signs: Journal of Women in Culture and Society* 16:3–26.

———, and Wendy McKenna. [1978] 1985. *Gender: an Ethnomethodological Approach.* Chicago: University of Chicago Press.

Kolata, Gina. 1992. Track federation urges end to gene test for femaleness. *New York Times,* 12 February.

Kramer, Pamela E., and Sheila Lehman. 1990. Mismeasuring women: A critique of research on computer ability and avoidance. *Signs: Journal of Women in Culture and Society* 16:158–72.

Laqueur, Thomas. 1990. *Making Sex: Body and Gender from the Greeks to Freud.* Cambridge, MA: Harvard University Press.

Levesque-Lopman, Louise. 1988. *Claiming Reality: Phenomenology and Women's Experience.* Totowa, NJ: Rowman & Littlefield.

MacKinnon, Catherine. 1987. *Feminism Unmodified.* Cambridge, MA: Harvard University Press.

Majors, Richard. 1990. Cool pose: Black masculinity in sports. In *Sport, Men, and the Gender Order: Critical Feminist Perspectives,* edited by Michael A. Messner and Donald F. Sabo. Champaign, IL: Human Kinetics.

Mangan, J. A., and Roberta J. Park. 1987. *From Fair Sex to Feminism: Sport and the Socialization of Women in the Industrial and Post-industrial Eras.* London: Frank Cass.

Messner, Michael A. 1988. Sports and male domination: The female athlete as contested ideological terrain. *Sociology of Sport Journal* 5:197–211.

———. 1992. *Power at Play: Sports and the Problem of Masculinity.* Boston: Beacon Press.

———, Margaret Carlisle Duncan, and Kerry Jensen. 1993. Separating the men from the girls: The gendered language of television sports. *Gender & Society* 7:121–37.

———, and Donald F. Sabo, eds., 1990. *Sport, Men, and the Gender Order: Critical Feminist Perspectives.* Champaign, IL: Human Kinetics.

Molotch, Harvey. 1988. The restroom and equal opportunity. *Sociological Forum* 3:128–32.

Money, John and Anke A. Ehrhardt. 1972. *Man & Woman, Boy & Girl.* Baltimore, MD: Johns Hopkins University Press.

Moran, Malcolm. 1992. Title IX: A 20-year search for equity. *New York Times* Sports Section, 21–23 June.

Naftolin, F., and E. Butz, eds. 1981. Sexual dimorphism. *Science* 211:1263–1324.

Olson, Wendy. 1990. Beyond Title IX: Toward an agenda for women and sports in the 1990s. *Yale Journal of Law and Feminism* 3:105–51.

Perry, Ruth, and Lisa Greber. 1990. Women and computers: An introduction. *Signs: Journal of Women in Culture and Society* 16:74–101.

Prior, Jerilynn C., Yvette M. Yigna, Martin T. Shechter, and Arthur E. Burgess. 1990. Spinal bone loss and ovulatory disturbances. *New England Journal of Medicine* 323:1221–27.

Richards, Renée, with Jack Ames. 1983. *Second Serve.* New York: Stein and Day.

Riley, Denise. 1988. *Am I that name? Feminism and the category of women in history.* Minneapolis: University of Minnesota Press.

Scharff, Virginia. 1991. *Taking the Wheel: Women and the Coming of the Motor Age.* New York: Free Press.

Slatton, Bonnie, and Susan Birrel. 1984. The politics of women's sport. *Arena Review* 8 (July).

Smith, Dorothy E. 1990. *The Conceptual Practices of Power: A Feminist Sociology of Knowledge.* Toronto: University of Toronto Press.

Spelman, Elizabeth. 1988. *Inessential Woman: Problems of Exclusion in Feminist Thought.* Boston: Beacon Press.

Theberge, Nancy. 1987. Sport and women's empowerment. *Women Studies International Forum* 10:387–93.

Vecsey, George. 1990. Cathy Rigby, unlike Peter, did grow up. *New York Times* Sports Section, 19 December.

Watson, Tracey. 1987. Women athletes and athletic women: The dilemmas and contradictions of managing incongruent identities. *Sociological Inquiry* 57:431–46.

Willis, Paul. 1982. Women in sport in ideology. In *Sport, Culture, and Ideology,* edited by Jennifer A. Hargreaves. London: Routledge & Kegan Paul.

Wright, Barbara Drygulski, Myra Marx Ferree, Gail O. Mellow, Linda H. Lewis, Maria-Luz Daza Samper, Robert Asher, and Kathleen Claspell, eds. 1987. *Women, Work, and Technology: Transformations.* Ann Arbor: University of Michigan Press.

Yoder, Janice D. 1989. Women at West Point: Lessons for token women in male-dominated occupations. In *Women: A Feminist Perspective,* edited by Jo Freeman. 4th ed. Palo Alto, CA: Mayfield.

Zimmerman, Jan, ed. 1983. *The Technological Woman: Interfacing with Tomorrow.* New York: Praeger.

ROBERT M. SAPOLSKY

Testosterone Rules

Face it, we all do it—we all believe in stereotypes about minorities. These stereotypes are typically pejorative and false, but every now and then they have a core of truth. I know, because I belong to a minority that lives up to its reputation. I have a genetic abnormality generally considered to be associated with high rates of certain socially abhorrent behaviors: I am male. Thanks to an array of genes that

This article is from *Discover,* March 1997, and is reprinted here with permission.

produce some hormone-synthesizing enzymes, my testes churn out a corrosive chemical and dump the stuff into my bloodstream, and this probably has behavioral consequences. We males account for less than 50 percent of the population, yet we generate a huge proportion of the violence. Whether it is something as primal as having an ax fight in a rain forest clearing or as detached as using computer-guided aircraft to strafe a village, something as condemned as assaulting a cripple or as glorified as killing someone wearing the wrong uniform, if it is violent, we males excel at it.

Why should this be? We all think we know the answer: something to do with those genes being expressed down in the testes. A dozen millennia ago or so, an adventurous soul managed to lop off a surly bull's testicles, thus inventing behavioral endocrinology. It is unclear from the historical records whether the experiment resulted in grants and tenure, but it certainly generated an influential finding: that the testes do something or other to make males aggressive pains in the ass.

That something or other is synthesizing the infamous corrosive chemical, testosterone (or rather, a family of related androgen hormones that I'll call testosterone for the sake of simplicity, hoping the androgen specialists won't take it the wrong way). Testosterone bulks up muscle cells—including those in the larynx, giving rise to operatic basses. It makes hair sprout here and there, undermines the health of blood vessels, alters biochemical events in the liver too dizzying to contemplate, and has a profound impact, no doubt, on the workings of cells in big toes. And it seeps into the brain, where it influences behavior in a way highly relevant to understanding aggression.

Genes are the hand behind the scene, directing testosterone's actions. They specify whether steroidal building blocks are turned into testosterone or estrogen, how much of each, and how quickly. They regulate how fast the liver breaks down circulating testosterone, thereby determining how long an androgenic signal remains in the bloodstream. They direct the synthesis of testosterone receptors—specialized proteins that catch hold of testosterone and allow it to have its characteristic effects on target cells. And genes specify how many such receptors the body has, and how sensitive they are. Insofar as testosterone alters brain function and produces aggression, and genes regulate how much testosterone is made and how effectively it works, this should be the archetypal case for studying how genes can control our behavior. Instead, however, it's the archetypal case for learning how little genes actually do so.

Some pretty obvious evidence links testosterone with aggression. Males tend to have higher testosterone levels in their circulation than do females, and to be more aggressive. Times of life when males are swimming in testosterone—for example, after reaching puberty—correspond to when aggression peaks. Among many species, testes are mothballed most of the year, kicking into action and pouring out testosterone only during a very circumscribed mating season—precisely the time when male-male aggression soars.

Impressive though they seem, these data are only correlative—testosterone found on the scene repeatedly with no alibi when some aggression has occurred. The proof comes with the knife, the performance of what is euphemistically known as a subtraction experiment. Remove the source of testosterone in species after species, and levels of aggression typically plummet. Reinstate normal testosterone levels afterward with injections of synthetic testosterone, and aggression returns.

The subtraction and replacement paradigm represents pretty damning proof that this hormone, with its synthesis and efficacy under genetic control, is involved in aggression. "Normal testosterone levels appear to be a prerequisite for normative levels of aggressive behavior" is the sort of catchy, hummable phrase the textbooks would use. That probably explains why you shouldn't mess with a bull moose during rutting season. But it's not why a lot of people want to understand this sliver of science. Does the action of testosterone tell us anything about individual differences in levels of aggression, anything about why some males—some human males—are exceptionally violent? Among an array of males, are the highest testosterone levels found in the most aggressive individuals?

Generate some extreme differences and that is precisely what you see. Castrate some of the well-paid study subjects, inject others with enough testosterone to quadruple the normal human levels, and the high-testosterone males are overwhelmingly likely to be the more aggressive ones. Obviously, extreme conditions don't tell us much about the real world, but studies of the normative variability in testosterone—in other words, seeing what everyone's natural levels are like without manipulating anything—also suggest that high levels of testosterone and high levels of aggression tend to go together. This would seem to seal the case that interindividual differences in levels of aggression among normal individuals are probably driven by differences in levels of testosterone. But that conclusion turns out to be wrong.

Here's why. Suppose you note a correlation between levels of aggression and levels of testosterone among normal males. It could be because (*a*) testosterone elevates aggression; (*b*) aggression elevates testosterone secretion; or (*c*) neither causes the other. There's a huge bias to assume option a, while b is the answer. Study after study has shown that if you examine testosterone levels when males are first placed together in the social group, testosterone levels predict nothing about who is going to be aggressive. The subsequent behavioral differences drive the hormonal changes, rather than the other way around.

Because of a strong bias among certain scientists, it has taken forever to convince them of this point. Suppose you're studying what behavior and hormones have to do with each other. How do you study the behavioral part? You get yourself a notebook, a stopwatch, a pair of binoculars. How do you measure the hormones and analyze the genes that regulate them? You need some gazillion-dollar machines; you muck around with radiation and chemicals, wear a lab coat, maybe even goggles—the whole nine yards. Which toys would you rather get for Christmas? Which facet of science are you going to believe in more? The higher the technology, goes the formula, the more scientific the discipline. Hormones seem to many to be more substantive than behavior, so when a correlation occurs, it must be because hormones regulate behavior, not the other way around.

This is a classic case of what is often called physics envy, a disease that causes behavioral biologists to fear their discipline lacks the rigor of physiology, physiologists to wish for the techniques of biochemists, biochemists to covet the clarity of the answers revealed by molecular geneticists, all the way down until you get to the physicists who confer only with God. Recently, a zoologist friend had obtained blood samples from the carnivores he studies and wanted some hormones in the samples tested in my lab. Although inexperienced with the technique, he offered to help in any way possible. I felt hesitant asking him to do anything tedious, but since he had offered, I tentatively said, "Well, if you don't mind some unspeakable drudgery, you could number about a thousand assay vials." And this scientist, whose superb work has graced the most prestigious science journals in the world, cheerfully answered, "That's okay. How often do I get to do real science, working with test tubes?"

Difficult though scientists with physics envy find it to believe, interindividual differences in testosterone levels don't predict subsequent differences in aggressive behavior among individuals. Similarly, fluctuations in testosterone levels within one individual over time don't predict subsequent changes in the levels of aggression in that one individual—get a hiccup in testosterone secretion one afternoon and that's not when the guy goes postal.

Look at our confusing state: normal levels of testosterone are a prerequisite for normal levels of aggression. Yet if one male's genetic makeup predisposes him to higher levels of testosterone than the next guy, he isn't necessarily going to be more aggressive. Like clockwork, that statement makes the students suddenly start coming to office hours in a panic, asking whether they missed something in their lecture notes.

Yes, it's going to be on the final, and it's one of the more subtle points in endocrinology—what's referred to as a hormone having a "permissive effect." Remove someone's testes and, as noted, the frequency of aggressive behavior is likely to plummet. Reinstate pre-castration levels of testosterone by injecting the hormone, and pre-castration levels of aggression typically return. Fair enough. Now, this time, castrate an individual and restore testosterone levels to only 20 percent of normal. Amazingly, normal pre-castration levels of aggression come back. Castrate and now introduce twice the testosterone levels from before castration, and the same level of aggressive behavior returns. You need some testosterone around for normal aggressive behavior. Zero levels after castration, and down it usually goes; quadruple levels (the sort of range generated in weight lifters abusing anabolic steroids), and aggression typically increases. But anywhere from roughly 20 percent of normal to twice normal and it's all the same. The brain can't distinguish among this wide range of basically normal values.

If you knew a great deal about the genetic makeup of a bunch of males, enough to understand how much testosterone they secreted into their bloodstream, you still couldn't predict levels of aggression among those individuals. Nevertheless, the subtraction and reinstatement data seem to indicate that, in a broad sort of way, testosterone causes aggressive behavior. But that turns out not to be true either, and the implications of this are lost on most people the first thirty times they hear about it. Those implications are important, however—so important that it's worth saying thirty-one times.

Round up some male monkeys. Put them in a group together and give them plenty of time to sort out where they stand with each other—grudges, affiliative friendships. Give them enough time to form a dominance hierarchy, the sort of linear ranking in which number 3, for example, can pass his day throwing around his weight with numbers 4 and 5, ripping off their monkey chow, forcing them to relinquish the best spots to sit in, but numbers 1 and 2 still expect and receive from him the most obsequious brownnosing.

Hierarchy in place, it's time to do your experiment. Take that third-ranking monkey and give him some testosterone. None of this within-the-normal-range stuff. Inject a ton of it, way higher than what you normally see in rhesus monkeys, give him enough testosterone to grow antlers and a beard on every neuron in his brain. And, no surprise, when you check the behavioral data, he will probably be participating in more aggressive interactions than before.

So even though small fluctuations in the levels of the hormone don't seem to matter much, testosterone still causes aggression, right? Wrong. Check out number 3 more closely. Is he raining aggressive terror on everyone in the group, frothing with indiscriminate violence? Not at all. He's still judiciously kowtowing to numbers 1 and 2 but has become a total bastard to numbers 4 and 5. Testosterone isn't causing aggression, it's exaggerating the aggression that's already there.

Another example, just to show we're serious. There's a part of your brain that probably has lots to do with aggression, a region called the amygdala. Sitting near it is the Grand Central Station of emotion-related activity in your brain, the hypothalamus. The amygdala communicates with the hypothalamus by way of a cable of neuronal connections called the stria terminalis. (No more jargon, I promise.) The amygdala influences aggression via that pathway, sending bursts of electrical excitation that ripple down the stria terminalis to the hypothalamus and put it in a pissy mood.

Once again, do your hormonal intervention: flood the area with testosterone. You can inject the hormone into the bloodstream, where it eventually makes its way to the amygdala. You can surgically microinject the stuff directly into the area. In a few years, you may even be able to construct animals with extra copies of the genes that direct testosterone synthesis, producing extra hormone that way. Six of one, half a dozen of the other. The key thing is what doesn't happen next. Does testosterone make waves of electrical excitation surge down the stria terminalis? Does it turn on that pathway? Not at all. If and only if the amygdala is already sending an excited volley down the stria terminalis, testosterone increases the rate of such activity by shortening the resting time between bouts. It's not turning on the pathway, it's increasing the volume of signaling if it is already turned on. It's not causing aggression, it's exaggerating the preexisting pattern of it, exaggerating the response to environmental triggers of aggression.

In every generation, it is the duty of behavioral biologists to try to teach this critical point, one that seems a maddening cliché once you get it. You take that hoary old dichotomy between nature and nurture, between intrinsic factors and extrinsic ones, between genes and environment, and regardless of which behavior and underlying biology you're studying, the dichotomy is a sham. No genes. No environment. Just the interaction between the two.

Do you want to know how important environment and experience are in understanding testosterone and aggression? Look back at how the effects of castration are discussed earlier. There were statements like "Remove the source of testosterone in species after species and levels of aggression typically plummet." Not "Remove the source . . . and aggression always goes to zero." On the average it declines, but rarely to zero, and not at all in some individuals. And the more social experience an individual had being aggressive prior to castration, the more likely that behavior persists sans cojones. In the right context, social conditioning can more than make up for the complete absence of the hormone.

A case in point: the spotted hyena. These animals are fast becoming the darlings of endocrinologists, sociobiologists, gynecologists, and tabloid writers because of their wild sex reversal system. Females are more muscular and more aggressive than males, and are socially dominant to them, rare traits in the mammalian world. And get this: females secrete more of certain testosterone-related hormones than the males do, producing muscles, aggression, and masculinized private parts that make it supremely difficult to tell the sex of a hyena. So high androgen levels would seem, again, to cause aggression and social dominance. But that's not the whole answer.

High in the hills above the University of California at Berkeley is the world's largest colony of spotted hyenas, massive bone-crunching beasts who fight each other for the chance to have their ears scratched by Laurence Frank, the zoologist who brought them over as infants from Kenya. Various scientists are studying their sex reversal system. The female hyenas are bigger and more muscular than the males and have the same weirdo genitals and elevated androgen levels as their female cousins back in the savanna. Everything is just as it is in the wild—except the social system. As those hyenas grew up, there was a very significant delay in the time it took for the females to begin socially dominating the males, even though the females were stoked on androgens. They had to grow up without the established social system to learn from.

When people first realize that genes have a great deal to do with behavior—even subtle, complex, human behavior—they are often struck with an initial evangelical enthusiasm, placing a convert's faith in the genetic components of the story. This enthusiasm is typically reductive—because of physics envy, because reductionism is so impressive, because it would be so nice if there were a single gene (or hormone or neurotransmitter or part of the brain) responsible for everything. But even if you completely understood how genes regulate all the important physical factors involved in aggression—testosterone synthesis and secretion, the brain's testosterone receptors, the amygdala neurons and their levels of transmitters, the favorite color of the hypothalamus—you still wouldn't be able to predict levels of aggression accurately in a group of normal individuals.

This is no mere academic subject. We are a fine species with some potential, yet we are racked by sickening amounts of violence. Unless we are hermits, we feel the threat of it, often every day, and should our leaders push the button, we will all be lost in a final global violence. But as we try to understand this feature of our sociality, it is critical to remember the limits of the biology. Knowing the genome, the complete DNA sequence, of some suburban teenager is never going to tell us why that kid, in his after-school chess club, has developed a particularly aggressive style with his bishops. And it certainly isn't going to tell us much about the teenager in some inner city hellhole who has taken to mugging people. "Testosterone equals aggression" is inadequate for those who would offer a simple biological solution to the violent male. And "testosterone equals aggression" is certainly inadequate for those who would offer the simple excuse that boys will be boys. Violence is more complex than a single hormone, and it is supremely rare that any of our behaviors can be reduced to genetic destiny. This is science for the bleeding-heart liberal: the genetics of behavior is usually meaningless outside the context of the social factors and environment in which it occurs.

PART 2

CULTURAL CONSTRUCTIONS OF GENDER

Biological evidence helps explain the ubiquity of gender difference and gender inequality, but social scientific evidence modifies both the universality and the inevitability implicit in biological claims. Cross-cultural research suggests that gender and sexuality are far more fluid, far more variable, than biological models would have predicted. If biological sex alone produced observed sex differences, Margaret Mead asked in the 1920s and 1930s, why did it produce such *different* definitions of masculinity and femininity in different cultures? In her path-breaking study, *Sex and Temperament in Three Primitive Societies*, Mead began an anthropological tradition of exploring and often celebrating the dramatically rich and varied cultural constructions of gender.

Anthropologists are more likely to locate the origins of gender difference and gender inequality in a sex-based division of labor, the near-universality of and the variations in the ways in which societies organize the basic provision and distribution of material goods. They've found that when women's and men's spheres are most distinctly divided—where women and men do different things in different places—women's status tends to be lower than when men and women share both work and workplaces.

Some researchers have explored the function of various cultural rituals and representations in creating the symbolic justification for gender differences and inequality based on this sex-based division of labor. For example, Gilbert Herdt describes a variety of "coming out" processes in a variety of cultures, thus demonstrating (1) the connections between sexual identity and gender identity, and (2) the dramatic variation among those identities.

Finally, Peggy Reeves Sanday explores the ways in which gender inequality is also a predictor for the likelihood that a culture will have either high or low rape rates. By locating the origins of rape in male domination—dramatic separation of spheres, gender inequality, low levels of male participation in child care—Sanday effectively lays to rest the facile biological argument that rape is the evolutionary sexual strategy of male "failures" in reproductive competition.

MARGARET MEAD

Sex and Temperament in Three Primitive Societies

We have now considered in detail the approved personalities of each sex among three primitive peoples. We found the Arapesh—both men and women—displaying a personality that, out of our historically limited preoccupations, we would call maternal in its parental aspects, and feminine in its sexual aspects. We found men, as well as women, trained to be co-operative, unaggressive, responsive to the needs and demands of others. We found no idea that sex was a powerful driving force either for men or for women. In marked contrast to these attitudes, we found among the Mundugumor that both men and women developed as ruthless, aggressive, positively sexed individuals, with the maternal cherishing aspects of personality at a minimum. Both men and women approximated to a personality type that we in our culture would find only in an undisciplined and very violent male. Neither the Arapesh nor the Mundugumor profit by a contrast between the sexes; the Arapesh ideal is the mild, responsive man married to the mild, responsive woman; the Mundugumor ideal is the violent aggressive man married to the violent aggressive woman. In the third tribe, the Tchambuli, we found a genuine reversal of the sex attitudes of our own culture, with the woman the dominant, impersonal, managing partner, the man the less responsible and the emotionally dependent person. These three situations suggest, then, a very definite conclusion. If those temperamental attitudes which we have traditionally regarded as feminine—such as passivity, responsiveness, and a willingness to cherish children—can so easily be set up as the masculine pattern in one tribe, and in another be outlawed for the majority of women as well as for the majority of men, we no longer have any basis for regarding such aspects of behaviour as sex-linked. And this conclusion becomes even stronger when we consider the actual reversal in Tchambuli of the position of dominance of the two sexes, in spite of the existence of formal patrilineal institutions.

The material suggests that we may say that many, if not all, of the personality traits which we have called masculine or feminine are as lightly linked to sex as are the clothing, the manners, and the form of head-dress that a society at a given period assigns to either sex. When we consider the behaviour of the typical Arapesh man or woman as contrasted with the behaviour of the typical Mundugumor man or woman, the evidence is overwhelmingly in favour of the strength of social conditioning. In no other way can we account for the almost complete uniformity with which Arapesh children develop into contented, passive, secure persons, while Mundugumor children develop as characteristically into violent, aggressive, insecure persons. Only to the impact of the whole of the integrated culture upon the growing child can we lay the formation of the contrasting types. There is no other explanation of race, or diet, or selection that can be adduced to explain them. We are forced to conclude that human nature is almost unbelievably malleable, responding accurately and contrastingly to contrasting cultural conditions. The differences between individuals who are members of different cultures, like the differences between individuals within a culture, are almost entirely to be laid to differences in conditioning, especially during early childhood, and the form of this conditioning is culturally determined. Standardized personality differences between the sexes are of this order, cultural creations to which each generation, male and female, is trained to conform. There remains, however, the problem of the origin of these socially standardized differences.

While the basic importance of social conditioning is still imperfectly recognized—not only in lay thought, but even by the scientist specifically concerned with such matters—to go beyond it and consider the possible influence of variations in hereditary equipment is a hazardous matter. The following pages will read very differently to one who has made a part of his thinking a recognition of the whole amazing mechanism of cultural conditioning—who has really accepted the fact that the same infant could be developed into a full participant in any one of these three cultures—than they will read to one who still believes that the minutiae of cultural behaviour are carried in the individual germ-plasm. If it is said, therefore, that when we have grasped the full significance of the malleability of the human organism and the preponderant importance of cultural conditioning, there are still further problems to solve, it must be remembered that these problems come *after* such a comprehension of the force of conditioning; they cannot precede it. The forces that make children born among the Arapesh grow up into typical Arapesh personalities are entirely social, and any discussion of the variations which do occur must be looked at against this social background.

With this warning firmly in mind, we can ask a further question. Granting the malleability of human nature, whence arise the differences between the standardized personalities that different cultures decree for all of their members, or which one culture decrees for the members of one sex as contrasted with the members of the opposite sex? If such differences are culturally created, as this material would most strongly suggest that they are, if the new-born child can be shaped with equal ease into an unaggressive Arapesh or an aggressive Mundugumor, why do these striking contrasts occur at all? If the clues to the different personalities decreed for men and women in Tchambuli do not lie in the physical constitution of the two sexes—an assumption that we must reject both for the Tchambuli and for our own society—where can we find the clues upon which the Tchambuli, the Arapesh, the Mundugumor, have built? Cultures are man-made, they are built of human materials; they are diverse but comparable structures within which human beings can attain full human stature. Upon what have they built their diversities?

We recognize that a homogeneous culture committed in all of its gravest institutions and slightest usages to a co-operative, unaggressive course can bend every child to that emphasis, some to a perfect accord with it, the majority to an easy acceptance, while only a few deviants fail to receive the cultural imprint. To consider such traits as aggressiveness or passivity to be sex-linked is not possible in the light of the facts. Have such traits, then, as aggressiveness or passivity, pride or humility, objectivity or a preoccupation with personal relationships, an easy response to the needs of the young and the weak or a hostility to the young and the weak, a tendency to initiate sex-relations or merely to respond to the dictates of a situation or another person's advances—have these traits any basis in temperament at all? Are they potentialities of all human temperaments that can be developed by different kinds of social conditioning and which will not appear if the necessary conditioning is absent?

When we ask this question we shift our emphasis. If we ask why an Arapesh man or an Arapesh woman shows the kind of personality that we have considered in the first section of this book, the answer is: Because of the Arapesh culture, because of the intricate, elaborate, and unfailing fashion in which a culture is able to shape each new-born child to the cultural image. And if we ask the same question about a Mundugumor man or woman, or about a Tchambuli man as compared with a Tchambuli woman, the answer is of the same kind. They display the personalities that are peculiar to the cultures in which they were born and educated. Our attention has been on the differences between Arapesh men and women as a group and Mundugumor men and women as a group. It is as if we had represented the Arapesh personality by a soft yellow, the Mundugumor by a deep red, while the Tchambuli female personality was deep orange, and that of the Tchambuli male, pale green. But if we now ask whence came the original direction in each culture, so that one now shows yellow, another red, the third orange and green by sex, then we must peer more closely. And learning closer to the picture, it is as if behind the bright consistent yellow of the Arapesh, and the deep equally consistent red of the Mundugumor, behind the orange and green that are Tchambuli, we found in each case the delicate, just discernible outlines of the whole spectrum, differently overlaid in each case by the monotone which covers it. This spectrum is the range of individual differences which lie back of the so much more conspicuous cultural emphases, and it is to this that we must turn to find the explanation of cultural inspiration, of the source from which each culture has drawn.

There appears to be about the same range of basic temperamental variation among the Arapesh and among the Mundugumor, although the violent man is a misfit in the first society and a leader in the second. If human nature were completely homogeneous raw material, lacking specific drives and characterized by no important constitutional differences between individuals, then individuals who display personality traits so antithetical to the social pressure should not reappear in societies of such differing emphases. If the variations between individuals were to be set down to accidents in the genetic process, the same accidents should not be repeated with similar frequency in strikingly different cultures, with strongly contrasting methods of education.

But because this same relative distribution of individual differences does appear in culture after culture, in spite of the divergence between the cultures, it seems pertinent to offer a hypothesis to explain upon what basis the personalities of men and women have been differently standardized so often in the history of the human race. This hypothesis is an extension of that advanced by Ruth Benedict in her *Patterns of Culture.* Let us assume that there are definite temperamental differences between human beings which if not entirely hereditary at least are established on a hereditary base very soon after birth. (Further than this we cannot at present narrow the matter.) These differences finally embodied in the character structure of adults, then, are the clues from which culture works, selecting one temperament, or a combination of related and congruent types, as desirable, and embodying this choice in every thread of the social fabric—in the care of the young child, the games the children play, the songs the people sing, the structure of political organization, the religious observance, the art and the philosophy.

Some primitive societies have had the time and the robustness to revamp all of their institutions to fit one extreme type, and to develop educational techniques which will ensure that the majority of each generation will show a personality congruent with this extreme emphasis. Other societies have pursued a less definitive course, selecting their models not from the most extreme, most highly differentiated individuals, but from the less marked types. In such societies the approved personality is less pronounced, and the culture often contains the types of inconsistencies that many human beings display also; one institution may be adjusted to the uses of pride, another to a casual humility that is congruent neither with pride nor with inverted pride. Such societies, which have taken the more usual and less sharply defined types as models, often show also a less definitely patterned social structure. The culture of such societies may be likened to a house the decoration of which has been informed by no definite and precise taste, no exclusive emphasis upon dignity or comfort or pretentiousness or beauty, but in which a little of each effect has been included.

Alternatively, a culture may take its clues not from one temperament, but from several temperaments. But instead of mixing together into an inconsistent hotchpotch the choices and emphases of different temperaments, or blending them together into a smooth but not particularly distinguished whole, it may isolate each type by making it the basis for the approved social personality for an age-group, a sex-group, a caste-group, or an occupational group. In this way society becomes not a monotone with a few discrepant patches of an intrusive colour, but a mosaic, with different groups displaying different personality traits. Such specializations as these may be based upon any facet of human endowment—different intellectual abilities, different artistic abilities, different emotional traits. So the Samoans decree that all young people must show the personality trait of unaggressiveness and punish with opprobrium the aggressive child who displays traits regarded as appropriate only in titled middle-aged men. In societies based upon elaborate ideas of rank, members of the aristocracy will be permitted, even compelled, to display a pride, a sensitivity to insult, that would be deprecated as inappropriate in members of the plebeian class. So also in professional groups or in religious sects some temperamental traits are selected and institutionalized, and taught to each new member who enters the profession or sect. Thus the physician learns the bedside manner, which is the natural behaviour of some temperaments and the standard behaviour of the general practitioner in the medical profession; the Quaker learns at least the outward behaviour and the rudiments of meditation, the capacity for which is not necessarily an innate characteristic of many of the members of the Society of Friends.

So it is with the social personalities of the two sexes. The traits that occur in some members of each sex are specially assigned to one sex, and disallowed in the other. The history of the social definition of sex-differences is filled with such arbitrary arrangements in the intellectual and artistic field, but because of the assumed congruence between physiological sex and emotional endowment we have been less able to recognize that a similar arbitrary selection is being made among emotional traits also. We have assumed that because it is convenient for a mother to wish to care for her child, this is a trait with which women have been more generously endowed by a carefully teleological process of evolution. We have assumed that because men have hunted, an activity requiring enterprise, bravery, and initiative, they have been endowed with these useful attitudes as part of their sex-temperament.

Societies have made these assumptions both overtly and implicitly. If a society insists that warfare is the major occupation for the male sex, it is therefore insisting that all male children display bravery and pugnacity. Even if the insistence upon the differential bravery of men and women is not made articulate, the difference in occupation makes this point implicitly. When, however, a society goes further and defines men as brave and women as timorous, when men are forbidden to show fear and women are indulged in the most flagrant display of fear, a more explicit element enters in. Bravery, hatred of any weakness, of flinching before pain or danger—this attitude which is so strong a component of *some human* temperaments has been selected as the key to masculine behaviour. The easy unashamed display of fear or suffering that is congenial to a different temperament has been made the key to feminine behaviour.

Originally two variations of human temperament, a hatred of fear or willingness to display fear, they have been socially translated into inalienable aspects of the personalities of the two sexes. And to that defined sex-personality every child will be educated, if a boy, to suppress fear, if a girl, to show it. If there has been no social selection in regard to this trait, the proud temperament that is repelled by any betrayal of feeling will display itself, regardless of sex, by keeping a stiff upper lip. Without an express prohibition of such behaviour the expressive unashamed man or woman will weep, or comment upon fear or suffering. Such attitudes, strongly marked in certain temperaments, may by social selection be standardized for everyone, or outlawed for everyone, or ignored by society, or made the exclusive and approved behaviour of one sex only.

Neither the Arapesh nor the Mundugumor have made any attitude specific for one sex. All of the energies of the culture have gone towards the creation of a single human type, regardless of class, age, or sex. There is no division into age-classes for which different motives or different moral attitudes are regarded as suitable. There is no class of seers or mediums who stand apart drawing inspiration from psychological sources not available to the majority of the people. The Mundugumor have, it is true, made one arbitrary selection, in that they recognize artistic ability only among individuals born with the cord about their necks, and firmly deny the happy exercise of artistic ability to those less unusually born. The Arapesh boy with a tinea infection has been socially selected to be a disgruntled, antisocial individual, and the society forces upon sunny co-operative children cursed with this affliction a final approximation to the behaviour appropriate to a pariah. With these two exceptions no emotional role is forced upon an individual because of birth or accident. As there is no idea of rank which declares that some are of high estate and some of low, so there is no idea of sex-difference which declares that one sex must feel differently from the other. One possible imaginative social construct, the attribution of different personalities to different members of the community classified into sex-, age-, or caste-groups, is lacking.

When we turn however to the Tchambuli, we find a situation that while bizarre in one respect, seems nevertheless more intelligible in another. The Tchambuli have at least made the point of sex-difference; they have used the obvious fact of sex as an organizing point for the formation of social personality, even though they seem to us to have reversed the normal picture. While there is reason to believe that not every Tchambuli woman is born with a dominating, organizing, administrative temperament, actively sexed and willing to initiate sex-relations, possessive, definite, robust, practical and impersonal in outlook, still most Tchambuli girls grow up to display these traits. And while there is definite evidence to show that all Tchambuli men are not, by native endowment, the delicate responsive actors of a play staged for the women's benefit, still most Tchambuli boys manifest this coquettish play-acting personality most of the time. Because the Tchambuli formulation of sex-attitudes contradicts our usual premises, we can see clearly that Tchambuli culture has arbitrarily permitted certain human traits to women, and allotted others, equally arbitrarily, to men.

GILBERT HERDT

Coming of Age and Coming Out Ceremonies Across Cultures

Coming of age and being socialized into the sexual lifeways of the culture through ceremonies and initiation rites are common in many cultures of the world. These traditions help to incorporate the individual—previously a child, possibly outside of the moral rules and sexual roles of the adult group—into the public institutions and practices that bring full citizenship. We have seen in prior chapters many examples of these transitions and ceremonial practices, and we are certainly justified in thinking of them as basic elements in the human condition. Coming of age or "puberty" ceremonies around the world are commonly assumed to introduce the young person to sexual life as a heterosexual. In both traditional and modern societies, ritual plays a role in the emergence of sexuality and the support of desires and relationships expected in later life.

Yet not all of this is seamless continuity, and in the study of homosexuality across cultures we must be aware of the gaps and barriers that exist between what is experienced in childhood or adolescence and the roles and customs in adulthood that may negate or oppose these experiences. Ruth Benedict (1938) stresses how development in a society may create cultural discontinuities in this sexual and gender cycle of identities and roles, necessitating rituals. She hints that homosexuality in particular may cause discontinuity of this kind, and the life stories of many gays and lesbians in western society reveal this problem. But in all societies, there is an issue of connecting childhood with adulthood, with the transition from sexual or biological immaturity to sexual maturity. In short, these transitions may create a "life crisis" that requires a social solution—and this is the aim of initiation ceremonies and rites of transition. Rituals may provide for the individual the necessary means to achieve difficult changes in sexual and gender status. Particularly in deeply emotional rituals, the energy of the person can be fully invested or bonded to the newfound group. This may create incredible attachments of the kind we have observed among the ancient Greeks, the feudal Japanese, and the Sambia of New Guinea, wherein the younger boy is erotically involved or partnered with an older male. In the conditions of a warrior society, homoerotic partnerships are particularly powerful when they are geared to the survival of the group.

The transition out of presumptive heterosexuality and secrecy and into the active process of self-identifying as gay or lesbian in the western tradition bears close comparison with these rites of passage. In the process of "coming out"—the current western concept of ritual passage—as gay or lesbian, a person undergoes emotional changes and a transformation in sexuality and gender that are remarkable and perhaps equal in their social drama to the initiation rites of small societies in New Guinea and Africa. Thus, the collective aspirations and desires of the adolescent or child going through the ritual to belong, participate in, and make commitments to communities of his or her own kind take on a new and broader scope.

Coming out is an implicit rite of passage for people who are in a crisis of identity that finds them "betwixt and between" being presumed to be heterosexual and living a totally secret and hidden life as a homosexual. Not until they enter into the gay or lesbian lifeway or the sexual culture of the gay and lesbian community will they begin to learn and be socialized into the rules, knowledge, and social roles and relationships of the new cultures. For many people, this experience is liberating; it is a highly charged, emotional, and dramatic process that changes them into adult gays or lesbians in all areas of their lives—with biological families, with coworkers, with friends or schoolmates, and with a sexual and romantic partner the same gender, possibly for the rest of their lives.

This transformation in the self and in social relations brings much that is new and sometimes frightening. An alternative moral system is opened up by the rituals. Why people who desire the same gender require a ritual when others in our society do not is painfully clear. Ritual is necessary because of the negative images, stigma, and intense social contamination that continue to exist in the stereotypes and antihomosexual laws of our society. To be homosexual is to be discredited as a full person in society; it is to have a spoiled identity—as a homosexual in society or as a frightened closet homosexual who may be disliked by openly gay and lesbian friends. But perhaps of greatest importance are the repression and social censorship involved: to have one's desires suppressed, to even experience the inner or "true" self as a secret.

It is hard to break through this taboo alone or without the support of a community because doing so exposes the person to all sorts of risk, requires considerable personal resources, and precipitates an emotional vulnerability that for many is very difficult to bear. But that is not all. For some people in our society, homosexuality is a danger and a source of pollution. Once the person's homosexuality is revealed, the stigma can also spread to the family, bringing the pollution of shame and dishonor to father and mother, clan and community. This is the old mask of the evil of homosexuality. . . . And this is what we have found in a study of these matters in Chicago (Herdt and Boxer 1996).

It is very typical to see an intense and negative reaction of family members to the declaration of same-sex desires by adolescents, even this late in the twentieth century. Society changes slowly and its myths even more slowly. For many people, homosexuality is an evil as frightening to the imagination as the monsters of bad Hollywood movies. Many people find it extremely difficult to deal with homosexuality and may exert strong pressures on their young to hide and suppress their feelings. Consequently, young people may feel that by declaring their same-sex desires, they will betray their families or the traditions of their sexual culture and its lifeways, which privilege marriage and the carrying on of the family name. And the younger person who desires the same gender may be afraid to come out for fear of dishonoring his or her ethnic community in the same way. To prevent these reactions, many people—closet homosexuals in the last century and many who fear the effects today—hide their basic feelings and all of their desires from their friends and families.

Here is where we may learn a lesson from other cultures. The mechanism of ritual helps to teach about the trials and ordeals of passages in other times and places, which in itself is a comfort, for it signals something basic in the human condition. To come out is to openly challenge sexual chauvinism, homophobia, and bias—refusing to continue the stigma and pollution of the past and opening new support and positive role models where before there were none. Through examples from New Guinea, the Mojave, and the Chicago gay and lesbian group, I examine these ideas in the following pages.

Many cultures around the world celebrate coming of age with a variety of events and rituals that introduce the person to sexual life. Indeed, initiation can be an introduction to sexual development and erotic life (Hart 1963). In Aboriginal Australia and New Guinea wherever the precolonial secret societies of the region flourished, the nature of all sexual interaction was generally withheld from prepubertal boys and girls until initiation. It often began their sense of sexual being, even if they had not achieved sexual puberty, since maturation often occurred late in these societies. Many of the Pacific societies actually disapproved of childhood sexual play, for this was felt to disrupt marriage and social regulation of premarital social relations. The Sambia are no different, having delayed sexual education until the initiation of boys and girls in different secret contexts for each. The stories of Sambia boys are clear in associating the awakening of their sexuality in late childhood with their initiation rites and fellatio debut with adolescent bachelor partners. The definition of social reality was thus opened up to same-gender sexuality.

SAMBIA BOYS' RITUAL INITIATION

The Sambia are a tribe numbering more than two thousand people in the Eastern Highlands of Papua New Guinea. Most elements of culture and social organization are constructed around the nagging destructive presence of warfare in the area. Descent is patrilineal and residence is patrilocal to maximize the cohesion of the local group as a warriorhood. Hamlets are composed of tiny exogamous patriclans that facilitate marriage within the group and exchange with other hamlets, again based on the local politics of warfare. Traditionally, all marriage was arranged; courtship is unknown, and social relationships between the sexes are not only ritually polarized but also often hostile. Like other Highlands societies of New Guinea, these groups are associated with a men's secret society that ideologically disparages women as dangerous creatures who can pollute men and deplete them of their masculine substance. The means of creating and maintaining the village-based secret society is primarily through the ritual initiation of boys beginning at ages seven through ten and continuing until their arranged and consummated marriages, many years later. The warriorhood is guaranteed by collective ritual initiations connecting neighboring hamlets. Within a hamlet, this warriorhood is locally identified with the men's clubhouse, wherein all initiated bachelors reside. Married men frequent the clubhouse constantly; and on occasion (during fight times, rituals, or their wives' menstrual periods) they sleep there. An account of Sambia culture and society has been published elsewhere and need not be repeated here (Herdt 1981).

Sambia sexual culture, which operates on the basis of a strongly essentializing model of sexual development, also incorporates many ideas of social support and cultural creation of the sexual; these ideas derive from the role of ritual and supporting structures of gendered ontologies throughout the life course of men and women. Sexual development, according to the cultural ideals of the Sambia life plan, is fundamentally distinct for men and women. Biological femaleness is considered "naturally" competent and innately complete; maleness, in contrast, is considered more problematic since males are believed incapable of achieving adult reproductive manliness without ritual treatment. Girls are born with female genitalia, a birth canal, a womb, and, behind that, a functional menstrual-blood organ, or *tingu*. Feminine behaviors such as gardening and mothering are thought to be by-products of women's natural *tingu* functioning. As the *tingu* and womb become engorged with blood, puberty and menarche occur; the menses regularly follow, and they are linked with women's child-bearing capacities. According to the canonical male view, all women then need is a penis (i.e., semen) in facilitating adult procreation by bestowing breast milk (transformed from semen), which prepares a woman for nursing her newborn. According to the women's point of view, however, women are biologically competent and can produce their own breast milk—a point of conflict between the two gendered ontologies. This gives rise to a notion that women have a greater internal resilience and health than males and an almost inexhaustible sexual appetite. By comparison, males are not competent biologically until they achieve manhood, and thus they require constant interventions of ritual to facilitate maturation.

The Sambia believe that boys will not "naturally" achieve adult competence without the interventions of ritual, an idea that may seem strange but is actually common throughout New Guinea, even in societies that do not practice boy-inseminating rites (Herdt 1993). Among the Sambia, the practice of age-structured homoerotic relations is a transition into adulthood. The insemination of boys ideally ends when a man marries and fathers a child. In fact, the vast majority of males—more than 90 percent—terminate their sexual relations with boys at that time. Almost all the men do so because of the taboos and, to a lesser degree, because they have "matured" to a new level of having exclusive sexual access to one or more wives, with genital sexual pleasure being conceived of as a greater privilege.

The sexual culture of the Sambia men instills definite and customary lifeways that involves a formula for the life course. Once initiated (before age ten), the boys undergo ordeals to have their "female" traces (left over from birth and from living with their mothers) removed; these ordeals involve painful rites, such as nose-bleedings, that are intended to promote masculinity and aggression. The boys are then in a ritually "clean" state that enables the treatment of their bodies and minds in new ways. These boys are regarded as "pure" sexual virgins, which is important for their insemination. The men believe that the boys are unspoiled because they have not been exposed to the sexual pollution of women, which the men greatly fear. It is thus through oral intercourse that the men receive a special kind of pleasure, unfettered by pollution, and the boys are thought to acquire semen for growth, becoming strong and fertile. All the younger males are thus inseminated by older bachelors, who were once themselves semen recipients.

The younger initiates are semen recipients until their third-stage "puberty" ceremony, around age fifteen. Afterward, they become semen donors to the younger boys. According to the men's sacred lore and the dogmas of their secret society, the bachelors are "married" to the younger recipient males—as symbolized by secret ritual flutes, made of bamboo and believed to be empowered by female spirits that are said to be hostile to women. During this time, the older adolescents are "bisexuals" who may inseminate their wives orally, in addition to the secret insemination of the boys. Eventually these youths have marriages arranged for them. After they become new fathers, they in turn stop sexual relations with boys. The men's family duties would be compromised by boy relations, the Sambia men say.

The growth of males is believed to be slower and more difficult than that of females. Men say that boys lack an endogenous means for creating manliness. Males do possess a *tingu* (menstrual blood) organ, but it is believed to be "dry" and nonfunctional. They reiterate that a mother's womb, menstrual blood, and vaginal fluids—all containing pollution—impede masculine growth for the boy until he is separated by initiation from mother and the women's world. Males also possess a semen organ (*keriku-keriku*), but unlike the female menstrual blood organ, it is intrinsically small, hard, and empty, containing no semen of its own. Although semen is believed to be the spark of human life and, moreover, the sole precipitant of biological maleness (strong bones and muscles and, later, male secondary-sex traits: a flat abdomen, a hairy body, a mature glans penis), the Sambia hold that the human body cannot naturally produce semen; it must be externally introduced. The purpose of ritual insemination through fellatio is to fill up the *keriku-keriku* (which then stores semen for adult use) and thereby masculinize the boy's body as well as his phallus. Biological maleness is therefore distinct from the mere possession of male genitalia, and only repeated inseminations begun at an early age and regularly continued for years confer the reproductive competence that culminates in sexual development and manliness.

There are four functions of semen exchange: (1) the cultural purpose of "growing" boys through insemination, which is thought to substitute for mother's milk; (2) the "masculinizing" of boys' bodies, again through insemination, but also through ritual ordeals meant to prepare them for warrior life; (3) the provision of "sexual play" or pleasure for the older youths, who have no other sexual outlet prior to marriage; and (4) the transmission of semen and soul substance from one generation of clansmen to the next, which is vital for spiritual and ritual power to achieve its rightful ends (Herdt 1984b). These elements of institutionalized boy-inseminating practices are the object of the most vital and secret ritual teachings in first-stage initiation, which occurs before puberty. The novices are expected to be orally inseminated during the rituals and to continue the practice on a regular basis for years to come. The semen transactions are, however, rigidly structured homoerotically: Novices may act only as fellators in private sexual interactions with older bachelors, who are typically seen as dominant and in control of the same-sex contacts. The adolescent youth is the erotically active party during fellatio, for his erection and ejaculation are necessary for intercourse, and a boy's oral insemination is the socially prescribed outcome of the encounter. Boys must never reverse roles with the older partners or take younger partners before the proper ritual initiations. The violation of such rules is a moral wrong that is sanctioned by a variety of punishments. Boy-inseminating, then, is a matter of sexual relations between unrelated kin and must be seen in the same light as the semen exchanges of delayed sister exchange marriage: Hamlets of potential enemies exchange women and participate in semen exchange of boys, which is necessary for the production of children and the maturation of new warriors.

Ritual initiation for boys is conducted every three or four years for a whole group of boys as an age-set from neighboring villages. This event lasts several months and consists of many ordeals and transitions, some of them frightening and unpleasant, but overall welcomed as the entry into honorable masculinity and access to social power. It culminates in the boys' entry into the men's clubhouse, which is forbidden to women and children. The boys change their identities and roles and live on their own away from their parents until they are grown up and married. The men's house thus becomes their permanent dormitory and secret place of gender segregation.

Sambia girls do not experience initiation until many years later, when they undergo a formal marriage ceremony. Based on what is known, it seems doubtful that the girls undergo a sexual period of same-gender relations like those of the boys, but I cannot be sure because I was not permitted to enter the menstrual hut, where the initiations of girls were conducted. Males begin their ritual careers and the change in their sexual lives early because the transformation expected of the boys is so great. Girls live on with their parents until they are married and achieve their first menstruation, which occurs very late, age nineteen on average for the Sambia and their neighbors. A secret initiation is performed for the girls in the menstrual hut. Only then can they begin to have sexual relations with their husbands and live with them in a new house built by husband and wife.

The first-stage initiation ceremonies begin the events of life crisis and change in identities for the boys. They are young. After a period of time they are removed to the forest, where the most critical rituals begin to introduce them to the secrets of the men's house and the secret society of the men's warriorhood. The key events involve blood-letting rituals and penis-and-flute rites, which we study here from observations of the initiation conducted in 1975 (Herdt 1982). Here the boys experience the revelation of sexuality and the basic elements of their transition into age-structured homoerotic relations.

On the first morning of the secret rituals in the forest, the boys have fierce and painful nosebleeding rituals performed on them. This is believed to remove the pollution of their mothers and the women's world that is identified with the boys' bodies. But it is also a testing ground to see how brave they are and the degree to which their fathers, older brothers, and the war leaders of the village can rely on the boys not to run and hide in times of war. Afterward, the boys are prepared by their ritual guardian, who is referred to as their "mother's brother," a kind of "male mother," for the main secret teaching that is to follow. They are dressed in the finest warrior decorations, which they have earned the right to wear through the initiation ordeals. And this begins their preparation for the rites of insemination that will follow. Now that their insides have been "cleansed" to receive the magical gift of manhood—semen—they are taken into the sacred chamber of a forest setting, and there they see for the first time the magical flutes, believed to be animated by the female spirit of the flute, which protects the men and the secrecy of the clubhouse and is thought to be hostile to women.

The key ceremony here is the penis-and-flutes ritual. It focuses on a secret teaching about boy insemination and is regarded by the men and boys alike as the most dramatic and awesome of all Sambia rituals. It begins with the older bachelors, the youths with whom the boys will engage in sexual relations later, who enter the chamber dressed up as the "female spirits of the flutes." The flute players appear, and in their presence, to the accompaniment of the wailing flutes, some powerful secrets of the men's cult are revealed. The setting is awesome: a great crowd waiting in silence as the mysterious sounds are first revealed; boys obediently lining up for threatening review by elders; and boys being told that secret fellatio exists and being taught how to engage in it. Throughout the ritual boys hear at close range the flute sounds associated since childhood with collective masculine power and mystery and pride. The flutes are unequivocally treated as phallic—as symbols of the penis and the power of men to openly flaunt their sexuality. The intent of the flutes' revelation is threatening to the boys as they begin to guess its meaning.

I have observed this flute ceremony during two different initiations, and although my western experience differs greatly from that of Sambia, one thing was intuitively striking to me: The men were revealing the *homoerotic meanings* of the sexual culture. This includes a great preoccupation with the penis and with semen but also with the mouth of the boy and penile erection, sexual impulses, homoerotic activities in particular, and the commencement of sexuality in its broadest sense for the boys. If there is a homoerotic core to the secret society of the Sambia, then this is surely where it begins. These revelations come as boys are enjoined to become fellators, made the sharers of ritual secrets, and threatened with death if they tell women or children what they have learned. They have to keep the secret forever.

Over the course of many years I collected the stories of the boys' experiences as they went through these rituals. The boys' comments indicated that they perceived several different social values bound up with the expression of homoerotic instruction in the flute ceremony. A good place to begin is with childhood training regarding shame about one's genitals. Here is Kambo, a boy who was initiated, talking about his own experience: "I thought—not good that they [elders] are lying or just playing a trick. That's [the penis] not for eating. . . . When I was a child our fathers said, 'This [penis] is not for handling; if you hold it you'll become lazy.' And because of that [at first in the cult house] I felt—it's not for sucking." Childhood experience is a contributing source of shame about fellatio: Children are taught to avoid handling their own genitals. In a wider sense Kambo's remark pertains to the taboo on masturbation, the sexual naïveté of children, and the boys' prior lack of knowledge about their fathers' homosexual activities.

Another key ritual story concerns the nutritive and "growth" values of semen. A primary source of this idea is men's ritual equation of semen with mother's breast milk, as noted before. The initiates take up this idea quickly in their own subjective orientations toward fellatio. (Pandanus nuts, like coconut, are regarded as another equivalent of semen.) The following remark by Moondi is a typical example of such semen identifications in the teachings of the flute ceremony: "The 'juice' of the pandanus nuts, . . . it's the same as the 'water' of a man, the same as a man's 'juice' [semen]. And I like to eat a lot of it [because it can give me more water], . . . for the milk of women is also the same as the milk of men. Milk [breast milk] is for when she carries a child—it belongs to the infant who drinks it." The association between semen and the infant's breast food is also explicit in this observation by Gaimbako, a second-stage initiate: "Semen is the same kind as that [breast milk] of women. . . . It's the very same kind as theirs, . . . the same as pandanus nuts too. . . . But when milk [semen] falls into my mouth [during fellatio], I think it's the milk of women." So the boys are taught beliefs that are highly motivating in support of same-gender sexual relations.

But the ritual also creates in boys a new awareness about their subordination to the older men. Kambo related this thought as his immediate response to the penis teaching of the flute ceremony: "I was afraid of penis. It's the same as mine—why should I eat it? It's the same kind; [our penises are] only one kind. We're men, not *different* kinds." This supposition is fundamental and implied in many boys' understandings. Kambo felt that males are of one kind, that is, "one sex," as distinct from females. This implies tacit recognition of the sameness of men, which ironically suggests that they should be not sexually involved but in competition for the other gender. Remember, too, the coercive character of the setting: The men's attempt to have boys suck the flutes is laden with overt hostility, much stronger than the latent hostility expressed in lewd homosexual jokes made during the preceding body decoration. The boys are placed in a sexually subordinate position, a fact that is symbolically communicated in the idiom that the novices are "married" to the flutes. (Novices suck the small flute, which resembles the mature glans penis, the men say.) The men thus place the boys in an invidious state of subordination during which the boys may sense that they are being treated too much like women. Sometimes this makes them panic and creates fear and shame. In time, however, a different feeling about the practice sets in.

Nearly all the novices perform their first act of fellatio during the days of initiation, and their story helps us to understand what happens later in their masculine development. Let me cite several responses of Moondi to this highly emotional act:

> I was wondering what they [elders] were going to do to us. And . . . I felt afraid. What will they do to us next? But they put the bamboo in and out of the mouth; and I wondered, what are they doing? Then, when they tried out our mouths, I began to understand . . . that they were talking about the penis. Oh, that little bamboo is the penis of the men. . . . My whole body was afraid, completely afraid, . . . and I was heavy, I wanted to cry.
>
> At that point my thoughts went back to how I used to think it was the *aatmwogwambu* [flute spirit], but then I knew that the men did it [made the sounds]. And . . . I felt a little better, for before [I thought that] the aatmwogwambu would get me. But now I saw that they [the men] did it.
>
> They told us the penis story. . . . Then I thought a lot, as my thoughts raced quickly. I was afraid—not good that the men "shoot" me [penetrate my mouth] and break my neck. Aye! Why should they put that [penis] inside our mouths! It's not a good thing. They all hide it [the penis] inside their grass skirts, and it's got lots of hair too!
>
> "You must listen well," the elders said. "You all won't grow by yourselves; if you sleep with the men you'll become a *strong* man." They said that; I was afraid. . . . And then they told us clearly: semen is inside—and when you hold a man's penis, you must put it inside your mouth—he can give you semen. . . . It's the same as your mother's breast milk.
>
> "This is no lie!" the men said. "You can't go tell the children, your sisters." . . . And then later I tried it [fellatio], and I thought: Oh, they told us about *aamoonaalyi* [breast milk; Moondi means semen]—it [semen] is in there.

Despite great social pressures, some boys evince a low interest in the practice from the start, and they seldom participate in fellatio. Some novices feverishly join in. Those are the extremes. The great majority of Sambia boys regularly engage in fellatio for years as constrained by taboo. Homoerotic activities are a touchy subject among males for many reasons. These activities begin with ceremony, it is true, but their occurrence and meaning fan out to embrace a whole secret way of life. What matters is that the boys become sharers of this hidden tradition; and we should expect them to acquire powerful feelings about bachelors, fellatio, semen, and the whole male sexual culture.

One story must stand for many in the way that the Sambia boys grow into this sexual lifeway. One day, while I was talking idly with Kambo, he mentioned singing to himself as he walked in the forest. I asked him what he sang about; and from this innocuous departure point, he said this: "When I think of men's name songs then I sing them: that of a bachelor who is sweet on me; a man of another line or my own line. When I sing the song of a creek in the forest I am happy about that place. . . . Or some man who sleeps with me—when he goes elsewhere, I sing his song. I think of that man who gave me a lot of semen; later, I must sleep with him. I feel like this: he gave me a lot of water [semen]. . . . Later, I will have a lot of water like him."

Here we see established in Kambo's thought the male emphasis on "accumulating semen" and the powerful homoerotic relationships that accompany it. Even a simple activity like singing can create a mood of subjective association with past fellatio and same-gender relationships with the older males. Kambo's last sentence contains a wish: that he will acquire abundant manliness, like that of the friend of whom he sings.

No issue in recent reviews has inspired more debate than the basic question of whether—or to what extent—sexual feelings and erotic desires are motives or consequences of these cultural practices. Does the Sambia boy desire sexual intercourse with the older male? Is the older male sexually attracted to the boy? Indeed, what does "erotic" or "sexual" mean in this context, and is "desire" the proper concept with which to gauge the ontology? Or do other factors, such as power or kinship, produce the sexual attraction and excitement (conscious or unconscious) necessary to produce arousal and uphold the tradition (Herdt 1991)?

Although Sambia culture requires that men eventually change their focus to marriage and give up boy-inseminating, some of the men continue to practice age-structured relations because they find them so pleasurable. A small number of individual men enjoy inseminating boys too much to give up the practice. They develop favorites among the boys and even resort to payment of meat when they find it difficult to obtain a boy who will service them. In our culture these men would probably be called homosexuals because of their preference for the boys, their desires, and their need to mask their activities within the secret domain of ritual. But such an identity of homosexual or gay does not exist for the Sambia, and we must be careful not to project these meanings onto them, for that would be ethnocentric. We can, however, see how they live and what it means to have such an experience—in the absence of the sexual identity system of western culture.

One of these men, Kalutwo, has been interviewed by me over a long period of time, and his sexual and social history reveals a pattern of broken, childless marriages and an exclusive attraction to boys. As he got older, he would have to "pay" the boys with gifts to engage in sex, but when he was younger, some of the boys were known to be fond of him as well (Herdt and Stoller 1990). Several other males are different from Kalutwo in liking boys but also liking women and being successfully married with children. They would be called bisexual in our society. They seem to enjoy sexual pleasure with women and take pride in making babies through their wives, yet they continue illicitly to enjoy oral sex with boys. But Kalutwo disliked women sexually and generally preferred the closeness, sexual intimacy, and emotional security of young men and boys. As he got older, it was increasingly difficult for him to obtain boys as sexual partners, and this seemed to make him feel depressed. Moreover, as he got older, he was increasingly at odds with his male peers socially and stood out from the crowd, having no wife or children, as expected of customary adult manhood. Some people made fun of him behind his back; so did some of the boys. In a society that had a homosexual role, Kalutwo might have found more social support or comfort and perhaps might have been able to make a different transition into middle age. But his village still accepts him, and he has not been turned away or destroyed—as might have occurred in another time had he lived in a western country.

Perhaps in these cases we begin to understand the culture of male camaraderie and emotional intimacy that created such deeply felt desire for same-gender relations in ancient Greece and Japan, in which sexual pleasures and social intimacies with the same gender were as prized as those of intercourse and family life with women. No difficulty was posed to society or to self-esteem so long as these men met their social and sexual obligations and were honorable in their relations with younger males. We know from the anthropological reports from New Guinea that such individuals existed elsewhere as well, and among the Malekula and Marind-anim tribes, for example, adult married men would continue such relations with boys even after reaching the age of being grandfathers in the group, for this was expected.

MOJAVE TWO-SPIRIT INITIATION

My reading of the gender-transformed role among American Indians has shown the importance of two spirits in Native American society for the broader understanding of alternative sexualities. What I have not established thus far is the development of the role in the life of the individual. Among the Mojave Indians, a special ceremony in late childhood marked a transition into the third-gender role that allowed for homoerotic relations so long as they were between people in different gender roles. The two spirit was the product of a long cultural history that involved myth and ceremonial initiation. The ceremonies were sacred and of such importance that their official charter was established in the origin myths of the tribe, known from time immemorial. The meanings of this transition deserve to be highlighted as another variation on coming of age ceremonies in nonwestern cultures.

The Mojave child was only about ten years old when he participated in the ceremony for determining whether a change to two spirit would occur. Perhaps this seems young for a coming of age ceremony; but it might be that the very degree of change and the special nature of the desires to become a man-woman required a childhood transition. In the Mojave case, it was said that a Mojave boy could act "strangely" at the time, turning away from male tasks and refusing the toys of his own sex. The parents would view this as a sign of personal and gender change. Recall that mothers had dreams that their sons would grow up to become two spirits. No doubt this spiritual sign helped to lend religious support for the ceremony. At any rate these signs of gender change were said by the Mojave to express the "true" intentions of the child to change into a man-woman. Nahwera, a Mojave elder, stated: "When there is a desire in a child's heart to become a transvestite that child will act different. It will let people become aware of that desire" (Devereux 1937, 503). Clearly, the child was beginning to act on desires that transgressed his role and required an adjustment, through ritual, to a new kind of being and social status in the culture.

Arrangements for the ceremony were made by the parents. The boy was reported to have been "surprised" by being offered "female apparel," whereon the relatives waited nervously to see his response. Devereux reported that this was considered both an initiation and an ultimate test of the child's true desires. "If he submitted to it, he was considered a genuine homosexual. . . . If the boy acted in the expected fashion during the ceremony he was considered an initiated homosexual, if not, the gathering scattered, much to the relief of the boy's family" (Devereux 1937, 508). The story suggests that the parents in general may have been ambivalent about this change and may not have wanted it. Nevertheless, true to Mojave culture, they accepted the actions of the boy and supported his decision to become a two-spirit person. The Mojave thus allowed a special combination of a child's ontological being and the support of the family to find its symbolic expression in a ready-made institutionalized cultural practice. It only awaited the right individual and circumstances for the two-spirit person to emerge in each community in each generation.

Both the Sambia example of age-structured relations and the Mojave illustration of gender-transformed homosexuality reveal transitions in late childhood up to age ten. What is magical about age ten? It may be that certain critical developmental changes begin to occur around this time—desires and attractions that indicate the first real sexuality and growing sense of becoming a sexual person. In fact, our study in Chicago revealed that nine and one-half years for boys and ten years for girls were the average age when they were first attracted to the same gender (Herdt and Boxer 1996).

COMING OUT—GAY AND LESBIAN TEENS IN AMERICA

Ours is a culture that defines male and female as absolutely different and then goes to great lengths to deny having done so; American culture reckons "heterosexual" and "homosexual" as fundamentally distinctive kinds of "human nature" but then struggles to find a place for both. Although such gender dimorphism is common in the thinking of nonwestern peoples, the latter idea is rare in, even absent from, many cultures—including our own cultural ancestors, the ancient Greeks. The Greeks described people's sexual behaviors but not their being as homosexual or heterosexual. As we have seen, the Greeks did not place people in categories of sexuality or create sexual classifications that erased all other cultural and personality traits. In our society today this kind of thinking is common and permeates the great symbolic types that define personal being and social action in most spheres of our lives. For many heterosexuals, their worldview and life course goals remain focused on the greatest ritual of reproduction: the church-ordained marriage. And this leads to parenting and family formation. Many think of this ritual process as "good" in all of its aspects. Others see same-gender desire as an attack on that reproductive and moral order, a kind of crisis of gender and sexuality that requires the assertion of a mythical "family values," descended from nineteenth-century ideals, that are seldom relevant to heterosexuals today, let alone to gays and lesbians.

Coming out is another form of ritual that intensifies change in a young person's sexual identity development and social being. It gives public expression to desires long felt to be basic to the person's sexual nature but formerly hidden because of social taboos and homophobia. The process leads to many events that reach a peak in the person's young adult years, especially in the development of gay or lesbian selves, roles, and social relations. Coming out continues to unfold across the entire course of life: There is never really an end to the process for the simple reason that as gay or lesbian people age and their social situations change, they continue to express in new, relevant ways what it means to be gay or lesbian. Such a social and existential crisis of identity—acted out on the stage of the lesbian and gay community—links the social drama of American youths' experiences with those of tribal initiations, such as those of the Sambia and Mojave, played out in the traditional communities. Of course, these two kinds of drama are different and should not be confused, but they share the issues of handling same-gender desires in cultural context.

Two different processes are involved. First is the secretive act of "passing" as heterosexual, involving the lone individual in largely hidden social networks and secret social spaces. . . . In many towns and cities, especially unsophisticated and traditionally conservative areas of the country, the possibilities are only now emerging for gay/lesbian identification and social action. Second is the coming out in adolescence or young adulthood.

Initially the gay or lesbian grows up with the assumption of being heterosexual. As an awareness of same-gender desires emerges, a feeling of having to hide these desires and pretend otherwise, of acting straight, leads to many moments of secrecy. Later, however, sexual and social experiences may yield a divergent awareness and a desire to be open. What follows is a process of coming out—typically begun in urban centers, sometimes in high school, sometimes later, after the young person has left home for college, work, or the service—that leads to self-identification as gay or lesbian. Through these ritual steps of disclosure all kinds of new socialization and opportunities emerge, including entrance into the gay and lesbian community.

Being and doing gay life are provisioned by the rituals of coming out, and they open significant questions for thinking about youths in search of positive same-gender roles. American teenagers may seem less exotic to the gay or lesbian reader; but they are more of an oddity to the heterosexual adult community as they come out. To many in our own society, these youths look "queer" and "strange" and "diseased," attitudes that reflect historical stereotypes and cultural homophobia.

The growing visibility of the lesbian and gay movement in the United States has made it increasingly possible for people to disclose their desires and "come out" at younger ages. Over the past quarter century, the evidence suggests that the average age of the declaration of same-gender desires has gotten earlier—a lot earlier, as much as ten years earlier than it was in the 1970s—and is for the first time in history a matter of adolescent development. It is not a matter for everyone, of course, but increasingly for those who become aware and are lucky to have the opportunities to begin a new life. In our study of gay and lesbian self-identified youths in Chicago, we found that the average age for boys and girls' "coming out" was sixteen. But we also found that the earliest awareness of same-gender attraction begins at about age ten, which suggests that the desires are a part of the deeper being of the gay or lesbian person.

Gay and lesbian teenagers are growing up with all of the usual problems of our society, including the political, economic, and social troubles of our country, as well as the sexual and social awakening that typifies the adolescent experience. I have already noted how American society and western cultures in general have changed in the direction of more positive regard for gays. This does not mean, however, that the hatred and homophobia of the past are gone or that the secrecy and fear of passing have faded away. People still fear, and rightly so, the effects of coming out on their lives and safety, their well-being and jobs, their social standing and community prestige. These youths are opting to come out as openly lesbian or gay earlier in the life course than ever before in our society. Yet they experience the troubles of feeling themselves attracted to the same gender, with its taboos and sorrows of stigma and shame, not knowing what to do about it. Fortunately, the gay and lesbian culture provides new contexts of support; these youths have institutions and media that talk about it; they learn from adult role models that they can live relatively happy and rewarding lives with their desires.

We can study how one group of adolescents in Chicago has struggled with these issues while preparing for socialization and coming out in the context of the lesbian and gay community. The study of gay, lesbian, and bisexual youths in Chicago was located in the largest gay social services agency of the city, Horizons Community Services. Horizons was created in the early 1970s out of the gay liberation movement, and by 1979 it had founded a gay and lesbian youth group, one of the first in the United States. The agency is based in the gay neighborhood of the city, and it depends on volunteers and the goodwill and interest of friends of the agency. In recent years the youths have lead the Gay and Lesbian Pride Day Parade in Chicago and have become a symbol of social and political progress in gay culture in the city.

The Horizons study was organized around the youth group, for ages thirteen to twenty, but the average age of the youths interviewed in depth was about eighteen. We interviewed a total of 202 male and female youths of all backgrounds from the suburbs and inner city, white and black and brown. Many people of color and of diverse ethnic subcultures in Chicago have experienced racism and many forms of homophobia, and these have effectively barred their coming out. The group tries to find a place for all of these diverse adolescents; no one is turned away. Group meetings are coordinated by lesbian and gay adults, esteemed role models of the teens. They facilitate a discussion of a variety of topics, particularly in matters of the coming out process, such as fears and homophobic problems at school or home, and issues of special interest to the teens. The youth group has an active social life as well, hosting parties and organizing social events, such as the annual alternative gay and lesbian prom, held on the weekend of high school proms in Chicago, for the youth members.

Protecting teens from the risk of infection from AIDS is another key goal of Horizons' sponsorship of the youth group. AIDS has become an increasingly important element of the youth group discussions. "Safe sex" is promoted through educational material and special public speakers. In general, the socialization rituals of the group prepare the youths for their new status in the gay and lesbian community, and the rituals culminate in marching in the Gay and Lesbian Pride Day Parade every June.

The lesbian or gay youth is in the throes of moving through the symbolic "death" of the heterosexual identity and role and into the "rebirth" of their social being as gay. As a life crisis and a passage between the past and future, the person is betwixt and between normal social states, that is, between the heterosexual worlds of parents and the cultural system of gay and lesbian adults. To the anthropologist, the youths are symbolically exiting what was once called "homosexuality" and entering what is now called "gay and lesbian." To the psychologist, their transition is from dependence and internalized homophobia to a more open and mature competence and pride in the sexual/gender domains of their lives. The transformative power contained in the rituals of coming out as facilitated by Horizons helps in the newfound development of the person. But it also helps in the lives of everyone touched by a youth who is coming out. As long as this process is blocked or resisted, the pull back into passing as heterosexual is very tempting.

Back in the 1960s, . . . coming out was a secret incorporation into the closet "homosexual" community. Studies at the time showed that the more visible contexts of engaging in same-sex contacts might lead to de facto coming out, but these were generally marginal and dangerous places, such as public toilets, where victimization and violence could occur. To come out in secret bars, the military, toilets, or bus depots did not create a positive identification with the category of gay/lesbian. There was generally no identity that positively accorded with gay or lesbian self-esteem as we think of it today. Thus, we can understand how many people found it revolutionary to fight back against homophobia and begin to march openly in parades in the 1970s. Nevertheless, the change was uneven and difficult.

People who continue to pass as straight when they desire people of the same gender and may in fact have sexual relations with them present a perplexing issue—not only for lesbians and gay men but also for society as a whole. This kind of person, through secrecy and passing, serves as a negative role model of what not to be. Alas, there are many movie stars, celebrities, and sports heroes who live closeted lives of this kind—until they are discovered or "outed" by someone. Many youths are frightened or intimidated when they discover adults they know and love, such as teachers, uncles, family friends, or pastors, who pass as heterosexual but have been discovered to desire the same gender. Adolescents can be angered to discover that a media person they admire has two lives, one publicly heterosexual and one privately homosexual. This is a cultural survival of the nineteenth-century system of closet homosexuality, with its hide-and-seek games to escape the very real dangers of homophobia. In contrast, positive role models provided by the largely white middle-class adult advisers at Horizons are the crucial source for learning how to enter the gay and lesbian community.

Cultural homophobia in high school is a powerful force against coming out. Learning to hide one's desires is crucial for the survival of some youths, especially at home and at school, the two greatest institutions that perpetuate homophobia in the United States. Our informants tell us that standard slurs to put people down in the schools remain intact. To be slurred as a "dyke" or a "faggot" is a real blow to social esteem. But "queer" is the most troubling epithet of all. To be targeted as a "queer" in high school is enormously troubling for the youths, somehow more alienating and isolating, an accusation not just of doing something "different" but of being something "unnatural." One seventeen-year-old eleventh grade boy remarked to us that he was secretive at school. "I'm hidden mostly—cause of the ways they'll treat you. Okay, there are lots of gangs. . . . They find out you're [what they call] a faggot and they beat on you and stuff. If they ask me I say it's none of their business." The role of secrecy, passing, and hiding continues the homophobia. Ironically, as Michelle Fine (1988, 36) notes in her study of black adolescent girls in New York City high schools, it was the gay and lesbian organization in the school that was the most open and safe environment in which young African-American girls could access their own feelings. They could, with the support of the lesbian and gay teenage group, start to become the agents of their *own* desires. Our study has shown that in Chicago most lesbian or gay youths have experienced harassment in school; and when this is combined with harassment and problems at home, it signals a serious mental health risk, especially for suicide. And the risk of suicide before lesbian or gay youths come to find the support of the Horizons group is very great.

The ritual of coming out means giving up the secrecy of the closet. This is a positive step toward mental health, for life in the closet involves not only a lot of hiding but also a good deal of magical thinking, which may be detrimental to the person's well-being. By magical thinking, I mean mainly contagious beliefs about homosexuality such as the common folk ideas of our culture that stereotype homosexuality as a disease that spreads, as well as the historical images of homosexuality as a mental illness or a crime against nature. These magical beliefs support homophobia and warn about the dangers of going to a gay community organization, whispering how the adolescent might turn into a monster or sex fiend or be raped or murdered or sold into slavery.

Another common contagious fear is the belief that by merely contacting other gays, the adolescent's "sin or disease" will spread to the self and will then unwittingly spread to others, such as friends and siblings. One of the common magical beliefs of many adults and parents is that the youth has merely to avoid other gay and lesbians in order to "go straight." This is surely another cultural "leftover" from the dark myth of homosexuality as evil. . . . If the adolescent will only associate with straights, the parent feels, this strange period of "confusion" will pass, and he or she will become heterosexual like everyone else. Such silly stereotypes are strongly associated with the false notion that all gay or lesbian teens are simply "confused," which was promoted by psychologists in the prior generation. This belief is based on the cultural myth that same-sex desires are "adolescent" desires of a transient nature that may be acquired or learned but can go away; and if the self ignores them, the desire for the opposite sex will grow in their place. Magical fears of contracting AIDS is a new and most powerful deterrent to coming out among some youths. Many youths fear their initial social contact with anyone gay because they think they might contagiously contract AIDS by being gay or lesbian or by interacting socially with gays.

The gender difference in the experience of coming out as a male or a female highlights the cultural pressures that are still exerted on teens to conform to the norm of heterosexuality in our society. Girls typically have more heterosexual experience in their histories, with two-thirds of the girls having had significant heterosexual contact before they came to Horizons. Since the age of our sample was about eighteen, it is easy to see that relatively early on, between the ages of thirteen and seventeen, girls were being inducted into sexual relations with boys. We face here the problem of what is socially necessary and what is preferred. Only one-third of the boys had had heterosexual experience, and fully two-fifths of them had had no sexual experience with girls. Note also that for many of the boys, their sexual contacts with girls were their lesbian-identified friends at the Horizons youth group. The boys tended to achieve sexual experiences earlier than the girls, by age sixteen, at which point the differences in development had evened out. Both genders were beginning to live openly lesbian or gay lives.

Clearly, powerful gender role pressures are exerted on girls to conform to the wishes of parents, siblings, peers, and boyfriends. Some of this, to use a phrase by Nancy Chodorow (1992) about heterosexuality as a compromise formation, results in a compromise of their desires, even of their personal integrity, in the development of their sexual and self-concept. But as we know from the work of Michele Fine (1992), who studied adolescent sexuality among African-American girls in the New York City schools, females were not able to explore and express their desires until they located a safe space that enabled them to think out loud. In fact, they could not become the agents of their own desires until they had located the gay and lesbian youth group in the high school! There, some of them had to admit, contrary to their stereotypes, they found the gay youths more accepting and open of variations than any of their peers or the adults. The lesson here is that when a cultural space is created, people can explore their own desires and better achieve their own identities and sociosexual goals in life.

We have found that four powerful magical beliefs exist in the implicit learning of homophobia and self-hatred among gay and lesbian youths. First is the idea that homosexuals are crazy and heterosexuals are sane. Unlearning this idea involves giving up the assumption of heterosexual normalcy in favor of positive attitudes and role models. Second is the idea that the problem with same-gender desires is in the self, not in society. Unlearning this belief means recognizing cultural homophobia and discovering that the problem with hatred lies not in the self but in society. Third is the magical belief that to have same-gender desires means giving up gendered roles as they were previously known and acting as a gender-transformed person, a boy acting or dressing as a girl, a girl living as a boy, or either living as an androgyne. There is nothing wrong with these transformations. What we have seen in the cross-cultural study, however, is that there are a variety of ways to organize same-gender desires. The old ways of gender inversion from the nineteenth century are only one of these. Unlearning gender reversal means accepting one's own gendered desires and enactments of roles, whatever these are, rather than living up to social standards—either in the gay or straight community.

Fourth is the belief that if one is going to be gay, there are necessary goals, rules, roles, and political and social beliefs that must be performed or expressed. This idea goes against the grain of American expressive individualism, in which we feel that each one of us is unique and entitled to "know thyself" as the means of social fulfillment. The key is that there is not one perfect way to be gay; there are many divergent ways. Nor is there any single event, or magic pill, that will enable the process of coming out. It is a lifelong process, as long as it takes to live and find a fulfilling social and spiritual lifeway in our culture.

Lesbian and gay youths have shown that coming out is a powerful means of confronting the unjust, false, wrongful social faces and values of prejudice in our culture. Before being out, youths are asking, "What can we be?" or "How can we fit into this society?" Emerging from the secrecy, these youths are making new claims on society to live up to its own standards of justice. The rituals of coming out are a way of unlearning and creating new learning about living with same-gender desires and creating a positive set of relationships around them. Surely the lesson of the gay movement is that hiding desires and passing as something other than what one is are no less injurious to the normal heart and the healthy mind of gay youths than was, say, passing as a Christian if one was a Jew in Nazi Germany or passing as white in the old South or in South Africa under apartheid.

Lesbian and gay youths are challenging society in ways that are no less revolutionary than discriminations based on skin color, gender, or religion. A new of kind of social and political activism has arisen; it goes beyond AIDS/HIV, but builds on the grief and anger that the entire generation feels about the impact of the pandemic on gay and lesbian culture. Some call this new generation queer. But others prefer lesbian or gay or bisexual or transgendered. Perhaps the word is less important than the commitment to building a rich and meaningful social world in which all people, including lesbians and gays, have a place to live and plan for the future.

We have seen in this chapter how a new generation of lesbian- and gay-identified youths has utilized transition rituals to find a place in the gay and lesbian community. It was the activism and social progress of the lesbian and gay culture that made this huge transformation possible. The emergence of a community enabled the support of youth groups and other institutions for the creation of a new positive role model and self-concept. Youths are beginning to take up new status rights and duties, having a new set of cultural ideas to create the moral voice of being gay, bisexual, lesbian, or queer. The rituals, such as the annual Gay and Lesbian Pride Day Parade, make these newly created traditions a lived reality; they codify and socialize gay and lesbian ideals, knowledge, and social roles, bonding past and future in a timeless present that will enable these youths to find a place in a better society.

References

Benedict, Ruth. 1938. "Continuities and discontinuities in cultural conditioning." *Psychiatry* 1:161–167.

Chodorow, Nancy J. 1992. "Heterosexuality as a Compromise Formation: Reflections on the Psychoanalytic Theory of Sexual Development." *Psychoanalysis and Contemporary Thought* 15:267–304.

Devereux, George. 1937. "Institutionalized Homosexuality Among the Mohave Indians." *Human Biology* 9:498–527.

Fine, Michelle. 1988. "Sexuality, Schooling, and Adolescent Females: The Missing Discourse of Desire." *Harvard Education Review* 58:29–53.

Hart, C. W. M. 1963. "Contrasts Between Prepubertal and Postpubertal Education" In *Education and Culture,* ed. G. Spindler, pp. 400–425. New York: Holt, Rinehart and Winston.

Herdt, Gilbert. 1981. *Guardians of the Flutes: Idioms of Masculinity.* New York: McGraw-Hill.

———. 1982. "Fetish and Fantasy in Sambia Initiation." In *Rituals of Manhood,* ed. G. Herdt., pp. 44–98. Berkeley and Los Angeles: University of California Press.

———. 1984b. "Semen Transactions in Sambia Culture." In *Ritualized Homosexuality in Melanesia,* ed. G. Herdt, pp. 167–210. Berkeley and Los Angeles: University of California Press.

———. 1991. "Representations of Homosexuality in Traditional Societies: An Essay on Cultural Ontology and Historical Comparison, Part II." *Journal of the History of Sexuality* 2:603–632.

———. 1993. "Introduction." In *Ritualized Homosexuality in Melanesia,* ed. G. Herdt, pp. vii–xliv. Berkeley and Los Angeles: University of California Press.

———, and Andrew Boxer. 1996. *Children of Horizons: How Gay and Lesbian Youth Are Forging a New Way Out of the Closet.* Boston: Beacon Press.

———, and Robert J. Stoller. 1990. *Intimate Communications: Erotics and the Study of Culture.* New York: Columbia University Press.

PEGGY REEVES SANDAY

Rape-Prone Versus Rape-Free Campus Cultures

In *Fraternity Gang Rape* (Sanday 1990) I describe the discourse, rituals, sexual ideology, and practices that make some fraternity environments rape prone. The reaction of fraternity brothers to the book was decidedly mixed. Individuals in some chapters were motivated to rethink their initiation ritual and party behavior. In sarcastic opinion pieces written for campus newspapers others dismissed the book on the grounds that I was "out to get" fraternities. As recently as December 1995, a young man wrote a letter to the editor of *The Washington Post* criticizing me for allegedly connecting hate speech and sexual crimes on college campuses with "single-sex organizations." Having set me up as the avenging witch, this young man then blames me for perpetuating the problem. My "[a]cross-the-board generalizations," he claims "only make it more difficult for supportive men to become involved and stay active in the fight against these attacks."

It is one of the tragedies of today's ideological warfare that this writer finds such an easy excuse to exempt himself from participating in the struggle to end violence against women. To make matters worse, his rationalization for opting out is based on a trumped-up charge. In the Introduction to my book, I carefully note that I am dealing with only "a few of the many fraternities at U. and on several other campuses." I state the case very clearly:

> The sexual aggression evident in these particular cases does not mean that sexual aggression is restricted to fraternities or that all fraternities indulge in sexual aggression. Sexist attitudes and the phallo-centric mentality associated with "pulling train" have a long history in Western society. For example, venting homoerotic desire in the gang rape of women who are treated as male property is the subject of several biblical stories. Susan Brownmiller describes instances of gang rape by men in war and in street gangs. Male bonding that rejects women and commodifies sex is evident in many other social contexts outside of universities. Thus, it would be wrong to place blame solely on fraternities. However, it is a fact also that most of the reported incidents of "pulling train" on campus have been associated with fraternities (Sanday 1990:19).

As an anthropologist interested in the particulars of sexual ideologies cross-culturally, I am very wary of generalizations of any sort. In 1975 I was very disturbed to read Susan Brownmiller's claim in the opening chapter of *Against Our Will* (1975:15) that rape is "a conscious process of intimidation by which all men keep all women in a state of fear." This statement was inconsistent with the compelling argument she presents in subsequent chapters that rape is culturally constructed and my own subsequent research on the sociocultural context of rape

Peggy Reeves Sanday, *Violence Against Women*, Vol. 2, No. 2, pp. 191–208, copyright © 1996 by Sage Publications, Inc. Reprinted by permission of Sage Publications, Inc.

cross-culturally, which provided evidence of rape-free as well as rape-prone societies.

In the following, I will briefly summarize what we know about rape-prone fraternity cultures and contrast this information with what a rape-free context might look like. Since the available data are sparse my goal here is mostly programmatic, namely to encourage studies of intra- campus and cross-campus variation in the rates and correlates of sexual assault.

RAPE-PRONE CAMPUS ENVIRONMENTS

The concept of rape-free versus rape-prone comes from my study of 95 band and tribal societies in which I concluded that 47% were rape free and 18% were rape prone (Sanday 1981). For this study I defined a rape-prone society as one in which the incidence of rape is reported by observers to be high, or rape is excused as a ceremonial expression of masculinity, or rape is an act by which men are allowed to punish or threaten women. I defined a rape-free society as one in which the act of rape is either infrequent or does not occur. I used the term "rape free" not to suggest that rape was entirely absent in a given society but as a label to indicate that sexual aggression is socially disapproved and punished severely. Thus, while there may be some men in all societies who might be potential rapists, there is abundant evidence from many societies that sexual aggression is rarely expressed.

Rape in tribal societies is part of a cultural configuration that includes interpersonal violence, male dominance, and sexual separation. Peallocentrism is a dominant psycho-sexual symbol in these societies and men "use the penis to dominate their women" as Yolanda and Robert Murphy say about the Mundurucu (Sanday 1981:25). Rape-prone behavior is associated with environmental insecurity and females are turned into objects to be controlled as men struggle to retain or to gain control of their environment. Behaviors and attitudes prevail that separate the sexes and force men into a posture of proving their manhood. Sexual violence is one of the ways in which men remind themselves that they are superior. As such, rape is part of a broader struggle for control in the face of difficult circumstances. Where men are in harmony with their environment, rape is usually absent.

In *Fraternity Gang Rape* I suggest that rape-prone attitudes and behavior on American campuses are adopted by insecure young men who bond through homophobia and "getting sex." The homoeroticism of their bonding leads them to display their masculinity through heterosexist displays of sexual performance. The phallus becomes the dominant symbol of discourse. A fraternity brother described to me the way in which he felt accepted by the brothers while he was a pledge.

> We . . . liked to share ridiculously exaggerated sexual boasting, such as our mythical "Sixteen Kilometer Flesh-Weapon". . . . By including me in this perpetual, hysterical banter and sharing laughter with me, they showed their affection for me. I felt happy, confident, and loved. This really helped my feelings

of loneliness and my fear of being sexually unappealing. We managed to give ourselves a satisfying substitute for sexual relations. We acted out all of the sexual tensions between us as brothers on a verbal level. Women, women everywhere, feminists, homosexuality, etc., all provided the material for the jokes (Sanday 1990: 140–41).

Getting their information about women and sex from pornography, some brothers don't see anything wrong with forcing a woman, especially if she's drunk. After the 1983 case of alleged gang rape I describe in the book one of the participants, a virgin at the time, told a news reporter:

We have this Select TV in the house, and there's soft porn on every midnight. All the guys watch it and talk about it and stuff, and [gang banging] didn't seem that odd because it's something that you see and hear about all the time. I've heard stories from other fraternities about group sex and trains and stuff like that. It was just like, you know, so this is what I've heard about, this is what it's like. . . . (Sanday 1990:34).

Watching their buddies have sex is another favorite activity in rape-prone campus environments. A woman is targeted at a party and brothers are informed who hide out on the roof outside the window, or secret themselves in a closet, or look through holes in the wall. Since the goal is to supply a live pornography show for their buddies, the perpetrators in these cases may easily overlook a woman's ability to consent. They certainly don't seek her consent to being watched. It is assumed that if she came to the house to party she is prepared for anything that might happen, especially if she gets drunk. On some campuses I have been told that this practice is called "beaching" or "whaling."

Taking advantage of a drunk woman is widely accepted. As a group of brothers said in a taped conversation in which they discussed the young woman in the 1983 case:

"She was drugged."
"She drugged herself."
"Yeah, she was responsible for her condition, and that just leaves her wide open . . . so to speak."
[laughter] (Sanday 1990:119)

In a 1990 talk show on which I appeared with the victim of gang rape a young man from a local university called up and admitted that the goal of all parties at his fraternity was "To get em drunk and go for it." In 1991, I read an article entitled, "Men, Alcohol, and Manipulation," in a campus newspaper from still another university. The author reported hearing several members of a fraternity talking with the bartender about an upcoming social event as follows:

Brother 1: Hey, don't forget—make the women's drinks really strong.
Bartender: Yeah, I won't forget. Just like usual.
Brother 2: We need to get them good and drunk.

Bartender: Don't worry, we'll take care of it.
Brother 3: That'll loosen up some of those inhibitions.

This is the kind of discourse I would classify as rape prone.

Getting a woman drunk to have sex in a show staged for one's buddies is tragically evident in the testimony heard in the St. Johns' sex case tried in Queens, New York, in 1991–92. This case involved six members of the St. Johns University lacrosse team who were indicted for acts ranging from unlawful imprisonment and sexual abuse to sodomy. A seventh defendant pleaded guilty and agreed to testify for immunity (see Sanday 1996 for a description of the case and the subsequent trial). From the testimony in the case and interviews with the complainant and members of the prosecution team, I reconstructed the following scenario.

A young, naive woman student, whom I call Angela (pseudonym), accepted a ride home from school from a male friend, Michael. On the way, he stopped at the house he shares with members of the St. Johns lacrosse team to get gas money and invited her inside. At first she refused to go in but upon his insistence accepted the invitation. Inside she met his roommates. Left alone in the third floor bedroom, she accepted a drink from Michael.

> The drink tasted terrible. It was bitter and stung her throat. When she asked what was in it, Michael said he put a little vodka in it. When she explained that she never drank, because drinking made her sick, Michael didn't listen. Then she tried to tell him that she hadn't eaten anything since lunch, But, this did not move him. "Vodka is a before dinner drink," he explained, insisting that she drink it.

> Finally, she gave into his pressure and downed the contents of the first cup in a few gulps because of the bitter taste. When she finished, Michael went over to the refrigerator and brought back a large container, which he said was orange soda with vodka. He placed the container on the floor beside her feet. When Michael poured another cup, she told him, "But Michael, I couldn't finish the first one. I don't think I will be able to finish another." Michael said again: "It's only vodka. It can't do anything to you, Angela." He also said, "You know, Angela, in college everyone does something, something wild they can look back on."

> "Something wild?" Angela asked quizzically.

> "Something wild," Michael said again. "Something you can look back on and talk about later in life." With the beer can that he was holding in his hand but never drank from, he hit her cup and said, "Here's to college life."

> Later, Angela blamed herself for accepting the drinks from Michael. She was caught between wanting to please the host and wanting to assert her own needs. She had tried to please him by finishing the first drink. Now, she drank the second.

> Then, he poured a third drink. When she balked at drinking this one, he started getting upset and annoyed. He told her it was a special drink, made just for

her. He accused her of making him waste it. He started pushing the drink up to her mouth. He put his hands over the cup and pushed it to her lips. He said, "Oh Angela, don't make me waste it. It's only vodka. A little vodka can't do anything to you."

By now, Angela felt dizzy and her hands were shaking. She felt lost, unable to move. She had spent a life time doing what she was told to avoid being punished. Here was Michael upset with her because she didn't want the drink he had made for her. She thought to herself, "If he wants me to drink it, I'll drink it for him." After she drank most of the third cup, Michael went to put the container back. Her head was spinning and she began to feel really sick, like she was going to vomit. She tried to tell Michael that she was sick, but he didn't seem interested in how she was feeling.

Michael sat next to her and massaged her shoulder. She would never forget his pseudo-seductive voice. She hardly knew him, and here he was talking to her like he really cared for her. It was so obviously a put on, she was shocked by the insincerity. He kept telling her, "You need to relax. You are too tense. If you relax, you will feel better." She tried to get up but she was too weak and she fell back down (Sanday 1996:11–12).

Testimony in the case revealed that after Angela passed out from Michael's drinks, three house members stood on the landing and watched as Michael engaged in oral sodomy. After Michael left the house, these three took their turns while visitors invited over from another lacrosse team house watched. At the trial these visitors testified that they left the room when Angela woke up and started screaming. One of the lead prosecutors speculated that they left because they realized only then that she was not consenting. They did not understand that the law applies to using drugs and alcohol as it does to using force.

CROSS-CAMPUS VARIATION IN RAPE AND SEXUAL COERCION

In his paper, Boeringer reports that 55.7% of the males in his study at a large southeastern university obtained sex by verbal harassment (i.e., "threatening to end a relationship unless the victim consents to sex, falsely professing love, or telling the victim lies to render her more sexually receptive," the variable labelled Coercion). One-quarter of the males in Boeringer's study reported using drugs or alcohol to obtain sex (Drugs/Alcohol) and 8.6% of the sample reported at least one use of force or threatened force to obtain sex (Rape.)

Schwartz and Nogrady found a much lower incidence of sexual coercion and assault at their research site, a large midwestern university. These authors (private communication) reported that 18.1% of the 116 males in their sample reported some form of unwanted sex: sex by pressure (6.9%); forced sex play/attempted rape (5.2%); or completed rape (6.0%). Of the 177 women interviewed 58.6% reported some form of unwanted sex; sex by pressure (24.1%); forced sex play/attempted rape (14.4%); and completed rape (20.1%).

The effect of fraternities is quite different on the two campuses. Boeringer found that fraternity men reported a higher overall use of coercion short of physical force to obtain sex. According to Boeringer, "fraternity members engage in significantly greater levels of sexual assault through drugging or intoxicating women to render them incapable of consent or refusal" (p. 9). Fraternity members are also more likely than independents to use "nonassaultative sexual coercion," or verbal pressure. "While not criminal in nature," Boeringer points out, "these verbally coercive tactics are nonetheless disturbing in that they suggest a more adversarial view of sexuality in which one should use deceit and guile to 'win favors' from a woman" (p. 10). From his study, Boeringer concludes that "fraternity members are disproportionately involved in some forms of campus sexual aggression." Like the prosecutor in the St. John's case mentioned above, he suggests that in all likelihood the process of "working a yes out" which I describe (Sanday 1990:113) is viewed by fraternity members as a "safer path to gaining sexual access to a reluctant, non-consenting woman than use of physical force" (p. 12).

Schwartz and Nogrady find no effect of fraternity membership. The most important predictor of sexual victimization in their study involves alcohol. It is not drinking per se that they found important, but whether or not a male perceives that his friends approve of getting a woman drunk for the purpose of having sex (the APPROVE variable). Also important is whether a male reports that he has friends that actually engage in this behavior (the GETDRUNK variable). The drinking variable that is the most influential in predicting a man's reported sexual assault is the intensity of his drinking, that is the number of drinks he consumes when he goes out drinking (DRINKS). Thus, the authors conclude that "the level of the perceived male peer support system for exploiting women through alcohol, plus the amount of alcohol actually consumed by men when they drink, are the primary predictors of whether they will report themselves as sexual victimizers of women."

The differences reported by Boeringer and Schwartz and Nogrady suggest not only that fraternities vary with respect to rape-prone behaviors but also that campuses vary with respect to overall rates of sexual assault. The latter result suggests that we need to look at cross-campus variation as well as at intra-campus variation. There are several problems that need to be addressed before either intra- or cross-campus variation can be established. First, in studying intra-campus variation we must be careful in reaching conclusions about the effect of such factors as drinking intensity or fraternity membership because the dependent variable is frequently lifetime prevalence rates rather than incidence in the past year.

Regarding cross-campus variation, there is the problem of comparability of studies. Boeringer (private communication), for example, measures prevalence rates in his study, while Schwartz and Nogrady (private communication) measure incidence. Since incidence rates are always lower, we cannot conclude that the campuses studied by these authors are that much different. Additionally, as noted by Schwartz and Nogrady as well as by Koss (1993), victimization rates from one study to another may not be comparable because of different methodologies, definitions, questions, and sampling procedures.

Nevertheless, some trends can be noticed. The available evidence against variation is seen in the fact that Koss's 15% completed rape prevalence rate in the national study of 32 campuses is replicated by other studies of college students on particular campuses. Koss and Cook (1993:109) note, for example, that estimates of completed rape frequency in the 12% range have been reported for two campuses and estimates "as high or higher than 12% for unwanted intercourse have been reported in more than 10 additional studies lacking representative sampling methods." According to these authors "there are no studies that have reported substantially lower or higher rates of rape among college students."

Evidence for variation comes from Koss's analysis of the relationship of prevalence rates to the institutional parameters used to design the sample (Koss 1988:11–12). She found that rates varied by region and by governance of the institution. Rates were twice as high at private colleges and major universities (14% and 17% respectively) than they were at religiously affiliated institutions (7%).

Ethnicity of the respondent (but, interestingly not the respondent's family income) was also associated with prevalence rates. More white women (16%) reported victimization than did Hispanic (12%), Black (10%), or Asian women (7%). These figures were almost reversed for men. Rape was reported by 4% of white men, 10% of black men, 7% of Hispanic men, and 2% of Asian men. Prevalence rates reported by men also differed by region of the country. More men in the Southeast region (6%) admitted to raping compared with men in the Plains states (3%) and those in the West (2%) (Koss 1988:12).

Intriguing evidence for cross-campus variation in rape rates and related variables comes from Koss's national study of 32 campuses. Using Koss's data I looked at prevalence and incidence rates for each of 30 campuses in her study (2 campuses were excluded because of the amount of missing information.) The results show a wide discrepancy when campuses are compared. For example the campus percentages of males admitting that they have used alcohol or force to obtain sex (Koss's 1988:11 rape variable) range from 0% to 10%. Campus percentages of males who admit to perpetrating unwanted sex in the past year (as opposed to since the age of 14) range from 6% to 22%. The latter percentages are higher because I computed them using all the sexual experience questions (excluding the two authority questions). Since the latter percentages are based on a question that measures incidence ("How many times in the past school year?") the results provide a measure of an dependent variable that can be compared with drinking intensity.

The Koss survey includes two questions that might be taken as measures of drinking intensity. Both questions are asked in such a fashion as to measure drinking intensity in the past year. One asks "How often do you drink to the point of intoxication or drunkenness"; the other asks "On a typical drinking occasion, how much do you usually drink?" The campus percentages of males checking the most extreme categories of the first question (1–2 or more times a week) ranges from 1% to 24%. The campus percentages of males checking the most extreme categories of the second question (more than 5 or 6 cans of beer or other alcoholic beverages) ranges from 6% to 71%. Since all studies—Schwartz, Boeringer, Koss and Gaines

(1993)—are unanimous on the effect of drinking this information, perhaps more than any other, is suggestive of variation in the rape-prone nature of campus environments.

THE CONCEPT OF A RAPE-FREE SOCIETY

Assuming that we could identify campuses on which both males and females reported a low incidence of rape and/or unwanted sex, the next question would be whether there is a significant difference in the sexual culture on these campuses compared to the more rape-prone campuses. My cross-cultural research which demonstrated differences in the character of heterosexual interaction in rape-free as opposed to rape-prone societies would suggest that the answer to this question is yes. The outstanding feature of rape-free societies is the ceremonial importance of women and the respect accorded the contribution women make to social continuity, a respect which places men and women in relatively balanced power spheres. Rape-free societies are characterized by sexual equality and the notion that the sexes are complementary. Although the sexes may not perform the same duties or have the same rights or privileges, each is indispensable to the activities of the other.

Since 1981 when this research was published, I spent approximately twenty-four months (extended over a period of fourteen years) doing ethnographic research among the Minangkabau, a rape-free Indonesian society. I chose the Minangkabau because of social factors that conformed with my profile of rape-free societies. The Minangkabau are the largest and most modern matrilineal society in the world today. Women play an undisputed role in Minangkabau symbol system and daily life, especially in the villages. Among the most populous of the ethnic groups of Indonesia, the Minangkabau are not an isolated tribal society in some far off corner of the world. Banks, universities, modern governmental buildings are found in two of the major cities of West Sumatra, the traditional homeland of the Minangkabau people. At the major universities, it is not uncommon to find Minangkabau Ph.D's trained in the U.S. People own cars and travel by bus throughout the province. Most children go to local schools, and many increasingly attend college.

The challenge facing me when I went to West Sumatra was first to find out whether the incidence of rape was low and if so to crack the cultural code that made it so. In the early years there was ample evidence from police reports and from interviews conducted all over the province that this was a rape-free society. Ethnographic research conducted in several villages provided confirmation. This research demonstrated that women are the mainstays of village life. The all-important family rice fields are inherited through the female line. Husbands live in their wives' houses. It is believed that this is the way it should be, because otherwise in the event of a divorce women and children would be left destitute. The main reason given for the matrilineal inheritance of property is that since women bear the infant and raise the child it is in keeping with the laws of nature to give women control of the ancestral property so that they will have the wherewithal to house and nurture the young.

Missing from the Minangkabau conception of sexuality is any show of interest in sex for the sake of sex alone. Sex is neither a commodity nor a notch in the male belt in this society. A man's sense of himself is not predicated by his sexual functioning. Although aggression is present, it is not linked to sex nor is it deemed a manly trait. The Minangkabau have yet to discover sex as a commodity or turn it into a fetish.

There is a cultural category for rape, which is defined as "forced sex" and is punishable by law. Rape is conceived as something that happens in the wild which places men who rape beyond the pale of society. In answer to my questions regarding the relative absence of rape among them compared to the United States, Minangkabau informants replied that rape was impossible in their society because custom, law, and religion forbade it and punished it severely. In the years that I worked in West Sumatra, I heard of only two cases of rape in the village where I lived. One case involved a group of males who ganged up on a young, retarded woman. In this case the leader of the group hanged himself the next day out of fear of avenging villagers. The rest of the assailants went to jail. The second case involved a local woman and a Japanese soldier during the Japanese occupation of the second world war and after. To this day people remember the case and talk about the horror of the Japanese occupation.

In the past few years, Indonesia's entrance into the global economy has been accompanied by an amazing shift in the eroticization of popular culture seen on TV. In 1995 the signs that this culture was filtering into Minangkabau villages were very evident. To the extent that commodification and eroticization breaks down the cultural supports for its matrilineal social system, the Minangkabau sexual culture will also change. Indeed, today in the provincial capital some argue that the Minangkabau are not rape free.

During my last field trip in 1995, I heard of many more reports of rape in the provincial capital. In the early 1990's, for example, there was a widely publicized acquaintance gang rape of a young woman by a group of boys. Interviewing court officers in the capital, I was told that this was the only case of its kind. Compared with similar cases in the U.S., such as the St. Johns case, the outcome was still very different. While the St. Johns defendants were either acquitted or got probation after pleading guilty, all the defendants in the Sumatran case were convicted and sent to jail. But, one may well ask whether the criminal justice system will continue to convict defendants as tolerance for sexual coercion begins to permeate popular beliefs.

RAPE-FREE CAMPUS CULTURES

A rape-free campus is relatively easy to imagine, but hard to find. Based on anecdotal information one candidate comes to mind. On this campus everyone, administrators, faculty, and students are on a first-name basis, which makes the atmosphere more egalitarian than most campuses. Decision making is by consensus and interpersonal interaction is guided by an ethic of respect for the individual. Those who are disrespectful of others are ostracized as campus life is motivated by a strong sense of community and the common good. No one group (such as fraternities, males, or athletes) dominates the social scene. Sexual assault is a serious offense treated with suspension or expulsion. Homophobic, racist, and sexist attitudes are virtually nonexistent. Individuals bond together in groups not to turn against others but because they are drawn together by mutual interests. Interviews suggest that the incidence of unwanted sex on this campus is low, however this must be corroborated by a campus-wide survey.

For information on a rape-free fraternity culture I turn to a description offered by a student who wrote a mini-ethnography on his fraternity for a class project. Corroboration of his description was offered by another brother in the same fraternity who read the ethnography and added additional information. In the following, the fraternity is referred to by the pseudonym QRS. With their permission, the fraternity brothers are identified by name.

Noel Morrison and Josh Marcus recognize that fraternities on their campus (called U.) "propagate sexist attitudes and provide a breeding ground for insecure acts of sexism, racism, and homophobia." According to Noel, U.'s fraternities "tend to be self-segregating entities which seek to maintain the inferior social position of women and minority students through exclusion" and social intolerance. QRS, however, consciously fights against this norm.

QRS is one of the oldest fraternities at U., going back at least 100 years. It was like all other fraternities at U. until 1977 when it was almost forced to disband due to insufficient numbers. At that time, a group of nine first year males pledged as a group knowing that their numbers would give them control of house decisions. They exercised this control by rewriting the house constitution and initiation rituals. Today the brothers are proud to say that they are "not a real fraternity." Interestingly, although both Joel and Noel treasure their lives in QRS (because of the fun, companionship of respected friends, and community the house offers), both feel that fraternities should be abolished.

Partly as a defense mechanism and partly to underscore their difference, QRS brothers stigmatize members of other fraternities as "jarheads." The word "jarhead" is used to refer to the "loud, obnoxious, sexist, racist, homophobic" members of U.'s fraternities. Most of the brothers in QRS do not participate in the campus inter-fraternity council and prefer to see themselves as "a group of friends," rather than as a fraternity, and their house as "a place to have concerts." Parties are always open to anyone and are either free to everyone or everyone pays, contrary to parties at other houses in which men pay and women are admitted for free.

At QRS heavy drinking is not a requisite for membership and is not a part of initiation. There are no drinking games and binge drinking does not occur. While some brothers drink to get drunk more than once a week, most don't. At parties there are always brothers who watch out for women or house members who have had too much to drink. Josh stressed that "it is clearly not acceptable for someone to take advantage of a drunk woman, because that's rape." There is no talk in the house about getting a girl drunk to have sex, he says. Members are very aware that where there is heavy drinking someone can be taken advantage of. If a female passes out or is very drunk she is watched or escorted home. Both Josh and Noel remember an incident during a party in the fraternity next door, in which several members of QRS came to the aid of a young woman whose shirt was above her waist and who had passed out on their porch, left there perhaps by friends from the party who had deserted her. Their intervention may have saved her life. When they were unable to get her to talk, they took her to the emergency room of a nearby hospital only to learn that she was in a coma and her heart had stopped. Fortunately, they were in time and she responded to treatment.

Women are not seen as sex objects in the house, but as friends. Unlike other fraternities at U., there is no distinction drawn between "girlfriends" and friends and there are no "party girls." Noel says that when he was rushing he would often hear women referred to as "sluts" in other fraternities. However, at QRS this is unheard of. According to Josh, a brother who acted "inappropriately" with a woman would be severely reprimanded, perhaps even expelled from the fraternity. The brothers are not afraid of strong women. There are women's studies students who are regulars at the house, along with outspoken feminists and activists. Noel quotes one of them:

> I guess there's a few brothers who make sexist jokes, but I don't know how seriously people take them. I remember last year in the middle of midterms I was studying late at night and was feeling sick and tired, and in a span of about five minutes, four people offered their beds to me, not as a sexual thing at all, but just because they cared.

One QRS brother started the Men's Association for Change and Openness (MAChO) and is an active participant in U's student peer-counseling group for sexual health. One brother displays a "Refuse and Resist" sticker on his door, proclaiming, "Date rape: cut it out or cut it off." In a 1993 pamphlet advertising QRS as the site of the National Anarchist gathering, the brothers wrote "Although QRS is a frat, it is generally a friendly place, along with being a safe haven for women."

Most interesting about QRS is its acceptance of homosexuality, and bisexuality. Homophobia does not become the basis for males to prove their virility to one another. Because of its openness about sex and acceptance of homosexuality, QRS has earned the reputation on campus of being "the gay frat" or "faggot house." Josh comments on this reputation and what it means to him:

> QRS's attitudes about homosexuality are complex, but fundamentally tolerant and respectful. Some brothers revel in rumors that we are the "gay frat." It is rumored that a few years ago a few of the brothers were involved sexually, and one of our most involved alumni is homosexual.

Although most fraternities have had or have a few homosexual brothers, this honest acceptance of homosexuality is unusual. QRS brothers are proud of being called the "gay frat." Evidence of this is the humorous statement in the letters given prospective pledges offering bids, which ends with the phrase "we are all gay."

CONCLUSION

The first step in the struggle against "hidden rape," which began in the late sixties with consciousness raising groups (see Sanday 1996, Chapter 8), was to recognize the problem and speak out against it. The next step was to change outmoded rape laws and assess the causes and frequency of sexual violence against women. Mary Koss's national survey of 1985 demonstrated that one in four women will experience rape or attempted rape in her lifetime. Since the eighties many other surveys have replicated her findings. The search for causes has been the subject of numerous studies, including those represented in this volume.

The next step is to go beyond the causes and study solutions. One approach would be to find naturally occurring rape-free environments on today's college campuses. QRS is one example. No rape-free campuses have been identified by research, yet I have heard descriptions from students that lead me to believe that such campuses exist. Identifying such campuses and seeking out environments like QRS is the next step for research. In this paper I have identified the kinds of problems such research must address. First, it is necessary to obtain incidence as well as prevalence data. Secondly, we need more subtle measures of the kinds of sociocultural correlates that have been discussed in this paper: drinking intensity; using pornography to learn about sex rather than talking with one's partner; bragging about sexual conquests; setting women up to display one's masculinity to other men; heterosexism; homophobia; and using pornography as a guide to female sexuality. Finally, we need to develop a consensus on the criteria for labelling a campus either rape free or rape prone. If at least one in five women on a given campus say they have experienced unwanted sex in the last year, I would label the campus rape prone. However, others may want to propose different criteria. Once a consensus is reached, the movement to make our campuses safe for women might include identifying rape-free and rape-prone campuses.

Note

This article has benefited from the comments of Mary P. Koss. I am also grateful to Koss for supplying me with the data on her 1986 study of 32 campuses. Martin D. Schwartz and Scot B. Boerginer graciously supplied me with additional data from their studies and answered my many questions. Noel Morrison played an important role by giving me permission to summarize his description of his fraternity. John Marcus, a brother in the same fraternity, was also helpful in corroborating Noel's observations and supplying a few of his own.

References

Brownmiller, S. (1975). *Against Our Will: Men, Women, and Rape*. New York: Simon and Schuster.

Koss, M. P. (1988). "Hidden rape: Sexual aggression and victimization in a national sample of students in higher education." In A.W. Burgess (ed.), *Rape and Sexual Assault II* (3–25). New York: Garland.

———. (1993). "Rape: Scope, impact, interventions, and public policy responses." *American Psychologist.* October 1062–1069.

Koss, M. P., & S. L. Cook. (1993). "Facing the facts: Date and acquaintance rape are significant problems for women." In R.J. Gelles and D.R. Loseke (eds.), *Current Controversies on Family Violence* (104–119). Newbury Park, CA: Sage.

Koss, M. P., & Gaines, J. A. (1993). "The prediction of sexual aggression by alcohol use, athletic participation, and fraternity affiliation." *Journal of Interpersonal Violence* 8, 94–108.

Sanday, P. R. (1981). "The socio-cultural context of rape: a cross-cultural study." *Journal of Social Issues*, 37, 5–27.

———. (1990). *Fraternity Gang Rape: Sex, Brotherhood and Privilege on Campus.* New York: New York University Press.

———. (1996). *A Woman Scorned: Acquaintance Rape on Trial.* New York: Doubleday.

PART 3 THE PSYCHOLOGY
OF SEX ROLES

Even if biology were destiny, the founder of psychoanalysis Sigmund Freud argued, the process by which biological males and females become gendered men and women does not happen naturally nor inevitably. Gender identity, he argued, is an achievement—the outcome of a struggle for boys to separate from their mothers and identify with their fathers, and of a parallel and complementary struggle for girls to reconcile themselves to their sexual inadequacy and therefore maintain their identification with their mothers.

Subsequent generations of psychologists have attempted to specify the content of that achievement of gender identity, and how it might be measured. In the early 1930s, Lewis Terman, one of the country's most eminent social psychologists, codified gender identity into a set of attitudes, traits, and behaviors that enabled researchers to pinpoint exactly where any young person was on a continuum between masculinity and femininity. If one had successfully acquired the "appropriate" collection of traits and attitudes, one (and one's parents) could rest assured that one would continue to develop "normally." Gender nonconformity—boys who scored high on the femininity side of the continuum, or girls who scored high on the masculine side—was a predictor, Terman argued, for sexual nonconformity. Homosexuality was the sexual behavioral outcome of a gender problem, of men who had not successfully mastered masculinity or women who had not successfully mastered femininity.

Though its origins lie in Freudian understandings of how the child acquires gender identity, this notion, that one can "read" sexuality—know whether someone is heterosexual or homosexual—by the way they enact gender has become a staple in American popular culture. Many contemporary psychologists have been uncomfortable with the ways in which traditional psychoanalytic models of gender identity and sexual orientation reproduced male domination and the "deviantization" of homosexuality as the outcome of gender problems. Kay Deaux and Brenda Major offer a psychodynamic perspective on gender difference that corrects the implicit problematization of female development, and stresses the ways in which gender inequality is part of gender socialization. Daryl Bem offers a more dynamic understanding that explains the origins of sexual orientation not through gender nonconformity, but through a process by which the child comes to eroticize what is different from his or her own sense of self. Far less normative than Terman or Freud—who believed that homosexuality was a problem to be explained by familial psychodynamics—Bem offers no value judgments about the person's eventual sexual orientation, but offers a psychological model of how he or she acquires it. Finally, James Garbarino underlines the ways in which these psychological processes affect boys' development by looking at codes of honor and violence among incarcerated youth.

KAY DEAUX AND BRENDA MAJOR

A Social-Psychological Model of Gender

Psychology's record of considering gender has been, with too few exceptions, a tradition of sex differences. Taking sexual dimorphism as a starting point, investigators have tried to establish, or in some cases refute, the existence of differences between women and men. Whichever conclusion is sought or reached, the debate has its origin in an implicit oppositional model.

This tendency to create oppositions between elements that can be dichotomized is a seductive feature of human thought. In a fascinating study by Barnes[1] parents were asked to describe their children. Parents who had three or more children described each child in separate terms: for example, Jane is intellectual, Bill is sociable, and Pamela is athletic. Parents of two children, in contrast, succumbed to oppositional thinking: If Jane was a leader, Bill was a follower; if Bill was more sociable, Jane was less sociable. This tendency toward bipolar contrasts is probably exaggerated in the case of males and females, where there is consensus as to what the two categories are and where the categories serve as significant markers in most societies. Dualistic assumptions about gender may also preclude other relevant categories—race, class, age—from entering the analysis.

Those who conclude that there are differences between women and men often assume that these differences are stable. This stability is implicit, we would argue, whether nature or nurture is invoked as the cause. The "different voice" that Carol Gilligan[2] describes with reference to moral reasoning, for example, is attributed primarily to differences in socialization experiences. Yet as the historian Joan Scott has suggested in analyzing the dualism expressed in this work, assumptions of differential experience often fall victim to a certain slippage, in which the original premise, namely, "Women are this way because of different experience," becomes "Women are this way because they are women." In Scott's words, "Implied in this line of reasoning is the ahistorical, if not essentialist, notion of women."[3]

As a group, psychologists have a pernicious tendency to develop a concept, devise a way to measure it, and then assume its reality. This reification creates a belief that people are, if their assessment scores so reveal, compulsive people, de-

From *Theoretical Perspectives on Sexual Difference*, edited by Deborah L. Rhode, pp. 89–99. Copyright © 1990 Yale University Press. Reprinted by permission of the publisher. Notes have been renumbered and edited.

pendent people, aggressive people, and the like. These descriptions, in turn, connote both generality across situations and stability across time (despite numerous disputes within the discipline as to whether those assumptions are justified). In addition, the hypothesized dimensions often take on causal properties, as they are used to explain and justify actions that may seem consistent with the characterization.

This general tendency to infer causality from stability is particularly evident in analyses of sex differences, for which the explanatory concepts tend to be global. As the prototypical case, the conceptualization of "masculinity" and "femininity" was intended to represent the psychological essence of being male and female. It was not linked directly to biological sex but was capable of predicting those behaviors that tend to be associated with gender. Slightly less broad at first glance, but equally pervasive in their implications, are such concepts as "instrumentality" and "expressiveness," or "justice" versus "caring." Like masculinity and femininity, these characteristics or behavioral styles are seen to reside primarily in one or the other sex and to dictate a wide range of outcomes and life choices.

Such diagnostic categories at most assess potentials and estimate probabilities. They do not dictate outcomes. As Hubbard suggests, human nature as an abstract concept means very little.[4] To give this concept meaning, we need to look at the things people actually do. The viewpoint this represents may be too behaviorist for some. Yet while pure behaviorism is as out of fashion in psychology as in the wider intellectual community, Hubbard's injunction provides a useful antidote to the more global diagnoses some psychological and psychoanalytic models make. The analysis of gender is ill served by a reliance on inflexible and often ephemeral conceptions of the nature of woman and man. Attention to actual behavior, in contrast, demands a model that recognizes variability and similarity—as well as stability and difference.

A SOCIAL-PSYCHOLOGICAL PERSPECTIVE ON GENDER

Our analysis is informed by a social-psychological perspective. In contrast to more traditional psychological analyses of gender that tend toward essentialism, a social-psychological perspective emphasizes the varying forces that influence women and men. Social psychology considers the situational influences on human behavior as a defining characteristic, assigning them a priority over individual traits and personality dispositions. From this perspective we ask quite different questions about sex differences in human behavior.

Our model takes as its point of departure the behavior of women and men in dyadic interaction. Such social interactions can involve many forms of behavior—for example, leadership, social influence, moral choices, cooperation, and competition. Although the basis for our analysis is the empirical literature of psychology, we believe that the implications of the analysis go considerably beyond this domain. The emphasis is not on structural constants that program behavior but on conditions that foster variability and change. In contrast to developmental models of gender that deal with the acquisition of gender-linked behavior, our model is concerned with gender as experienced and enacted in a particular social context. The model is intended to supplement, not supplant, earlier theoretical models that stress the origins of specifiable tendencies and habits.

Fundamental to our perspective is the assumption that gender-related behavior is marked by flexibility, fluidity, and variability. Without denying that there may be some regularities in male and female behavior that are the result of biological propensity or socialization experience, we believe it is essential to recognize evidence of changes over time and circumstance. Acknowledging this variation makes the task of analysis more complex—but it is a complexity we need to confront.

A second assumption that underlies the current perspective is that women and men make choices in their actions. In contrast to the deterministic models offered by both psychoanalysis and behaviorism, our framework presumes a repertoire of possibilities from which individual men and women choose different responses on varying occasions with varying degrees of self-consciousness. In other words, gender-related behaviors are a process of individual and social construction. A number of commentators in other disciplines have argued a similar position. Scott, as one recent example, states that "there is room for a concept of human agency as the attempt (at least partially rational) to construct an identity, a life, a set of relationships, a society with certain sets of limits and with language."[5] The sociologists Gerson and Peiss describe gender as a set of "socially constructed relationships which are produced and reproduced through people's actions."[6] In both of these statements, as in our own model, an active dynamic replaces a passive determinism.

To assume flexibility and choice in an analysis of gender requires an appreciation of context. Choices are not made in a vacuum but are shaped by such transitory factors as the other people involved and the prevailing societal norms. In the present analysis, we reflect our disciplinary bias by emphasizing the immediate interpersonal context. Within such situations, individuals simultaneously react to others and present themselves. Social interaction can be viewed as a process of identity negotiation where individuals pursue particular goals for the interaction.

Our view of gender-related behavior in terms of negotiated social interaction draws heavily on two theoretical perspectives in social psychology. Research on expectancy confirmation—sometimes called self-fulfilling prophecy—focuses on the active role of observers in maintaining or creating social reality through their cognitions or behaviors toward a particular individual. This process involves a sequence in which individuals take actions on the basis of their beliefs, and these actions then influence the behavior of the recipient, leading to a confirmation of the initial belief. In applying this analysis here, we consider how the gender belief system of another can impact upon the individual woman, channeling her behavior in ways that support the stereotypic beliefs.

A second theoretical tradition concerns the factors that motivate an individual to vary how she presents herself to others. On the one hand, concerns with self-verification may lead the person to emphasize those underlying beliefs and characteristics that define a stable self-identity. On the other, external pressures may encourage the choice of self-presentation strategies that increase the likelihood of positive reactions from another. In either case the person shows a freedom of choice to select some facet of self from among a number of possible alternatives.

The model that we are developing attempts to deal both with the variation between people and with the variation in a given individual across situations and time. Clearly people confronted with the same situational pressures vary in their responses. Similarly, a single person may take a different course of action depending on the context in which the choice occurs. Dyadic interaction is our chosen testing ground, although our model has implications for other domains as well. In the model, two individuals bring specific beliefs and identities to an interaction, and their interaction occurs within a specifiable context. We do not assume that gender is always salient in these interactions. One of the objectives of our formulation is to specify and to predict just when gender substantially shapes the course of an interaction and when its influence is more muted. To make these predictions, we look at three influences: first, the individual woman or man; second, other individuals with whom the person interacts; and third, the context or setting in which the interaction takes place.

GENDER IDENTITY AND GENDER-BASED ACTION

Gender identity, as the term is typically used by psychologists, refers to a "fundamental, existential sense of one's maleness or femaleness, an acceptance of one's gender as a social-psychological construction that parallels acceptance of one's biological sex."[7] This sense of maleness or femaleness is acquired early in most people's lives. As Spence has stated, "It is inarguable . . . that gender is one of the earliest and most central components of the self concept and serves as an organizing principle through which many experiences and perceptions of self and other are filtered."[8]

Although the concept of gender identity is universal, substantial individual differences occur in the characteristics of these identities. First, people differ in the degree to which gender is a salient aspect of their identity. Chodorow, for example, has suggested that gender identity is differentially important to women and to men.[9] Data from a recent study of self-definition support this suggestion. When asked what identities were important to them, women were more likely than men either to mention gender spontaneously or to acknowledge gender as a central identity when questioned by the interviewer. (Such findings are consistent with the argument that dominant groups have less need to be self-reflective than do groups who must define themselves vis-à-vis a more powerful other.)

A second way in which gender identities differ among individuals concerns the particular features associated with those identities. People may think of themselves as womanly, feminine, or feminist; within any of these general categories, the beliefs and behaviors associated with the label can differ dramatically. Two individuals who are equally conscious of their identities as women may, by virtue of experience or belief, have markedly different conceptions of what that identity means.

The influence of gender on social interaction depends heavily on the degree to which associations with gender are invoked, either consciously or unconsciously. In cognitive psychologists' terms, we can talk about the *accessibility* of gender identity—the degree to which concepts of gender are actively involved in a particular experience or are part of what has been called the "working self-concept."[10] Accessibility is affected by at least two sets of factors: the strength or centrality of that aspect of the self and features of the immediate situation that make gender salient.

For some people, gender will always be part of the working self-concept, an ever-present filter for experience. Individuals differ in how much gender is a chronically accessible aspect of self, and the prominence of gender identity can differ for the same individual across different situations and stages of life. Gender is more likely to shape a woman's experience, for example, when she has her first child or when she receives a diagnosis of breast cancer than it is on other less gender-linked occasions.

External cues can also evoke gender identity, moving it into the working self-concept. In a laboratory demonstration of gender awareness, for example, college students mentioned gender more often when their sex was a minority in a group situation than when it was a majority. Kanter has vividly described how in other work environments gender becomes salient for the individual who is a token in an organizational setting.[11]

Not always recognized in feminist analyses is the fact that people have identities other than gender. A person may think of herself not only as a woman, but as a Black, a professor, an Easterner, or any of numerous other identities. These various senses of self may exist as independent units having little implication for each other. Or two identities may have different implications for action in the same setting and hence prove contradictory. Which identity is dominant in a situation in which both might be accessible depends both on the individual (the relative prominence of a particular identity in some hierarchy of identities) and on the situation (the degree to which circumstances make a particular identity salient). Gender is most likely to dominate interaction, by this account, when it is an identity of primary importance and when the situation contrives to make gender relevant.

Awareness of gender does not automatically dictate action. Instead people choose how to present themselves to others, with the choices reflecting a variety of motivations. Choices may be based on conscious intentions to present a particular stance or to convey a particular image; individuals may act for the sake of goals that are not clearly recognized in conscious thought. The motives of actions vary. One line of psychological investigation has stressed the degree to which individuals act to verify self-concepts, choosing actions that will be consistent with previous definitions of self. An alternative perspective stresses the degree to which people are sensitive to the social significance of their conduct and strive to present themselves in ways that will ensure social rewards. These two processes are not necessarily contradictory. Rather, concerns with self-verification and self-presentation may be interwoven in any social interaction, as the individual uses both internal and external standards to monitor and shape behavioral choice.

Some empirical investigations have shown how gender concerns can alter the image one presents. In one study, for example, women presented descriptions of themselves to a man who was believed to hold either traditional or liberal views of the appropriate roles for women and men. When the target of their presentation was a man possessing socially desirable characteristics (e.g., not in a steady dating relationship, attractive, wealthy), women modified their presentation to approximate the man's alleged views. In contrast, when the man was described as having traits that would presumably not motivate goals of continued interaction (e.g., currently engaged, unattractive, limited career goals), the women did not alter their presentation from what it had been at an earlier assessment. Such alterations are evident in men confronting women as well. Another empirical study of self-presentational shifts found that women ate fewer available snacks when they were interacting with a desirable male partner as compared to a less desirable one. In extending their analysis, the investigators suggested that such eating disorders as anorexia and bulimia might be linked to self-presentational concerns, as women attempting to appear feminine choose behaviors that they believe are consistent with societal norms of femininity.[12]

THE INFLUENCE OF OTHERS

Social interaction occurs in a context in which certain expectations are conveyed by participants toward each other. Within a given setting, whether the dyadic case emphasized in our model or in a larger arena, the individual is generally aware of what is expected, prescribed, or typical in that setting. These expectations can shape the interaction so as to constitute a self-fulfilling prophecy. People interacting with each other may come to manifest the previously held beliefs of their companions.

We know, from both extensive research and common observation, that gender stereotypes are pervasive. People typically believe that men and women differ in a wide range of personality traits, physical characteristics, role behaviors, and occupational positions. Traits related to instrumentality, dominance, and assertiveness, for example, are believed more characteristic of men, while such traits as warmth, expressiveness, and concern for other people are thought more characteristic of women. These beliefs are not all-or-nothing ascriptions; rather, people make judgments about the relative likelihood that women and men will exhibit various characteristics.

People not only have beliefs about women and men at the most general level. They also have clear images of certain types of women and men, such as business-women or blue-collar working men. These types correspond to roles that men and women occupy in society and are often described in terms of physical features as well as personality traits. A macho man, for example, is most frequently characterized as being muscular, having a hairy chest and a moustache. Images of sexy women include references to the woman's hair, figure, clothes, facial appearance, and nail polish. These beliefs, operating at various levels of specificity, serve as a framework or orientation for the individual approaching any particular interaction, and because information about physical appearance is both readily available and prominently coded, stereotypic thinking may be triggered quite early in initial encounters.

Of course individuals differ in the degree to which they endorse these beliefs and in the attributes they associate with gender categories. Some people may, as Bem has argued, be gender schematic, readily imposing stereotypical beliefs and making sharp distinctions between male and female. Aschematic people eschew such distinctions.[13] More generally, one can think of people as varying along a range of stereotypy, showing greater or lesser propensity to endorse the pervasive cultural beliefs. It seems quite unlikely, however, that many people in contemporary society are unencumbered by some gender-linked expectations and beliefs.

As in the case of self, we do not believe that gender is always salient to the observer or that gender-related beliefs are necessarily activated in social interaction. Yet the obviousness of a person's sex in most instances makes it very likely to influence implicit assumptions. Kessler and McKenna argue that gender attribution is universal, taking precedence over many other forms of categorization.[14]

Both parties in an interaction can influence the likelihood of gender schemata's being activated. Specific features of a person's appearance can trigger a subset of gender beliefs in the mind of the observer, for example, shifting the expectancies from those associated with women and men in general to those linked to more particular subtypes. A woman with a briefcase elicits different associations for most people than does a woman in an apron and housedress. A woman with a low-cut blouse, slit skirt, and high-heeled shoes elicits more attributions of sexiness and seductiveness than does her more conservatively dressed counterpart. Predispositions in the observer may lower the threshold for seeing gender relevance or influence the way in which a particular behavior is interpreted. Men, for example, are more likely than women to assume sexual intent in the friendly behavior of a woman. An analysis of these beliefs is important because of their consequences. The expectancy confirmation sequence describes processes linking beliefs to actions. This link manifests itself in a number of ways, including active avoidance or termination of an interaction. A person can avoid individuals who are presumed undesirable, and such avoidance allows the retention of beliefs in the (untested) attributes of the undesirable one. More typically, perhaps, expectancies shape the form of interaction that occurs. To take an example from the employment realm, consider the case of a female manager whose supervisor believes her to be unfit for leadership positions. The supervisor might engage in such actions toward the woman as shunting her into a subordinate role that allows no room for the display of leadership qualities. The woman's subordinate behavior would then confirm the supervisor's initial belief independent of the woman's actual qualities.

SITUATION AND CONTEXT

The context in which an interaction takes place, like the characters of the actors, shapes the outcome. Context can be considered at many levels, from cultural norms and societal structures to the more immediate circumstances of an interaction. Although our analysis emphasizes immediate circumstances, we do not suggest that others are insignificant, for these more general forces shape, modify, and often limit the range of behaviors available to the individual actor.

Certain situations make gender more salient, increasing the likelihood that each of the participants will bring gender scripts to bear. Some environments, such as a nursery school or an automobile repair shop, are closely linked to gender. Other situations make gender salient because of the particular participants, as Kanter's analysis of tokenism illustrates.[15] Established norms can make gender more or less appropriate as an organizing principle.

To predict whether sex differences will be the rule or the exception, one must analyze the total set of influencing factors. The actual behavior of women and men in a situation depends on the relative weight of the three elements: the self-definitions and goals of each participant, the beliefs and expectations of the other, and the context in which the interaction takes place. By this analysis, sex differences, that is, observed differences in the actions of women and men, are one of several possible outcomes. In most cases this outcome could be altered relatively easily if one or more elements were changed.

The most straightforward predictions for observed behavior are possible when all forces press toward the same outcome. Using as an example a pair of entry-level managers in a corporation, we can describe conditions of maximal and minimal likelihood for the appearance of sex differences. Sex differences will be most likely, according to our analysis, when:

1. The man and the woman have different conceptions of themselves as managers and different goals for their corporate experience.
2. The supervisor holds strong stereotypic beliefs about women and men and is prone to act on those beliefs, creating different experiences for women and men.
3. The situation is one in which men and women have traditionally assumed different roles and in which the organizational structure is based on a premise of different activities for women and men.

In contrast, sex differences should be rare when the opposite influences prevail. If women and men bring similar experiences and self-conceptions to a situation, if they aspire to the same outcomes, and if they are acting in a context within which sex discrimination is minimal, relatively few differences should be observed.

Both of these scenarios represent pure cases, in which the various influences converge toward a single outcome. In reality cases are rarely that simple. Women with identities and aspirations that match men's encounter situations that press for differentiation. Contexts that are seemingly neutral may still provide a venue for display of sharp differences between particular women and men. When two sources of influence produce contradictory pressures—one fostering difference and the other stressing similarity—what form does behavior take?

To deal with the complexity of frequently conflicting messages and pressures, we turn to a microlevel analysis of the social-psychological process involved in interaction. Rather than offering general statements of sex difference or similarity, we suggest that many dynamic factors must be considered. In each general domain—individual self-systems, expectancies of others, and contextual influences—the range of alternatives is great. With reference to the self-system, for example, people vary in the importance they attach to pleasing others versus verifying internal truths. If pleasing others is more important, situational factors should be much more influential. Characteristics of the other's expectancy that can be important include the desirability of the advocated behavior for the individual and the certainty with which that message is sent. *Who* is conveying the expectation also matters a great deal. A person is far more likely to confirm the expectations of those who are powerful, likable, and control rewards and outcomes than of those whose resources are more limited. Confirmation of another person's expectancies is more likely in public situations than in private, and more common in novel situations than in familiar ones.

The enactment of gender is a dynamic, not a static, phenomenon. People choose (although not necessarily at a conscious level) to act out gender-related behaviors and to vary their behavior with circumstances. Their choices reflect the joint contribution of cognitive factors like the accessibility of relevant beliefs and self-definitions, and motivational factors that relate to one's objectives for a particular interaction. Although we use observable behavior as a criterion, we *recognize* the determinants of these behaviors in mental acts. The actions of individual women and men cannot be understood without reference to social context. Changes in context mean changes in outcome, belying the stability of male-female differences so often posited.

The present analysis is more microlevel than some. We are concerned less with human nature than with human actions; with where the repertoires of behavior come from than with how people make choices within those repertoires. Our framework does not deny the usefulness of other formulations, but we believe that the social-psychological perspective is a valuable one. It offers little in the way of ultimatums. What it does, and does in a way lacking in many previous accounts, is to affirm the range of human behavior available to both women and men. By so doing, it moves us away from the oppositional thought that has guided so much previous work.

Notes

1. This study is reported in an unpublished doctoral dissertation from the Harvard Graduate School of Education (W. S. Barnes, "Sibling Influences within Family and School Contexts," 1984) and is described in Deborah Belle, "Ironies in the Contemporary Study of Gender," *Journal of Personality* 53 (June 1985): 400–5.

2. Carol Gilligan, *In a Different Voice* (Cambridge: Harvard University Press, 1982).

3. Joan W. Scott, "Gender: A Useful Category of Historical Analysis," *American Historical Review* 91 (1986): 1053–75, 1065.

4. Ruth Hubbard, "The Political Nature of 'Human Nature,'" in Deborah Rhode, ed., *Theoretical Perspectives on Sexual Difference* (New Haven: Yale University Press, 1990): 63–73.

5. Scott, "Gender," 1067.

6. Judith M. Gerson and Kathy Peiss, "Boundaries, Negotiation, Consciousness: Reconceptualizing Gender Relations," *Social Problems* 32 (April 1985): 327.

7. Janet T. Spence, "Masculinity, Femininity, and Gender-Related Traits: A Conceptual Analysis and Critique of Current Research," *Progress in Experimental Personality Research* 13 (1984): 84. For more traditional discussions of gender identity, see Richard Green, *Sexual Identity Conflict in Children and Adults* (New York: Basic, 1974); John Money and Anke A. Ehrhardt, *Man and Woman, Boy and Girl* (Baltimore: Johns Hopkins University Press, 1972); Robert J. Stoller, *Sex and Gender: On the Development of Masculinity and Femininity* (New York: Science House, 1968).

8. Janet T. Spence, "Gender Identity and Its Implications for Concepts of Masculinity and Femininity," in T. Sondregger, ed., *Nebraska Symposium on Motivation* (Lincoln: University of Nebraska Press, 1985).

9. Nancy Chodorow, "What is the Relation Between Psychoanalytic Feminism and the Psychoanalytic Psychology of Women?" In Deborah Rhode, ed., *Theoretical Perspectives on Sex Differences* (New Haven: Yale University Press, 1990).

10. For more discussion, see E. Tory Higgins and Gillian King, "Accessibility of Social Constructs: Information-Processing Consequences of Individual and Contextual Variability," in Nancy Cantor and John F. Kihlstrom, eds., *Personality, Cognition, and Social Behavior* (Hillsdale, N.J.: Lawrence Erlbaum, 1981), 69–121; also Hazel Markus and Ziva Kunda, "Stability and Malleability of the Self-Concept," *Journal of Personality and Social Psychology* 51 (October 1986): 858–66.

11. Rosabeth Moss Kanter, *Men and Women of the Corporation* (New York: Basic, 1977).

12. DeAnna Mori, Shelly Chaiken, and Patricia Pliner, "'Eating Lightly' and the Self-Presentation of Femininity," *Journal of Personality and Social Psychology* 53 (October 1987): 693–702.

13. Sandra L. Bem, "Gender Schema Theory: A Cognitive Account of Sex Typing, *Psychological Review* 88 (July 1981): 354–64.

14. Suzanne J. Kessler and Wendy McKenna, *Gender: An Ethnomethodological Approach* (New York: John Wiley, 1978).

15. Kanter, *Men and Women of the Corporation*.

DARYL J. BEM

The Exotic-Becomes-Erotic Theory of Sexual Orientation

The question "What causes homosexuality?" is both politically suspect and scientifically misconceived. Politically suspect because it is so frequently motivated by an agenda of prevention and cure. Scientifically misconceived because it presumes that heterosexuality is so well understood—so obviously the "natural" evolutionary consequence of reproductive advantage—that only deviations from it are theoretically problematic. Accordingly, the theory described in this article addresses the question "What causes sexual orientation?" and proposes the same basic account for both opposite-sex and same-sex desire. In particular, Figure 1 displays the proposed temporal sequence of events that leads to sexual orientation for most men and women in a gender-polarizing culture like ours—a culture that emphasizes the differences between the sexes by pervasively organizing both the perceptions and realities of communal life around the male/female dichotomy. The sequence begins at the top of the figure with biological variables (labeled A) and ends at the bottom with erotic/romantic attraction (F).

$A \rightarrow B$: Biological variables such as genes or prenatal hormones do not code for sexual orientation per se, but for childhood temperaments, such as aggression or activity level.

$B \rightarrow C$: Children's temperaments predispose them to enjoy some activities more than others. One child will enjoy rough-and-tumble play and competitive team sports (male-typical activities); another will prefer to socialize quietly or play jacks or hopscotch (female-typical activities). Children will also prefer to play with peers who share their activity preferences. Children who prefer sex-typical activities and same-sex playmates are referred to as "gender conforming"; children who prefer sex-atypical activities and opposite-sex playmates are referred to as "gender nonconforming."

$C \rightarrow D$: Gender-conforming children will feel different from opposite-sex peers, perceiving them as unfamiliar and exotic. Similarly, gender-nonconforming children will perceive same-sex peers as unfamiliar and exotic.

$D \rightarrow E$: These feelings of unfamiliarity produce heightened physiological arousal. For the male-typical child, it may be felt as antipathy toward girls; for the female-typical child, it may be felt as timidity or apprehension in the presence of boys. A particularly clear example is provided by the "sissy" boy who is taunted by male peers for his gender nonconformity and, as a result, is likely to experience the strong physiological arousal of fear and anger in their presence. The theory claims, however, that every child, conforming or nonconforming, experiences heightened nonspecific physiological arousal in the presence of peers from whom

A revised and shortened version of Daryl Bem, "Exotic Becomes Erotic: A Developmental Theory of Sexual Orientation," in *Psychological Review*, Vol. 103, no. 2 (1996). Copyright © 1997 by Daryl Bem. Reprinted by permission. All rights reserved. Notes have been renumbered and edited.

The Exotic-Becomes-Erotic Theory of Sexual Orientation

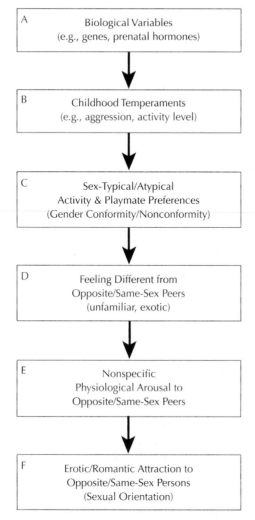

Figure 1. The Temporal Sequence of Events Leading to Sexual Orientation for Most Men and Women in a Gender-Polarizing Culture.

he or she feels different. In this most common case, the arousal will not necessarily be affectively toned or consciously felt.

$E \rightarrow F$: This physiological arousal is transformed in later years into erotic/romantic attraction. Steps $D \rightarrow E$ and $E \rightarrow F$ thus encompass specific psychological mechanisms that transform exotic into erotic ($D \rightarrow F$). For brevity, the entire sequence outlined in Figure 1 will be referred to as the "EBE (exotic becomes erotic)" theory of sexual orientation.

As noted above, Figure 1 does not describe an inevitable, universal path to sexual orientation but, rather, the most common path followed by men and women in a gender-polarizing culture like ours. Individual variations, alternative

Table 1.

Percentage of Respondents Reporting Gender-Nonconforming Preferences and Behaviors During Childhood

	Men		Women	
Response	Gay (n = 686)	Heterosexual (n = 337)	Lesbian (n = 293)	Heterosexual (n = 140)
Had not enjoyed sex-typical activities	63	10	63	15
Had enjoyed sex-atypical activities	48	11	81	61
Atypically sex-typed (masculinity/femininity)	56	8	80	24
Most childhood friends were opposite sex	42	13	60	40

Note: All chi-square comparisons between gay and heterosexual subgroups are significant at $p < .0001$.

paths, and cultural influences on sexual orientation are discussed later in the chapter.

EVIDENCE FOR THE THEORY

Evidence for EBE theory is organized into the following narrative sequence: gender conformity or nonconformity in childhood is a causal antecedent of sexual orientation in adulthood ($C \rightarrow F$). This is so because gender conformity or nonconformity causes a child to perceive opposite or same-sex peers as exotic ($C \rightarrow D$), and the exotic class of peers subsequently becomes erotically or romantically attractive to him or her ($D \rightarrow F$). This occurs because exotic peers produce heightened physiological arousal ($D \rightarrow E$) which is subsequently transformed into erotic/romantic attraction ($E \rightarrow F$). This entire sequence of events can be initiated, among other ways by biological factors that influence a child's temperaments ($A \rightarrow B$), which in turn, influence his or her preferences for gender-conforming or gender nonconforming activities and peers ($B \rightarrow C$).

Gender Conformity or Nonconformity in Childhood Is a Causal Antecedent of Sexual Orientation ($C \rightarrow F$)

In a study designed to test hypotheses about the development of sexual orientation, researchers conducted intensive interviews with approximately 1,000 gay men and lesbians and with 500 heterosexual men and women in the San Francisco Bay Area. The study (hereinafter, the San Francisco study) found that childhood gender conformity or nonconformity was not only the strongest, but also the only significant, childhood predictor of later sexual orientation for both men and women. As Table 1 shows, the effects were large and significant.[1]

For example, gay men were significantly more likely than heterosexual men to report that as children they had not enjoyed boys' activities (e.g., baseball and football), had enjoyed girls' activities (e.g., hopscotch, playing house, and jacks), and had been nonmasculine. These were the three variables that defined gender nonconformity in the study. Additionally, gay men were more likely than heterosexual men to have had girls as childhood friends. The corresponding comparisons between lesbian and heterosexual women were also large and significant.

It is also clear from the table that relatively more women than men had enjoyed sex-atypical activities and had opposite-sex friends during childhood. (In fact, more heterosexual women than gay men had enjoyed boys' activities as children—61 percent versus 37 percent, respectively.)

Many other studies have also shown that gay men and lesbians are more likely than heterosexual men and women to have gender-nonconforming behaviors and interests in childhood, including some studies that began with children and followed them into adulthood. The largest of these reported that approximately 75 percent of gender-nonconforming boys became bisexual or homosexual in adulthood, compared with only 4 percent of gender-conforming boys.[2]

Gender Conformity and Nonconformity Produce Feelings of Being Different from Opposite- and Same-Sex Peers, Respectively (C → D)

EBE theory proposes that gender-nonconforming children will come to feel different from their same-sex peers. In the San Francisco study, 70 percent of gay men and lesbians reported that they had felt different from same-sex peers in childhood, compared with only 38 percent and 51 percent of heterosexual men and women, respectively ($p < .0005$ for both gay/heterosexual comparisons). They further reported that they had felt this way throughout childhood and adolescence.

When asked in what way they had felt different from same-sex peers, gay men were most likely to say that they did not like sports; lesbians were most likely to say that they were more interested in sports or were more masculine than other girls. In contrast, those heterosexual men and women who had felt different from their same-sex peers typically cited differences unrelated to gender, such as being poorer, more intelligent, or more introverted. Heterosexual women frequently cited differences in physical appearance.

Exotic Becomes Erotic (D → F)

The heart of EBE theory is the proposition that individuals become erotically or romantically attracted to those who were unfamiliar to them in childhood. We have already seen some evidence for this in Table 1: those who played more with girls in childhood, gay men and heterosexual women, preferred men as sexual/romantic partners in later years; those who played more with boys in childhood, lesbian women and heterosexual men, preferred women as sexual/romantic partners in later years. Moreover, it has long been known that childhood familiarity is antithetical to later erotic or romantic attraction. For example, Westermarck observed over a century ago that married couples who had been betrothed in childhood experienced problematic sexual relationships when the girl had been taken in by the future husband's family and treated like one of the siblings.

A contemporary example is provided by children on Israeli kibbutzim, who are raised communally with age-mates in mixed-sex groups and exposed to one another constantly during their entire childhood. Sex play is not discouraged and is quite intensive during early childhood. After childhood, there is no formal or informal pressure or sanction against heterosexual activity within the peer group from educators, parents, or members of the peer group itself. Yet despite all this, there is a virtual absence of erotic attraction between peer group members in adolescence or adulthood. A review of nearly 3,000 marriages contracted by second-generation adults in all Israeli kibbutzim revealed that there was not a single case of an intrapeer group marriage.[3]

The Sambian culture in New Guinea illustrates the phenomenon in a homosexual context. Sambian males believe that boys cannot attain manhood without ingesting semen from older males. At seven years of age, Sambian boys are removed from the family household and initiated into secret male rituals, including ritualized homosexuality. For the next several years, they live in the men's clubhouse and regularly fellate older male adolescents. When they reach sexual maturity, they reverse roles and are fellated by younger initiates. During this entire time, they have no sexual contact with girls or women. And yet, when it comes time to marry and father children in their late teens or early twenties, all but a small minority of Sambian males become exclusively heterosexual. Although Sambian boys enjoy their homosexual activities, the context of close familiarity in which it occurs apparently prevents the development of strongly charged homo-erotic feelings.[4]

How Does Exotic Become Erotic? (D → E → F): The Extrinsic Arousal Effect

In his first-century Roman handbook, *The Art of Love,* Ovid advised any man who was interested in sexual seduction to take the woman in whom he was interested to a gladiatorial tournament, where she would more easily be aroused to passion. He did not say why this should be so, however, and it was not until 1887 that an elaboration appeared in the literature:

> Love can only be excited by strong and vivid emotion, and it is almost immaterial whether these emotions are agreeable or disagreeable. The Cid wooed the proud heart of Donna Ximene, whose father he had slain, by shooting one after another of her pet pigeons.[5]

A contemporary explanation of this effect is that it is a special case of the two-factor theory of emotion. That theory states that the physiological arousal of our autonomic nervous system provides the cues that we are feeling emotional but that the more subtle judgment of which emotion we are feeling often depends on our cognitive appraisal of the surrounding circumstances. Thus, the experience of passionate love or erotic/romantic attraction results from the conjunction of physiological arousal and the cognitive causal attribution (or misattribution) that the arousal has been elicited by the potential lover.

There is now extensive experimental evidence that an individual who has been physiologically aroused will show heightened sexual responsiveness to an appropriate target stimulus. In one set of studies, male participants were physiologically aroused by running in place, by hearing an audiotape of a comedy routine, or by hearing an audiotape of a grisly killing. They then viewed a taped interview with a physically attractive woman. Finally, they rated the woman's attractiveness, sexiness, and the degree to which they would like to date or kiss her. No matter how the arousal had been elicited, participants were more erotically responsive to the attractive woman than were control participants who had not been aroused.[6]

This extrinsic arousal effect can also be detected physiologically. In a pair of studies, men or women watched a sequence of two videotapes. The first portrayed either an anxiety-inducing or nonanxiety-inducing scene; the second videotape portrayed a nude heterosexual couple engaging in sexual foreplay. Preexposure to the anxiety-inducing scene produced greater penile tumescence in men and greater vaginal blood volume increases in women in response to the erotic scene than did preexposure to the nonanxiety-inducing scene.[7]

In short, physiological arousal, regardless of its source or affective tone, can subsequently be experienced cognitively, emotionally, and physiologically as erotic/romantic attraction. At that point, it is erotic/romantic attraction. The pertinent question, then, is whether this effect can account for the link between the hypothesized "exotic" physiological arousal in childhood and the erotic/romantic attraction later in life. One difficulty is that the effect occurs in the laboratory over brief time intervals, whereas the proposed developmental process spans several years. The time gap may be more apparent than real, however. As noted earlier, an individual sense of being different from same- or opposite-sex peers is not a one-time event, but a protracted and sustained experience throughout the childhood and adolescent years. This implies that the arousal will also be present throughout that time, ready to be converted into erotic or romantic attraction whenever the maturational, cognitive, and situational factors coalesce to provide the defining moment.

In fact, the laboratory experiments may actually underestimate the strength and reliability of the effect in real life. In the experiments, the arousal is deliberately elicited by a source extrinsic to the intended target, and there is disagreement over whether the effect even occurs when participants are aware of that fact. But in the real-life scenario envisioned by EBE theory, the physiological arousal is genuinely elicited by the class of individuals to which the erotic/romantic attraction develops. The exotic arousal and the erotic arousal are thus likely to be subjectively indistinguishable to the individual.

The Biological Connection: $(A \rightarrow F)$ versus $(A \rightarrow B)$

In recent years, researchers, the mass media, and segments of the lesbian/gay/bisexual community have rushed to embrace the thesis that a homosexual orientation is coded in the genes or determined by prenatal hormones and brain neuroanatomy. In contrast, EBE theory proposes that biological factors influence sexual orientation only indirectly, by intervening earlier in the chain of events to determine a child's temperaments and subsequent activity preferences.

One technique used to determine whether a trait is correlated with an individual's genotype (inherited characteristics) is to compare monozygotic (identical) twins, who share all their genes, with dizygotic (fraternal) twins, who, on average, share only 50 percent of their genes. If a trait is more highly correlated across monozygotic pairs of twins than across dizygotic pairs, this provides evidence for a correlation between the trait and the genotype. Using this technique, researchers have recently reported evidence for a correlation between an individual's genotype and his or her sexual orientation. For example, in a sample of gay men who had male twins, 52 percent of monozygotic twin brothers were also gay compared with only 22 percent of dizygotic twin brothers. In a comparable sample of lesbians, 48 percent of monozygotic twin sisters were also lesbian compared with only 16 percent of dizygotic twin sisters. A more systematic study of nearly 5,000 twins who had been drawn from a twin registry confirmed the genetic correlation for men but not for women.[8]

But these same studies provide even stronger evidence for the link proposed by EBE theory between an individual's genotype and his or her childhood gender nonconformity—even when sexual orientation is held constant. For example, in the 1991 twin study of gay men, the correlation on gender nonconformity in which both brothers were gay was .76 for monozygotic twins but only .43 for gay dizygotic twins, implying that gender conformity is significantly correlated with the genotype. Childhood gender nonconformity was also significantly correlated with the genotype for both men and women in the large twin registry study, even though sexual orientation itself was not correlated for the women. These studies are thus consistent with the link specified by EBE theory between the genotype and gender nonconformity ($A \rightarrow C$).

EBE theory further specifies that this link is composed of two parts; a link between the genotype and childhood temperaments ($A \rightarrow B$) and a link between those temperaments and gender nonconformity ($B \rightarrow C$). The temperaments most likely to be involved are aggression—and its benign cousin, rough-and-tumble play—and activity level. There is now substantial evidence that boys' play shows higher levels of rough-and-tumble play and activity than girls' play, that gender-nonconforming children of both sexes are sex-atypical on both traits, and that both traits are significantly correlated with the genotype.

In addition to these empirical findings, there are, I believe, conceptual grounds for preferring the EBE account to the competing hypothesis that there is a direct link between biology and sexual orientation. First, no theoretical rationale for a direct link between the genotype and sexual orientation has been clearly articulated, let alone established. At first glance, the theoretical rationale would appear to be nothing less than the powerful and elegant theory of evolution. The belief that sexual orientation is coded in the genes would appear to be just the general case of the implicit assumption, mentioned in the introduction, that heterosexuality is the obvious "natural" evolutionary consequence of reproductive advantage. But if that is true, then a homosexual orientation is an evolutionary anomaly that requires an explanation of how lesbians and gay men would pass on their "homosexual genes" to successive generations. Although several hypothetical scenarios have been suggested, they have been faulted on both theoretical and empirical grounds.

But the main problem with the direct-link hypothesis is that it fails to spell out any developmental process through which an individual's genotype actually gets transformed into his or her sexual orientation—which is precisely what EBE theory attempts to do. It is not that an argument for a direct link has been made and found wanting; it is that it has not yet been made.

I am certainly willing to concede that heterosexual behavior is reproductively advantageous, but it does not follow that it must therefore be sustained through genetic transmission. In particular, EBE theory suggests that heterosexuality is the most common outcome across time and culture because virtually all human societies polarize the sexes to some extent, setting up a sex-based division of labor and power, emphasizing or exaggerating sex differences, and, in general, superimposing the male/female dichotomy on virtually every aspect of communal life. These gender-polarizing practices ensure that most boys and girls will grow up seeing the other sex as unfamiliar and exotic—and, hence, erotic.

The more general point is that as long as the environment supports or promotes a reproductively successful behavior sufficiently often, it will not necessarily get programmed into the genes. For example, it is presumably reproductively advantageous for ducks to mate with other ducks, but as long as most baby ducklings first meet—and get imprinted on—other ducks, evolution can simply implant the imprinting process itself into the species rather than the specific content of what, reproductively speaking, needs to be imprinted. Analogously, because most cultures ensure that the two sexes will see each other as exotic, it would be sufficient for evolution to implant exotic-becomes-erotic processes into our species rather than heterosexuality per se. In fact, ethological studies of birds show that an exotic-becomes-erotic mechanism is actually a component of sexual imprinting. If ducks, which are genetically free to mate with any moving object, have not perished from the earth, then neither shall we.

In general, any biological factor that correlates with one or more of the intervening processes proposed by EBE theory could also emerge as a correlate of sexual orientation. Even if EBE theory turns out to be wrong, the more general point, that a mediating personality variable could account for observed correlations between biological variables and sexual orientation, still holds.

INDIVIDUAL VARIATIONS AND ALTERNATIVE PATHS

As noted earlier, Figure 1 is not intended to describe an inevitable, universal path to sexual orientation but only the path followed by most men and women in a gender-polarizing culture. Individual variations can arise in several ways. First, different individuals might enter the EBE path at different points in the sequence. For example, a child might come to feel different from same-sex peers not because of a temperamentally induced preference for gender-nonconforming activities, but because of an atypical lack of contact with same-sex peers or a physical disability. In general, EBE theory predicts that the effect of any childhood variable on an individual's sexual orientation depends on whether it prompts him or her to feel more similar to or more different from same-sex or opposite-sex peers.

Individual variations can also arise from differences in how individuals interpret the "exotic" arousal emerging from the childhood years, an interpretation that is inevitably guided by social norms and expectations. For example, girls might be more socially primed to interpret the arousal as romantic attraction, whereas boys might be more primed to interpret it as sexual arousal. Certainly, most individuals in our culture are primed to anticipate, recognize, and interpret opposite-sex arousal as erotic or romantic attraction and to ignore, repress, or differently interpret comparable same-sex arousal. In fact, the heightened visibility of gay men and lesbians in our society is now prompting individuals who experience same-sex arousal to recognize it, label it, and act on it at earlier ages than in previous years.[9]

In some instances, the EBE process itself may be supplemented or even superseded by processes of conditioning or social learning, both positive and negative. Such processes could also produce shifts in an individual's sexual orientation over the life course. For example, the small number of bisexual respondents in the San Francisco study appeared to have added same-sex erotic attraction to an already established heterosexual orientation after adolescence. Similar findings were reported in a more extensive study of bisexual individuals, with some respondents adding heterosexual attraction to a previously established homosexual orientation. This same study also showed that different components of an individual's sexual orientation need not coincide; for example, some of the bisexual respondents were more erotically attracted to one sex but more romantically attracted to the other.

Finally, some women who would otherwise be predicted by the EBE model to have a heterosexual orientation might choose for social or political reasons to center their lives around other women. This could lead them to avoid seeking out men for sexual or romantic relationships, to develop affectional and erotic ties to other women, and to self-identify as lesbians or bisexuals. In general, issues of sexual orientation identity are beyond the formal scope of EBE theory.

DECONSTRUCTING THE CONCEPT OF SEXUAL ORIENTATION

Nearly fifty years ago, Alfred Kinsey took a major step in deconstructing or redefining the concept of sexual orientation by construing it as a bipolar continuum, ranging from exclusive heterosexuality, through bisexuality, to exclusive homosexuality. Because many of the studies cited in this chapter have selected their respondents on the basis of Kinsey-like scales, EBE theory has necessarily been couched in that language: but the theory itself is not constrained by such bipolar dimensions. In fact, Figure 1 actually treats sexual orientation as two separate dimensions—a heteroerotic dimension and a homoerotic dimension—and EBE theory describes the processes that determine an individual's location on each of the two dimensions.

Conceptually, the two paths are independent, thereby allowing for a panoply of individual differences, including several variants of bisexuality (e.g., being erotically attracted to one sex and romantically attracted to the other). Empirically, however, the two dimensions are likely to be negatively correlated in a gender-polarizing culture in which most individuals come to be familiar with one sex while being estranged from the other. EBE theory predicts that this should be especially true for men in American society because, as shown in Table 1, boys are less likely than girls to have childhood friends of both sexes. This prediction is supported in a survey of a national probability sample of Americans. When asked to whom they were sexually attracted, men were likely to report that either they were exclusively heterosexual or exclusively homosexual. In contrast, women were more likely to report that they were bisexual than that they were exclusively homosexual.[10]

Culture influences not only the structure and distribution of sexual orientation in a society, but also how its natives, including its biological and behavioral scientists, conceptualize sexual orientation. Like the natives of any gender-polarizing culture, we have learned to look at the world through the lenses of gender, to impose the male/female dichotomy on virtually every aspect of life, especially sexuality. Which brings us to the most deeply embedded cultural assumption of all: that sexual orientation is necessarily based on sex. As Sandra Bem remarked,

> I am not now and never have been a "heterosexual." But neither have I ever been a "lesbian" or a "bisexual." . . . The sex-of-partner dimension implicit in the three categories . . . seems irrelevant to my own particular pattern of erotic attractions and sexual experiences. Although some of the (very few) individuals to whom I have been attracted . . . have been men and some have been women, what those individuals have in common has nothing to do with either their biological sex or mine—from which I conclude, not that I am attracted to both sexes, but that my sexuality is organized around dimensions other than sex.[11]

This statement also suggests the shape that sexual orientation might assume in a nongender-polarizing culture, a culture that did not systematically estrange its children from either opposite-sex or same-sex peers. Such children would not grow up to be asexual; rather, their erotic and romantic preferences would simply crystallize around a more diverse and idiosyncratic variety of attributes. Gentlemen might still prefer blonds, but some of those gentlemen (and some ladies) would prefer blonds of any sex. In the final deconstruction, then, EBE theory reduces to but one "essential" principle: exotic becomes erotic.

A POLITICAL POSTSCRIPT

Biological explanations of homosexuality have become more popular with the public in the 1990s, and many members of the lesbian/gay/bisexual community welcome this trend. For example, *The Advocate,* a national gay and lesbian news-magazine, reported that 61 percent of its readers believed that "it would mostly help gay and lesbian rights if homosexuality were found to be biologically determined."[12]

Because EBE theory proposes that an individual's sexual orientation is more directly the result of childhood experiences than of biological factors, it has prompted concerns that it could encourage an antigay agenda of prevention and "cure." In particular, the theory appears to suggest that parents could prevent their gender-nonconforming children from becoming gay or lesbian by encouraging sex-typical activities and same-sex friendships and by discouraging sex-atypical activities and opposite-sex friendships.

Of course, our society hardly needed EBE theory to suggest such a strategy. The belief that childhood gender nonconformity leads to later homosexuality is already so widely believed that many parents (especially fathers) already discourage their children (especially sons) from engaging in gender-nonconforming behaviors lest they become homosexual. And, if EBE theory is correct in positing that both homosexuality and heterosexuality derive from the same childhood processes, then it is clear that a gender-polarizing society like ours is already spectacularly effective in producing heterosexuality: 85–95 percent of all men and women in the United States are exclusively heterosexual.

But this same figure suggests that those children who continue to express sex-atypical preferences despite such cultural forces must have their gender nonconformity strongly determined by their basic inborn temperaments—as EBE theory proposes. Forcing such children to engage exclusively in sex-typical activities is unlikely to diminish their feelings of being different from same-sex peers and, hence, is unlikely to diminish their subsequent erotic attraction to those peers.

Empirical support for this hypothesis emerges from the longitudinal study of gender-nonconforming boys, cited earlier. About 27 percent of these boys had been entered by their parents into some kind of therapy, including behavioral therapy specifically designed to prevent a homosexual orientation from developing. Compared with parents of other gender-nonconforming boys, these parents were more worried about their sons' later sexuality, which suggests that they probably tried to discourage their sons' gender nonconformity in many other ways as well. All of this effort was for naught: 75 percent of their sons emerged as homosexual or bisexual, slightly more than the percentage of boys whose more laid-back parents had not entered them into therapy.[13] In the context of our society's current gender-polarizing practices, then, EBE theory does not provide a successful strategy for preventing gender-nonconforming children from becoming homosexual adults.

In general, I suggest that biological explanations of homosexuality are no more likely to promote gay-positive attitudes and practices than experienced-based explanations. For example, whenever new evidence for a "gay gene" is announced in the media, the researchers receive inquiries about techniques for detecting pregay children before they are born—presumably so that such children could be aborted. This chilling prevention strategy should disabuse us of the optimistic notion that biological explanations of homosexuality necessarily promote tolerance. Historically, of course, biological theories of human differences have tended to produce the least tolerant attitudes and the most conservative, even draconian, public policies—as in Nazi Germany.

Even more generally, I do not believe that attitudes toward homosexuality are substantially influenced by beliefs about causality; on the contrary, I believe that an individual's beliefs about causality are influenced by his or her preexisting attitudes toward homosexuality: people tend to find most credible those beliefs that best rationalize their attitudes. In short, EBE theory does not threaten the interests of the lesbian/gay/bisexual community any more than does a biological theory.

Notes

1. Alan P. Bell, Martin S. Weinberg, and Sue Kiefer Hammersmith, *Sexual Preference: Its Development in Men and Women* (Bloomington: Indiana University Press, 1981). The percentages in Table 10.1 have been calculated from the data given in the separately published appendix: Alan P. Bell, Martin S. Weinberg, and Sue Kiefer Hammersmith, *Sexual Preference: Its Development in Men and Women: Statistical Appendix* (Bloomington: Indiana University Press, 1981), 74–75, 77.

2. A summary review of retrospective studies appears in J. Michael Bailey, and Kenneth J. Zucker, "Childhood Sex-Typed Behavior and Sexual Orientation: A Conceptual Analysis and Quantitative Review," *Developmental Psychology*, 31 (1995) 43–55. Seven prospective studies are summarized in Kenneth J. Zucker and Richard Green, "Psychological and Familial Aspects of Gender Identity Disorder," *Child and Adolescent Psychiatric Clinics of North America*, 2(1993): 513–542. The largest of these is fully reported in Richard Green, The 'Sissy Boy Syndrome' and the Development of Homosexuality (New Haven: Yale University Press, 1987).

3. Edward A. Westermarck, *The History of Human Marriage*, (London: Macmillan, 1891). Observations on children of the kibbutzim will be found in Bruno Bettelheim, *The Children of the Dream* (New York: Macmillan, 1969); Albert Israel Rabin, *Growing Up in a Kibbutz* (New York: Springer, 1965); Joseph Shepher, "Mate Selection among Second Generation Kibbutz Adolescents and Adults: Incest Avoidance and Negative Imprinting," *Archives of Sexual Behavior* (1971): 1, 293–307; Melford E. Spiro, *Children of the Kibbutz* (Cambridge, MA: Harvard University Press, 1958); and Y. Talmon, "Mate Selection in Collective Settlements," *American Sociological Review* (1964): 29, 481–508.

4. Gilbert Herdt, *Sambia: Ritual and Gender in New Guinea* (New York: Holt, Rinehart and Winston, 1987).

5. Horwicz, quoted in Henry Theophilus Finck, *Romantic Love and Personal Beauty: Their Development, Causal Relations, Historic and National Peculiarities* (London: Macmillan, 1887).

6. Gregory L. White and Thomas D. Kight, "Misattribution of Arousal and Attraction: Effects of Salience of Explanations for Arousal," *Journal of Experimental Social Psychology*, (1984): 20, 55–64.

7. Peter W. Hoon, John P. Wincze, and Emily Franck Hoon, "A Test of Reciprocal Inhibition: Are Anxiety and Sexual Arousal in Women Mutually Inhibitory?" *Journal of Abnormal Psychology*, 86 (1977): 65–74; Sharlene A. Wolchik, Vicki E. Beggs, John P. Wincze, David K. Sakheim, David H., Barlow, and Matig Mavissakalian, "The Effect of Emotional Arousal on Subsequent Sexual Arousal in Men," *Journal of Abnormal Psychology*, 89 (1980): 595–598.

8. The twin studies are J. Michael Bailey and Richard C. Pillard, "A Genetic Study of Male Sexual Orientation," *Archives of General Psychiatry*, 48 (1991): 1089–1096; J. Michael Bailey, Richard C. Pillard, Michael C. Neale, and Yvonne Agyei, "Heritable Factors Influence Sexual Orientation in Women," *Archives of General Psychiatry*, 50 (1993): 217–223; and J. Michael Bailey and N. G. Martin, "A Twin Registry Study of Sexual Orientation," Paper presented at the annual meeting of the International Academy of Sex Research, Provincetown, MA, September, 1995.

9. Ronald C. Fox, "Bisexual Identities," in Anthony R. D'Augelli and Charlotte J. Petterson, eds., *Lesbian, Gay and Bisexual Identities Over the Lifespan* (New York: Oxford University Press, 1995), 48–86.

10. Edward I. Laumann, John H. Gagnon, Robert T. Michael, and Stuart Michaels, *The Social Organization of Sexuality: Sexual Practices in the United States* (Chicago: University of Chicago Press, 1994).

11. Sandra Lipsitz Bem, "The Lenses of Gender: Transforming the Debate on Sexual Inequality" (New Haven, CT: Yale University Press, 1993), vii.

12. "*Advocate* Poll results." *The Advocate*, February 6, 1996, 8.

13. Green, "Psychological and Familial Aspects," 318.

JAMES GARBARINO

A Boy's Code of Honor: Frustrated Justice and Fractured Morality

MAKING MORAL SENSE IS DIFFICULT

Making moral sense of their behavior is probably the most difficult challenge in dealing with kids who kill. When I appeared on a radio talk show in the days after Kip Kinkel's shootings in Springfield, Oregon, one of the callers said, "Surely, by the time a child reaches the age of four years, he knows the difference between right and wrong!" How can we understand the acts of lethal violence committed by violent boys in a way that helps us not only help them but prevents other kids from doing the same in the years to come? Do these actions make *any* moral sense? Are these boys without moral sense? Are they simply immoral? We need answers to these questions if we are to complete our understanding of the chain of events that begins in the disrupted relationships and rejections experienced in infancy and early childhood, that includes the bad behavior and aggression we see in later childhood, and that culminates in lethal violence in adolescence.

Sixteen-year-old Taylor is in prison for stabbing a priest. How did it happen, and why did he do it? Generally, Taylor doesn't like to talk about it. Now, looking

From *Lost Boys: Why Our Sons Turn Violent and How We Can Save Them*, chapter 5. Copyright © 1999 by James Garbarino. Reprinted by permission of the author.

back on it during an interview with me, he seems a bit ashamed. When he is finally willing to tell me the story, it comes out like this: "I needed money. I used to go to the church—lot of good it did me—so I knew there was money in the church. So I went there to take it. You know, from the collection box. Anyway, I needed the money, and I was working on the box with a screwdriver, you know, opening it, when this priest comes in and yells at me to stop. I started to run and he came after me, so I stabbed him, you know, with the screwdriver. Then I ran."

It seems hard to fathom any moral framework in which stabbing a priest makes sense. But is it really any more or less sensible than killing your classmates? Or shooting a convenience store clerk because he stuttered and was slow to get the money out of the cash register? Or killing a stranger on the street who insulted you? Or shooting a cop to death because he stopped you on the street? The violent boys I know have done all these things and more. Do any of these acts make moral sense?

What strikes us about many of the kids who kill is that their actions don't seem to make any moral sense. And so we readily conclude that these boys *have* no moral sense. But things are not always as obvious upon reflection as they seem to be at first—both for the kids who kill and for all of us who judge them. To these boys and their peers, their acts often do make moral sense. Or perhaps they don't see their acts as either moral or immoral at all but, rather, as necessary for survival, or as simple entitlements. This latter point is worth reflecting upon.

Regardless of its origins, the action of many violent boys conveys a kind of arrogance, or what journalist Edward Helmore, writing in *The Guardian* in 1997, calls "deadly petulance." "I needed money," says Taylor, as if that is justification enough. "He insulted me," says Conneel, as if that is sufficient to warrant a death sentence. In this these two are not alone: many of the shooters in the small-town and suburban school attacks offer what appear to be similarly self-centered explanations. Luke Woodham feels like an outcast and reported, "I just couldn't take it anymore." Michael Carneal says he felt mad about the way other kids treated him. Mitchell Johnson says, "Everyone that hates me, everyone I don't like is going to die." According to newspaper accounts, Andrew Wurst is reported to have said he hated his parents and his teachers and was mad about not being successful with girls.

Just hearing these few words from boys who kill does seem to cast their actions as grandiose, egotistical, and arrogant. Who the hell are they to take a human life because they feel insulted, frustrated, or teased or just because they need money? At this level they do sound like simply rotten kids. But there is much more to the story. The sense of their actions and the scope of their moral framework emerges from the details, rather than the headlines, of the story when we place these details in the larger context of their lives. It comes from their being lost in the world.

LOOKING IN THE MORAL MIRROR

Before we look closely at the boys, however, we must begin with ourselves. For starters, we need to recognize that most people accept killing as a necessity. The issue for most of us is not the wrongness of killing in general but killing outside the boundaries of society's rules and values. The critical point is how we define immoral killing.

Many of us can understand killing when we can see and sympathize with the moral justification behind it. There is no better example than the death penalty—judicially justified homicide. State governments throughout the United States impose the death penalty, and they do so with the support of a majority of the voters. Yet many Americans see this brand of killing as immoral, and once you get beyond our national borders, many more people are amazed that we condone it at all. In addition to our widespread acceptance of the death penalty, most of us accept as justifiable a killing committed in personal self-defense. Killing someone who attacks us is killing too, but it is accepted legally and morally as self-defense.

In recent years this moral and legal legitimacy has even been extended to include the actions of some battered women who kill their husbands after enduring years of extremely violent, nonlethal assault. This kind of killing has come to make moral sense to us after decades of public education about the psychological dynamics and cultural implications of domestic violence. But not so long ago, many men believed that a marriage license was a license to beat their wives and knew that institutions—police, courts, social services—accepted that right. Until recently, battered women who killed their abusive husbands could expect to be treated like eighteenth-century slaves in revolt: while the excessiveness of the victimizer's behavior was recognized, that behavior alone was not considered enough to justify radically violent action that challenged the status quo. It was particularly easy to apply this attitude to battered wives when it was assumed that they "asked for it" in the first place. Now, as we understand better what it means to live inside an abusive relationship, and as women have gained in status generally, we are beginning to see the moral sense when a woman sets her abusive husband's bed on fire or shoots him while he sleeps or poisons him at dinnertime. Again, we see this type of killing as justifiable homicide.

Most of us saw the moral sense in the killing of innocent civilians in Iraq. We saw it as a necessary side effect of prosecuting the Gulf War in 1992, and again in 1998 and 1999, as *politically justifiable* homicide. The same is true of our support for antigovernment forces in Nicaragua and elsewhere in the world throughout the 1980s. Killing seems to make some sense to people when it is politically sanctioned. Just how many absolute pacifists are there among us who would not justify almost any killing act when committed by a legally constituted government in pursuit of national security? Or, more broadly, how many pacifists are there when it comes to interpersonal violence on the streets, at school, or at home?

THE MORAL CIRCLE

All of us have a *moral circle* when it comes to violence; some acts are inside the circle of moral justification while other acts are outside that circle. Would you kill an intruder in your home? Would you kill a terminally ill relative? Would you abort a third-trimester pregnancy? Would you agree to the assassination of Saddam Hussein? Would you kill a relative if he were sexually abusing your child? Would you kill a raccoon that bit your son? What if there was a remote possibility the animal had rabies and killing it was the only way to find out for sure? Would you kill it? Killing a raccoon is not the same as killing a human being. Nor is killing Saddam Hussein the same as killing Martin Luther King. Stabbing an abuser is different from stabbing a stranger. Where does one draw the line, and how does one determine which killings make moral sense and which do not?

Cultures and societies set different standards for the morality of killing. Watching the film *Seven Years in Tibet* about the youthful Dalai Lama, many of us were amused to watch the lengths to which Tibetan Buddhists went to avoid killing worms while digging the foundation for a new building. Their reverence for life extends their moral circle very widely. Most of us would put worms *outside* our moral circle when it comes to killing. Does that make us immoral, or does it make much of the killing we do amoral (in the sense that few Americans can relate to the killing of worms as a *moral* issue at all)? Yet any four-year-old Tibetan Buddhist child knows the wrongness of killing any living being, worms included. How many Christian, Jewish, or Muslim children appreciate *this* moral distinction? Are worms inside the moral circle of these children?

What about dogs and cats? Most of us would put dogs and cats inside the circle, particularly if they are household pets (less so if they are strays). Thus, most Americans would have moral qualms about killing a dog or a cat but not a cow, a pig, or a chicken. How and where do we draw these lines? Is vegetarianism more moral than carnivorousness? Is cannibalism absolutely different from the killing and eating of our fellow mammals? Let us start by keeping these complicated moral distinctions in mind as we look deeper into the stories of young people who commit murder. Let's walk a bit in the lost boys' shoes before we judge them.

Most of us can morally justify some form of killing when it seems necessary. Most of us legitimize violence when we see no moral alternatives and denounce it when we believe alternatives are available. In this sense, necessity is the moral mother of murder. And that is the key to understanding boys who kill and their legitimization of violence. At the moment of crisis they don't see positive alternatives, because of who they are and their emotional history, and where they come from and how they see the world. They do what they have to do—*as they see it.* Understanding this horrible reality is very difficult; it requires a kind of openheartedness and openmindedness that is hard for anyone to achieve, particularly in today's political and emotional climate. But achieve it we must if we are to understand the motivations and experiences that drive boys to commit acts of lethal violence and then marshal our resources to prevent this from happening with other troubled boys.

STRUGGLING TO UNDERSTAND

I face my own personal struggle to understand when the incarcerated boys I interview talk about killing. It is my third interview with Conneel, and although the official topic of discussion is "his neighborhood," we end up talking about violence, specifically, his "first homicide." We are talking about girls, and Conneel says in passing, "They really started coming around after my first homicide." He says it so casually that I think it would be a good time to hear the whole story, particularly since other boys (such as Kip Kinkel) echo this theme; namely, that some girls find violent boys attractive.

Conneel tells his tale rather matter-of-factly, a narrative style common to the boys I have interviewed in prison. The discourse leading up to the description of the killing itself sounds rather chilling despite—or perhaps because of—the nature of the story. In this account, fifteen-year-old Conneel rounds a corner in his Brooklyn neighborhood and sees a nineteen-year-old standing on the street in front of his building; he is surrounded by other kids, most of whom Conneel knows from dealing drugs. Recognizing the gold chain around his neck as the one this youth had stolen from him at gunpoint two weeks earlier, Conneel approaches, gun drawn, and demands the chain back. The nineteen-year-old at first yells out that he doesn't know "what the fuck" Conneel is talking about, but then gives up the chain after seeing Conneel's gun. With the chain now in his left hand, Conneel puts the gun to the nineteen-year-old's head and pulls the trigger. The boy dies instantly.

Why on earth did he kill him when the chain was recovered? For Conneel it was simply, "I did what I had to do." What does that mean in moral terms? It means that this was a matter of retributive justice and an act of preemptive violence that made moral sense to Conneel because by robbing him in the first place the boy he killed had placed himself outside of Conneel's moral circle. Conneel calculated that if he didn't kill the other boy at that moment, he would be exposing himself to danger in the future, so he "did what he had to do." In Conneel's eyes, the boy deserved the death penalty for threatening him, and executing him was a morally justified act of punishment, deterrence, and self-preservation. The fact that in Conneel's eyes the shooting was morally justified doesn't mean it was right. I must say that I feel the same way about those who favor the execution of kids who kill. They offer a moral justification, but they are not right.

Consider Dennis, whose parents abused and then abandoned him to his grandmother when he was four years old. When his grandmother died only four years later, the perceived injustice of this abandonment and death was too great for Dennis to bear. And so he "declared war on the world" (his words), and we all know that "all's fair in love and war."

Violent boys operate in a particular moral universe. They often have moral circles much more circumscribed than those of other kids their age. Sometimes these moral circles shrink so as to virtually disappear, which produces what seems from the outside to be unlimited legitimization of aggression. However, all but those with the most profound psychological damage do have a moral circle.

The world that Dennis lives in is filled with violence, but it does have rules. In fact, it is highly moralistic in many ways. Malcolm lives in that same world. I learned this when he spoke of his response when he learned that his pregnant girlfriend had been shot. It was clear that in his moral system, the shooting of his girlfriend violated the rules. He perceived this act very differently from the way he saw what appeared to me to be similar acts in his world. As I sat with him, Malcolm was filled with outrage that someone would shoot a *girl*, even more so a pregnant one (with his male child). And he had some very clear ideas about how the shooting fit into the social life of his community. "Has to be outside people coming in. Has to be, 'cause you can't be in the same neighborhood and do something like that." "What is going to happen next?" I asked. Malcolm was pretty clear on that score, expecting that his friends and relatives would see to it that his son's death was avenged. And it was. Within two weeks, the boys who had done the shooting were identified, tracked down, and killed.

THE LURE OF THE DARK SIDE

There are individuals who are so profoundly damaged that they are literally amoral, that is, without any morality whatsoever when it comes to interpersonal aggression and violence. As Yale University psychiatrist Dorothy Otnow-Lewis reports in her book *Guilty by Reason of Insanity*, some of the most notorious serial killers are so psychologically damaged that they approximate this state of pure amorality. But such individuals are very, very few in number, and even most of them do have some small area of morality in which they suspend their lethal behavior—for a dog, a cat, a bird, a rat, a lizard, or even a child.

Complete amorality is extremely rare. We have encountered a couple of boys in our work who are so profoundly damaged that they seem to have no moral circle at all. The psychiatric term for these individuals is *psychopath*. Their psychopathy is chilling. Stanley, for example, speaks coolly and casually about sexual violence, about self-mutilation, about animals and people he has killed, and about his plans to continue killing when the opportunity arises. It is chilling to hear. It takes your breath away and it makes your skin crawl. It makes you glad there is someone observing through the interview room's window. When Stanley notices the reaction he is eliciting, he smiles and asks rhetorically, "Does this bother you?"

Few boys ever get to this point, where they are beyond morality. But some boys do come close to achieving this final state, particularly when they are operating in the war-zone mentality of a conventional youth prison, where honor and the preservation of some modicum of dignity is a constant battle. Some get there when they are immersed in some sort of negative ideology, such as Satanism, in which they adopt a profound nihilism, believing only in the darkest of the dark side.

A study done by psychologists Kelly Damphousse and Ben Crouch revealed that nearly 10 percent of juvenile offenders in the Texas system reported some level of involvement in Satanism. These boys were characterized by a low level of attachment to conventional society, as represented by parents and schools; a high level of attachment to peers; higher than average intelligence; and a sense of life being out of their control. The fourteen-year-old shooter in Edinboro, Pennsylvania, Andrew Wurst, was nicknamed Satan by his schoolmates. Kip Kinkel in Springfield, Oregon, was involved in the dark, violent imagery of "heavy metal" music. Luke Woodham, the sixteen-year-old shooter in Pearl, Mississippi, was part of an avowed Satanist group of boys in his community.

The culture of the dark side has a special draw for troubled boys, alienated boys, and boys who are outside the orbit of the positive features of American life. When this attraction combines with the power of negative peer groups, the result can be very dangerous. Social worker Ronald Feldman has studied the impact of peer group composition on adolescent behavior for decades. He finds that the tipping point in an adolescent peer group, from positive to negative, can come with only a minority of the individuals being predisposed to negative behavior. Once these negative peers take over the group, the positive boys either leave or are driven out or go along with the negative agenda. Today boys can become members of negative peer groups without even leaving home (e.g., through Internet chat groups).

PERCEIVED INJUSTICE AND THE MORAL CODE OF VIOLENCE

Malcolm spoke about his time in a youth prison that was out of adult control and that had deteriorated into a savage battle for physical and psychological survival. He reports, "I was fighting every day. If a person looked at me wrong, I'd reach across the table and hit him. If he touched something on my tray, I'd hit him. If he reached over at my food, I'd hit him. That's how it was. I had the mind of a savage. I didn't have self-discipline. I couldn't just let little stuff ride, because if I did I felt like nobody respected me. So I tried to inflict pain on them and serve justice. But it wasn't justice. I know that now."

Much more common than truly amoral boys are boys within whom a stunted or otherwise troubled emotional life combines with a narrow and intense personal need for justice. These impulses come to dominate a boy's moral thinking to the exclusion of other considerations, such as social conventions about right and wrong, consequences, empathy, and even personal survival.

I learned this lesson about the links between perceived injustice and the moral code of violence first from the work of psychiatrist James Gilligan. For many years Gilligan worked in the mental health system of the state prisons of Massachusetts, dealing with violent boys grown into full, psychologically impoverished manhood. Gilligan achieved the incredible openness of heart and mind required to understand men who commit lethal violence. He worked ceaselessly at knowing them, with an unprejudiced understanding of what violence is about in the lives of these highly criminal, highly dangerous men. As he did so, he came to understand that almost all acts of violence are related to perceived injustice, the subjective experience of frustrated justice, and an attempt to redress injustice. Deadly petulance usually hides some deep emotional wounds, a way of compensating through an exaggerated sense of grandeur for an inner sense of violation, victimization, and injustice.

When boys kill, they are seeking justice—*as they see it, through their eyes*. What makes these acts appear senseless to us is often the fact that we either don't see the connection between the original injustice and the eventual lethal act or don't understand why the boy perceived injustice in the first place. This latter point is sometimes easily dispelled if it results from our lack of understanding of the boy's experience.

Consider Stephen, for example, an eighteen-year-old who killed a police officer. Stephen is a polite young man with an engaging smile and a shy manner. Words don't come easy for him, but when they do come they often tell volumes about his desperate efforts to escape his physically and psychologically abusive mother in the years after his father died, when Stephen was eight years old.

I see little evidence in the reports of his social workers and psychologists that they recognized the injustice he experienced at home at the hands of a mother who rejected him while she accepted his brother, a mother who whipped his back raw while she rewarded his compliant brother and who told him that he was like his "no-good father" and that his brother "favored" her side of the family. Interestingly, what comes across in Stephen's records is just a boy who after losing his father grew into an ungrateful teenager who caused his mother embarrassment and inconvenience.

But I have had a chance to see and hear the real story, from the inside out. What did Stephen want more than anything in the world? He wanted to be loved and accepted by his mother. In this he is no different from any of us. Is there any greater injustice for a child than to be unloved, rejected, and abused? Failing to receive, or perceive, that love and acceptance, what did he want? He wanted to be free of the imprisonment he felt at home, where, he told me, his greatest fear was that he would strike out at his abusive mother. And when I asked him if he thought God would forgive her for what she did to him, he responded, "I hope so."

Of course, not all the lost boys are so forgiving. Boys do commit parricide. In fact, kids kill their parents with alarming frequency, almost always in response to feeling they have been rejected and abused. In his book on the topic, *When a Child Kills*, lawyer Paul Mones presents numerous examples. Even when the initial story paints the child as an ungrateful or crazed monster, further investigation often (but, admittedly, not always) reveals that the killing took place as the culmination of years of deteriorating family relationships and, most often, abuse.

I met one boy from such a situation, a fifteen-year-old who had killed his abusive stepfather. Abandoned emotionally by his mother, Terry was left behind in the supposed care of her former husband. His humiliation of Terry was unceasing, but the boy had nowhere else to go. After nearly two years of escalating anger and sadness, Terry reached his limit when his stepfather casually slapped Terry's nephew across the face so hard that the two-year-old went sprawling across the floor. "I just wasn't going to take it any more," Terry told me. "I knew I would have to pay the price for what I did, but I didn't care. The man had to be stopped. So I went into the bedroom and got his shotgun. Both barrels. Then I called the cops."

Terry was sentenced to twenty-five years in prison. Killings such as Terry's are easier to make sense of than what Stephen did. Even if we think Terry's response was extreme and impulsive, most of us can at least imagine his moral framework: retributive justice, vengeance, and a desperate attempt to escape from an emotionally intolerable situation. But what about Stephen?

WHEN BEING WRONGED BECOMES INTOLERABLE

Stephen killed when he was stopped on the street by the police. Why was he out on the street? He needed to escape from home. Why did he kill that night on the street? He was carrying a gun and he was out on bail awaiting sentencing on a weapons charge; he was hoping for a brief sentence on that charge, but he knew that if he was picked up carrying a gun, the sentence would be lengthened substantially. At the moment he was stopped by police, he was caught by the injustice of his situation. Stephen needed freedom more than anything else (except love), and here was a threat to that freedom in the form of two cops who were stopping him on the street "for no good reason." As a result of this unfair action, he knew he would lose his freedom. He felt he had no choice but to prevent this injustice from going any further. He shot at the cops—he says to scare them so that he could run away. But after he shot twice, they started shooting at him. More injustice. Stephen returned the fire, and the result was a dead cop and his wounded partner—and one boy facing the death penalty.

In Paducah, Kentucky, fifteen-year-old Michael Carneal was tired of being teased and picked on by his schoolmates. Luke Woodham of Pearl, Mississippi, said, "No one truly loved me." Overweight and bespectacled, he had been picked on since kindergarten. His note said, "I killed because people like me are mistreated every day." Perceived injustice. No, make that real injustice.

This intolerability is an important aspect of the psychological situation faced by kids who kill. It often reflects their sense of honor and dishonor. This is a very American attitude. New Hampshire's state motto is "Live free or die." Soldiers are taught the code of "death before dishonor." Boys incorporate this code. Evidence of this is their belief in divine punishment and their frequent recourse to suicide as a means of escaping. James Gilligan reminds us that adult killers are much more likely to kill themselves than to be killed by the state.

Kids see death as a way out, too. One of the two brave schoolmates who wrestled Kip Kinkel to the ground and put a stop to his shooting spree reported that he heard the boy plead, "Shoot me." According to the classmate who wrestled Michael Carneal to the ground as he stopped shooting momentarily to reload, the boy said, "Kill me now." Stephen has said that he wants the death penalty if the alternative is life in prison, and Malcolm told me he would rather die than submit to any more abuse.

DEATH BEFORE DISHONOR: SHAME AND VIOLENCE

While there is an inner circle of compassion in Malcolm's life, outside that circle it is all tooth and claw. For example, he once nearly killed a man who molested his younger cousin. The crime for which he is presently serving time is another example:

As his sister opened the door of a neighborhood convenience store, a young man named Clifton burst out the door, knocking her and her two-year-old son to the ground, causing the little boy to suffer a concussion. Without apologizing, Clifton laughed and walked off. Malcolm tracked him down to demand an apology for the insult and blatant disrespect of his sister and her child. First he studied Clifton's movements, waiting until he was sure he could confront him one-on-one. Then he arranged for Clifton's girlfriend to set him up for a meeting. Then he had his brother pull his car in behind Clifton's car in the girl's driveway so that there would be no possibility of escape. Having made these preparations, Malcolm confronted Clifton, gun in hand, and gave him an opportunity to apologize. Clifton laughed in his face. This response was intolerable. Malcolm hit him in the head with his fist and again demanded an apology. Clifton declined and reached down for his own gun. When he did, Malcolm opened fire. Two shots. Luckily for both of them, neither was fatal.

Many of the acts of lethal violence committed by boys are deliberate and sometimes even meticulously planned, rather than spur-of-the-moment explosions of rage. I think this is significant, because it highlights the importance of understanding that boys think about violence as a solution to their problems. More than just the result of an uncontrollable urge, these violent acts are related to Gilligan's idea of frustrated justice. This is particularly true of the boys who committed the school shootings in the 1997–1998 school year:

In Kentucky, Michael Carneal timed his assault so that it would occur during the regular morning prayer meeting at his high school. In Arkansas, thirteen-year-old Mitchell Johnson and eleven-year-old Andrew Golden developed an elaborate plan involving a false fire alarm to draw students out into the line of fire they had set up, like soldiers preparing an ambush; they succeeded in killing students and a teacher. In Oregon, Kip Kinkel carried his arsenal into the school cafeteria at just the right time in the morning and was able to shoot twenty-four classmates, two fatally.

What produces this intolerable state of being in which violent boys live? James Gilligan believes that injustice produces shame, and it is shame that generates the intolerability of existence. Shame imposes the fear that one will cease to exist, the prospect of psychic annihilation. Nothing seems to threaten the human spirit more than rejection, brutalization, and lack of love. Nothing—not physical deformity, not debilitating illness, not financial ruin, not academic failure—can equal insults to the soul. Nothing compares with the trauma of this profound assault on the psyche.

Those who are shamed are vulnerable to committing violence and aggression, because they know that acts of violence against self or others are a reliable method for reasserting existence when life experience has denied it. "I hurt, therefore I am." A colleague of mine reports that an adult prisoner once told her, "I'd rather be wanted for murder than not wanted at all." A grim assessment but ringing with truth. Acts of violence and aggression confirm existence. And, paradoxically, acts of violence against the self may serve the same purpose, particularly for children; as they contemplate suicide or actually engage in a suicide attempt, many youth seem to think, "That will show them. They'll be sorry when I'm gone."

Remember that adolescents are theatrical, viewing the world as a stage, with themselves playing the leading roles. And their plays are often melodramas and, on occasion, even tragedies. Many of us can recall thinking suicidal thoughts, but most of us had the inner resources and outer supports to leave it at that. Of course, tens of thousands of kids each year can't leave it at that and do attempt suicide.

The greatest danger comes when the crisis of perceived impending psychic annihilation is melodramatically merged with the idea of addressing intolerable injustice with violence. The two go together, because in our society the idea of retribution through violence is a basic article of faith. Vengeance is not confined to some small group of psychologically devastated individuals. It is normal for us, a fact of value in our culture.

It isn't surprising that those of us who feel unjustly treated—by our mother or father, a spouse or lover, a friend or acquaintance, even a child or society itself—resort to violence to redress that sense of injustice. The most vulnerable members of our community show us where the negative values in our culture lead, show us how things really look at the extremes. The actions of violent boys show us what comes of our society's poisonous belief that "revenge is sweet." We would all do better to heed the ancient proverb "When you begin a journey of revenge, start by digging two graves, one for your enemy and one for yourself."

The links between injustice and shame operate inside families in their most devastating forms, but they also operate outside the family in the larger community, particularly at the intersection of race and class. Ethologist Desmond Morris said many years ago, "The viciousness with which children are treated is a measure of the dominant pressures imposed upon their tormentors." It is a message worth repeating today: If you want peace, work for justice—in the world and on the playground.

MAKING MORAL MISTAKES

Illuminating the role of shame and perceived injustice in the lives of violent boys provides a good beginning to making some moral sense of their violent actions. But there is more to tell. One of the most difficult things to understand about the lost boys is their use of the word *mistake* to describe what others define as an immoral act. Few aspects of youth violence elicit such a negative response as this one does. As Stanton Samenow, a psychologist who has worked with criminals for many years, puts it, "They may have left a long trail of injury behind them, may even admit that they have done harm, caused horrible problems, but if you ask if they think they are bad people, they will say no. A rapist will say, 'I'm basically a good guy, though I have made some mistakes'—imagine calling rape a mistake!"

I've heard it, too. Lost boys use the term *mistake* to refer to deliberate, intentional acts of violence that achieve their conscious goal. Is there any way to understand how they can regard these immoral acts as mistakes without resorting to explanations that hinge upon the assumption that they are simply lying or engaging in self-protective denial?

Studies of moral reasoning generally focus on the development of sophisticated thinking as the hallmark of moral development, yet sophisticated thinking is but one side of a triangle. The other two are sophisticated feelings and behavior. Thus, the moral person is one who does more than reason about dilemmas. Such a person has moral character. As character education expert Tom Lickona puts it, being a moral person involves "knowing the good, desiring the good, and doing the good."

The standard for efforts to assess the thinking part of morality or moral reasoning grew out of the work of Harvard psychologist Lawrence Kohlberg. Kohlberg's approach has been adopted and adapted by many investigators as a strategy for identifying how well kids are doing in applying their intellect to the task of figuring out moral dilemmas. His system has three levels, each of which contains two stages representing more sophisticated reasoning and more abstract principles than the levels and stages that come before it. The three main levels are "preconventional moral reasoning," "conventional moral reasoning," and "postconventional moral reasoning." At the preconventional level, the emphasis is on fear of punishment, desire for rewards, and the trade-offs between the two that alternative courses of action will produce. At the conventional level, the focus is on doing what "good people" do and respecting family and society's rules. At the postconventional level, the key is an attempt to live by more universal principles, that is, principles that go beyond specific times and places and people.

Most violent boys stand mostly at Level 1 in Kohlberg's classification system, preconventional moral reasoning. Systematic studies of juvenile delinquents responding to moral dilemmas of the type used by Kohlberg also identify such kids as primitive thinkers. For example, psychologists James Nelson, Deborah Smith, and John Dodd have reported that juvenile delinquents in general tend to operate at Level 1, where the concern is with the pragmatics of reward and punishment and getting what one wants. A boy at this level responds to the rightness and wrongness of alternative courses of action on the basis of what and how each possibility will cost and benefit him. Few violent youths are at Level 2, where right and wrong are couched in terms of what helps people meet their legitimate needs. For these boys, "wrong" equals "mistake." Thus, when they say they made a mistake in committing their crimes, often this is an indication of unsophisticated moral reasoning, not amorality per se.

In the wake of the Jonesboro shootings, in the spring of 1998, I ask Conneel about the two boys who committed the murders. Conneel has already admitted to me that he himself was responsible for several deaths and has amassed a substantial arsenal that is hidden in the basement of his apartment building. When I ask him to tell me what he thinks about an appropriate punishment for Mitchell Johnson and Andrew Golden, he starts out with the thought that they might deserve the death penalty. But then he quickly pulls back from that position, reminding me that he is concerned that the death penalty may be imposed upon *him* for *his* lethal acts. He thinks for a while, and then continues. "They're responsible for what they did," he says. "They shot innocent victims—girls," he reasons, "and they should go to prison for that. I'd say at least fifteen years in jail so they can change." When it comes to judging *others,* Conneel is about normal for an American. Of course, like many of us, he has trouble applying those standards to himself. His killings were not of innocent people, he is quick to point out. But isn't that always the point? Do any violent offenders see the target of their lethal violence as innocent?

To an outsider, the violence that lost boys commit often seems to make no sense or to evidence a total breakdown in morality. But this is not the case when we see the world through their eyes. These boys often commit acts of violence on the basis of a "moral" idea in their heads, usually something to do with revenge or injustice or wounded pride or glory. Pressures build as they ruminate on the injustice done to them, usually some specific insult or disappointment set within a bigger picture of resentment. In this way, there is no such thing as a "senseless act of violence." This does not mean that we simply accept their analysis as legitimate, of course, but it does force us to look beyond our shock, horror, and indignation to see the roots of the problem.

MORALITY DEVELOPS IF NURTURED

Boys who kill tend to operate at a low level of sophistication in their moral judgments. But these levels of reasoning are not fixed. They reflect how a boy has adapted to date, not what is possible for him in the future. Indeed, one of the goals for any program to succeed with them is its ability to elevate their moral thinking and help them believe that they can live in a world where something other than survival ethics rules. More on that later.

Another way of looking at moral development is through the development of conscience. Psychologist Barbara Stilwell and her colleagues have explored this process, and they, too, offer a system of levels to convey the progression through which children move morally. Conscience is an individual's sense of listening to a moral voice (the image of Pinocchio's Jiminy Cricket comes to my mind). Stilwell reports two findings particularly useful to understanding the lost boys.

First, the average fifteen-year-old exhibits a "confused conscience," meaning that he is trying to deal with competing and sometimes incompatible moral messages coming from inside and outside his head. This is relevant because it highlights the idea that the confusion lost boys display is to some degree normal; it is the nature of the issues they face that is abnormal. It is one thing to be a fifteen-year-old confused about cheating on a math exam and quite another to be confused about killing someone who threatens you with violence. I can recall the first from my adolescence, but I had no experience with the latter. This is not a demonstration of my moral and developmental superiority but, rather, of the relative social health of my childhood environment. . . .

Second, Stilwell and her colleagues report that conscience development is a big problem for children with Conduct Disorder, which we have seen afflicts the majority of violent boys. As one nine-year-old boy in her study put it, "a conscience is a little guy inside you that tells you right from wrong, but I ain't got one of them." Interestingly, at this stage of what Stilwell calls external conscience, what the child needs to progress developmentally is "emotional attachment, supervision, clarity of rules, and limit setting"—just what most violent boys don't receive most of the time.

CONSCIENCE UNDER CONSTRUCTION

Eleven-to-fifteen-year-olds are as much children as they are adolescents, and their ability to engage in reality-based moral thinking is still very much "under construction." Some children have erected a solid internal monitor, a prosocial conscience, by the time they enter adolescence. But, again, as psychologist Barbara Stilwell's research shows, most teens actually have to deal with a "confused conscience." Some are still mainly responding to external messages about what is right and what is wrong. And some have a great emotional emptiness inside that drives them to seek extreme solutions to their problems. Some of this emptiness is personal, as we see from the individual life histories, but some of it is social and cultural in its origins.

But whether they exhibit conscience or not, boys are not yet adults, and their ability to appreciate the consequences of their behavior is often quite limited. This has a bearing on what we should do with juvenile killers. The fact that they are capable of committing lethal, adult-like crimes does not mean that they are adults. The two things are quite separate and distinct. The common belief that "if you can do the crime, you can do the time" is offered to justify the prosecution and incarceration of kids as if they were adults, but this approach has no basis in the realities of child development.

FEELING FOR YOURSELF IS THE FOUNDATION OF FEELING FOR OTHERS

When it comes to the feeling part of morality, boys who kill are at a special disadvantage. The key to moral feeling is empathy, which is an openness to the feelings of others that allows a person to appreciate what an action means emotionally to someone else. But when a boy's own emotional life is closed off and locked away, when he can't accurately and openly feel his own feelings, it is unlikely that he has much of a basis for being empathic with others. Of course, this is a problem for males generally in our society, as Terrence Real's work so vividly demonstrates. In this sense, the emotional blockage so characteristic of violent boys is partly a result of their maleness in American culture.

But added to this generic problem is the fact that most violent boys have specific unresolved issues of trauma from experiences of abuse and rejection at home, in addition to their exposure to violence and victimization in the community, on the streets, and through the mass media. In psychological terms, this means many have a history of dissociation, the emotionally self-protective strategy of choice for children facing trauma. This adaptation shuts off and compartmentalizes feelings, and very likely inhibits empathy.

Twenty years ago, a study by Gregory Jurkovic and his colleagues found that the most dangerous violent juvenile delinquents display very little empathy. In his widely read book *Emotional Intelligence,* Daniel Goleman defines emotional intelligence as the ability to read emotions in others, to communicate effectively in the nonverbal realm, to manage the ups and downs of day-to-day life, and to have appropriate expectations for relationships. Empathy is one of the foundations for emotional intelligence, and emotional intelligence is at least as important for life success as intellectual intelligence. Goleman puts it this way: "The empathic attitude is engaged again and again in moral judgments, for moral dilemmas involve potential victims." A boy who has organized his inner life around the need to protect himself from his feelings of victimization and unworthiness is unlikely to pay attention effectively to the feelings of others, especially to their feelings as victims. This psychological defense mechanism is an important source of deadly petulance, that arrogant stance in which an individual feels justified in responding to insult with lethal violence. Violent boys are so desperately defensive that they over-compensate with arrogance. It's not because deep down they really feel superior to everyone else that they assume the prerogative of deciding who lives and who dies, but because deep down they feel so empty and worthless.

In talking with violent boys, I find validation for this interpretation. For example, although the youth prisons program offers "victim awareness" programs, the boys find it hard to make use of these programs because their own victimization remains largely unacknowledged and certainly unaddressed. Conneel says, "What about me, man? What about what I have gone through? I mean, I want to talk about what hurts me, and all they want to talk about is the people I hurt. I won't do it. The whole program stinks."

A WORLD WHERE MORALITY IS IRRELEVANT?

Perhaps one clue to the moral universe of violent boys comes from listening to someone like Kareem talk at length about the personal characteristics and attributes required to become a successful architect versus a successful gangster. He says, "You got to be smart for both, you know. It don't come easy. You got to work hard and be tough. You got to take advantage of your opportunities and figure out the best way to get what you want. You need knowledge, lots of knowledge; it's just different kinds of knowledge. You got to be ambitious and go for it. Nobody's going to hand it to you, you got to take it."

As he elaborates on this theme, the focus of his discussion is the similarities. You need to be intelligent. You need to be emotionally controlled. You need to work hard. You need to be competitive. You need to be able to "read" people. When I ask him if there is any moral difference between the two careers, he seems at first puzzled, then replies, "No. That's not the point."

Of course, for most everyone else that would be the point; being an architect is socially acceptable whereas being a gangster is immoral and illegal. Of course, there is a large measure of hypocrisy and duplicity on both sides of this equation. *Kareem* knows that being a gangster is different from being an architect, and *we* know that there is a lot of immoral behavior committed by people in the legally legitimate world.

Before he killed his classmates in Oregon, Kip Kinkel telegraphed his intentions to friends at school the day before he did the shooting. He reportedly said, "I am going to do something stupid tomorrow." Notice that he didn't say, "I am going to do something *wrong* tomorrow." He said "stupid." His choice of words is consistent with how these boys see the world. I think what he said relates to the sense of inevitability that some boys have about their violent actions. It flows from the conclusions they have drawn about the nature of morality as they have come to know it.

Boys often see the pure exercise of power. This is a particular problem for boys who develop patterns of bad behavior and aggression early in their lives. Maltreated boys are likely to develop a "hypervigilance" to negative social cues and a relative inability to see the positive social cues. They do live in a different world from those of us fortunate enough to have grown up loved, accepted, and treated well. Their social maps chart the same physical territory, but it is as if they are color-blind—not because they were born that way but because their early experiences stunted the development of color vision. They see the negative but not the positive. They learn early that power is what counts and that conventional morality often masks and justifies abuse. For example, the values espoused by Stephen's abusive mother look good on paper but not on his back. I believe these early lessons are one important reason why the morality of violent boys often appears as primitive and "truncated" (usually Level 1 in Kohlberg's scheme). It is primitive because it reflects the lessons they have learned from their experiences in the world.

ADOLESCENT MELODRAMA HAS MORAL IMPLICATIONS

As children pass into adolescence they are particularly vulnerable to melodrama and sentimentality. This finds benign expression in their attraction to stories of doomed lovers. This is why so many adolescents saw the movie *Titanic* over and over again and why Shakespeare's *Romeo and Juliet* is a perennial favorite among teenagers. Thirty years ago when I taught in a junior high school, we took the entire ninth-grade class to see the Zeffirelli version. The tears flowed, even among the most delinquent kids in the class—in fact, *particularly* among the most delinquent kids in the class. And this melodramatic sentimentality can actually be a resource in dealing with children. More than one child therapist of my acquaintance has reported that they found their work with girls enhanced when they were able to make use of *Titanic* as a parable, as a reference point in discussing their client's own life. Boys like *Titanic*, too, but they are much more likely to find their parables in *Rambo, Blade, Boyz in the Hood, Terminator,* and *Dirty Harry.*

Impulsiveness and self-centered thinking are the other hallmarks of adolescence. Teenagers do act rashly, and they do see the world as if it revolved around them. By and large, they do believe, with Shakespeare, that "all the world's a stage." But teenagers more than adults tend to believe that they are always the star of the show. This is why teenagers find it nearly impossible to leave home for school in the morning without carefully considering their appearance. After all, *everyone* will be looking at them. Sociologist Erving Goffman identified this "imaginary audience" as an important influence in adolescent behavior. Most of the time, in most teenagers, this self-centeredness ranges from cute to exasperating, but when the script of the play in which the teenager is a star is a violent tragedy, people die. The lost boys are teenagers, but they are starring in a horror show while more fortunate teens are starring in situation comedies or championship games. Television shows and movies play a role in providing teenagers with the scenarios for their performances.

BOYS NEED PROTECTION AND MORAL TEACHING

Once youngsters get melodramatic moral ideas into their heads, they need the moderating influence of adults to bring them back to moral reality. Many American kids, troubled or healthy, don't receive that protection. There is a breakdown in childhood protection all around us, a breakdown that hits violent boys hardest because they are most in need of protection.

In some cases this breakdown takes the form of adults who care for kids by training them to shoot down living beings—albeit usually with the intention that they limit their shooting to animals. The breakdown also comes when adults saturate kids with vivid media images glorifying violence as the legitimate solution to all problems and provide them with point-and-shoot video games that desensitize them to the act of killing. It comes when adults fail to take seriously and respond effectively to early signs of trouble that often are quite dramatic—for example, threatening statements, revenge fantasies, and acts of cruelty to animals. And finally, the breakdown in childhood protection comes when adults leave children too much to their own devices—home alone, either literally or figuratively. All this leads to a breakdown of adult authority and greater reliance by kids on peer influences and the violent culture of the mass media, a recipe for moral retardation. When this happens to boys in general the result is sad, taking the form of alienation, aggression, and the obnoxiousness that we so commonly refer to as disrespect for one's elders. But, most dangerously, when it happens to vulnerable boys, it exposes them to a do-it-yourself morality. And when it occurs in the context of shame and existential crisis, killing becomes the right thing to do "on stage" for such a boy's imaginary audience, no matter how big a mistake it may be offstage, where the real-world consequences must be faced.

Moral development is the process through which children learn the rules of conduct in their society and learn to act upon these rules. But this learning must take place in the heart as well as in the head. Without adequate adult buffering and limit setting, the moral behavior of children is left in the hands of children themselves, where their own feelings and thoughts are the last line of defense.

What can adults do to protect boys from negative moral development and teach them good moral sense? Let me outline a few positive steps here:

- First, adults can *stimulate the development of empathy.* To behave morally, children need to develop empathy, the ability to feel what others are feeling. Empathy helps them to connect abstract principles of morality with real-life situations and feelings. Without empathy there is always the danger that morality will become moralistic, a caricature of caring in which an individual's distorted perspective on what is right and wrong becomes a self-justifying rationale for violence. After the shooting stops, the fallacy of their moral reasoning often becomes clear to kids who kill, but by then it is too late.

- Second, adults can *protect boys from degrading, dehumanizing, and desensitizing images.* Go to almost any movie theater showing an R-rated film full of horrible violence and aggressive sexuality, and you can see young boys entering the theater. This exposure is a corrupting influence on the foundations of moral development.

- Third, adults can *stimulate and support the spiritual development of boys.* While going to a church or synagogue is no guarantee of receiving caring moral instruction designed to increase empathy, a boy's involvement in a non-punitive religious institution does help. Psychologist Andrew Weaver at the University of Hawaii has reviewed the evidence linking religious and spiritual experience to adolescent behavior and development, and he has found that this experience does buffer children from the cultural and social poisons of modern life. It is important that the religious experience be nonpunitive, that is, that it put the message of love center stage.

I remember as a teenager reading something that the great humanitarian Albert Schweitzer wrote about morality. Schweitzer said that if a farmer is plowing his fields to raise food to feed his family and destroys ten thousand flowers, that's morally acceptable. But if on the way home he gratuitously destroys one flower, that's a moral crime. I think there is something very important in this idea, something that is critical to an understanding of the moral calculus of violent boys, whose imperatives of necessity are driven by very primitive forces because their basic emotional needs are so grievously unmet. Caring is the basis for expanding their moral circles.

EXPANDING THE MORAL CIRCLE THROUGH THE EXPERIENCE OF CARING

Over the months that I interviewed Malcolm, his moral calculus began to change concerning the pit bulls he used in the dogfights he staged for profit. When we started, there were very clear boundaries about which dogs were inside and which were outside his circle of caring. He didn't use all his pit bulls, he used only those he had included in his world of expediency. He held back the few that were his pets, including them in his circle of caring. The change was this: after five months of our conversations, Malcolm volunteered the information that he had decided he could no longer put *any* of his dogs in the ring and was giving them up. He had opened up to the emotional meaning of his relationship with the dogs. Nevertheless, he was ambivalent about this course of action: on the one hand, he sounded proud of himself for making this decision, but he was sad about giving up the money and the status that came with his position as owner of the fighting dogs.

In my own life I have undergone a similar development. As I began to explore the links between animal abuse and child abuse, I found myself befriending a bird, a lizard, and a rat, adding them to my circle of caring, which already included a dog and a cat. Eventually I had to give up my childhood hobby of fishing—I became morally incapable of it (though I miss it sometimes). That same expanding circle of caring moved me toward vegetarianism. I do occasionally miss veal and hamburgers. Sometimes morality is inconvenient.

But where does caring stop? Violent boys experience the world as a dangerous place, often because they face physical threats, but always because they feel psychologically beleaguered. Can they afford to expand their circles of caring beyond what they bring with them into adolescence? For some, the dangers of expansion are physical: on the mean streets of the most socially poisoned environments, those who care may appear weak and thus invite exploitation. The same is true of life in a conventional prison. The boys speak of this often, when given a chance.

Sixteen-year-old Arnell gives me a short course in how to act on the street and in the prison beyond the privacy of the interview room. He demonstrates how to walk tough, how to look tough, and how to talk tough. "You take any crap from anyone," he says, "and you get marked as a pussy. Know what I mean? And if you get marked as a pussy, your life is hell. Man, you could get to a point where you rather die than live that way."

How do the ethics of survival and the circle of caring negotiate a settlement? For some boys the danger is purely psychological. They feel so very vulnerable because of rejection and shame that they come to fear anything that lowers their guard. They may feel they cannot afford the risk of stretching, of reaching beyond what survival ethics demand. It is their psychological vulnerability that keeps them at Kohlberg's Level 1.

All of us operate in two moral systems: one set of ethical principles for the people we consider insiders, a second set for outsiders. But troubled, violence-prone boys differ from most of us in how they decide who is inside and who is outside the circle, in where they draw the line. Where they draw the line is a matter of personal history and circumstances as much as, or perhaps more than, it is a matter of choice. Incarcerated boys often remark that when they were on the streets, they lived to survive and behaved accordingly but that now they are (safely) institutionalized, they can afford to consider other moral options. They may find it scary to switch moral systems, because doing so requires that they have trust and faith. Though often in short supply, neither is totally absent. Building trust and faith in the first place is the foundation for preventing youth violence. Finding ways to nurture it in boys who have already killed is the key to their moral rehabilitation.

PART 4 THE SOCIAL CONSTRUCTION OF GENDER RELATIONS

To sociologists, the psychological discussion of sex roles—that collection of attitudes, traits and behaviors that are normative for either boys or girls—exposes the biological sleight of hand that suggests that what is normative—enforced, socially prescribed—is actually normal. But psychological models themselves do not go far enough, unable to fully explain the variations *among* men or women based on class, race, ethnicity, sexuality, age, or to explain the ways in which one gender consistently enjoys power over the other. And, most importantly to sociologists, psychological models describe how individuals acquire sex role identity, but then assume that these gendered individuals enact their gendered identities in institutions that are gender-neutral.

Sociologists have taken up each of these themes in exploring (1) how the institutions in which we find ourselves are also gendered, (2) the ways in which those psychological prescriptions for gender identity reproduce *both* gender difference and male domination, and (3) the ways in which gender is accomplished and expressed in everyday interaction.

In their essay, Judith Gerson and Kathy Peiss provide a conceptual mapping of the field of gender relations based on asymmetries of power and inequality between women and men. Using the terms *boundaries, negotiation,* and *consciousness,* they re-navigate the study of gender toward a model that explains both difference and domination, as well as establishing the foundations for resistance.

James Messerschmidt offers a careful explanation of very different types of masculinities, which enables us to locate the ways in which masculinity is situational, contextual, and not simply a "thing" that a person carries with him or herself into all situations in the same way. Taking a different approach toward similar ends, Candace West and Don Zimmerman make it clear that gender is not a property of the individual, something that one *has,* but rather is a process that one *does* in everyday interaction with others.

JUDITH M. GERSON AND KATHY PEISS

Boundaries, Negotiation, Consciousness: Reconceptualizing Gender Relations

Over the last fifteen years research on sex and gender has examined the role of women in the past and present, recovered neglected human experiences, and transformed social analysis. A key contribution of this work—one that directly confronts traditional interpretations of women—is that gender is a primary social category which cannot be subsumed under such analytical categories as class and caste. Conceptualizing gender, however, remains a problem. Questions of how gender systems operate, their cultural construction, and their relation to individual and social interactions often are implicit in the analysis of women's experience. As a result, calls for greater definitional and theoretical clarity have been issued and scholars in this field increasingly have asserted the need to understand gender as a system of social relations.

This formulation of gender asserts that gender is defined by socially constructed relationships between women and men, among women, and among men in social groups. Gender is not a rigid or reified analytic category imposed on human experience, but a fluid one whose meaning emerges in specific social contexts as it is created and recreated through human actions. Analysis of gender relations necessarily goes beyond comparisons of the status and power of the sexes, involving examination of the dynamic, reciprocal, and interdependent interactions between and among women and men. In these relationships—those, for example, which construct the sexual division of labor and the social organization of sexuality and reproduction—women and men constitute distinct social groups.

While the problems of conceptualization remain significant, scholars have identified and elaborated several major constructs central to an analysis of gender as a system of social relations: (1) separate spheres; (2) domination of women; and (3) sex-related consciousness. The first, separate spheres, has allowed scholars to examine the different material and ideological worlds in which women and men work, live, and think. The literature on domination explains the forms and processes of physical intimidation, economic exploitation, and ideological control to which women are subjected. Lastly, women's consciousness as well as feminist consciousness have been analyzed as rooted in women's distinctive experiences as a social category.

Our aim in this paper is to recast these basic constructs in several ways, by reconsidering gender relations in terms of boundaries, processes of negotiation as well as domination, and gender consciousness as an interactive and multidimensional process. The concept of boundaries describes the complex structures—physical, social, ideological, and psychological—which establish the differences

From *Social Problems*, Vol. 32, no. 4 (April 1985), pp. 317–331. Copyright © 1985 by The Society for the Study of Social Problems. Reprinted by permission of University of California Press. References have been edited.

and commonalities between women and men, among women, and among men, shaping and constraining the behavior and attitudes of each gender group. The reciprocal processes of negotiation and domination elucidate the ways in which women and men act to support and challenge the existing system of gender relations. Domination describes the systems of male control and coercion, while negotiation addresses the processes by which men and women bargain for privileges and resources. Each group has some assets which enable it to cooperate with or resist existing social arrangements, although clearly these resources and the consequent power are unequal. Finally, although women's consciousness is grounded conceptually in shared female experiences, it is also an interactive and multidimensional process, developing dialectically in the social relations of the sexes, and involving different forms of awareness among individuals and social groups. We argue that thinking about gender in this way provides a set of more sensitive and complex analytical tools for understanding women's experiences.

BOUNDARIES

The development of the idea of separate spheres in the social science literature has stressed the assignment of women to the domestic realm, men to the public one, the physical separation between both spheres, and the social prestige attached to the public domain. Research on sex and gender has been influenced profoundly by the description of this basic structural division between the sexes, the apparent universality of the concept, and its explanatory power in the analysis of women's experience. Concurrently, the concept of separate spheres has been criticized for its tendency to reify the division of social experience into public/male and private/female worlds, and to overlook the interactions between them.

The use of the "separate spheres" formulation becomes increasingly problematic in the analysis of contemporary society. Unlike 19th century social life with its rigid social, physical, and ideological separation of the sexes, American society today is marked by the blurring of the public and private spheres, as women have entered the workforce in larger numbers, and men seemingly have become more involved in family life. At the same time, considerable social and cultural distance remains. Women's positions in the marketplace are neither secure nor taken for granted, while men's household roles are often marginal and limited. The dichotomy of separate spheres tends to simplify and reduce social life to two discrete physical environments without capturing the complexity of social and cultural divisions. Moreover, the concept has been used in a relatively static way, as a descriptive tool to chronicle and compare women's and men's activities. Only rarely have scholars gone beyond this approach to analyze the interactions between women and men (and among them) as they are influenced by and in turn shape these spheres.

We need a conceptualization that will allow us to express a basic commonality in the division(s) between the sexes and also to encompass definitions of changing patterns of social relations. Refocusing the analysis of gender divisions by using the concept of boundaries has several distinct advantages. First, it overcomes the problem of universality in the "separate spheres" formulation. Boundary is a more generic term which simultaneously allows us to see specific commonalities and discern actual differences in historical and current patterns of gender-based experiences. Second, the concept of boundaries allays the problem of bifurcating gender relations through the assignment of women and men to separate spheres. There are many more boundaries which mark people's lives than the public-private dichotomy suggests. There are boundaries which divide women and men in leisure and work activities, as well as in face-to-face interactions. There are also smaller boundaries within larger ones. In the workplace, for example, gender difference may be maintained by an overall segmentation of the labor force by sex, denoted by the allocation of social space and privileges (e.g., typing pools vs. executive offices, different dining facilities, etc.) and reinforced by limitations on interpersonal behavior (e.g., unidirectional patterns of touch and naming). Finally, the concept of boundaries also suggests permeability, whereas the image of spheres connotes comparatively autonomous environments. Boundaries mark the social territories of gender relations, signalling who ought to be admitted or excluded. There are codes and rules which guide and regulate traffic, with instructions on which boundaries may be transversed under what conditions. As a consequence, boundaries are an important place to observe gender relations; these intersections reveal the normal, acceptable behaviors and attitudes as well as deviant, inappropriate ones. At the same time, boundaries highlight the dynamic quality of the structures of gender relations, as they influence and are shaped by social interactions.

Describing the nature of boundaries and analyzing their congruence or lack of congruence will reveal a complex picture of gender arrangements. This approach should be particularly useful in comparative studies across time and in different cultures. In some periods and places, boundaries are mutually reinforcing or complementary, while in other instances they come into conflict. Within the American middle class in the 19th century, for example, the growing physical boundary between home and workplace was reinforced by a hegemonic ideological boundary, the cult of domesticity, as well as smaller social and cultural distinctions. While some women crossed these boundaries, and entered the public arena of education and voluntary association, most did so within the dynamics of their assignment to the home, rationalizing their activities as an extension of women's mission to protect and uplift the family. A somewhat similar ideological boundary marked the 1950s, in the set of ideas and images Betty Friedan (1963) labelled the "feminine mystique." Unlike the 19th century, however, other boundaries operated at cross-purposes. Physical boundaries between home and workplace become less salient in the mid-20th century as middle-class women entered the labor force in large numbers. Moreover, the ideology of companionate marriage cut across the feminine mystique with its assertion of mutuality, togetherness and male involvement in family life. Examination of the different relationships between boundaries may provide descriptive categories for viewing gender relations over time and in different settings.

The analysis of boundaries—their congruence and contradictions—may be useful in assessing stability and change in a system of gender relations. The above example suggests that mutually reinforcing boundaries will be indicators of relatively stable gender relations, while those that are contradictory may promote or reflect social change. An analysis of such change raises two important questions: How are boundaries reconstituted as existing boundaries are challenged and lose importance? What boundaries become or remain significant in defining gender difference and asymmetry as macro-level divisions become less distinct over time?

The boundaries between home and work provide examples of such changes. How is womens' place redefined when family/work divisions become less rigid and women are no longer anomalies as wage-earners? One consequence is that boundaries *within* the workplace (e.g., occupational segregation) and interactional, micro-level boundaries assume increased significance in defining the subordinate position of women. Occupational segregation sets up divisions within the labor force which reduce women to secondary status; with low-paying, low-status jobs and their continued assignment to the home, women retain their primary definition as housewives. For women entering nontraditional occupations, other boundaries maintain women's marginal and subordinate place. Micro-level phenomena—the persistence of informal group behavior among men (e.g., after-work socializing, the uses of male humor, modes of corporate attire)—act to define insiders and outsiders thus maintaining gender-based distinctions.

A similar definition of boundaries may be seen in the current debate over men's growing role in the household. Men's household labor appears to have increased somewhat in recent years, while ideological support for it (e.g., public discussion of paternity leaves) has grown. At the same time, women and men continue to define male household activity as secondary and marginal, taking the form of "helping out." The bulk of housework, childrearing and caretaking remains women's work.

In both these examples, boundaries shift in small but important ways, indicating a change in gender relations and the ways individual women and men may experience them. At the same time, challenges to the stability of patriarchal social arrangements may be met by concessions which in effect readjust the boundaries, but allow the overall system of male dominance to persist.

Since gender involves the accentuation of human difference into dichotomous categories of femininity and masculinity, the social divisions between women and men constitute the primary boundary of gender relations. On the micro level of analysis, what happens at the boundaries between sexes is frequently evidence of exaggerated gender-specific behavior, as compared with same-sex behavior. Perhaps the most common example of this phenomenon is heterosexual dating behavior, with women and men often playing out traditional stereotypical feminine and masculine roles. On a broader level of analysis, the primacy of the heterosocial boundary is assured by the sexual division of labor and the enforcement of compulsory heterosexuality, both of which assert women's difference from men, their subordinate position, and their dependency.

The concept of boundaries should help delineate the interaction between homosocial and heterosocial relationships, and their role in the construction of gender. Recent research has identified the significance of female friendships, networks, and cultures in providing women with varying degrees of autonomy, support, and influence. Similarly, scholars have documented the same-sex bonding in the realms of business, sports, and the military which supply men with resources, skills, solidarity, and power. Such homosocial relations are influenced by the boundaries between the sexes, and in turn shape these same boundaries. Among 19th century middle-class women, for example, friendships centered on the home, kinship, and ritualistic events; these constituted a separate "female world," which owed its emergence to the rigid structural differentiation between male/public and female/private domains. At the same time, the dynamics of female solidarity led some women into political agitation and reform activities, crossing and subverting this primary boundary. On the other hand, homosocial bonds among men may operate to strengthen the boundaries between the sexes, as they have in the world of sports. Women may pursue individual athletic activities which conflict least with social definitions of femininity, but they do not participate in team sports characterized by masculine rituals. Such rituals not only affirm male dominance through the exclusion of women, but they also promote group bonding, teamwork, and skills at negotiation and conflict resolution, qualities which help build and reinforce men's power in other realms of life.

At the same time, there are boundaries within same-sex groups which influence and in turn are shaped by the division between women and men. For example, the historical barriers between prostitutes and "respectable" married women have reinforced the double standard by strengthening male sexual privilege while dividing women on the basis of sexual morality. In contemporary society, aging is a boundary which separates younger and older women according to standards of physical attractiveness and youth, standards not applied to men. This in turn reinforces competition among women for men thus buttressing the institutional heterosexuality which constructs the primary male-female division and women's subordination.

Boundaries between the sexes and within each sex, in their respective spatial, social, and psychological dimensions, delineate the structure of gender relations at a given time and place. However, to explain how and why boundaries change, we must uncover the ways in which individuals make and reshape their social worlds. Thus, the interpretation of gender relations must involve a theory of social process and consciousness. First we examine the social interactions between individuals and groups which establish, maintain, and potentially subvert boundaries; these are the processes of negotiation and domination.

PROCESSES OF NEGOTIATION AND DOMINATION

A major contribution of scholarship on gender has been the analysis of *domination* in explaining the subordinate position of women. In numerous studies of sex and gender, researchers have documented the ways in which men as a group have power over women as a group. Theorists have raised fundamental questions about the sources of domination and have proposed strategies for changing extant power relations. Analyses of social life in the past and present reveal the extent of male control through physical coercion, reproductive policies, the institution of heterosexuality, economic exploitation, and ideology.

Although this analysis is essential for understanding the dynamics of gender arrangements, it nevertheless has an inherent conceptual shortcoming. Regardless of the theoretical orientation, the assumption is made that women are the passive victims of a system of power or domination. While women are not responsible for their own oppression and exploitation, at the same time they are not fully passive either. We need to explore the various ways women participate in setting up, maintaining, and altering the system of gender relations. This statement does not presume that women somehow ask for the sexism they experience. Rather we are suggesting that there is more than one process going on, perhaps simultaneously. Domination explains the ways women are oppressed and either accommodate or resist, while negotiation describes the ways women and men bargain for privileges and resources. Given the considerable scholarship about domination, we focus our discussion on the process of negotiation, recognizing that the two processes are interdependent and exist concurrently.

The concept of negotiation suggests human agency. Both women and men are active participants, sometimes asking or inviting, sometimes demanding that resources be shared or real located. Implicit in this formulation is the recognition that both women and men have some resources they initially control. In addition, this conceptualization suggests that both parties to a negotiation must somehow agree in order for it to take effect. Not only must there be mutuality in consent, but the process of negotiation is reciprocal. Though men seem to do most of the inviting, women also have done the asking and made demands. Furthermore, the heterosocial negotiations which occur usually involve crossing a boundary, however small. The negotiations which do take place may act to either maintain or change structural boundaries.

The entry of women into the office as clerical workers provides one such example of gender negotiation. Margery Davies (1982) has shown that women were allowed into the office only after the invention of the typewriter and its popular acceptance as a tool for low-paid, unskilled labor. In other words, women were "invited" into the office as clerical workers, crossing a boundary that years earlier they could not have trespassed. Office work for women appeared to be a real asset to them since other opportunities for wage earning were limited. Women may choose to participate because they perceive possibilities for economic gains or status enhancement. While we can speak of individual women being invited into the office by individual male bosses, it is important to remember that the processes of invitation and negotiation operate on the level of social groups.

Women also have the resources to negotiate with men for access to privileges and opportunities. Micaela di Leonardo (1984) has demonstrated that women do the kin work—the labor involved in sustaining and nurturing ties and affiliations among family kin. Her sample, a group of Italian American families living in California, showed a pattern in which women had greater knowledge about kin, had stronger familial ties, and did more of the planning of kin gatherings than did the men. These women derived not only responsibilities and obligations from these duties, but prerogatives and power as well. As a result, women had control over a set of kin-based resources and permitted men access to those resources only if and when the women so desired.

While these examples demonstrate that women and men actively participate in negotiations, they also suggest a fundamental asymmetry in the process of negotiation which is integrally tied to the process of domination. Women's dependency is ensured through domination in many forms, including exploitation in the system of wage labor, structured through occupational segregation. Given their low economic status, most women are in some way ultimately dependent on men's work, a dependency reinforced by the ideology and material conditions of compulsory heterosexuality. Given their relative lack of structural power, women have fewer resources with which to negotiate, experience fewer situations in which they can set up negotiations, and derive fewer advantages from their negotiations.

What then is the effect of these negotiations on the system of gender relations? On the one hand, they may permit the system to continue in "dynamic stasis," with reciprocal negotiations between women and men reifying structural boundaries in daily life. The traditional act of marriage exemplifies this form of negotiation, being a "free" exchange of obligations and responsibilities which reinforce heterosexuality and the sexual division of labor. However, an alternative consequence might be an adjustment in the boundaries either proceeded, accompanied, or followed by an alteration in consciousness. Men inviting women to cross a boundary or vice versa will not necessarily lead to lasting structural change. Indeed, ample evidence suggests that boundaries may be transversed and consciousness reconstructed in such a way that a changed status for women is largely cosmetic or minimal. When women were invited into the office, for example, a change in consciousness occurred (i.e., it was then considered proper for women to be secretaries), but the boundaries merely shifted to incorporate the precise change without seriously disrupting the dominant system of gender relations. One could even argue that the system was strengthened, since the ideological and material conditions of secretarial work reinforced women's role in the family.

A similar pattern emerges for women in traditionally male occupations. Women are now "invited" to enter the corporation, but the consequences of the negotiation are contradictory: by insisting that women be "male" in their job performance (i.e., have managerial ability) while retaining their "femaleness," the rules insure that women will remain outsiders. The popular literature on dress for success and assertiveness training exemplifies forms of negotiation that may lead to a change in some women's behaviors and consciousness, but not to lasting changes in the structure of opportunity, achievement and power for all women.

At the same time, changes in consciousness and shifts in boundaries arising from negotiations, however small, may have real and direct consequences in people's lives, even if they do not result in a major change in women's status or in the system of gender relations. To understand the creation and impact of those changes, it is necessary to explore the realm of consciousness. At the most general of levels, consciousness may be depicted in a reciprocal and dynamic relation to social structure. The structural location of a person or group in a social system (i.e., boundaries) as well as individual or collective acts (i.e., social processes), both shape and are shaped by social consciousness.

CONSCIOUSNESS

Traditionally when researchers have studied gender consciousness, they have focussed their efforts essentially on one of two questions. Either they have investigated the conditions and consequences of feminist consciousness or they have considered the foundations and components of female consciousness. Studies of feminist consciousness have concentrated on the social and historical context which gives rise to an active awareness and visible consequences of that awareness. For example, DuBois (1978) has chronicled the relationship between the anti-slavery movement and the subsequent movement for women's suffrage; Eisenstein (1983) has traced the growth of feminist consciousness in women's groups. Studies such as these generally situate feminist consciousness in an active social movement, associating consciousness with those people participating in the movement and conversely attributing a lack of feminist consciousness to those outside it. One of the tendencies of this research, therefore, is to understand feminist consciousness as an either/or phenomenon—either you have it or you do not.

Scholars working on the content of female consciousness have proposed a similar formulation. They understand female consciousness as the outcome of women's unique set of experiences. Whether as the primary caretakers of children or more generally because of their social roles which are distinct from men's, women apprehend the world in ways that are unique to them. This female consciousness replicates the same dichotomy apparent in the treatment of feminist consciousness. Women share a common culture, ostensibly autonomous from the male world, from which they derive their consciousness. Comparable to the problem with feminist consciousness, female consciousness is understood as a dichotomous, discrete variable.

One shortcoming of these formulations is that the possible varieties of feminist and female consciousness often remain unexplored. We know very little about the actual forms of nascent consciousness and which factors help explain the means by which that consciousness develops or recedes. Moreover, if gender relations shape women's experience then it is necessary to consider both the interaction of women and men as social groups as well as the dynamics within "women's culture" if we are to apprehend the formation of female and feminist consciousness. We propose that viewing forms of gender consciousness along a continuum produces a more useful conception of consciousness, while examining gender-based interactions allows us to explain how these forms of consciousness develop and change.

Our analysis of consciousness distinguishes among three types—gender awareness, female/male consciousness, feminist/anti-feminist consciousness—that represent three points along a continuum. The first, gender awareness, is basic to the development of the subsequent two forms—female/male and feminist/anti-feminist consciousness. Social scientists studying child development and socialization consistently report that very young children understand that they are either a girl or a boy and that this understanding has actual consequences for what they may or may not do. This form of consciousness which we label gender awareness is the most basic type. In this culture gender awareness is virtually universal past infancy, although it is neither infantile nor restricted to youngsters; it is present in parallel or reciprocal forms among both females and males. Gender awareness permeates most facets of everyday life in either real or symbolic ways. People continue to believe in a dimorphic world, even though the research on sex differences has shown that no quality or trait is associated exclusively with one sex or the other, except primary sex characteristics. Women are still thought of as weak or dependent, although we routinely encounter women who "objectively" are strong and independent. In fact gender attribution is so strong that it frequently distorts the empirical phenomenon.

Gender awareness involves a non-critical description of the existing system of gender relations, whereby people accept the current social definitions of gender as natural and inevitable. Gender awareness, then, means that people may associate or correlate certain phenomena with one gender group or another, but there is no evaluation of the ultimate significance or meaning of these attributions. For example, while a person's awareness of gender might indicate that women, in contrast to men, tend to be more sensitive and nurturant, this awareness would not enable her or him to discern the causes or effects of these traits. This form of gender consciousness ultimately involves a statement about the status quo, a remark concerning the ways things are for males and females. Moreover, as gender awareness is characterized by a basic acceptance of gender arrangements, any lingering or residual dissatisfaction with the status quo is individualized as a personal trouble. Being overly sensitive is seen as a personal female shortcoming; there is no social context for this problem. Similarly, a woman's failure to gain a job in the skilled trades is perceived as a result of her personal shortcomings, not an outcome of sexist hiring practices. Small dissatisfactions with gender arrangements may arise, but they do not result in a questioning of that system or one's place within it.

The second form of gender consciousness female or male consciousness, is based on gender awareness but goes beyond the descriptive attributions to a recognition of the rights and obligations associated with being female or male. These privileges and responsibilities are socially constructed and specific to a particular culture at a given point in time. The gender-linked traits which are descriptive of women and men at the level of gender awareness come to be vested with a sense of reciprocal rights and responsibilities at the level of female or male consciousness.

Kaplan (1982) defines female consciousness as acceptance of a society's gender system. Female consciousness ". . . emerges from the division of labor by sex, which assigns women the responsibility of preserving life. But, accepting this task, women with female consciousness demand the rights that their obligations entail" (Kaplan, 1982:545). While we agree with Kaplan, we want to offer two refinements. First, our understanding of boundaries tells us that the sexual division of labor represents a sum total of several more discrete boundaries. Thus, our model suggests that the source of this form of consciousness is more accurately depicted as a person's specific location in a system of gender arrangements. Second, we want to emphasize a notion implicit in Kaplan's definition. By demanding rights, the conceptualization of female consciousness connotes the idea that this consciousness is dynamic and malleable. Female consciousness is the outcome of processes of negotiation and domination, and their reciprocal interaction, as well as the result of women's structural location. Moreover, female consciousness influences processes of negotiation and domination, and ultimately, the boundaries shaping gender relations.

Recent research suggests the general dimensions of female consciousness: First, women are concerned with immediate material reality. The sexual division of labor situates women in the position of child bearers, responsible for sustaining life as well. As such, women are obligated and feel responsible for meeting survival needs of their families. Women, therefore, behave in accordance with normative expectations and act to further support those expectations. Concerns for the necessities of everyday life take numerous forms. Women concerned about food, shelter, and well-being, for example, have organized and protested when state regulations made it difficult if not impossible for them to feed their families.

At a more general level, responsibility for everyday life has meant that women are more apt to apprehend phenomena concretely rather than abstractly. In part because of their heightened responsibility for others, women act as mediators. Gilligan (1982:147) discusses women's complex negotiation between the ethic of self sacrifice and the sense of moral responsibility: "Thus morality, rather than being opposed to integrity or to an ideal of agreement, is aligned with 'the kind of integrity' that comes from 'making decisions after working through everything you think is involved and important in the situation,' and taking resposibility for choice." Finally, the constraints women experience in their daily lives lead to a consciousness of female inferiority. In comparison with men, women learn intellectual, moral, emotional, and physical inferiority. This generalized sense of inferiority leads women to believe that they are incomplete and inadequate without a man—father, husband, etc. Moreover, because of their perceived inabilities and the existence of real threats, women learn fear and have an ingrained sense of curfew and exclusion.

As Kaplan (1982) clearly documents in her research, female consciousness has both a progressive or revolutionary potential as well as a conservative or reactionary one. When women act to protest or disrupt the existing social order because they cannot satisfactorily fulfill their obligations, they challenge existing powers. The eventual outcome of such protests depends on a larger social context, but at a minimum underscores the value women place on maintaining social life (Kaplan, 1982). We would want to know what the relationship is between clearly demarcated boundaries of gender and the development of female consciousness.

An understanding of female consciousness and more broadly, gender relations, must entail an analysis of male consciousness. Is it identical to or even comparable to female consciousness? Given the differences in structural locations and social processes between women and men, male consciousness appears to be profoundly distinct from female consciousness. Male consciousness is characterized by the value placed on individual autonomy, a sense of entitlement, and a relative superiority to women. Men's moral judgments are guided by abstract principles rather than the concrete dimensions of everyday life. Recently Ehrenreich (1983) has chronicled some of the changes in male consciousness over the last thirty years. Her analysis is instructive but raises additional questions central to our concerns here. For example, what is the effect of relative power, and differences in the type or form of power, on consciousness? In what way is consciousness heightened or diminished by such power? Further research into the relationship between female and male consciousness, and its consequences for the system of gender relations is needed.

Finally, female/male consciousness must be distinguished from consciousness that is explicitly feminist or antifeminist/masculinist. To paraphrase Marx, we need to understand the formation of a gender *for* itself. Feminist and antifeminist consciousness involves a highly articulated challenge to or defense of the system of gender relations in the form of ideology, as well as a shared group identity and a growing politicization resulting in a social movement. Recent research extensively explores this issue, documenting the origins, organizational development, and ideology of the first and second waves of feminism. It also has examined the circumstances in which feminist consciousness reinforced or conflicted with other forms of consciousness based on class, race, ethnicity or sexual preference. In investigating the circumstances in which women define their interests as gender-based, it is necessary to examine the areas of female assertion and power, and the ways women move from female to feminist consciousness. At the same time, the formation of feminist consciousness must be seen in relation to antifeminist ideology and activity. The rise of feminism occurs in a dialectical context, in which the feminist challenge to the existing system of gender arrangements evokes an organized response, which in turn influences the nature of feminist consciousness and practice. This process has become particularly apparent in the New Right's movement against feminist demands for legal equality, economic justice and reproductive rights; it may also be seen in earlier historical periods such as the organized opposition to suffrage in the late 19th century. The dynamics of gender-conscious groups, particularly in the last one hundred years, have forcefully shaped gender relations, contributing to the changing definition of boundaries and rules for negotiation and domination.

CONCLUSIONS

In this paper we have argued that gender relations can be fruitfully understood by recasting our conceptual framework. These redefinitions should focus our attention on several issues which have consequences for future research on sex and gender.

From a definitional perspective, the conception of gender as a set of socially constructed relationships which are produced and reproduced through people's actions is central. Such a view highlights social interaction rather than more unidirectional processes of socialization, adaptation, and/or oppression. This emphasis suggests that we appreciate women as the active creators of their own destines within certain constraints, rather than as passive victims or objects. At the same time, this suggests that feminist scholars must avoid analyzing men as one-dimensional, omnipotent oppressors. Male behavior and consciousness emerge from a complex interaction with women as they at times initiate and control, while at other times, cooperate or resist the action of women. Clearly researchers need to examine men in the context of gender relations more precisely and extensively than they have at the present time.

This conceptualization also urges us to examine stasis and change in a more consistent and comprehensive fashion, thereby avoiding the mistake of studying change as an either/or phenomenon. We want to identify the mechanisms which perpetuate existing gender arrangements and those which tend to elicit change. Changes in gender relations occur along the three dimensions of boundaries, negotiation/domination, and consciousness; change in any one variable elicits change in the other two. For example, there cannot be a boundary shift unless it is preceded, accompanied, or followed by changes in negotiation/domination and consciousness. The sequencing of such changes, both in terms of patterns and timing, needs further study. In addition to these questions we also need to look at the magnitude of change. Large versus small-scale change in gender arrangements must be evaluated in terms of the number and proportion of groups affected, their centrality and susceptibility to change, and the degree and suddenness of change. We are also interested in the durability of change. Which kinds of changes are resistant to counter-vailing forces, and which seem to be more tentative, temporary, or makeshift? How are changes in gender relations challenged or co-opted? With the nature of change specified, we will be able to compare more precisely systems of gender relations across historical time and across cultures.

Grounding our research in these dimensions also will facilitate comparisons of systems of gender relations with other systems of domination. Such comparative work is important as it yields a greater understanding of the dynamics of domination. We can distinguish the forms of oppression that are unique to gender from those that are common to all systems of oppression.

Recently, scholars have pointed to the concepts of gender, gender relations, and sex/gender systems as potentially integrating the wide-ranging empirical research on women. Toward this end, our approach has been to redefine three concrete categories for the analysis of gender. These categories offer both a conceptu-

al framework and a research strategy which recommend greater specificity and comparability in examining gender relations. We hope that this framework will encourage researchers to clarify and extend their analyses of gender relations along both empirical and theoretical dimensions.

References

Bernard, Jessie. 1981. The Female World. New York: Free Press.

Davies, Margery. 1982. Women's Place Is at the Typewriter. Office Work and Office Workers 1870–1930. Philadelphia: Temple University Press.

di Leonardo, Micaela. 1984. The Varieties of Ethnic Experience: Kinship, Class and Gender Among Italian Americans in Northern California. Ithaca: Cornell University Press.

DuBois, Ellen Carol. 1978. Feminism and Suffrage: The Emergence of an Independent Women's Movement in America 1848–1869. Ithaca: Cornell University Press.

Ehrenreich, Barbara. 1983. The Hearts of Men: American Dreams and the Flight from Commitment. Garden City, NY: Anchor/Doubleday.

Eisenstein, Hester. 1983. Contemporary Feminist Thought. Boston: G. K. Hall & Co.

Friedan, Betty. 1963. The Feminine Mystique. New York: Dell.

Gilligan, Carol. 1982. In a Different Voice: Psychological Theory and Women's Development. Cambridge: Harvard University Press.

Kaplan, Temma. 1982. "Female consciousness and collective action: The case of Barcelona, 1910–1918." Signs 7:545–66.

JAMES MESSERSCHMIDT
Varieties of "Real Men"

It was a theoretical breakthrough in social theory when the family came to be recognized generally as both gendered and political. Feminist work has now begun to reveal theoretically what we have known for some time in practice—that other social milieux, such as the street and workplace, are not only political but also gendered (Acker 1990; Connell 1987; Cockburn 1983). I extend this theoretical insight through an analysis of how the social structures of labor, power, and sexuality constrain and enable social action within three specific social settings: the street, the workplace, and the family. I focus on how some men, within particular social situations, can make use of certain crimes to construct various public and private adult masculinities.

Research reveals that men construct masculinities in accord with their posi-

From *Masculinities and Crime: Critique and Reconceptualization of Theory,* Rowman and Littlefield Publishers, 1993, pp. 199–53 (edited). Reprinted by permission of the publisher.

tion in social structures and, therefore, their access to power and resources. Because men situationally accomplish masculinity in response to their socially structured circumstances, various forms of crime can serve as suitable resources for doing masculinity within the specific social contexts of the street, the workplace, and the family. Consequently, I emphasize the significant differences among men and how men utilize different types of crimes to situationally construct distinct forms of masculinities. We begin with the street and an examination of pimping.

THE STREET

Middle-class, working-class, and lower-working-class young men exhibit unique types of public masculinities that are situationally accomplished by drawing on different forms of youth crime. Moreover, class and race structure the age-specific form of resources employed to construct the cultural ideals of hegemonic masculinity. Such public arenas as the school and street are lush with gendered meanings and signals that evoke various styles of masculinity and femininity. Another type of public masculinity found in the social setting of the street is that of the adult pimp. This particularized form of masculinity is examined here within the context of "deviant street networks."

The Pimp and His Network

Eleanor Miller's (1986, 35–43) respected work *Street Woman* reports that in Milwaukee, Wisconsin, African American men in their mid to late twenties and early thirties dominate what she calls "deviant street networks." Deviant street networks are groups of men and women assembled to conduct such illegal profit-making ventures as prostitution, check and credit-card fraud, drug trafficking, burglary, and robbery. Although both men and women engage in various aspects of these "hustling activities," gender relations are unequal, reflecting the social structures of labor, power, and normative heterosexuality. Miller (p. 37) found that a major source of continuous income in these networks "derives from the hustling activity of women who turn their earnings over to the men in exchange for affection, an allowance, the status of their company, and some measure of protection." Commonly referred to as "pimps," the men act as agents and/or companions of these women, substantially profiting from their labor. Miller found that to work as street hustlers, it is essential that women have a "male" sponsor and protector. However, this "essential." has not always existed in the history of prostitution.

Throughout the 1800s, U.S. prostitution was condemned but not classified as a criminal offense, and was conducted primarily under the direction of a "madam" in brothels located in specific red-light districts (Rosen 1982, 27–30). In an attempt to halt prostitution, state legislatures enacted laws in the early 1900s in order to close down these red-light districts and, contemporaneously, women-controlled brothels. Predictably, rather than halting prostitution, new forms of prostitution emerged from this attempt at legislating morality. As Rosen (p. 32) shows in *The Lost Sisterhood*, the closing of the brothels simply increased street-walking for women; because prostitutes could no longer receive "johns" "in the semiprotected environment of the brothel or district, . . . they had to search for business in public places—hotels, restaurants, cabarets, or on the street." This search for customers in public places exposed prostitutes to violent clients and police harassment. Consequently, these women turned to men for help in warding off dangers, providing legal assistance, and offering some emotional support. Eventually, the overall prostitution business came to be dominated by individual pimp entrepreneurs or masculine-dominated syndicated crime.

In today's deviant street network, the pimp usually controls two to three women (labeled "wives-in-law") on the street (Miller 1986, 37–38). The women turn over their earnings to the pimp and he decides how it will be spent. The disciplinarian of the network, the pimp also "decides upon and metes out the punishment" (Romenesko and Miller 1989, 120). Indeed, as Romenesko and Miller (p. 117) show in their interviews with street hustlers, the pimp demands unquestioned respect:

> Showing respect for "men" means total obedience and complete dedication to them. Mary reports that in the company of "men" she had to "talk mainly to the women—try not to look at the men if possible at all—try not to have conversations with them." Rita, when asked about the rules of the street, said, "Just basic, obey. Do what he wants to do. Don't disrespect him. . . . I could not disrespect him in any verbal or physical way. I never attempted to hit him back. Never." And, in the same vein, Tina said that when her "man" had others over to socialize, the women of the family were relegated to the role of servant. "We couldn't speak to them when we wasn't spoken to, and we could not foul up on orders. And you cannot disrespect them."

This authority and control exercised by pimps over women is also clearly exemplified in biographies of pimp life (Malcolm X 1965; Slim 1967). Christina Milner and Richard Milner (1972, 52–53) reported a similar form of gendered power in their study of African American pimps in San Francisco:

> First and foremost, the pimp must be in complete control of his women; this control is made conspicuous to others by a series of little rituals which express symbolically his woman's attitude. When in the company of others she must take special pains to treat him with absolute deference and respect. She must light his cigarettes, respond to his every whim immediately, and never, never, contradict him. In fact, a ho [prostitute] is strictly not supposed to speak in the company of pimps unless spoken to.

Gender is a situated accomplishment in which we produce forms of behavior seen by others in the same immediate situation as masculine or feminine. Within the confines and social setting of the street, economically marginal men and women create street networks for economic survival, yet simultaneously "do gender" in the process of surviving. In this manner, deviant street networks become the condition that produces material survival as well as the social setting that reaffirms one's gender. The result is a gendered, deviant street network in which men and women do masculinity and femininity, albeit in a distinct manner.

In short, the division of street network labor is concerned both with rationally assigning specific tasks to network members and with the symbolic affirmation and assertion of specific forms of masculinity and femininity (discussed further below). Consequently, pimps simultaneously do pimping and masculinity. As marginalized men, street pimps choose pimping in preference to unemployment and routine labor for "the man." Lacking other avenues and opportunities for accomplishing gender, the pimp lifestyle is a survival strategy that is exciting and rewarding for them as men. The deviant street network provides the context within which to construct one's "essential nature" as a man and to survive as a human being.

The Cool Pose of the Badass

African American street pimps engage in specific practices (constrained by class and race) intended to construct a specific "cool pose" as an important aspect of their specific type of masculinity (Majors 1986; Majors and Billson 1992). In the absence of resources that signify other types of masculinity, sex category is held more accountable and physical presence, personal style, and expressiveness take on an increased importance (Messner 1989, 82). Consequently, as Richard Majors (1986, 5) argues, many "black males have learned to make great use of 'poses' and 'postures' that connote control, toughness and detachment," adopting a specific carriage that exemplifies an expressive and distinct assertion of masculinity.

The often flamboyant, loud, and ostentatious style of African American pimps signifies aspects of this cool pose. The exaggerated display of luxury (for example, in the form of flashy clothing) is also a specific aspect of the cool pose distinctively associated with African American pimps. Majors and Billson (1992, 81–84) argue that the "sharp" and "clean" look of pimps is intended to upstage other men in the highly competitive arena of the street where they earn street applause for their style, providing an "antidote to invisibility." Pimps literally prance above their immediate position in the class and race divisions of labor and power, thereby constructing a specific masculine street upper-crust demeanor.

Notwithstanding, this cool presence complements an intermittent and brutal comportment to construct masculinity and, in the process, show that the pimp means business. In other words, the African American pimp must always be prepared to employ violence both for utilitarian reasons and for constructing and maintaining a formidable, portentious profile (Katz 1988, 97). The following account by Milner and Milner (1972, 232) illustrates this unpredictable use of violence:

> One ho known as Birthday Cake said she worked for a pimp for four years, gave him a new Cadillac every year, and one night came home from work with her money "funny" and got the beating of her life. She walked in and handed over the money; he counted it and said, "That's all right, honey," drew her a

bath, laid her down afterwards on the bed, went to the closet and got a tire iron and beat her senseless with it. She showed us the long scars which required hundreds of stitches and demonstrated her permanent slight limp.

This "badass" form of masculinity (Katz 1988, 80–113) is also publicly displayed for, and supported by, other pimps. Milner and Milner (1972, 56) discuss how a pimp took one of "his" prostitutes (who was also a dancer) into the dancer's dressing room and "began to shout at her and slap her around" loud enough for everyone in the bar to hear. "The six pimps sitting at the back of the bar near the dressing room began to clap and whistle loudly," seemingly for the current dancer, "but in reality to cover the noise of the beating from the ears of the straight customers" (p. 56). Emerging from the dressing room and joining the others, the pimp exclaimed, "Well, I took care of that bitch." Then they all began to "joke around." In contrast, when the prostitute emerged, not "one of them (pimps) felt it proper to comfort her in any way" (p. 56). Such violence, neither out-of-control nor ungovernable, is situationally determined and regulated. Thus, pimp violence becomes a means of disciplining the prostitute and of constructing a badass public masculinity.

The combined cool pose and badass identity of African American pimps clearly represent a specialized means with which to transcend class and race domination. Yet, it also demonstrates the socially constrained nature of social action, and how African American pimps rework the ideals of hegemonic masculinity as a vehicle for achieving that transcendence. Pimping, then, is a resource for surmounting oppressive class and race conditions and for reasserting the social dominance of men. Moreover, like other men, pimps associate masculinity with work, with authority and control, and with explicit heterosexuality.

Within deviant street networks, the prostitute/pimp relationship represents a reworking of these hegemonic masculine ideals under specifically structured social possibilities/constraints. Through their authority and control within deviant street networks, pimps create a class- and race-specific type of masculine meaning and configuration, resulting in a remodeling of heterosexual monogamy in which the pimp provides love, money, and an accompanying sense of security for his "wives-in-law" (Romenesko and Miller 1989, 123).

Normative heterosexuality is the major focus of activities: wives-in-law are expected to be sexually seductive to men, receptive to the sexual "drives" and special "needs" of men (including the pimp), and to work for men who "protect" them and negotiate the "rough spots."[1] Pimping, as a resource for demonstrating that one is a "real man," distinguishes pimps from prostitutes in a specific way. Within the social context of the deviant street network, this pimp type of masculinity is sustained by means of collective and gendered practices that subordinate women, manage the expression of violence against women, and exploit women's labor and sexuality. Indeed, the individual style of the pimp is somewhat meaningless outside the group (Connell 1991, 157); it is the deviant street network that provides meaning and currency for this type of masculinity.[2] Pimping, in short, is a practice that facilitates a particular gender strategy.

In spite of the above, in attempting to transcend oppressive social structures,

African American pimps ultimately reproduce them. Their masculine style is at once repugnant to "conventionality"—their source of wealth anathema to traditional morality (Katz 1988, 97)—yet simultaneously reactionary and reproductive of the gendered social order. In other words, African American pimps respond in a gender-specific manner to race and class oppression, which in turn locks them into the very structured constraints they attempt to overcome. Thus, pimping becomes a form of social action that ultimately results in the reproduction of the gender divisions of labor and power as well as normative heterosexuality.

The following section examines two distinct types of masculinity constructed in the workplace.

THE WORKPLACE

The gender divisions of labor and power and normative heterosexuality structure gender relations in the workplace. The workplace not only produces goods and provides services but is the site of gendered control and authority. Because women historically have been excluded from paid work or segregated within it, today the gender division in the workplace is both horizontally and vertically segregated (Walby 1986; Reskin and Roos 1987; Game and Pringle 1984).[3] The result is that women are concentrated overwhelmingly at the lower levels of the occupational hierarchy in terms of wages and salary, status, and authority. Indeed, a recent study of nearly four hundred firms revealed that the vast majority of women were either completely or nearly completely segregated by gender (Bielby and Baron 1986). Consequently, gender relations throughout much of the paid-labor market—like gender relations in schools, youth groups, and deviant street networks—embody relations of power: the domination of men and the subordination of women. Moreover, the creation of "male" and "female" jobs helps to maintain and reproduce this power relationship. Accordingly, gender differences are maintained through gender segregation, and occupational segregation is born of practices ultimately based on conceptions of what constitutes the "essential" natures of men and women.

In addition, the concepts "worker" and "a job" are themselves gendered. As Joan Acker (1990) recently demonstrated, these concepts embody the gender divisions of labor and power. Historically, the idea of a job and who works it has assumed a specific gendered organization of public and private life: a man's life centers on full-time work at a job outside the household; a woman's life focuses on taking care of all his other needs. Consequently, as the abstract worker is masculinized (p. 152):

> it is the man's body, his sexuality, minimal responsibility in procreation, and conventional control of emotions that pervades work and organizational processes. Women's bodies—female sexuality, their ability to procreate and their pregnancy, breast feeding, childcare, menstruation, and mythic "emotionality"—are suspect, stigmatized, and used as grounds for control and exclusion.

Because organization and sexuality occur simultaneously, the workplace is sexualized and normative heterosexuality actually conditions work activities (Hearn and Parkin 1987). As Rosemary Pringle (1989, 162) recently reported, heterosexuality in the workplace is actively perpetuated in a range of practices and interactions exemplified in "dress and self-presentation, in jokes and gossip, looks and flirtations, secret affairs and dalliances, in fantasy and in the range of coercive behaviors that we now call sexual harassment."

Within the social situation of gendered segregation, power, and normative heterosexuality, men and women in the paid-labor market actively construct specific types of masculinity and femininity, depending upon their position in the workplace. In other words, social action is patterned in the workplace in terms of a distinction between masculine and feminine. Regarding men specifically, a power hierarchy exists in the workplace among men and, not surprisingly, different forms of masculinity correspond to particular positions in this hierarchy.

Let us now look at two differing forms of masculinity in the workplace: (1) workers and their relation to a specific type of sexual harassment and (2) corporate executives and their involvement in a variant form of sexual harassment. In each case, I demonstrate how specific crimes are a resource for constructing particularized representations of private masculinity—those that are occluded from the vision, company, or intervention of outsiders.

Workers and Sexual Harassment

Studies highlight the persistence and dominance of normative heterosexuality on the shop floor—such practices as exhibiting men's sexuality as biologically driven and perpetually incontinent, whereas women are the objects of a sexuality that precipitates men's "natural urges" (Willis 1979; Cockburn 1983; Hearn 1985; Gray 1987). This macho sexual prowess, mediated through bravado and sexist joking, is constructed and encouraged on the shop floor (Collinson and Collinson 1989, 95–98). Moreover, failure to participate in this specific interaction raises serious questions about one's masculinity. In this way, situationally specific notions of heterosexuality are reproduced through the construction of shop-floor masculinity and center on men's insistence on exercising power over women.

Under such conditions, when women enter the shop floor as coworkers, a threatening situation (for the men, that is) results. In this situation, some shop-floor men are likely to engage in forms of interaction quite different from their interaction with women outside the workplace. Not surprising, sexual harassment is more prevalent in this type of social setting. For example, one study of a manufacturing firm (in which the vast majority of manual laborers were men) found (DiTomaso 1989, 81):

> the men in the plant acted differently than they would if they interacted with these women in any other context. Their behavior, in other words, was very much related to the work context itself. It appeared to provide a license for offensive behavior and an occasion for attempting to take advantage of many of the women in the plant.

In DiTomaso's study, the younger women on the shop floor were perceived by the men as the most threatening because they were competing directly for the same kinds of jobs as were the men. Consequently, these women were more likely than other women to be subjected to demeaning forms of social interaction: the men's behavior was more likely to exceed simple flirtation and to involve specific forms of sexual harassment. The following are comments from several women in the plant (pp. 80–81):

> "The men are different here than on the street. It's like they have been locked up for years."

> "It's like a field day."

> "A majority of the men here go out of their way to make you feel uneasy about being inside the plant and being a female; nice guys are a minority."

Research reveals that sexual harassment occurs at all levels in the workplace—from shop floor to management. However, sexual harassment by men on the shop floor generally is twice as serious and persistent, and is different from sexual harassment by managers (Hearn 1985, 121). In the shop-floor setting (where men are the majority), sexual harassment is "a powerful form of economic protection and exclusion from men's territory. Women workers are perceived as a threat to solidarity between men" (pp. 121–122). Studies of shop-floor sexual harassment suggest that 36 to 53 percent of women workers report some type of sexual harassment (Gruber and Bjorn 1982); furthermore, a recent study of workplace sexual assault suggests that manual workers (as opposed to other men in the firm) committed the overwhelming majority of both attempted and completed assaults within the entire firm (Schneider 1991, 539).

Notwithstanding, the most common types of sexual harassment on the shop floor involve such demeaning acts as sexual slurs, pinches or grabs, and public displays of derogatory images of women (Schneider 1991, 539; Carothers and Crull 1984, 222). Perceptively, women shop-floor coworkers are more likely than women coworkers in other occupational settings to describe this sexual harassment as designed to label them as "outsiders." The "invasion" of women on the shop floor poses a threat to men's monopoly over these jobs, and one way to discourage women from attempting to compete in this domain is to remind them, through remarks and behavior, of their "female fragility" (Carothers and Crull 1984, 224). In this way, then, shop-floor men attempt to secure the "maleness" of the job by emphasizing the "femaleness" of women coworkers (DiTomaso 1989, 88).

Although most shop-floor workers clearly do not engage in sexual harassment, the unique social setting of the shop floor increases the likelihood that this particular type of sexual harassment will occur. Indeed, this specific shop-floor sexual harassment must be seen as a practice communicating anger against women for invading a "male" bastion and for threatening the economic and social status of men (Carothers and Crull 1984, 224). In addition, however, the shop floor is an ideal arena for differentiating between masculinity and femininity—performing manual labor demonstrates to others that such workers are "real men." The presence of women on the shop floor dilutes this gender distinction: if women can do what "real men" do, the value of the practice for accomplishing masculinity is effectively challenged. Because "doing gender" means creating differences between men and women, by maintaining and emphasizing the "femaleness" of women coworkers, shop-floor men are attempting to distinguish clearly between women and men manual laborers, thus preserving the peculiar masculinity of the shop floor. This type of sexual harassment serves as an effective (albeit primitive) resource for solidifying, strengthening, and validating a specific type of heterosexual shop-floor masculinity, while simultaneously excluding, disparaging, and ridiculing women (Segal, 1990: 211).[4]

Moving from shop floor to boardroom, we will next consider how a different type of sexual harassment provides certain white corporate executives with resources for constructing a specific form of private masculinity.

White Corporate Executives and Sexual Harassment

Sexual harassment is a resource available to corporate executives for constructing a specific type of masculinity. Because of their subordinate position in the corporation, women "are vulnerable to the whim and fancy of male employers or organizational superiors, who are in a position to reward or punish their female subordinate economically" (Box 1983, 152). In other words, corporate-executive men are in a unique position to sexually exploit, if they desire, women subordinates. Executive exploitation of sexuality is often a means of reinforcing men's power at the same time as making profits. For example, secretaries frequently are treated as conspicuous "possessions"; therefore, by hiring the "best looking" instead of the most competent secretary, managers exploit secretarial sexuality to "excite the envy of colleagues, disarm the opposition and obtain favors from other departments" (Hearn 1985, 118). Thus, as Jeff Hearn (p. 118) points out, exploitation of secretarial sexuality is not only a matter of directly objectifying women but also of using their sexuality for the eyes of other men. Economic and gender relations are produced simultaneously through the same ongoing sexual practices.

In addition to this direct exploitation of secretarial sexuality, corporate executives sometimes engage in specific types of sexual harassment. While shop-floor men who engage in sexual harassment are more likely to undertake practices that create a sexually demeaning work environment characterized by slurs, pictures, pinches, and grabs, white corporate-executive men are more likely to threaten women workers and lower-level managers who refuse to comply with demands for sexual favors with the loss of their jobs (Carothers and Crull 1984, 222). One secretary described this type of sexual harassment from a corporate executive as follows (cited in Carothers and Crull 1984, 222):

> He always complimented me on what I wore. I thought he was just being nice. It got to the place that every time he buzzed for me to come into his office for dictation, my stomach turned. He had a way of looking at me as if he were un-

dressing me. This time as his eyes searched up and down my body and landed on my breast, he said. "Why should your boyfriend have all the fun. You could have fun with me and it could pay off for you. Good jobs are really scarce these days."

The harassment of women in subordinate positions by an executive man more likely involves hints and requests for dates or sexual favors, which, when rejected, are likely followed by work retaliation (p. 224). Essentially, this particular type of sexual harassment involves economic threats by white, corporate-executive men such that if a women employee or would-be employee refuses to submit, she will, on the one hand, not be hired, retained, or promoted or, on the other hand, will be fired, demoted, or transferred to a less-pleasant work assignment. Assuming that the woman employee or potential employee does not desire a sexual relationship with the executive, such threats are extremely coercive. Given the economic position of many of these women, termination, demotion, or not being hired is economically devastating. When women depend on men for their economic well-being, some men take advantage of their economic vulnerability and engage in this particular practice of sexual harassment.

Although the imbalance of corporate gender power can be exercised coercively, sexual harassment is by no means automatic. Women often enter into genuine and humane relationships with men in the workplace, notwithstanding the fact that these men may be in supervisory positions vis-à-vis the woman.[5] Nevertheless, the general power imbalance within the corporation often creates conditions such that men in supervisory positions may exercise economic coercion to gain sexual access without genuine overt consent. Indeed, the corporate structural position of white executive men ensures that such exploitation will more likely be manipulative than violent.

One recent study of workplace assaults found that shop-floor workers utilized physical force more often than other forms of coercion because they lack the institutionalized economic means with which to force compliance. Corporate executives are much more likely to use economic coercion than physical force as a means with which to obtain sexual access to women subordinates (Schneider 1991). Two women who experienced this type of sexual assault stated in part (cited in MacKinnon 1979, 32):

"If I wasn't going to sleep with him, I wasn't going to get my promotion."

"I was fired because I refused to give at the office."

When women refuse to "give at the office," some corporate executives retaliate by exercising their power over women's careers. In one case, an executive, "following rejection of his elaborate sexual advances, barraged the woman with unwarranted reprimands about her job performance, refused routine supervision or task direction, which made it impossible for her to do her job, and then fired her for poor work performance" (MacKinnon 1979, 35).

The social construction of masculinity/femininity in the executive/secretary relationship shows clearly how this specific type of sexual harassment comes about. A secretary is often expected to nurture the executive by stroking his ego, making his coffee, cleaning the office, and ensuring he is presentable (Sokoloff 1980, 220). Secretaries are often symbolically hired as "office wives." In one case, an executive had his secretary do all his grocery shopping and even go to his home and take his washing off the line! (Pringle 1989, 169–170).

Rosabeth Moss Kanter (1977, 88) noted some time ago that a "tone of emotional intensity" pervades the relationship between secretary and executive. The secretary comes to "feel for" the executive, "to care deeply about what happens to him and to do his feeling for him." In fact, according to Kanter (p. 88), secretaries are rewarded for their willingness "to take care of bosses' personal needs." In other words, women subordinates construct a specific type of femininity by performing an extensive nurturing service for the executive.[6] Women do in the workplace what they traditionally have done in the home. It should come as no surprise that some executives come to expect such nurturance from women subordinates, just as they do from their wives, and that some take this nurturance further to include sexual nurturing. The result is that some women are coerced to exchange sexual services for material survival. As Carothers and Crull (1984, 223) observe in their important study of sexual harassment:

> The male boss can use his power over women within the organizational structure to impose sexual attentions on a woman, just as he can coerce her into getting his coffee. They both know that if she does not go along, she is the one who will lose in terms of job benefits.

Corporate-executive harassment and sexual coercion are practices that simultaneously construct a specific form of masculinity. This type of sexual harassment arrogantly celebrates hegemonic masculinity, its presumed heterosexual urgency, and the "normality" of pursuing women aggressively. In an attempt to "score" with his secretary, the corporate-executive sexual harasser strengthens gender hierarchy, thereby "affirming in men a shared sense of themselves as the dominant, assertive and active sex" (Segal 1990, 244). The corporate executive enjoys an immediate sensation of power derived from this practice, power that strengthens his masculine self-esteem.

In this way, in addition to normative heterosexuality, white, corporate-executive sexual harassers attempt to reproduce their gender power. Through the practice of corporate sexual harassment, executives exhibit, as MacKinnon (1979, 162) argues, "that they can go this far any time they wish and get away with it." White, corporate-executive sexual harassment, constructed differently than by shop-floor men, provides a resource for constructing this specific type of heterosexual masculinity that centers on the "driven" nature of "male" sexuality and "male" power.

Although clearly most corporate executives do not engage in sexual harassment, the social setting of the executive/secretary relationship increases the probability that this specific form of sexual harassment will occur. Corporate executives engage in sexual harassment to reinforce their power by sexualizing women subordinates, creating "essential" differences between women and men by constructing this particular type of masculinity.

THE FAMILY

In addition to the street and the workplace, the divisions of labor and power frame social interactions and practices in the contemporary nuclear family where, for example, women remain responsible primarily for unpaid housework and child care while men remain responsible primarily for paid labor. Indeed, the gender division of household labor defines not only who does most of the unpaid household labor but also the kind of household labor assigned to men and women. Moreover, the sociological evidence indicates clearly that in Western industrialized societies gender asymmetry in the performance of household labor continues to exist (Andersen 1988, 141–145; Messerschmidt 1986, 74; Hartmann 1981; Berk 1985; Hochschild 1989, 1992) and women share less in the consumption of household goods (from food to leisure time) than do men (Walby 1989, 221).

It is true that barely 10 percent of all U.S. heterosexual households consist of a husband and wife with two children living at home, where the husband is the sole breadwinner (Messerschmidt 1986, 74). Further, as fertility is delayed or declines, and with more and more women working during pregnancy and child-rearing years, active motherhood is shrinking as a component of most women's lives (Petchesky 1984, 246). Nevertheless, evidence indicates that women continue to perform most of the household labor, even as these demographic changes occur and women's participation in the paid-labor market increases dramatically. Indeed, Arlie Hochschild (1992, 512) concluded in her study of fifty-two heterosexual couples over an eight-year period that just as "there is a wage gap between men and women in the work place, there is a 'leisure gap' between them in the home. Most women work one shift at the office or factory and a 'second shift' at home."

This gender division of labor embodies the husband's power to define the household setting in his terms. While conscious efforts are being made in many households to dismantle familial power relations (Connell 1987, 124), especially in the middle class (Ehrenreich 1983), for most couples the capacity of each spouse to determine the course of their shared life is unequal: men alone make the "very important" decisions in the household; women alone make few "important" decisions (Komter 1989). In many dual-career families, men's power is deemed authentic and an acceptable part of social relations. This legitimized power in the family provides men with considerably greater authority (Komter 1989; Pahl 1992; Bernard 1982). Concomitantly, the marital sexual relationship, as with other aspects of marriage, likely embodies power, unless consciously dismantled, and "in most cases it is the husband who holds the initiative in defining sexual practice" (Connell 1987, 123).

The concept of patriarchy has lost its strength and usefulness as a theoretical starting point for comprehending gender inequality in Western industrialized societies. Nevertheless, the concept is helpful to describe a certain type of masculinity that persists today: some men are simply *patriarchs* in the traditional sense. Patriarchs fashion configurations of behavior and pursue a gender strategy within the family setting that control women's labor and/or sexuality. Moreover, these men will most likely use violence against women in the family. In the final section of this chapter, the discussion focuses on two forms of violence against women in the family—wife beating and wife rape—and analyzes how these crimes serve as a resource for the construction of specific types of patriarchal masculinities.

Wife Beating and Battering Rape

Victimization surveys indicate that in the home, wives are assaulted much more often by their husbands than husbands are by their wives (less than 5 percent of domestic violence involves attacks on husbands by their wives) and women are much more likely than men to suffer injury from these assaults (Dobash, Dobash, Wilson, and Daly 1992).[7] Wife beating also develops within a setting of prolonged and persistent intimidation, domination, and control over women (Dobash et al. 1992; Dobash and Dobash 1984; Pagelow 1984). Accordingly, wife beating is the "chronic battering of a person of inferior power who for that reason cannot effectively resist" (Gordon 1988, 251).

Violence by men in the household derives from the domestic authority of men and is intimately linked to the traditional patriarchal expectation (1) that men are the credible figures within monogamous relationships and (2) that men possess the inherent right to control those relationships. As Susan Schechter (1982, 222) argues, "a man beats to remind a woman that the relationship will proceed in the way he wants or that ultimately he holds the power."

Katz's (1988, 18–31) discussion of "righteous slaughter"—killing among family members, friends, and acquaintances—by men aids in understanding how this focus on household authority and control results in wife beating as a resource for masculine construction. Katz argues that for the typical killer, murder achieves *Good* by obliterating *Bad*. Moreover, the killer has no capacity to "ignore a fundamental challenge" to his self-worth and identity. From the killer's perspective, the victim teases, dares, defies, or pursues the killer. Accordingly, the killer sees himself as simply "defending his rights." In other words, the killer's identity and self-worth have been taken away—by an insult, losing an argument, an act of infidelity—and such events attack an "eternal human value" that calls for a "last stand in defense of his basic worth." The "eternally humiliating situation" is transformed into a blinding rage and the compulsion to wipe away the stigmatizing stain through the act of murder. And the rage is not random and chaotic but, rather, "coherent, disciplined action, cunning in its moral structure" (p. 30). The killer "does not kill until and unless he can fashion violence to convey the situational meaning of defending his rights" (p. 31).

Investigations of wife beating indicate further the application of the notion "defending his rights." Violence is regarded by the husband as achieving *Good* by pulverizing *Bad*; such men engage in a coherent and disciplined rage to defend what they consider to be their rights. According to interviews with wife beaters, their wife is perceived as not "performing well," not accomplishing what her "essential nature" enjoins and stipulates. Women are beaten for not cooking "up to standards," for not being obeisant and deferential, and for not completing or performing housework sufficiently—for not being a "good wife" (Ptacek 1988, 147). According to the offender, the "privileges of male entitlement have been unjustly denied" because the wife is not submissive and, therefore, not conforming to his standards of "essential femininity" (p. 148). Irene Frieze's (1983, 553) interviews with wife beaters found that they believe "it is their right as men to batter wives who disobey them."

Dobash and Dobash (1984, 274) similarly found that most wife beating is precipitated by verbal confrontations centering on possessiveness and jealousy on the part of the husband and a husband's demand concerning domestic labor and services. During an argument over such issues, "the men were most likely to become physically violent at the point when the woman could be perceived to be questioning his authority or challenging the legitimacy of his behavior or at points when she asserted herself in some way" (p. 274). In other words, wife beating arises not solely from gendered subordination but also from women actively contesting that subordination (Gordon 1988, 286). In such situations, the wife beater is punishing "his wife" for her failure to fulfill adequately her "essential" obligations in the gender division of labor and power and for her challenge to his dominance. The wife beater perceives that he has an inherent patriarchal right to punish "his woman" for her alleged wrongdoing.

Wife beaters are piously sure of their righteousness, and thus fashion their violence to communicate the situational meaning of defending their patriarchal rights. Indeed, the more traditional the gender division of labor (regardless of class and race position) the greater the likelihood of wife beating (Edleson, Eisikovits, and Guttman 1986; Messerschmidt 1986; Smith 1990a). In such traditional patriarchal households, both husband and wife tend to perceive the lopsided gender division of labor and power as "fair" (Berk 1985). Linda Gordon's (1988, 260–261) historical study of family violence found that in households where wife beating is prevalent:

> Women as well as men professed allegiance to male-supremacist understandings of what relations between the sexes should be like. These shared assumptions, however, by no means prevented conflict. Women's assumptions of male dominance did not mean that they quit trying to improve their situations.

The wife beater attempts to resolve in his way what he regards as a conflict over this "fair" arrangement, even when the wife is not actively or consciously contesting that "fair" household organization.[8] Accordingly, as West and Zimmerman (1987, 144) argue, "It is not simply that household labor is designated as 'women's work,' but that a woman to engage in it and a man not to engage in it is to draw on and exhibit the 'essential nature' of each." By engaging in practices that maintain gender divisions of labor and power, husbands and wives do not simply produce household goods and services, but also produce gender. Indeed, husbands and wives develop gendered rationalizations and justifications for this asymmetrical household labor. What follows are selected but representative examples (Komter 1989, 209):

By wives:
"He has no feeling for it."
"He is not born to it."
"It does not fit his character."

By husbands:
"She has more talent for it."
"It is a woman's natural duty."

When this asymmetry is questioned (whether consciously or not), the wife beater assumes that his "essential rights" are being denied—an injustice has occurred, a violation of the "natural" order of things. The "essential nature" of wife beaters is that they control familial decision making and thus dominate the family division of labor and power. When wives "question" this decision making, through words or actions, they threaten their husband's control of the gender division of labor and power. In other words, the husband interprets such behavior as a threat to his "essential nature"—control and domination of the household. Because spousal domestic labor is a symbolic affirmation of a patriarch's masculinity and his wife's femininity, such men are extremely vulnerable to disappointment when that labor is not performed as they expect (Gordon 1988, 268).

According to the wife beater, it is his duty to determine, for example, what constitutes a satisfactory meal, how children are cared for, when and how often sexual relations occur, and the nature of leisure activities (Ferraro 1988, 134). Women are beaten for some of the most insignificant conduct imaginable: for example, preparing a casserole instead of a meat dish for dinner, wearing their hair in a ponytail, or remarking that they do not like the pattern on the wallpaper. Kathleen Ferraro (p. 135) discusses a case in which even the issue of wearing a particular piece of clothing was perceived by the husband as a threat to his control:

> On her birthday, she received a blouse from her mother that she put on to wear to a meeting she was attending without Steven. He told her she could not wear the blouse, and after insisting that she would, Steven beat her. It was not only her insistence on wearing the blouse that evening that triggered Steven's abuse. It was the history of his symbolic control, through determining her appearance that was questioned by wearing the new blouse.

Wife beaters (regardless of class and race position) presume they have the patriarchal right—because it is part of their "essential nature"—to dominate and control their wives, and wife beating serves both to ensure continued compliance with their commands and as a resource for constructing a "damaged" patriarchal masculinity. Thus, wife beating increases (or is intended to do so) their control over women and, therefore, over housework, child care, and sexual activity.

Yet wife beating is related not only to the husband's control over familial decision making, but also develops from another form of control, possessiveness. For some wife beaters, spousal demonstration of loyalty is a focal concern and is closely monitored. For instance, time spent with friends may be interpreted by a wife beater simply as disloyalty. Indeed, sexual jealousy of friends is a common theme in the literature on wife beating (Dobash and Dobash 1979, 1984; Ferraro 1988; Frieze 1983), and indicates the importance of the social structure of normative heterosexuality to understanding wife beating. The wife's uncommitted wrong is the potential to be unfaithful, which to her husband is not only a serious challenge to his patriarchal ideology, but his very real fear that his wife will choose another man and, thereby, judge him less "manly" than his "competitor." Thus, because time spent with friends endangers his ongoing interest in heterosexual performance, wife beating reassures him that his wife is his to possess sexually.

Moreover, not only potential sexual competitors can threaten a patriarchal husband, but relatives may also pose threats to a wife's loyalty. Pregnancy, for example, is closely associated with wife beating, and reflects the husband's resentment of the fetal intruder (Ferraro 1988). Walker (1979, 83–84) offers an example of a husband and wife who planned to spend the day together, but the wife broke off the plans, choosing instead to baby-sit her three-year-old granddaughter. Her husband (Ed) seems to have interpreted this choice as disloyal behavior and a challenge to his ultimate control:

> Ed became enraged. He began to scream and yell that I didn't love him, that I only loved my children and grandchildren. I protested and said, "Maybe you would like to come with me," thinking that if he came, he might feel more a part of the family. He just became further enraged. I couldn't understand it. . . . He began to scream and yell and pound me with his fists. He threw me against the wall and shouted that he would never let me leave, that I had to stay with him and could not go. I became hysterical and told him that I would do as I saw fit. . . . Ed then became even further enraged and began beating me even harder.

Thus, under conditions where labor services are "lacking" and possessiveness is "challenged," a wife beater's masculinity is threatened. In such a scenario, predictably, the wife beater attempts to reestablish control by reconstructing his patriarchal masculinity through the practice of wife beating.

Approximately 30 to 40 percent of battered women are also victims of wife rape (Walker 1979; Russell 1982; Frieze 1983). These "battering rapes," as Finkelhor and Yllö (1985) describe them, do not result from marital conflicts over sex; rather, the rape is an extension of other violence perpetrated on the victim. The wife beating/rape represents punishment and degradation for challenging his authority and, thus, the traditional division of labor and power. In fact, although wife beating and battering rapes extend across all classes and races (for the reasons discussed above), they occur most frequently in working-class and lower-working-class households wherein the traditional patriarchal gender division of labor and power—husband decision maker and wife caretaker—is strongest (Straus, Gelles, and Steinmetz 1980; Finkelhor and Yllö 1985; Smith 1990b; Walker 1977–78; Messerschmidt 1986, 144). Research consistently shows that class conditions are associated with wife beating: for example, low-income (Straus et al. 1980; DeKeseredy and Hinch 1991) and working-class wives are approximately twice as likely as middle-class wives to experience wife beating (Smith 1990a; Stets and Straus 1989). Moreover, among couples in which the husband is unemployed or employed part-time, the level of husband-to-wife violence is three times as high as the level among couples in which the husband is fully employed (Straus et al. 1980; DeKeseredy and Hinch 1991).

Finally, Michael Smith's (1990b, 49) study of risk factors in wife beating found that "the lower the income, the higher the probability of abuse." This same study went on to report that the chances of a low-income woman being severely battered during marriage exceed those of a middle-class woman by a factor of ten. Smith's (1990a, 267) data reveals that "men with relatively low incomes, less educated men, and men in low-status jobs were significantly more likely than their more privileged counterparts to subscribe to an ideology of familial patriarchy. These men were also more likely to have beaten their wives."

Although at work he is individually powerless, at home the working-class battering rapist is a patriarch endowed with individual authority. His ability to earn money (if available) "authorizes" his patriarchal power as husband/father. But his masculine identity depends on the demarcation of public and private responsibility; consequently, any challenge to the status quo in the home is taken personally as a confrontation (Tolson 1977, 70). In seeking to sustain this specific type of patriarchal masculinity, working-class men develop an intense emotional dependency on the family/household (Donaldson 1987), demanding nurturance, services, and comfort on their terms when at home. As Lynne Segal (1990, 28) points out, "the sole site of authority" for such men is in the home. And when their power and authority are threatened or perceived to be threatened at home, working-class men are more likely than other men to employ battering rapes to accomplish gender and reestablish their control. As Harris and Bologh (1985, 246) point out in their examination of "blue collar battering," "If he can establish an aura of aggression and violence, then he may be able to pass as a 'real man,' for surely it is admirable to use violence in the service of one's honor."

Battering in this sense is a resource for affirming "maleness." Because of their structural position in the class division of labor, working-class men—in particular, lower-working-class men—lack traditional resources for constructing their masculinity and, as a result, are more likely than are middle-class men to forge a particular type of masculinity that centers on ultimate control of the domestic setting through the use of violence. Moreover, unemployment and low occupational status undermine the patriarchal breadwinner/good provider masculinity: he cannot provide for his wife and children. Such men are more likely than are economically advantaged husbands to engage in wife beating and battering rapes to reestablish their masculinity. As Kathleen Ferraro (1988, 127) puts it, "for men who lack any control in the civil realm, dominance within the private realm of the home becomes their sole avenue for establishing a sense of self in control of others."[9]

In sum, most working- and lower-working-class husbands do not abuse their wives, nor is this particular type of abuse limited to this class of men. Nevertheless, the peculiar social conditions prevalent in working- and lower-working-class families increase the incidence of this type of abuse. For these men; power is exercised in the home in ways that hegemonic masculinity approves: men are allowed to be aggressive and sexual. Lacking dominance over others at work or the ability to act out a breadwinner (or even economic contributor) masculinity, sex category is particularly important, and working- and lower-working-class men are more likely to express their masculinity as patriarchs, attempting to control the labor and sexuality of "their women." Consequently, when patriarchal relations are "challenged," their taken-for-granted "essential nature" is undermined and, accordingly, doing masculinity requires extra effort. Wife beating/rape is a specific practice designed with an eye to one's accountability as a "real man" and, therefore, serves as a suitable resource for simultaneously accomplishing gender and affirming patriarchal masculinity.

Force-only Rape

However, wife rape is not limited to the victims of wife beating. Indeed, in Finkelhor and Yllö's (1985) study, 40 percent of their sample were "force-only rapes"—situations in which husbands use only the force necessary to coerce their wives into submission. The perpetrators and victims of force-only rapes were significantly more educated than those of battering rapes, more often middle-class, and almost half held business- or professional-level jobs.[10] Moreover, the perpetrators and victims of force-only rapes were much less likely to have been in a relationship based on the traditional gender divisions of labor and power. Sex was usually the issue in force-only rapes, and the offenders were "acting on some specifically sexual complaint," such as how often to have sex or what were acceptable sexual activities (p. 46).

In some sectors of the "progressive" middle class, there have been serious attempts to become truly equal marriage partners, where the wife has a career and where the husband participates equally in child care and housework. However, the greater the income differential between husbands and wives, the less involved some husbands are in parenting and housework, and there exists greater equality in dual-career families than in dual-income families (Segal 1990, 38). Consequently, as Barbara Ehrenreich (1989, 218–220; see also 1983, 1984) argues, a new heterosexual masculinity on the part of certain progressive, middle-class men has emerged, consisting of choosing a mate who can "pull her own weight" economically and who is truly committed to sharing household labor equally.

Notwithstanding, this progressive "dual-career" relationship is not supplemented, in many cases, by a progressive sexual relationship. As Andrew Tolson (1977, 121) argued as early as 1977, for many progressive, middle-class men, sexual passion is "still acted out in familial terms of masculine 'conquest'—to which women could only 'respond.'" Although many progressive, middle-class men seriously seek "free women" who live for themselves and their careers (Ehrenreich 1984), in bed they continue to demand submission and the affirmation of masculinity through heterosexual performance (Tolson 1977, 121). That is, many progressive, middle-class men continue to adhere to the hegemonic masculine ideology that "entitles" them to sex with their wives whenever they want it. For example, Finkelhor and Yllö (1985, 62–70) discuss the case of Ross, a middle-class businessman who somewhat represents this progressive middle class, yet who frequently raped his wife. Ross describes below how one such rape occurred during an argument over sex that his wife was winning (p. 66):

> She was standing there in her nightie. The whole thing got me somewhat sexually stimulated, and I guess subconsciously I felt she was getting the better of me. It dawned on me to just throw her down and have at her . . . which I did. I must have reached out and grabbed at her breast. She slapped my hand away. So I said, "Lay down. You're going to get it." She replied, "Oh, no, you don't," so I grabbed her by the arms and she put up resistance for literally fifteen seconds and then just resigned herself to it. There were no blows or anything like that. It was weird. I felt very animalistic, and I felt very powerful. I had the best erection I'd had in years. It was very stimulating. . . . I walked around with a smile on my face for three days.

Ross believed his wife not only controlled the sexuality in their lives, but that she had "completely and totally emasculated" him (p. 68). The rape was both a way to overcome that loss of power in his life and a means to construct a specific type of patriarchal masculinity centering on heterosexual performance and the domination and control of women's sexuality.

Another businessman, Jack, stated to Finkelhor and Yllö (p. 72), "When she would not give it freely, I would take it." He felt that his wife did not have the right to deny sex, he had the right to sex when he pleased, and it was her duty to satisfy his sexual needs. Similarly, in Irene Frieze's (1983, 544, 553) study of wife rape, the vast majority of wife rapists engaged in this form of violence in order to prove their "manhood," believing "that their wives were obligated to service them sexually in whatever ways they desired."

Thus, in force-only rapes, the assaults are practices of masculine control based on expectations that sex is a right. Both battering and force-only rapists consciously choose such violent action to facilitate a patriarchal gender strategy and to protect what they view as their "essential" privileges. The resulting masculine construction is not only an exhibition of their "essential nature," but also illustrates the seductive quality of violence for displaying that "essential nature." For these men, masculine authority is quite simply expressed through the violent control of women.

Nevertheless, such personal choices become enigmatic when detached from social structures. In battering rapes, because the traditional division of labor and power is prevalent and the struggle is over authority and control of that division, these men construct a patriarchal form of masculinity that punishes and degrades the wife for deviating from her "essential" duties. In force-only rapes, however, the gender division of labor is not the issue: this is the classic, middle-class, dual-career family in which both partners participate in decision making and household tasks, and in which the husband accepts, in a general way, his wife's autonomous right to develop her own interests. However, the force-only rapist feels specifically wronged, cheated, and deprived in the sexual realm. Some progressive, middle-class men simply adhere to the hegemonic masculine ideology that entitles them to sex whenever they want it. Sex is considered a marriage right by which gender is accomplished through effective performance in the sexual realm. Like sexual harassment, a similar type of crime, wife rape can be a resource for accomplishing masculinity differently. And as the social setting within the nuclear family changes, so does the conceptualization of what is normative masculine behavior. Different social settings generate different masculinities, even when the particular resource (crime) is similar.

In sum, the structure of the gender division of labor and power and normative heterosexuality impinges on the construction of masculinity. These structural features both preclude and permit certain forms of crime as resources that men may use to pursue a gender strategy and construct their masculinity. Although both battering and force-only rapists try to control their wives, they do so in qualitatively different ways. The social relations extant within their respective gender divisions of labor and power are different, and different options exist for maintaining their control. The choices made by each type of rapist, and the resources available to carry out those choices, develop in response to the specific social circumstances in which they live. For these reasons, then, these men employ different forms of violence to construct different types of private masculinities.

This chapter has attempted to demonstrate that men produce specific configurations of behavior that can be seen by others within the same immediate social setting as "essentially male." These different masculinities emerge from practices that utilize different resources, and class and race relations structure the resources available to construct specific masculinities. Pimps, workers, executives, and patriarchs generate situationally accomplished, unique masculinities by drawing on different types of crime indigenous to their distinct positions within the structural divisions of labor and power. Because men experience their everyday world from a uniquely individualistic position in society, they construct the cultural ideals of hegemonic masculinity in different ways.

Social structures are framed through social action and, in turn, provide resources for constructing masculinity. As one such resource, specific types of crime ultimately are based on these social structures. Thus, social structures both enable and constrain social action and, therefore, masculinities and crime.

Notes

1. Prostitutes, or "wives-in-law," are constructing a femininity that both confirms and violates stereotypical "female" behavior. In addition to the conventional aspects of femininity just mentioned, prostitute femininity also ridicules conventional morality by advocating sex outside marriage, sex for pleasure, anonymous sex, and sex that is not limited to reproduction and the domesticated couple. This construction of a specific type of femininity clearly challenges, in certain respects, stereotypical femininity. Nevertheless, the vast majority of prostitutes do not consider themselves feminists: they know very little about the feminist movement, do not share its assumptions, and believe men and women are "naturally" suited for different types of work (Miller 1986, 160).

2. The masculinity constructed by African American pimps is fittingly comparable to the masculinity associated with men (usually from working-class backgrounds) who are members of white motorcycle gangs. The men in such groups act extremely racist and similarly

exploit the sexuality and labor of "biker women." However, biker men do not display a "cool pose" with an accompanying show of luxury in the form of flashy clothing and exotic hairstyles. On the contrary, a biker usually has long unkempt hair, a "rough" beard, and his "colors" consist of black motorcycle boots, soiled jeans, and a simple sleeveless denim jacket with attached insignia (see Hopper and Moore 1990; Willis 1978).

3. Horizontal segregation allocates men and women to different types of jobs; vertical segregation concentrates men and women in different occupations at different steps in an occupational hierarchy.

4. Nevertheless, it should be pointed out that increasing numbers of men are attempting to counter sexism on the shop floor and, therefore, reconstruct shop-floor masculinity. For an excellent example, see Gray 1987.

5. Indeed, office romances seem to be flourishing because women more routinely work beside men in professional and occupational jobs (Ehrenreich 1989, 219).

6. This particular form of femininity has been explored by Pringle (1988).

7. Despite devastating criticisms of the Conflict Tactics Scale as a methodological tool (Dobash, Dobash, Wilson, and Daly 1992), some researchers (remarkably) continue to use it to guide their work, concluding that women are about as violent as men in the home (Straus and Gelles 1990) or even, in some cases, that more men are victimized in the home than are women (McNeely and Mann 1990).

8. Unfortunately, there is scant research on wife beating in racial-minority households. Nevertheless, what evidence there is on African American households suggests that when violence does occur, both husband and wife are likely to accept the traditional patriarchal division of labor and power as natural and that complete responsibility for the battering, when questioned, "lies with white society" (Richie 1985, 42; see also Asbury 1987). Consequently, I am forced to concentrate solely on class and wife beating.

9. This is not to deny that many middle-class men engage in wife beating for the reasons discussed earlier in this section. What I suggest, following Segal (1990, 255) and others, is that it is clearly less common in middle-class households because such men have access to other resources, possibly more effective resources, through which they exert control over women without employing violence.

10. Because Finkelhor and Yllö (1985, 9) found no significantly higher rate of marital rape among African Americans than among whites, I do not distinguish by race.

References

Acker, Joan. (1990). "Hierarchies, Jobs, Bodies: A Theory of Gendered Organization." *Gender and Society* 4(2): 139–58.

Andersen, Margaret. (1988). *Thinking About Women*. New York: Macmillan.

Asbury, Jo-Ellen. (1987). "African-American Women in Violent Relationships: An Exploration of Cultural Differences." In *Violence in the Black Family*, ed. Robert L. Hampton, 89–105. Lexington, KY: Lexington Books.

Berk, Sarah Fenstermaker. (1985). *The Gender Factory: The Apportionment of Work in American Households*. New York: Plenum Press.

Bernard, Jessie. (1982). *The Future of Marriage*. New Haven, CT: Yale University Press.

Bielby, William, and James N. Baron. (1986). "A Woman's Place Is with Other Women: Sex

Segregation within Organizations." In *Sex Segregation in the Workplace: Trends, Explanations, Remedies,* ed. Barbara Reskin, 27–55. Washington, DC: National Academy Press.

Box, Steven. (1983). *Power, Crime and Mystification.* New York: Tavistock.

Carothers, Suzanne C., and Peggy Crull. (1984). "Contrasting Sexual Harassment in Female- and Male-Dominated Occupations." In *My Troubles Are Going to Have Trouble with Me,* ed. Karen Brodkin Sacks and Dorothy Remy, 219–28. New Brunswick, NJ: Rutgers University Press.

Cockburn, Cynthia. (1983). *Brothers: Male Dominance and Technological Change.* London: Pluto Press.

Collinson, David L., and Margaret Collinson. (1989). "Sexuality in the Workplace: The Domination of Men's Sexuality." In *The Sexuality of Organization,* ed. Jeff Hearn, Deborah L. Sheppard, Peta Tancred-Sheriff, and Gibson Burrell, 91–109. Newbury Park, CA: Sage.

Connell, R. W. (1991). "Live Fast and Die Young: The Construction of Masculinity among Young Working-Class Men on the Margin of the Labour Market." Australian and New Zealand Journal of Sociology 27 (2): 141–71.

———. (1987). *Gender and Power.* Stanford, CA: Stanford University Press.

DeKeseredy, Walter, and Ronald Hinch. (1991). *Woman Abuse: Sociological Perspectives.* Lewiston, NY: Thompson Educational Pub. Inc.

DiTomaso, Nancy. (1989). "Sexuality in the Workplace: Discrimination and Harassment." In *The Sexuality of Organization,* eds. Jeff Hearn, Deborah L. Sheppard, Peta Tancred-Sheriff, and Gibson Burrell, 71–90. Newbury Park, CA: Sage.

Dobash, R. Emerson, and Russell P. Dobash. (1984). "The Nature and Antecedents of Violent Events." *British Journal of Criminology* 24 (3): 269–88.

Dobash, Russell P., R. Emerson Dobash, Margo Wilson, and Martin Daly. (1992). "The Myth of Sexual Symmetry in Marital Violence." *Social Problems* 39 (1): 71–91.

Donaldson, Mike. (1987). "Labouring Men: Love, Sex and Strife." *Australian and New Zealand Journal of Sociology* 23 (2): 165–84.

Edleson, Jeffrey L., Zvi Eisikovits, and Edna Guttman. (1986). "Men Who Batter Women: A Critical Review of the Evidence." *Journal of Family Issues* 6 (2): 229–47.

Ehrenreich, Barbara. (1989). *Fear of Falling.* New York: Pantheon.

———. (1984). "A Feminist's View of the New Man." *New York Times Magazine,* May 20, 1984: 36–48.

———. (1983). *The Hearts of Men.* New York: Double-day.

Ferraro, Kathleen J. (1989). "The Legal Response to Woman Battering in the United States." In *Women, Policing and Male Violence,* ed. Jalna Hanmer, Jill Radford, and Elizabeth A. Stanko, 155–84. New York: Routledge.

———. (1988). "An Existential Approach to Battering." In *Family Abuse and Its Consequences,* ed. Gerald T. Hotaling, David Finkelhor, John T. Kirkpatrick, and Murray Straus, 126–3 Newbury Park, CA: Sage.

Finkelhor, David, and Kristi Yllö. (1985). *License to Rape: Sexual Abuse of Wives.* New York: Holt, Rinehart and Winston.

Frieze, Irene H. (1983). "Investigating the Causes and Consequences of Marital Rape." *Signs* 8 (3): 532–53.

Game, Ann, and Rosemary Pringle. (1984). *Gender at Work.* Boston: Allen and Unwin.

Gordon, Linda. (1988). *Heroes of Their Own Lives.* New York: Viking.

Gray, Stan. (1987). "Sharing the Shop Floor." In *Beyond Patriarchy,* ed. Michael Kaufman, 216–34. New York: Oxford University Press.

Gruber, James, and Lars Bjorn. (1982). "Blue Collar Blues: The Sexual Harassment of Women Autoworkers." *Work and Occupations* (3): 271–98.

Harris, Richard N., and Roslyn Wallach Bologh. (1985). "The Dark Side of Love: Blue and White Collar Wife Abuse." *Victimology* 10 (1–4): 242–52.

Hartmann, Heidi. (1981). "The Unhappy Marriage of Marxism and Feminism: Towards a More Progressive Union." In *Women and Revolution,* ed. Lydia Sargent, 1–41. Boston: South End Press.

Hearn, Jeff. (1985). "Men's Sexuality at Work." In The *Sexuality of Men* ed. Andy Metcalf and Martin Humphries, 110–28. London: Pluto Press.

Hearn, Jeff, and Wendy Parkin. (1987). *"Sex" at "Work."* New York: St. Martin's Press.

Hochschild, Arlie. (1992). "The Second Shift: Employed Women Are Putting in Another Day of Work at Home." In *Men's Lives,* ed. Michael S. Kimmel and Michael A. Messner, 511–15. New York: Macmillan.

———. (1989). *The Second Shift.* New York: Viking.

Hopper, Columbus, and Johnny Moore. (1990). "Women in Outlaw Motorcycle Gangs." *Journal of Contemporary Ethnography* 18 (4): 363–87.

Kanter, Rosabeth Moss. (1977). *Men and Women of the Corporation.* New York: Basic Books.

Katz, Jack. (1988). *Seductions of Crime: Moral and Sensual Attractions in Doing Evil.* New York: Basic Books.

Komter, Aafke. (1989). "Hidden Power in Marriage." *Gender and Society* 3 (2): 187–216.

MacKinnon, Catherine A. (1979). *Sexual Harassment of Working Women.* New Haven, CT: Yale University Press.

McNeely, R. L., and CoraMae Richey Mann. (1990). "Domestic Violence Is a Human Issue." *Journal of Interpersonal Violence* 5 (1): 129–32.

Majors, Richard. (1986). "Cool Pose: The Proud Signature of Black Survival." *Changing Men* 17: 5–6.

Majors, Richard, and Janet Mancini Billson. (1992). *Cool Pose: The Dilemma's of Black Manhood in America.* New York: Macmillan.

Malcolm X. (1965). *The Autobiography of Malcolm X.* New York: Grove Press.

Messerschmidt, James W. (1986). *Capitalism, Patriarchy and Crime: Toward a Socialist Feminist Criminology.* Totowa, NJ: Rowman Littlefield.

Messner, Michael. (1989). "Masculinities and Athletic Careers." *Order and Society* 3 (1): 71–88.

Miller, Eleanor. (1986). *Street Woman.* Philadelphia: Temple University Press.

Milner, Christina, and Richard Milner. (1972). *Black Players: The Secret World of Black Pimps.* Boston: Little, Brown.

Pagelow, Mildred D. (1984). *Family Violence.* New York: Praeger.

Pahl, Jan. (1992). "Money and Power in Marriage." In *Gender, Power, and Sexuality,* ed. Pamela Abbott and Claire Wallace, 41–57. London: Macmillan.

Petchesky, Rosalind. (1984). *Abortion and Woman's Choice.* New York: Longman.

Pringle, Rosemary. (1989). "Bureaucracy, Rationality and Sexuality: The Case of Secretaries." In *The Sexuality of Organization,* ed. Jeff Hearn, Deborah L. Sheppard, Peta Tancred-Sheriff, and Gibson Burell, 158–77. Newbury Park, CA: Sage.

———. (1988). *Secretaries Talk: Sexuality, Power and Work.* New York: Verso.

Placek, James. (1988). "Why Do Men Batter Their Wives?" In *Feminist Perspectives on Wife Abuse,* ed. Kersti Yllö and Michele Bogard, 133–57. Newbury Park, CA: Sage.

Reskin, Barbara, and Patricia Roos. (1987). "Status Hierarchies and Sex Segregation." In *Ingredients for Women's Employment Poll* ed. Christine Bose and Glenna Spitze, 3–21. Albany: State University of New York Press.

Richie, Beth. (1985). "Battered Black Women: A Challenge for the Black Community." *The Black Scholar* 16 (2): 40–44.

Romenesko, Kim, and Eleanor M. Miller. (1989). "The Second ??? in Double Jeopardy: Appropriating the Labor of Female Street Hustlers." *Crime and Delinquency* 35 (1): 109–35.

Rosen, Ruth. (1982). *The Lost Sisterhood: Prostitution in America, 1900–1918.* Baltimore: John Hopkins University Press.

Russell, Diana E. H. (1982). *Rape in Marriage,* New York: Macini.

Schechter, Susan. (1982). *Women and Male Violence.* Boston: South End Press.

Schneider, Beth E. (1991). "Put Up and Shut Up: Workplace Sexual Assaults." *Gender and Society* 5 (4): 533–48.

Segal, Lynne. (1990). *Slow Motion: Changing Masculinities, Changing Men.* New Brunswick, NJ: Rutgers University Press.

Slim, Iceberg. (1967). *Pimp: The Story of My Life.* Los Angeles: Holloway House.

Smith, Michael D. (1990a). "Patriarchal Ideology and Wife Beating: A Test of a Feminist Hypothesis." *Violence and Victims* 5: 257–73.

———. (1990b). "Sociodemographic Risk Factors in Wife Abuse: Results from a Survey of Toronto Women." *Canadian Journal of Sociology.* 15 (1): 39–58.

Stets, Jan E., and Murray A. Straus. (1989). "The Marriage License as a Hitting License: A Comparison of Assaults in Dating, Cohabitating and Married Couples." In *Violence in Dating Relationships,* ed. Maureen A. Pirog-Good and Jan E. Stets, 38–52. New York: Praeger.

Straus, Murray A., and Richard J. Gelles. (1990). "How Violent Are American Families? Estimates from the National Family Violence Survey and Other Studies." In *Physical Violence in American Families,* ed. Murray A. Straus and Richard J. Gelles, 95–112. New Brunswick, NJ: Transaction.

Straus, Murray A., Richard J. Gelles, and Susan Steinmetz. (1980). *Behind Closed Doors.* New York: Doubleday.

Tolson, Andrew. (1977). *The Limits of Masculinity.* New York: Harper and Row.

Walby, Sylvia. (1989). "Theorizing Patriarchy." *Sociology* 23 (2): 213–34.

———. (1986). *Patriarchy at Work: Patriarchal and Capitalist Relations in Employment.* Minneapolis: University of Minnesota Press.

Walker, Lenore E. (1979). *The Battered Woman.* New York: Harper and Row.

———. (1977–78). "Battered Women and Learned Helplessness." *Victimology* 2 (4): 525–34.

West, Candace, and Don H. Zimmerman. (1987). "Doing Gender." *Gender and Society* 1 (2): 125–51.

Willis, Paul E. (1979). "Shop Floor Culture, Masculinity and the Wage Form." In *Working Class Culture,* ed. John Clarke, Chas Critcher, and Richard Johnson, 185–98. London: Hutchinson.

———. (1978). *Profane Culture.* London: Routledge & Kegan Paul.

CANDACE WEST AND DON H. ZIMMERMAN

Doing Gender

In the beginning, there was sex and there was gender. Those of us who taught courses in the area in the late 1960s and early 1970s were careful to distinguish one from the other. Sex, we told students, was what was ascribed by biology: anatomy, hormones, and physiology. Gender, we said, was an achieved status: that which is constructed through psychological, cultural, and social means. To introduce the difference between the two, we drew on singular case studies of hermaphrodites and anthropological investigations of "strange and exotic tribes."

Inevitably (and understandably), in the ensuing weeks of each term, our students became confused. Sex hardly seemed a "given" in the context of research that illustrated the sometimes ambiguous and often conflicting criteria for its ascription. And gender seemed much less an "achievement" in the context of the anthropological, psychological, and social imperatives we studied—the division of labor, the formation of gender identities, and the social subordination of women by men. Moreover, the received doctrine of gender socialization theories conveyed the strong message that while gender may be "achieved," by about age five it was certainly fixed, unvarying, and static—much like sex.

Since about 1975, the confusion has intensified and spread far beyond our individual classrooms. For one thing, we learned that the relationship between biological and cultural processes was far more complex—and reflexive—than we previously had supposed. For another, we discovered that certain structural arrangements, for example, between work and family, actually produce or enable some capacities, such as to mother, that we formerly associated with biology. In the midst of all this, the notion of gender as a recurring achievement somehow fell by the wayside.

Our purpose in this article is to propose an ethnomethodologically informed, and therefore distinctively sociological, understanding of gender as a routine, methodical, and recurring accomplishment. We contend that the "doing" of gender is undertaken by women and men whose competence as members of society is hostage to its production. Doing gender involves a complex of socially guided

From *Gender & Society,* Vol. 1, no. 2 (June 1987), pp. 125–151. Copyright © 1987 by Sociologists for Women in Society. Reprinted by permission of publisher. References have been edited.

perceptual, interactional, and micropolitical activities that cast particular pursuits as expressions of masculine and feminine "natures."

When we view gender as an accomplishment, an achieved property of situated conduct, our attention shifts from matters internal to the individual and focuses on interactional and, ultimately, institutional arenas. In one sense, of course, it is individuals who "do" gender. But it is a situated doing, carried out in the virtual or real presence of others who are presumed to be oriented to its production. Rather than as a property of individuals, we conceive of gender as an emergent feature of social situations: both as an outcome of and a rationale for various social arrangements and as a means of legitimating one of the most fundamental divisions of society.

To advance our argument, we undertake a critical examination of what sociologists have meant by *gender*, including its treatment as a role enactment in the conventional sense and as a "display" in Goffman's (1976) terminology. Both *gender role* and *gender display* focus on behavioral aspects of being a woman or a man (as opposed, for example, to biological differences between the two). However, we contend that the notion of gender as a role obscures the work that is involved in producing gender in everyday activities, while the notion of gender as a display relegates it to the periphery of interaction. We argue instead that participants in interaction organize their various and manifold activities to reflect or express gender, and they are disposed to perceive the behavior of others in a similar light.

To elaborate our proposal, we suggest at the outset that important but often overlooked distinctions be observed among *sex, sex category*, and *gender. Sex* is a determination made through the application of socially agreed upon biological criteria for classifying persons as females or males. The criteria for classification can be genitalia at birth or chromosomal typing before birth, and they do not necessarily agree with one another. Placement in a *sex category* is achieved through application of the sex criteria, but in everyday life, categorization is established and sustained by the socially required identificatory displays that proclaim one's membership in one or the other category. In this sense, one's sex category presumes one's sex and stands as proxy for it in many situations, but sex and sex category can vary independently; that is, it is possible to claim membership in a sex category even when the sex criteria are lacking. *Gender,* in contrast, is the activity of managing situated conduct in light of normative conceptions of attitudes and activities appropriate for one's sex category. Gender activities emerge from and bolster claims to membership in a sex category.

We contend that recognition of the analytical independence of sex, sex category, and gender is essential for understanding the relationships among these elements and the interactional work involved in "being" a gendered person in society. While our primary aim is theoretical, there will be occasion to discuss fruitful directions for empirical research following from the formulation of gender that we propose.

We begin with an assessment of the received meaning of gender, particularly in relation to the roots of this notion in presumed biological differences between women and men.

PERSPECTIVES ON SEX AND GENDER

In Western societies, the accepted cultural perspective on gender views women and men as naturally and unequivocally defined categories of being with distinctive psychological and behavioral propensities that can be predicted from their reproductive functions. Competent adult members of these societies see differences between the two as fundamental and enduring—differences seemingly supported by the division of labor into women's and men's work and an often elaborate differentiation of feminine and masculine attitudes and behaviors that are prominent features of social organization. Things are the way they are by virtue of the fact that men are men and women are women—a division perceived to be natural and rooted in biology, producing in turn profound psychological, behavioral, and social consequences. The structural arrangements of a society are presumed to be responsive to these differences.

Analyses of sex and gender in the social sciences, though less likely to accept uncritically the naive biological determinism of the view just presented, often retain a conception of sex-linked behaviors and traits as essential properties of individuals. The "sex differences approach" is more commonly attributed to psychologists than to sociologists, but the survey researcher who determines the "gender" of respondents on the basis of the sound of their voices over the telephone is also making trait-oriented assumptions. Reducing gender to a fixed set of psychological traits or to a unitary "variable" precludes serious consideration of the ways it is used to structure distinct domains of social experience.

Taking a different tack, role theory has attended to the social construction of gender categories, called "sex roles" or, more recently, "gender roles" and has analyzed how these are learned and enacted. Beginning with Linton (1936) and continuing through the works of Parsons (Parsons 1951; Parsons and Bales 1955) and Komarovsky (1946, 1950), role theory has emphasized the social and dynamic aspect of role construction and enactment. But at the level of face-to-face interaction, the application of role theory to gender poses problems of its own. Roles are *situated* identities—assumed and relinquished as the situation demands—rather than *master identities,* such as sex category, that cut across situations. Unlike most roles, such as "nurse," "doctor," and "patient" or "professor" and "student," gender has no specific site or organizational context.

Moreover, many roles are already gender marked, so that special qualifiers—such as "female doctor" or "male nurse"—must be added to exceptions to the rule. Thorne (1980) observes that conceptualizing gender as a role makes it difficult to assess its influence on other roles and reduces its explanatory usefulness in discussions of power and inequality. Drawing on Rubin (1975), Thorne calls for a reconceptualization of women and men as distinct social groups, constituted in "concrete, historically changing—and generally unequal—social relationships" (Thorne 1980, p. 11).

We argue that gender is not a set of traits, nor a variable, nor a role, but the product of social doings of some sort. What then is the social doing of gender? It is more than the continuous creation of the meaning of gender through human actions. We claim that gender itself is constituted through interaction. To develop the implications of our claim, we turn to Goffman's (1976) account of "gender display." Our object here is to explore how gender might be exhibited or portrayed through interaction, and thus be seen as "natural," while it is being produced as a socially organized achievement.

GENDER DISPLAY

Goffman contends that when human beings interact with others in their environment, they assume that each possesses an "essential nature"—a nature that can be discerned through the "natural signs given off or expressed by them" (1976, p. 75). Femininity and masculinity are regarded as "prototypes of essential expression—something that can be conveyed fleetingly in any social situation and yet something that strikes at the most basic characterization of the individual" (1976, p. 75). The means through which we provide such expressions are "perfunctory, conventionalized acts" (1976, p. 69), which convey to others our regard for them, indicate our alignment in an encounter, and tentatively establish the terms of contact for that social situation. But they are also regarded as expressive behavior, testimony to our "essential natures."

Goffman (1976, pp. 69–70) sees *displays* as highly conventionalized behaviors structured as two-part exchanges of the statement-reply type, in which the presence or absence of symmetry can establish deference or dominance. These rituals are viewed as distinct from but articulated with more consequential activities, such as performing tasks or engaging in discourse. Hence, we have what he terms the "scheduling" of displays at junctures in activities, such as the beginning or end, to avoid interfering with the activities themselves. Goffman (1976, p. 69) formulates *gender display* as follows:

> If gender be defined as the culturally established correlates of sex (whether in consequence of biology or learning), then gender display refers to conventionalized portrayals of these correlates.

These gendered expressions might reveal clues to the underlying, fundamental dimensions of the female and male, but they are, in Goffman's view, optional performances. Masculine courtesies may or may not be offered and, if offered, may or may not be declined (1976, p. 71). Moreover, human beings "themselves employ the term 'expression,' and conduct themselves to fit their own notions of expressivity" (1976, p. 75). Gender depictions are less a consequence of our "essential sexual natures" than interactional portrayals of what we would like to convey about sexual natures, using conventionalized gestures. Our human nature gives us the ability to learn to produce and recognize masculine and feminine gender displays—"a capacity [we] have by virtue of being persons, not males and females" (1976, p. 76).

Upon first inspection, it would appear that Goffman's formulation offers an engaging sociological corrective to existing formulations of gender. In his view, gender is a socially scripted dramatization of the culture's *idealization* of feminine and masculine natures, played for an audience that is well schooled in the presentational idiom. To continue the metaphor, there are scheduled performances presented in special locations, and like plays, they constitute introductions to or time out from more serious activities.

There are fundamental equivocations in this perspective. By segregating gender display from the serious business of interaction, Goffman obscures the effects of gender on a wide range of human activities. Gender is not merely something that happens in the nooks and crannies of interaction, fitted in here and there and not interfering with the serious business of life. While it is plausible to contend that gender displays—construed as conventionalized expressions—are optional, it does not seem plausible to say that we have the option of being seen by others as female or male.

It is necessary to move beyond the notion of gender display to consider what is involved in doing gender as an ongoing activity embedded in everyday interaction. Toward this end, we return to the distinctions among sex, sex category, and gender introduced earlier.

SEX, SEX CATEGORY, AND GENDER

Garfinkel's (1967, pp. 118–40) case study of Agnes, a transsexual raised as a boy who adopted a female identity at age 17 and underwent a sex reassignment operation several years later, demonstrates how gender is created through interaction and at the same time structures interaction. Agnes, whom Garfinkel characterized as a "practical methodologist," developed a number of procedures for passing as a "normal, natural female" both prior to and after her surgery. She had the practical task of managing the fact that she possessed male genitalia and that she lacked the social resources a girl's biography would presumably provide in everyday interaction. In short, she needed to display herself as a woman, simultaneously learning what it was to be a woman. Of necessity, this full-time pursuit took place at a time when most people's gender would be well-accredited and routinized. Agnes had to consciously contrive what the vast majority of women do without thinking. She was not "faking" what "real" women do naturally. She was obliged to analyze and figure out how to act within socially structured circumstances and conceptions of femininity that women born with appropriate biological credentials come to take for granted early on. As in the case of others who must "pass," such as transvestites, Kabuki actors, or Dustin Hoffman's "Tootsie," Agnes's case makes visible what culture has made invisible—the accomplishment of gender.

Garfinkel's (1967) discussion of Agnes does not explicitly separate three analytically distinct, although empirically overlapping, concepts—sex, sex category, and gender.

Sex

Agnes did not possess the socially agreed upon biological criteria for classification as a member of the female sex. Still, Agnes regarded herself as a female, albeit a female with a penis, which a woman ought not to possess. The penis, she insisted, was a "mistake" in need of remedy (Garfinkel 1967, pp. 126–27, 131–32). Like other competent members of our culture, Agnes honored the notion that there are "essential" biological criteria that unequivocally distinguish females from males. However, if we move away from the commonsense viewpoint, we discover that the reliability of these criteria is not beyond question. Moreover, other cultures have acknowledged the existence of "cross-genders" and the possibility of more than two sexes.

More central to our argument is Kessler and McKenna's (1978, pp. 1–6) point that genitalia are conventionally hidden from public inspection in everyday life; yet we continue through our social rounds to "observe" a world of two naturally, normally sexed persons. It is the *presumption* that essential criteria exist and would or should be there if looked for that provides the basis for sex categorization. Drawing on Garfinkel, Kessler and McKenna argue that "female" and "male" are cultural events—products of what they term the "gender attribution process"— rather than some collection of traits, behaviors, or even physical attributes. Illustratively they cite the child who, viewing a picture of someone clad in a suit and a tie, contends, "It's a man, because he has a pee-pee" (Kessler and McKenna 1978, p. 154). Translation: "He must have a pee-pee [an essential characteristic] because I see the *insignia* of a suit and tie." Neither initial sex assignment (pronouncement at birth as a female or male) nor the actual existence of essential criteria for that assignment (possession of a clitoris and vagina or penis and testicles) has much—if anything—to do with the identification of sex category in everyday life. There, Kessler and McKenna note, we operate with a moral certainty of a world of two sexes. We do not think, "Most persons with penises are men, but some may not be" or "Most persons who dress as men have penises." Rather, we take it for granted that sex and sex category are congruent—that knowing the latter, we can deduce the rest.

Sex Categorization

Agnes's claim to the categorical status of female, which she sustained by appropriate identificatory displays and other characteristics, could be *discredited* before her transsexual operation if her possession of a penis became known and after by her surgically constructed genitalia. In this regard, Agnes had to be continually alert to actual or potential threats to the security of her sex category. Her problem was not so much living up to some prototype of essential femininity but preserving her categorization as female. This task was made easy for her by a very powerful resource, namely, the process of commonsense categorization in everyday life.

The categorization of members of society into indigenous categories such as "girl" or "boy," or "woman" or "man," operates in a distinctively social way. The act of categorization does not involve a positive test, in the sense of a well-defined set of criteria that must be explicitly satisfied prior to making an identification. Rather, the application of membership categories relies on an "if-can" test in everyday interaction. This test stipulates that if people *can be seen* as members of relevant categories, *then categorize them that way.* That is, use the category that seems appropriate, except in the presence of discrepant information or obvious features that would rule out its use. This procedure is quite in keeping with the attitude of everyday life, which has us take appearances at face value unless we have special reason to doubt. It should be added that it is precisely when we have special reason to doubt that the issue of applying rigorous criteria arises, but it is rare, outside legal or bureaucratic contexts, to encounter insistence on positive tests.

Agnes's initial resource was the predisposition of those she encountered to take her appearance (her figure, clothing, hair style, and so on), as the undoubted appearance of a normal female. Her further resource was our cultural perspective on the properties of "natural, normally sexed persons." Garfinkel (1967, pp. 122–28) notes that in everyday life, we live in a world of two—and only two—sexes. This arrangement has a moral status, in that we include ourselves and others in it as "essentially, originally, in the first place, always have been, always will be, once and for all, in the final analysis, either 'male' or 'female'" (Garfinkel 1967, p. 122).

Consider the following case:

> This issue reminds me of a visit I made to a computer store a couple of years ago. The person who answered my questions was truly a *salesperson*. I could not categorize him/her as a woman or a man. What did I look for? (1) Facial hair: She/he was smooth skinned, but some men have little or no facial hair. (This varies by race, Native Americans and Blacks often have none.) (2) Breasts: She/he was wearing a loose shirt that hung from his/her shoulders. And, as many women who suffered through a 1950s' adolescence know to their shame, women are often flat-chested. (3) Shoulders: His/hers were small and round for a man, broad for a woman. (4) Hands: Long and slender fingers, knuckles a bit large for a woman, small for a man. (5) Voice: Middle range, unexpressive for a woman, not at all the exaggerated tones some gay males affect. (6) His/her treatment of me: Gave off no signs that would let me know if I were of the same or different sex as this person. There were not even any signs that he/she knew his/her sex would be difficult to categorize and I wondered about that even as I did my best to hide these questions so I would not embarrass him/her while we talked of computer paper. I left still not knowing the sex of my salesperson, and was disturbed by that unanswered question (child of my culture that I am). (Diane Margolis, personal communication)

What can this case tell us about situations such as Agnes's or the process of sex categorization in general? First, we infer from this description that the computer salesclerk's identificatory display was ambiguous, since she or he was not dressed or adorned in an unequivocally female or male fashion. It is when such a display *fails* to provide grounds for categorization that factors such as facial hair or tone of voice are assessed to determine membership in a sex category. Second, beyond the fact that this incident could be recalled after "a couple of years," the customer was not only "disturbed" by the ambiguity of the salesclerk's category but also assumed that to acknowledge this ambiguity would be embarrassing to the salesclerk. Not only do we want to know the sex category of those around us (to see it at a glance, perhaps), but we presume that others are displaying it for us, in as decisive a fashion as they can.

Gender

Agnes attempted to be "120 percent female" (Garfinkel 1967, p. 129), that is, unquestionably in all ways and at all times feminine. She thought she could protect herself from disclosure before and after surgical intervention by comporting herself in a feminine manner, but she also could have given herself away by overdoing her performance. Sex categorization and the accomplishment of gender are not the same. Agnes's categorization could be secure or suspect, but did not depend on whether or not she lived up to some ideal conception of femininity. Women can be seen as unfeminine, but that does not make them "unfemale." Agnes faced an ongoing task of being a woman—something beyond style of dress (an identificatory display) or allowing men to light her cigarette (a gender display). Her problem was to produce configurations of behavior that would be seen by others as normative gender behavior.

Agnes's strategy of "secret apprenticeship," through which she learned expected feminine decorum by carefully attending to her fiancé's criticisms of other women, was one means of masking incompetencies and simultaneously acquiring the needed skills (Garfinkel 1967, pp. 146–47). It was through her fiancé that Agnes learned that sunbathing on the lawn in front of her apartment was "offensive" (because it put her on display to other men). She also learned from his critiques of other women that she should not insist on having things her way and that she should not offer her opinions or claim equality with men (Garfinkel 1967, pp. 147–48). (Like other women in our society, Agnes learned something about power in the course of her "education.")

Popular culture abounds with books and magazines that compile idealized depictions of relations between women and men. Those focused on the etiquette of dating or prevailing standards of feminine comportment are meant to be of practical help in these matters. However, the use of any such source *as a manual of procedure* requires the assumption that doing gender merely involves making use of discrete, well-defined bundles of behavior that can simply be plugged into interactional situations to produce recognizable enactments of masculinity and femininity. The man "does" being masculine by, for example, taking the woman's arm to guide her across a street, and she "does" being feminine by consenting to be guided and not initiating such behavior with a man.

Agnes could perhaps have used such sources as manuals, but, we contend, doing gender is not so easily regimented. Such sources may list and describe the sorts of behaviors that mark or display gender, but they are necessarily incomplete. And to be successful, marking or displaying gender must be finely fitted to situations and modified or transformed as the occasion demands. Doing gender consists of managing such occasions so that, whatever the particulars, the outcome is seen and seeable in context as gender-appropriate or, as the case may be, gender-*in*appropriate, that is, *accountable.*

GENDER AND ACCOUNTABILITY

As Heritage (1984, pp. 136–37) notes, members of society regularly engage in "descriptive accountings of states of affairs to one another," and such accounts are both serious and consequential. These descriptions name, characterize, formulate, explain, excuse, excoriate, or merely take notice of some circumstance or activity and thus place it within some social framework (locating it relative to other activities, like and unlike).

Such descriptions are themselves accountable, and societal members orient to the fact that their activities are subject to comment. Actions are often designed with an eye to their accountability, that is, how they might look and how they might be characterized. The notion of accountability also encompasses those actions undertaken so that they are specifically unremarkable and thus not worthy of more than a passing remark, because they are seen to be in accord with culturally approved standards.

Heritage (1984, p. 179) observes that the process of rendering something accountable is interactional in character:

> [This] permits actors to design their actions in relation to their circumstances so as to permit others, by methodically taking account of circumstances, to recognize the action for what it is.

The key word here is *circumstances*. One circumstance that attends virtually all actions is the sex category of the actor. As Garfinkel (1967, p. 118) comments:

> [T]he work and socially structured occasions of sexual passing were obstinately unyielding to [Agnes's] attempts to routinize the grounds of daily activities. This obstinacy points to the *omnirelevance* of sexual status to affairs of daily life as an invariant but unnoticed background in the texture of relevances that compose the changing actual scenes of everyday life. (italics added)

If sex category is omnirelevant (or even approaches being so), then a person engaged in virtually any activity may be held accountable for performance of that activity as a *woman* or a *man*, and their incumbency in one or the other sex category can be used to legitimate or discredit their other activities. Accordingly, virtually any activity can be assessed as to its womanly or manly nature. And note, to "do" gender is not always to live up to normative conceptions of femininity or masculinity; it is to engage in behavior *at the risk of gender assessment*. While it is individuals who do gender, the enterprise is fundamentally interactional and institutional in character, for accountability is a feature of social relationships and its idiom is drawn from the institutional arena in which those relationships are enacted. If this be the case, can we ever *not* do gender? Insofar as a society is partitioned by "essential" differences between women and men and placement in a sex category is both relevant and enforced, doing gender is unavoidable.

RESOURCES FOR DOING GENDER

Doing gender means creating differences between girls and boys and women and men, differences that are not natural, essential, or biological. Once the differences have been constructed, they are used to reinforce the "essentialness" of gender. In a delightful account of the "arrangement between the sexes," Goffman (1977) observes the creation of a variety of institutionalized frameworks through which our "natural, normal sexedness" can be enacted. The physical features of social setting provide one obvious resource for the expression of our "essential" differences. For example, the sex segregation of North American public bathrooms distinguishes "ladies" from "gentlemen" in matters held to be fundamentally biological, even though both "are somewhat similar in the question of waste products and their elimination" (Goffman 1977, p. 315). These settings are furnished with dimorphic equipment (such as urinals for men or elaborate grooming facilities for women), even though both sexes may achieve the same ends through the same means (and apparently do so in the privacy of their own homes). To be stressed here is the fact that:

> The *functioning* of sex-differentiated organs is involved, but there is nothing in this functioning that biologically recommends segregation; that arrangement is a totally cultural matter . . . toilet segregation is presented as a natural consequence of the difference between the sex-classes when in fact it is a means of honoring, if not producing, this difference. (Goffman 1977, p. 316)

Standardized social occasions also provide stages for evocations of the "essential female and male natures." Goffman cites organized sports as one such institutionalized framework for the expression of manliness. There, those qualities that ought "properly" to be associated with masculinity, such as endurance, strength, and competitive spirit, are celebrated by all parties concerned—participants, who may be seen to demonstrate such traits, and spectators, who applaud their demonstrations from the safety of the sidelines (1977, p. 322).

Assortative mating practices among heterosexual couples afford still further means to create and maintain differences between women and men. For example, even though size, strength, and age tend to be normally distributed among females and males (with considerable overlap between them), selective pairing ensures couples in which boys and men are visibly bigger, stronger, and older (if not "wiser") than the girls and women with whom they are paired. So, should situations emerge in which greater size, strength, or experience is called for, boys and men will be ever ready to display it and girls and women, to appreciate its display.

Gender may be routinely fashioned in a variety of situations that seem conventionally expressive to begin with, such as those that present "helpless" women next to heavy objects or flat tires. But, as Goffman notes, heavy, messy, and precarious concerns can be constructed from *any* social situation, "even though by standards set in other settings, this may involve something that is light, clean, and safe" (Goffman 1977, p. 324). Given these resources, it is clear that any interactional situation sets the stage for depictions of "essential" sexual natures. In sum, these situations "do not so much allow for the expression of natural differences as for the production of that difference itself" (Goffman 1977, p. 324).

Many situations are not clearly sex categorized to begin with, nor is what transpires within them obviously gender relevant. Yet any social encounter can be pressed into service in the interests of doing gender. Thus, Fishman's (1978) research on casual conversations found an asymmetrical "division of labor" in talk between hetero-sexual intimates. Women had to ask more questions, fill more silences, and use more attention-getting beginnings in order to be heard. Her conclusions are particularly pertinent here:

> Since interactional work is related to what constitutes being a woman, with what a woman is, the idea that it is work is obscured. The work is not seen as what women do, but as part of what they are. (Fishman 1978, p. 405)

We would argue that it is precisely such labor that helps to constitute the essential nature of women as women in interactional contexts.

Individuals have many social identities that may be donned or shed, muted or made more salient, depending on the situation. One may be a friend, spouse, professional, citizen, and many other things to many different people—or, to the same person at different times. But we are always women or men—unless we shift into another sex category. What this means is that our identificatory displays will provide an ever-available resource for doing gender under an infinitely diverse set of circumstances.

Some occasions are organized to routinely display and celebrate behaviors that are conventionally linked to one or the other sex category. On such occasions, everyone knows his or her place in the interactional scheme of things. If an individual identified as a member of one sex category engages in behavior usually associated with the other category, this routinization is challenged. Hughes (1945, p. 356) provides an illustration of such a dilemma:

> [A] young woman . . . became part of that virile profession, engineering. The designer of an airplane is expected to go up on the maiden flight of the first plane built according to the design. He [sic] then gives a dinner to the engineers and workmen who worked on the new plane. The dinner is naturally a stag party. The young woman in question designed a plane. Her co-workers urged her not to take the risk—for which, presumably, men only are fit—of the maiden voyage. They were, in effect, asking her to be a lady instead of an engineer. She chose to be an engineer. She then gave the party and paid for it like a man. After food and the first round of toasts, she left like a lady.

On this occasion, parties reached an accommodation that allowed a woman to engage in presumptively masculine behaviors. However, we note that in the end, this compromise permitted demonstration of her "essential" femininity, through accountably "ladylike" behavior.

Hughes (1945, p. 357) suggests that such contradictions may be countered by managing interactions on a very narrow basis, for example, "keeping the relationship formal and specific." But the heart of the matter is that even—perhaps, especially—if the relationship is a formal one, gender is still something one is accountable for. Thus a woman physician (notice the special qualifier in her case) may be accorded respect for her skill and even addressed by an appropriate title. Nonetheless, she is subject to evaluation in terms of normative conceptions of appropriate attitudes and activities for her sex category and under pressure to prove that she is an "essentially" feminine being, despite appearances to the contrary. Her sex category is used to discredit her participation in important clinical activities, while her involvement in medicine is used to discredit her commitment to her responsibilities as a wife and mother. Simultaneously, her exclusion from the physician colleague community is maintained and her accountability *as a woman* is ensured.

In this context, "role conflict" can be viewed as a dynamic aspect of our current "arrangement between the sexes" (Goffman 1977), an arrangement that provides for occasions on which persons of a particular sex category can "see" quite clearly that they are out of place and that if they were not there, their current troubles would not exist. What is at stake is, from the standpoint of interaction, the management of our "essential" natures, and from the standpoint of the individual, the continuing accomplishment of gender. If, as we have argued, sex category is omnirelevant, then any occasion, conflicted or not, offers the resources for doing gender.

We have sought to show that sex category and gender are managed properties of conduct that are contrived with respect to the fact that others will judge and respond to us in particular ways. We have claimed that a person's gender is not simply an aspect of what one is, but, more fundamentally, it is something that one does, and *does* recurrently, in interaction with others.

What are the consequences of this theoretical formulation? If, for example, individuals strive to achieve gender in encounters with others, how does a culture instill the need to achieve it? What is the relationship between the production of gender at the level of interaction and such institutional arrangements as the division of labor in society? And, perhaps most important, how does doing gender contribute to the subordination of women by men?

RESEARCH AGENDAS

To bring the social production of gender under empirical scrutiny, we might begin at the beginning, with a reconsideration of the process through which societal members acquire the requisite categorical apparatus and other skills to become gendered human beings.

Recruitment to Gender Identities

The conventional approach to the process of becoming girls and boys has been sex-role socialization. In recent years, recurring problems arising from this approach have been linked to inadequacies inherent in role theory *per se*—its emphasis on "consensus, stability and continuity" (Stacey and Thorne 1985, p. 307), its a historical and depoliticizing focus (Thorne 1980, p. 9; Stacey and Thorne 1985, p. 307), and the fact that its "social" dimension relies on "a general assumption that people choose to maintain existing customs" (Connell 1985, p. 263).

In contrast, Cahill (1982, 1986a, 1986b) analyzes the experiences of preschool children using a social model of recruitment into normally gendered identities. Cahill argues that categorization practices are fundamental to learning and displaying feminine and masculine behavior. Initially, he observes, children are primarily concerned with distinguishing between themselves and others on the basis of social competence. Categorically, their concern resolves itself into the opposition of "girl/boy" classification versus "baby" classification (the latter designating children whose social behavior is problematic and who must be closely supervised). It is children's concern with being seen as socially competent that evokes their initial claims to gender identities:

> During the exploratory stage of children's socialization . . . they learn that only two social identities are routinely available to them, the identity of "baby," or, depending on the configuration of their external genitalia, either "big boy" or "big girl." Moreover, others subtly inform them that the identity of "baby" is a discrediting one. When, for example, children engage in disapproved behavior, they are often told "You're a baby" or "Be a big boy." In effect, these typical verbal responses to young children's behavior convey to them that they must behaviorally choose between the discrediting identity of "baby" and their anatomically determined sex identity. (Cahill 1986a, p. 175)

Subsequently, little boys appropriate the gender ideal of "efficaciousness," that is, being able to affect the physical and social environment through the exercise of physical strength or appropriate skills. In contrast, little girls learn to value "appearance," that is, managing themselves as ornamental objects. Both classes of children learn that the recognition and use of sex categorization in interaction are not optional, but mandatory.

Being a "girl" or a "boy" then, is not only being more competent than a "baby," but also being competently female or male, that is, learning to produce behavioral displays of one's "essential" female or male identity. In this respect, the task of four- to five-year-old children is very similar to Agnes's:

> For example, the following interaction occurred on a preschool playground. A 55-month-old boy (D) was attempting to unfasten the clasp of a necklace when a preschool aide walked over to him.
>
> A: Do you want to put that on?
>
> D: No. It's for girls.
>
> A: You don't have to be a girl to wear things around your neck.

> Kings wear things around their necks. You could pretend you're a king.

> D: I'm not a king. I'm a boy. (Cahill 1986a, p. 176)

As Cahill notes of this example, although D may have been unclear as to the sex status of a king's identity, he was obviously aware that necklaces are used to announce the identity "girl." Having claimed the identity "boy" and having developed a behavioral commitment to it, he was leery of any display that might furnish grounds for questioning his claim.

In this way, new members of society come to be involved in a *self-regulating process* as they begin to monitor their own and others' conduct with regard to its gender implications. The "recruitment" process involves not only the appropriation of gender ideals (by the valuation of those ideals as proper ways of being and behaving) but also *gender identities* that are important to individuals and that they strive to maintain. Thus gender differences, or the sociocultural shaping of "essential female and male natures," achieve the status of objective facts. They are rendered normal, natural features of persons and provide the tacit rationale for differing fates of women and men within the social order.

Additional studies of children's play activities as routine occasions for the expression of gender-appropriate behavior can yield new insights into how our "essential natures" are constructed. In particular, the transition from what Cahill (1986a) terms "apprentice participation" in the sex-segregated worlds that are common among elementary school children to "bona fide participation" in the heterosocial world so frightening to adolescents is likely to be a keystone in our understanding of the recruitment process.

Gender and the Division of Labor

Whenever people face issues of *allocation*—who is to do what, get what, plan or execute action, direct or be directed, incumbency in significant social categories such as "female" and "male" seems to become pointedly relevant. How such issues are resolved conditions the exhibition, dramatization, or celebration of one's "essential nature" as a woman or man.

Berk (1985) offers elegant demonstration of this point in her investigation of the allocation of household labor and the attitudes of married couples toward the division of household tasks. Berk found little variation in either the actual distribution of tasks or perceptions of equity in regard to that distribution. Wives, even when employed outside the home, do the vast majority of household and childcare tasks. Moreover, both wives and husbands tend to perceive this as a "fair" arrangement. Noting the failure of conventional sociological and economic theories to explain this seeming contradiction, Berk contends that something more complex is involved than rational arrangements for the production of household goods and services:

> Hardly a question simply of who has more time, or whose time is worth more, who has more skill or more power, it is clear that a complicated relationship be-

tween the structure of work imperatives and the structure of normative expectations attached to work as *gendered* determines the ultimate allocation of members' time to work and home. (Berk 1985, pp. 195–96)

She notes, for example, that the most important factor influencing wives' contribution of labor is the total amount of work demanded or expected by the household; such demands had no bearing on husbands' contributions. Wives reported various rationales (their own and their husbands') that justified their level of contribution and, as a general matter, underscored the presumption that wives are essentially responsible for household production.

Berk (1985, p. 201) contends that it is difficult to see how people "could rationally establish the arrangements that they do solely for the production of household goods and services"—much less, how people could consider them "fair." She argues that our current arrangements for the domestic division of labor support *two* production processes: household goods and services (meals, clean children, and so on) and, at the same time, gender. As she puts it:

> Simultaneously, members "do" gender, as they "do" housework and child care, and what [has] been called the division of labor provides for the joint production of household labor and gender; it is the mechanism by which both the material and symbolic products of the household are realized. (1985, p. 201)

It is not simply that household labor is designated as "women's work," but that for a woman to engage in it and a man not to engage in it is to draw on and exhibit the "essential nature" of each. What is produced and reproduced is not merely the activity and artifact of domestic life, but the material embodiment of wifely and husbandly roles, and derivatively, of womanly and manly conduct. What are also frequently produced and reproduced are the dominant and subordinate statuses of the sex categories.

How does gender get done in work settings outside the home, where dominance and subordination are themes of overarching importance? Hochschild's (1983) analysis of the work of flight attendants offers some promising insights. She found that the occupation of flight attendant consisted of something altogether different for women than for men:

> As the company's main shock absorbers against "mishandled" passengers, their own feelings are more frequently subjected to rough treatment. In addition, a day's exposure to people who resist authority in a woman is a different experience than it is for a man. . . . In this respect, it is a disadvantage to be a woman. And in this case, they are not simply women in the biological sense. They are also a highly visible distillation of middle-class American notions of femininity. They symbolize Woman. Insofar as the category "female" is mentally associated with having less status and authority, female flight attendants are more readily classified as "really" females than other females are. (Hochschild 1983, p. 175)

In performing what Hochschild terms the "emotional labor" necessary to maintain airline profits, women flight attendants simultaneously produce enactments of their "essential" femininity.

Sex and Sexuality

What is the relationship between doing gender and a culture's prescription of "obligatory heterosexuality"? As Frye (1983, p. 22) observes, the monitoring of sexual feelings in relation to other appropriately sexed persons requires the ready recognition of such persons "before one can allow one's heart to beat or one's blood to flow in erotic enjoyment of that person." The appearance of heterosexuality is produced through emphatic and unambiguous indicators of one's sex, layered on in ever more conclusive fashion (Frye 1983, p. 24). Thus, lesbians and gay men concerned with passing as heterosexuals can rely on these indicators for camouflage; in contrast, those who would avoid the assumption of heterosexuality may foster ambiguous indicators of their categorical status through their dress, behaviors, and style. But "ambiguous" sex indicators are sex indicators nonetheless. If one wishes to be recognized as a lesbian (or heterosexual woman), one must first establish a categorical status as female. Even as popular images portray lesbians as "females who are not feminine" (Frye 1983, p. 129), the accountability of persons for their "normal, natural sexedness" is preserved.

Nor is accountability threatened by the existence of "sex-change operations"—presumably, the most radical challenge to our cultural perspective on sex and gender. Although no one coerces transsexuals into hormone therapy, electrolysis, or surgery, the alternatives available to them are undeniably constrained:

> When the transsexual experts maintain that they use transsexual procedures only with people who ask for them, and who prove that they can "pass," they obscure the social reality. Given patriarchy's prescription that one must be *either* masculine or feminine, free choice is conditioned. (Raymond 1979, p. 135, italics added)

The physical reconstruction of sex criteria pays ultimate tribute to the "essentialness" of our sexual natures—as women *or* as men.

GENDER, POWER, AND SOCIAL CHANGE

Let us return to the question: Can we avoid doing gender? Earlier, we proposed that insofar as sex category is used as a fundamental criterion for differentiation, doing gender is unavoidable. It is unavoidable because of the social consequences of sex-category membership: the allocation of power and resources not only in the domestic, economic, and political domains but also in the broad arena of interpersonal relations. In virtually any situation, one's sex category can be relevant, and one's performance as an incumbent of that category (i.e., gender) can be subjected to evaluation. Maintaining such pervasive and faithful assignment of lifetime status requires legitimation.

But doing gender also renders the social arrangements based on sex category accountable as normal and natural, that is, legitimate ways of organizing social life. Differences between women and men that are created by this process can then be portrayed as fundamental and enduring dispositions. In this light, the institutional arrangements of a society can be seen as responsive to the differences—the social order being merely an accommodation to the natural order. Thus if, in doing gender, men are also doing dominance and women are doing deference, the resultant social order, which supposedly reflects "natural differences," is a powerful reinforcer and legitimator of hierarchical arrangements. Frye observes:

> For efficient subordination, what's wanted is that the structure not appear to be a cultural artifact kept in place by human decision or custom, but that it appear *natural*—that it appear to be quite a direct consequence of facts about the beast which are beyond the scope of human manipulation. . . . That we are trained to behave so differently as women and men, and to behave so differently toward women and men, itself contributes mightily to the appearance of extreme dimorphism, but also, the *ways* we act as women and men, and the *ways* we act toward women and men, mold our bodies and our minds to the shape of subordination and dominance. We do become what we practice being. (Frye 1983, p. 34)

If we do gender appropriately, we simultaneously sustain, reproduce, and render legitimate the institutional arrangements that are based on sex category. If we fail to do gender appropriately, we as individuals—not the institutional arrangements—may be called to account (for our character, motives, and predispositions).

Social movements such as feminism can provide the ideology and impetus to question existing arrangements, and the social support for individuals to explore alternatives to them. Legislative changes, such as that proposed by the Equal Rights Amendment, can also weaken the accountability of conduct to sex category, thereby affording the possibility of more widespread loosening of accountability in general. To be sure, equality under the law does not guarantee equality in other arenas. As Lorber (1986, p. 577) points out, assurance of "scrupulous equality of categories of people considered essentially different needs constant monitoring." What such proposed changes can do is provide the warrant for asking why, if we wish to treat women and men as equals, there needs to be two sex categories at all.

The sex category/gender relationship links the institutional and interactional levels, a coupling that legitimates social arrangements based on sex category and reproduces their asymmetry in face-to-face interaction. Doing gender furnishes the interactional scaffolding of social structure, along with a built-in mechanism of social control. In appreciating the institutional forces that maintain distinctions between women and men, we must not lose sight of the interactional validation of those distinctions that confers upon them their sense of "naturalness" and "rightness."

Social change, then, must be pursued both at the institutional and cultural level of sex category and at the interactional level of gender. Such a conclusion is hardly novel. Nevertheless, we suggest that it is important to recognize that the analytical distinction between institutional and interactional spheres does not pose an either/or choice when it comes to the question of effecting social change. Reconceptualizing gender not as a simple property of individuals but as an integral dynamic of social orders implies a new perspective on the entire network of gender relations:

> [T]he social subordination of women, and the cultural practices which help sustain it; the politics of sexual object-choice, and particularly the oppression of homosexual people; the sexual division of labor, the formation of character and motive, so far as they are organized as femininity and masculinity; the role of the body in social relations, especially the politics of childbirth; and the nature of strategies of sexual liberation movements. (Connell 1985, p. 261)

Gender is a powerful ideological device, which produces, reproduces, and legitimates the choices and limits that are predicated on sex category. An understanding of how gender is produced in social situations will afford clarification of the interactional scaffolding of social structure and the social control processes that sustain it.

References

Berk, Sarah F. 1985. *The Gender Factory: The Apportionment of Work in American Households.* New York: Plenum.

Cahill, Spencer E. 1982. "Becoming Boys and Girls." Ph.D. dissertation, Department of Sociology, University of California, Santa Barbara.

———. 1986a. "Childhood Socialization as Recruitment Process: Some Lessons from the Study of Gender Development." Pp. 163–86 in *Sociological Studies of Child Development*, edited by P. Adler and P. Adler. Greenwich, CT: JAI Press.

———. 1986b. "Language Practices and Self-Definition: The Case of Gender Identity Acquisition." *The Sociological Quarterly* 27:295–311.

Connell, R.W. 1985. "Theorizing Gender." *Sociology* 19:260–72.

Fishman, Pamela. 1978. "Interaction: The Work Women Do." *Social Problems* 25:397–406.

Frye, Marilyn. 1983. *The Politics of Reality: Essays in Feminist Theory.* Trumansburg, NY: The Crossing Press.

Garfinkel, Harold. 1967. *Studies in Ethnomethodology.* Englewood Cliffs, NJ: Prentice-Hall.

Goffman, Erving. 1976. "Gender Display." *Studies in the Anthropology of Visual Communication* 3:69–77.

———. 1977. "The Arrangement Between the Sexes." *Theory and Society* 4:301–31.

Heritage, John. 1984. *Garfinkel and Ethnomethodology.* Cambridge, England: Polity Press.

Hochschild, Arlie R. 1983. *The Managed Heart. Commercialization of Human Feeling.* Berkeley: University of California Press.

Hughes, Everett C. 1945. "Dilemmas and Contradictions of Status." *American Journal of Sociology* 50:353–59.

Kessler, Suzanne J., and Wendy McKenna. 1978. *Gender: An Ethnomethodological Approach.* New York: Wiley.

Komarovsky, Mirra. 1946. "Cultural Contradictions and Sex Roles." *American Journal of Sociology* 52:184–89.

———. 1950. "Functional Analysis of Sex Roles." *American Sociological Review* 15:508–16.

Linton, Ralph. 1936. *The Study of Man*. New York: Appleton-Century.

Lorber, Judith. 1986. "Dismantling Noah's Ark." *Sex Roles* 14:567–80.

Parsons, Talcott. 1951. *The Social System*. New York: Free Press.

———, and Robert F. Bales. 1955. *Family, Socialization and Interaction Process*. New York: Free Press.

Raymond, Janice G. 1979. *The Transsexual Empire*. Boston: Beacon.

Rossi, Alice. 1984. "Gender and Parenthood." *American Sociological Review* 49:1–19.

Rubin, Gayle. 1975. "The Traffic in Women: Notes on the 'Political Economy' of Sex." Pp. 157–210 in *Toward an Anthropology of Women*, edited by R. Reiter. New York: Monthly Review Press.

Stacey, Judith, and Barrie Thorne. 1985. "The Missing Feminist Revolution in Sociology." *Social Problems* 32:301–16.

Thorne, Barrie. 1980. "Gender . . . How Is It Best Conceptualized?" Unpublished manuscript.

PART 5 THE GENDERED FAMILY

The current debates about the "crisis" of the family—a traditional arrangement that some fear is collapsing under the weight of contemporary trends ranging from relaxed sexual attitudes, increased divorce, women's entry into the labor force, to rap music and violence in the media—actually underscores how central the family is to the reproduction of social life—and to gender identity. If gender identity were biologically "natural," we probably wouldn't need such strong family structures to make sure that everything turned out all right.

Though the "typical" family of the 1950s television sitcom—breadwinner father, housewife mother, and 2.5 happy and well-adjusted children—is the empirical reality for less than 10 percent of all households, it remains the cultural ideal against which contemporary family styles are measured. And some, such as sociologist David Popenoe, would like to see us "return" as close as possible to that imagined idealized model—perhaps by restricting access to easy divorce, or restricting women's entry into the labor force, or by promoting sexual abstinence and delegitimating homosexuality.

Others, though, see the problem differently. Sociologist Lillian Rubin provides a careful portrait of the ways in which different groups of Americans—based on class, race, ethnicity—are struggling to make family life coherent and meaningful, while sociologist Scott Coltrane notices a relationship between the housework and child care and the status of women in society. The more housework and child care women do, the lower their status. Thus, he suggests that sharing housework and child care is not only a way for husbands and wives to enact more egalitarian relationships, but also a way to ensure that the next generation will have more egalitarian attitudes.

DAVID POPENOE

Modern Marriage: Revising the Cultural Script

Of all the parts in the cultural scripts of modern societies, few have become more vague and uncertain than those concerning marriage and marital gender roles. Should we even bother to marry? And if and when we do marry and have children, who should do what—within the home and outside of it? Throughout history the answers to both of these questions have been relatively clear. Marriage is one of the few universal social institutions found in every known culture. And in most historical cultures the scripts for marital gender roles have been unambiguously formulated; indeed, in the world's remaining premodern societies the prescription of marital gender roles is a principal cultural focal point.

In the industrialized nations today, marriage is becoming deinstitutionalized. Growing numbers of people are cohabiting outside of marriage. The assigned roles for husband and wife are endlessly negotiated, especially with regard to the allocation of work and child care responsibilities. You work now, I'll work later—no, let's both work. I'll take care of the kids while you work—no, let's both take care of the kids. One may call it the growth of personal freedom and self-fulfillment, and for many women it has been just that. But such endless negotiation is no way to run a family—or a culture. The whole point of a cultural script, or in sociological terms an institutionalized set of social norms, is to provide people in common situations with social expectations for behavior that are geared to maintaining long-term societal well-being and promoting generational continuity.

Is there not some way out of this predicament? With full realization that I am climbing out on a long limb, I believe that a new set of role expectations for marriage and marital gender roles can be established which is adapted to the new conditions of modern life and which, in a balanced and fair manner, maximizes the life experiences of men, women, and children, helps to maintain social order, and represents a "best fit" with biosocial reality. The purpose of this chapter is to review the sociocultural and biological bases for a new set of marital norms and to put forth for discussion some tenets toward establishing these norms.

AN ASSUMPTION AND SOME ALTERNATIVES

If the family trends of recent decades are extended into the future, the result will be not only growing uncertainty within marriage but the gradual elimination of marriage in favor of casual liaisons oriented to adult expressiveness and self-fulfillment. The problem with this scenario is that children will be harmed, adults

From *Promises to Keep: The Decline and Renewal of Marriage in America*, edited by David Popenoe, Jean Bethke Elshtain, and David Blankenhorn, chapter 11. Copyright © 1996 by the Institute for American Values. Reprinted by permission of David Popenoe and the Institute for American Values. Notes have been renumbered and edited.

will probably be no happier, and the social order could collapse. For this chapter, therefore, I hold the assumption that marriage is a good and socially necessary institution worthy of being preserved in some form, and that the alternative of "letting things go on as they are" should be rejected.

In considering what marriage path modern societies should take instead, several broad alternatives have been widely discussed. We could try to restore the traditional nuclear family of bread-winning husband and full-time housewife that flourished in the 1950s (a time when marriage rates were at an all-time high). This alternative, I suggest, is neither possible nor desirable. We could encourage married women to shift to the traditional marital role of men, centered on a full-time career and involving a high level of detachment from the home, leaving the children to be raised by someone else. This would mean, however, that large numbers of children would face the highly undesirable prospect of being raised in institutional day care. Or we could encourage married men to shift to the so-called "new man" role in which, based on the ideal of social androgyny, men and women in marriage fully share both outside work and child care on an exactly fifty-fifty basis. There are a variety of problems with this solution, which I will discuss.

In place of these alternatives, what is needed is a marriage pattern and set of marital gender-role expectations that will feel "comfortable" yet be reasonably fair and equitable to both men and women, that stands the best chance of generating an enduring marriage, and that will benefit children. (Of these factors, the generation of a lasting marriage is often overlooked, yet it is wisely said that the very best thing parents can give their children is a strong marriage.) Obviously, this is a tall order, and there are some basically conflicting needs that must be reconciled—those of men, of women, of children, and of society as a whole.

SETTING THE SCENE: TODAY'S CONFUSION OVER MARITAL ROLES

For about 150 years, from the early eighteenth century to the 1960s, what we now call the traditional nuclear family was the prevailing family ideal in American culture. The main distinguishing characteristics of this family form were a legally and culturally dominant breadwinning husband and an economically dependent full-time housewife; both parents were devoted to raising their children, but the wife played the role of primary nurturer and teacher. Marital gender-role expectations were unequivocally clear.

At least in its distribution across the American population, this family form had its apogee in the 1950s. More adults were able to live up to these family expectations in "the '50s" than at any other period of our history. Part of the reason is demographic. For women born between the periods of 1830 to 1920, maternal and child mortality rates steadily declined and marriage rates increased. A high point was reached in America by the mid-twentieth century in the percentage of women who married, bore children who survived, and had husbands who lived jointly with them until at least the age of fifty. This was a time when death rates had dropped sharply, leaving many fewer widows, and divorce rates had not reached their current high levels. Another reason is economic. The 1950s in America was an era of unparalleled affluence and economic growth, enabling many families to live comfortably on the income of a single wage earner.

Then, with the coming of age of the baby boom generation in the 1960s, traditional family expectations began to falter. Associated with this faltering was what many today see as "family decline," not just a shift to some different family form but a manifest weakening of the family as an institution—especially as regards the care of children. Today, even though many Americans would probably still claim the traditional nuclear family as their family ideal, a sizable segment of the younger generation—especially the college educated—has largely rejected it.

Much confusion over family expectations and marital gender roles now exists. To the degree that they think about such things, young people coming into adulthood today are highly uncertain about the kind of marital gender roles they want, although almost everyone plans to marry eventually and nearly 90 percent are likely to do so if current age-specific rates continue. Many men still tend to prefer the traditional family form, yet a growing number would also like their wives to work in order to bring in a second income. At the same time, most men believe that childrearing is fundamentally a woman's responsibility. Many women plan to work after they are married and have children, often believing that they will have to in order to make ends meet. And many college-educated women desire to have full-blown work careers combined with marriage. Among women, both ordinary workers and careerists are uncertain about how they will mesh work goals with family responsibilities and child care.

Some women (and a few men), especially those influenced by left-feminist thinking, hold to a new ideal of coequal and fully-shared breadwinning and parenting, what can be called social androgyny. Believing that primary authority for child care should rest with women, however, this is an arrangement that few men seem prepared to accept. Some women and men intend to rely heavily on day care to raise children, thus lessening the direct child-care responsibilities of both parents (for single parents, of course, this is sometimes a necessity). In general, women expect their husbands to play a larger role than earlier generations of fathers did in the home and with children. And, although resistance among men is seemingly widespread, the evidence points to a growing, albeit still modest, equalization of gender roles in this respect.

Before children arrive, marital gender roles across all segments of society now tend to be relatively similar to one another, or "egalitarian." Typically, both partners work outside the home, and both share in the domestic responsibilities. Cooking, for example, can be done by either sex. Moreover, with ever-increasing median ages at first marriage and at the birth of the first child, such marital role similarity takes up an ever-longer portion of each person's life, especially if one includes the stage of premarital cohabitation that precedes more than half of all formal marriages today. Indeed, males and females living together with similar roles and no children has become a formative period of young adulthood, a far cry from the days when women (especially) lived with their parents until they married, and then had children soon thereafter.

If people today never moved beyond this stage of life, the present chapter would not have to be written. With the coming of children, however, the situation of marital-role similarity suddenly changes. Far from bringing joy to the new parents, an abundance of scholarly studies has shown that the least happy time in the life course of recently married couples is when they have young children. A major reason is that the division of labor within the household abruptly shifts, and gender-role expectations become uncertain; it is no longer clear who should do what. Marital gender-role expectations not only become ambiguous, but they typically revert to their traditional family form—with wife at home taking care of the children and husband becoming the sole breadwinner—to a degree far beyond anything anticipated by either party.

The marital-role stresses that arise from this sudden change can be enormous, especially after the couple have settled in with their new infant. Frequently, the wife becomes resentful and the husband becomes angry. The wife becomes resentful because she has had to leave her job while her husband is still occupationally progressing and because her husband doesn't help out enough. Often, in addition, she herself has had little preparation for the trials and tribulations that come with infant care. Also, she suddenly finds herself economically dependent (and perhaps guilty about not contributing financially), vulnerable, and stuck at home doing a job that has low status in our society. The husband, meanwhile, is angry because of his sudden new responsibilities and loss of freedom and because he has diminished sexual access to his wife and no longer receives as much of her attention. The baby has become the important figure in the home and the new focus of the wife's affections. While having young children (especially sons) slightly retards the chances of divorce, the animosities set up during this period are often long lasting and can lead to eventual breakup. The animosities negatively impact not only the marriage, of course, but also the children.

Probably the most common piece of advice now offered to young people at this stage of life is that "every situation is different," and they will simply have to work things out for themselves—find what is best for them. But this is not "cultural advice"; it is an unthoughtful reaction in an over-optioned society. It does forcefully raise the question, however: If not the marital roles of the traditional nuclear family, then what? The traditional roles were at least clear cut: the wife's job in life was childrearing, and the husband's was to provide economically for the mother-child unit.

THE TRADITIONAL NUCLEAR FAMILY: WHY WE CANNOT RETURN

While some are tempted to think that a return to the era of the traditional nuclear family would provide a solution to this set of problems, there are powerful reasons why this is neither desirable nor possible. To understand these reasons, we must consider why the traditional nuclear family fell into decline in the first place. Although most readers are probably well aware of the causes for this decline, they are worth a moment's reflection.

Social change of the past few centuries has affected women's roles much more than men's. Throughout history, the role of married men has principally been that of provider and protector of the mother-child unit. And, in virtually every known human society, the main role of married women has been that of child nurturer. Unlike today, however, married women almost never undertook the childrearing task all by themselves. Many others were around to help, especially older children, parents, and other close relatives. Most mothers were involved as well in what was the equivalent in preindustrial times of today's paid labor force where "productive work" took place, the typical work being home-generated agricultural production.

It was not until economic conditions permitted, mainly after the industrial revolution, that women left the labor force and became full-time mothers. Although most American women in the last century were in the labor market sometime during their lives, the pattern was typically this: They finished school at fourteen or fifteen and only worked until they got married in their early twenties. They then soon had children, and for the rest of their lives (shorter than today) they played the role of mother of at-home children. At the turn of the twentieth century, less than 10 percent of married women were gainfully employed, and the chances were that a woman would die before her last child left home.

But by the late 1940s, the Bureau of Labor Statistics listed nearly half of all American women as "essentially idle." They did not have children under eighteen, did not work in the labor force, and were not aged or infirm, a combination leading to the proverbial "bored housewife." In what represents a major historical shift, only about one-third of the adult life of the average married women today will be spent as the mother of at-home children. This is because of later ages at first marriage and birth of the first child, average family sizes of less than two children, and a much longer life span. Thus, even if one were to assume that a woman's main purpose in life was to be a mother, that role today clearly would no longer take up more than a fraction of her adult years. Moreover, because of the high divorce rate, a woman may well spend one-half to two-thirds of her adulthood not only without children but also without a husband to care for and to rely on economically, forcing her to rely on her own resources.

With such a steep reduction in the portion of women's lives that is taken up by marriage and childrearing, is it any wonder that women have been looking more to their own careers as separate individuals, and attaching less importance to their domestic roles? Under the new social circumstances, the demographers Kingsley Davis and Pietronella van den Oever have noted, "for best results [women] must choose an occupation early in order to get the necessary training, and they must enter employment while young and remain employed consistently in order to build up experience, seniority, reputation, and whatever other cumulative benefit comes from occupational commitment."[1]

The Downside

"Once under way," Davis and van den Oever continue,

> the system of change exhibits a dynamic of its own. Insofar as demographic trends lead women to downgrade marriage and stress employment, they also

lead them to reduce not only their dependence on their husbands but also their service to them. Men, in turn, are induced to reconsider the costs and benefits of marriage. They sense that, at older ages, men are increasingly scarce compared with women, that they do not have to marry to enjoy female company, and that if they do marry, their role as father and family head has somehow been eroded. Not surprisingly, the divorce rate rises to unprecedented levels, making marriage less secure and therefore less valuable for both sexes. Marriage undergoes attrition in two ways: it is postponed or not undertaken at all, and when it is undertaken, it is increasingly brittle.[2]

The available evidence suggests that, for durable demographic and economic reasons, this scenario of "family decline" has largely come to pass and it has been accompanied by some devastating personal and social consequences. First, more families have broken up, fatherlessness has rapidly increased, and parents have had less time to spend with their children. Such family instability has undoubtedly been an important factor in the decline of child well-being in recent years, as indicated by numerous statistics. Second, women have not entirely been well served. There is substantial evidence that almost all women deeply want not just a job or a career or financial independence, but also to be a mother and to have a strong and hopefully lasting relationship with a man. And while women's financial independence has improved, their family relationships have deteriorated. Third, and least widely discussed, there have been important negative repercussions for men. Despite the great importance for cultures to direct men into family roles (men gain tremendously in health and happiness from marriage and fatherhood, and single men are a universal social problem), any "new men" have probably been more than offset by men who have largely abandoned family life.

In all, society has suffered. Such trends are surely a major component in the view of most adult Americans today that, in many ways, "things are not as good as they were when I was growing up."

THE NUCLEAR FAMILY: ELEMENTS TO BE MAINTAINED

If the era of the traditional nuclear family must be recognized as a thing of the past, and if we should not continue in the direction we are headed, then what? Rather than the alternatives of institutional day care or androgynous gender roles in marriage, a strong case can be made for the maintenance of relatively traditional marital gender roles—*but only at the stage of marriage when children are young.* This case is based on the requirements of optimal child development, on the biological differences between men and women, and on what is ultimately personally fulfilling for men and women and what they "really want" out of marriage.

Childrearing Requirements

No one has spoken more eloquently about the requirements for optimum child development than Urie Bronfenbrenner. He recently summarized the main findings of the "scientific revolution" that has occurred in the study of human development. Two of his findings bear special attention:[3]

1. In order to develop—intellectually, emotionally, socially, and morally—a child requires participation in progressively more complex reciprocal activity, on a regular basis over an extended period in the child's life, with one or more persons with whom the child develops a strong, mutual, irrational attachment and who is committed to the child's well-being and development, preferably for life.

2. The establishment and maintenance of patterns of progressively more complex interaction and emotional attachment between caregiver and child depend in substantial degree on the availability and involvement of another adult, a third party, who assists, encourages, spells off, gives status to, and expresses admiration and affection for the person caring for and engaging in joint activity with the child.

Here we have not just the "main findings of the scientific revolution," but a statement of a relatively traditional division of labor in marriages between husbands and wives. Note that as they stand the statements are gender neutral, but we shall turn to that issue below.

The key element in proposition number one is the "irrational attachment" of the child with at least one caretaker. Empirical support for this proposition has grown enormously in recent years, mostly stemming from the many psychological studies that have upheld "attachment theory"—the theory that infants have a biosocial necessity to have a strong, enduring socioemotional attachment to a caretaker, especially during the first year of life. This is what pioneering attachment theorist John Bowlby has called starting life with "a secure base."[4] Empirical studies have shown that failure to become attached, to have a secure base, can have devastating consequences for the child, and that patterns of attachment developed in infancy and childhood largely stay with the individual in adulthood, affecting one's relationships and sense of well-being.

The work on attachment theory has been paralleled by research showing some negative effects of placing infants in group care. While still controversial, a widely discussed finding is that extensive (more than twenty hours per week) nonparental care initiated during the first year of life is likely to cause attachment problems (insecurity, aggression, and noncompliance) in children. Some recent evidence suggests that negative consequences may also occur from nonparental care during the second year of life. None of this research is conclusive; social science research seldom is. But it certainly supports what almost every grandmother would have told us from the outset—that there is considerable risk during the first few years of life in the reduction of infant-parent contacts and in nonparental child-rearing.

After the child reaches age three, on the other hand, there is little or no evidence that limited, high quality day care has any ill effects on children. Indeed, American children have long gone to "nursery school" at ages three and four, and group care at these ages is common in most other industrialized nations, including Japan.

Why is close contact with a parent so important in the first few years of life? Because parents are typically motivated, like no one else, to provide warm and supportive care for their children. The task of parenting could be, and occasionally is, successfully accomplished by a nonrelated caretaker, such as a full-time nanny. But attachment is much less likely in group settings where there is normally a high caretaker-child ratio and also a very high turnover of staff members.

But why should the primary parent of young children ordinarily be a mother and not a father? There is now a substantial body of evidence that fathers can do the job "if they are well-trained and strongly motivated." Some scholars have turned this research into the message that "daddies make good mommies, too," holding that the two roles might really be interchangeable. Yet it is much harder to train and motivate men than women for child care. Most dads do not want to be moms, and they do not feel comfortable being moms. And, in my opinion, neither children nor society in general benefits from such androgyny. To understand why the sexes are not interchangeable with one another in child care, it is necessary to review the biological differences between them.

Biological Differences Between the Sexes

No society in the world has ever been known to exist in which men were the primary caretakers of young children, and the reason for this certainly has much to do with the biological nature of males and females. Unfortunately, any discussion of biologically influenced sex differences has in recent years been fraught with peril. As historian Carl Degler has noted, the idea of a biological rootedness to human nature was almost universally accepted at the turn of the twentieth century, only to all but vanish from social thought as the century wore on, mainly due to the vigorous (and reasonably successful) battle against sexism (and racism).[5] Understandably, this knowledge blackout on the discussion of sex differences was associated with the need to challenge centuries-old stereotypes about the capacities of women, and to overcome strong resistances to a more forceful and equal role for women in economic and public life. The result was, however, that about the only sex differences that everyone within the academic community has been willing to accept over the past few decades are that women menstruate and are capable of becoming pregnant, giving birth, and lactating and that men are on average taller and muscularly stronger. But, when they have been discussed at all, the behavioral implications of even these differences are left vague.

Today, the full recognition of biological influences on human behavior is returning, albeit very slowly. Although the idea is still foreign, even inimical, to most social scientists, in probably no other area has the idea of biological roots to human nature become more widely discussed than in the field of sex and gender. A cover story in *Time* on "Sizing Up the Sexes" began, "Scientists are discovering that gender differences have as much to do with the biology of the brain as with the way we are raised."[6]

Having been trained as a sociologist, I have long been partial to sociocultural explanations. But I must say, quite apart from the scientific evidence, that after a lifetime of experiences which consisted, in part, of growing up in a family of four boys and fathering a family of two girls, I would be utterly amazed if someone were to prove that biology is unimportant in gender differences. The "natural and comfortable" way that most males think, feel, and act seems to me fundamentally different from the way most women think, feel, and act, and I have encountered these differences across the world's societies. (I probably need add that I don't believe one way is better than the other; indeed, I find symmetry and complementarity remarkable, even astonishing.)

It is not that biology is "determinant" of human behavior; that is a poorly chosen word. All human behavior represents a combination of biological and sociocultural forces, and it makes little sense, as sociologist Alice Rossi has stressed, to view them "as separate domains contesting for election as primary causes."[7] Also, the case can certainly be made, in the promotion of female equality, for a culture's not accentuating the biological differences that do exist. (Cultures differ radically in this respect; consider the difference in gender roles between Arab cultures and Nordic cultures.) Yet in my judgment a stronger case should be presented at this time, one of declining family stability and personal well-being, for a more frank acknowledgement of the very real differences between men and women. More acknowledgement by both sexes of the differences between them in sexual motives, cognitive styles, and communication patterns, for example, would probably make for stronger marriages, and recognition that the roles of father and mother are not interchangeable would probably make for better parenting.

Differences between men and women have universally been found with respect to four behavioral/psychological traits: aggression and general activity level, cognitive skills, sensory sensitivity, and sexual and reproductive behavior. That differences are universally found does not unequivocally mean they are heavily influenced by biology, but it seems to me that the implication is stronger than for most other scientific findings about human affairs. Moreover, a large body of evidence points to the fact that many universally found differences are rooted in a distinct "wiring" of male and female brains, and in a pronounced hormotial variation between the sexes.

What some call the greatest behavioral difference is in aggression. From birth onward, boys tend to be more aggressive and, in general, to have a higher physical activity level than girls. To a large degree, this accounts for the male dominance that universally has been prevalent in human societies. Differences in male and female cognitive skills are less well known and perhaps not as large as aggressive behavior, but they are now widely confirmed by empirical studies. From early adolescence onward, males tend to have greater visual-spatial and mathematical ability than females, and females tend to have greater verbal ability than males. (Spatial ability refers to being able to mentally picture physical objects in terms of their shape, position, geography, and proportion.) Also, there is a female superiority in being more sensitive to all sensory stimuli. Females typically receive a wider array of sensory information, are able to communicate it better, and place a primacy on personal relationships within which such information is communicated.

In brief, while male strengths rest with "things and theorems," female strengths rest with personal relationships. Even shortly after birth, girls are more interested than boys in people and faces, whereas boys "just seem as happy with an object dangled in front of them."[8] That these differences become accentuated at adolescence strongly suggests the role of hormones, specifically testosterone in men and estrogen in women. The role of hormones gains further support from the fact that the behavioral differences decline at older age levels, when hormonal levels are dropping. It is also worth noting that males are the best and the worst with respect to several of these traits. Males, for example, disproportionately make up math geniuses, but also math dysfunctionals.

Not all of these behavioral differences, however, could be expected to have a direct effect on family behavior. Most important for family behavior are differences that stem from the dissimilar role of males and females in sexual activity and the reproductive process. The differential "sexual strategies" of men and women have long been commented on; in popular terminology, they roughly boil down to the fact that women give sex to get love, and men give love to get sex. The world over, sex is something that women have that men want, rather than vice versa, while relationships and intimacy are the special province of women.

Probably the most compelling explanation for male-female differences in sexuality and sexual strategies comes from the field of evolutionary psychology. It goes something like this: In evolutionary terms, the goal of each individual's life is to perpetuate one's genes through reproduction and maximize the survival of all those with the same genes. In the mammalian world, the primary reproductive function is for males to inseminate and for females to harbor the growing fetus. Since sperm is common and eggs are rare (both being the prime genetic carriers), a different sexual or reproductive strategy is most adaptive for males and females, with males having more incentive to spread their sperm more widely among many females, and females having a strong incentive to bind males to themselves for the long-term care of their offspring.

Thus males universally are the more sexually driven and promiscuous while females are universally the more relationship oriented, setting up a continuing tension between the sexes. One psychologist found, for example, that the strongest predictor of sexual dissatisfaction for American males was "sexual withholding by the wife," and for females was "sexual aggressiveness by the husband."[9] And, according to the plausible explanation of evolutionary psychologists, men tend to be far more upset by their mate's sexual infidelity than vice versa because a man can never be certain that a child borne by his mate is really his, while women tend to be much more upset by the loss of their mate's emotional fidelity, which threatens long-term commitment and support.

Male promiscuity *à la* the tom cat is not characteristic of humankind, however. Wide variation in male sexual strategies can be found, ranging from the relatively promiscuous and low-paternal-investment "cad" approach, in which sperm is widely distributed with the hope that more offspring will survive to reproduce, to the "dad" approach, in which a high paternal investment is made in a limited number of offspring. But in every society the biological fathers of children are identified if possible, and required to hold some responsibility for their children's upbringing. In fact, compared to other species, human beings are noted for a relatively high paternal investment because human children have a long period of dependency and require extensive cultural training to survive, and because the character of human female sexuality (loss of estrus) encourages men to stay around.

Culture, of course, has a major say in which sexual strategies are institutionalized, and in all industrialized societies a very high paternal-investment strategy is the culturally expected one for males. Monogamy is strongly encouraged in these societies (although "serial monogamy" has become the norm in many nations, especially the United States), polygamy is outlawed, and male promiscuity is somewhat contained. Because it promotes high paternal investment, monogamy is well suited to modern social conditions.

Whatever the sexual strategies, our underlying biological nature dictates that every society faces the problem of how to keep men in the reproductive pair-bond. Especially for males, sex is rather ill-designed for lasting marriages. Margaret Mead is once purported to have said that there is no society in the world where men will stay married for very long unless culturally required to do so. This is not to suggest that marriage isn't "good" for men, only that their inherited biological propensities push them in another direction.

Biologically, male attachment to the mother-child pair is said to be largely through the sexual relationship with the mother. Many anthropologists have noted that motherhood is a biological necessity while fatherhood is mainly a cultural invention. Because it is not so biologically based as the mother's, a father's attachment to the children must be culturally fostered. Cross-cultural comparisons have shown that men are most likely to take active care of their children "if they are sure they are the fathers, if they are not needed as warriors and hunters, if mothers contribute to food resources, and if male parenting is encouraged by women."[10] Fortunately, these conditions largely prevail in modern societies. But bear in mind that it is not male care of infants that is at issue here. Universally, men have almost never been highly involved in child care at the early stages of life.

Sex Differences and Modern Family Behavior

What is the relevance for modern marriage and family behavior of all this biological and anthropological information? There is much evidence suggesting that men make a significant contribution to child development, especially in the case of sons, and that the absence of a male presence typically poses a handicap for the child. Indeed, men's assistance to women in childrearing may be more important now than ever before because mothers have become so isolated from their traditional support systems. Even more than in the past, it is crucial to maintain cultural measures that induce men to take an active interest in their families. It should be recognized, however, that the parenting of young infants is not a "natural" activity for males, and to perform well they require much training and experience plus encouragement from their wives.

All this said, there appear to be some dangers in moving too far in the direction of androgynous marital gender roles. Especially in American circumstances one hates to say anything that could possibly be used to feed stereotypes and to deter men from providing more help at home, yet it is important to point out that fully androgynous roles in marriage may not be best for child development, and they may not be the kind of personal relationships that men and women really want.

Regarding child development, a large body of evidence suggests that, while females may not have a "maternal instinct," hormonal changes occur after child-birth that strongly motivate women (but not men) to care for their new-born children. These hormonal changes are linked, in part, to the woman's capacity to breast-feed. Also, a number of the female sex differences noted above are directly related to this stage of the reproductive process. "In caring for a nonverbal, fragile infant," it has been noted, "women have a head start in reading an infant's facial expressions, smoothness of body motions, ease in handling a tiny creature with tactile gentleness, and soothing through a high, soft, rhythmic use of the voice."[11] Such evidence provides a strong case for women, rather than men, being the primary caretakers of infants.

Men seem better able to perform the parental role after children reach the age of 18 months, by which age children are more verbal and men don't have to rely so much on a wide range of senses.[11] Yet even at that age many studies have shown that men interact with children in a different way than women, suggesting that the father's mode of parenting is not interchangeable with that of the mother's; for example, men emphasize "play" more than "caretaking," and their play is more likely to involve a "rough-and-tumble" approach. Moreover, there is evidence to support the value of reasonably sex-typed parenting in which mothers are "responsive" and fathers are "firm"; one research review determined that "children of sex-typed parents are somewhat more competent than children of androgynous parents."[12] As social psychologist Willard W. Hartup has concluded, "The importance of fathers, then, may be in the degree to which their interactions with their children do not duplicate the mother's and in the degree to which they support maternal caregiving rather than replicate it."[13]

Less widely discussed, but probably no less important, is the effect of androgyny on the marriage relationship. The most common idea cited in this connection is that many men, being of a more independent spirit, will simply avoid marrying and having children if they are going to be asked to give up their independence and over-engage in "unnatural" nurturing and caretaking roles. And it is not as if they have few alternatives. Under the old system the marital exchange of sex for love was largely operative: if a man wanted regular sex (other than with prostitutes) he had to marry. Today, with permissive sexual standards and the availability of a huge pool of single and divorced women (to say nothing of married women), men obviously have abundant opportunities for sex outside of permanent attachments, much less those attachments which involve extensive child care responsibilities. Such a sociocultural reality may help to explain men's current delay of marriage, and the growing complaint of women that "men will not commit."

Nevertheless, most men eventually do marry and have children, and when they do they receive enormous personal benefits. My real concern, therefore, is not with men's delay of marriage (it is largely to the good) but rather with what happens to the marriage after it takes place. If it is the case that the best thing parents can do for their children is to stay together and have a good marriage, one serious problem with the "new man" alternative, in which dad tries to become mom, is that there is some evidence that marriages which follow this alternative are not very happy and have a high likelihood of divorce, especially those marriages in which a "role-reversal" has taken place. This is a most significant consequence that is seldom discussed by "new man" proponents.

Why should marriages in which the husband is doing "just what he thought his wife always wanted" have a high breakup rate? The answer concerns the fundamental nature of modern marriages. Marriages today are based on two basic principles: companionship, by which husbands and wives are expected to be each other's close friends, and romantic love based on sexual attraction, by which husbands and wives are expected to be each other's exclusive sexual partners. The joining of these two different principles is not without problems. For a good companion, you want someone who is as much like yourself as possible. But for a sexual partner, people tend to be attracted to the differences in the other. Therein lies a continuing tension that must be resolved if the modern marriages are to endure—the partners must be similar enough to remain best friends, but different enough so that sexual attraction is maintained.

The basis of sexual and emotional attraction between men and women is based not on sameness but on differences. If we closely examine the marital roles of childrearing couples who have been able to stay together and remain interested in each other for a long period of time (an important area for new research), I doubt that we will find such couples relentlessly pursuing the ideal of social androgyny.

SEVEN TENETS FOR ESTABLISHING NEW MARITAL NORMS

What I propose as a remedy for society's confusion over marital gender-role expectations, in conclusion, is a pattern of late marriage followed, in the early childrearing years, by what one could call a "modified traditional nuclear family." The main elements of this pattern can be summarized as follows. (I recognize, of course, that this pattern—being a set of normative expectations—is not something to which everyone can or should conform.)

1. Girls, as well as boys, should be trained according to their abilities for a socially useful paid job or career. It is important for women to be able to achieve the economic, social, and psychic rewards of the workplace that have long been reserved for men. It is important for society that everyone be well educated, and that they make an important work contribution over the course of their lives.

2. Young people should grow up with the expectation that they will marry, only once and for a lifetime, and that they will have children. Reproduction is a fundamental purpose of life, and marriage is instrumental to its success. Today,

close to 90 percent of Americans actually marry and about the same percentage of American women have children; although these figures have been dropping, the social expectation in these respects is currently quite well realized. Lifetime monogamy is not so well realized, however, with the divorce rate now standing at over 50 percent.

3. Young adults should be encouraged to marry later in life than is common now, with an average age at time of marriage in the late twenties or early thirties (the average ages currently are twenty-six for men and twenty-four for women). Even later might be better for men, but at older ages than this for women who want children, the "biological clock" becomes a growing problem.

From society's viewpoint, the most important reasons why people should be encouraged to marry relatively late in life is that they are more mature, they know better what they want in a mate, they are more established in their jobs or careers, and the men have begun to "settle down" sexually (partly due to a biological diminution of their sex drive). Age at marriage has proven to be the single most important predictor of eventual divorce, with the highest divorce rates found among those who marry in their teenage years. But we must also recognize that both women and men want to have time, when they are young, to enjoy the many opportunities for personal expression and fulfillment that modern, affluent societies are able to provide.

We should anticipate that many of these years of young adulthood will be spent in nonmarital cohabitation, an arrangement that often makes more sense than the alternatives to it, especially living alone or continuing to live with one's family of origin. I am not implying, much less advocating, sexual promiscuity here, but rather serious, caring relationships which may involve cohabitation.

4. From the perspective of promoting eventual family life, however, the downside to late age of marriage is that people live for about a decade or more in a non-family, "singles" environment which reinforces their personal drive for expressive individualism and conceivably reduces their impulse toward carrying out eventual family obligations, thus making the transition to marriage and child-rearing more difficult. To help overcome the anti-family impact of these years, young unmarried adults should be encouraged to save a substantial portion of their income for a "family fund" with an eye toward offsetting the temporary loss of the wife's income after marriage and childbirth.

5. Once children are born, wives should be encouraged to leave the labor market and become substantially full-time mothers for a period of at least a year to eighteen months per child. The reason for this is that mother-reared infants appear to have distinct advantages over those reared apart from their mothers. It is desirable for children to have full-time parenting up to at least age three, but after eighteen months—partly because children by then are more verbal—it is appropriate for fathers to become the primary caretakers, and some men may wish to avail themselves of the opportunity. At age three, there is no evidence

that children in quality group care suffer any disadvantages (in fact, for most children there are significant advantages). Once children reach that age, therefore, the average mother could resume working part-time until the children are at least of school age, and preferably in their early to middle teen years, at which point she could resume work full-time. Alternatively, when the children reach the age of three the father could stay home part-time, and the mother could resume work full-time.

For women, this proposal is essentially the strategy known as "sequencing." The main difficulty with it, as sociologist Phyllis Moen has noted, "is that child-nurturing years are also the career-nurturing years. What is lost in either case cannot be 'made up' at a later time."[14] Yet I would argue that it is possible to "make up" for career loss, but impossible to make up for child-nurturing loss. To make it economically more possible for a family with young children to live on a single income, we should institute (in addition to the "family fund") what virtually every other industrialized society already has in place—parental leave and child allowance programs. And, to help compensate women for any job or career setbacks due to their time out of the labor force, we should consider the development of "veterans benefits" type programs that provide mothers with financial subsidies and job priorities when they return to the paid work force. In general, women must be made to feel that caring for young children is important work, respected by the working community.

6. According to this proposal, the mother and not the father ordinarily would be the primary caretaker of infants. This is because of fundamental biological differences between the sexes that assume great importance in childrearing, as discussed above. The father should be an active supporter of the mother-child bond during this period, however, as well as auxiliary homemaker and care provider. Fathers should expect to spend far more time in domestic pursuits than their own fathers did. Their work should include not only the male's traditional care of the house as a physical structure and of the yard and car, but in many cases cooking, cleaning, and child care, the exact distribution of such activities depending on the individual skills and talents of the partners. And, as noted above, after children reach age eighteen months it may be desirable for the father and not the mother to become the primary caretaker. This means that places of employment must make allowances for substantial flex-time and part-time job absence for fathers as well as for mothers.

7. It should be noted that there is some balancing out of domestic and paid-work roles between men and women over the course of life. Under current socioeconomic conditions husbands, being older, retire sooner than their wives. Also, in later life some role switching occurs, presumably caused in part by hormonal changes, in which women become more work-oriented and men become more domestic. Given current male-female differences in longevity, of course, the average woman can expect to spend an estimated seven years of her later life as a widow.

CONCLUDING REMARKS

Later marriage, together with smaller families, earlier retirement, and a longer life in a society of affluence, provide both men and women in modern societies an historically unprecedented degree of freedom to pursue personal endeavors. Yet what David Gutmann has called the "parental imperative"[15] is also a necessary and important part of life, and during the parental years expressive freedom for adults must be curtailed in the interest of social values, especially the welfare of children.

Male bread winning and female childrearing have been the pattern of social life throughout history, albeit not always in quite so extreme a form as found in modern societies over the past century and a half. Except perhaps for adult pair-bonds in which no young children are involved, where much social experimentation is possible, it is foolhardy to think that the nuclear family can or should be entirely scrapped. When children become a part of the equation, fundamental biological and social constraints come into play—such as the importance of mothers to young children—and central elements of the nuclear family are dismissed at society's peril. Rather than strive for androgyny and be continuously frustrated and unsettled by our lack of achievement of it, we would do much better to more readily acknowledge, accommodate, and appreciate the very different needs, sexual interests, values, and goals of each sex. And rather than the unisex pursuit of "freedom with a male bias," we should be doing more to foster a culture in which the traditional female values of relationship and caring are given a higher priority and respect.

In a much modified form, then, traditional marital gender roles are necessary if the good of society—and of individuals—is to be advanced. But the period of time in which these gender roles still apply has become a relatively short phase of life, and not adult life in its entirety as once was the case. This leaves individuals abundant time for the pursuit of self-fulfillment through social roles of their own choosing.

Notes

1. Kingsley Davis and Pietronella van den Oever, "Demographic Foundations of New Sex Roles." *Population and Development Review* 8, no. 3 (1982): 495–511, 508.

2. Ibid.

3. Urie Bronfenbrenner, "Discovering What Families Do," in *Rebuilding the Nest*, ed. David Blankenhorn, Steven Bayme, and Jean Bethke Elshtain (Milwaukee: Family Service America, 1990), 27–38.

4. John Bowlby, *Attachment and Loss*, 3 vols. (New York: Basic Books, 1969–77).

5. Carl N. Degler, In *Search of Human Nature* (New York: Oxford University Press, 1991).

6. *Time*, January 20, 1992: 42.

7. Alice Rossi, "Parenthood in Transition: From Lineage to Child to Self-Orientation." in *Parenting Across the Life Span: Biosocial Dimensions*, ed. Jane B. Lancaster et al. (New York: Aldine de Gruyter, 1987), 31–81, quote from 64.

8. Moir and Jessel, *Brain Sex*, 17.

9. David M. Buss, "Conflict Between the Sexes," *Journal of Personality and Social Psychology* 56 (May 1989), cited in Degler, *In Search of Human Nature*, 305.

10. M. M. West and M. L. Konner, "The Role of the Father: An Anthropological Perspective," in *The Role of the Father in Child Development*, 1st ed., ed. Michael E. Lamb (New York: Wiley-Interscience, 1976), 185–218, cited in Rossi, "Parenthood in Transition," 67–68.

11. Alice S. Rossi, "Parenthood In Transition: From Lineage to child to self-orientation." In *Parenting Across The Life Span: Biosocial Dimensions*. Jane B. Lancaster et al., eds. (New York: Aldine de Gruyter, 1987): 56–61.

12. Diana Baumrind, "Are Androgynous Individuals More Effective Persons and Parents?" *Child Development* 53 (1982): 44–75. In another study of adolescent outcomes, it was found that the most effective parenting was that which was both highly demanding and highly responsive, a difficult task for either a man or a woman to combine. Diana Baumrind, "The Influence of Parenting Style on Adolescent Competence and Substance Use," *Journal of Early Adolescence* 11, no. 1 [1991]: 56–95). See also Frances K. Grossman, William S. Pollack, and Ellen Golding, "Fathers and Children: Predicting the Quality and Quantity of Fathering," *Developmental Psychology* 24, no. 1 (1988): 82–92.

13. Willard W. Hartup, "Social Relationships and Their Developmental Significance," *American Psychologist*, February 1989: 120–26, quote from 122.

14. Phyllis Moen, *Women's Two Roles: A Contemporary Dilemma* (New York: Auburn House, 1992), 133.

15. David Gutmann, "Men, Women, and the Parental Imperative," *Commentary* 56, no. 5 (1973): 59–64.

SCOTT COLTRANE

Household Labor and the Routine Production of Gender

Motherhood is often perceived as the quintessence of womanhood. The everyday tasks of mothering are taken to be "natural" expressions of femininity, and the routine care of home and children is seen to provide opportunities for women to express and reaffirm their gendered relation to men and to the world. The traditional tasks of fatherhood, in contrast, are limited to begetting, protecting, and providing for children. While fathers typically derive a gendered sense of self from these activities, their masculinity is even more dependent on *not* doing the things that mothers do. What happens, then, when fathers share with mothers those tasks that we define as expressing the true nature of womanhood?

This chapter describes how a sample of twenty dual-earner couples talk about sharing housework and child care. Since marriage is one of the least script-

From *Social Problems*, Vol. 36, no. 5 (December 1989), pp. 473–490. Copyright © 1989 by The Society for the Study of Social Problems. Reprinted by permission of University of California Press. References have been edited.

ed or most undefined interaction situations, the marital conversation is particularly important to a couple's shared sense of reality. I investigate these parents' construction of gender by examining their talk about negotiations over who does what around the house; how these divisions of labor influence their perceptions of self and other; how they conceive of gender-appropriate behavior; and how they handle inconsistencies between their own views and those of the people around them. Drawing on the parents' accounts of the planning, allocation, and performance of child care and housework, I illustrate how gender is produced through everyday practices and how adults are socialized by routine activity.

GENDER AS AN ACCOMPLISHMENT

Candace West and Don Zimmerman (1987) suggest that gender is a routine, methodical, and recurring accomplishment. "Doing gender" involves a complex of socially guided perceptual, interactional, and micropolitical activities that cast particular pursuits as expressions of masculine and feminine "natures." Rather than viewing gender as a property of individuals, West and Zimmerman conceive of it as an emergent feature of social situations that results from and legitimates gender inequality. Similarly, Sarah Fenstermaker Berk (1985, 204, emphasis in original) suggests that housework and child care

> can become the occasion for producing commodities (e.g., clean children, clean laundry, and new light switches) and a reaffirmation of one's *gendered* relation to the work and to the world. In short, the "shoulds" of gender ideals are fused with the "musts" of efficient household production. The result may be something resembling a "gendered" household-production function.

If appropriately doing gender serves to sustain and legitimate existing gender relations, would inappropriate gender activity challenge that legitimacy? Or, as West and Zimmerman (1987, 146) suggest, when people fail to do gender appropriately, are their individual characters, motives, and predispositions called into question? If doing gender is unavoidable and people are held accountable for its production, how might people initiate and sustain atypical gender behaviors?

By investigating how couples share child care and housework, I explore (1) the sorts of dyadic and group interactions that facilitate the sharing of household labor; (2) how couples describe the requirements of parenting and how they evaluate men's developing capacities for nurturing; and (3) the impact of sharing domestic labor on conceptions of gender.

THE SAMPLE

To find couples who shared child care, I initially contacted schools and day care centers in several suburban California communities. Using snowball sampling techniques, I selected twenty moderate- to middle-income dual-earner couples with children. To compensate for gaps in the existing literature and to enhance comparisons between sample families, I included couples if they were the biological parents of at least two school-aged children, they were both employed at least half time, and both identified the father as assuming significant responsibility for routine child care. I observed families in their homes and interviewed fathers and mothers separately at least once and as many as five times. I recorded the interviews and transcribed them for coding and constant comparative analysis.

The parents were primarily in their late thirties and had been living together for an average of ten years. All wives and 17 of 20 husbands attended some college and most couples married later and had children later than others in their birth cohort. The median age at marriage for the mothers was 23; for fathers, 26. Median age at first birth for mothers was 27; for fathers, 30. Fifteen of 20 fathers were at least one year older than their wives. Median gross annual income was $40,000, with three families under $25,000 and three over $65,000. Sixteen of the couples had two children and four had three children. Over two-thirds of the families had both sons and daughters, but four families had two sons and no daughters, and two families had two daughters and no sons. The children's ages ranged from four to fourteen, with 80 percent between the ages of five and eleven and with a median age of seven.

Mothers were more likely than fathers to hold professional or technical jobs, although most were employed in female-dominated occupations with relatively limited upward mobility and moderate pay. Over three-quarter held jobs in the "helping" professions: seven mothers were nurses, five were teachers, and four were social workers or counselors. Other occupations for the mothers were administrator, laboratory technician, filmmaker, and bookbinder. Sample fathers held both blue-collar and white collar jobs, with concentrations in construction (3), maintenance (2), sales (3), business (3), teaching (3), delivery (4), and computers (2). Like most dual-earner wives, sample mothers earned, on average, less than half of what their husband's did, and worked an average of eight fewer hours per week. Eleven mothers (55 percent), but only five fathers (25 percent) were employed less than 40 hours per week. In nine of twenty families, mothers were employed at least as many hours as fathers, but in only four families did the mother's earnings approach or exceed those of her husband.

DEVELOPING SHARED PARENTING

Two-thirds of the parents indicated that current divisions of labor were accomplished by making minor practical adjustments to what they perceived as an already fairly equal division of labor. A common sentiment was expressed by one father who commented.

> Since we've both always been working since we've been married, we've typically shared everything as far as all the working—I mean all the housework responsibilities as well as child care responsibilities. So it's a pattern that was set up before the kids were even thought of.

Nevertheless, a full three-quarters of the couples reported that the mother performed much more of the early infant care. All of the mothers and only about half of the fathers reported that they initially reduced their hours of employment after having children. About a third of the fathers said they increased their employment hours to compensate for the loss of income that resulted from their wives taking time off work before or after the births of their children.

In talking about becoming parents, most of the fathers stressed the importance of their involvement in conception decisions, the birth process, and early infant care to later assumption of child care duties. Most couples planned the births of their children jointly and intentionally. Eighty percent reported that they mutually decided to have children, with two couples reporting that the wife desired children more than the husband and two reporting that the husband was more eager than the wife to become a parent. For many families, the husband's commitment to participate fully in childrearing was a precondition of the birth decision. One mother described how she and her husband decided to have children.

> Shared parenting was sort of part of the decision. When we decided to have children, we realized that we were both going to be involved with our work, so it was part of the plan from the very beginning. As a matter of fact, I thought that we only could have the one and he convinced me that we could handle two and promised to really help (laughs), which he really has, but two children is a lot more work than you realize (laughs).

By promising to assume partial responsibility for childrearing, most husbands influenced their wives' initial decision to have children, the subsequent decision to have another child, and the decision of whether and when to return to work. Almost all of the mothers indicated that they had always assumed that they would have children, and most also assumed that they would return to paid employment before the children were in school. Half of the mothers did return to work within six months of the birth of their first child.

All but one of the fathers were present at the births of their children and most talked about the importance of the birth experience, using terms like "incredible," "magical," "moving," "wonderful," and "exciting." While most claimed that they played an important part in the birth process by providing emotional support to their wives or acting as labor coaches, a few considered their involvement to be inconsequential. Comments included, "I felt a little bit necessary and a lot unnecessary," and "I didn't bug her too much and I might have helped a little." Three quarters of the fathers reported that they were "very involved" with their newborns, even though the mother provided most of the daily care for the first few months. Over two-thirds of the mothers breastfed their infants. Half of the fathers reported that they got up in the night to soothe their babies, and many described their early infant care experience in terms that mothers typically use to describe "bonding" with newborns. The intensity of father-infant interaction was discussed by fathers as enabling them to experience a new and different level of intimacy and was depicted as "deep emotional trust," "very interior," "drawing me in," and "making it difficult to deal with the outside world."

About half of the fathers referred to the experience of being involved in the delivery and in early infant care as a necessary part of their assuming responsibility for later child care. Many described a process in which the actual performance of caretaking duties provided them with the self-confidence and skills to feel that they knew what they were doing. They described their time alone with the baby as especially helpful in building their sense of competence as a shared primary caretaker. One man said,

> I felt I needed to start from the beginning. Then I learned how to walk them at night and not be totally p.o'ed at them and not feel that it was an infringement. It was something I *got* to do in some sense, along with changing diapers and all these things. It was certainly not repulsive and in some ways I really liked it a lot. It was not something innate, it was something to be learned. I managed to start at the beginning. If you *don't* start at the beginning then you're sort of left behind.

This father, like almost all of the others, talked about having to learn how to nurture and care for his children. He also stressed how important it was to "start at the beginning." While all fathers intentionally shared routine child care as the children approached school age, only half of the fathers attempted to assume a major share of daily infant care, and only five couples described the father as an equal caregiver for children under one year old. These early caregiving fathers described their involvement in infant care as explicitly planned:

> She nursed both of them completely, for at least five or six months. So, my role was—we agreed on this—my role was the other direct intervention, like changing, and getting them up and walking them, and putting them back to sleep. For instance, she would nurse them but I would bring them to the bed afterward and change them if necessary, and get them back to sleep. . . . I really initiated those other kinds of care aspects so that I could be involved. I continued that on through infant and toddler and preschool classes that we would go to, even though I would usually be the only father there.

This man's wife offered a similar account, commenting that "except for breast-feeding, he always provided the same things that I did—the emotional closeness and the attention."

Another early caregiving father described how he and his wife "very consciously" attempted to equalize the amount of time they spent with their children when they were infants: "In both cases we very consciously made the decision that we wanted it to be a mutual process, so that from the start we shared, and all I didn't do was breastfeed. And I really would say that was the only distinction." His wife also described their infant care arrangements as "equal," and commented that other people did not comprehend the extent of his participation:

> I think that nobody really understood that Jennifer had two mothers. The burden of proof was always on me that he was literally being a mother. He wasn't nursing, but he was getting up in the night to bring her to me, to change her

poop, which is a lot more energy than nursing in the middle of the night. You have to get up and do all that, I mean get awake. So his sleep was interrupted, and yet within a week or two, at his work situation, it was expected that he was back to normal, and he never went back to normal. He was part of the same family that I was.

This was the only couple who talked about instituting, for a limited time, an explicit record-keeping system to ensure that they shared child care equally.

[Father]: We were committed to the principle of sharing and we would have schedules, keep hours, so that we had a pretty good sense that we were even, both in terms of the commitment to the principle as well as we wanted to in fact be equal. We would keep records in a log—one might say in a real compulsive way—so that we knew what had happened when the other person was on.

[Mother]: When the second one came we tried to keep to the log of hours and very quickly we threw it out completely. It was too complex.

PRACTICALITY AND FLEXIBILITY

Both early- and later-sharing families identified practical considerations and flexibility as keys to equitable divisions of household labor. Most did not have explicit records or schedules for child care or housework. For example, one early involved father reported that practical divisions of labor evolved "naturally":

Whoever cooks doesn't have to do the dishes. If for some reason she cooks and I don't do the dishes, she'll say something about it, certainly. Even though we never explicitly agreed that's how we do it, that's how we do it. The person who doesn't cook does the dishes. We don't even know who's going to cook a lot of the time. We just get it that we can do it. We act in good faith.

Couples who did not begin sharing routine child care until after infancy were even more likely to describe their division of labor as practical solutions to shortages of time. For example, one mother described sharing household tasks as "the only logical thing to do," and her husband said, "It's the only practical way we could do it." Other fathers describe practical and flexible arrangements based on the constraints of employment scheduling:

Her work schedule is more demanding and takes up a lot of evening time, so I think I do a lot of the every day routines, and she does a lot of the less frequent things. Like I might do more of the cooking and meal preparation, but she is the one that does the grocery shopping. An awful lot of what gets done gets done because the person is home first. That's been our standing rule for who fixes dinner. Typically, I get home before she does so I fix dinner, but that isn't a fixed rule. She gets home first, then she fixes dinner. Making the beds and doing the laundry just falls on me because I've got more time during the day to do it. And the yardwork and cuttin' all the wood, I do that. And so I'm endin' up doin' more around here than her just because I think I've got more time.

While mothers were more likely than fathers to report that talk was an important part of sharing household labor, most couples reported that they spent little time planning or arguing about who was going to do what around the house. Typical procedures for allocating domestic chores were described as "ad hoc," illustrated by one mother's discussion of cooking:

> Things with us have happened pretty easily as far as what gets done by who. It happened without having to have a schedule or deciding—you know—like cooking. We never decided that he would do all the cooking; it just kind of ended up that way. Every once in a while when he doesn't feel like cooking he'll say, "Would you cook tonight?" "Sure, fine." but normally I don't offer to cook. I say, "What are we having for dinner?"

In general, divisions of labor in sample families were described as flexible and changing. One mother talked about how routine adjustments in task allocation were satisfying to her: "Once you're comfortable in your roles and division of tasks for a few months then it seems like the needs change a little bit and you have to change a little bit and you have to regroup. That's what keeps it interesting. I think that's why it's satisfying."

UNDERLYING IDEOLOGY

While ad hoc divisions of labor were described as being practical solutions to time shortages, there were two major ideological underpinnings to the sharing of housework and child care: child-centeredness and equity ideals. While those who attempted to share infant care tended to have more elaborate vocabularies for talking about these issues, later sharing couples also referred to them. For instance, all couples provided accounts that focused on the sanctity of childhood and most stressed the impossibility of mothers "doing it all."

Couples were child-centered in that they placed a high value on their children's well-being, defined parenting as an important and serious undertaking, and organized most of their nonemployed hours around their children. For instance, one father described how his social life revolved around his children:

> Basically if the other people don't have kids and if they aren't involved with the kids, then we aren't involved with them. It's as simple as that. The guys I know at work that are single or don't have children my age don't come over because then we have nothing in common. They're kind of the central driving force in my life.

While about half of the couples (11 of 20) had paid for ongoing out-of-home child care, and three-quarters had regularly used some form of paid child care, most of the parents said that they spent more time with their children than the other dual-earner parents in their neighborhoods. One father commented that he and his wife had structured their lives around personally taking care of their children:

> An awful lot of the way we've structured our lives has been based around our reluctance to have someone else raise our children. We just really didn't want the kids to be raised from 7:30 in the morning 'till 4:30 or 5:00 in the afternoon by somebody else. So we've structured the last ten years around that issue.

Many parents also advocated treating children as inexperienced equals or "little people," rather than as inferior beings in need of authoritarian training. For example, an ex-military father employed in computer research stated, "We don't discipline much. Generally the way it works is kind of like bargaining. They know that there are consequences to whatever actions they take, and we try and make sure they know what the consequences are before they have a chance to take the action." Another father described his moral stance concerning children's rights:

> I'm not assuming—when I'm talking about parent-child stuff—that there's an inequality. Yes, there are a lot of differences in terms of time spent in this world, but our assumption has been, with both children, that we're peers. And so that's how we are with them. So, if they say something and they're holding fast to some position, we do not say, "You do this because we're the parent and you're the child."

About half of the parents talked directly about such equity ideals as applied to children.

Concerning women's rights, 80 percent of fathers and 90 percent of mothers agreed that women were disadvantaged in our society, but only two mothers and one father mentioned equal rights or the women's movement as motivators for sharing household labor. Most did not identify themselves as feminists, and a few offered derogatory comments about "those women's libbers." Nevertheless, almost all parents indicated that no one should be forced to perform a specific task because they were a man or a woman. This implicit equity ideal was evidenced by mothers and fathers using time availability, rather than gender, to assign most household tasks.

DIVISIONS OF HOUSEHOLD LABOR

Contributions to 64 household tasks were assessed by having fathers and mothers each sort cards on a five-point scale to indicate who most often performed them (see Table 1). Frequently performed tasks, such as meal preparation, laundry, sweeping, or putting children to bed, were judged for the two weeks preceding the interviews. Less frequently performed tasks, such as window washing, tax preparation, or car repair, were judged as to who typically performed them.

Some differences occurred between mothers' and fathers' accounts of household task allocation, but there was general agreement on who did what.

Table 1.

Household Tasks by Person Most Often Performing Them

Mother More	Fathers and Mother Equally	Father More
Cleaning		
Mopping	Vacuuming	Taking out trash
Sweeping	Cleaning tub/shower	Cleaning porch
Dusting	Making beds	
Cleaning bathroom sink	Picking up toys	
Cleaning toilet	Tidying living room	
	Hanging up clothes	
	Washing windows	
	Spring cleaning	
Cooking		
Planning menus	Preparing lunch	Preparing breakfast
Grocery shopping	Cooking dinner	
Baking	Making snacks	
	Washing dishes	
	Putting dishes away	
	Wiping kitchen counters	
	Putting food away	
Clothes		
Laundry	Shoe care	
Hand laundry		
Ironing		
Sewing		
Buying clothes		
Household		
	Running errands	Household repairs
	Decorating	Exterior painting
	Interior painting	Car maintenance
	General yardwork	Car repair
	Gardening	Washing car
		Watering lawn
		Mowing lawn
		Cleaning rain gutters
Finance, Social		
Writing or phoning	Deciding major purchases	Investments
Relatives/friends	Paying bills	
	Preparing taxes	
	Handling insurance	
	Planning couple dates	
Children		
Arranging baby-sitters	Waking children	
	Helping children dress	
	Helping children bathe	
	Putting children to bed	
	Supervising children	
	Disciplining children	
	Driving children	
	Taking children to doctor	
	Caring for sick children	
	Playing with children	
	Planning outings	

Note: Tasks were sorted separately by fathers and mothers according to relative frequency of performance: (1) Mother mostly or always, (2) Mother more than father, (3) Father and mother about equal, (4) Father more than mother, (5) Father mostly or always, For each task a mean ranking by couple was computed with 1.00–2.49 = Mother, 2.50–3.50 = Shared, 3.51–5.0 = Father. If over 50 percent of families ranked a task as performed by one spouse more than the other, the task is listed under that spouse, otherwise tasks are listed as shared. N = 20 couples.

Table 1 shows that in the majority of families, most household tasks were seen as shared. Thirty-seven of 64 tasks (58 percent), including all direct child care, most household business, meal preparation, kitchen clean-up, and about half of other housecleaning tasks were reported to be shared about equally by fathers and mothers. Nevertheless, almost a quarter (15) of the tasks were performed principally by the mothers, including most clothes care, meal planning, kin-keeping, and some of the more onerous repetitive housecleaning. Just under one-fifth (12) of the tasks were performed principally by the fathers. These included the majority of the occasional outside chores such as home repair, car maintenance, lawn care, and taking out the trash. As a group, sample couples can thus be characterized as sharing an unusually high proportion of housework and child care, but still partially conforming to a traditional division of household labor. The fathers and mothers in this study are pioneers in that they divided household tasks differently than their parents did, differently from most others in their age cohort, and from most families studied in time-use research.

MANAGING VERSUS HELPING

Household divisions of labor in these families also can be described in terms of who takes responsibility for planning and initiating various tasks. In every family there were at least six frequently performed household chores over which the mother retained almost exclusive managerial control. That is, mothers noticed when the chore needed doing and made sure that someone adequately performed it. In general, mothers were more likely than fathers to act as managers for cooking, cleaning, and child care, but over half of the couples shared responsibility in these areas. In all households the father was responsible for initiating and managing at least a few chores traditionally performed by mothers.

Based on participants' accounts of strategies for allocating household labor, I classified twelve couples as sharing responsibility for household labor and eight couples as reflecting manager-helper dynamics. Helper husbands often waited to be told what to do, when to do it, and how it should be done. While they invariably expressed a desire to perform their "fair share" of housekeeping and child-rearing, they were less likely than the other fathers to assume responsibility for anticipating and planning these activities. Manager-helper couples sometimes referred to the fathers' contributions as "helping" the mother.

When asked what they liked most about their husband's housework, about half of the mothers focused on their husband's selfresponsibility: voluntarily doing work without being prodded. They commented, "He does the everyday stuff" and "I don't have to ask him." The other mothers praised their husbands for particular skills with comments such as "I love his spaghetti" or "He's great at cleaning the bathroom." In spite of such praise, three-fourths of the mothers said that what bothered then most about their husband's housework was the need to remind him to perform certain tasks, and some complained of having to "train him" to correctly perform the chores. About a third of the fathers complained that their wives either didn't notice when things should be done or that *their* standards were too low. Although the extent of domestic task sharing varied considerably among couples, 90 percent of both mothers and fathers independently reported that their divisions of labor were "fair."

Some mothers found it difficult to share authority for household management. For instance, one mother said, "There's a certain control you have when you do the shopping and the cooking and I don't know if I'm ready to relinquish that control." Another mother who shares most child care and housework with her husband admitted that "in general, household organization is something that I think I take over." In discussing how they divide housework, she commented on how she notices more than her husband does:

> He does what he sees needs to be done. That would include basic cleaning kinds of things. However, there are some detailed kinds of things that he doesn't see that I feel need to be done, and in those cases I have to ask him to do things. He thinks some of the details are less important and I'm not sure, that might be a difference between men and women.

Like many of the mothers who maintained a managerial position in the household, this mother attributed an observed difference in domestic perceptiveness to an essential difference between women and men. By contrast, mothers who did not act as household managers were unlikely to link housecleaning styles to essential gender differences.

Many mothers talked about adjusting their housecleaning standards over the course of their marriage and trying to feel less responsible for being "the perfect homemaker." By partially relinquishing managerial duties and accepting their husband's housecleaning standards, some mothers reported that they were able to do less daily housework and focus more on occasional thorough cleaning or adding "finishing touches." A mother with two nursing jobs whose husband delivered newspapers commented:

> He'll handle the surface things no problem, and I get down and do the nitty gritty. And I do it when it bugs me or when I have the time. It's not anything that we talk about usually. Sometimes if I feel like things are piling up, he'll say "Well, make me a list," and I will. And he'll do it. There are some things that he just doesn't notice and that's fine: he handles the day-to-day stuff. He'll do things, like for me cleaning off the table—for him it's getting everything off it; for me it's putting the tablecloth on, putting the flowers on, putting the candles on. That's the kind of stuff I do and I like that; it's not that I want him to start.

This list-making mother illustrates that responsibility for managing housework sometimes remained in the mother's domain, even if the father performed more of the actual tasks.

Responsibility for managing child care, on the other hand, was more likely to be shared. Planning and initiating "direct" child care, including supervision, discipline and play, was typically an equal enterprise. Sharing responsibility for "indirect" child care, including clothing, cleaning, and feeding, was less common, but was still shared in over half of the families. When they cooked, cleaned, or tended to the children, fathers in these families did not talk of "helping" the mother; they spoke of fulfilling their responsibilities as equal partners and parents. For example, one father described how he and his wife divided both direct and indirect child care:

> My philosophy is that they are my children and everything is my responsibility, and I think she approaches it the same way too. So when something needs to be done, it's whoever is close does it . . . whoever it is convenient for. And we do keep a sense of what the other's recent efforts are, and try to provide some balance, but without actually counting how many times you've done this and I've done that.

In spite of reported efforts to relinquish total control over managing home and children, mothers were more likely than fathers to report that they would be embarrassed if unexpected company came over and the house was a mess (80 percent vs. 60 percent). When asked to compare themselves directly to their spouse, almost two-thirds of both mothers and fathers reported that the mother would be more embarrassed than the father. Some mothers reported emotional reactions to the house being a mess that were similar to those they experienced when their husbands "dressed the kids funny." The women were more likely to focus on the children "looking nice," particularly when they were going to be seen in public. Mothers' greater embarrassment over the kemptness of home or children might reflect their sense of mothering as part of women's essential nature.

ADULT SOCIALIZATION THROUGH CHILDREARING

Parents shared in creating and sustaining a worldview through the performance and evaluation of childrearing. Most reported that parenting was their primary topic of conversation, exemplified by one father's comment: "That's what we mostly discuss when we're not with our kids—either when we're going to sleep or when we have time alone—is how we feel about how we're taking care of them." Others commented that their spouse helped them to recognize unwanted patterns of interaction by focusing on parenting practices. For instance, one father remarked,

> I'm not sure I could do it as a one-parent family, cause I wouldn't have the person, the other person saying, "Hey, look at that, that's so much like what you do with your own family." In a one-parent family, you don't have that, you don't have the other person putting out that stuff, you have to find it all out on your own and I'm not sure you can.

Usually the father was described as being transformed by the parenting experience and developing increased sensitivity. This was especially true of discourse between parents who were trying to convert a more traditional division of family labor into a more egalitarian one. A self-employed construction worker said his level of concern for child safety was heightened after he rearranged his work to do half of the parenting:

> There's a difference in being at the park with the kids since we went on the schedule. Before it was, like, "Sure, jump off the jungle bars." But when you're totally responsible for them, and you know that if they sprained an ankle or something you have to pick up the slack, it's like you have more investment in the kid and you don't want to see them hurt and you don't want to see them crying. I find myself being a lot more cautious.

Mothers also reported that their husbands began to notice subtle cues from the children as a result of being with them on a regular basis. The wife of the construction worker quoted above commented that she had not anticipated many of the changes that emerged from sharing routine child care.

> I used to worry about the kids a lot more. I would say in the last year it's evened itself out quite a bit. That was an interesting kind of thing in sharing that started to happen that I hadn't anticipated. I suppose when you go into this your expectations about what will happen—that you won't take your kids to day care, that they'll be with their dad, and they'll get certain things from their dad and won't that be nice, and he won't have to worry about his hours— but then it starts creeping into other areas that you didn't have any way of knowing it was going to have an impact. When he began to raise issues about the kids or check in on them at school when they were sick, I thought, "Well, that's my job, what are you talking about that for?" or, "Oh my god. I didn't notice that!" Where did he get the intuitive sense to know what needed to be done? It wasn't there before. A whole lot of visible things happened.

Increased sensitivity on the part of the fathers, and their enhanced competence as parents, was typically evaluated by adopting a vocabulary of motives and feelings similar to the mothers', created and sustained through an ongoing dialogue about the children: a dialogue that grew out of the routine child care practices. Another mother described how her husband had "the right temperament" for parenting, but had to learn how to notice the little things that she felt her daughters needed:

> When it comes to the two of us as parents, I feel that my husband's parenting skills are probably superior to mine, just because of his calm rationale. But maybe that's not what little girls need all the time. He doesn't tend to be the one that tells them how gorgeous they look when they dress up, which they really like, and I see these things, I see when they're putting in a little extra effort. He's getting better as we grow in our relationship, as the kids grow in their relationship with him.

Like many fathers in this study, this one was characterized as developing sensitivity to the children by relying on interactions with his wife. She "see things" which he has to learn to recognize. Thus, while he may have "superior" parenting skills, he must learn something subtle from her. His reliance on her expertise suggests that his "calm rationale" is insufficient to make him "maternal" in the way that she is. Her ability to notice things, and his inattention to them, serves to render them both accountable: parenting remains an essential part of her nature, but is a learned capacity for him. Couples talked about fathers being socialized, as adults, to become nurturing parents. This talking with their wives about child care helped husbands construct and sustain images of themselves as competent fathers.

Greater paternal competence was also reported to enhance marital interaction. Fathers were often characterized as paying increased attention to emotional cues from their wives and engaging in more reciprocal communication. Taking responsibility for routine household labor offered some men the opportunity to better understand their mother's lives as well. For instance, one involved father who did most of the housework suggested that he could sometimes derive pleasure from cleaning the bathroom or picking up a sock if he looked at it as an act of caring for his family:

> It makes it a different job, to place it in a context of being an expression of caring about a collective life together. It's at that moment that I'm maybe closest to understanding what my mother and other women of my mother's generation, and other women now, have felt about being housewives and being at home, being themselves. I think I emotionally understand the satisfaction and the gratification of being a homemaker.

More frequently, however, sharing child care and housework helped fathers understand its drudgery. One father who is employed as a carpenter explained how assuming more responsibility for housework motivated him to encourage his wife to buy whatever she needs to make housework easier.

> It was real interesting when I started doing more housework. Being in construction, when I needed a tool, I bought the tool. And when I vacuum floors, I look at this piece of shit, I mean I can't vacuum the floor with this and feel good about it, it's not doing a good job. So I get a good vacuum system. So I have more appreciation for housecleaning. When I clean the tubs, I want something that is going to clean the tubs; I don't want to work extra hard. You know I have a kind of sponge to use for cleaning the tubs. So I have more of an appreciation for what she had to do. I tell her "If you know of something that's going to make it easier, let's get it."

Most sample fathers reported that performance of child care, in and of itself, increased their commitment to both parenting and housework. All of the fathers had been involved in some housework before the birth of their children, but many indicated that their awareness and performance of housework increased in conjunction with their involvement in parenting. They reported that as they spent more time in the house alone with their children, they assumed more responsibility for cooking and cleaning. Fathers also noted that as they became more involved in the daily aspects of parenting, and in the face of their wives' absence and relinquishment of total responsibility for housekeeping, they became more aware that certain tasks needed doing and they were more likely to perform them.

This was conditioned by the amount of time fathers spent on the job, but more than half reported that they increased their contributions to household labor when their children were under ten years old. This did not always mean that fathers' relative proportion of household tasks increased, because mothers were also doing more in response to an expanding total household workload.

GENDER ATTRIBUTIONS

Approximately half of both mothers and fathers volunteered that men and women brought something unique to child care, and many stressed that they did not consider their own parenting skills to be identical to those of their spouse. One mother whose husband had recently increased the amount of time he spent with their school-aged children commented: "Anybody can slap together a cream cheese and cucumber sandwich and a glass of milk and a few chips and call it lunch, but the ability to see that your child is troubled about something, or to be able to help them work through a conflict with a friend, that is really much different." A list-making mother who provided less child care and did less housework than her husband described herself as "more intimate and gentle," and her husband as "rough and out there." Like many others she emphasized that mothers and fathers provide "a balance" for their children. She described how she had to come to terms with her expectations that her husband would "mother" the way that she did:

> One of the things that I found I was expecting from him when he started doing so much here and I was gone so much, I was expecting him to mother the kids. And you know, I had to get over that one pretty quick and really accept him doing the things the way he did them as his way, and that being just fine with me. He wasn't mothering the kids, he was fathering the kids. It was just that he was the role of the mother as far as the chores and all that stuff.

A mother who managed and performed most of the housework and child care used different reasoning to make similar claims about essential differences between women and men. In contrast to the mothers quoted above, this mother suggested that men could nurture, but not perform daily child care:

> Nurturance is one thing, actual care is another thing. I think if a father had to— like all of a sudden the wife was gone, he could nurture it with the love that it needed. But he might not change the diapers often enough, or he might not give 'em a bath often enough and he might not think of the perfect food to feed. But as far as nurturing, I think he's capable of caring . . . If the situation is the mother is there and he didn't have to, then he would trust the woman to.

This mother concluded, "The woman has it more in her genes to be more equipped for nurturing" Thus many of the manager-helper couples legitimated their divisions of labor and reaffirmed the "naturalness" of essential gender differences.

Parents who equally shared the responsibility for direct and indirect child care, on the other hand, were more likely to see similarities in their relationships with their children. They all reported that their children were emotionally "close" to both parents. When asked who his children went to when they were hurt or upset, one early- and equal-sharing father commented: "They'll go to either of us, that is pretty indistinguishable." Mothers and fathers who equally shared most direct child care reported that their children typically called for the parent with whom they had most recently spent time, and frequently called her mother "daddy" or the father "mommy," using the gendered form to signify "parent." Most often, parents indicated that their children would turn to "whoever's closest" or "whoever they've been with," thus linking physical closeness with emotional closeness. In-home observations of family interactions confirmed such reports.

The central feature of these and other parental accounts is that shared activities formed an emotional connection between parent and child. Shared activities were also instrumental in constructing images of fathers as competent, nurturing care givers. Two-thirds of both mothers and fathers expressed the belief that men could care for children's emotional needs as well as women. When asked whether men, in general, could nurture like women, mothers used their husbands as examples. One said, "I don't necessarily think that that skill comes with a sex type. Some women nurture better than others, some men nurture better than other men. I think that those skills can come when either person is willing to have the confidence and commitment to prioritize them."

However, the parents who were the most successful at sharing child care were the most likely to claim that men could nurture like women. Those who sustained manager-helper dynamics in child care tended to invoke the images of "maternal instincts" and alluded to natural differences between men and women. In contrast, more equal divisions of household labor were typically accompanied by an ideology of gender *similarity* rather than gender difference. The direction of causality is twofold: (1) those who believed that men could nurture like women seriously attempted to share all aspects of child care, and (2) the successful practice of sharing child care facilitated the development of beliefs that men could nurture like women.

NORMALIZING ATYPICAL BEHAVIOR

Mothers and fathers reported that women friends, most of whom were in more traditional marriages or were single, idealized their shared-parenting arrangements. About two-thirds of sample mothers reported that their women friends told them that they were extremely fortunate, and labeled their husbands "wonderful," "fantastic," "incredible," or otherwise out of the ordinary. Some mothers said that women friends were "jealous," "envious," or "amazed," and that they "admired" and "supported" their efforts at sharing domestic chores.

Both mothers and fathers said that the father received more credit for his family involvement than the mother did, because it was expected that she would perform child care and housework. Since parenting is assumed to be "only natural" for women, fathers were frequently praised for performing a task that would go unnoticed if a mother had performed it:

> I think I get less praise because people automatically assume that, you know, the mother's *supposed* to do the child care. And he gets a lot of praise because he's the visible one. Oh, I think that he gets far more praise. I can bust my butt at that school and all he has to do is show up in the parking lot and everybody's all *gah gah* over him. I don't get resentful about that—think it's funny and I think it's sad.

While the fathers admitted that they enjoyed such praise, many indicated that they did not take these direct or implied compliments very seriously.

> I get more credit than she does, because it's so unusual that the father's at home and involved in the family. I realize what it is: it's prejudice. The strokes feel real nice, but I don't take them too seriously. I'm sort of proud of it in a way that I don't really like. It's nothing to be proud of, except that I'm glad to be doing it and I think it's kind of neat because it hasn't been the style traditionally. I kind of like that, but I know that it means nothing.

These comments reveal that fathers appreciated praise, but actively discounted compliments received from those in dissimilar situations. The fathers's everyday parenting experiences led them to view parenthood as drudgery as well as fulfillment. They described their sense of parental responsibility as taken-for-granted and did not consider it to be out of the ordinary or something worthy of special praise. Fathers sometimes reported being puzzled by compliments from their wives' acquaintances and judged them to be inappropriate. When I asked one what kinds of reactions he received when his children were infants, he said,

> They all thought it was really wonderful. They thought she'd really appreciate how wonderful it was and how different that was from her to father. They'd say, "You ought to know how lucky you are, he's doing so much." I just felt like I'm doing what any person should do. Just like shouldn't anybody be this interested in their child? No big deal.

Another father said he resented all the special attention he received when he was out with his infant son:

> Constant going shopping and having women stop me and say "Oh it's so good to see you fathers." I was no longer an individual: I was this generic father who was now a liberated father who could take care of his child. I actually didn't like it. I felt after a while that I wanted the time and the quality of my relationship with my child at that point, what was visible in public, to simply be accepted as what you do. It didn't strike me as worthy of recognition, and it pissed me off a lot that women in particular would show this sort of appreciation, which I think is well-intentioned, but which also tended to put a frame around the whole thing as though somehow this was an experience that could be extracted from one's regular life. It wasn't. It was going shopping with my

son in a snuggly or on the backpack was what I was doing. It wasn't somehow this event that always had to be called attention to.

Thus fathers discounted and normalized extreme reactions to their divisions of labor and interpreted them in a way that supported the "natural" character of what they were doing.

One mother commented on a pattern that was typically mentioned by both parents: domestic divisions of labor were "normal" to those who were attempting something similar, and "amazing" to those who were not: "All the local friends here think it's amazing. They call him 'Mr. Mom' and tell me how lucky I am. I'm waiting for someone to tell him how lucky *he* is. I have several friends at work who have very similar arrangements and they just feel that it's normal."

Because fathers assumed traditional mothering functions, they often had more social contact with mothers than with other fathers. They talked about being the only fathers at children's lessons, parent classes and meetings, at the laundromat, or in the market. One father said it took mothers there a while before they believed he really shared a range of household tasks.

At first they ask me, "Is this your day off?" And I say, "If it's the day off for me, why isn't it the day off for you?" "Well, I work 24 hours a day!" And I say, "Yeah, right. I got my wash done and hung out and the beds made." It takes the mother a couple of times to realize that I really do that stuff.

In general, fathers resisted attempts by other people to compare them to traditional fathers, and often compared themselves directly to their wives, or to other mothers.

Fathers tended to be employed in occupations predominantly composed of men, and in those settings were often discouraged from talking about family or children. Several fathers reported that people at their place of employment could not understand why they did "women's work," and a few mentioned that coworkers would be disappointed when they would repeatedly turn down invitations to go out "with the boys" for a drink. One of three self-employed carpenters in the study said that he would sometimes conceal that he was leaving work to do something with his children because he worried about negative reactions from employers or coworkers:

I would say reactions that we've got—in business, like if I leave a job somewhere that I'm on and mention that I'm going to coach soccer, my son's soccer game, yeah. I have felt people kind of stiffen, like, I was more shirking my job, you know, such a small thing to leave work for, getting home, racing home for. I got to the point with some people where I didn't necessarily mention what I was leaving for, just because I didn't need for them to think that I was being irresponsible about their work, I mean, I just decided it wasn't their business. If I didn't know them well enough to feel that they were supportive. I would just say, "I have to leave early today"—never lie, if they asked me a question. I'd tell them the answer—but not volunteer it. And, maybe in some cases, I feel like, you know, you really have to be a little careful about being too *groovy* too, that what it is that you're doing is just so wonderful. "I'm a father, I'm going to go be with my children." It isn't like that, you know. I don't do it for what people think of me; I do it because I enjoy it.

Some fathers said their talk of spending time with their children was perceived by coworkers as indicating they were not "serious" about their work. They reported receiving indirect messages that *providing* for the family was primary and *being with* the family was secondary. Fathers avoided negative workplace sanctions by selectively revealing the extent of their family involvement.

Many fathers selected their current jobs because the work schedule was flexible, or so they could take time off to care for their children. For instance, even though most fathers worked full-time, two-thirds had some daytime hours off, as exemplified by teachers, mail carriers, and self-employed carpenters. Similarly, most fathers avoided extra, work-related tasks or overtime hours in order to maximize time spent with their children. One computer technician said that he was prepared to accept possible imputations of nonseriousness:

> I kind of tend to choose my jobs. When I go to a job interview, I explain to people that I have a family and the family's very important to me. Some companies expect you to work a lot of overtime or work weekends, and I told them that I don't have to accept that sort of thing. I may not have gotten all the jobs I ever might have had because of it, but it's something that I bring up at the job interview and let them know that my family comes first.

The same father admitted that it is sometimes a "blessing" that his wife works evenings at a local hospital, because it allows him to justify leaving his job on time:

> At five o'clock or five thirty at night, when there are a lot of people that are still going to be at work for an hour or two more. I go "Adios!" [laughs]. I mean, I *can't* stay. I've gotta pick up the kids. And there are times when I feel real guilty about leaving my fellow workers behind when I know they're gonna be there for another hour or so. About a block from work I go "God, this is great!" [laughs].

Over half of the study participants also indicated that their own mothers or fathers reacted negatively to their divisions of labor. Parents were described as "confused," "bemused," and "befuddled," and it was said that they "lack understanding" or "think it's a little strange." One mother reported that her parents and in-laws wouldn't "dare to criticize" their situation because "times have changed," but she sensed their underlying worry and concern:

> I think both sides of the family think it's fine because it's popular now. They don't dare—I mean if we were doing this thirty years ago, they would dare to criticize. In a way, now they don't. I think both sides feel it's a little strange. I thought my mom was totally sympathetic and no problem, but when I was going to go away for a week and my husband was going to take care of the kids, she said something to my sister about how she didn't think I should do it. There's a little underlying tension about it, I think.

Other study participants reported that disagreements with parents were common, particularly if they revolved around trying to change childrearing practices their own parents had used.

Many couples reported that initial negative reactions from parents turned more positive over time as they saw that the children were "turning out all right," that the couple was still together after an average of ten years, and that the men were still employed. This last point, that parents were primarily concerned with their son's or son-in-law's provider responsibilities, highlights how observers typically evaluated the couple's task sharing. A number of study participants mentioned that they thought their parents wanted the wife to quit work and stay home with the children and that the husband should "make up the difference." Most mentioned, however, that parents were more concerned that the husband continue to be the provider than they were that the wife made "extra money" or that the husband "helped out" at home.

> In the beginning there was a real strong sense that I was in the space of my husband's duty. That came from his parents pretty strongly. The only way that they have been able to come to grips with this in any fashion is because he has also been financially successful. If he had decided, you know, "Outside work is not for me, I'm going to stay home with the kids and she's going to work." I think there would have been a whole lot more talk than there was. I think it's because he did both and was successful that it was okay.

Another mother noted that parental acceptance of shared parenting did not necessarily entail acceptance of the woman as provider:

> There is a funny dynamic that happens. It's not really about child care, where I don't think in our families—with our parents—I don't get enough credit for being the breadwinner. Well they're still critical of him for not earning as much money as I do. In a way they've accepted him as being an active parenting father more than they've accepted me being a breadwinner.

Here again, the "essential nature" of men is taken to be that of provider. If the men remain providers, they are still accountable as men, even if they take an active part in child care.

DISCUSSION

This brief exploration into the social construction of shared parenting in twenty dualearner families illustrates how more equal domestic gender relations arise and under what conditions they flourish. All couples described flexible and practical task-allocation procedures that were responses to shortages of time. All families were child-centered in that they placed a high value on their children's well-being, defined parenting as an important and serious undertaking, and organized most of their nonemployed time around their children. Besides being well-educated and delaying childbearing until their late twenties or early thirties, couples who shared most of the responsibility for household labor tended to involve the father in routine child care from the children's early infancy. As Sara Rudduck (1982) has noted, the everyday aspects of child care and housework help share ways of thinking, feeling, and acting that become associated with what it means to be a mother. My findings suggest that when domestic activities are equally shared, "maternal thinking" develops in fathers, too, and the social meaning of gender begins to change. This deemphasizes notions of gender as personality and locates it in social interaction.

To treat gender as the "cause" of household division of labor overlooks its emergent character and fails to acknowledge how it is in fact implicated in precisely such routine practices.

References

Berk, Sarah Fenstermaker. 1985. *The Gender Factory.* New York: Plenum.

Ruddick, Sara. 1982. "Maternal thinking." In *Rethinking the Family,* ed. Barrie Thorne and Marilyn Yalom, 76–94. New York: Longman.

West, Candace, and Don H. Zimmerman. 1987. "Doing gender." *Gender & Society* 1:125–51.

LILLIAN RUBIN

The Transformation of Family Life

"I know my wife works all day, just like I do," says Gary Braunswig, a twenty-nine-year-old white drill press operator, "but it's not the same. She doesn't *have* to do it. I mean, she *has* to because we need the money, but it's different. It's not really her job to have to be working; it's mine." He stops, irritated with himself because he can't find exactly the words he wants, and asks, "Know what I mean? I'm not saying it right; I mean, it's the man who's supposed to support his family, so I've got to be responsible for that, not her. And that makes one damn big difference.

"I mean, women complain all the time about how hard they work with the house and the kids and all. I'm not saying it's not hard, but that's her responsibility, just like the finances are mine."

"But she's now sharing that burden with you, isn't she?" I remark.

"Yeah, and I do my share around the house, only she doesn't see it that way. Maybe if you add it all up, I don't do as much as she does, but then she doesn't bring in as much money as I do. And she doesn't always have to be looking for overtime to make an extra buck. I got no complaints about that, so how come she's always complaining about me? I mean, she helps me out financially, and I help her out with the kids and stuff. What's wrong with that? It seems pretty equal to me."

Cast that way, his formulation seems reasonable: They're each responsible for one part of family life; they each help out with the other. But the abstract formula doesn't square with the lived reality. For him, helping her adds relatively little to the burden of household tasks he *must* do each day. A recent study by University of Wisconsin researchers, for example, found that in families where both wife and husband work full-time, the women average over twenty-six hours a week in household labor, while the men do about ten.[1] That's because there's nothing in the family system to force him to accountability or responsibility on a daily basis. He may "help her out with the kids and stuff" one day and be too busy or preoccupied the next.

But for Gary's wife, Irene, helping him means an extra eight hours every working day. Consequently, she wants something more consistent from him than a helping hand with a particular task when he has the time, desire, or feels guilty enough. "Sure, he helps me out," she says, her words tinged with resentment. "He'll give the kids a bath or help with the dishes. But only when I ask him. He doesn't have to *ask* me to go to work every day, does he? Why should I have to ask him?"

"Why should I have to ask him?"—words that suggest a radically different consciousness from the working-class women I met twenty years ago. Then, they counted their blessings. "He's a steady worker; he doesn't drink; he doesn't hit me," they told me by way of explaining why they had "no right to complain."[2] True, these words were reminders to themselves that life could be worse, that they shouldn't take these things for granted—reminders that didn't wholly work to obscure their discontent with other aspects of the marriage. But they were nevertheless meaningful statements of value that put a brake on the kinds of demands they felt they could make of their men, whether about the unequal division of household tasks or about the emotional content of their lives together.

Now, the same women who reminded themselves to be thankful two decades ago speak openly about their dissatisfaction with the role divisions in the family. Some husbands, especially the younger ones, greet their wives' demands sympathetically. "I try to do as much as I can for Sue, and when I can't, I feel bad about it," says twenty-nine-year-old Don Dominguez, a Latino father of three children, who is a construction worker.

Others are more ambivalent. "I don't know, as long as she's got a job, too, I guess it's right that I should help out in the house. But that doesn't mean I've got to like it," says twenty-eight-year-old Joe Kempinski, a white warehouse worker with two children.

Some men are hostile, insisting that their wives' complaints are unreasonable, unjust, and oppressive. "I'm damn tired of women griping all the time; it's nothing but nags and complaints," Ralph Danesen, a thirty-six-year-old white factory worker and the father of three children, says indignantly. "It's enough! You'd think they're the only ones who've got it hard. What about me? I'm not living in a bed of roses either.

"Christ, what does a guy have to do to keep a wife quiet these days? What does she want? It's not like I don't do anything to help her out, but it's never enough."

In the past there was a clear understanding about the obligations and entitlements each partner took on when they married. He was obliged to work outside the home; she would take care of life inside. He was entitled to her ministrations, she to his financial support. But this neat division of labor with its clear-cut separation of rights and obligations no longer works. Now, women feel obliged to hold up their share of the family economy—a partnership men welcome. In return, women believe they're entitled to their husband's full participation in domestic labor. And here is the rub. For while men enjoy the fruits of their wives' paid work outside the home, they have been slow to accept the reciprocal responsibilities—that is, to become real partners in the work inside the home.

The women, exhausted from doing two days' work in one, angry at the need to assume obligations without corresponding entitlements, push their men in ways unknown before. The men, battered by economic uncertainty and by the escalating demands of their wives, feel embattled and victimized on two fronts—one outside the home, the other inside. Consequently, when their wives seem not to see the family work they do, when they don't acknowledge and credit it, when they fail to appreciate them, the men feel violated and betrayed. "You come home and you want to be appreciated a little. But it doesn't work that way, leastwise not here anymore," complains Gary Braunswig, his angry words at odds with sadness in his eyes. "There's no peace, I guess that's the real problem; there's no peace anywhere anymore."

The women often understand what motivates their husbands' sense of victimization and even speak sympathetically about it at times. But to understand and sympathize is not to condone, especially when they feel equally assaulted on both the home and the economic fronts. "I know I complain a lot, but I really don't ask for that much. I just want him to help out a little more," explains Ralph Danesen's wife, Helen, a thirty-five-year-old office worker. "It isn't like I'm asking him to cook the meals or anything like that. I know he can't do that, and I don't expect him to. But every time I try to talk to him, you know, to ask him if I couldn't get a little more help around here, there's a fight."

One of the ways the men excuse their behavior toward family work is by insisting that their responsibility as breadwinner burdens them in ways that are alien to their wives. "The plant's laying off people left and right; it could be me tomorrow. Then what'll we do? Isn't it enough I got to worry about that? I'm the one who's got all the worries; she doesn't. How come that doesn't count?" demands Bob Duckworth, a twenty-nine-year-old factory worker.

But, in fact, the women don't take second place to their men in worrying about what will happen to the family if the husband loses his job. True, the burden of finding another one that will pay the bills isn't theirs—not a trivial difference. But the other side of this truth is that women are stuck with the reality that the financial welfare of the family is out of their control, that they're helpless to do anything to prevent its economic collapse or to rectify it should it happen. "He thinks I've got it easy because it's not my job to support the family," says Bob's wife, Ruthanne. "But sometimes I think it's worse for me. I worry all the time that he's going to get laid off, just like he does. But I can't do anything about it. And if I try to talk to him about it, you know, like maybe make a plan in case it happens, he won't even listen. How does he think *that* makes me feel? It's my life, too, and I can't even talk to him about it."

Not surprisingly, there are generational differences in what fuels the conflict around the division of labor in these families. For the older couples—those who grew up in a different time, whose marriages started with another set of ground rules—the struggle is not simply around how much men do or about whether they take responsibility for the daily tasks of living without being pushed, prodded, and reminded. That's the overt manifestation of the discord, the trigger that starts the fight. But the noise of the explosion when it comes serves to conceal the more fundamental issue underlying the dissension: legitimacy. What does she have a *right* to expect? "What do I know about doing stuff around the house?" asks Frank Moreno, a forty-eight-year-old foreman in a warehouse. "I wasn't brought up like that. My pop, he never did one damn thing, and my mother never complained. It was her job; she did it and kept quiet. Besides, I work my ass off every day. Isn't that enough?"

For the younger couples, those under forty, the problem is somewhat different. The men may complain about the expectation that they'll participate more fully in the care and feeding of the family, but talk to them about it quietly and they'll usually admit that it's not really unfair, given that their wives also work outside the home. In these homes, the issue between husband and wife isn't only who does what. That's there, and it's a source of more or less conflict, depending upon what the men actually do and how forceful their wives are in their demands. But in most of these families there's at least a verbal consensus that men *ought* to participate in the tasks of daily life. Which raises the next and perhaps more difficult issue in contest between them: Who feels responsible for getting the tasks done? Who regards them as a duty, and for whom are they an option? On this, tradition rules.

Even in families where husbands now share many of the tasks, their wives still bear full responsibility for the organization of family life. A man may help cook the meal these days, but a woman is most likely to be the one who has planned it. He may take the children to child care, but she virtually always has had to arrange it. It's she also who is accountable for the emotional life of the family, for monitoring the emotional temperature of its members and making the necessary corrections. It's this need to be responsible for it all that often feels as burdensome as the tasks themselves. "It's not just doing all the stuff that needs doing," explains Maria Jankowicz, a white twenty-eight-year-old assembler in an electronics factory. "It's worrying all the time about everything and always having to arrange everything, you know what I mean. It's like I run the whole show. If I don't stay on top of it all, things fall apart because nobody else is going to do it. The kids can't and Nick, well, forget it," she concludes angrily.

If, regardless of age, life stage, or verbal consensus, women usually still carry the greatest share of the household burdens, why is it important to notice that younger men grant legitimacy to their wives' demands and older men generally do not? Because men who believe their wives have a right to expect their participation tend to suffer guilt and discomfort when they don't live up to those expectations. And no one lives comfortably with guilt. "I know I don't always help enough, and I feel bad about it, you know, guilty sometimes," explains Bob Beardsley, a thirty-year-old white machine operator, his eyes registering the discomfort he feels as he speaks.

"Does it change anything when you feel guilty?" I ask.

A small smile flits across his face, and he says, "Sometimes. I try to do a little more, but then I get busy with something and forget that she needs me to help out. My wife says I don't pay attention, that's why I forget. But I don't know. Seems like I've just got my mind on other things."

It's possible, of course, that the men who speak of guilt and rights are only trying to impress me by mouthing the politically correct words. But even if true, they display a sensitivity to the issue that's missing from the men who don't speak those words. For words are more than just words. They embody ideas; they are the symbols that give meaning to our thoughts; they shape our consciousness. New ideas come to us on the wings of words. It's words that bring those ideas to life, that allow us to see possibilities unrecognized before we gave them words. Indeed, without words, there is no conscious thought, no possibility for the kind of self-reflection that lights the path of change.[3]

True, there's often a long way between word and deed. But the man who feels guilty when he disappoints his wife's expectations has a different consciousness than the one who doesn't—a difference that usually makes for at least some small change in his behavior. Although the emergence of this changing male consciousness is visible in all the racial groups in this study, there also are differences among them that are worthy of comment.

Virtually all the men do some work inside the family—tending the children, washing dishes, running the vacuum, going to the market. And they generally also remain responsible for those tasks that have always been traditionally male—mowing the lawn, shoveling the snow, fixing the car, cleaning the garage, doing repairs around the house. Among the white families in this study, 16 percent of the men share the family work relatively equally, almost always those who live in families where they and their wives work different shifts or where the men are unemployed. "What choice do I have?" asks Don Bartlett, a thirty-year-old white handyman who works days while his wife is on the swing shift. "I'm the only one here, so I do what's got to be done."

Asian and Latino men of all ages, however, tend to operate more often on the old male model, even when they work different shifts or are unemployed, a finding that puzzled me at first. Why, I wondered, did I find only two Asian men and one Latino who are real partners in the work of the family? Aren't these men subject to the same social and personal pressures others experience?

The answer is both yes and no. The pressures are there but, depending upon where they live, there's more or less support for resisting them. The Latino and Asian men who live in ethnic neighborhoods—settings where they are embedded in an intergenerational community and where the language and culture of the home country is kept alive by a steady stream of new immigrants—find strong support for clinging to the old ways. Therefore, change comes much more slowly in those families. The men who live outside the ethnic quarter are freer from the mandates and constraints of these often tight-knit communities, therefore are more responsive to the winds of change in the larger society.

These distinctions notwithstanding, it's clear that Asian and Latino men generally participate least in the work of the household and are the least likely to believe they have much responsibility there beyond bringing home a paycheck. "Taking care of the house and kids is my wife's job, that's all," says Joe Gomez flatly.

"A Chinese man mopping a floor? I've never seen it yet," says Amy Lee angrily. Her husband, Dennis, trying to make a joke of the conflict with his wife, says with a smile, "In Chinese families men don't do floors and windows. I help with the dishes sometimes if she needs me to or," he laughs, "if she screams loud enough. The rest, well, it's pretty much her job."

The commonly held stereotype about black men abandoning women and children, however, doesn't square with the families in this study. In fact, black men are the most likely to be real participants in the daily life of the family and are more intimately involved in raising their children than any of the others. True, the men's family work load doesn't always match their wives', and the women are articulate in their complaints about this. Nevertheless, compared to their white, Asian, or Latino counterparts, the black families look like models of egalitarianism.

Nearly three-quarters of the men in the African-American families in this study do a substantial amount of the cooking, cleaning, and child care, sometimes even more than their wives. All explain it by saying one version or another of: "I just figure it's my job, too." Which simply says what is, without explaining how it came to be that way.

To understand that, we have to look at family histories that tell the story of generations of African-American women who could find work and men who could not, and to the family culture that grew from this difficult and painful reality. "My mother worked six days a week cleaning other people's houses, and my father was an ordinary laborer, when he could find work, which wasn't very often," explains thirty-two-year-old Troy Payne, a black waiter and father of two children. "So he was home a lot more than she was, and he'd do what he had to do around the house. The kids all had to do their share, too. It seemed only fair, I guess."

Difficult as the conflict around the division of labor is, it's only one of the many issues that have become flash points in family life since mother went to work. Most important, perhaps, is the question: Who will care for the children? For the lack of decent, affordable facilities for the care of the children creates unbearable problems and tensions for these working-class families.

It's hardly news that child care is an enormous headache and expense for all two-job families. In many professional middle-class families, where the child-care bill can be $1,500–2,000 a month, it competes with the mortgage payment as the biggest single monthly expenditure. Problematic as this may be, however, these families are the lucky ones when compared to working-class families, many of whom don't earn much more than the cost of child care in these upper middle-class families. Even the families in this study at the highest end of the earnings scale, those who earn $42,000 a year, can't dream of such costly arrangements.

For most working-class families, therefore, child care often is patched together in ways that leave parents anxious and children in jeopardy. "Care for the little ones, that's a real big problem," says Beverly Waldov, a thirty-year-old white mother of three children, the youngest two, products of a second marriage, under three years old. "My oldest girl is nine, so she's not such a problem. I hate the idea of her being a latchkey kid, but what can I do? We don't even have the money to put the little ones in one of those good day-care places, so I don't have any choice with her. She's just *got* to be able to take care of herself after school," she says, her words a contest between anxiety and hope.

"We have a kind of complicated arrangement for the little kids. Two days a week, my mom takes care of them. We pay her, but at least I don't have to worry when they're with her; I know it's fine. But she works the rest of the time, so the other days we take them to this woman's house. It's the best we can afford, but it's not great because she keeps too many kids, and I know they don't get good attention. Especially the little one; she's just a baby, you know." She pauses and looks away, anguished. "She's so clingy when I bring her home; she can't let go of me, like nobody's paid her any mind all day. But it's not like I have a choice. We barely make it now; if I stop working, we'd be in real trouble."

Even such makeshift solutions don't work for many families. Some speak of being unable to afford day care at all. "We couldn't pay our bills if we had to pay for somebody to take care of the kids."

Some say they're unwilling to leave the children in the care of strangers. "I just don't believe someone else should be raising our kids, that's all."

Some have tried a variety of child-care arrangements, only to have them fail in a moment of need. "We tried a whole bunch of things, and maybe they work for a little while," says Faye Ensey, a black twenty-eight-year-old office worker. "But what happens when your kid gets sick? Or when the baby sitter's kids get sick? I lost two jobs in a row because my kids kept getting sick and I couldn't go to work. Or else I couldn't take my little one to the baby sitter because her kids were sick. They finally fired me for absenteeism. I didn't really blame them, but it felt terrible anyway. It's such a hassle, I sometimes think I'd be glad to just stay home. But we can't afford for me not to work, so we had to figure out something else."

For such families, that "something else" is the decision to take jobs on different shifts—a decision made by one-fifth of the families in this study. With one working days and the other on swing or graveyard, one parent is home with the children at all times. "We were getting along okay before Daryl junior was born, because Shona, my daughter, was getting on. You know, she didn't need somebody with her all the time, so we could both work days," explains Daryl Adams, a black thirty-year-old postal clerk with a ten-year-old daughter and a nine-month-old son. "I used to work the early shift—seven to three—so I'd get home a little bit after she got here. It worked out okay. But then this here big surprise came along." He stops, smiles down fondly at his young son and runs his hand over his nearly bald head.

"Now between the two of us working, we don't make enough money to pay for child care and have anything left over, so this is the only way we can manage. Besides, both of us, Alesha and me, we think it's better for one of us to be here, not just for the baby, for my daughter, too. She's growing up and, you know, I think maybe they need even more watching than when they were younger. She's coming to the time when she could get into all kinds of trouble if we're not here to put the brakes on."

But the cost such arrangements exact on a marriage can be very high. When I asked these husbands and wives when they have time to talk, more often than not I got a look of annoyance at a question that, on its face, seemed stupid to them. "Talk? How can we talk when we hardly see each other?" "Talk? What's that?" "Talk? Ha, that's a joke."

Mostly, conversation is limited to the logistics that take place at shift-changing time when children and chores are handed off from one to the other. With children dancing around underfoot, the incoming parent gets a quick summary of the day's or night's events, a list of reminders about things to be done, perhaps about what's cooking in the pot on the stove. "Sometimes when I'm coming home and it's been a hard day, I think: Wouldn't it be wonderful if I could just sit down with Leon for half an hour and we could have a quiet beer together?" thirty-one-year-old Emma Guerrero, a Latina baker, says wistfully.

But it's not to be. If the arriving spouse gets home early enough, there may be an hour when both are there together. But with the pressures of the workday fresh for one and awaiting the other, and with children clamoring for parental attention, this isn't a promising moment for any serious conversation. "I usually get home about forty-five minutes or so before my wife has to leave for work," says Ralph Jo, a thirty-six-year-old Asian repairman whose children, ages three and five, are the product of a second marriage. "So we try to take a few minutes just to make contact. But it's hard with the kids and all. Most days the whole time gets spent with taking care of business—you know, who did what, what the kids need, what's for supper, what bill collector was hassling her while I was gone—all the damn garbage of living. It makes me nuts."

Most of the time even this brief hour isn't available. Then the ritual changing of the guard takes only a few minutes—a quick peck on the cheek in greeting, a few words, and it's over. "It's like we pass each other. He comes in; I go out; that's it."

Some of the luckier couples work different shifts on the same days, so they're home together on weekends. But even in these families there's so little time for normal family life that there's hardly any room for anyone or anything outside. "There's so much to do when I get home that there's no time for anything but the chores and the kids," says Daryl's wife, Alesha Adams. "I never get to see anybody or do anything else anymore and, even so, I'm always feeling upset and guilty because there's not enough time for them. Daryl leaves a few minutes after I get home, and the rest of the night is like a blur—Shona's homework, getting the kids fed and down for the night, cleaning up, getting everything ready for tomorrow. I don't know; there's always something I'm running around doing. I sometimes feel like—What do you call them?—one of those whirling dervishes, rushing around all the time and never getting everything done.

"Then on the weekends, you sort of want to make things nice for the kids—and for us, too. It's the only time we're here together, like a real family, so we always eat with the kids. And we try to take them someplace nice one of the days, like to the park or something. But sometimes we're too tired, or there's too many other catch-up things you have to do. I don't even get to see my sister anymore. She's been working weekends for the last year or so, and I'm too busy week nights, so there's no time.

"I don't mean to complain; we're lucky in a lot of ways. We've got two great kids, and we're a pretty good team, Daryl and me. But I worry sometimes. When you live on this kind of schedule, communication's not so good."

For those whose days off don't match, the problems of sustaining both the couple relationship and family life are magnified enormously. "The last two years have been hell for us," says thirty-five-year-old Tina Mulvaney, a white mother of two teenagers. "My son got into bad company and had some trouble, so Mike and I decided one of us had to be home. But we can't make it without my check, so I can't quit.

"Mike drives a cab and I work in a hospital, so we figured one of us could transfer to nights. We talked it over and decided it would be best if I was here during the day and he was here at night. He controls the kids, especially my son, better than I do. When he lays down the law, they listen." She interrupts her narrative to reflect on the difficulty of raising children. "You know, when they were little, I used to think about how much easier it would be when they got older. But now I see it's not true; that's when you really have to begin to worry about them. This is when they need someone to be here all the time to make sure they stay out of trouble."

She stops again, this time fighting tears, then takes up where she left off. "So now Mike works days and I work graveyard. I hate it, but it's the only answer; at least this way somebody's here all the time. I get home about 8:30 in the morning. The kids and Mike are gone. It's the best time of the day because it's the only time I have a little quiet here. I clean up the house a little, do the shopping and the laundry and whatever, then I go to sleep for a couple of hours until the kids come home from school.

"Mike gets home at five; we eat; then he takes over for the night, and I go back to sleep for another couple of hours. I try to get up by 9 so we can all have a little time together, but I'm so tired that I don't make it a lot of times. And by 10, he's sleeping because he has to be up by 6 in the morning. So if I don't get up, we hardly see each other at all. Mike's here on weekends, but I'm not. Right now I have Tuesday and Wednesday off. I keep hoping for a Monday-Friday shift, but it's what everybody wants, and I don't have the seniority yet. It's hard, very hard; there's no time to live or anything," she concludes with a listless sigh.

Even in families where wife and husband work the same shift, there's less time for leisure pursuits and social activities than ever before, not just because both parents work full-time but also because people work longer hours now than they did twenty years ago.[4] Two decades ago, weekends saw occasional family outings, Friday-evening bowling, a Saturday trip to the shopping mall, a Sunday with extended family, once in a while an evening out without the children. In summer, when the children weren't in school, a week night might find the family paying a short visit to a friend, a relative, or a neighbor. Now almost everyone I speak with complains that it's hard to find time for even these occasional outings. Instead, most off-work hours are spent trying to catch up with the dozens of family and household tasks that were left undone during the regular work week. When they aren't doing chores, parents guiltily try to do in two days a week what usually takes seven—that is, to establish a sense of family life for themselves and their children.

"Leisure," snorts Peter Pittman, a twenty-eight-year-old African-American father of two, married six years. "With both of us working like we do, there's no time for anything. We got two little kids; I commute better than an hour each way to my job. Then we live here for half rent because I take care of the place for the landlord. So if somebody's got a complaint, I've got to take care of it, you know, fix it myself or get the landlord to get somebody out to do it if I can't. Most things I can do myself, but it takes time. I sometimes wonder what this life's all about, because this sure ain't what I call living. We don't go anyplace; we don't do anything; Christ, we hardly have time to go to the toilet. There's always some damn thing that's waiting that you've got to do."

Clearly, such complaints aren't unique to the working class. The pressures of time, the impoverishment of social life, the anxieties about child care, the fear that children will live in a world of increasing scarcity, the threat of divorce—all these are part of family life today, regardless of class. Nevertheless, there are important differences between those in the higher reaches of the class structure and the families of the working class. The simple fact that middle-class families have more discretionary income is enough to make a big difference in the quality of their social life. For they generally have enough money to pay for a baby-sitter once in a while so that parents can have some time to themselves; enough, too, for a family vacation, for tickets to a concert, a play, or a movie. At $7.50 a ticket in a New York or San Francisco movie house, a working-class couple will settle for a $3.00 rental that the whole family can watch together.

Finding time and energy for sex is also a problem, one that's obviously an issue for two-job families of any class. But it's harder to resolve in working-class families because they have so few resources with which to buy some time and privacy for themselves. Ask about their sex lives and you'll be met with an angry, "What's that?" or a wistful, "I wish." When it happens, it is, as one woman put it, "on the run"—a situation that's particularly unsatisfactory for most women. For them, the pleasure of sex is related to the whole of the interaction—to a sense of intimacy and connection, to at least a few relaxed, loving moments. When they can't have these, they're likely to avoid sex altogether—a situation the men find equally unsatisfactory.

"Sex?" asks Lisa Scranton, a white twenty-nine-year-old mother of three who feigns a puzzled frown, as if she doesn't quite know the meaning of the word. "Oh yeah, that; I remember now," she says, her lips smiling, her eyes sad. "At the beginning, when we first got together, it was WOW, real hot, great. But after a while it cools down, doesn't it? Right now, it's down the toilet. I wonder, does it happen to everybody like that?" she asks dejectedly.

"I guess the worst is when you work different shifts like we do and you get to see each other maybe six minutes a day. There's no time for sex. Sometimes we try to steal a few minutes for ourselves but, I don't know, I can't get into it that way. He can. You know how men are; they can do it any time. Give them two minutes, and they can get off. But it takes me time; I mean, I like to feel close, and you can't do that in three minutes. And there's the kids; they're right here all the time. I don't want to do it if it means being interrupted. Then he gets mad, so sometimes I do. But it's a problem, a real problem."

The men aren't content with these quick sexual exchanges either. But for them it's generally better than no sex at all, while for the women it's often the other way around. "You want to talk about sex, huh?" asks Lisa's husband, Chuck, his voice crackling with anger. "Yeah, I don't mind; it's fine, only I got nothing to talk about. Far as I'm concerned, that's one of the things I found out about marriage. You get married, you give up sex. We hardly ever do it anymore, and when we do, it's like she's doing me a favor.

"Christ, I know the way we've got to do things now isn't great," he protests, running a hand through his hair agitatedly. "We don't see each other but a few minutes a day, but I don't see why we can't take five and have a little fun in the sack. Sure, I like it better when we've got more time, too. But for her, if it can't be perfect, she gets all wound and uptight and it's like . . ." He stops, groping for words, then explodes, "It's like screwing a cold fish."

She isn't just a "cold fish," however. The problems they face are deeper than that. For once such conflicts arise, spontaneity takes flight and sex becomes a problem that needs attention rather than a time out for pleasure and renewal. Between times, therefore, he's busy calculating how much time has passed: "It's been over two weeks"; nursing his wounds: "I don't want to have to beg her"; feeling deprived and angry: "I don't know why I got married." When they finally do come together, he's disappointed. How could it be otherwise, given the mix of feelings he brings to the bed with him—the frustration and anger, the humiliation of feeling he has to beg her, the wounded sense of manhood.

Meanwhile, she, too, is preoccupied with sex, not with thoughts of pleasure but with figuring out how much time she has before, as she puts it, "he walks around with his mouth stuck out. I know I'm in real big trouble if we don't do it once a week. So I make sure we do, even if I don't want to." She doesn't say those words to him, of course. But he knows. And it's precisely this, the knowledge that she's servicing him rather than desiring him that's so hard for him to take.

The sexual arena is one of the most common places to find a "his and her" marriage—one marriage, two different sex lives.[5] Each partner has a different story to tell; each is convinced that his or her version is the real one. A husband says mournfully, "I'm lucky if we get to make love once a week." His wife reports with irritation, "It's two, sometimes three times a week." It's impossible to know whose account is closest to the reality. And it's irrelevant. It that's what they were after, they could keep tabs and get it straight. But facts and feelings are often at war in family life. And nowhere does right or wrong, true or false count for less than in their sexual interactions. It isn't that people arbitrarily distort the truth. They simply report their experience, and it's feeling, not fact, that dominates that experience; feeling, not fact, that is their truth.

But it's also true that, especially for women, the difference in frequency of sexual desire can be a response—sometimes conscious, sometimes not—to other conflicts in the marriage. It isn't that men never withhold sex as a weapon in the family wars, only that they're much more likely than women to be able to split sex from emotion, to feel their anger and still experience sexual desire. For a man, too, a sexual connection with his wife can relieve the pressures and tensions of the day, can make him feel whole again, even if they've barely spoken a word to each other.

For a woman it's different. What happens—or, more likely, what doesn't happen—in the kitchen, the living room, and the laundry room profoundly affects what's possible in the bedroom. When she feels distant, unconnected, angry; when her pressured life leaves her feeling fragmented; when she hasn't had a real conversation with her husband for a couple of days, sex is very far from either her mind or her loins. "I run around busy all the time, and he just sits there, so by the time we go to bed, I'm too tired," explains Linda Bloodworth, a white thirty-one-year-old telephone operator.

"Do you think your lack of sexual response has something to do with your anger at your husband's refusal to participate more fully in the household?" I ask.

Her eyes smoldering, her voice tight, she snaps, "No, I'm just tired, that's all." Then noticing something in my response, she adds, "I know what you're thinking; I saw that look. But really, I don't think it's *because* I'm angry; I really am tired. I have to admit, though, that I tell him if he helped more, maybe I wouldn't be so tired all the time. And," she adds defiantly, "maybe I wouldn't be."

Some couples, of course, manage their sexual relationship with greater ease. Often that's because they have less conflict in other areas of living. But whether they accommodate well or poorly, for all two-job families, sex requires a level of attention and concern that leaves most people wanting much of the time. "It's a problem, and I tell you, it has to be well planned," explains thirty-four-year-old Dan Stolman, a black construction worker. "But we manage okay; we make dates or try to slip it in when the baby's asleep and my daughter's out with a friend or something. I don't mean things are great in that department. I'm not always satisfied and neither is Lorraine. But what can you do? We try to do the best we can. Sex isn't all there is to a marriage, you know. We get along really well, so that makes up for a lot.

"What I really miss is that we don't ever make love anymore. I mean, we have sex like I said, but we don't have the kind of time you need to make love. We talk about getting away for an overnight by ourselves once in a while. Lorraine's mother would come watch the kids if we asked her; the problem is we don't have any extra cash to spare right now."

Time and money—precious commodities in short supply. These are the twin plagues of family life, the missing ingredients that combine to create families that are both frantic and fragile. Yet there's no mystery about what would alleviate the crisis that now threatens to engulf them: A job that pays a living wage, quality child-care facilities at rates people can pay, health care for all, parental leave, flexible work schedules, decent and affordable housing, a shorter work week so that parents and children have time to spend together, tax breaks for those in need rather than for those in greed, to mention just a few. These are the policies we need to put in place if we're to have any hope of making our families stable and healthy.

What we have, instead, are families in which mother goes to work to relieve financial distress, only to find that time takes its place next to money as a source of strain, tension, and conflict. Time for the children, time for the couple's relationship, time for self, time for social life—none of it easily available for anyone in two-job families, not even for the children, who are hurried along at every step of the way.[6] And money! Never enough, not for the clothes children need, not for the doctor's bill, not for a vacation, not even for the kind of child care that would allow parents to go to work in peace. But large as these problems loom in the lives of working-class families, difficult as they are to manage, they pale beside those they face when unemployment strikes, especially if it's father who loses his job.

Notes

1. James Sweet, Larry Bumpass, and Vaugn Call, *National Survey of Families and Households* (Madison, Wisc.: Center for Demography and Ecology, University of Wisconsin, 1988). This study featured a probability sample of 5,518 households and included couples with and without children. See also Joseph Pleck, *Working Wives/Working Husbands* (Beverly Hills: Sage Publications, 1985), who summarizes time-budget studies; and Iona Mara-Drita, "The Effects of Power, Ideology, and Experience on Men's Participation in Housework," unpublished paper (1993), whose analysis of Sweet, Bumpass, and Call's data shows that when housework and employment hours are added together, a woman's work week totals 69 hours, compared to 52 hours for a man.

2. Lillian B. Rubin, *Worlds of Pain* (New York: Basic Books, 1976), p. 93.

3. See Daniel Stern, *The Interpersonal World of the Infant* (New York: Basic Books, 1985), who argues that a child's capacity for self-reflection coincides with the development of language

4. For an excellent analysis of the increasing amount of time Americans spend at work and the consequences to family and social life, see Juliet B. Schor, *The Over-worked American* (New York: Basic Books, 1992). See also Carmen Sirianni and Andrea Walsh, "Through the Prism of Time: Temporal Structures in Postindustrial America," in Alan Wolfe, ed., *America at Century's End* (Berkeley: University of California Press, 1991), for their discussion of the "time famine."

5. For the origin of the term "his and her marriage," see Jessie Bernard, *The Future of Marriage* (New York: Bantam Books, 1973).

6. David Elkind, *The Hurried Child* (New York: Addison-Wesley, 1981).

THE GENDERED CLASSROOM

Along with the family, educational institutions—from primary schools to secondary schools, colleges, universities, and professional schools—are central arenas in which gender is reproduced. Students learn more than the formal curriculum—they learn what the society considers appropriate behavior for men and women. And for adults, educational institutions are gendered workplaces, where the inequalities found in other institutions are also found.

From the earliest grades, students' experiences in the classroom differ by gender. Boys are more likely to interrupt, to be called upon by teachers, and to have any misbehavior overlooked. Girls are more likely to remain obedient and quiet and to be steered away from math and science. As Myra and David Sadker, Lynn Fox, and Melinda Salata show, in this summary of the findings of their path-breaking book, *Failing at Fairness*, every arena of elementary and secondary education reproduces both gender difference and gender inequality. Ellen Jordan and Angela Cowan explore the ways in which children's play reinforces traditional gender stereotypes. It is in both the classroom and on the playground that gender boundaries become most rigidly enforced. And the article by Michael Kimmel takes on the current political question "what about the boys?" and examines the kinds of arguments—and the motivations for them—that lie behind these polemics.

MYRA SADKER, DAVID SADKER, LYNN FOX, AND
MELINDA SALATA

Gender Equity in the Classroom:
The Unfinished Agenda

*"In my science class the teacher never calls on me, and I feel like I
don't exist. The other night I had a dream that I vanished."*[1]

Our interviews with female students have taught us that it is not just in science
class that girls report the "disappearing syndrome" referred to above. Female
voices are also less likely to be heard in history and math classes, girls' names are
less likely to be seen on lists of national merit finalists, and women's contributions
infrequently appear in school textbooks. Twenty years after the passage of Title IX,
the law prohibiting gender discrimination in U.S. schools, it is clear that most girls
continue to receive a second-class education.

The very notion that women should be educated at all is a relatively recent
development in U.S. history. It was not until late in the last century that the concept of educating girls beyond elementary school took hold. Even as women were
gradually allowed to enter high school and college, the guiding principle in education was separate and unequal. Well into the twentieth century, boys and girls
were assigned to sex-segregated classes and prepared for very different roles in
life.

In 1833 Oberlin became the first college in the United States to admit women;
but these early female college students were offered less rigorous courses and required to wait on male students and wash their clothes. Over the next several
decades, only a few colleges followed suit in opening their doors to women. During the nineteenth century, a number of forward-thinking philanthropists and educators founded postsecondary schools for women—Mount Holyoke, Vassar, and
the other seven-sister colleges. It was only in the aftermath of the Civil War that
coeducation became more prevalent on campuses across the country, but even
here economics and not equity was the driving force. Since the casualties of war
meant the loss of male students and their tuition dollars, many universities turned
to women to fill classrooms and replace lost revenues. In 1870 two-thirds of all
universities still barred women. By 1900 more than two-thirds admitted them. But
the spread of coeducation did not occur without a struggle. Consider that as late
as the 1970s the all-male Ivy League colleges did not admit women, and even now
state-supported Virginia Military Institute fights to maintain both its all-male status and its state funding.

CYCLE OF LOSS

Today, most female and male students attend the same schools, sit in the same classrooms, and read the same books; but the legacy of inequity continues beneath the veneer of equal access. Although the school door is finally open and girls are inside the building, they remain second-class citizens.

In the early elementary school years, girls are ahead of boys academically, achieving higher standardized test scores in every area but science. By middle school, however, the test scores of female students begin a downward spiral that continues through high school, college, and even graduate school. Women consistently score lower than men on the Graduate Record Exams as well as on entrance tests for law; business, and medical schools. As a group, women are the only students who actually lose ground the longer they stay in school.

Ironically, falling female performance on tests is not mirrored by lower grades. Some have argued that women's grade-point averages are inflated because they tend not to take the allegedly more rigorous courses, such as advanced mathematics and physics. Another hypothesis suggests that female students get better grades in secondary school and college as a reward for effort and better behavior rather than a mastery of the material. Another possibility is that the standardized tests do not adequately measure that female students know and what they are really able to do. Whatever the reason, course grades and test grades paint very different academic pictures.

Lower test scores handicap girls in the competition for places at elite colleges. On average, girls score 50 to 60 points less than boys on the Scholastic Aptitude Test (SAT), recently renamed the Scholastic Assessment Test, which is required for admission to most colleges. Test scores also unlock scholarship money at 85 percent of private colleges and 90 percent of the public ones. For example, in 1991, boys scored so much higher on the Preliminary SAT/National Merit Scholarship Qualifying Test (PSAT/NMSQT) that they were nominated for two-thirds of the Merit Scholarships—18 thousand boys compared to 8 thousand girls in 1991.

The drop in test scores begins around the same time that another deeply troubling loss occurs in the lives of girls: self-esteem. There is a precipitous decline from elementary school to high school. Entering middle school, girls begin what is often the most turbulent period in their young lives. According to a national survey sponsored by the American Association of University Women, 60 percent of elementary school girls agreed with the statement "I'm happy the way I am," while only 37 percent still agreed in middle school. By high school, the level had dropped an astonishing 31 points to 29 percent, with fewer than three out of every 10 girls feeling good about themselves. According to the survey, the decline is far less dramatic for boys: 67 percent report being happy with themselves in elementary school, and this drops to 46 percent in high school.

Recent research points to the relationship between academic achievement and self-esteem. Students who do well in school feel better about themselves; and in turn, they then feel more capable. For most female students, this connection has a negative twist and a cycle of loss is put into motion. As girls feel less good about themselves, their academic performance declines, and this poor performance further erodes their confidence. This pattern is particularly powerful in math and science classes, with only 18 percent of middle school girls describing themselves as good in these subjects, down from 31 percent in elementary school. It is not surprising that the testing gap between boys and girls is particularly wide in math and science.

INEQUITY IN INSTRUCTION

During the past decade, Myra and David Sadker have investigated verbal interaction patterns in elementary, secondary, and college classrooms in a variety of settings and subject areas. In addition, they have interviewed students and teachers across the country. In their new book, *Failing at Fairness: How America's Schools Cheat Girls,* they expose the microinequities that occur daily in classrooms across the United States—and they show how this imbalance in attention results in the lowering of girls' achievement and self-esteem. Consider the following:

- From grade school to graduate school, girls receive less teacher attention and less useful teacher feedback.
- Girls talk significantly less than boys do in class. In elementary and secondary school, they are eight times less likely to call out comments. When they do, they are often reminded to raise their hands while similar behavior by boys is accepted.
- Girls rarely see mention of the contributions of women in the curricula; most textbooks continue to report male worlds.
- Too frequently female students become targets of unwanted sexual attention from male peers and sometimes even from administrators and teachers.

From omission in textbooks to inappropriate sexual comments to bias in teacher behavior, girls experience a powerful and often disabling education climate. A high school student from an affluent Northeastern high school describes her own painful experience:

> My English teacher asks the class, "What is the purpose of the visit to Johannesburg?" . . . I know the answer, but I contemplate whether I should answer the question. The boys in the back are going to tease me like they harass all the other girls in our class . . . I want to tell them to shut up. But I stand alone. All of the other girls don't even let themselves be bold. Perhaps they are all content to be molded into society's image of what a girl should be like—submissive, sweet, feminine . . . In my ninth period class, I am actually afraid—of what [the boys] might say . . . As my frustration builds, I promise myself that I will yell back at them. I say that everyday . . . and I never do it.[2]

Teachers not only call on male students more frequently than on females; they also allow boys to call out more often. This imbalance in instructional attention is greatest at the college level. Our research shows that approximately one-half of the students in college classrooms are silent, having no interaction whatsoever with the professor. Two-thirds of these silent students are women. This verbal domination is further heightened by the gender segregation of many of today's classes. Sometimes teachers seat girls and boys in different sections of the room, but more often students segregate themselves. Approximately one-half of the elementary and high school classrooms and one-third of the coeducational college classrooms that the Sadkers visited are sex-segregated. As male students talk and call out more, teachers are drawn to the noisier male sections of the class, a development that further silences girls.

Not only do male students interact more with the teacher but at all levels of schooling they receive a higher quality of interaction. Using four categories of teacher responses to student participation—praise, acceptance, remediation, and criticism—the Sadkers' studies found that more than 50 percent of all teacher responses are mere acceptances, such as "O.K." and "uh huh." These nonspecific reactions offer little instructional feedback. Teachers use remediation more than 30 percent of the time, helping students correct or improve answers by asking probing questions or by phrases such as "Try again." Only 10 percent of the time do teachers actually praise students, and they criticize them even less. Although praise, remediation, and criticism provide more useful information to students than the neutral acknowledgment of an "O.K." these clearer, more precise teacher comments are more often directed to boys.

Who gets taught—and how—has profound consequences. Student participation in the classroom enhances learning and self-esteem. Thus, boys gain an educational advantage over girls by claiming a greater share of the teacher's time and attention. This is particularly noteworthy in science classes, where, according to the AAUW report, *How Schools Shortchange Girls,* boys perform 79 percent of all student-assisted demonstrations. When girls talk less and do less, it is little wonder that they learn less. Even when directing their attention to girls, teachers sometimes short-circuit the learning process. For example, teachers frequently explain how to focus a microscope to boys but simply adjust the microscope for the girls. Boys learn the skill; girls learn to ask for assistance.

When female students do speak in class, they often preface their statements with self-deprecating remarks such as, "I'm not sure this is right," or "This probably isn't what you're looking for." Even when offering excellent responses, female students may begin with this self-criticism. Such tentative forms of speech project a sense of academic uncertainty and self-doubt—almost a tacit admission of lesser status in the classroom.

Women are not only quiet in classrooms; they are also missing from the pages of textbooks. For example, history textbooks currently in use at middle and high schools offer little more than 2 percent of their space to women. Studies of music textbooks have found that 70 percent of the figures shown are male. A recent content analysis of five secondary school science textbooks revealed that more than two-thirds of all drawings were of male figures and that not a single female scientist was depicted. Furthermore, all five books used the male body as the model for the human body, a practice that continues even in medical school texts. At the college level, too, women rarely see themselves reflected in what they study. For example, the two-volume *Norton Anthology of English Literature* devotes less than 15 percent of its pages to the works of women. Interestingly, there was greater representation of women in the first edition of the anthology in 1962 than in the fifth edition published in 1986.

PRESENCE AND POWER

Not only are women hidden in the curriculum and quiet in the classroom, they are also less visible in other school locations. Even as early as the elementary grades, considered by some to be a distinctly feminine environment, boys tend to take over the territory. At recess time on playgrounds across the country, boys grab bats and balls as they fan out over the school yard for their games. Girls are likely to be left on the sideline—watching. In secondary school, male students become an even more powerful presence. In *Failing at Fairness,* high school teachers and students tell these stories:

> A rural school district in Wisconsin still has the practice of having the cheerleaders (all girls, of course) clean the mats for the wrestling team before each meet. They are called the "Mat Maidens."

> In our local high school, boys' sports teams received much more support from the school system and the community. The boys' team got shoes, jackets, and played on the best-maintained grounds. The girls' softball team received no clothes and nobody took care of our fields. Cheerleaders did not cheer for us. When we played, the bleachers were mostly empty.

Sports are not the only fields where women lose ground. In many secondary schools, mathematics, science, and computer technology remain male domains. In the past, girls were actively discouraged or even prohibited from taking the advanced courses in these fields. One woman, now a college professor, recalls her high school physics class:

> I was the only girl in the class. The teacher often told off-color jokes and when he did he would tell me to the leave the room. My great regret today is that I actually did it.

Today, we hope such explicitly offensive behavior is rare, yet counselors and teachers continue to harbor lower expectations for girls and are less likely to encourage them to take advanced classes in math and science. It is only later in life that women realize the price they paid for avoiding these courses as they are screened out of lucrative careers in science and technology.

By the time they reach college, male students' control of the environment is visible. Male students are more likely to hold positions of student leadership on campus and to play in heavily funded sports programs. College presidents and deans are usually men, as are most tenured professors. In a sense, a "glass wall" divides today's college campus. On one side of the glass wall are men, comprising 70 percent of all students majoring in chemistry, physics, and computer science. The percentage is even higher in engineering. While the "hard sciences" flourish on the men's side of the campus, the women's side of the glass wall is where education, psychology, and foreign languages are taught. These gender walls not only separate programs, they also indicate social standing. Departments with higher male enrollment carry greater campus prestige and their faculty are often paid higher salaries.

These gender differences can be seen outside academic programs, in peer relationships both at college and in high school. In 1993 a national survey sponsored by the AAUW and reported in *Hostile Hallways* found that 76 percent of male students and 85 percent of female students in the typical high school had experienced sexual harassment. What differed dramatically for girls and boys was not the occurrence of unwanted touching or profane remarks but their reaction to them. Only 28 percent of the boys, compared to 70 percent of the girls, said they were upset by these experiences. For 33 percent of the girls, the encounters were so troubling that they did not want to talk in class or even go to school. On college campuses problems range from sexist comments and sexual propositions to physical assault. Consider the following incidents:

- A UCLA fraternity manual found its way into a campus magazine. Along with the history and bylaws were songs the pledges were supposed to memorize. The lyrics described sexual scenes that were bizarre, graphic, and sadistic.
- One fraternity on a New England campus hosted "pig parties" where the man bringing the female date voted the ugliest wins.
- A toga party on the campus of another elite liberal arts college used for decoration the torso of a female mannequin hung from the balcony and splattered with paint to look like blood. A sign below suggested the female body was available for sex.

When one gender is consistently treated as less important and less valuable, the seeds of contempt take root and violence can be the result.

STRATEGIES FOR CHANGE

One of the ironies of gender bias in schools is that so much of its goes unnoticed by educators. While personally committed to fairness, many are unable to see the microinequities that surround them. The research on student-teacher interactions led the Sadkers to develop training programs to enable teachers and administrators to detect this bias and create equitable teaching methods. Program evaluations indicate that biased teaching patterns can be changed, and teachers can achieve equity in verbal interactions with their students. Research shows that for elementary and secondary school teachers, as well as college professors, this training leads not only to more equitable teaching but to more effective teaching as well.

During the 1970s, content analysis research showed women missing from schoolbooks. Publishers issued guidelines for equity and vowed to reform. But recent studies show that not all publishing companies have lived up to the promise of their guidelines. The curriculum continues to present a predominately male model of the world. Once again publishers and authors must be urged to incorporate women into school texts. Teachers and students need to become aware of the vast amount of excellent children's literature, including biographies that feature resourceful girls and strong women. *Failing at Fairness* includes an extensive list of these resources for both elementary and secondary schools.

In postsecondary education, faculty members typically select instructional materials on the basis of individual preference. Many instructors would benefit from programs that alert them to well-written, gender-fair books in their academic fields. And individual professors can enhance their own lectures and discussions by including works by and about women.

Education institutions at every level have a responsibility for students in and beyond the classroom. Harassing and intimidating behaviors that formerly might have been excused with the comment "boys will be boys" are now often seen as less excusable and less acceptable. Many schools offer workshops for students and faculty to help eliminate sexual harassment. While controversy surrounds the exact definition of sexual harassment, the education community must take this issue seriously and devise strategies to keep the learning environment open to all.

After centuries of struggle, women have finally made their way into our colleges and graduate schools, only to discover that access does not guarantee equity. Walls of subtle bias continue to create different education environments, channeling women and men toward separate and unequal futures. To complete the agenda for equity, we must transform our education institutions and empower female students for full participation in society.

Notes

1. M. Sadker and D. Sadker, *Failing at Fairness: How America's Schools Cheat Girls* (New York: Charles Scribner's Sons, 1994). The research for this article as well as the anecdotes are drawn from this book.

2. L. Kim, "Boys Will Be Boys . . . Right?" *The Lance*, Livingston High School (June 1993), 32:5.

ELLEN JORDAN AND ANGELA COWAN

Warrior Narratives in the Kindergarten Classroom: Renegotiating the Social Contract?

Since the beginning of second wave feminism, the separation between the public (masculine) world of politics and the economy and the private (feminine) world of the family and personal life has been seen as highly significant in establishing gender difference and inequality (Eisenstein 1984). Twenty years of feminist research and speculation have refined our understanding of this divide and how it has been developed and reproduced. One particularly striking and influential account is that given by Carole Pateman in her book *The Sexual Contract* (1988).

Pateman's broad argument is that in the modern world, the world since the Enlightenment, a "civil society" has been established. In this civil society, patriarchy has been replaced by a fratriarchy, which is equally male and oppressive of women. Men now rule not as fathers but as brothers, able to compete with one another, but presenting a united front against those outside the group. It is the brothers who control the public world of the state, politics, and the economy. Women have been given token access to this world because the discourses of liberty and universalism made this difficult to refuse, but to take part they must conform to the rules established to suit the brothers.

This public world in which the brothers operate together is conceptualized as separate from the personal and emotional. One is a realm where there is little physicality—everything is done rationally, bureaucratically, according to contracts that the brothers accept as legitimate. Violence in this realm is severely controlled by agents of the state, except that the brothers are sometimes called upon for the supreme sacrifice of dying to preserve freedom. The social contract redefines the brawling and feuding long seen as essential characteristics of masculinity as deviant, even criminal, while the rest of physicality—sexuality, reproduction of the body, daily and intergenerationally—is left in the private sphere. Pateman quotes Robert Unger, "The dichotomy of the public and private life is still another corollary of the separation of understanding and desire. . . . When reasoning, [men] belong to a public world. . . . When desiring, however, men are private beings" (Pateman 1989, 48).

This is now widely accepted as the way men understand and experience their world. On the other hand, almost no attempt has been made to look at how it is that they take these views on board, or why the public/private divide is so much more deeply entrenched in their lived experience than in women's. This article looks at one strand in the complex web of experiences through which this is achieved. A major site where this occurs is the school, one of the institutions par-

Ellen Jordan and Angela Cowan, *Gender & Society*, Vol. 9 No. 6, pp. 727–43, copyright © 1995 by Sage Publications, Inc. Reprinted by permission of Sage Publications, Inc.

ticularly characteristic of the civil society that emerged with the Enlightenment (Foucault 1980, 55–7). The school does not deliberately condition boys and not girls into this dichotomy, but it is, we believe, a site where what Giddens (1984, 10–3) has called a cycle of practice introduces little boys to the public/private division.

The article is based on weekly observations in a kindergarten classroom. We examine what happens in the early days of school when the children encounter the expectations of the school with their already established conceptions of gender. The early months of school are a period when a great deal of negotiating between the children's personal agendas and the teacher's expectations has to take place, where a great deal of what Genovese (1972) has described as accommodation and resistance must be involved.

In this article, we focus on a particular contest, which, although never specifically stated, is central to the children's accommodation to school: little boys' determination to explore certain narratives of masculinity with which they are already familiar—guns, fighting, fast cars—and the teacher's attempts to outlaw their importation into the classroom setting. We argue that what occurs is a contest between two definitions of masculinity: what we have chosen to call "warrior narratives" and the discourses of civil society—rationality, responsibility, and decorum—that are the basis of school discipline.

By "warrior narratives," we mean narratives that assume that violence is legitimate and justified when it occurs within a struggle between good and evil. There is a tradition of such narratives, stretching from Hercules and Beowulf to Superman and Dirty Harry, where the male is depicted as the warrior, the knight-errant, the superhero, the good guy (usually called a "goody" by Australian children), often supported by brothers in arms, and always opposed to some evil figure, such as a monster, a giant, a villain, a criminal, or, very simply, in Australian parlance, a "baddy." There is also a connection, it is now often suggested, between these narratives and the activity that has come to epitomize the physical expression of masculinity in the modern era: sport (Crosset 1990; Duthie 1980, 91–4; Messner 1992, 15). It is as sport that the physicality and desire usually lived out in the private sphere are permitted a ritualized public presence. Even though the violence once characteristic of the warrior has, in civil society and as part of the social contract, become the prerogative of the state, it can still be reenacted symbolically in countless sporting encounters. The mantle of the warrior is inherited by the sportsman.

The school discipline that seeks to outlaw these narratives is, we would suggest, very much a product of modernity. Bowles and Gintis have argued that "the structure of social relations in education not only inures the student to the discipline of the work place, but develops the types of personal demeanor, modes of self-presentation, self-image, and social-class identifications which are the crucial ingredients of job adequacy" (1976, 131). The school is seeking to introduce the children to the behavior appropriate to the civil society of the modern world.

An accommodation does eventually take place, this article argues, through a recognition of the split between the public and the private. Most boys learn to accept that the way to power and respectability is through acceptance of the conventions of civil society. They also learn that warrior narratives are not a part of this world; they can only be experienced symbolically as fantasy or sport. The outcome, we will suggest, is that little boys learn that these narratives must be left behind in the private world of desire when they participate in the public world of reason.

THE STUDY

The school where this study was conducted serves an old-established suburb in a country town in New South Wales, Australia. The children are predominantly Australian born and English speaking, but come from socioeconomic backgrounds ranging from professional to welfare recipient. We carried out this research in a classroom run by a teacher who is widely acknowledged as one of the finest and most successful kindergarten teachers in our region. She is an admired practitioner of free play, process writing, and creativity. There was no gender definition of games in her classroom. Groups composed of both girls and boys had turns at playing in the Doll Corner, in the Construction Area, and on the Car Mat.

The research method used was nonparticipant observation, the classic mode for the sociological study of children in schools (Burgess 1984; Goodenough 1987; Thorne 1986). The group of children described came to school for the first time in February 1993. The observation sessions began within a fortnight of the children entering school and were conducted during "free activity" time, a period lasting for about an hour. At first we observed twice a week, but then settled to a weekly visit, although there were some weeks when it was inconvenient for the teacher to accommodate an observer.

The observation was noninteractive. The observer stationed herself as unobtrusively as possible, usually seated on a kindergarten-sized chair, near one of the play stations. She made pencil notes of events, with particular attention to accurately recording the words spoken by the children, and wrote up detailed narratives from the notes, supplemented by memory, on reaching home. She discouraged attention from the children by rising and leaving the area if she was drawn by them into any interaction.

This project thus employed a methodology that was ethnographic and open-ended. It was nevertheless guided by certain theories, drawn from the work on gender of Jean Anyon, Barrie Thorne, and R. W. Connell, of the nature of social interaction and its part in creating personal identity and in reproducing the structures of a society.

Anyon has adapted the conceptions of accommodation and resistance developed by Genovese (1972) to understanding how women live with gender. Genovese argued that slaves in the American South accommodated to their contradictory situation by using certain of its aspects, for example, exposure to the Christian religion, to validate a sense of self-worth and dignity. Christian beliefs then allowed them to take a critical view of slavery, which in turn legitimated certain forms of resistance (Anyon 1983, 21). Anyon lists a variety of ways in which women accommodate to and resist prescriptions of appropriate feminine behavior, arguing for a significant level of choice and agency (Anyon 1983, 23–6).

Thorne argues that the processes of social life, the form and nature of the interactions, as well as the choices of the actors, should be the object of analysis. She writes, "In this book I begin not with individuals, although they certainly appear in the account, but with *group life*—with social relations, the organization and meanings of social situations, the collective practices through which children ad adults create and recreate gender in their daily interactions" (1993, 4).

These daily interactions, Connell (1987, 139–41) has suggested mesh to form what Giddens (1984, 10–3) has called "cyclical practices." Daily interactions are neither random nor specific to particular locations. They are repeated and recreated in similar settings throughout a society. Similar needs recur, similar discourses are available, and so similar solutions to problems are adopted; thus, actions performed and discourses adopted to achieve particular ends in particular situations have the unintended consequence of producing uniformities of gendered behavior in individuals.

In looking at the patterns of accommodation and resistance that emerge when the warrior narratives that little boys have adapted from television encounter the discipline of the classroom, we believe we have uncovered one of the cyclical practices of modernity that reveal the social contract to these boys.

WARRIOR NARRATIVES IN THE DOLL CORNER

In the first weeks of the children's school experience, the Doll Corner was the area where the most elaborate acting out of warrior narratives was observed. The Doll Corner in this classroom was a small room with a door with a glass panel opening off the main area. Its furnishings—stove, sink, dolls' cots, and so on—were an attempt at a literal re-creation of a domestic setting, revealing the school's definition of children's play as a preparation for adult life. It was an area where the acting out of "pretend" games was acceptable.

Much of the boys' play in the area was domestic:

> Jimmy and Tyler were jointly ironing a table-cloth. "Look at the sheet is burnt, I've burnt it," declared Tyler, waving the toy iron above his head. "I'm telling Mrs. Sandison," said Jimmy worriedly. "No, I tricked you. It's not really burnt. See," explained Tyler, showing Jimmy the black pattern on the cloth. (February 23, 1993)

> "Where is the baby, the baby boy?" Justin asked, as he helped Harvey and Malcolm settle some restless teddy babies. "Give them some potion." Justin pretended to force feed a teddy, asking "Do you want to drink this potion?" (March 4, 1993)

On the other hand, there were attempts from the beginning by some of the boys and one of the girls to use this area for nondomestic games and, in the case of the boys, for games based on warrior narratives, involving fighting, destruction, goodies, and baddies.

> The play started off quietly, Winston cuddled a teddy bear, then settled it in a bed. Just as Winston tucked in his bear, Mac snatched the teddy out of bed and swung it around his head in circles. "Don't hurt him, give him back," pleaded Winston, trying vainly to retrieve the teddy. The two boys were circling the small table in the center of the room. As he ran, Mac started to karate chop the teddy on the arm, and then threw it on the floor and jumped on it. He then snatched up a plastic knife, "This is a sword. Ted is dead. They all are." He sliced the knife across the teddy's tummy, repeating the action on the bodies of two stuffed dogs. Winston grabbed the two dogs, and with a dog in each hand, staged a dog fight. "They are alive again." (February 10, 1993)

> Three boys were busily stuffing teddies into the cupboard through the sink opening. "They're in jail. They can't escape," said Malcolm. "Let's pour water over them." "Don't do that. I'll hurt them," shouted Winston, rushing into the Doll Corner. "Go away, Winston. You're not in our group," said Malcolm. (February 12, 1993)

The boys even imported goodies and baddies into a classic ghost scenario initiated by one of the girls:

> "I'm the father," Tyler declared. "I'm the mother," said Alanna. "Let's pretend it's a stormy night and I'm afraid. Let's pretend a ghost has come to steal the dog." Tyler nodded and placed the sheet over his head. Tyler moaned, "ooooOOOOOOOAHHHH!!!" and moved his outstretched arms toward Alanna. Jamie joined the game and grabbed a sheet from the doll's cradle, "I'm the goody ghost." "So am I," said Tyler. They giggled and wrestled each other to the floor. "No! you're the baddy ghost," said Jamie. Meanwhile, Alanna was making ghostly noises and moving around the boys. "Did you like the game? Let's play it again," she suggested. (February 23, 1993)

In the first two incidents, there was some conflict between the narratives being invoked by Winston and those used by the other boys. For Winston, the stuffed toys were the weak whom he must protect knight-errant style. For the other boys, they could be set up as the baddies whom it was legitimate for the hero to attack. Both were versions of a warrior narrative.

The gender difference in the use of these narratives has been noted by a number of observers (Clark 1989, 250–2; Paley 1984; Thorne 1993, 98–9). Whereas even the most timid, least physically aggressive boys—Winston in this study is typical—are drawn to identifying with the heroes of these narratives, girls show almost no interest in them at this early age. The strong-willed and assertive girls in our study, as in others (Clark 1990, 83–4; Walkerdine 1990, 10–2), sought power by commandeering the role of mother, teacher, or shopkeeper, while even the highly imaginative Alanna, although she enlivened the more mundane fantasies of the other children with ghosts, old widow women, and magical mirrors, seems not to have been attracted by warrior heroes.[1]

Warrior narratives, it would seem, have a powerful attraction for little boys, which they lack for little girls. Why and how this occurs remains unexplored in early childhood research, perhaps because data for such an explanation are not available to those doing research in institutional settings. Those undertaking ethnographic research in preschools find the warrior narratives already in possession in these sites (Davies 1989, 91–2; Paley 1984, 70–3, 116). In this research, gender difference in the appeal of warrior narratives has to be taken as a given—the data gathered are not suitable for constructing theories of origins; thus, the task of determining an explanation would seem to lie within the province of those investigating and theorizing gender differentiation during infancy, and perhaps, specifically, of those working in the tradition of feminist psychoanalysis pioneered by Dinnerstein (1977) and Chodorow (1978). Nevertheless, even though the cause may remain obscure, there can be little argument that in the English-speaking world for at least the last hundred years—think of Tom Sawyer playing Robin Hood and the pirates and Indians in J. M. Barrie's *Peter Pan*—boys have built these narratives into their conceptions of the masculine.

ACCOMMODATION THROUGH *BRICOLAGE*

The school classroom, even one as committed to freedom and self-actualization as this, makes little provision for the enactment of these narratives. The classroom equipment invites children to play house, farm, and shop, to construct cities and roads, and to journey through them with toy cars, but there is no overt invitation to explore warrior narratives.

In the first few weeks of school, the little boys un-self-consciously set about redressing this omission. The method they used was what is known as *bricolage*—the transformation of objects from one use to another for symbolic purposes (Hebdige 1979, 103). The first site was the Doll Corner. Our records for the early weeks contain a number of examples of boys rejecting the usages ascribed to the various Doll Corner objects by the teacher and by the makers of equipment and assigning a different meaning to them. This became evident very early with their use of the toy baby carriages (called "prams" in Australia). For the girls, the baby carriages were just that, but for many of the boys they very quickly became surrogate cars:

> Mac threw a doll into the largest pram in the Doll Corner. He walked the pram out past a group of his friends who were playing "crashes" on the Car Mat. Three of the five boys turned and watched him wheeling the pram toward the classroom door. Mac performed a sharp three-point turn; raced his pram past the Car Mat group, striking one boy on the head with the pram wheel. (February 10, 1993)

> "Brrrrmmmmmm, brrrrrmmmmmm," Tyler's revving engine noises grew louder as he rocked the pram back and forth with sharp jerking movements. The engine noise grew quieter as he left the Doll Corner and wheeled the pram around the classroom. He started to run with the pram when the teacher could not observe him. (March 23, 1993)

The boys transformed other objects into masculine appurtenances: knives and tongs became weapons, the dolls' beds became boats, and so on.

> Mac tried to engage Winston in a sword fight using Doll Corner plastic knives. Winston backed away, but Mac persisted. Winston took a knife but continued to back away from Mac. He then put down the knife, and ran away half-screaming (semi-seriously, unsure of the situation) for his teacher. (February 10, 1993)

In the literature on youth subcultures, bricolage is seen as a characteristic of modes of resistance. Hebdige writes:

> It is through the distinctive rituals of consumption, through style, that the sub-culture at once reveals its "secret" identity and communicates its forbidden meanings. It is predominantly the way commodities are used in subculture which mark the subculture off from more orthodox cultural formations. . . . The concept of *bricolage* can be used to explain how subcultural styles are constructed. (1979, 103)

In these early weeks, however, the boys did not appear to be aware that they were doing anything more than establishing an accommodation between their needs and the classroom environment.

This mode of accommodation was rejected by the teacher, however, who practiced a gentle, but steady, discouragement of such bricolage. Even though the objects in this space are not really irons, beds, and cooking pots, she made strong efforts to assert their cultural meaning, instructing the children in the "proper" use of the equipment and attempting to control their behavior by questions like "Would you do that with a tea towel in your house?" "Cats never climb up on the benches in *my* house." It was thus impressed upon the children that warrior narratives were inappropriate in this space.

The children, our observations suggest, accepted her guidance, and we found no importation of warrior narratives into the Doll Corner after the first few weeks. There were a number of elaborate and exciting narratives devised, but they were all to some degree related to the domestic environment. For example, on April 20, Justin and Nigel used one of the baby carriages as a four-wheel drive, packed it with equipment and went off for a camping trip, setting out a picnic with Doll Corner tablecloths, knives, forks, and plates when they arrived. On May 18, Matthew, Malcolm, Nigel, and Jonathan were dogs being fed in the Doll Corner. They then complained of the flies, and Jonathan picked up the toy telephone and said, "Flycatcher! Flycatcher! Come and catch some flies. They are everywhere." On June 1, the following was recorded:

> "We don't want our nappies [diapers] changed," Aaron informed Celia, the mum in the game. "I'm poohing all over your clothes mum," Mac declared, as he grunted and positioned himself over the dress-up box. Celia cast a despairing glance in Mac's direction, and went on dressing a doll. "I am too; poohing all over your clothes mum," said Aaron. "Now mum will have to clean it all up

and change my nappy," he informed Mac, giggling. He turned to the dad [Nigel], and said in a baby voice, "Goo-goo; give him [Mac] the feather duster." "No! give him the feather duster; he did the longest one all over the clothes," Mac said to Nigel. (June 1, 1993)

Although exciting and imaginative games continued, the bricolage virtually disappeared from the Doll Corner. The intention of the designer of the Doll Corner equipment was increasingly respected. Food for the camping trip was bought from the shop the teacher had set up and consumed using the Doll Corner equipment. The space invaded by flies was a domestic space, and appropriate means, calling in expert help by telephone, were used to deal with the problem. Chairs and tables were chairs and tables, clothes were clothes and could be fouled by appropriate inhabitants of a domestic space, babies. Only the baby carriages continued to have an ambiguous status, to maintain the ability to be transformed into vehicles of other kinds.

The warrior narratives—sword play, baddies in jail, pirates, and so on—did not vanish from the boys' imaginative world, but, as the later observations show, the site gradually moved from the Doll Corner to the Construction Area and the Car Mat. By the third week in March (that is, after about six weeks at school), the observer noticed the boys consistently using the construction toys to develop these narratives. The bricolage was now restricted to the more amorphously defined construction materials.

Tyler was busy constructing an object out of five pieces of plastic straw (clever sticks). "This is a water pistol. Everyone's gonna get wet," he cried as he moved into the Doll Corner pretending to wet people. The game shifted to guns and bullets between Tyler and two other boys. "I've got a bigger gun," Roger said, showing off his square block object. "Mine's more longer. Ehehehehehehehe, got you," Winston yelled to Roger, brandishing a plastic straw gun. "I'll kill your gun," Mac said, pushing Winston's gun away. "No Mac. You broke it. No," cried Winston. (March 23, 1993)

Two of the boys picked up swords made out of blue- and red-colored plastic squares they had displayed on the cupboard. "This is my sword," Jamie explained to Tyler. "My jumper [sweater] holds it in. Whichever color is at the bottom, well that's the color it shoots out. Whoever is bad, we shoot with power out of it." "Come on Tyler," he went on. "Get your sword. Let's go get some baddies." (March 30, 1993)

The toy cars on the Car Mat were also pressed into the service of warrior narratives:

Justin, Brendan, and Jonathan were busy on the Car Mat. The game involved police cars that were chasing baddies who had drunk "too much beers." Justin explained to Jonathan why his car had the word "DOG" written on the front. "These are different police cars, for catching robbers taking money." (March 4, 1993)

Three boys, Harvey, Maurice, and Marshall, were on the Car Mat. "Here comes the baddies," Harvey shouted, spinning a toy car around the mat. "Crasssshhhhh everywhere." He crashed his car into the other boys' cars and they responded with laughter. "I killed a baddie everyone," said Maurice, crashing his cars into another group of cars. (May 24, 1993)

A new accommodation was being proposed by the boys, a new adaptation of classroom materials to the needs of their warrior narratives.

CLASSROOM RULES AND RESISTANCE

Once again the teacher would not accept the accommodation proposed. Warrior narratives provoked what she considered inappropriate public behavior in the miniature civil society of her classroom. Her aim was to create a "free" environment where children could work independently, learn at their own pace, and explore their own interests, but creating such an environment involved its own form of social contract, its own version of the state's appropriation of violence. From the very first day, she began to establish a series of classroom rules that imposed constraints on violent or disruptive activity.

The belief underlying her practice was that firmly established classroom rules make genuine free play possible, rather than restricting the range of play opportunities. Her emphasis on "proper" use of equipment was intended to stop it being damaged and consequently withdrawn from use. She had rules of "no running" and "no shouting" that allowed children to work and play safely on the floor of the classroom, even though other children were using equipment or toys that demanded movement, and ensured that the noise level was low enough for children to talk at length to one another as part of their games.

One of the outcomes of these rules was the virtual outlawing of a whole series of games that groups of children usually want to initiate when they are playing together, games of speed and body contact, of gross motor self-expression and skill. This prohibition affected both girls and boys and was justified by setting up a version of public and private spaces: The classroom was not the proper place for such activities, they "belong" in the playground.[2] The combined experience of many teachers has shown that it is almost impossible for children to play games involving car crashes and guns without violating these rules; therefore, in this classroom, as in many others (Paley 1984, 71, 116), these games were in effect banned.

These rules were then policed by the children themselves, as the following interchange shows:

"Eeeeeeheeeeeeheeeeh!" Tyler leapt about the room. A couple of girls were saying, "Stop it Tyler" but he persisted. Jane warned, "You're not allowed to have guns." Tyler responded saying, "It's not a gun. It's a water pistol, and that's not a gun." "Not allowed to have water pistol guns," Tony reiterated to Tyler. "Yes, it's a water pistol," shouted Tyler. Jane informed the teacher, who responded stating, "NO GUNS, even if they are water pistols." Tyler made a spear out of Clever Sticks, straight after the banning of gun play. (March 23, 1993)

The boys, however, were not prepared to abandon their warrior narratives. Unlike gross motor activities such as wrestling and football, they were not prepared to see them relegated to the playground, but the limitations on their expression and the teacher disapproval they evoked led the boys to explore them surreptitiously; they found ways of introducing them that did not violate rules about running and shouting.

As time passed, the games became less visible. The warrior narratives were not so much acted out as talked through, using the toy cars and the construction materials as a prompt and a basis:

Tyler was showing his plastic straw construction to Luke. "This is a Samurai Man and this is his hat. A Samurai Man fights in Japan and they fight with the Ninja. The bad guys who use cannons and guns. My Samurai is captain of the Samurai and he is going to kill the sergeant of the bad guys. He is going to sneak up on him with a knife and kill him." (June 1, 1993)

Malcolm and Aaron had built boats with Lego blocks and were explaining the various components to Roger. "This ship can go faster," Malcolm explained. "He [a plastic man] is the boss of the ship. Mine is a goody boat. They are not baddies." "Mine's a steam shovel boat. It has wheels," said Aaron. "There it goes in the river and it has to go to a big shed where all the steam shovels are stopping." (June 11, 1993)

It also became apparent that there was something covert about this play. The cars were crashed quietly. The guns were being transformed into water pistols. Swords were concealed under jumpers and only used when the teacher's back was turned. When the constructed objects were displayed to the class, their potential as players in a fighting game was concealed under a more mundane description. For example:

Prior to the free play, the children were taking turns to explain the Clever Stick and Lego Block constructions they had made the previous afternoon. I listened to Tyler describe his Lego robot to the class: "This is a transformer robot. It can do things and turn into everything." During free play, Tyler played with the same robot explaining its capacities to Winston: "This is a terminator ship. It can kill. It can turn into a robot and the top pops off." (March 23, 1993)

Children even protested to one another that they were not making weapons, "This isn't a gun, it's a lookout." "This isn't a place for bullets, it's for petrol."

The warrior narratives, it would seem, went underground and became part of a "deviant" masculine subculture with the characteristic "secret" identity and hidden meanings (Hebdige 1979, 103). The boys were no longer seeking accommodation but practicing hidden resistance. The classroom, they were learning, was not a place where it was acceptable to explore their gender identity through fantasy.

This, however, was a message that only the boys were receiving. The girls' gender-specific fantasies (Davies 1989, 118–22; Paley 1984, 106–8) of nurturing and self-display—mothers, nurses, brides, princesses—were accommodated easily within the classroom. They could be played out without contravening the rules of the miniature civil society. Although certain delightful activities—eating, running, hugging, and kissing (Best 1983, 110)—might be excluded from this public sphere, they were not ones by means of which their femininity, and thus their subjectivity, their conception of the self, was defined.

MASCULINITY, THE SCHOOL REGIME, AND THE SOCIAL CONTRACT

We suggest that this conflict between warrior narratives and school rules is likely to form part of the experience of most boys growing up in the industrialized world. The commitment to such narratives was not only nearly 100 percent among the boys we observed, but similar commitment is, as was argued above, common in other sites. On the other hand, the pressure to preserve a decorous classroom is strong in all teachers (with the possible exception of those teaching in "alternative" schools) and has been since the beginnings of compulsory education. Indeed, it is only in classrooms where there is the balance of freedom and constraint we observed that such narratives are likely to surface at all. In more formal situations, they would be defined as deviant and forced underground from the boys' first entry into school.

If this is a widely recurring pattern, the question then arises: Is it of little significance or is it what Giddens (1984, 10–3) would call one of the "cyclical practices" that reproduce the structures of our society? The answer really depends on how little boys "read" the outlawing of their warrior narratives. If they see it as simply one of the broad constraints of school against which they are continually negotiating, then perhaps it has no significance. If, on the other hand, it has in their minds a crucial connection to the definition of gender, to the creation of their own masculine identity, to where they position particular sites and practices on a masculine to feminine continuum, then the ostracism of warrior narratives may mean that they define the school environment as feminine.

There is considerable evidence that some primary school children do in fact make this categorization (Best 1983, 14–5; Brophy 1985, 118; Clark 1990, 36), and we suggest here that the outlawry of the masculine narrative contributes to this. Research by Willis (1977) and Walker (1988) in high schools has revealed a culture of resistance based on definitions of masculinity as *antagonistic* to the demands of the school, which are construed as feminine by the resisters. It might therefore seem plausible to see the underground perpetuation of the warrior narrative as an early expression of this resistance and one that gives some legitimacy to the resisters' claims that the school is feminine.

Is the school regime that outlaws the warrior narratives really feminine? We would argue, rather, that the regime being imposed is based on a male ideal, an outcome of the Enlightenment and compulsory schooling. Michel Foucault has pointed out that the development of this particular regime in schools coincided with the emergence of the prison, the hospital, the army barracks, and the factory (Foucault 1980, 55–7). Although teachers in the first years of school are predominantly female, the regime they impose is perpetuated by male teachers (Brophy 1985, 121), and this preference is endorsed by powerful and influential males in the society at large. The kind of demeanor and self-management that teachers are trying to inculcate in the early school years is the behavior expected in male-dominated public arenas like board-rooms, courtrooms, and union mass meetings.[3]

Connell (1989, 291) and Willis (1977, 76, 84) provide evidence that by adolescence, boys from all classes, particularly if they are ambitious, come to regard acquiescence in the school's demands as compatible with constructing a masculine identity. Connell writes:

> Some working class boys embrace a project of mobility in which they construct a masculinity organized around themes of rationality and responsibility. This is closely connected with the "certification" function of the upper levels of the education system and to a key form of masculinity among professionals. (1989, 291)

Rationality and responsibility are, as Weber argued long ago, the primary characteristics of the modern society theorized by the Enlightenment thinkers as based on a social contract. This prized rationality has been converted in practice into a bureaucratized legal system where "responsible" acceptance by the population of the rules of civil society obviates the need for individuals to use physical violence in gaining their ends or protecting their rights, and where, if such violence is necessary, it is exercised by the state (Weber 1978, 341–54). In civil society, the warrior is obsolete, his activities redefined bureaucratically and performed by the police and the military.

The teacher in whose classroom our observation was conducted demonstrated a strong commitment to rationality and responsibility. For example, she devoted a great deal of time to showing that there was a cause and effect link between the behavior forbidden by her classroom rules and classroom accidents. Each time an accident occurred, she asked the children to determine the cause of the accident, its result, and how it could have been prevented. The implication throughout was that children must take responsibility for the outcomes of their actions.

> Mac accidentally struck a boy, who was lying on the floor, in the head with a pram wheel. He was screaming around with a pram, the victim was playing on the Car Mat and lying down to obtain a bird's eye view of a car crash. Mac rushed past the group and collected Justin on the side of the head. Tears and confusion ensued. The teacher's reaction was to see to Justin, then stop all play and gain children's attention, speaking first to Mac and Justin plus Justin's group:

T.	How did Justin get hurt?
M.	[No answer]
T.	Mac, what happened?

M.	I was wheeling the pram and Justin was in the way.
T.	Were you running?
M.	I was wheeling the pram.

The teacher now addresses the whole class:

| T. | Stop working everyone, eyes to me and listen. Someone has just been hurt because someone didn't remember the classroom rules. What are they, Harvey? |

(Harvey was listening intently and she wanted someone who could answer the question at this point).

H.	No running in the classroom.
T.	Why?

Other children offer an answer.

Chn.	Because someone will get hurt.
T.	Yes, and that is what happened. Mac was going too quickly with the pram and Justin was injured. Now how can we stop this happening next time?
Chn.	No running in the classroom, only walk. (February 10, 1993)

Malcolm, walking, bumped Winston on the head with a construction toy. The teacher intervened.

T.	[To Malcolm and Winston] What happened?
W.	Malcolm hit me on the head.
M.	But it was an accident. I didn't mean it. I didn't really hurt him.
T.	How did it happen?
M.	It was an accident.
W.	He [Malcolm] hit me.
T.	Malcolm, I know you didn't mean to hurt Winston, so how did it happen?
M.	I didn't mean it.
T.	I know you didn't mean it, Malcolm, but why did Winston get hurt?
Chn.	Malcolm was running.
M.	No I wasn't.
T.	See where everyone was sitting? There is hardly enough room for children to walk. Children working on the floor must remember to leave a walking path so that other children can move safely around the room. Otherwise someone will be hurt, and that's what has happened today. (February 23, 1993)

This public-sphere masculinity of rationality and responsibility, of civil society, of the social contract is not the masculinity that the boys are bringing into the classroom through their warrior narratives. They are using a different, much older version—not the male as responsible citizen, the producer and consumer who keeps the capitalist system going, the breadwinner, and caring father of a family. Their earliest vision of masculinity is the male as warrior, the bonded male who goes out with his mates and meets the dangers of the world, the male who attacks and defeats other males characterized as baddies, the male who turns the natural products of the earth into weapons to carry out these purposes.

We would argue, nevertheless, that those boys who aspire to become one of the brothers who wield power in the public world of civil society ultimately realize that conformity to rationality and responsibility, to the demands of the school, is the price they must pay. They realize that although the girls can expect one day to become the brides and mothers of their pretend games, the boys will never, except perhaps in time of war, be allowed to act out the part of warrior hero in reality.

On the other hand, the school softens the transition for them by endorsing and encouraging the classic modern transformation and domestication of the warrior narrative, sport (Connell 1987, 177; Messner 1992, 10–2). In the school where this observation was conducted, large playground areas are set aside for lunchtime cricket, soccer, and basketball; by the age of seven, most boys are joining in these games. The message is conveyed to them that if they behave like citizens in the classroom, they can become warriors on the sports oval.

Gradually, we would suggest, little boys get the message that resistance is not the only way to live out warrior masculinity. If they accept a public/private division of life, it can be accommodated within the private sphere; thus, it becomes possible for those boys who aspire to respectability, figuring in civil society as one of the brothers, to accept that the school regime and its expectations are masculine and to reject the attempts of the "resisters" to define it (and them) as feminine. They adopt the masculinity of rationality and responsibility as that appropriate to the public sphere, while the earlier, deeply appealing masculinity of the warrior narratives can still be experienced through symbolic reenactment on the sports field.

CONCLUSION

We are not, of course, suggesting that this is the only way in which the public/private division becomes part of the lived awareness of little boys. We do, however, believe that we have teased out one strand of the manner in which they encounter it. We have suggested that the classroom is a major site where little boys are introduced to the masculinity of rationality and responsibility characteristic of the brothers in civil society; we have been looking at a "cycle of practice" where, in classroom after classroom, generation after generation, the mode of masculinity typified in the warrior narratives is first driven underground and then transferred to the sports field. We are, we would suggest, seeing renegotiated for each generation and in each boy's own life the conception of the "social contract" that is characteristic of the era of modernity, of the Enlightenment, of democracy, and of capitalism. We are watching reenacted the transformation of violence and power as exercised by body over body, to control through surveillance and rules (Foucault 1977, 9; 1984, 66–7), the move from domination by individual superiors to acquiescence in a public sphere of decorum and rationality (Pateman 1988).

Yet, this is a social *contract*, and there is another side to the bargain. Although they learn that they must give up their warrior narratives of masculinity in the public sphere, where rationality and responsibility hold sway, they also learn that in return they may preserve them in the private realm of desire as fantasy, as bricolage, as a symbolic survival that is appropriate to the spaces of leisure and self-indulgence, the playground, the backyard, the television set, the sports field. Although this is too large an issue to be explored in detail here, there may even be a reenactment in the school setting of what Pateman (1988, 99–115) has defined as the sexual contract, the male right to dominate women in return for accepting the constraints of civil society. Is this, perhaps, established for both boys and girls by means of the endemic misogyny—invasion of girls' space (Thorne 1986, 172; 1993, 63–88), overt expressions of aversion and disgust (D'Arcy 1990, 81; Goodenough 1987, 422), disparaging sexual innuendo (Best 1983, 129; Clark 1990, 38–46; Goodenough, 1987, 433)—noted by so many observers in the classrooms and playgrounds of modernity? Are girls being contained by the boys' actions within a more restricted, ultimately a private, sphere because, in the boys' eyes, they have not earned access to the public sphere by sharing their ordeal of repression, resistance, and ultimate symbolic accommodation of their gender-defining fantasies?

Notes

Authors' Note: The research on which this article is based was funded by the Research Management Committee of the University of Newcastle. The observation was conducted at East Maitland Public School and the authors would like to thank the principal, teachers, and children involved for making our observer so welcome.

1. Some ethnographic studies describe a "tomboy" who wants to join in the boys' games (Best 1983, 95–7; Davies 1989, 93, 123; Thorne 1993, 127–9), although in our experience, such girls are rare, rarer even than the boys who play by choice with girls. The girls' rejection of the warrior narratives does not appear to be simply the result of the fact that the characters are usually men. Bronwyn Davies, when she read the role-reversal story *Rita the Rescuer* to preschoolers, found that many boys identified strongly with Rita ("they flex their muscles to show how strong they are and fall to wrestling each other on the floor to display their strength"), whereas for most girls, Rita remained "other" (Davies 1989, 57–8).

2. This would seem to reverse the usual parallel of outdoor/indoor with public/private. This further suggests that the everyday equation of "public" with "visible" may not be appropriate for the specialized use of the term in sociological discussions of the public/private division. Behavior in the street may be more visible than what goes on in a courtroom, but it is nevertheless acceptable for the street behavior to be, to a greater degree, personal, private, and driven by "desire."

3. There are some groups of men who continue to reject these modes of modernity throughout their lives. Andrew Metcalfe, in his study of an Australian mining community, has identified two broad categories of miner, the "respectable," and the "larrikin" (an Australian slang expression carrying implications of nonconformism, irreverence, and impudence). The first are committed to the procedural decorums of union meetings, sporting and hobby clubs, welfare groups, and so on; the others relate more strongly to the less disciplined masculinity of the pub, the brawl, and the racetrack (Metcalfe, 1988, 73–125). This distinction is very similar to that noted by Paul Willis in England between the "ear'oles" and the "lads" in a working-class secondary school (Willis, 1977). It needs to be noted that this is not a *class* difference and that demographically the groups are identical. What distinguishes them is, as Metcalfe points out, their relative commitment to the respectable modes of accommodation and resistance characteristic of civil society of larrikin modes with a much longer history, perhaps even their acceptance or rejection of the social contract.

References

Anyon, Jean. 1983. Intersections of gender and class: Accommodation and resistance by working-class and affluent females to contradictory sex-role ideologies. In *Gender, class and education,* edited by Stephen Walker and Len Barton. Barcombe, Sussex: Falmer.

Best, Raphaela. 1983. *We've all got scars: What girls and boys learn in elementary school.* Bloomington: Indiana University Press.

Bowles, Samuel, and Herbert Gintis. 1976. *Schooling in capitalist America: Educational reform and the contradictions of economic life.* London: Routledge and Kegan Paul.

Brophy, Jere E. 1985. Interactions of male and female students with male and female teachers. In *Gender influences in classroom interaction,* edited by L. C. Wilkinson and C. B. Marrett. New York: Academic Press.

Burgess, R. G., ed. 1984. *The research process in educational settings: Ten case studies.* Lewes: Falmer.

Chodorow, Nancy. 1978. *The reproduction of mothering: Psychoanalysis and the sociology of gender.* Berkeley: University of California Press.

Clark, Margaret. 1989. Anastasia is a normal developer because she is unique. *Oxford Review of Education* 15:243–55.

———. 1990. *The great divide: Gender in the primary school.* Melbourne: Curriculum Corporation.

Connell, R. W. 1987. *Gender and power: Society, the person and sexual politics.* Sydney: Allen and Unwin.

———. 1989. Cool guys, swots and wimps: The interplay of masculinity and education. *Oxford Review of Education* 15:291–303.

Crosset, Todd. 1990. Masculinity, sexuality, and the development of early modern sport. In *Sport, men and the gender order,* edited by Michael E. Messner and Donald F. Sabo. Champaign, IL: Human Kinetics Books.

D'Arcy, Sue. 1990. Towards a non-sexist primary classroom. In *Dolls and dungarees: Gender issues in the primary school curriculum,* edited by Eva Tutchell. Milton Keynes: Open University Press.

Davies, Bronwyn. 1989. *Frogs and snails and feminist tales: Preschool children and gender.* Sydney: Allen and Unwin.

Dinnerstein, Myra. 1977. *The mermaid and the minotaur: Sexual arrangements and human malaise.* New York: Harper and Row.

Duthie, J. H. 1980. Athletics: The ritual of a technological society? In *Play and culture,* edited by Helen B. Schwartzman. West Point, NY: Leisure.

Eisenstein, Hester. 1984. *Contemporary feminist thought.* London: Unwin Paperbacks.

Foucault, Michel. 1977. *Discipline and punish: The birth of the prison.* Translated by Alan Sheridan. New York: Pantheon.

———. 1980. Body/power. In *power/knowledge: Selected interviews and other writings 1972–1977,* edited by Colin Gordon. Brighton: Harvester

———. 1984. Truth and power. In *The Foucault reader,* edited by P. Rabinow. New York: Pantheon.

Genovese, Eugene E. 1972. *Roll, Jordan, roll: The world the slaves made.* New York: Pantheon.

Giddens, Anthony. 1984. *The constitution of society. Outline of the theory of structuration.* Berkeley: University of California Press.

Goodenough, Ruth Gallagher. 1987. Small group culture and the emergence of sexist behaviour: A comparative study of four children's groups. In *Interpretive ethnography of education,* edited by G. Spindler and L. Spindler. Hillsdale, NJ: Lawrence Erlbaum.

Hebdige, Dick. 1979. *Subculture: The meaning of style.* London: Methuen.

Messner, Michael E. 1992. *Power at play: Sports and the problem of masculinity.* Boston: Beacon.

Metcalfe, Andrew. 1988. *For freedom and dignity: Historical agency and class structure in the coalfields of NSW.* Sydney: Allen and Unwin.

Paley, Vivian Gussin. 1984. *Boys and girls: Superheroes in the doll corner.* Chicago: University of Chicago Press.

Pateman, Carole. 1988. *The sexual contract.* Oxford: Polity.

———. 1989. The fraternal social contract. In *The disorder of women.* Cambridge: Polity.

Thorne, Barrie. 1986. Girls and boys together . . . but mostly apart: Gender arrangements in elementary schools. In *Relationships and development,* edited by W. W. Hartup and Z. Rubin. Hillsdale, NJ: Lawrence Erlbaum.

———. 1993. *Gender play: Girls and boys in school.* New Brunswick, NJ: Rutgers University Press.

Walker, J. C. 1988. *Louts and legends: Male youth culture in an inner-city school.* Sydney: Allen and Unwin.

Walkerdine, Valerie. 1990. *Schoolgirl fictions.* London: Verso.

Weber, Max. 1978. *Selections in translation.* Edited by W. G. Runciman and translated by Eric Matthews. Cambridge: Cambridge University Press.

Willis, Paul. 1977. *Learning to labour: How working class kids get working class jobs.* Farnborough: Saxon House.

MICHAEL S. KIMMEL

"What About the Boys?" What the Current Debates Tell Us—and Don't Tell Us—About Boys in School

I've placed the question contained in my title—"what about the boys?"—in quotation marks. In that way, I can pose two different questions to frame the discussion of boys in school. First, the question within the quotation marks is the empirical one: What *about* the boys? What's going on with them? The second question, expressed by the question *and* the quotation marks, is cultural and political: Why is

Michael S. Kimmel, *Michigan Feminist Studies*, Vol. 14, pp. 1–28, copyright © 1999 by Michael S. Kimmel.

the question "what about the boys?" such a pressing question on the cultural agenda? Why is the question popping up increasingly in the cultural conversation about gender? Why has it become one of the litany of questions that compose the backlash against feminism?

I believe that the answers to both questions are linked. But first let's look at each separately.

WHAT ABOUT THE BOYS?

Are boys in trouble in school? At first glance, the statistics would suggest that they are. Boys drop out of school, are diagnosed as emotionally disturbed, and commit suicide four times more often than girls; they get into fights twice as often; they murder ten times more frequently and are 15 times more likely to be the victims of a violent crime. Boys are six times more likely to be diagnosed with Attention Deficit Disorder (see, for example, Knickerbocker).

If they can manage to sit still and not get themselves killed, the argument seems to go, boys get lower grades on standardized tests of reading and writing, and have lower class rank and fewer honors than girls (Kleinfeld).

Finally, if they succeed in dodging the Scylla of elementary and high school, they're likely to dash themselves against the Charybdis of collegiate male bashing. We read that women now constitute the majority of students on college campuses, passing men in 1982, so that in eight years women will earn 58 percent of bachelor's degrees in U.S. colleges. One reporter tells us that if present trends continue, "the graduation line in 2068 will be all females." (That's like saying that if the enrollment of black students at Ol' Miss was 1 in 1964, 24 in 1968 and 400 in 1988, that by 1994 there should have been no more white students there.) Doomsayers lament that women now outnumber men in the social and behavioral sciences by about three to one, and that they've invaded such traditionally male bastions as engineering, where they now make up about 20 percent of all students, and biology and business, where the genders are virtually on par (see Lewin; Koerner).

So, the data might seem to suggest that there are fewer and fewer boys, getting poorer grades, with increasing numbers of behavioral problems. Three phenomena—numbers, achievement and behavior—compose the current empirical discussion about where the boys are and what they are doing.

"WHAT ABOUT THE BOYS?"

These three themes—numbers, grades, behavior—frame the political debate about boys as well. (Now I'm going to include the quotation marks.) Given these gender differences, it's not surprising that we're having a national debate. After all, boys seem not only to be doing badly, but they are also doing worse than girls. What may be surprising, though, is the way the debate is being framed.

To hear some tell it, there's a virtual war against boys in America. Best-sellers' subtitles counsel us to "protect" boys, to "rescue" them. Inside these books, we read how boys are failing at school, where their behavior is increasingly seen as a problem. We read that boys are depressed, suicidal, emotionally shut down. Therapists advise anguished parents about boys' fragility, their hidden despondence and depression, and issue stern warnings about the dire consequences if we don't watch our collective cultural step.

But if there is a "war against boys" who has declared it? What are the sides of the conflict? Who is to blame for boys' failures? What appears to be a concern about the plight of boys actually masks a deeper agenda—a critique of feminism. And I believe that in the current climate, boys need defending against precisely those who claim to defend them; they need rescuing from precisely those who would rescue them.

The arguments of these jeremiads go something like this: First, we hear, feminism has already succeeded in developing programs for girls, enabling and encouraging girls to go into the sciences, to continue education, to imagine careers outside the home. But, in so doing, feminists have over-emphasized the problems of girls, and distorted the facts. Particularly objectionable are the findings of the American Association of University Women (AAUW) reports on the "chilly classroom climate." According to these critics, the salutary effects of paying attention to girls have been offset by the increasing problematization of boys. It was feminists, we hear, who pitted girls against boys, and in their efforts to help girls, they've "pathologized" boyhood.

Elementary schools, we hear, are "anti-boy," emphasizing reading and restricting the movements of young boys. They "feminize" boys, forcing active, healthy and naturally rambunctious boys to conform to a regime of obedience, "pathologizing what is simply normal for boys," as psychologist Michael Gurian put it (qtd. in Zachary 1). In *The Wonder of Boys,* Gurian argues that with testosterone surging through their little limbs, we demand that they sit still, raise their hands, and take naps. We're giving them the message, he says, that "boyhood is defective" (qtd. in Zachary 1).

In many ways, these discussions rehearse debates we've had several times before in our history. At the turn of the century, for example, cultural critics were concerned that the rise of white collar businesses meant increasing indolence for men and the separation of spheres meant that women—as mothers, teachers, and Sunday school teachers—had taken primary responsibility for the socialization of children, both boys and girls. With women teaching boys to become men, a generation of effeminate dandies were being produced. Then, as now, the solutions were to find arenas in which boys could simply be boys, and where men could be men as well. At the turn of the century, fraternal lodges offered men a homosocial sanctuary, and dude ranches and sports provided a place where these sedentary men could experience what Theodore Roosevelt called "the strenuous life." Boys, in danger of feminization by female teachers, Sunday school teachers and mothers could troop off with the Boys Scouts, designed as a fin-de-siecle "boys' liberation movement." Modern society, was turning hardy robust boys into, as the Boy Scouts' founder Ernest Thompson Seton put it, "a lot of flat chested cigarette smokers with shaky nerves and doubtful vitality" (qtd. in Kimmel, *Manhood in America* 170).

Today, women teachers are still to blame for boys' feminization. "It's teachers' job to create a classroom environment that accommodates both male and female energy, not just mainly female energy," explains the energetic therapist Michael Gurian (qtd. in Knickerbocker 2). Since women also may run those boy scout troops and may actually run circles around the boys on the soccer field, men may be feeling a tad defensive these days. Not to worry—we can always retreat into our den to watch "The Man Show" and read *Men's Health* magazine.

In this way, the problem of boys is a problem caused entirely by women who both feminize the boys and pathologize them in their rush to help girls succeed. I'll return to these issues later, but for now, let me turn to what I see are the chief problems with the current "what about the boys?" debate.

WHAT'S WRONG WITH THE "WHAT ABOUT THE BOYS?" DEBATE

First, it creates a false opposition between girls and boys, pretending that the educational reforms undertaken to enable girls to perform better actually hindered boys' educational development. But these reforms—new initiatives, classroom configurations, teacher training, increased attentiveness to students' processes and individual learning styles—actually enable larger numbers of boys to get a better education.

And since, as Susan McGee Bailey and Patricia Campbell point out in their comment on "The Gender Wars in Education" in the January, 2000 issue of the *WCW Research Report*, "gender stereotypes, particularly those related to education, hurt both girls and boys," the challenging of those stereotypes, decreased tolerance for school violence and bullying, and increased attention to violence at home actually enables *both* girls *and* boys to feel safer at school (13).

Second, the critics all seem to be driven to distraction by numbers—the increasing percentages of women in high education and the growing gender gap in test scores. But here's a number they don't seem to factor in: zero—as in zero dollars of *any* new public funding for school programs for the past twenty years, the utter dearth of school bond issues that have passed, money from which might have developed remedial programs, intervention strategies, and teacher training. Money that might have prevented cutting school sports programs and after-school extra-curricular activities. Money that might have enabled teachers and administrators to do more than "store" problem students in separate classes.

Nor do the critics mention managed care health insurance, which virtually demands that school psychologists diagnose problem behavior as a treatable medical condition so that drugs may be substituted for costly, "unnecessary" therapy. These numbers—numbers of dollars—don't seem to enter the discussion about boys, and yet they provide the foundation for everything else. But even the numbers they *do* discuss—numbers and test scores—don't add up. For one thing, more *people* are going to college than ever before. In 1960, 54 percent of boys and 38 percent of girls went directly to college; today the numbers are 64 percent of boys and 70 percent of girls (Mortenson).

And while some college presidents fret that to increase male enrollments they'll be forced to lower standards (which is, incidentally, exactly the opposite of what they worried about 25 years ago when they all went coeducational) no one seems to find gender disparities going the other way all that upsetting. Of the top colleges and universities in the nation, only Stanford sports a 50–50 gender balance. Harvard and Amherst enroll 56 percent men, Princeton and Chicago 54 percent men, Duke and Berkeley 52 percent and Yale 51 percent. And that doesn't even begin to approach the gender disparities at Cal Tech (65 percent male, 35 percent female) or MIT (62 percent male, 38 percent female) (Gose "Liberal Arts Colleges Ask"). Nor does anyone seem driven to distraction about the gender disparities in nursing, social work, or education. Did somebody say "what about the girls?" Should we lower standards to make sure they're gender balanced?

In fact, much of the great gender difference we hear touted is actually what sociologist Cynthia Fuchs Epstein calls a "deceptive distinction," a difference that appears to be about gender but is actually about something else—in this case, class or race (see Epstein *Deceptive Distinctions*). Girls' vocational opportunities are far more restricted than boys' are. Their opportunities are from the service sector, with limited openings in manufacturing or construction. A college-educated woman earns about the same as a high-school educated man, $35,000 to $31,000 (Gose "Colleges Look for Ways").

The shortage of male college students is also actually a shortage of *non-white* males. The gender gap between college-age white males and white females is rather small, 51 percent women to 49 percent men. But only 37 percent of black college students are male, and 63 percent female, and 45 percent of Hispanic students are male, compared with 55 percent female (Lewin). (If this is a problem largely of class and race, why do the books that warn of this growing crisis have cute little white boys on their covers?)

These differences among boys—by race, or class, for example—do not typically fall within the radar of the cultural critics who would rescue boys. These differences are incidental because, in their eyes, all boys are the same: aggressive, competitive, rambunctious little devils. And this is perhaps the central problem and contradiction in the work of those who would save boys. They argue that it's testosterone that makes boys into boys, and a society that paid attention to boys would have to acknowledge testosterone. We're making it impossible for boys to be boys.

This facile biologism mars the apologists' often insightful observations about the sorry state of boyhood. "Testosterone equals vitality," writes Australian men's movement guru Steve Biddulph, "and it's our job to honor it and steer it into healthy directions" (54). Feminists, Gurian argues, only make the problem worse, with an unyielding critique of the very masculinity that young boys are trying so desperately to prove (*A Fine Young Man*).

This over-reliance on biology leads to a celebration of all things masculine as the simple product of that pubescent chemical elixir. Gurian, for example, celebrates all masculine rites of passage, "like military boot camp, fraternity hazings, graduation day, and bar mitzvah" as "essential parts of every boy's life" (*A Fine*

Young Man 151). Excuse me? Hazing and bar mitzvahs in the same breath? I've read of no reports of boys dying at the hands of other boys on their bar mitzvahs.

Feminist emphases on gender discrimination, sexual harassment, or date rape only humiliate boys and distract us from intervening constructively. These misdiagnoses lead to some rather chilling remedies. Gurian suggests reviving corporal punishment, both at home and at school—but only when administered privately with cool indifference and never in the heat of adult anger. He calls it "spanking responsibly" (*A Fine Young Man* 175), though school boards and child welfare agencies might call it child abuse.

Permit me a brief digression about testosterone. On the surface, the experiments on testosterone and aggression appear convincing. Males have higher levels of testosterone and higher rates of aggressive behavior. What's more, if you increase the level of testosterone in a normal male, his level of aggression will increase. Castrate him—or at least a rodent proxy of him—and his aggressive behavior will cease. Though this might lead one to think that testosterone is the cause of the aggression, Stanford neurobiologist Robert Sapolsky warns against such leaps of logic. He explains that if you take a group of five male monkeys arranged in a dominance hierarchy from 1–5, then you can pretty much predict how everyone will behave toward everyone else. (The top monkey's testosterone level will be higher than the ones below him and levels will decrease down the line.) Number 3, for example, will pick fights with numbers 4 and 5, but will avoid and run away from numbers 1 and 2. If you give number 3 a massive infusion of testosterone, he will likely become more aggressive—but only toward numbers 4 and 5, with whom he has now become an absolute violent torment. He will still avoid numbers 1 and 2, demonstrating that the "testosterone isn't causing aggression, it's exaggerating the aggression that's already there" (155).

It turns out that testosterone has what scientists call a "permissive effect" on aggression: It doesn't cause it, but it does facilitate and enable the aggression that is already there. What's more, testosterone is produced *by* aggression. In studies of tennis players, medical students, wrestlers, nautical competitors, parachutists, and officer candidates, winning and losing determined levels of testosterone, so that the levels of the winners rose dramatically, while those of the losers dropped or remained the same. This was true of women's testosterone levels as well (Kemper; Kling).

What these experiments tell us, I think, is that the presence or absence of testosterone is not the critical issue—but rather the presence or absence of social permission for aggression. Thus, arguments to let boys be boys are likely to exacerbate precisely the problems they attempt to alleviate.

If the cause of the problem is not feminists' deliberately ignoring or raging against male hormones, then it must be the result of that other current social calamity—fatherlessness. It must be, we hear, that boys today lack adequate role models because their fathers are either at work all the time or divorced with limited custody and visitation privileges. Discussions of boys' problems almost invariably circle back to fathers, or rather, the lack of them.

Contemporary jeremiads about fatherlessness remind us how central fathers are to family life, and how fatherlessness is the single cause of innumerable social problems, from crime, delinquency, to drug taking, sexual irresponsibility, poverty and the like. Fathers bring something irreplaceable to the family, something, "inherently masculine" notes Wade Horn, director of the National Fatherhood Initiative (qtd. in Knickerbocker 18).

Unfortunately, we never hear exactly what the cause of all this fatherlessness is. To be sure, we hear about unwed mothers, single-parent families, babies having babies, and punitive and vindictive ex-wives (and their equally punitive and wealthy lawyers) who prevent men from being more present in the lives of their children. They *would* be there, if only women would let them.

"Fortunately," writes Australian Steve Biddulph, "fathers are fighting their way back into family life" (74). Fighting against whom exactly? Women? Feminist women have been pleading with men to come home and share housework and child care—let alone to help raise their sons—for what, 150 years?!

As role models, fathers would provide a model of decisiveness, discipline, and ability to control one's emotions—which would be useful for their naturally aggressive, testosterone-juiced sons at school. But how do these same biologically driven, rambunctious, boys magically grow up to be strong, silent, decisive and controlled fathers?

Easy—by women doing what they are biologically programmed to do: stay home and raise boys (but not for too long) and constrain the natural predatory, aggressive and lustful impulses of their men. In leaving the home and going to work, women abandoned their naturally prescribed role of sexual constraint. Presto: a debate about fatherhood and boyhood, becomes a debate not about masculinity, but about feminism.

WHAT'S MISSING FROM THE DEBATE ABOUT BOYS

I believe that it is *masculinity* that is missing in the discussions of both fathers and sons. Though we hear an awful lot about *males,* we hear very little about *masculinity,* about the cultural meanings of the biological fact of maleness. Raising the issue of masculinity, I believe, will enable us to resolve many of these debates.

When I say that masculinity is invisible in the discussion, what could I possibly mean? How is masculinity invisible? Well, let me ask you this: when I say the word "gender," what gender do you think of? In our courses and our discourses, we act as if women alone "had" gender. This is political; this is central.

Let me tell you a story about that invisibility, one that will also reveal the ways that invisibility is political. (I take this from Kimmel *Manhood in America*). In the early 1980s, I participated in a small discussion group on feminism. In one meeting, in a discussion between two women, I first confronted this invisibility of gender to men. A white woman and a black woman were discussing whether all women were, by definition, "sisters," because they all had essentially the same experiences and because all women faced a common oppression by men. The white woman asserted that the fact that they were both women bonded them, in spite of racial differences. The black woman disagreed.

"When you wake up in the morning and look in the mirror, what do you see?" she asked.

"I see a woman," replied the white woman.

"That's precisely the problem," responded the black woman. "I see a *black* woman. To me, race is visible every day, because race is how I am *not* privileged in our culture. Race is invisible to you, because it's how you are privileged. It's why there will always be differences in our experience."

As I witnessed this exchange, I was startled, and groaned—more audibly, perhaps, than I had intended. Being the only man in the room, someone asked what my response had meant.

"Well," I said, "when I look in the mirror, I see a human being. I'm universally generalizable. As a middle-class white man, I have no class, no race, no gender. I'm the generic person!"

Sometimes, I like to think that it was on that day that I *became* a middle-class, white man. Sure, I had been all that before, but these identities had not meant much to me. Since then, I've begun to understand that race, class, and gender don't refer only to other people, who were marginalized by race, class or gender privilege. Those terms also described me. I enjoyed the privilege of invisibility. The very processes that confer privilege to one group and not another group are often invisible to those upon whom that privilege is conferred. What makes us marginal or powerless are the processes we see, partly because others keep reminding us of them. Invisibility is a privilege in a double sense—describing both the power relations that are kept in place by the very dynamics of invisibility, and in the sense of privilege as luxury. It is a luxury that only white people have in our society not to think about race every minute of their lives. It is a luxury that only men have in our society to pretend that gender does not matter.

Let me give you another example of how power is so often invisible to those who have it. Many of you have email addresses, and you write email messages to people all over the world. You've probably noticed that there is one big difference between email addresses in the United States and email addresses of people in other countries: their addresses have "country codes" at the end of the address. So, for example, if you were writing to someone in South Africa, you'd put "za" at the end, or "jp" for Japan, or "uk" for England or "de" for Germany. But when you write to people in the United States, the email address ends with "edu" for an educational institution, "org" for an organization, "gov" for a federal government office, or "com" or "net" for commercial internet providers. Why is it that the United States doesn't have a country code? It is because when you are the dominant power in the world, everyone else needs to be named. When you are "in power," you needn't draw attention to yourself as a specific entity, but, rather, you can pretend to be the generic, the universal, the generalizable. From the point of view of the United States, all other countries are "other" and thus need to be named, marked, noted. Once again, privilege is invisible. Only an American could write a song titled "We are the World."

There are consequences to this invisibility: privilege, as well as gender, remains invisible. And it is hard to generate a politics of inclusion from invisibility. The invisibility of privilege means that many men, like many white people, become defensive and angry when confronted with the statistical realities or the human consequences of racism or sexism. Since our privilege is invisible, we may become defensive. Hey, we may even feel like victims ourselves.

Let me give you two more illustrations of this that are quite a bit closer to our topic. In a recent article about the brutal homophobic murder of Mathew Shepard, the reporter for the *New York Times* writes that "[y]oung men account for 80 percent to 90 percent of people arrested for 'gay bashing' crimes, says Valerie Jenness, a sociology professor who teaches a course on hate crimes" at U. C. Irvine. Then the reporter quotes Professor Jenness directly: "'This youth variable tells us they are working out identity issues, making the transition away from home into adulthood'" (Brooke A16). Did you hear it disappear? The *Times* reporter says "young men" account for . . . ," the sociologist, the expert, is quoted as saying, "this youth variable." That is what invisibility looks like.[1]

And finally, here's one more illustration of the invisibility of masculinity in the discussion of young boys, and how that invisibility almost always plays out as a critique of feminism. Asked to comment on the school shootings at Columbine and other high schools, House Majority Leader Tom DeLay said that guns "have little or nothing to do with juvenile violence" but rather, that the causes were daycare, the teaching of evolution, and "working mothers who take birth control pills" (qtd. in *The Nation* 5).

Some of the recent boy books do get it; they get that masculinity—not feminism, not testosterone, not fatherlessness, and not the teaching of evolution—is the key to understanding boyhood and its current crisis. For example, in *Raising Cain,* Dan Kindlon and Michael Thompson write that male peers present a young boy with a "culture of cruelty" in which they force him to deny emotional neediness, "routinely disguise his feelings," and end up feeling emotionally isolated (89). And in *Real Boys,* therapist William Pollack calls it the "boy code" and the "mask of masculinity"—a kind of swaggering posture that boys embrace to hide their fears, suppress dependency and vulnerability, and present a stoic, impervious front.

What exactly is that "boy code?" Twenty-five years ago, psychologist Robert Brannon described the four basic rules of manhood:

1. "No Sissy Stuff"—one can never do anything that even remotely hints of femininity; masculinity is the relentless repudiation of the feminine.

2. "Be a Big Wheel"—Wealth, power, status are markers of masculinity. We measure masculinity by the size of one's pay-check. In the words of that felicitous Reagan-era phrase, "He who has the most toys when he dies, wins."

3. "Be a Sturdy Oak"—what makes a man a man is that he is reliable in a crisis, and what makes a man reliable in a crisis is that he resembles an inanimate object. Rocks, pillars, trees are curious masculine icons.

4. "Give em Hell!"—exude an aura of daring and aggression. Live life on the edge. Take risks (Brannon and David).

Of course, these four rules are elaborated by different groups of men and boys in different circumstances. There are as sizable differences among different groups of men as there are differences between women and men. Greater in fact. Just because we make masculinity visible doesn't mean that we make other categories of experience—race, class, ethnicity, sexuality, age—invisible. What it means to be a 71 year-old, black, gay man in Cleveland is probably radically different from what it means to a 19 year-old, white, heterosexual farm boy in Iowa.

Forget that biology and testosterone stuff: there's plenty of evidence that boys are not just boys everywhere and in the same way. Few European nations would boast of such violent, homophobic, and misogynist adolescent males. If it's all so biological, why are Norwegian or French or Swiss boys so different? Are they not boys?

One cannot speak of masculinity in the singular, but of *masculinities,* in recognition of the different definitions of manhood that we construct. By pluralizing the term, we acknowledge that masculinity means different things to different groups of men at different times. But, at the same time, we can't forget that all masculinities are not created equal. All American men must also contend with a singular vision of masculinity, a particular definition that is held up as the model against which we all measure ourselves. We thus come to know what it means to be a man in our culture by setting our definitions in opposition to a set of "others"—racial minorities, sexual minorities, and, above all, women. As the sociologist Erving Goffman once wrote:

> In an important sense there is only one complete unblushing male in America: a young, married, white, urban, northern, heterosexual, Protestant, father, of college education, fully employed, of good complexion, weight, and height, and a recent record in sports. . . . Any male who fails to qualify in any one of these ways is likely to view himself—during moments at least—as unworthy, incomplete, and inferior. (128)

I think it's crucial to listen carefully to those last few words. When men feel that they do not measure up, Goffman argues, they are likely to feel "unworthy, incomplete and inferior." It is, I believe, from this place of unworthiness, incompleteness and inferiority that boys begin their efforts to prove themselves as men. And the ways they do it—based on misinformation and disinformation—is what is causing the problems for girls and boys in school.

HOW DOES THE PERSPECTIVE ON MASCULINITY TRANSFORM THE DEBATE?

Introducing masculinities into the discussion alleviates several of the problems with the "what about the boys?" debate. It enables us to explore the ways in which class and race complicate the picture of boys' achievement and behaviors, for one thing. For another, it reveals that boys and girls are on the same side in this struggle, not pitted against each other.

For example, when Kindlon and Thompson describe the things that *boys* need, they are really describing what *children* need. Adolescent boys, Kindlon and

Thompson inform us, want to be loved, get sex, and not be hurt (195–6). And girls don't? Parents are counseled to: allow boys to have their emotions (241); accept a high level of activity (245); speak their language and treat them with respect (247); teach that empathy is courage (249); use discipline to guide and build (253); model manhood as emotionally attached (255); and teach the many ways a boy can be a man (256). Aside from the obvious tautologies, what they advocate is exactly what feminist women have been advocating for girls for some time.

Secondly, a focus on masculinity explains what is happening to those boys in school. Consider again the parallel for girls. Carol Gilligan's astonishing and often moving work on adolescent girls describes how these assertive, confident and proud young girls "lose their voices" when they hit adolescence (see, for example, Brown and Gilligan). At the same moment, William Pollack notes, boys become *more* confident, even beyond their abilities. You might even say that boys *find* their voices, but it is the inauthentic voice of bravado, of constant posturing, of foolish risk-taking and gratuitous violence. The "boy code" teaches them that they are supposed to be in power, and thus begin to act like it. They "ruffle in a manly pose," as William Butler Yeats once put it, "for all their timid heart."

What's the cause of all this posturing and posing? It's not testosterone, but privilege. In adolescence, both boys and girls get their first real dose of gender inequality: girls suppress ambition, boys inflate it.

Recent research on the gender gap in school achievement bears this out. Girls are more likely to undervalue their abilities, especially in the more traditionally "masculine" educational arenas such as math and science. Only the most able and most secure girls take such courses. Thus, their numbers tend to be few, and their grades high. Boys, however, possessed of this false voice of bravado (and many facing strong family pressure) are likely to *over-value* their abilities, to remain in programs though they are less qualified and capable of succeeding. This difference, and not some putative discrimination against boys, is the reason that girls' mean test scores in math and science are now, on average, approaching that of boys. Too many boys who over-value their abilities remain in difficult math and science courses longer than they should; they pull the boys' mean scores down. By contrast, few girls, whose abilities and self-esteem are sufficient to enable them to "trespass" into a male domain, skew female data upwards.

A parallel process is at work in the humanities and social sciences. Girls' mean test scores in English and foreign languages, for example, also outpace boys. But this is not the result of "reverse discrimination"; rather, it is because the boys bump up against the norms of masculinity. Boys regard English as a "feminine" subject. Pioneering research in Australia by Wayne Martino found that boys are uninterested in English because of what it might say about their (inauthentic) masculine pose (see, for example, Martino "Gendered Learning Practices," "'Cool Boys'"; see also Yates "Gender Equity", "The 'What About the Boys' Debate"; Lesko). "Reading is lame, sitting down and looking at words is pathetic," commented one boy. "Most guys who like English are faggots" (Martino "Gendered Learning Practices" 132). The traditional liberal arts curriculum is seen as feminizing: as Catharine Stimpson recently put it sarcastically, "real men don't speak French" (qtd. in Lewin A26).

Boys tend to hate English and foreign languages for the same reasons that girls love it. In English, they observe, there are no hard and fast rules, but rather one expresses one's opinion about the topic and everyone's opinion is equally valued. "The answer can be a variety of things, you're never really wrong," observed one boy. "It's not like math and science where there is one set answer to everything." Another boy noted:

> I find English hard. It's because there are no set rules for reading texts . . . English isn't like math where you have rules on how to do things and where there are right and wrong answers. In English you have to write down how you feel and that's what I don't like. (Martino "Gendered Learning Practices" 133)

Compare this to the comments of girls in the same study:

> I feel motivated to study English because . . . you have freedom in English—unlike subjects such as math and science—and your view isn't necessarily wrong. There is no definite right or wrong answer and you have the freedom to say what you feel is right without it being rejected as a wrong answer. (Martino "Gendered Learning Practices" 134)

It is not the school experience that "feminizes" boys, but rather the ideology of traditional masculinity that keeps boys from wanting to succeed. "The work you do here is girls' work," one boy commented to a researcher. "It's not real work" (Mac an Ghaill 59; for additional research on this, see Lesko).

ARE SINGLE-SEX SCHOOLS THE ANSWER?

So, are single-sex schools the answer? There are many people who think so. It's true that there is some evidence that single-sex schools are beneficial to women. There has even been some evidence that men's achievement was improved by attending a single-sex college. Empirically, however, these findings are not persuasive, since the effects typically vanish when social class and boys' secondary school experiences were added to the equation.

In their landmark book, *The Academic Revolution,* sociologists Christopher Jencks and David Riesman write:

> The all male-college would be relatively easy to defend if it emerged from a world in which women were established as fully equal to men. But it does not. It is therefore likely to be a witting or unwitting device for preserving tacit assumptions of male superiority. . . . Thus while we are not against segregation of the sexes under all circumstances, we are against it when it helps preserve sexual arrogance.[2] (300, 298)

In short, what women often learn at all-women's colleges is that they can do anything that men can do. By contrast, what men learn at all-men's colleges is that they (women) cannot do what they (the men) do. In this way, women's colleges may constitute a challenge to gender inequality, while men's colleges reproduce that inequality.

Consider an analogy with race here. One might justify the continued existence of historically all-black colleges on the grounds that such schools challenge racist ideas that black students could not achieve academically and provide a place where black students are free of everyday racism and thus free to become serious students. But one would have a more difficult time justifying maintaining an all-white college, which would, by its very existence, reproduce racist inequality. Returning to gender, as psychologist Carol Tavris concludes, "there is a legitimate place for all-women's schools if they give young women a stronger shot at achieving self-confidence, intellectual security, and professional competence in the workplace." On the other hand, since coeducation is based "on the premise that there are few genuine differences between men and women, and that people should be educated as individuals, rather than as members of a gender," the question is "not whether to become coeducational, but rather when and how to undertake the process" (Tavris 127; see also Priest, Vitters and Prince, 1978 590).

Single-sex education for women often perpetuates detrimental attitudes and stereotypes about women, that "by nature or situation girls and young women cannot become successful or learn well in coeducational institutions" (Epstein "Myths and Justifications" 191). Even when supported by feminist women, the idea that women cannot compete equally with men in the same arena, that they need "special" treatment, signals an abandonment of hope, the inability or unwillingness to make the creation of equal and safe schools a national priority. "Since we cannot do that," we seem to be telling girls, "we'll do the next best thing— separate you from those nasty boys who will only make your lives a living hell."

Such proposals also seem to be based on faulty understandings of the differences between women and men, the belief in an unbridgeable chasm between "them" and "us" based on different styles of learning, qualities of mind, structures of brains, and ways of knowing, talking, or caring. John Dewey, perhaps America's greatest theorist of education, and a fierce supporter of women's equal rights, was infuriated at the contempt for women suggested by such programs. In 1911, Dewey scoffed at "'female botany,' 'female algebra,' and for all I know a 'female multiplication table,'" (59). "Upon no subject has there been so much dogmatic assertion based on so little scientific evidence, as upon male and female types of mind." Coeducation, Dewey argued, was beneficial to women, opening up opportunities previously unattainable. Girls, he suggested, became less manipulative, and acquired "greater self-reliance and a desire to win approval by deserving it instead of by 'working' others. Their narrowness of judgment, depending on the enforced narrowness of outlook, is overcome; their ultra-feminine weaknesses are toned up" (60).

What's more, Dewey claimed, coeducation was beneficial to men. "Boys learn gentleness, unselfishness, courtesy; their natural vigor finds helpful channels of expression instead of wasting itself in lawless boisterousness," he wrote (60). Another social and educational reformer, Thomas Wentworth Higginson, also opposed single-sex schools: "Sooner or later, I am persuaded, the human race will look upon all these separate collegiate institutions as most American travelers now look at the vast monastic establishments of Southern Europe; with respect for the pious motives of their founders, but with wonder that such a mistake should ever have been made" (1).

Ultimately, I believe that we're going to have to do this together. Single-sex schools for women may challenge male domination, but single-sex schools for men tend to perpetuate it. Single-sex schools for women also perpetuate the idea that women can't do well without extra assistance and that masculinity is so impervious to change that it would be impossible to claim an education with men around. I believe this insults both women and men.

THE REAL BOY CRISIS IS A CRISIS OF MASCULINITY

Making masculinity visible enables us to understand what I regard as the *real* boy crisis in America. The real boy crisis usually goes by another name. We call it "teen violence," "youth violence," "gang violence," "suburban violence," "violence in the schools." Just who do we think are doing it—girls?

Imagine if all the killers in the schools in Littleton, Pearl, Paducah, Springfield, and Jonesboro were all black girls from poor families who lived instead in New Haven, Newark, or Providence. We'd be having a national debate about inner-city, poor, black girls. The entire focus would be on race, class, and gender. The media would invent a new term for their behavior, as with "wilding" a decade ago. We'd hear about the culture of poverty, about how living in the city breeds crime and violence, about some putative natural tendency among blacks towards violence. Someone would even blame feminism for causing girls to become violent in a vain imitation of boys. Yet the obvious fact that these school killers were all middle-class, white boys seems to have escaped everyone's notice.

Let's face facts: Men and boys are responsible for 95 percent of all violent crimes in this country. Every day 12 boys and young men commit suicide—seven times the number of girls. Every day 18 boys and young men die from homicide— ten times the number of girls (see Kimmel *The Gendered Society*). From an early age, boys learn that violence is not only an acceptable form of conflict resolution, but one that is admired. Four times more teenage boys than teenage girls think fighting is appropriate when someone cuts into the front of a line. Half of all teenage boys get into a physical fight each year.

And it's been that way for many years. No other culture developed such a violent "boy culture," as historian E. Anthony Rotundo calls it in his book, *American Manhood*. Where else did young boys, as late as the 1940s, actually carry little chips of wood on their shoulders daring others to knock it off so that they might have a fight? It may be astonishing to readers that "carrying a chip on your shoulder" is literally true—a test of manhood for adolescent boys.

In what other culture did some of the reigning experts of the day actually *prescribe* fighting for young boys' healthy masculine development? The celebrated psychologist, G. Stanley Hall, who invented the term "adolescence," believed that a non-fighting boy was a "nonentity," and that it was "better even an occasional nose dented by a fist . . . than stagnation, general cynicism and censoriousness, bodily and psychic cowardice" (154).

And his disciples vigorously took up the cause. Here, for example is J. Adams Puffer in 1912, from his successful parental advice book, *The Boy and His Gang:*

> There are times when every boy must defend his own rights if he is not to be-come a coward, and lose the road to independence and true manhood. . . . The strong willed boy needs no inspiration to combat, but often a good deal of guidance and restraint. If he fights more than, let us say, a half-dozen times a week—except of course, during his first week at a new school—he is probably over-quarrelsome and needs to curb. (91)

Boys are to fight an average of once a day, except during the first week at a new school, during which, presumably they would have to fight more often!

From the turn of the century to the present day, violence has been part of the meaning of manhood, part of the way men have traditionally tested, demonstrat-ed and proved their manhood. Without another cultural mechanism by which young boys can come to think of themselves as men, they've eagerly embraced vi-olence as a way to become men.

I remember one little childhood game called "Flinch" that we played in the school yard. One boy would come up to another and pretend to throw a punch at his face. If the second boy flinched—as any *reasonable* person would have done—the first boy shouted "you flinched" and proceeded to punch him hard on the arm. It was his right; after all, the other boy had failed the test of masculinity. Being a man meant never flinching.

In the recent study of youthful violent offenders, psychologist James Garbari-no locates the origins of men's violence in the ways boys swallow anger and hurt. Among the youthful offenders he studied, "[d]eadly petulance usually hides some deep emotional wounds, a way of compensating through an exaggerated sense of grandeur for an inner sense of violation, victimization, and injustice" (128). In other words, as that famous Reagan-era bumper-sticker put it, "I don't just get mad, I get even." Or, as one prisoner said, "I'd rather be wanted for mur-der than not wanted at all" (132).

James Gilligan is even more specific. In his book *Violence,* one of the most in-sightful studies of violence I've ever read, he argues that violence has its origins in "the fear of shame and ridicule, and the overbearing need to prevent others from laughing at oneself by making them weep instead" (77).

Recall those words by Goffman again—"unworthy, incomplete, inferior." Now listen to these voices: First, here is Evan Todd, a 255-pound defensive line-man on the Columbine football team, an exemplar of the jock culture that Dylan Klebold and Eric Harris—the gunmen at Columbine High School—found to be such an interminable torment: "Columbine is a clean, good place, except for those rejects," Todd says. "Sure we teased them. But what do you expect with kids who come to school with weird hairdos and horns on their hats? It's not just jocks; the whole school's disgusted with them. They're a bunch of homos, grabbing each others' private parts. If you want to get rid of someone, usually you tease 'em. So the whole school would call them homos" (qtd. in Gibbs and Roche 50–51). Harris says people constantly made fun of "my face, my hair, my shirts" (44). Klebold adds, "I'm going to kill you all. You've been giving us s____ for years" (44).

OUR CHALLENGE

If we really want to rescue boys, protect boys, promote boyhood, then our task must be to find ways to reveal and challenge this ideology of masculinity, to disrupt the facile "boys will be boys" model, and to erode boys' sense of entitlement. Because the reality is that it is this ideology of masculinity that is the problem for *both* girls *and* boys. And seen this way, our strongest ally, it seems to me, is the women's movement.

To be sure, feminism opened the doors of opportunity to women and girls. And it's changed the rules of conduct: in the workplace, where sexual harassment is no longer business as usual; on dates, where attempted date rape is no longer "dating etiquette"; and in schools, where both subtle and overt forms of discrimination against girls—from being shuffled off to Home Economics when they want to take physics, excluded from military schools and gym classes, to anatomy lectures using pornographic slides—have been successfully challenged. And let's not forget the legal cases that have confronted bullying, and sexual harassment by teachers and peers.

More than that, feminism has offered a blueprint for a new boyhood and masculinity based on a passion for justice, a love of equality, and expression of a fuller emotional palette. So naturally, feminists will be blamed for male bashing— feminists imagine that men (and boys) can do better (see, for example, Miedzian; Silverstein and Rashbaum).

And to think feminists are accused of male bashing! Actually, I think the anti-feminist right wing are the real male bashers. Underneath the anti-feminism may be perhaps the most insulting image of masculinity around. Males, you see, are savage, predatory, sexually omnivorous, violent creatures, who will rape, murder and pillage unless women perform their civilizing mission and act to constrain us. "Every society must be wary of the unattached male, for he is universally the cause of numerous social ills," writes David Popenoe (12). When they say that boys will be boys, they mean boys will be uncaged, uncivilized animals. Young males, conservative critic Charles Murray wrote recently, are "essentially barbarians for whom marriage . . . is an indispensible civilizing force" (23). And what of evolutionary psychologist Robert Wright, who recently "explained" that women and men are hard-wired by evolutionary imperatives to be so different as to come from different planets. "Human males," he wrote, "are by nature oppressive, possessive, flesh-obsessed pigs" (22). Had any radical feminist said these words, anti-feminist critics would howl with derision about how feminists hated men!

And here's that doyenne of talk radio, Dr. Laura Schlesinger: "Men would not do half of what they do if women didn't let them," she told an interviewer for *Modern Maturity* magazine recently. "That a man is going to do bad things is a fact.

That you keep a man who does bad things in your life is your fault" (qtd. in Goodman 68).

Now it seems to me that the only rational response to these insulting images of an unchangeable, hard-wired, violent manhood is, of course, to assume they're true. Typically when we say that boys will be boys, we assume that propensity for violence is innate, the inevitable fruition of that prenatal testosterone cocktail. So what? That only begs the question. We still must decide whether to organize society so as to maximize boy's "natural" predisposition toward violence, or to minimize it. Biology alone cannot answer that question, and claiming that boys will be boys, helplessly shrugging our national shoulders, abandons our political responsibility.

Besides, one wants to ask, which biology are we talking about? Therapist Michael Gurian demands that we accept boy's "hard wiring." This "hard wiring," he informs us, is competitive and aggressive. "Aggression and physical risk taking are hard wired into a boy," he writes. Gurian claims that he likes the kind of feminism that "is not anti-male, accepts that boys are who they are, and chooses to love them rather than change their hard wiring" (*A Fine Young Man* 53–4).

That's too impoverished a view of feminism—and of boys—for my taste. I think it asks far too little of us, to simply accept boys and this highly selective definition of their hard-wiring. Feminism asks more of us—that we *not* accept those behaviors that are hurtful to boys, girls, and their environment—because we can do better than what this *part* of our hard wiring might dictate. We are also, after all, hard-wired towards compassion, nurturing and love, aren't we?

Surely we wouldn't insult men the way the right-wing insults men, by arguing that only women are hard-wired for love, care-giving, nurturing, and love, would we? (I am sure that those legions of men's rights types, demanding custody wouldn't dare do so!) I'm reminded of a line from Kate Millett's path-breaking book, *Sexual Politics*, more than thirty years ago:

> Perhaps nothing is so depressing an index of the inhumanity of the male supremacist mentality as the fact that the more genial human traits are assigned to the underclass: affection, response to sympathy, kindness, cheerfulness. (324–6)

The question, to my mind, is not whether or not we're hard wired, but rather which hard wiring elements we choose to honor and which we choose to challenge.

I remember one pithy definition that feminism was the radical idea that women are people. Feminists also seem to believe the outrageous proposition that, if given enough love, compassion and support, boys—as well as men—can also be people. That's a vision of boyhood I believe is worth fighting for.

Notes

This paper began as the keynote address at the 6th annual K–12 Gender Equity in Schools Conference, Wellesley College Center for Research on Women, Wellesley College, January,

2000. A revised version was also presented at The Graduate School of Education, Harvard University, May, 2000. Although modified and revised, I have tried to retain the language and feeling of the original oral presentation. I am grateful to Susan McGee Bailey and Carol Gilligan for inviting me, and to Amy Aronson, Peggy McIntosh, Martin Mills, and Nan Stein, for their comments and support, and to the editors at *Michigan Feminist Studies*, and especially Laura Citrin, for their patience and editorial precision.

1. In fairness to Professor Jenness, whose work on gay bashing crimes I admire, it is possible that her quotation was only part of what she said, and that it was the newspaper, not the expert, who again rendered masculinity invisible.

2. Despite his own findings, Riesman supported the continuation of VMI and Citadel's single sex policy and testified on their behalf. See David Riesman.

References

Adams, Lorraine, and Dale Russakoff. "Dissecting Columbine's Cult of the Athlete." *The Washington Post*, 15 July 1999.

American Association of University Women. *How Schools Shortchange Girls: The AAUW Report, A Study of Major Findings on Girls and Education.* Washington, DC: American Association of University Women Educational Foundation, 1992.

———. *Gender Gaps: Where Schools Still Fail Our Children.* New York: Marlowe and Co., 1999.

Bailey, Susan McGee, and Patricia B. Campbell, "The Gender Wars in Education." *WCW Research Report*. Wellesley, MA: Wellesley Center for Research on Women, 1999/2000.

Biddulph, Steve. *Raising Boys.* Berkeley: Ten Speed P, 1999.

Brannon, Robert, and Deborah David. "Introduction" to *The Forty-Nine Per Cent Majority.* Reading, MA: Addison, Wesley, 1976.

Brooke, James. "Men Held in Beating Lived on the Fringes." *The New York Times.* 16 October 1998: A16.

Brown, Lyn Mikeal, and Carol Gilligan. *Meeting at the Cross-roads.* New York: Ballantine, 1992.

Connell, R. W. "Teaching the Boys: New Research on Masculinity, and Gender Strategies for Schools." *Teachers College Record*, 98 (2), Winter 1996.

Dewey, John. "Is Coeducation Injurious to Girls?" *Ladies Home Journal.* 11 June 1911.

Epstein, Cynthia Fuchs. *Deceptive Distinctions.* New Haven: Yale UP, 1988.

———. "The Myths and Justifications of Sex Segregation in Higher Education: VMI and the Citadel." *Duke Journal of Gender Law and Policy* 4, 1997.

Garbarino, James. *Lost Boys: Why Our Sons Turn Violent and How We Can Save Them.* New York: The Free P, 1999.

Gibbs, Nancy and Timothy Roche. "The Columbine Tapes." *Time* 154 (25), 20 December 1999: 40–51.

Gilbert, Rob, and Pam Gilbert. *Masculinity Goes to School.* London: Routledge, 1998.

Gilligan, Carol. *In a Different Voice.* Cambridge: Harvard UP, 1982.

Gilligan, James. *Violence.* New York: Vintage, 1997.

Goffman, Erving. *Stigma: Notes on the Management of Spoiled Identity.* Englewood Cliffs, NJ: Prentice-Hall, 1963.

Goodman, Susan. "Dr. No." *Modern Maturity,* September-October, 1999.

Gose, Ben. "Liberal Arts Colleges Ask: Where Have the Men Gone?" *Chronicle of Higher Education.* 6 June 1997: A35–6.

———. "Colleges Look for Ways to Reverse a Decline in Enrollment of Men." *Chronicle of Higher Education.* 26 November 1999: A73.

Gurian, Michael. *A Fine Young Man: What parents, mentors, and educators can do to shape adolescent boys into exceptional men.* New York: Jeremy P. Tarcher/Putnam, 1998.

———. *The Wonder of Boys: What parents, mentors, and educators can do to shape boys into exceptional men.* New York: Jeremy P. Tarcher/Putnam, 1996.

Hall, G. Stanley. "The Awkward Age." *Appleton's Magazine.* August 1900.

Higginson, Thomas Wentworth. "Sex and Education." *The Woman's Journal.* 1874. Reprinted in *History of Woman Suffrage,* Vol. 3, S. B. Anthony, E. C. Stanton, and M. J. Gage, Eds. New York: Woman Suffrage Association Press, n.d.

Jencks, Christopher, and David Riesman. *The Academic Revolution.* Chicago: U of Chicago P, 1977.

Kemper, Theodore. *Testosterone and Social Structure.* New Brunswick, NJ: Rutgers UP, 1990.

Kimmel, Michael. *The Gendered Society.* New York: Oxford UP, 2000.

———. *Manhood in America: A Cultural History.* New York: The Free P, 1996.

Kindlon, Dan, and Michael Thompson. *Raising Cain: Protecting the Emotional Life of Boys.* New York: Ballantine, 1999.

Kleinfeld, Judith. "Student Performance: Males Versus Females." *The Public Interest.* Winter 1999.

Kling, Arthur. "Testosterone and Aggressive Behavior in Man and Non-human Primates." Eds. B. Eleftheriou and R. Sprott. *Hormonal Correlates of Behavior.* New York: Plenum, 1975.

Knickerbocker, Brad. "Young and Male in America: It's Hard Being a Boy." *Christian Science Monitor.* 29 April 1999.

Koerner, Brendan. "Where the Boys Aren't." *U.S. News and World Report.* 8 February 1999.

Lesko, Nancy, ed. *Masculinities and Schools.* Newbury Park, CA: Sage Publications, 2000.

Lewin, Tamar. "American Colleges Begin to Ask, Where Have All the Men Gone?" *The New York Times.* 6 December 1998.

Lingard, Bob. "Masculinity Politics, Myths and Boys' Schooling: A Review Essay." *British Journal of Educational Studies,* 45 (3), September 1997.

Mac an Ghaill, Mairtin. *The Making of Men: Masculinities, Sexualities and Schooling.* London: Open UP, 1994.

———. "'What About the Boys?': Schooling, Class and Crisis Masculinity." *Sociological Review,* 44 (3), 1996.

Martino, Wayne. "Gendered Learning Practices: Exploring the Costs of Hegemonic Masculinity for Girls and Boys in Schools." *Gender Equity: A Framework for Australian Schools.* Canberra: np, 1997.

———. "'Cool Boys,' 'Party Animals', 'Squids,' and 'Poofters': Interrogating the Dynamics and Politics of Adolescent Masculinities in School." *British Journal of Sociology of Education,* 20 (2), 1999.

Miedzian, Myriam. *Boys will be Boys: Breaking the Link Between Masculinity and Violence.* New York: Doubleday, 1991.

Millett, Kate. *Sexual Politics.* New York: Random House, 1969.

Mills, Martin. "Disrupting the 'What About the Boys?' Discourse: Stories from Australia" paper presented at the Men's Studies Conference, SUNY at Stony Brook, 6 August 1998.

Mortenson, Thomas. "Where Are the Boys? The Growing Gender Gap in Higher Education." *The College Board Review,* 188, August 1999.

Murray, Charles. "The Emerging British Underclass." London: IEA Health and Welfare Unit, 1990.

The Nation. "News of the Week in Review." 15 November 1999.

Pollack, William. *Real Boys: Rescuing Our Sons from the Myths of Boyhood.* New York: Henry Holt, 1998.

Popenoe, David. *Life Without Father.* New York: The Free P, 1996.

Priest, R., A. Vitters, and H. Prince, "Coeducation at West Point." *Armed Forces and Society,* 4 (4), 1978.

Puffer, J. Adams. *The Boy and His Gang.* Boston: Houghton, Mifflin, 1912.

Riesman, David. "A Margin of Difference: The Case for Single-Sex Education." Eds. J. R. Blau and N. Goodman. *Social Roles and Social Institutions: Essays in Honor of Rose Laub Coser.* Boulder: Westview P, 1991.

Rotundo, E. Anthony. *American Manhood: Transformations of Masculinity from the Revolution to the Present Era.* New York: BasicBooks, 1993.

Salisbury, Jonathan, and David Jackson. *Challenging Macho Values: Practical Ways of Working with Adolescent Boys.* London: The Falmer P, 1996.

Sapolsky, Robert. *The Trouble with Testosterone.* New York: Simon and Schuster, 1997.

Silverstein, Olga, and Beth Rashbaum. *The Courage to Raise Good Men.* New York: Penguin, 1995.

Tavris, Carol. *The Mismeasure of Woman.* New York: Simon and Schuster, 1992.

Wright, Robert. "The Dissent of Woman: What Feminists can Learn from Darwinism." *Matters of Life and Death: Demos Quarterly,* 10, 1996.

Yates, Lyn. "Gender Equity and the Boys Debate: What Sort of Challenge Is It?" *British Journal of Sociology of Education,* 18 (3), 1997.

———. "The 'What About the Boys?' Debate as a Public Policy Issue." Ed. Nancy Lesko. *Masculinities and Schools.* Newbury Park, CA: Sage Publications, 2000.

Zachary, G. Pascal. "Boys Used to Be Boys, But Do Some Now See Boyhood as a Malady." *The Wall Street Journal,* 2 May 1997.

PART 7 THE GENDERED WORKPLACE

Perhaps the most dramatic social change in industrial countries in the twentieth century has been the entry of women into the workplace. The nineteenth-century ideology of "separate spheres"—the breadwinner husband and the homemaker wife—has slowly and steadily evaporated. While only 20 percent of women, and only 4 percent of married women, worked outside the home in 1900, more than three-fourths did so by 1995, including 60 percent of married women. In the first decade of the twenty-first century, 80 percent of the new entrants into the labor force will be women, minorities, and immigrants.

Despite the collapse of the doctrine of separate spheres—work and home—the workplace remains a dramatically divided world, where women and men rarely do the same jobs in the same place for the same pay. Occupational sex segregation, persistent sex discrimination, wage disparities—all these are problems faced by working women. As the article by Barbara Reskin demonstrates, workplace inequality is among the most persistent and pernicious forms of gender discrimination. And the article by Joan Acker places the question of gender and work in a larger framework of organizations-as-gendered.

Even women who are seeking to get ahead by entering formerly all-male fields frequently bump into the "glass ceiling"—a limit on how high they can rise in any organization. On the other hand, as Christine Williams argues, men who do "women's work"—taking occupations such as nurse, nursery school teacher, librarian—not only avoid the glass ceiling but actually glide up a "glass escalator"—finding greater opportunities at the higher, better paying levels of their professions than women.

And even when women are protected by a variety of laws that promise comparable worth for equal work, wage and salary parity, and no occupational sex segregation, they still face myriad psychological and interpersonal struggles, such as sexual harassment, the creation of a "hostile environment" that keeps them in their place.

JOAN ACKER

Hierarchies, Jobs, Bodies: A Theory of Gendered Organizations

Most of us spend most of our days in work organizations that are almost always dominated by men. The most powerful organizational positions are almost entirely occupied by men, with the exception of the occasional biological female who acts as a social man. Power at the national and world level is located in all-male enclaves at the pinnacle of large state and economic organizations. These facts are not news, although sociologists paid no attention to them until feminism came along to point out the problematic nature of the obvious. Writers on organizations and organizational theory now include some consideration of women and gender, but their treatment is usually cursory, and male domination is, on the whole, not analyzed and not explained.

Among feminist social scientists there are some outstanding contributions on women and organizations, such as the work of Kanter (1977), Feldberg and Glenn (1979), MacKinnon (1979), and Ferguson (1984). In addition, there have been theoretical and empirical investigations of particular aspects of organizational structure and process, and women's situations have been studied using traditional organizational ideas. Moreover, the very rich literature, popular and scholarly, on women and work contains much material on work organizations. However, most of this new knowledge has not been brought together in a systematic feminist theory of organizations.

A systematic theory of gender and organizations is needed for a number of reasons. First, the gender segregation of work, including divisions between paid and unpaid work, is partly created through organizational practices. Second, and related to gender segregation, income and status inequality between women and men is also partly created in organizational processes; understanding these processes is necessary for understanding gender inequality. Third, organizations are one arena in which widely disseminated cultural images of gender are invented and reproduced. Knowledge of cultural production is important for understanding gender construction. Fourth, some aspects of individual gender identity, perhaps particularly masculinity, are also products of organizational processes and pressures. Fifth, an important feminist project is to make large-scale organizations more democratic and more supportive of humane goals.

In this article, I begin by speculating about why feminist scholars have not debated organizational theory. I then look briefly at how those feminist scholars who have paid attention to organizations have conceptualized them. In the main part of the article, I examine organizations as gendered processes in which both gender and sexuality have been obscured through a gender-neutral, asexual discourse, and suggest some of the ways that gender, the body, and sexuality are part of the

From *Gender & Society*, Vol. 4, no. 2 (June 1990), pp. 139–158. Copyright © 1990 by Sociologists for Women in Society. Reprinted by permission of the author. References have been edited.

processes of control in work organizations. Finally, I point to some directions for feminist theory about this ubiquitous human invention.

WHY SO LITTLE FEMINIST DEBATE ON ORGANIZATIONS?

The early radical feminist critique of sexism denounced bureaucracy and hierarchy as male-created and male-dominated structures of control that oppress women. The easiest answer to the "why so little debate" question is that the link between masculinity and organizational power was so obvious that no debate was needed. However, experiences in the feminist movement suggest that the questions are not exhausted by recognizing male power.

Part of the feminist project was to create nonhierarchical, egalitarian organizations that would demonstrate the possibilities of nonpatriarchal ways of working. Although many feminist organizations survived, few retained this radical-democratic form. Others succumbed to the same sorts of pressures that have undermined other utopian experiments with alternative work forms, yet analyses of feminist efforts to create alternative organizations were not followed by debates about the feasibility of nonpatriarchal, nonhierarchical organization or the relationship of organizations and gender. Perhaps one of the reasons was that the reality was embarrassing; women failing to cooperate with each other, taking power and using it in oppressive ways, creating their own structures of status and reward were at odds with other images of women as nurturing and supportive.

Another reason for feminist theorists' scant attention to conceptualizing organizations probably lies in the nature of the concepts and models at hand. As Dorothy Smith (1979) has argued, the available discourses on organizations, the way that organizational sociology is defined as an area or domain "is grounded in the working worlds and relations of men, whose experience and interests arise in the course of and in relation to participation in the ruling apparatus of this society" (p. 148). Concepts developed to answer managerial questions, such as how to achieve organizational efficiency, were irrelevant to feminist questions, such as why women are always concentrated at the bottom of organizational structures.

Critical perspectives on organizations, with the notable exception of some of the studies of the labor process, although focusing on control, power, exploitation, and how these relations might be changed, have ignored women and have been insensitive to the implications of gender for their own goals. The active debate on work democracy, the area of organizational exploration closest to feminist concerns about oppressive structures, has been almost untouched by feminist insights. For example, Carole Pateman's influential book, *Participation and Democratic Theory* (1970), critical in shaping the discussions on democratic organization in the 1970s, did not consider women or gender. More recently, Pateman (1983a, 1983b, 1988) has examined the fundamental ideas of democracy from a feminist perspective, and other feminist political scientists have criticized theories of democracy, but on the whole, their work is isolated from the main discourse on work organization and democracy.

Empirical research on work democracy has also ignored women and gender.

For example, in the 1980s, many male Swedish researchers saw little relation between questions of democracy and gender equality with a few exceptions. Other examples are studies of Mondragon, a community in the Spanish Basque country, which is probably the most famous attempt at democratic ownership, control, and organization. Until Sally Hacker's feminist study (1987), researchers who went to Mondragon to see this model of work democracy failed to note the situation of women and asked no questions about gender. In sum, the absence of women and gender from theoretical and empirical studies about work democracy provided little material for feminist theorizing.

Another impediment to feminist theorizing is that the available discourses conceptualize organizations as gender neutral. Both traditional and critical approaches to organizations originate in the male, abstract intellectual domain and take as reality the world as seen from that standpoint. As a relational phenomenon, gender is difficult to see when only the masculine is present. Since men in organizations take their behavior and perspectives to represent the human, organizational structures and processes are theorized as gender neutral. When it is acknowledged that women and men are affected differently by organizations, it is argued that gendered attitudes and behavior are brought into (and contaminate) essentially gender-neutral structures. This view of organizations separates structures from the people in them.

Current theories of organization also ignore sexuality. Certainly, a gender-neutral structure is also asexual. If sexuality is a core component of the production of gender identity, gender images, and gender inequality, organizational theory that is blind to sexuality does not immediately offer avenues into the comprehension of gender domination. Catharine MacKinnon's (1982) compelling argument that sexual domination of women is embedded within legal organizations has not to date become part of mainstream discussions. Rather, behaviors such as sexual harassment are viewed as deviations of gendered actors, not, as MacKinnon (1979) might argue, as components of organizational structure.

FEMINIST ANALYSES OF ORGANIZATIONS

The treatment of women and gender most assimilated into the literature on organizations is Rosabeth Moss Kanter's *Men and Women of the Corporation* (1977). Kanter sets out to show that gender differences in organizational behavior are due to structure rather than to characteristics of women and men as individuals (1977, 291–92). She argues that the problems women have in large organizations are consequences of their structural placement, crowded in dead-end jobs at the bottom and exposed as tokens at the top. Gender enters the picture through organizational roles that "carry characteristic images of the kinds of people that should occupy them" (p. 250). Here, Kanter recognizes the presence of gender in early models of organizations:

> A "masculine ethic" of rationality and reason can be identified in the early image of managers. This "masculine ethic" elevates the traits assumed to belong

to men with educational advantages to necessities for effective organizations: a tough-minded approach to problems; analytic abilities to abstract and plan; a capacity to set aside personal, emotional considerations in the interests of task accomplishment; a cognitive superiority in problem-solving and decision making. (1974, 43)

Identifying the central problem of seeming gender neutrality, Kanter observes: "While organizations were being defined as sex-neutral machines, masculine principles were dominating their authority structures" (1977, 46).

In spite of these insights, organizational structure, not gender, is the focus of Kanter's analysis. In posing the argument as structure *or* gender, Kanter also implicitly posits gender as standing outside of structure, and she fails to follow up her own observations about masculinity and organizations (1977, 22). Kanter's analysis of the effects of organizational position applies as well to men in low-status positions. Her analysis of the effect of numbers, or the situation of the "token" worker, applies also to men as minorities in women-predominant organizations, but fails to account for gender differences in the situation of the token. In contrast to the token woman, white men in women-dominated workplaces are likely to be positively evaluated and to be rapidly promoted to positions of greater authority. The specificity of male dominance is absent in Kanter's argument, even though she presents a great deal of material that illuminates gender and male dominance.

Another approach, using Kanter's insights but building on the theoretical work of Hartmann (1976), is the argument that organizations have a dual structure, bureaucracy and patriarchy (Ressner 1987). Ressner argues that bureaucracy has its own dynamic, and gender enters through patriarchy, a more or less autonomous structure, that exists alongside the bureaucratic structure. The analysis of two hierarchies facilitates and clarifies the discussion of women's experiences of discrimination, exclusion, segregation, and low wages. However, this approach has all the problems of two systems theories of women's oppression: the central theory of bureaucratic or organizational structure is unexamined, and patriarchy is added to allow the theorist to deal with women. Like Kanter, Ressner's approach implicitly accepts the assumption of mainstream organizational theory that organizations are gender-neutral social phenomena.

Ferguson, in *The Feminist Case Against Bureaucracy* (1984), develops a radical feminist critique of bureaucracy as an organization of oppressive male power, arguing that it is both mystified and constructed through an abstract discourse on rationality, rules, and procedures. Thus, in contrast to the implicit arguments of Kanter and Ressner, Ferguson views bureaucracy itself as a construction of male domination. In response to this overwhelming organization of power, bureaucrats, workers, and clients are all "feminized," as they develop ways of managing their powerlessness that at the same time perpetuate their dependence. Ferguson argues further that feminist discourse, rooted in women's experiences of caring and nurturing outside bureaucracy's control, provides a ground for opposition to bureaucracy and for the development of alternative ways of organizing society.

However, there are problems with Ferguson's theoretical formulation. Her argument that feminization is a metaphor for bureaucratization not only uses a stereotype of femininity as oppressed, weak, and passive, but also, by equating the experience of male and female clients, women workers, and male bureaucrats, obscures the specificity of women's experiences and the connections between masculinity and power. Ferguson builds on Foucault's (1979) analysis of power as widely diffused and constituted through discourse, and the problems in her analysis have their origin in Foucault, who also fails to place gender in his analysis of power. What results is a disembodied, and consequently gender-neutral, bureaucracy as the oppressor. That is, of course, not a new vision of bureaucracy, but it is one in which gender enters only as analogy, rather than as a complex component of processes of control and domination.

In sum, some of the best feminist attempts to theorize about gender and organizations have been trapped within the constraints of definitions of the theoretical domain that cast organizations as gender neutral and asexual. These theories take us only part of the way to understanding how deeply embedded gender is in organizations. There is ample empirical evidence: We know now that gender segregation is an amazingly persistent pattern and that the gender identity of jobs and occupations is repeatedly reproduced, often in new forms. The reconstruction of gender segregation is an integral part of the dynamic of technological and organizational change. Individual men and particular groups of men do not always win in these processes, but masculinity always seems to symbolize self-respect for men at the bottom and power for men at the top, while confirming for both their gender's superiority. Theories that posit organization and bureaucracy as gender neutral cannot adequately account for this continual gendered structuring. We need different theoretical strategies that examine organizations as gendered processes in which sexuality also plays a part.

ORGANIZATION AS GENDERED PROCESSES

The idea that social structure and social processes are gendered has slowly emerged in diverse areas of feminist discourse. Feminists have elaborated gender as a concept to mean more than a socially constructed, binary identity and image. This turn to gender as an analytic category is an attempt to find new avenues into the dense and complicated problem of explaining the extraordinary persistence through history and across societies of the subordination of women. Scott, for example, defines gender as follows: "The core of the definition rests on an integral connection between two propositions; gender is a constitutive element of social relationships based on perceived differences between the sexes, and gender is a primary way of signifying relationships of power" (1986, 1067).

New approaches to the study of waged work, particularly studies of the labor process, see organizations as gendered, not as gender neutral and conceptualize organizations as one of the locations of the inextricably intertwined production of both gender and class relations. Examining class and gender, I have argued that class is constructed through gender and that class relations are always gendered.

The structure of the labor market, relations in the workplace, the control of the work process, and the underlying wage relation are always affected by symbols of gender, processes of gender identity, and material inequalities between women and men. These processes are complexly related to and powerfully support the reproduction of the class structure. Here, I will focus on the interface of gender and organizations, assuming the simultaneous presence of class relations.

To say that an organization, or any other analytic unit, is gendered means that advantage and disadvantage, exploitation and control, action and emotion, meaning and identity, are patterned through and in terms of a distinction between male and female, masculine and feminine. Gender is not an addition to ongoing processes, conceived as gender neutral. Rather, it is an integral part of those processes, which cannot be properly understood without an analysis of gender. Gendering occurs in at least five interacting processes that, although analytically distinct, are, in practice, parts of the same reality.

First is the construction of divisions along lines of gender—divisions of labor, of allowed behaviors, of locations in physical space, of power, including the institutionalized means of maintaining the divisions in the structures of labor markets, the family, the state. Such divisions in work organizations are well documented as well as often obvious to casual observers. Although there are great variations in the patterns and extent of gender division, men are almost always in the highest positions of organizational power. Managers' decisions often initiate gender divisions, and organizational practices maintain them—although they also take on new forms with changes in technology and the labor process. For example, Cynthia Cockburn (1983, 1985) has shown how the introduction of new technology in a number of industries was accompanied by a reorganization, but not abolition, of the gendered division of labor that left the technology in men's control and maintained the definition of skilled work as men's work and unskilled work as women's work.

Second is the construction of symbols and images that explain, express, reinforce, or sometimes oppose those divisions. These have many sources or forms in language, ideology, popular and high culture, dress, the press, television. For example, as Kanter (1975), among others, has noted, the image of the top manager or the business leader is an image of successful, forceful masculinity. In Cockburn's studies, men workers' images of masculinity linked their gender with their technical skills; the possibility that women might also obtain such skills represented a threat to that masculinity.

The third set of processes that produce gendered social structures, including organizations, are interactions between women and men, women and women, men and men, including all those patterns that enact dominance and submission. For example, conversation analysis shows how gender differences in interruptions, turn taking, and setting the topic of discussion recreate gender inequality in the flow of ordinary talk. Although much of this research has used experimental groups, qualitative accounts of organizational life record the same phenomena: Men are the actors, women the emotional support.

Fourth, these processes help to produce gendered components of individual identity, which may include consciousness of the existence of the other three aspects of gender, such as, in organizations, choice of appropriate work, language use, clothing, and presentation of self as a gendered member of an organization.

Finally, gender is implicated in the fundamental, ongoing processes of creating and conceptualizing social structures. Gender is obviously a basic constitutive element in family and kinship, but, less obviously, it helps to frame the underlying relations of other structures, including complex organizations. Gender is a constitutive element in organizational logic, or the underlying assumptions and practices that construct most contemporary work organizations. Organizational logic appears to be gender neutral; gender-neutral theories of bureaucracy and organizations employ and give expression to this logic. However, underlying both academic theories and practical guides for managers is a gendered substructure that is reproduced daily in practical work activities and, somewhat less frequently, in the writings of organizational theorists.

Organizational logic has material forms in written work rules, labor contracts, managerial directives, and other documentary tools for running large organizations, including systems of job evaluation widely used in the comparable-worth strategy of feminists. Job evaluation is accomplished through the use and interpretation of documents that describe jobs and how they are to be evaluated. These documents contain symbolic indicators of structure; the ways that they are interpreted and talked about in the process of job evaluation reveals the underlying organizational logic. I base the following theoretical discussion on my observations of organizational logic in action in the job-evaluation component of a comparable-worth project.

Job evaluation is a management tool used in every industrial country, capitalist and socialist, to rationalize the organizational hierarchy and to help in setting equitable wages. Although there are many different systems of job evaluation, the underlying rationales are similar enough so that the observation of one system can provide a window into a common organizational mode of thinking and practice.

In job evaluation, the content of jobs is described and jobs are compared on criteria of knowledge, skill, complexity, effort, and working conditions. The particular system I observed was built incrementally over many years to reflect the assessment of managers about the job components for which they were willing to pay. Thus today this system can be taken as composed of residues of these judgments, which are a set of decision rules that, when followed, reproduce managerial values. But these rules are also the imagery out of which managers construct and reconstruct their organizations. The rules of job evaluation, which help to determine pay differences between jobs, are not simply a compilation of managers' values or sets of beliefs, but are the underlying logic or organization that provides at least part of the blueprint for its structure. Every time that job evaluation is used, that structure is created or reinforced.

Job evaluation evaluates jobs, not their incumbents. The job is the basic unit in a work organization's hierarchy, a description of a set of tasks, competencies, and responsibilities represented as a position on an organizational chart. A job is separate from people. It is an empty slot, a reification that must continually be reconstructed, for positions exist only as scraps of paper until people fill them. The rationale for evaluating jobs as devoid of actual workers reveals further the organizational logic—the intent is to assess the characteristics of the job, not of their incumbents who may vary in skill, industriousness, and commitment. Human beings are to be motivated, managed, and chosen to fit the job. The job exists as a thing apart.

Every job has a place in the hierarchy, another essential element in organizational logic. Hierarchies, like jobs, are devoid of actual workers and based on abstract differentiations. Hierarchy is taken for granted, only its particular form is at issue. Job evaluation is based on the assumption that workers in general see hierarchy as an acceptable principle, and the final test of the evaluation of any particular job is whether its place in the hierarchy looks reasonable. The ranking of jobs within an organization must make sense to managers, but it is also important that most workers accept the ranking as just if the system of evaluation is to contribute to orderly working relationships.

Organizational logic assumes a congruence between responsibility, job complexity, and hierarchical position. For example, a lower-level position, the level of most jobs filled predominantly by women, must have equally low levels of complexity and responsibility. Complexity and responsibility are defined in terms of managerial and professional tasks. The child-care worker's responsibility for other human beings or the complexity facing the secretary who serves six different, temperamental bosses can only be minimally counted if the congruence between position level, responsibility, and complexity is to be preserved. In addition, the logic holds that two jobs at different hierarchical levels cannot be responsible for the same outcome; as a consequence, for example, tasks delegated to a secretary by a manager will not raise her hierarchical level because such tasks are still his responsibility, even though she has the practical responsibility to see that they are done. Levels of skill, complexity, and responsibility, all used in constructing hierarchy, are conceptualized as existing independently of any concrete worker.

In organizational logic, both jobs and hierarchies are abstract categories that have no occupants, no human bodies, no gender. However, an abstract job can exist, can be transformed into a concrete instance, only if there is a worker. In organizational logic, filling the abstract job is a disembodied worker who exists only for the work. Such a hypothetical worker cannot have other imperatives of existence that impinge upon the job. At the very least, outside imperatives cannot be included within the definition of the job. Too many obligations outside the boundaries of the job would make a worker unsuited for the position. The closest the disembodied worker doing the abstract job comes to a real worker is the male worker whose life centers on his full-time, life-long job, while his wife or another woman takes care of his personal needs and his children. While the realities of life in industrial capitalism never allowed all men to live out this ideal, it was the goal for labor unions and the image of the worker in social and economic theory. The woman worker, assumed to have legitimate obligations other than those required by the job, did not fit with the abstract job.

The concept "a job" is thus implicitly a gendered concept, even though organizational logic presents it as gender neutral. "A job" already contains the gender-based division of labor and the separation between the public and the private sphere. The concept of "a job" assumes a particular gendered organization of domestic life and social production. It is an example of what Dorothy Smith has called "the gender subtext of the rational and impersonal" (1988, 4).

Hierarchies are gendered because they also are constructed on these underlying assumptions: Those who are committed to paid employment are "naturally" more suited to responsibility and authority; those who must divide their commitments are in the lower ranks. In addition, principles of hierarchy, as exemplified in most existing job-evaluation systems, have been derived from already existing gendered structures. The best-known systems were developed by management consultants working with managers to build methods of consistently evaluating jobs and rationalizing pay and job classifications. For example, all managers with similar levels of responsibility in the firm should have similar pay. Job-evaluation systems were intended to reflect the values of managers and to produce a believable ranking of jobs based on those values. Such rankings would not deviate substantially from rankings already in place that contain gender typing and gender segregation of jobs and the clustering of women workers in the lowest and the worst-paid jobs. The concrete value judgments that constitute conventional job evaluation are designed to replicate such structures. Replication is achieved in many ways; for example, skills in managing money, more often found in men's than in women's jobs, frequently receive more points than skills in dealing with clients or human relations skills, more often found in women's than in men's jobs.

The gender-neutral status of "a job" and of the organizational theories of which it is a part depend upon the assumption that the worker is abstract, disembodied, although in actuality both the concept of "a job" and real workers are deeply gendered and "bodied." Carole Pateman (1986), in a discussion of women and political theory, similarly points out that the most fundamental abstraction in the concept of liberal individualism is "the abstraction of the 'individual' from the body. In order for the individual to appear in liberal theory as a universal figure, who represents anyone and everyone, the individual must be disembodied" (p. 8). If the individual were not abstracted from bodily attributes, it would be clear that the individual represents one sex and one gender, not a universal being. The political fiction of the universal "individual" or "citizen," fundamental to ideas of democracy and contract, excluded women, judging them lacking in the capacities necessary for participation in civil society. Although women now have the rights of citizens in democratic states, they still stand in an ambiguous relationship to the universal individual who is "constructed from a male body so that his identity is always masculine" (Pateman 1988, 223). The worker with "a job" is the same universal "individual" who in actual social reality is a man. The concept of a universal worker excludes and marginalizes women who cannot, almost by definition, achieve the qualities of a real worker because to do so is to become like a man.

ORGANIZATIONAL CONTROL, GENDER, AND THE BODY

The abstract, bodiless worker, who occupies the abstract, gender-neutral job has no sexuality, no emotions, and does not procreate. The absence of sexuality, emotionality, and procreation in organizational logic and organizational theory is an additional element that both obscures and helps to reproduce the underlying gender relations.

New work on sexuality in organizations, often indebted to Foucault (1979), suggests that this silence on sexuality may have historical roots in the development of large, all-male organizations that are the primary locations of societal power. The history of modern organizations includes, among other processes, the suppression of sexuality in the interests of organization and the conceptual exclusion of the body as a concrete living whole.

In a review of historical evidence on sexuality in early modern organizations, Burrell (1984, 98) suggests that "the suppression of sexuality is one of the first tasks the bureaucracy sets itself." Long before the emergence of the very large factory of the nineteenth century, other large organizations, such as armies and monasteries, which had allowed certain kinds of limited participation of women, were more and more excluding women and attempting to banish sexuality in the interests of control of members and the organization's activities. Active sexuality was the enemy of orderly procedures, and excluding women from certain areas of activity may have been, at least in part, a way to control sexuality. As Burrell (1984) points out, the exclusion of women did not eliminate homosexuality, which has always been an element in the life of large all-male organizations, particularly if members spend all of their time in the organization. Insistence on heterosexuality or celibacy were ways to control homosexuality. But heterosexuality had to be practiced outside the organization, whether it was an army or a capitalist workplace. Thus the attempts to banish sexuality from the workplace were part of the wider process that differentiated the home, the location of legitimate sexual activity, from the place of capitalist production. The concept of the disembodied job symbolizes this separation of work and sexuality.

Similarly, there is no place within the disembodied job or the gender-neutral organization for other "bodied" processes, such as human reproduction or the free expression of emotions. Sexuality, procreation, and emotions all intrude upon and disrupt the ideal functioning of the organization, which tries to control such interferences. However, as argued above, the abstract worker is actually a man, and it is the man's body, its sexuality, minimal responsibility in procreation, and conventional control of emotions that pervades work and organizational processes. Women's bodies—female sexuality, their ability to procreate and their pregnancy, breast-feeding, and child care, menstruation, and mythic "emotionality"—are suspect, stigmatized, and used as grounds for control and exclusion.

The ranking of women's jobs is often justified on the basis of women's identification with childbearing and domestic life. They are devalued because women are assumed to be unable to conform to the demands of the abstract job. Gender segregation at work is also sometimes openly justified by the necessity to control sexuality, and women may be barred from types of work, such as skilled blue-collar work or top management, where most workers are men, on the grounds that potentially disruptive sexual liaisons should be avoided. On the other hand, the gendered definition of some jobs "includes sexualization of the woman worker as a part of the job" (MacKinnon 1979, 18). These are often jobs that serve men, such as secretaries, or a largely male public.

The maintenance of gendered hierarchy is achieved partly through such often-tacit controls based on arguments about women's reproduction, emotionality, and sexuality, helping to legitimate the organizational structures created through abstract, intellectualized techniques. More overt controls, such as sexual harassment, relegating childbearing women to lower-level mobility tracks, and penalizing (or rewarding) their emotion management also conform to and reinforce hierarchy. MacKinnon (1979), on the basis of an extensive analysis of legal cases, argues that the willingness to tolerate sexual harassment is often a condition of the job, both a consequence and a cause of gender hierarchy.

While women's bodies are ruled out of order, or sexualized and objectified, in work organizations, men's bodies are not. Indeed, male sexual imagery pervades organizational metaphors and language, helping to give form to work activities. For example, the military and the male world of sports are considered valuable training for organizational success and provide images for teamwork, campaigns, and tough competition. The symbolic expression of male sexuality may be used as a means of control over male workers, too, allowed or even encouraged within the bounds of the work situation to create cohesion or alleviate stress. Management approval of pornographic pictures in the locker room or support for all-male work and play groups where casual talk is about sexual exploits or sports are examples. These symbolic expressions of male dominance also act as significant controls over women in work organizations because they are per se excluded from the informal bonding men produce with the "body talk" of sex and sports.

Symbolically, a certain kind of male heterosexual sexuality plays an important part in legitimating organizational power. Connell (1987) calls this hegemonic masculinity, emphasizing that it is formed around dominance over women and in opposition to other masculinities, although its exact content changes as historical conditions change. Currently, hegemonic masculinity is typified by the image of the strong, technically competent, authoritative leader who is sexually potent and attractive, has a family, and has his emotions under control. Images of male sexual function and patriarchal paternalism may also be embedded in notions of what the manager does when he leads his organization. Women's bodies cannot be adapted to hegemonic masculinity; to function at the top of male hierarchies requires that women render irrelevant everything that makes them women.

The image of the masculine organizational leader could be expanded, without altering its basic elements, to include other qualities also needed, according to many management experts, in contemporary organizations, such as flexibility and sensitivity to the capacities and needs of subordinates. Such qualities are not necessarily the symbolic monopoly of women. For example, the wise and experienced coach is empathetic and supportive to his individual players and flexibly leads his team against devious opposition tactics to victory.

The connections between organizational power and men's sexuality may be even more deeply embedded in organizational processes. Sally Hacker (1989) argues that eroticism and technology have common roots in human sensual pleasure and that for the engineer or the skilled worker, and probably for many other kinds of workers, there is a powerful erotic element in work processes. The pleasures of technology, Hacker continues, become harnessed to domination, and passion becomes directed toward power over nature, the machine, and other people, particularly women, in the work hierarchy. Hacker believes that men lose a great deal in this transformation of the erotic into domination, but they also win in other ways. For example, many men gain economically from the organizational gender hierarchy. As Crompton and Jones (1984) point out, men's career opportunities in white-collar work depend on the barriers that deny those opportunities to women. If the mass of female clerical workers were able to compete with men in such work, promotion probabilities for men would be drastically reduced.

Class relations as well as gender relations are reproduced in organizations. Critical, but nonfeminist, perspectives on work organizations argue that rational-technical systems for organizing work, such as job classification and evaluation systems and detailed specification of how work is to be done, are parts of pervasive systems of control that help to maintain class relations. The abstract "job," devoid of a human body, is a basic unit in such systems of control. The positing of a job as an abstract category, separate from the worker, is an essential move in creating jobs as mechanisms of compulsion and control over work processes. Rational-technical, ostensibly gender-neutral, control systems are built upon and conceal a gendered substructure (Smith 1988) in which men's bodies fill the abstract jobs. Use of such abstract systems continually reproduces the underlying gender assumptions and the subordinated or excluded place of women. Gender processes, including the manipulation and management of women's and men's sexuality, procreation, and emotion, are part of the control processes of organizations, maintaining not only gender stratification but contributing also to maintaining class and, possibly, race and ethnic relations. Is the abstract worker white as well as male? Are white-male-dominated organizations also built on underlying assumptions about the proper place of people with different skin colors? Are racial differences produced by organizational practices as gender differences are?

CONCLUSION

Feminists wanting to theorize about organizations face a difficult task because of the deeply embedded gendering of both organizational processes and theory. Commonsense notions, such as jobs and positions, which constitute the units managers use in making organizations and some theorists use in making theory, are posited upon the prior exclusion of women. This underlying construction of a way of thinking is not simply an error, but part of processes of organization. This exclusion in turn creates fundamental inadequacies in theorizing about gender-neutral systems of positions to be filled. Creating more adequate theory may come only as organizations are transformed in ways that dissolve the concept of the abstract job and restore the absent female body.

Such a transformation would be radical in practice because it would probably require the end of organizations as they exist today, along with a redefinition of work and work relations. The rhythm and timing of work would be adapted to the rhythms of life outside of work. Caring work would be just as important and well rewarded as any other; having a baby or taking care of a sick mother would be as valued as making an automobile or designing computer software. Hierarchy would be abolished, and workers would run things themselves. Of course, women and men would share equally in different kinds of work. Perhaps there would be some communal or collective form of organization where work and intimate relations are closely related, children learn in places close to working adults, and workmates, lovers, and friends are all part of the same group. Utopian writers and experimenters have left us many possible models (Hacker 1989). But this brief listing begs many questions, perhaps the most important of which is how, given the present organization of economy and technology and the pervasive and powerful, impersonal, textually mediated relations of ruling (Smith 1988), so radical a change could come about.

Feminist research and theorizing, by continuing to puzzle out how gender provides the subtext for arrangements of subordination, can make some contributions to a future in which collective action to do what needs doing—producing goods, caring for people, disposing of the garbage—is organized so that dominance, control, and subordination, particularly the subordination of women, are eradicated, or at least minimized, in our organization life.

References

Burrell, Gibson. 1984. Sex and organizational analysis. *Organization Studies* 5:97–118.

Cockburn, Cynthia. 1983. *Brothers: Male dominance and technological change.* London: Pluto Press.

———. 1985. *Machinery of dominance.* London: Pluto Press.

Connell, R. W. 1987. *Gender and power.* Stanford, CA: Stanford University Press.

Crompton, Rosemary, and Gareth Jones. 1984. *White-collar proletariat: deskilling and gender in clerical work.* Philadelphia: Temple University Press.

Feldberg, Roslyn, and Evelyn Nakano Glenn. 1979. Male and female: Job versus gender models in the sociology of work. *Social Problems* 26:524–38.

Ferguson, Kathy E. 1984. *The feminist case against bureaucracy.* Philadelphia: Temple University Press.

Foucault, Michel. 1979. *The history of sexuality,* Vol. 1. London: Allen Lane.

Hacker, Sally. 1987. Women workers in the Mondragon system of industrial cooperatives. *Gender & Society* 1:358–79.

———. 1989. *Pleasure, power and technology.* Boston: Unwin Hyman.

Hartmann, Heidi. 1976. Capitalism, patriarchy and job segregation by sex. *Signs* 1:137–70.

Kanter, Rosabeth Moss. 1975. Women and the structure of organizations: Explorations in theory and behavior. In *Another voice,* edited by Rosabeth Kanter and Marcia Millman. New York: Doubleday.

———. 1977. *Men and women of the corporation.* New York: Basic Books.

MacKinnon, Catharine A. 1979. *Sexual harassment of working women.* New Haven, CT: Yale University Press.

———. 1982. Feminism, Marxism, method and the state: An agenda for theory. *Signs* 7:515–44.

Pateman, Carole. 1970. *Participation and democratic theory.* Cambridge: Cambridge University Press.

———. 1983a. Feminist critiques of the public private dichotomy. In *Public and private in social life,* edited by S. I. Benn and G. F. Gaus. Beckenham, Kent: Croom Helm.

———. 1983b. Feminism and democracy. In *Democratic theory and practice,* edited by Graeme Duncan. Cambridge: Cambridge University Press.

———. 1986. Introduction: The theoretical subversiveness of feminism. In *Feminist challenges,* edited by Carole Pateman and Elizabeth Gross. Winchester, MA: Allen & Unwin.

———. 1988. *The sexual contract.* Cambridge, MA: Polity.

Ressner, Ulla. 1986. Review of K. Ferguson, *The feminist case against bureaucracy. Economic and Industrial Democracy* 7:130–34.

———. 1987. *The hidden hierarchy.* Aldershot: Gower.

Scott, Joan. 1986. Gender: A useful category of historical analysis. *American Historical Review* 91:1053–75.

Smith, Dorothy E. 1979. A sociology for women. In *The prism of sex: Essays in the sociology of knowledge,* edited by Julia A. Sherman and Evelyn Torten Beck. Madison: University of Wisconsin Press.

———. 1988. *The everyday world as problematic.* Boston: Northeastern University Press.

BARBARA F. RESKIN

Bringing the Men Back In: Sex Differentiation and the Devaluation of Women's Work

One of the most enduring manifestations of sex inequality in industrial and postindustrial societies is the wage gap. In 1986, as in 1957, among full-time workers in the United States, men earned 50 percent more per hour than did women. This disparity translated to $8,000 a year in median earnings, an all-time high bonus for being male. Most sociologists agree that the major cause of the wage gap

From *Gender & Society,* Vol. 2, no. 1 (March 1988), pp. 58–81. Copyright © 1988 by Sociologists for Women in Society. Reprinted by permission of Sage Publications. References have been edited.

is the segregation of women and men into different kinds of work. Whether or not women freely choose the occupations in which they are concentrated, the outcome is the same: the more proportionately female an occupation, the lower its average wages. The high level of job segregation means that the 1963 law stipulating equal pay for equal work did little to reduce the wage gap.

This "causal model"—that the segregation of women and men into different occupations causes the wage gap—implies two possible remedies. One is to equalize men and women on the causal variable—occupation—by ensuring women's access to traditionally male occupations. The other is to replace occupation with a causal variable on which women and men differ less, by instituting comparable-worth pay policies that compensate workers for the "worth" of their job regardless of its sex composition.

I contend, however, that the preceding explanation of the wage gap is incorrect because it omits variables responsible for the difference between women and men in their distribution across occupations. If a causal model is incorrect, the remedies it implies may be ineffective. Lieberson's (1985, p. 185) critique of causal analysis as it is commonly practiced explicates the problem by distinguishing between *superficial* (or surface) causes that *appear* to give rise to a particular outcome and *basic* causes that *actually* produce the outcome. For example, he cites the belief that the black-white income gap is due to educational differences and thus can be reduced by reducing the educational disparity. As Lieberson pointed out, this analysis misses the fact that "the dominant group . . . uses its dominance to advance its own position" (p. 166), so that eliminating race differences in education is unlikely to reduce racial inequality in income because whites will find another way to maintain their income advantage. In other words, what appear in this example to be both the outcome variable (the black-white income gap) and the imputed causal variable (the black-white educational disparity) may stem from the same basic cause (whites' attempt to maintain their economic advantage). If so, then if the disparity in education were eliminated, some other factor would arise to produce the same economic consequence.

Dominant groups remain privileged because they write the rules, and the rules they write "enable them *to continue to write the rules*" (Lieberson 1985, p. 167; emphasis added). As a result, they can change the rules to thwart challenges to their position. Consider the following example. Because Asian American students tend to outscore occidentals on standard admissions tests, they are increasingly overrepresented in some university programs. Some universities have allegedly responded by imposing quotas for Asian students or weighing more heavily admissions criteria on which they believe Asian Americans do less well.

How can one tell whether a variable is a superficial or a basic cause of some outcome? Lieberson offered a straightforward test: Does a change in that variable lead to a change in the outcome? Applying this rule to the prevailing causal theory of the wage gap, we find that between 1970 and 1980 the index of occupational sex segregation declined by 10 percent, but the wage gap for full-time workers declined by just under 2 percent. Although its meaning may be equivocal, this finding is consistent with other evidence that attributing the wage gap to job segregation misses its basic cause: men's propensity to maintain their privileges. This claim is neither novel nor specific to men. Marxist and conflict theory have long recognized that dominant groups act to preserve their position. Like other dominant groups, men are reluctant to give up their advantages (Goode 1982). To avoid having to do so, they construct "rules" for distributing rewards that guarantee them the lion's share (see also Epstein 1985, p. 30). In the past, men cited their need as household heads for a "family wage" and designated women as secondary earners. Today, when millions of women who head households would benefit from such a rule, occupation has supplanted it as the principle for assigning wages.

Neoclassical economic theory holds that the market is the mechanism through which wages are set, but markets are merely systems of rules that dominant groups establish for their own purposes. When other groups, such as labor unions, amassed enough power, they modified the "market" principle. Steinberg (1987) observed that when consulted in making comparable-worth adjustments, male-dominated unions tended to support management over changes that would raise women's salaries.

In sum, the basic cause of the income gap is not sex segregation but men's desire to preserve their advantaged position and their ability to do so by establishing rules to distribute valued resources in their favor. Figure 1 represents this more complete causal model. Note that currently segregation is a superficial cause of the income gap, in part through "crowding," but that some other distributional system such as comparable-worth pay could replace it with the same effect.

With respect to income, this model implies that men will resist efforts to close the wage gap. Resistance will include opposing equalizing women's access to jobs because integration would equalize women and men on the current superficial

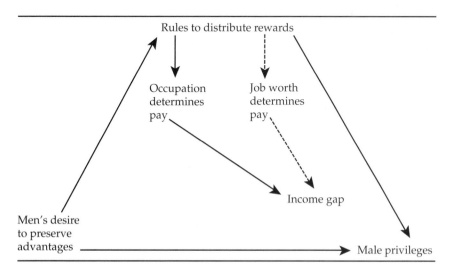

Figure 1.   Heuristic Model of the Wage Gap

cause of the wage gap—occupation. Men may also try to preserve job segregation because it is a central mechanism through which they retain their dominance in other spheres, and because many people learn to prefer the company of others like them. My theory also implies that men will resist efforts to replace occupation with alternative principles for assigning pay that would mitigate segregation's effect on women's wages (as pay equity purports to do).

Before I offer evidence for these claims, let us examine how dominant groups in general and men in particular maintain their privileged position. I formulate my analysis with reference to dominant groups to emphasize that the processes I discuss are not specific to sex classes. It also follows that, were women the dominant sex, the claims I make about men's behavior should hold for women.

DIFFERENTIATION, DEVALUATION, AND HIERARCHY

Differentiation—the practice of distinguishing categories based on some attribute—is the fundamental process in hierarchical systems, a logical necessity for differential evaluation and differential rewards. But differentiation involves much more than merely acting on a preexisting difference. In a hierarchical context, differentiation assumes, amplifies, and even creates psychological and behavioral differences in order to ensure that the subordinate group differs from the dominant group, "because the systematically differential delivery of benefits and deprivations require[s] making no mistake about who was who" (MacKinnon 1987, p. 40) and because "differences are inequality's post hoc excuse" (MacKinnon 1987, p. 8).

Differentiated status characteristics influence evaluations of people's behavior and their overall worth. In hierarchical systems in which differentiation takes the form of an Aristotelian dichotomy, individuals are classified as either A ("the subject") or Not-A ("the other"). But these two classes are not construed as natural opposites that both have positive qualities; instead, A's characteristics are valued as normal or good and Not-A's as without value or negative.

The official response to the influx of south- and central-eastern European immigrants to the United States early in this century, when people assumed that each European country represented a distinct biological race, illustrates differentiation's central role in dominance systems. A congressionally mandated immigration commission concluded that "innate, ineradicable race distinctions separated groups of men from one another" and agreed on the

> necessity of classifying these races to know which were most worthy of survival. The immediate problem was to ascertain "whether there may not be certain races that are inferior to other races . . . to discover some test to show whether some may be better fitted for American citizenship than others."
> (Lieberson 1980, pp. 2–26)

Thus differentiation in all its forms supports dominance systems by demonstrating that superordinate and subordinate groups differ in essential ways and that such differences are natural and even desirable.

"Sex Differentiation" Versus "Gender Differentiation": A Note on Terminology

Scholars speak of both "sex" and "gender" differentiation: the former when bio-logical sex or the "sex category" into which people are placed at birth is the *basis for* classification and differential treatment; the latter to refer to the *result* of that differential treatment. In order to emphasize that the initial biological difference (mediated through sex category) is the basis for differential treatment, I use the terms *sex differentiation* and *sex segregation*. This usage should not obscure the fact that the process of converting sex category into gender is a social one or that most differences that are assumed to distinguish the sexes are socially created. I agree with Kessler and McKenna (1978) that the "gender attribution process" assumes dimorphism and seeks evidence of it to justify classifying people as male and fe-male and treating them unequally. This article examines how and why those dif-ferences are produced.

Sex Differentiation and Devaluation

Probably no system of social differentiation is as extensive as that based on sex category. Its prevalence led anthropologist Gayle Rubin to claim that there is "a taboo against the sameness of men and women, a taboo dividing the sexes into two mutually exclusive categories, a taboo which exacerbates the biological differ-ences between the sexes and thereby *creates* gender" (1975, p. 178). Moreover, al-though femaleness is not always devalued, its deviation from maleness in a cul-ture that reserves virtues for men has meant the devaluation of women. Bleier's research on biological scientists' study of sex differences illustrates this point: the "search for the truth about differences, [implies] that difference means *different from the white male norm and, therefore, inferior*" (1987, p. 2; emphasis added). In con-sequence, men's activities are typically valued above women's, regardless of their content or importance for group survival, and both sexes come to devalue wo-men's efforts. Thus it should be no surprise that women's occupations pay less at least partly *because* women do them.

In short, differentiation is the sine qua non of dominance systems. Because of its importance, it is achieved through myriad ways:

> To go for a walk with one's eyes open is enough to demonstrate that humanity is divided into two classes of individuals whose clothes, faces, bodies, smiles, gaits, interests and occupations are manifestly different. (de Beauvoir 1953, p. xiv)

We differentiate groups in their location, appearance, and behavior, and in the tasks they do. Now let us turn to how these mechanisms operate to differentiate women and men.

PHYSICAL SEGREGATION

Dominant groups differentiate subordinate groups by physically isolating them—in ghettos, nurseries, segregated living quarters, and so on. Physical segregation fosters unequal treatment, because physically separate people can be treated differently and because it spares members of the dominant group the knowledge of the disparity and hides it from the subordinate group. Although women and men are integrated in some spheres, physical separation continues to differentiate them.

Cohn's (1985) vivid account of women's physical segregation in the British Foreign Office in the nineteenth century illustrates the extent to which organizations have gone to separate the sexes. The Foreign Office hid its first female typists in an attic, but it failed to rescind the requirement that workers collect their pay on the ground floor. When payday came, managers evacuated the corridors, shut all the doors, and then sent the women running down the attic stairs to get their checks and back up again. Only after they were out of sight were the corridors reopened to men.

This account raises the question of *why* managers segregate working men and women. What licentiousness did the Foreign Office fear would occur in integrated hallways? Contemporary answers are markedly similar to turn-of-the-century fears. Compare the scenario expressed in a 1923 editorial in the *Journal of Accountancy* ("any attempt at heterogeneous personnel [in after-hours auditing of banks] would hamper progress and lead to infinite embarrassment" [p. 151]) with recent reactions to the prospect of women integrating police patrol cars, coal mines, and merchant marine vessels (e.g., Martin 1980). At or just below the surface lies the specter of sexual liaisons. For years, McDonald's founder Ray Kroc forbade franchisees to hire women counter workers because they would attract "the wrong type" of customers. The U.S. Army ended sex-integrated basic training to "facilitate toughening goals," and the Air Force reevaluated whether women could serve on two-person Minuteman missile-silo teams because "it could lead to stress."

My thesis offers a more parsimonious alternative to these ad hoc explanations—men resist allowing women and men to work together *as equals* because doing so undermines differentiation and hence male dominance.

BEHAVIORAL DIFFERENTIATION

People's behavior is differentiated on their status-group membership in far too many ways for me to review the differences adequately here. I concentrate in this section on differentiation of behaviors that occur in the workplace: task differentiation and social differentiation.

Task differentiation assigns work according to group membership. It was expressed in the extreme in traditional Hindu society in which caste virtually determined life work. Task assignment based on sex category—the sexual division of labor—both prescribes and proscribes assorted tasks to each sex, and modern societies still assign men and women different roles in domestic work, labor-market work, and emotional and interpersonal work. Task differentiation generally assigns to lower-status groups the least desirable, most poorly rewarded work: menial, tedious, and degraded tasks, such as cleaning, disposing of waste, and caring for the dying. This practice symbolizes and legitimates the subordinate group's low status, while making it appear to have an affinity for these undesirable tasks.

As an added benefit, members of the dominant group don't have to do them! Important to discussions of the wage gap, because modern law and custom permit unequal pay for different work, task differentiation justifies paying the subordinate group lower wages, thereby ensuring their economic inferiority. Women's assignment to child care, viewed as unskilled work in our society, illustrates these patterns. Women are said to have a "natural talent" for it and similar work; men are relieved from doing it; society obtains free or cheap child care; and women are handicapped in competing with men. As researchers have shown, sex-based task differentiation of both nonmarket and market work legitimates women's lower pay, hinders women's ability to succeed in traditionally male enterprises, and, in general, reinforces men's hegemony.

Social differentiation is achieved through norms that set dominant and subordinate groups apart in their appearance (sumptuary rules) or behavior. When applied to sex, Goffman's (1976) concept of "gender display" encompasses both. Sumptuary rules require certain modes of dress, diet, or life-style of members of subordinate groups as emblems of their inferior status, and reserve other modes to distinguish the dominant group. For example, Rollins (1985) discovered that white female employers preferred black domestic employees to dress shabbily to exaggerate their economic inferiority. Sex-specific sumptuary rules are epitomized in norms that dictate divergent dress styles that often exaggerate physical sex differences and sometimes even incapacitate women. An extreme example is the *burqua* fundamentalist Muslim women wear as a symbol of their status and as a portable system of segregation.

Etiquette rules support differentiation by requiring subordinate group members to display ritualized deference toward dominants Relations between enlistees and officers or female domestic workers and their employers illustrate their role. Although typically it is the subordinate group that must defer, gender etiquette that requires middle- and upper-class men to display deference to women of the same classes preserves differentiation by highlighting women's differentness. Women who do not express gratitude or who refuse to accept the deference are faced with hostility, shattering the fiction that women hold the preferred position.

Physical segregation, behavioral differentiation, social separation, and even hierarchy are functional alternatives for satisfying the need for differentiation in domination systems. For example, when their physical integration with the dominant group means that a subordinate group's status differences might otherwise be invisible, special dress is usually required of them, as servants are required to wear uniforms. Physical separation can even compensate for the absence of hierarchy, a point acknowledged in the black folk saying that southern whites don't care how close blacks get if they don't get too high, and northern whites don't care how high blacks get if they don't get too close.

This substitutability explains why men will tolerate women in predominantly male work settings if they work in "women's" jobs and accept women doing "men's" jobs in traditionally female settings, but resist women doing traditionally male jobs in male work settings. Physical proximity per se is not threatening as long as another form of differentiation sets women apart. But the absence of *any* form of differentiation precludes devaluation and unequal rewards and hence threatens the sex-gender hierarchy. Because of the centrality of differentiation in domination systems, dominant groups have a considerable stake in maintaining it.

DOMINANTS' RESPONSE TO CHALLENGES

Dominants respond to subordinates' challenges by citing the group differences that supposedly warrant differential treatment. Serious challenges often give rise to attempts to demonstrate biological differences scientifically.

The nineteenth-century antislavery and women's rights movements led reputable scientists to try to prove that women's and blacks' brains were underdeveloped. The Great Migration to the United States in the first two decades of this century fueled a eugenics movement that purported to establish scientifically the inferiority of south- and central-eastern Europeans. The civil rights movement of the 1960s stimulated renewed efforts to establish racial differences in intelligence. And we are once again witnessing a spate of allegedly scientific research seeking a biological basis for presumed sex differences in cognitive ability and, specifically, for boys' higher average scores on math questions in some standardized tests. As Bleier pointed out, "The implication if not purposes of [such] research is to demonstrate that the structure of society faithfully reflects the natural order of things." According to Bleier, reputable journals have published studies that violate accepted standards of proof, and the scientific press has given dubious findings considerable attention (as in the news story in *Science* that asked, "Is There a Male Math Gene?"). Although subsequently these studies have been discredited, the debate serves its purpose by focusing attention on how groups differ.

MEN'S RESPONSE TO OCCUPATIONAL INTEGRATION

An influx of women into male spheres threatens the differentiation of men and women, and men resist. One response is to bar women's entry. Women have had to turn to the courts to win entry into Little League sports, college dining clubs, private professional clubs, and the Rotary. Recently, University of North Carolina trustees decried the fact that women are now a majority of UNC students, and some proposed changing the weights for certain admission criteria to restore the male majority. Twice since a shortage of male recruits forced the army to lift its quota on women, it has reduced the number of jobs open to women.

Numerous studies have documented men's resistance to women entering "their" jobs. Sometimes the resistance is simply exclusion; at other times it is subtle barriers that block women's advancement or open harassment. Now that more women hold managerial jobs, one hears of "a glass ceiling" that bars middle-management women from top-level positions, and Kanter (1987) claimed that organizations are changing the rules of what one must do to reach the top in order to make it more difficult for women to succeed.

My thesis implies that men will respond to women's challenge in the workplace by emphasizing how they differ from men. Especially common are reminders of women's "natural" roles as wife, mother, or sexual partner. Witness the recent—and subsequently disputed—claims that women who postponed marriage and childbearing to establish their careers had a negligible chance of finding husbands and were running the risk that their "biological clocks" would prevent pregnancy, and accounts of women dropping out of middle management to spend more time with their children.

Men who cannot bar women from "male" jobs can still preserve differentiation in other spheres. Their attempts to do so may explain why so few husbands of wage-working women share housework, as well as elucidating Wharton and Baron's (1987) finding that among men working in sex-integrated jobs, those whose wives were employed were more dissatisfied than unmarried men or men married to homemakers.

Another response to women's challenge is to weaken the mechanisms that have helped women advance in the workplace. Since 1980, the Reagan administration has sought to undermine equal-opportunity programs and affirmative-action regulations, and the campaign has partly succeeded. Efforts to dilute or eliminate Equal Employment Opportunity (EEO) programs are advanced by claims that sex inequality has disappeared (or that men now experience "reverse discrimination"). For example, the *New York Times* recently described the Department of Commerce announcement that women now compose the majority in professional occupations as a "historic milestone," adding that "the barriers have fallen."

THE ILLUSION OF OCCUPATIONAL INTEGRATION

If male resistance is so pervasive, how can we explain the drop in the index of occupational sex segregation in the 1970s and women's disproportionate gains in a modest number of male-dominated occupations? In order to answer this question, Patricia Roos and I embarked on a study of the changing sex composition of occupations. The results of our case studies of a dozen traditionally male occupations in which women made disproportionate statistical gains during the 1970s cast doubt on whether many women can advance economically through job integration.

The case studies revealed two general patterns. First, within many occupations nominally being integrated, men and women remain highly segregated, with men concentrated in the highest-status and best-paying jobs. For example, although women's representation in baking grew from 25 percent in 1970 to 41 percent in 1980, men continue to dominate production baking. The increase in women bakers is due almost wholly to their concentration in proliferating "in-store" bakeries. Although women now make up the majority of residential real estate salespersons, men still monopolize commercial sales.

The second pattern shows that women often gained access to these occupations after changes in work content and declines in autonomy or rewards made the work less attractive to men. In some occupations, the growth of functions already socially labeled as "women's work" (e.g., clerical, communications, or emotional work) spurred the change. For example, computerization and the ensuing clericalization prompted women's entry into typesetting and composing and insurance adjusting and examining. An increasing emphasis on communicating and interpersonal or emotional work contributed to women's gains in insurance sales, insurance adjusting and examining, systems analysis, public relations, and bank and financial management.

Brief summaries of our findings for two occupations illustrate these process-es. First, women's disproportionate gains in pharmacy have been largely confined to the retail sector (male pharmacists work disproportionately in research and management) and occurred after retail pharmacists lost professional status and entrepreneurial opportunities. After drug manufacturers took over the com-pounding of drugs, pharmacists increasingly resembled retail sales clerks; their primary duties became dispensing and record keeping. As chain and discount-store pharmacies supplanted independently owned pharmacies, retail pharmacy no longer offered a chance to own one's own business, reducing another tradition-al attraction for men. The resulting shortages of male pharmacy graduates eased women's access to training programs and retail jobs.

Second, book editing illustrates how declining autonomy and occupational prestige contributed to feminization of an occupation. For most of this century, the cultural image of publishing attracted bright young men and women despite very low wages. But during the 1970s, multinational conglomerates entered book pub-lishing, with profound results. Their emphasis on the bottom line robbed publish-ing of its cultural aura, and the search for blockbusters brought a greater role for marketing people in acquisition decisions, thereby eroding editorial autonomy. As a result, editing could no longer compete effectively for talented men who could choose from better opportunities. Because women's occupational choices are more limited than men's, editing still attracted them, and the occupation's sex composi-tion shifted accordingly.

In sum, although sex integration appears to have occurred in the 1970s among census-designated detailed occupations, our findings indicate that within these occupations, women are segregated into certain specialties or work settings and that they gained entry because various changes made the occupations less at-tractive to men. The nominal integration that occurred in the 1970s often masks within-occupation segregation or presages resegregation of traditionally male oc-cupations as women's work. In short, the workplace is still overwhelmingly dif-ferentiated by sex. Moreover, our preliminary results suggest that real incomes in the occupations we are studying declined during the 1970s; so reducing segrega-tion at the occupational level appears to have been relatively ineffective in reduc-ing the wage gap—and certainly not the remedy many experts predicted. This brings us to the other possible remedy for the wage gap—comparable worth.

IMPLICATIONS FOR COMPARABLE WORTH

The comparable-worth movement calls for equal pay for work of equal worth. Worth is usually determined by job-evaluation studies that measure the skill, ef-fort, and responsibility required, but in practice, assessing worth often turns on how to conceptualize and measure skill.

Although some objective criteria exist for assessing skill (e.g., how long it takes a worker to learn the job, typically the designation of work as skilled is socially negotiated. Workers are most likely to win it when they control social resources that permit them to press their claims, such as a monopoly over a labor supply or authority based on their personal characteristics such as education, training, or sex. As a result, the evaluation of "skill" is shaped by and confounded with workers' sex.

Groups use the same power that enabled them to define their work as skilled to restrict competition by excluding women (among others) from training for and practicing their trade or profession, as Millicent Fawcett recognized almost a hundred years ago when she declared, "Equal pay for equal work is a fraud for women." Because men use their power to keep women "from obtaining equal skills, their work [cannot be] equal" (Hartmann 1976, p. 157). Roos's (1986) case history of the effect of technological change on women's employment in typesetting illustrates these points. When a Linotype machine was developed that "female typists could operate," the International Typographical Union (ITU) used its labor monopoly to force employers to agree to hire as operators only skilled printers who knew *all* aspects of the trade. By denying women access to apprenticeships or other channels to become fully skilled and limiting the job of operating the Linotype to highly skilled printers, the ITU effectively barred women from the new Linotype jobs. In short, the ITU used its monopoly power both to restrict women's access to skills and credentials and to define its members as "uniquely skilled" to operate the Linotype.

Excluded from occupations male workers define as skilled, women are often unable, for several reasons, to press the claim that work in traditionally female occupations is skilled. First, as I have shown, the devaluation of women's work leads whatever work women do to be seen as unskilled. Second, women's powerlessness prevents their successfully defining their work—caring for children, entering data, assembling microelectronic circuits—as skilled. Third, because many female-dominated occupations require workers to acquire skills before employment, skill acquisition is less visible and hence unlikely to be socially credited. Fourth, the scarcity of apprenticeship programs for women's jobs and women's exclusion from other programs denies women a credential society recognizes as denoting skill. Finally, "much of women's work involves recognizing and responding to subtle cues" (Feldberg 1984, p. 321), but the notion of "women's intuition" permits men to define such skills as inborn and hence not meriting compensation. Thus women are both kept from acquiring socially valued skills and not credited for those they do acquire. As a result, the sex of the majority of workers in an occupation influences whether or not their work is classified as skilled.

In view of these patterns, how effective can comparable worth be in reducing the wage gap? As with the Equal Pay Act, implementing it has symbolic value. Moreover, it would bar employers from underpaying women relative to their job-evaluation scores, the practice alleged in *AFSCME v. Washington State* (1985). But setting salaries according to an occupation's worth will reduce the wage gap only to the extent that (1) women have access to tasks that society values, (2) evaluators do not take workers' sex into account in determining a job's worth, and (3) implementers do not sacrifice equity to other political agendas.

Neither of the first two conditions holds. As I have shown, men already dominate jobs society deems skilled. Moreover, the tendency to devalue women's work is embedded in job-evaluation techniques that define job worth; so such techniques may yield biased evaluations of traditionally female jobs and lower their job-evaluation scores. Beyond these difficulties is the problem of good-faith implementation. Acker (1987), Brenner (1987), and Steinberg (1987) have documented the problems in implementing comparable-worth pay adjustments. According to Steinberg (p. 8), New York State's proposed compensation model *negatively* values working with difficult clients, work performed in historically female and minority jobs (in other words, workers lose pay for doing it!), and Massachusetts plans to establish separate comparable-worth plans across sex-segregated bargaining units. For these reasons, the magnitude of comparable-worth adjustments have been about half of what experts expected—only 5 percent to 15 percent of salaries (Steinberg 1987).

Moreover, to the extent that equity adjustments significantly raise salaries in women's jobs, men can use their power to monopolize them. It is no accident that the men who integrated the female semiprofessions moved rapidly to the top. The recent experience of athletic directors provides an additional illustration. Title IX required college athletic programs to eliminate disparities in resources between women's and men's programs including salaries. Within ten years the proportion of coaches for women's programs who were male grew from 10 percent to 50 percent. Finally, men as the primary implementers of job evaluation have a second line of defense—they can and do subvert the process of job evaluation.

CONCLUSION

Integrating men's jobs and implementing comparable-worth programs have helped some women economically and, more fully implemented, would help others. But neither strategy can be broadly effective because both are premised on a flawed causal model of the pay gap that assigns primary responsibility to job segregation. A theory that purports to explain unequal outcomes without examining the dominant group's stake in maintaining them is incomplete. Like other dominant groups, men make rules that preserve their privileges. With respect to earnings, the current rule—that one's job or occupation determines one's pay—has maintained white men's economic advantage because men and women and whites and nonwhites are differently distributed across jobs.

Changing the allocation principle from occupation to job worth would help nonwhites and women if occupation were the pay gap's basic cause. But it is not. As long as a dominant group wants to subordinate others' interests to its own and is able to do so, the outcome—distributing more income to men than women—is, in a sense, its own cause, and tinkering with superficial causes will not substantially alter the outcome. Either the rule that one's occupation determines one's wages exists *because* men and women hold different occupations, or men and women hold different occupations because we allocate wages according to one's occupation. Obviously the dominant group will resist attempts to change the rules. In *Lemon v. City and County of Denver* (1980), the court called comparable worth "pregnant with the possibility of disrupting the entire economic system" (Steinberg 1987). "Disrupting the entire white-male dominance system" would have been closer to the mark.

If men's desire to preserve their privileges is the basic cause of the wage gap, then how can we bring about change? The beneficiaries of hierarchical reward systems yield their privileges only when failing to yield is more costly than yielding. Increasing the costs men pay to maintain the status quo or rewarding men for dividing resources more equitably may reduce their resistance.

As individuals, many men will gain economically if their partners earn higher wages. Of course, these men stand to lose whatever advantages come from out-earning one's partner. But more important than individual adjustments are those achieved through organizations that have the power to impose rewards and penalties. Firms that recognize their economic stake in treating women equitably (or can be pressed by women employees or EEO agencies to act as if they do) can be an important source of pressure on male employees. Employers have effectively used various incentives to overcome resistance to affirmative action (e.g., rewarding supervisors for treating women fairly [Shaeffer and Lynton 1979; Walshok 1981]). Employers are most likely to use such mechanisms if they believe that regulatory agencies are enforcing equal-opportunity rules. We can attack men's resistance through political pressure on employers, the regulatory agencies that monitor them, and branches of government that establish and fund such agencies.

Analyses of sex inequality in the 1980s implicitly advance a no-fault concept of institutionalized discrimination rather than fixing any responsibility on men. But men *are* the dominant group, the makers and the beneficiaries of the rules. Of course, most men do not consciously oppose equality for women or try to thwart women's progress. When men and women work together, both can gain, as occurred when the largely male blue-collar union supported the striking Yale clerical and technical workers. But as a rule, this silent majority avoids the fray, leaving the field to those who do resist to act on behalf of all men. It is time to bring men back into our theories of economic inequality. To do so does not imply that women are passive agents. The gains we have made in the last two decades in the struggle for economic equality—redefining the kinds of work women can do, reshaping young people's aspirations, and amassing popular support for pay equity despite opponents' attempt to write it off as a "loony tune" idea—stand as testimony to the contrary. Just as the causal model I propose views the dominant group's self-interest as the source of unequal outcomes, so too does it see subordinate groups as the agents of change.

References

Acker, Joan. 1987. "Sex Bias in Job Evaluation: A Comparable-Worth Issue." Pp. 183–96 in *Ingredients for Women's Employment Policy,* edited by Christine Bose and Glenna Spitze. Albany: SUNY University Press.

AFSCME v. *State of Washington.* 1985. 770 F.2d 1401. 9th Circuit.

Bleier, Ruth. 1987. "Gender Ideology: The Medical and Scientific Construction of Women." Lecture presented at the University of Illinois, Urbana.

Brenner, Johanna. 1987. "Feminist Political Discourses: Radical vs. Liberal Approaches to the Feminization of Poverty and Comparable Worth." *Gender & Society* 1:447–65.

Cohn, Samuel. 1985. *The Process of Occupational Sex Typing.* Philadelphia: Temple University Press.

de Beauvoir, Simone. 1953. *The Second Sex.* New York: Knopf.

Epstein, Cynthia F. 1985. "Ideal Roles and Real Roles or the Fallacy of Misplaced Dichotomy." *Research on Social Stratification and Mobility* 4:29–51.

Feldberg, Roslyn L. 1984. "Comparable Worth: Toward Theory and Practice in the U.S." *Signs: Journal of Women in Culture and Society* 10:311–28.

Goffman, Erving. 1976. "Gender Display." *Studies in the Anthropology of Visual Communication* 3:69–77.

Goode, William C. 1964. *The Family.* Englewood Cliffs, NJ: Prentice Hall.

Hartmann, Heidi. 1976. "Capitalism, Patriarchy, and Job Segregation by Sex." *Signs: Journal of Women in Culture and Society* 1 (Part 2):137–69.

Kanter, Rosabeth Moss. 1987. "Men and Women of the Change Master Corporation (1977–1987 and Beyond): Dilemmas and Consequences of Innovations of Organizational Structure." Paper presented at Annual Meetings, Academy of Management, New Orleans.

Kessler, Suzanne and Wendy McKenna. 1978. *Gender: An Ethnomethodological Approach.* New York: John Wiley.

Lieberson, Stanley. 1980. *A Piece of the Pie.* Berkeley: University of California Press.

———. 1985. *Making It Count.* Berkeley: University of California Press.

MacKinnon, Catharine. 1987. *Feminism Unmodified.* Cambridge, MA: Harvard University Press.

Martin, Susan E. 1980. *Breaking and Entering.* Berkeley: University of California Press.

Rollins, Judith. 1985. *Between Women.* Philadelphia: Temple University Press.

Roos, Patricia A. 1986. "Women in the Composing Room: Technology and Organization as the Determinants of Social Change." Paper presented at Annual Meetings, American Sociological Association, New York.

Rubin, Gayle. 1975. "The Traffic in Women: Notes on the 'Political Economy' of Sex." Pp. 157–210 in *Toward an Anthropology of Women,* edited by Rayna R. Reiter. New York: Monthly Review Press.

Shaeffer, Ruth Gilbert and Edith F. Lynton. 1979. *Corporate Experience in Improving Women's Job Opportunities.* Report no. 755. New York: The Conference Board.

Steiger, Thomas. 1987. "Female Employment Gains and Sex Segregation: The Case of Bakers." Paper presented at Annual Meetings, American Sociological Association, Chicago.

Steinberg, Ronnie J. 1987. "Radical Challenges in a Liberal World: The Mixed Successes of Comparable Worth." *Gender & Society* 1:466–75.

Walshok, Mary Lindenstein. 1981. "Some Innovations in Industrial Apprenticeship at General Motors." Pp. 173–82 in *Apprenticeship Research: Emerging Findings and Future Trends* edited by Vernon M. Briggs, Jr., and Felician Foltman. Ithaca: New York State School of Industrial Relations.

CHRISTINE L. WILLIAMS

The Glass Escalator: Hidden Advantages for Men in the "Female" Professions

The sex segregation of the U.S. labor force is one of the most perplexing and tenacious problems in our society. Even though the proportion of men and women in the labor force is approaching parity (particularly for younger cohorts of workers), men and women are still generally confined to predominantly single-sex occupations. Forty percent of men or women would have to change major occupational categories to achieve equal representation of men and women in all jobs, but even this figure underestimates the true degree of sex segregation. It is extremely rare to find specific jobs where equal numbers of men and women are engaged in the same activities in the same industries.

Most studies of sex segregation in the work force have focused on women's experiences in male-dominated occupations. Both researchers and advocates for social change have focused on the barriers faced by women who try to integrate predominantly male fields. Few have looked at the "flip-side" of occupational sex segregation: the exclusion of men from predominantly female occupations. But the fact is that men are less likely to enter female sex-typed occupations than women are to enter male-dominated jobs. Reskin and Roos, for example, were able to identify 33 occupations in which female representation increased by more than nine percentage points between 1970 and 1980, but only three occupations in which the proportion of men increased as radically (1990).

In this paper, I examine men's underrepresentation in four predominantly female occupations—nursing, librarianship, elementary school teaching, and social work. Throughout the twentieth century, these occupations have been identified with "women's work"—even though prior to the Civil War, men were more likely to be employed in these areas. These four occupations, often called the female "semi-professions," today range from 5.5 percent male (in nursing) to 32 percent male (in social work). (See Table 1.) These percentages have not changed substantially in decades. In fact, as Table 1 indicates, two of these professions—librarianship and social work—have experienced declines in the proportions of men since 1975. Nursing is the only one of the four experiencing noticeable changes in sex composition, with the proportion of men increasing 80 percent between 1975 and 1990. Even so, men continue to be a tiny minority of all nurses.

From *Social Problems*, Vol. 39, no. 3 (August 1992), pp. 253–267. Copyright © 1992 by The Society for the Study of Social Problems. Reprinted by permission of University of California Press. References have been edited.

Table 1.
Percent Male in Selected Occupations, Selected Years

Profession	1990	1980	1975
Nurses	5.5	3.5	3.0
Elementary teachers	14.8	16.3	14.6
Librarians	16.7	14.8	18.9
Social workers	31.8	35.0	39.2

Source: U.S. Department of Labor. Bureau of Labor Statistics. *Employment and Earnings* 38:1 (January 1991), Table 22 (Employed civilians by detailed occupation), 185; 28:1 (January 1981), Table 23 (Employed persons by detailed occupation), 180; 22:7 (January 1976), Table 2 (Employed persons by detailed occupation), 11.

Although there are many possible reasons for the continuing preponderance of women in these fields, the focus of this paper is discrimination. Researchers examining the integration of women into "male fields" have identified discrimination as a major barrier to women. This discrimination has taken the form of laws or institutionalized rules prohibiting the hiring or promotion of women into certain job specialties. Discrimination can also be "informal," as when women encounter sexual harassment, sabotage, or other forms of hostility from their male co-workers resulting in a poisoned work environment. Women in nontraditional occupations also report feeling stigmatized by clients when their work puts them in contact with the public. In particular, women in engineering and blue-collar occupations encounter gender-based stereotypes about their competence which undermine their work performance. Each of these forms of discrimination—legal, informal, and cultural—contributes to women's underrepresentation in predominantly male occupations.

The assumption in much of this literature is that any member of a token group in a work setting will probably experience similar discriminatory treatment. Kanter (1977), who is best known for articulating this perspective in her theory of tokenism, argues that when any group represents less than 15 percent of an organization, its members will be subject to predictable forms of discrimination. Likewise, Jacobs argues that "in some ways, men in female-dominated occupations experience the same difficulties that women in male-dominated occupations face" (1989:167), and Reskin contends that any dominant group in an occupation will use their power to maintain a privileged position (1988:62).

However, the few studies that have considered men's experience in gender atypical occupations suggest that men may not face discrimination or prejudice when they integrate predominantly female occupations. Zimmer (1988) and Martin (1988) both contend that the effects of sexism can outweigh the effects of tokenism when men enter nontraditional occupations. This study is the first to systematically explore this question using data from four occupations. I examine the barriers to men's entry into these professions; the support men receive from their supervisors, colleagues and clients; and the reactions they encounter from the public (those outside their professions).

METHODS

I conducted in-depth interviews with 76 men and 23 women in four occupations from 1985–1991. Interviews were conducted in four metropolitan areas: San Francisco/Oakland, California; Austin, Texas; Boston, Massachusetts; and Phoenix, Arizona. These four areas were selected because they show considerable variation in the proportions of men in the four professions. For example, Austin has one of the highest percentages of men in nursing (7.7 percent), whereas Phoenix's percentage is one of the lowest (2.7 percent). The sample was generated using "snowballing" techniques. Women were included in the sample to gauge their feelings and responses to men who enter "their" professions.

Like the people employed in these professions generally, those in my sample were predominantly white (90 percent). Their ages ranged from 20 to 66 and the average age was 38. The interview questionnaire consisted of several open-ended questions on four broad topics: motivation to enter the profession; experiences in training; career progression; and general views about men's status and prospects within these occupations. I conducted all the interviews, which generally lasted between one and two hours. Interviews took place in restaurants, my home or office, or the respondent's home or office. Interviews were tape-recorded and transcribed for the analysis.

Data analysis followed the coding techniques described by Strauss (1987). Each transcript was read several times and analyzed into emergent conceptual categories. Likewise, Strauss' principle of theoretical sampling was used. Individual respondents were purposively selected to capture the array of men's experiences in these occupations. Thus, I interviewed practitioners in every specialty, oversampling those employed in the *most* gender atypical areas (e.g., male kindergarten teachers). I also selected respondents from throughout their occupational hierarchies—from students to administrators to retirees. Although the data do not permit within-group comparisons, I am reasonably certain that the sample does capture a wide range of experiences common to men in these female-dominated professions. However, like all findings based on qualitative data, it is uncertain whether the findings generalize to the larger population of men in nontraditional occupations.

In this paper, I review individuals' responses to questions about discrimination in hiring practices, on-the-job rapport with supervisors and co-workers, and prejudice from clients and others outside their profession.

DISCRIMINATION IN HIRING

Contrary to the experience of many women in the male-dominated professions, many of the men and women I spoke to indicated that there is a *preference* for hiring men in these four occupations. A Texas librarian at a junior high school said that his school district "would hire a male over a female."

I: Why do you think that is?

R: Because there are so few, and the . . . ones that they do have, the library directors seem to really . . . think they're doing great jobs. I don't know, maybe they just feel they're being progressive or something, [but] I have had a real sense that they really appreciate having a male, particularly at the junior high. . . . As I said, when seven of us lost our jobs from the high schools and were redistributed, there were only four positions at junior high, and I got one of them. Three of the librarians, some who had been here longer than I had with the school district, were put down in elementary school as librarians. And I definitely think that being male made a difference in my being moved to the junior high rather than an elementary school.

Many of the men perceived their token status as males in predominantly female occupations as an *advantage* in hiring and promotions. I asked an Arizona teacher whether his specialty (elementary special education) was an unusual area for men compared to other areas within education. He said,

> Much more so. I am extremely marketable in special education. That's not why I got into the field. But I am extremely marketable because I am a man.

In several cases, the more female-dominated the specialty, the greater the apparent preference for men. For example, when asked if he encountered any problem getting a job in pediatrics, a Massachusetts nurse said,

> No, no, none. . . . I've heard this from managers and supervisory-type people with men in pediatrics: "It's nice to have a man because it's such a female-dominated profession."

However, there were some exceptions to this preference for men in the most female-dominated specialties. In some cases, formal policies actually barred men from certain jobs. This was the case in some rural Texas school districts, which refused to hire men in the youngest grades (K–3). Some nurses also reported being excluded from positions in obstetrics and gynecology wards, a policy encountered more frequently in private Catholic hospitals.

But often the pressures keeping men out of certain specialties were more subtle than this. Some men described being "tracked" into practice areas within their professions which were considered more legitimate for men. For example, one Texas man described how he was pushed into administration and planning in social work, even though "I'm not interested in writing policy; I'm much more interested in research and clinical stuff." A nurse who is interested in pursuing graduate study in family and child health in Boston said he was dissuaded from entering the program specialty in favor of a concentration in "adult nursing." A kindergarten teacher described the difficulty of finding a job in his specialty after graduation: "I was recruited immediately to start getting into a track to become an administrator. And it was men who recruited me. It was men that ran the system at that time, especially in Los Angeles."

This tracking may bar men from the most female-identified specialties within these professions. But men are effectively being "kicked upstairs" in the process. Those specialties considered more legitimate practice areas for men also tend to be the most prestigious, better paying ones. A distinguished kindergarten teacher, who had been voted city-wide "Teacher of the Year," told me that even though people were pleased to see him in the classroom, "there's been some encouragement to think about administration, and there's been some encouragement to think about teaching at the university level or something like that, or supervisory-type position." That is, despite his aptitude and interest in staying in the classroom, he felt pushed in the direction of administration.

The effect of this "tracking" is the opposite of that experienced by women in male-dominated occupations. Researchers have reported that many women encounter a "glass ceiling" in their efforts to scale organizational and professional hierarchies. That is, they are constrained by invisible barriers to promotion in their careers, caused mainly by sexist attitudes of men in the highest positions (Freeman 1990). In contrast to the "glass ceiling," many of the men I interviewed seem to encounter a "glass escalator." Often, despite their intentions, they face invisible pressures to move up in their professions. As if on a moving escalator, they must work to stay in place.

A public librarian specializing in children's collections (a heavily female-dominated concentration) described an encounter with this "escalator" in his very first job out of library school. In his first six-months' evaluation, his supervisors commended him for his good work in storytelling and related activities, but they criticized him for "not shooting high enough."

> Seriously. That's literally what they were telling me. They assumed that because I was a male—and they told me this—and that I was being hired right out of graduate school, that somehow I wasn't doing the kind of management-oriented work that they thought I should be doing. And as a result, really they had a lot of bad marks, as it were, against me on my evaluation. And I said I couldn't believe this!

Throughout his ten-year career, he has had to struggle to remain in children's collections.

The glass escalator does not operate at all levels. In particular, men in academia reported some gender-based discrimination in the highest positions due to their universities' commitment to affirmative action. Two nursing professors reported that they felt their own chances of promotion to deanships were nil because their universities viewed the position of nursing dean as a guaranteed female appointment in an otherwise heavily male-dominated administration. One California social work professor reported his university canceled its search for a dean because no minority male or female candidates had been placed on their short list. It was rumored that other schools on campus were permitted to go forward with their searches—even though they also failed to put forward names of minority candidates—because the higher administration perceived it to be "easier" to fulfill affirmative action goals in the social work school. The interviews provide greater evidence of the "glass escalator" at work in the lower levels of these professions.

Of course, men's motivations also play a role in their advancement to higher professional positions. I do not mean to suggest that the men I talked to all resented the informal tracking they experienced. For many men, leaving the most female-identified areas of their professions helped them resolve internal conflicts involving their masculinity. One man left his job as a school social worker to work in a methadone drug treatment program not because he was encouraged to leave by his colleagues, but because "I think there was some macho shit there, to tell you the truth, because I remember feeling a little uncomfortable there. . . ; it didn't feel right to me." Another social worker, employed in the mental health services department of a large urban area in California, reflected on his move into administration:

> The more I think about it, through our discussion, I'm sure that's a large part of why I wound up in administration. It's okay for a man to do the administration. In fact, I don't know if I fully answered a question that you asked a little while ago about how did being male contribute to my advancing in the field. I was saying it wasn't because I got any special favoritism as a man, but . . . I think . . . because I'm a man, I felt a need to get into this kind of position. I may have worked harder toward it, may have competed harder for it, than most women would do, even women who think about doing administrative work.

Elsewhere I have speculated on the origins of men's tendency to define masculinity through single-sex work environments. Clearly, personal ambition does play a role in accounting for men's movement into more "male-defined" arenas within these professions. But these occupations also structure opportunities for males independent of their individual desires or motives.

The interviews suggest that men's under-representation in these professions cannot be attributed to discrimination in hiring or promotions. Many of the men indicated that they received preferential treatment because they were men. Although men mentioned gender discrimination in the hiring process, for the most part they were channelled into the more "masculine" specialties within these professions, which ironically meant being "tracked" into better paying and more prestigious specialties.

SUPERVISORS AND COLLEAGUES: THE WORKING ENVIRONMENT

Researchers claim that subtle forms of work place discrimination push women out of male-dominated occupations. In particular, women report feeling excluded from informal leadership and decision-making networks, and they sense hostility from their male co-workers, which makes them feel uncomfortable and unwanted. Respondents in this study were asked about their relationships with supervisors and female colleagues to ascertain whether men also experienced "poisoned" work environments when entering gender atypical occupations.

A major difference in the experience of men and women in nontraditional occupations is that men in these situations are far more likely to be supervised by a member of their own sex. In each of the four professions I studied, men are overrepresented in administrative and managerial capacities, or, as in the case of nursing, their positions in the organizational hierarchy are governed by men. Thus, unlike women who enter "male fields," the men in these professions often work under the direct supervision of other men.

Many of the men interviewed reported that they had good rapport with their male supervisors. Even in professional school, some men reported extremely close relationships with their male professors. For example, a Texas librarian described an unusually intimate association with two male professors in graduate school:

> I can remember a lot of times in the classroom there would be discussions about a particular topic or issue, and the conversation would spill over into their office hours, after the class was over. And even though there were . . . a couple of the other women that had been in on the discussion, they weren't there. And I don't know if that was preferential or not . . . it certainly carried over into personal life as well. Not just at the school and that sort of thing. I mean, we would get together for dinner . . .

These professors explicitly encouraged him because he was male:

> I: Did they ever offer you explicit words of encouragement about being in the profession by virtue of the fact that you were male? . . .
>
> R: Definitely. On several occasions. Yeah. Both of these guys, for sure, including the Dean who was male also. And it's an interesting point that you bring up because it was, oftentimes, kind of in a sign, you know. It wasn't in the classroom, and it wasn't in front of the group, or if we were in the student lounge or something like that. It was . . . if it was just myself or maybe another one of the guys, you know, and just talking in the office. It's like . . . you know, kind of an opening-up and saying, "You know, you are really lucky that you're in the profession because you'll really go to the top real quick, and you'll be able to make real definite improvements and changes. And you'll have a real influence," and all this sort of thing. I mean, really, I can remember several times.

Other men reported similar closeness with their professors. A Texas psychotherapist recalled his relationships with his male professors in social work school:

> I made it a point to make a golfing buddy with one of the guys that was in administration. He and I played golf a lot. He was the guy who kind of ran the research training, the research part of the master's program. Then there was a sociologist who ran the other part of the research program. He and I developed a good friendship.

This close mentoring by male professors contrasts with the reported experience of women in nontraditional occupations. Others have noted a lack of solidarity among women in nontraditional occupations. Writing about military academies, for example, Yoder describes the failure of token women to mentor succeeding generations of female cadets. She argues that women attempt to play down their gender difference from men because it is the source of scorn and derision.

> Because women felt unaccepted by their male colleagues, one of the last things they wanted to do was to emphasize their gender. Some women thought that, if they kept company with other women, this would highlight their gender and would further isolate them from male cadets. These women desperately wanted to be accepted as cadets, not as *women* cadets. Therefore, they did everything from not wearing skirts as an option with their uniforms to avoiding being a part of a group of women. (Yoder 1989:532)

Men in nontraditional occupations face a different scenario—their gender is construed as a *positive* difference. Therefore, they have an incentive to bond together and emphasize their distinctiveness from the female majority.

Close, personal ties with male supervisors were also described by men once they were established in their professional careers. It was not uncommon in education, for example, for the male principal to informally socialize with the male staff, as a Texas special education teacher describes:

> Occasionally I've had a principal who would regard me as "the other man on the campus" and "it's us against them," you know? I mean, nothing really that extreme, except that some male principals feel like there's nobody there to talk to except the other man. So I've been in that position.

These personal ties can have important consequences for men's careers. For example, one California nurse, whose performance was judged marginal by his nursing supervisors, was transferred to the emergency room staff (a prestigious promotion) due to his personal friendship with the physician in charge. A Massachusetts teacher acknowledged that his principal's personal interest in him landed him his current job.

> I: You had mentioned that your principal had sort of spotted you at your previous job and had wanted to bring you here [to this

> school]. Do you think that has anything to do with the fact that you're a man, aside from your skills as a teacher?
>
> R: Yes, I would say in that particular case, that was part of it. . . . We have certain things in common, certain interests that really lined up.
>
> I: Vis-à-vis teaching?
>
> R: Well, more extraneous things—running specifically, and music. And we just seemed to get along real well right off the bat. It is just kind of a guy thing; we just liked each other . . .

Interviewees did not report many instances of male supervisors discriminating against them, or refusing to accept them because they were male. Indeed, these men were much more likely to report that their male bosses discriminated against the *females* in their professions. When asked if he thought physicians treated male and female nurses differently, a Texas nurse said:

> I think yeah, some of them do. I think the women seem like they have a lot more trouble with the physicians treating them in a derogatory manner. Or, if not derogatory, then in a very paternalistic way than the men [are treated]. Usually if a physician is mad at a male nurse, he just kind of yells at him. Kind of like an employee. And if they're mad at a female nurse, rather than treat them on an equal basis, in terms of just letting their anger out at them as an employee, they're more paternalistic or there's some sexual harassment component to it.

A Texas teacher perceived a similar situation where he worked:

> I've never felt unjustly treated by a principal because I'm a male. The principals that I've seen that I felt are doing things that are kind of arbitrary or not well thought out are doing it to everybody. In fact, they're probably doing it to the females worse than they are to me.

Openly gay men may encounter less favorable treatment at the hands of their supervisors. For example, a nurse in Texas stated that one of the physicians he worked with preferred to staff the operating room with male nurses exclusively— as long as they weren't gay. Stigma associated with homosexuality leads some men to enhance, or even exaggerate their "masculine" qualities, and may be another factor pushing men into more "acceptable" specialties for men.

Not all men who work in these occupations are supervised by men. Many of the men interviewed who had female bosses also reported high levels of acceptance—although levels of intimacy with women seemed lower than with other men. In some cases, however, men reported feeling shut-out from decision making when the higher administration was constituted entirely by women. I asked an Arizona librarian whether men in the library profession were discriminated against in hiring because of their sex:

> Professionally speaking, people go to considerable lengths to keep that kind of thing out of their [hiring] deliberations. Personally, is another matter. It's pretty common around here to talk about the "old girl network." This is one of the few libraries that I've had any intimate knowledge of which is actually controlled by women. . . . Most of the department heads and upper level administrators are women. And there's an "old girl network" that works just like the "old boy network," except that the important conferences take place in the women's room rather than on the golf course. But the political mechanism is the same, the exclusion of the other sex from decision making is the same. The reasons are the same. It's somewhat discouraging. . . .

Although I did not interview many supervisors, I did include 23 women in my sample to ascertain their perspectives about the presence of men in their professions. All of the women I interviewed claimed to be supportive of their male colleagues, but some conveyed ambivalence. For example, a social work professor said she would like to see more men enter the social work profession, particularly in the clinical specialty (where they are underrepresented). Indeed, she favored affirmative action hiring guidelines for men in the profession. Yet, she resented the fact that her department hired "another white male" during a recent search. I questioned her about this ambivalence:

> *I:* I find it very interesting that, on the one hand, you sort of perceive this preference and perhaps even sexism with regard to how men are evaluated and how they achieve higher positions within the profession, yet, on the other hand, you would be encouraging of more men to enter the field. Is that contradictory to you, or . . .?
>
> *R:* Yeah, it's contradictory.

It appears that women are generally eager to see men enter "their" occupations. Indeed, several men noted that their female colleagues had facilitated their careers in various ways (including mentorship in college). However, at the same time, women often resent the apparent ease with which men advance within these professions, sensing that men at the higher levels receive preferential treatment which closes off advancement opportunities for women.

But this ambivalence does not seem to translate into the "poisoned" work environment described by many women who work in male-dominated occupations. Among the male interviewees, there were no accounts of sexual harassment. However, women do treat their male colleagues differently on occasion. It is not uncommon in nursing, for example, for men to be called upon to help catheterize male patients, or to lift especially heavy patients. Some librarians also said that women asked them to lift and move heavy boxes of books because they were men.

Teachers sometimes confront differential treatment as well, as described by this Texas teacher:

> As a man, you're teaching with all women, and that can be hard sometimes. Just because of the stereotypes, you know. I'm real into computers . . . and all the time people are calling me to fix their computer. Or if somebody gets a flat tire, they come and get me. I mean, there are just a lot of stereotypes. Not that I mind doing any of those things, but it's . . . you know, it just kind of bugs me that it is a stereotype, "A man should do that." Or if their kids have a lot of discipline problems, that kiddo's in your room. Or if there are kids that don't have a father in their home, that kid's in your room. Hell, nowadays that'd be half the school in my room (laughs). But you know, all the time I hear from the principal or from other teachers, "Well, this child really needs a man . . . a male role model" (laughs). So there are a lot of stereotypes that . . . men kind of get stuck with.

This special treatment bothered some respondents. Getting assigned all the "discipline problems" can make for difficult working conditions, for example. But many men claimed this differential treatment did not cause distress. In fact, several said they liked being appreciated for the special traits and abilities (such as strength) they could contribute to their professions.

Furthermore, women's special treatment sometimes enhanced—rather than poisoned—the men's work environments. One Texas librarian said he felt "more comfortable working with women than men" because "I think it has something to do with control. Maybe it's that women will let me take control more than men will." Several men reported that their female colleagues often cast them into leadership roles. Although not all savored this distinction, it did enhance their authority and control in the work place. In subtle (and not-too-subtle) ways, then, differential treatment contributes to the "glass escalator" men experience in nontraditional professions.

Even outside work, most of the men interviewed said they felt fully accepted by their female colleagues. They were usually included in informal socializing occasions with the women—even though this frequently meant attending baby showers or Tupperware parties. Many said that they declined offers to attend these events because they were not interested in "women's things," although several others claimed to attend everything: The minority men I interviewed seemed to feel the least comfortable in these informal contexts. One social worker in Arizona was asked about socializing with his female colleagues:

> I: So in general, for example, if all the employees were going to get together to have a party, or celebrate a bridal shower or whatever, would you be invited along with the rest of the group?
>
> R: They would invite me, I would say, somewhat reluctantly. Being a black male, working with all white females, it did cause some outside problems. So I didn't go to a lot of functions with them . . .

I: You felt that there was some tension there on the level of your acceptance . . .?

R: Yeah. It was OK working, but on the outside, personally, there was some tension there. It never came out, that they said, "Because of who you are we can't invite you" (laughs), and I wouldn't have done anything anyway. I would have probably respected them more for saying what was on their minds. But I never felt completely in with the group.

Some single men also said they felt uncomfortable socializing with married female colleagues because it gave the "wrong impression." But in general, the men said that they felt very comfortable around their colleagues and described their work places as very congenial for men. It appears unlikely, therefore, that men's under-representation in these professions is due to hostility towards men on the part of supervisors or women workers.

DISCRIMINATION FROM "OUTSIDERS"

The most compelling evidence of discrimination against men in these professions is related to their dealings with the public. Men often encounter negative stereotypes when they come into contact with clients or "outsiders"—people they meet outside of work. For instance, it is popularly assumed that male nurses are gay. Librarians encounter images of themselves as "wimpy" and asexual. Male social workers describe being typecast as "feminine" and "passive." Elementary school teachers are often confronted by suspicions that they are pedophiles. One kindergarten teacher described an experience that occurred early in his career which was related to him years afterwards by his principal:

> He indicated to me that parents had come to him and indicated to him that they had a problem with the fact that I was a male. . . . I recall almost exactly what he said. There were three specific concerns that the parents had: One parent said, "How can he love my child; he's a man." The second thing that I recall, he said the parent said, "He has a beard." And the third thing was, "Aren't you concerned about homosexuality?"

Such suspicions often cause men in all four professions to alter their work behavior to guard against sexual abuse charges, particularly in those specialties requiring intimate contact with women and children.

Men are very distressed by these negative stereotypes, which tend to undermine their self-esteem and to cause them to second-guess their motivations for entering these fields. A California teacher said,

> If I tell men that I don't know, that I'm meeting for the first time, that that's what I do, . . . sometimes there's a look on their faces that, you know, "Oh, couldn't get a real job?"

When asked if his wife, who is also an elementary school teacher, encounters the same kind of prejudice, he said,

> No, it's accepted because she's a woman. . . . I think people would see that as a . . . step up, you know. "Oh, you're not a housewife, you've got a career. That's great . . . that you're out there working. And you have a daughter, but you're still out there working. You decided not to stay home, and you went out there and got a job." Whereas for me, it's more like I'm supposed to be out working anyway, even though I'd rather be home with [my daughter].

Unlike women who enter traditionally male professions, men's movement into these jobs is perceived by the "outside world" as a step down in status. This particular form of discrimination may be most significant in explaining why men are underrepresented in these professions. Men who otherwise might show interest in and aptitudes for such careers are probably discouraged from pursuing them because of the negative popular stereotypes associated with the men who work in them. This is a crucial difference from the experience of women in nontraditional professions: "My daughter, the physician," resonates far more favorably in most people's ears than "My son, the nurse."

Many of the men in my sample identified the stigma of working in a female-identified occupation as the major barrier to more men entering their professions. However, for the most part, they claimed that these negative stereotypes were not a factor in their own decisions to join these occupations. Most respondents didn't consider entering these fields until well into adulthood, after working in some related occupation. Several social workers and librarians even claimed they were not aware that men were a minority in their chosen professions. Either they had no well-defined image or stereotype, or their contacts and mentors were predominantly men. For example, prior to entering library school, many librarians held part-time jobs in university libraries, where there are proportionally more men than in the profession generally. Nurses and elementary school teachers were more aware that mostly women worked in these jobs, and this was often a matter of some concern to them. However, their choices were ultimately legitimized by mentors, or by encouraging friends or family members who implicitly reassured them that entering these occupations would not type-cast them as feminine. In some cases, men were told by recruiters there were special advancement opportunities for men in these fields, and they entered them expecting rapid promotion to administrative positions.

> I: Did it ever concern you when you were making the decision to enter nursing school, the fact that it is a female-dominated profession?
>
> R: Not really. I never saw myself working on the floor. I saw myself pretty much going into administration, just getting the background and then getting a job someplace as a supervisor and then working, getting up into administration.

Because of the unique circumstances of their recruitment, many of the respondents did not view their occupational choices as inconsistent with a male gender role, and they generally avoided the negative stereotypes directed against men in these fields.

Indeed, many of the men I interviewed claimed that they did not encounter negative professional stereotypes until they had worked in these fields for several years. Popular prejudices can be damaging to self-esteem and probably push some men out of these professions altogether. Yet, ironically, they sometimes contribute to the "glass escalator" effect I have been describing. Men seem to encounter the most vituperative criticism from the public when they are in the most female-identified specialties. Public concerns sometimes result in their being shunted into more "legitimate" positions for men. A librarian formerly in charge of a branch library's children's collection, who now works in the reference department of the city's main library, describes his experience:

> R: Some of the people [who frequented the branch library] complained that they didn't want to have a man doing the story-telling scenario. And I got transferred here to the central library in an equivalent job . . . I thought that I did a good job. And I had been told by my supervisor that I was doing a good job.
>
> I: Have you ever considered filing some sort of lawsuit to get that other job back?
>
> R: Well, actually, the job I've gotten now . . . well, it's a reference librarian; it's what I wanted in the first place. I've got a whole lot more authority here. I'm also in charge of the circulation desk. And I've recently been promoted because of my new stature, so . . . no, I'm not considering trying to get that other job back.

The negative stereotypes about men who do "women's work" can push men out of specific jobs. However, to the extent that they channel men into more "legitimate" practice areas, their effects can actually be positive. Instead of being a source of discrimination, these prejudices can add to the "glass escalator effect" by pressuring men to move *out* of the most female-identified areas, and *up* to those regarded more legitimate and prestigious for men.

CONCLUSION: DISCRIMINATION AGAINST MEN

Both men and women who work in nontraditional occupations encounter discrimination, but the forms and consequences of this discrimination are very different. The interviews suggest that unlike "nontraditional" women workers, most of the discrimination and prejudice facing men in the "female professions" emanates from outside those professions. The men and women interviewed for the most part believed that men are given fair—if not preferential—treatment in hiring and promotion decisions, are accepted by supervisors and colleagues, and are well-integrated into the work place subculture. Indeed, subtle mechanisms seem to enhance men's position in these professions—a phenomenon I refer to as the "glass escalator effect."

The data lend strong support for Zimmer's (1988) critique of "gender neutral theory" (such as Kanter's [1977] theory of tokenism) in the study of occupational segregation. Zimmer argues that women's occupational inequality is more a consequence of sexist beliefs and practices embedded in the labor force than the effect of numerical underrepresentation per se. This study suggests that token status itself does not diminish men's occupational success. Men take their gender privilege with them when they enter predominantly female occupations: this translates into an advantage in spite of their numerical rarity.

This study indicates that the experience of tokenism is very different for men and women. Future research should examine how the experience of tokenism varies for members of different races and classes as well. For example, it is likely that informal work place mechanisms similar to the ones identified here promote the careers of token whites in predominantly black occupations. The crucial factor is the social status of the token's group—not their numerical rarity—that determines whether the token encounters a "glass ceiling" or a "glass escalator."

However, this study also found that many men encounter negative stereotypes from persons not directly involved in their professions. Men who enter these professions are often considered "failures," or sexual deviants. These stereotypes may be a major impediment to men who otherwise might consider careers in these occupations. Indeed, they are likely to be important factors whenever a member of a relatively high status group crosses over into a lower status occupation. However, to the extent that these stereotypes contribute to the "glass escalator effect" by channeling men into more "legitimate" (and higher paying) occupations, they are not discriminatory.

Women entering traditionally "male" professions also face negative stereotypes suggesting they are not "real women." However, these stereotypes do not seem to deter women to the same degree that they deter men from pursuing nontraditional professions. There is ample historical evidence that women flock to male-identified occupations once opportunities are available. Not so with men. Examples of occupations changing from predominantly female to predominantly male are very rare in our history. The few existing cases—such as medicine—suggest that redefinition of the occupations as appropriately "masculine" is necessary before men will consider joining them.

Because different mechanisms maintain segregation in male- and female-dominated occupations, different approaches are needed to promote their integration. Policies intended to alter the sex composition of male-dominated occupations—such as affirmative action—make little sense when applied to the "female professions." For men, the major barriers to integration have little to do with their treatment once they decide to enter these fields. Rather, we need to address the social and cultural sanctions applied to men who do "women's work" which keep men from even considering these occupations.

One area where these cultural barriers are clearly evident is in the media's representation of men's occupations. Women working in traditionally male professions have achieved an unprecedented acceptance on popular television shows. Women are portrayed as doctors ("St. Elsewhere"), lawyers ("The Cosby Show," "L.A. Law"), architects ("Family Ties"), and police officers ("Cagney and Lacey"). But where are the male nurses, teachers and secretaries? Television rarely portrays men in nontraditional work roles, and when it does, that anomaly is made the central focus—and joke—of the program. A comedy series (1991–92) about a male elementary school teacher ("Drexell's Class") stars a lead character who *hates children!* Yet even this negative portrayal is exceptional. When a prime time hospital drama series ("St. Elsewhere") depicted a male orderly striving for upward mobility, the show's writers made him a "physician's assistant," not a nurse or nurse practitioner—the much more likely "real life" possibilities.

Presenting positive images of men in nontraditional careers can produce limited effects. A few social workers, for example, were first inspired to pursue their careers by George C. Scott, who played a social worker in the television drama series, "Eastside/Westside." But as a policy strategy to break down occupational segregation, changing media images of men is no panacea. The stereotypes that differentiate masculinity and femininity, and degrade that which is defined as feminine, are deeply entrenched in culture, social structure, and personality. Nothing short of a revolution in cultural definitions of masculinity will effect the broad scale social transformation needed to achieve the complete occupational integration of men and women.

Of course, there are additional factors besides societal prejudice contributing to men's underrepresentation in female-dominated professions. Most notably, those men I interviewed mentioned as a deterrent the fact that these professions are all underpaid relative to comparable "male" occupations, and several suggested that instituting a "comparable worth" policy might attract more men. However, I am not convinced that improved salaries will substantially alter the sex composition of these professions unless the cultural stigma faced by men in these occupations diminishes. Occupational sex segregation is remarkably resilient, even in the face of devastating economic hardship. During the Great Depression of the 1930s, for example, "women's jobs" failed to attract sizable numbers of men. In her study of American Telephone and Telegraph (AT&T) workers, Epstein (1989) found that some men would rather suffer unemployment than accept relatively high paying "women's jobs" because of the damage to their identities this would cause. She quotes one unemployed man who refused to apply for a female-identified telephone operator job:

> I think if they offered me $1000 a week tax free, I wouldn't take that job. When I . . . see those guys sitting in there [in the telephone operating room], I wonder what's wrong with them. Are they pansies or what? (Epstein 1989:577)

This is not to say that raising salaries would not affect the sex composition of these jobs. Rather, I am suggesting that wages are not the only—or perhaps even the major—impediment to men's entry into these jobs. Further research is needed to explore the ideological significance of the "woman's wage" for maintaining occupational stratification.

At any rate, integrating men and women in the labor force requires more than dismantling barriers to women in male-dominated fields. Sex segregation is a two-way street. We must also confront and dismantle the barriers men face in predominantly female occupations. Men's experiences in these nontraditional occupations reveal just how culturally embedded the barriers are, and how far we have to travel before men and women attain true occupational and economic equality.

References

Epstein, Cynthia Fuchs. 1989. "Workplace boundaries: Conceptions and creations." *Social Research* 56: 571–590.

Freeman, Sue J. M. 1990. *Managing Lives: Corporate Women and Social Change.* Amherst, Mass.: University of Massachusetts Press.

Jacobs, Jerry. 1989. *Revolving Doors: Sex Segregation and Women's Careers.* Stanford, Calif.: Stanford University Press.

Kanter, Rosabeth Moss. 1977. *Men and Women of the Corporation.* New York: Basic Books.

Martin, Susan E. 1980. *Breaking and Entering: Police Women on Patrol.* Berkeley, Calif.: University of California Press.

———. 1988. "Think like a man, work like a dog, and act like a lady: Occupational dilemmas of police-women." In *The Worth of Women's Work: A Qualitative Synthesis,* ed. Anne Statham, Eleanor M. Miller, and Hans O. Mauksch, 205–223. Albany, N.Y.: State University of New York Press.

Reskin, Barbara. 1988. "Bringing the men back in: Sex differentiation and the devaluation of women's work." *Gender & Society* 2: 58–81.

Reskin, Barbara, and Patricia Roos. 1990. *Job Queues, Gender Queues: Explaining Women's Inroads into Male Occupations.* Philadelphia: Temple University Press.

Strauss, Anselm L. 1987. *Qualitative Analysis for Social Scientists.* Cambridge, England: Cambridge University Press.

Yoder, Janice D. 1989. "Women at West Point: Lessons for token women in male-dominated occupations." In *Women: A Feminist Perspective,* ed. Jo Freeman, 523–537. Mountain View, Calif.: Mayfield Publishing Company.

Zimmer, Lynn. 1988. "Tokenism and women in the workplace." *Social Problems* 35: 64–77.

PART 8

~

THE GENDERED BODY

Perhaps nothing is more deceptive than the "naturalness" of our bodies. We experience what happens to our bodies, what happens *in* our bodies, as utterly natural, physical phenomena.

Yet to the social scientist, nothing could be farther from the truth. Our bodies are themselves shaped and created, and interpreted and understood by us, in entirely gendered ways. How we look, what we feel, and what we think about how our bodies look and feel, are the products of the ways our society defines what bodies should look like and feel. Thus, for example, cultural standards of beauty, musculature, and aesthetics are constantly changing—and with them our feelings about how we look stacked up against those images.

Take, for example, women's notions of beauty. Feminist writer Naomi Wolf argued that "the beauty myth"—constantly shifting and unrealizable cultural ideals of beauty—trap women into endless cycles of diets, fashion, and consumer spending that render them defenseless. Fortunes are made by companies that purvey the beauty myth, who remind women that they do not measure up to these cultural standards, and then providing products that will help them try. By such logic, women who experience eating disorders are not deviant, nonconformists, but rather overconformists to unrealizable norms of femininity. Feminist philosopher Susan Bordo's essay reminds us of the ways in which cultural conceptions of women's bodies articulate with notions of femininity.

A parallel process engages men. While women can never be thin enough, men can never be pumped up enough. Musculature remains the most visible signifier of masculinity, according to sociologist Barry Glassner.

Equally true, the ways in which we engage with our bodies reproduce gender relations. Men have far lower rates of health-seeking behavior—it's more manly to ignore health problems and live with pain—and there are gender differences in rates of various illnesses.

There is even some evidence that the "truth" of our bodies may be quite deceiving. Transgendered people, intersexed people, people with ambiguous genitalia all throw into stark relief the ways in which our assumptions that gender adheres to a specific body may not hold in all circumstances.

SUSAN BORDO

The Body and the Reproduction
of Femininity

RECONSTRUCTING FEMINIST DISCOURSE ON THE BODY

The body—what we eat, how we dress, the daily rituals through which we attend to the body—is a medium of culture. The body, as anthropologist Mary Douglas has argued, is a powerful symbolic form, a surface on which the central rules, hierarchies, and even metaphysical commitments of a culture are inscribed and thus reinforced through the concrete language of the body.[1] The body may also operate as a metaphor for culture. From quarters as diverse as Plato and Hobbes to French feminist Luce Irigaray, an imagination of body morphology has provided a blueprint for diagnosis and/or vision of social and political life.

The body is not only a *text* of culture. It is also, as anthropologist Pierre Bourdieu and philosopher Michel Foucault (among others) have argued, a *practical*, direct locus of social control. Banally, through table manners and toilet habits, through seemingly trivial routines, rules, and practices, culture is *"made* body," as Bourdieu puts it—converted into automatic, habitual activity. As such it is put "beyond the grasp of consciousness . . . [untouchable] by voluntary, deliberate transformations."[2] Our conscious politics, social commitments, strivings for change may be undermined and betrayed by the life of our bodies—not the craving, instinctual body imagined by Plato, Augustine, and Freud, but what Foucault calls the "docile body," regulated by the norms of cultural life.[3]

Throughout his later "genealogical" works (*Discipline and Punish, The History of Sexuality*), Foucault constantly reminds us of the primacy of practice over belief. Not chiefly through ideology, but through the organization and regulation of the time, space, and movements of our daily lives, our bodies are trained, shaped, and impressed with the stamp of prevailing historical forms of selfhood, desire, masculinity, femininity. Such an emphasis casts a dark and disquieting shadow across the contemporary scene. For women, as study after study shows, are spending more time on the management and discipline of our bodies than we have in a long, long time. In a decade marked by a reopening of the public arena to women, the intensification of such regimens appears diversionary and subverting. Through the pursuit of an ever-changing, homogenizing, elusive ideal of femininity—a pursuit without a terminus, requiring that women constantly attend to minute and often whimsical changes in fashion—female bodies become docile bodies—bodies whose forces and energies are habituated to external regulation, subjection, transformation, "improvement." Through the exacting and normalizing disciplines of diet, makeup, and dress—central organizing principles of time and space in the day of many women—we are rendered less socially oriented and more centripetally focused on self-modification. Through these disciplines, we continue to memorize on our bodies the feel and conviction of lack, of insufficiency, of never being good enough. At the farthest extremes, the practices of femininity may lead us to utter demoralization, debilitation, and death.

Viewed historically, the discipline and normalization of the female body—perhaps the only gender oppression that exercises itself, although to different degrees and in different forms, across age, race, class, and sexual orientation—has to be acknowledged as an amazingly durable and flexible strategy of social control. In our own era, it is difficult to avoid the recognition that the contemporary preoccupation with appearance, which still affects women far more powerfully than men, even in our narcissistic and visually oriented culture, may function as a backlash phenomenon, reasserting existing gender configurations against any attempts to shift or transform power relations.[4] Surely we are in the throes of this backlash today. In newspapers and magazines we daily encounter stories that promote traditional gender relations and prey on anxieties about change: stories about latch-key children, abuse in day-care centers, the "new woman's" troubles with men, her lack of marriageability, and so on. A dominant visual theme in teenage magazines involves women hiding in the shadows of men, seeking solace in their arms, willingly contracting the space they occupy. The last, of course, also describes our contemporary aesthetic ideal for women, an ideal whose obsessive pursuit has become the central torment of many women's lives. In such an era we desperately need an effective political discourse about the female body, a discourse adequate to an analysis of the insidious, and often paradoxical, pathways of modern social control.

Developing such a discourse requires reconstructing the feminist paradigm of the late 1960s and early 1970s, with its political categories of oppressors and oppressed, villains and victims. Here I believe that a feminist appropriation of some of Foucault's later concepts can prove useful. Following Foucault, we must first abandon the idea of power as something possessed by one group and leveled against another; we must instead think of the network of practices, institutions, and technologies that sustain positions of dominance and subordination in a particular domain.

Second, we need an analytics adequate to describe a power whose central mechanisms are not repressive, but *constitutive:* "a power bent on generating forces, making them grow, and ordering them, rather than one dedicated to impeding them, making them submit, or destroying them." Particularly in the realm of femininity, where so much depends on the seemingly willing acceptance of various norms and practices, we need an analysis of power "from below," as Foucault puts it; for example, of the mechanisms that shape and proliferate—rather than repress—desire, generate and focus our energies, construct our conceptions of normalcy and deviance.[5]

And, third, we need a discourse that will enable us to account for the subversion of potential rebellion, a discourse that, while insisting on the necessity of objective analysis of power relations, social hierarchy, political backlash, and so forth, will nonetheless allow us to confront the mechanisms by which the subject at times becomes enmeshed in collusion with forces that sustain her own oppression.

This essay will not attempt to produce a general theory along these lines. Rather, my focus will be the analysis of one particular arena where the interplay of these dynamics is striking and perhaps exemplary. It is a limited and unusual arena, that of a group of gender-related and historically localized disorders: hysteria, agoraphobia, and anorexia nervosa.[6] I recognize that these disorders have also historically been class- and race-biased, largely (although not exclusively) occurring among white middle- and upper-middle-class women. Nonetheless, anorexia, hysteria, and agoraphobia may provide a paradigm of one way in which potential resistance is not merely undercut but *utilized* in the maintenance and reproduction of existing power relations.[7]

The central mechanism I will describe involves a transformation (or, if you wish, duality) of meaning, through which conditions that are objectively (and, on one level, experientially) constraining, enslaving, and even murderous, come to be experienced as liberating, transforming, and life-giving. I offer this analysis, although limited to a specific domain, as an example of how various contemporary critical discourses may be joined to yield an understanding of the subtle and often unwitting role played by our bodies in the symbolization and reproduction of gender.

THE BODY AS A TEXT OF FEMININITY

The continuum between female disorder and "normal" feminine practice is sharply revealed through a close reading of those disorders to which women have been particularly vulnerable. These, of course, have varied historically: neurasthenia and hysteria in the second half of the nineteenth century; agoraphobia and, most dramatically, anorexia nervosa and bulimia in the second half of the twentieth century. This is not to say that anorectics did not exist in the nineteenth century—many cases were described, usually in the context of diagnoses of hysteria[8]—or that women no longer suffer from classical hysterical symptoms in the twentieth century. But the taking up of eating disorders on a mass scale is as unique to the culture of the 1980s as the epidemic of hysteria was to the Victorian era.[9]

The symptomatology of these disorders reveals itself as textuality. Loss of mobility, loss of voice, inability to leave the home, feeding others while starving oneself, taking up space, and whittling down the space one's body takes up—all have symbolic meaning, all have *political* meaning under the varying rules governing the historical construction of gender. Working within this framework, we see that whether we look at hysteria, agoraphobia, or anorexia, we find the body of the sufferer deeply inscribed with an ideological construction of femininity emblematic of the period in question. The construction, of course, is always homogenizing and normalizing, erasing racial, class, and other differences and insisting that all women aspire to a coercive, standardized ideal. Strikingly, in these disorders the construction of femininity is written in disturbingly concrete, hyperbolic terms: exaggerated, extremely literal, at times virtually caricatured presentations of the ruling feminine mystique. The bodies of disordered women in this way offer themselves as an aggressively graphic text for the interpreter—a text that insists, actually demands, that it be read as a cultural statement, a statement about gender.

Both nineteenth-century male physicians and twentieth-century feminist critics have seen, in the symptoms of neurasthenia and hysteria (syndromes that became increasingly less differentiated as the century wore on), an exaggeration of stereotypically feminine traits. The nineteenth-century "lady" was idealized in terms of delicacy and dreaminess, sexual passivity, and a charmingly labile and capricious emotionality.[10] Such notions were formalized and scientized in the work of male theorists from Acton and Krafft-Ebing to Freud, who described "normal," mature femininity in such terms.[11] In this context, the dissociations, the drifting and fogging of perception, the nervous tremors and faints, the anesthesias, and the extreme mutability of symptomatology associated with nineteenth-century female disorders can be seen to be concretizations of the feminine mystique of the period, produced according to rules that governed the prevailing construction of femininity. Doctors described what came to be known as the hysterical personality as "impressionable, suggestible, and narcissistic; highly labile, their moods changing suddenly, dramatically, and seemingly for inconsequential reasons . . . egocentric in the extreme . . . essentially asexual and not uncommonly frigid"[12]—all characteristics normative of femininity in this era. As Elaine Showalter points out, the term *hysterical* itself became almost interchangeable with the term *feminine* in the literature of the period.[13]

The hysteric's embodiment of the feminine mystique of her era, however, seems subtle and ineffable compared to the ingenious literalism of agoraphobia and anorexia. In the context of our culture this literalism makes sense. With the advent of movies and television, the rules for femininity have come to be culturally transmitted more and more through standardized visual images. As a result, femininity itself has come to be largely a matter of constructing, in the manner described by Erving Goffman, the appropriate surface presentation of the self.[14] We are no longer given verbal descriptions or exemplars of what a lady is or of what femininity consists. Rather, we learn the rules directly through bodily discourse: through images that tell us what clothes, body shape, facial expression, movements, and behavior are required.

In agoraphobia and, even more dramatically, in anorexia, the disorder presents itself as a virtual, though tragic, parody of twentieth-century constructions of femininity. The 1950s and early 1960s, when agoraphobia first began to escalate among women, was a period of reassertion of domesticity and dependency as the feminine ideal. *Career woman* became a dirty word, much more so than it had been during the war, when the economy depended on women's willingness to do "men's work." The reigning ideology of femininity, so well described by Betty Friedan and perfectly captured in the movies and television shows of the era, was childlike, nonassertive, helpless without a man, "content in a world of bedroom and kitchen, sex, babies and home."[15] The housebound agoraphobic lives this construction of femininity literally. "You want me in this home? You'll have me in this home—with a vengeance!" The point, upon which many therapists have commented, does not need belaboring. Agoraphobia, as I. G. Fodor has put it, seems "the logical—albeit extreme—extension of the cultural sex-role stereotype for wo-men" in this era.[16]

The emaciated body of the anorectic, of course, immediately presents itself as a caricature of the contemporary ideal of hyper-slenderness for women, an ideal that, despite the game resistance of racial and ethnic difference, has become the norm for women today. But slenderness is only the tip of the iceberg, for slender-ness itself requires interpretation. "C'est le sens qui fait vendre," said Barthes, speaking of clothing styles—it is meaning that makes the sale.[17] So, too, it is mean-ing that makes the body admirable. To the degree that anorexia may be said to be "about" slenderness, it is about slenderness as a citadel of contemporary and his-torical meaning, not as an empty fashion ideal. As such, the interpretation of slen-derness yields multiple readings, some related to gender, some not. For the pur-poses of this essay I will offer an abbreviated, gender-focused reading. But I must stress that this reading illuminates only partially, and that many other currents not discussed here—economic, psychosocial, and historical, as well as ethnic and class dimensions—figure prominently.[18]

We begin with the painfully literal inscription, on the anorectic's body, of the rules governing the construction of contemporary femininity. That construction is a double bind that legislates contradictory ideals and directives. On the one hand, our culture still widely advertises domestic conceptions of femininity, the ideolog-ical moorings for a rigorously dualistic sexual division of labor that casts woman as chief emotional and physical nurturer. The rules for this construction of femi-ninity (and I speak here in a language both symbolic and literal) require that women learn to feed others, not the self, and to construe any desires for self-nurturance and self-feeding as greedy and excessive.[19] Thus, women must devel-op a totally other-oriented emotional economy. In this economy, the control of fe-male appetite for food is merely the most concrete expression of the general rule governing the construction of femininity: that female hunger—for public power, for independence, for sexual gratification—be contained, and the public space that women be allowed to take up be circumscribed, limited. Figure 1, which appeared in a women's magazine fashion spread, dramatically illustrates the degree to which slenderness, set off against the resurgent muscularity and bulk of the cur-rent male body-ideal, carries connotations of fragility and lack of power in the face of a decisive male occupation of social space. On the body of the anorexic woman such rules are grimly and deeply etched.

On the other hand, even as young women today continue to be taught tradi-tionally "feminine" virtues, to the degree that the professional arena is open to them they must also learn to embody the "masculine" language and values of that arena—self-control, determination, cool, emotional discipline, mastery, and so on. Female bodies now speak symbolically of this necessity in their slender spare shape and the currently fashionable men's-wear look. (A contemporary clothing line's clever mirror-image logo, shown in Figure 2, offers women's fashions for the "New Man," with the model posed to suggest phallic confidence combined with female allure.) Our bodies, too, as we trudge to the gym every day and fiercely re-sist both our hungers and our desire to soothe ourselves, are becoming more and more practiced at the "male" virtues of control and self-mastery. Figure 3 il-

Figure 1

lustrates this contemporary equation of physical discipline with becoming the "captain" of one's soul. The anorectic pursues these virtues with single-minded, unswerving dedication. "Energy, discipline, my own power will keep me going," says ex-anorectic Aimee Liu, recreating her anorexic days. "I need nothing and no one else. . . . I will be master of my own body, if nothing else, I vow."[20]

The ideal of slenderness, then, and the diet and exercise regimens that have become inseparable from it offer the illusion of meeting, through the body, the contradictory demands of the contemporary ideology of femininity. Popular images reflect this dual demand. In a single issue of *Complete Woman* magazine, two articles appear, one on "Feminine Intuition," the other asking, "Are You the New Macho Woman?" In *Vision Quest,* the young male hero falls in love with the heroine, as he says, because "she has all the best things I like in girls and all the best things I like in guys," that is, she's tough and cool, but warm and alluring. In the enormously popular *Aliens,* the heroine's personality has been deliberately constructed, with near-comic book explicitness, to embody traditional nurturant femininity alongside breathtaking macho prowess and control; Sigourney Weaver, the actress who portrays her, has called the character "Rambolina."

Figure 2

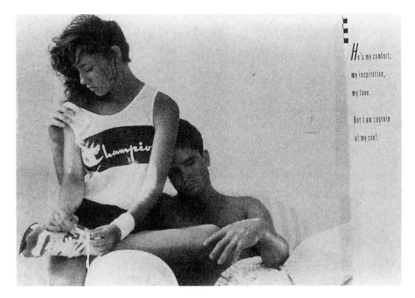

Figure 3

In the pursuit of slenderness and the denial of appetite the traditional construction of femininity intersects with the new requirement for women to embody the "masculine" values of the public arena. The anorectic, as I have argued, embodies this intersection, this double bind, in a particularly painful and graphic way.[21] I mean *double bind* quite literally here. "Masculinity" and "femininity," at least since the nineteenth century and arguably before, have been constructed through a process of mutual exclusion. One cannot simply add the historically feminine virtues to the historically masculine ones to yield a New Woman, a New Man, a new ethics, or a new culture. Even on the screen or on television, embodied in created characters like the *Aliens* heroine, the result is a parody. Unfortunately, in this image-bedazzled culture, we find it increasingly difficult to discriminate between parodies and possibilities for the self. Explored as a possibility for the self, the "androgynous" ideal ultimately exposes its internal contradiction and becomes a war that tears the subject in two—a war explicitly thematized, by many anorectics, as a battle between male and female sides of the self.[22]

PROTEST AND RETREAT IN THE SAME GESTURE

In hysteria, agoraphobia, and anorexia, then, the woman's body may be viewed as a surface on which conventional constructions of femininity are exposed starkly to view, through their inscription in extreme or hyperliteral form. They are written, of course, in languages of horrible suffering. It is as though these bodies are speaking to us of the pathology and violence that lurks just around the corner, waiting at the horizon of "normal" femininity. It is no wonder that a steady motif in the feminist literature on female disorder is that of pathology as embodied *protest*—unconscious, inchoate, and counterproductive protest without an effective language, voice, or politics, but protest nonetheless.

American and French feminists alike have heard the hysteric speaking a language of protest, even or perhaps especially when she was mute. Dianne Hunter interprets Anna O.'s aphasia, which manifested itself in an inability to speak her native German, as a rebellion against the linguistic and cultural rules of the father and a return to the "mother-tongue": the semiotic babble of infancy, the language of the body. For Hunter, and for a number of other feminists working with Lacanian categories, the return to the semiotic level is both regressive and, as Hunter puts it, an "expressive" communication "addressed to patriarchal thought," "a self-repudiating form of feminine discourse in which the body signifies what social conditions make it impossible to state linguistically."[23] "The hysterics are accusing; they are pointing," writes Catherine Clément in *The Newly Born Woman*; they make a "mockery of culture."[24] In the same volume, Hélène Cixous speaks of "those wonderful hysterics, who subjected Freud to so many voluptuous moments too shameful to mention, bombarding his mosaic statute/law of Moses with their carnal, passionate body-words, haunting him with their inaudible thundering denunciations." For Cixous, Dora, who so frustrated Freud, is "the core example of the protesting force in women."[25]

The literature of protest includes functional as well as symbolic approaches.

Robert Seidenberg and Karen DeCrow, for example, describe agoraphobia as a "strike" against "the renunciations usually demanded of women" and the expectations of housewifely functions such as shopping, driving the children to school, accompanying their husband to social events.[26] Carroll Smith-Rosenberg presents a similar analysis of hysteria, arguing that by preventing the woman from functioning in the wifely role of caretaker of others, of "ministering angel" to husband and children, hysteria "became one way in which conventional women could express—in most cases unconsciously—dissatisfaction with one or several aspects of their lives."[27] A number of feminist writers, among whom Susie Orbach is the most articulate and forceful, have interpreted anorexia as a species of unconscious feminist protest. The anorectic is engaged in a "hunger strike," as Orbach calls it, stressing that this is a political discourse, in which the action of food refusal and dramatic transformation of body size "expresses with [the] body what [the anorectic] is unable to tell us with words"—her indictment of a culture that disdains and suppresses female hunger, makes women ashamed of their appetites and needs, and demands that women constantly work on the transformation of their body.[28]

The anorectic, of course, is unaware that she is making a political statement. She may, indeed, be hostile to feminism and any other critical perspectives that she views as disputing her own autonomy and control or questioning the cultural ideals around which her life is organized. Through embodied rather than deliberate demonstration she exposes and indicts those ideals, precisely by pursuing them to the point at which their destructive potential is revealed for all to see.

The same gesture that expresses protest, moreover, can also signal retreat; this, indeed, may be part of the symptom's attraction. Kim Chernin, for example, argues that the debilitating anorexic fixation, by halting or mitigating personal development, assuages this generation's guilt and separation anxiety over the prospect of surpassing our mothers, of living less circumscribed, freer lives.[29] Agoraphobia, too, which often develops shortly after marriage, clearly functions in many cases as a way to cement dependency and attachment in the face of unacceptable stirrings of dissatisfaction and restlessness.

Although we may talk meaningfully of protest, then, I want to emphasize the counterproductive, tragically self-defeating (indeed, self-deconstructing) nature of that protest. Functionally, the symptoms of these disorders isolate, weaken, and undermine the sufferers; at the same time they turn the life of the body into an all-absorbing fetish, beside which all other objects of attention pale into unreality. On the symbolic level, too, the protest collapses into its opposite and proclaims the utter capitulation of the subject to the contracted female world. The muteness of hysterics and their return to the level of pure, primary bodily expressivity have been interpreted, as we have seen, as rejecting the symbolic order of the patriarchy and recovering a lost world of semiotic, maternal value. But *at the same time,* of course, muteness is the condition of the silent, uncomplaining woman—an ideal of patriarchal culture. Protesting the stifling of the female voice through one's own voicelessness—that is, employing the language of femininity to protest the conditions of the female world—will always involve ambiguities of this sort. Perhaps this is why symptoms crystallized from the language of femininity are so perfectly suited to express the dilemmas of middle-class and upper-middle-class women living in periods poised on the edge of gender change, women who have the social and material resources to carry the traditional construction of femininity to symbolic excess but who also confront the anxieties of new possibilities. The late nineteenth century, the post–World War II period, and the late twentieth century are all periods in which gender becomes an issue to be discussed and in which discourse proliferates about "the Woman Question," "the New Woman," "What Women Want," "What Femininity Is."

COLLUSION, RESISTANCE, AND THE BODY

The pathologies of female protest function, paradoxically, as if in collusion with the cultural conditions that produce them, reproducing rather than transforming precisely that which is being protested. In this connection, the fact that hysteria and anorexia have peaked during historical periods of cultural backlash against attempts at reorganization and redefinition of male and female roles is significant. Female pathology reveals itself here as an extremely interesting social formation through which one source of potential for resistance and rebellion is pressed into the service of maintaining the established order.

In our attempt to explain this formation, objective accounts of power relations fail us. For whatever the objective social conditions are that create a pathology, the symptoms themselves must still be produced (however unconsciously or inadvertently) by the subject. That is, the individual must invest the body with meanings of various sorts. Only by examining this productive process on the part of the subject can we, as Mark Poster has put it, "illuminate the mechanisms of domination in the processes through which meaning is produced in everyday life"; that is, only then can we see how the desires and dreams of the subject become implicated in the matrix of power relations.[30]

Here, examining the context in which the anorexic syndrome is produced may be illuminating. Anorexia will erupt, typically, in the course of what begins as a fairly moderate diet regime, undertaken because someone, often the father, has made a casual critical remark. Anorexia *begins in,* emerges out of, what is, in our time, conventional feminine practice. In the course of that practice, for any number of individual reasons, the practice is pushed a little beyond the parameters of moderate dieting. The young woman discovers what it feels like to crave and want and need and yet, through the exercise of her own will, to triumph over that need. In the process, a new realm of meanings is discovered, a range of values and possibilities that Western culture has traditionally coded as "male" and rarely made available to women: an ethic and aesthetic of self-mastery and self-transcendence, expertise, and power over others through the example of superior will and control. The experience is intoxicating, habit-forming.

At school the anorectic discovers that her steadily shrinking body is admired, not so much as an aesthetic or sexual object, but for the strength of will and self-control it projects. At home she discovers, in the inevitable battles her parents fight to get her to eat, that her actions have enormous power over the lives of those around her. As her body begins to lose its traditional feminine curves, its breasts and hips and rounded stomach, begins to feel and look more like a spare, lanky male body, she begins to feel untouchable, out of reach of hurt, "invulnerable, clean and hard as the bones etched into my silhouette," as one student described it in her journal. She despises, in particular, all those parts of her body that continue to mark her as female. "If only I could eliminate [my breasts]," says Liu, "cut them off if need be."[31] For her, as for many anorectics, the breasts represent a bovine, unconscious, vulnerable side of the self. Liu's body symbolism is thoroughly continuous with dominant cultural associations. Brett Silverstein's studies on the "Possible Causes of the Thin Standard of Bodily Attractiveness for Women"[32] testify empirically to what is obvious from every comedy routine involving a dramatically shapely woman: namely, our cultural association of curvaceousness with incompetence. The anorectic is also quite aware, of course, of the social and sexual vulnerability involved in having a female body; many, in fact, were sexually abused as children.

Through her anorexia, by contrast, she has unexpectedly discovered an entry into the privileged male world, a way to become what is valued in our culture, a way to become safe, to rise above it all—for her, they are the same thing. She has discovered this, paradoxically, by pursuing conventional feminine behavior—in this case, the discipline of perfecting the body as an object—to excess. At this point of excess, the conventionally feminine deconstructs, we might say, into its opposite and opens onto those values our culture has coded as male. No wonder the anorexia is experienced as liberating and that she will fight family, friends, and therapists in an effort to hold onto it—fight them to the death, if need be. The anorectic's experience of power is, of course, deeply and dangerously illusory. To reshape one's body into a male body is *not* to put on male power and privilege. To *feel* autonomous and free while harnessing body and soul to an obsessive bodypractice is to serve, not transform, a social order that limits female possibilities. And, of course, for the female to become male is only for her to locate herself on the other side of a disfiguring opposition. The new "power look" of female bodybuilding, which encourages women to develop the same hulklike, triangular shape that has been the norm for male body-builders, is no less determined by a hierarchical, dualistic construction of gender than was the conventionally "feminine"norm that tyrannized female body-builders such as Bev Francis for years.

Although the specific cultural practices and meanings are different, similar mechanisms, I suspect, are at work in hysteria and agoraphobia. In these cases too, the language of femininity, when pushed to excess—when shouted and asserted, when disruptive and demanding—deconstructs into its opposite and makes available to the woman an illusory experience of power previously forbidden to her by virtue of her gender. In the case of nineteenth-century femininity, the forbidden experience may have been the bursting of fetters—particularly moral and emotional fetters. John Conolly, the asylum reformer, recommended institutionalization for women who "want that restraint over the passions without which the female character is lost."[33] Hysterics often infuriated male doctors by their lack of precisely this quality. S. Weir Mitchell described these patients as "the despair of physicians," whose "despotic selfishness wrecks the constitution of nurses and devoted relatives, and in unconscious or half-conscious self-indulgence destroys the comfort of everyone around them."[34] It must have given the Victorian patient some illicit pleasure to be viewed as capable of such disruption of the staid nineteenth-century household. A similar form of power, I believe, is part of the experience of agoraphobia.

This does not mean that the primary reality of these disorders is not one of pain and entrapment. Anorexia, too, clearly contains a dimension of physical addiction to the biochemical effects of starvation. But whatever the physiology involved, the ways in which the subject understands and thematizes her experience cannot be reduced to a mechanical process. The anorectic's ability to live with minimal food intake allows her to feel powerful and worthy of admiration in a "world," as Susie Orbach describes it, "from which at the most profound level [she] feels excluded" and unvalued.[35] The literature on both anorexia and hysteria is strewn with battles of will between the sufferer and those trying to "cure" her; the latter, as Orbach points out, very rarely understand that the psychic values she is fighting for are often more important to the woman than life itself.

TEXTUALITY, PRAXIS, AND THE BODY

The "solutions" offered by anorexia, hysteria, and agoraphobia, I have suggested, develop out of the practice of femininity itself, the pursuit of which is still presented as the chief route to acceptance and success for women in our culture. Too aggressively pursued, that practice leads to its own undoing, in one sense. For if femininity is, as Susan Brownmiller has said, at its core a "tradition of imposed limitations,"[36] then an unwillingness to limit oneself, even in the pursuit of femininity, breaks the rules. But, of course, in another sense the rules remain fully in place. The sufferer becomes wedded to an obsessive practice, unable to make any effective change in her life. She remains, as Toril Moi has put it, "gagged and chained to [the] feminine role," a reproducer of the docile body of femininity.[37]

This tension between the psychological meaning of a disorder, which may enact fantasies of rebellion and embody a language of protest, and the practical life of the disordered body, which may utterly defeat rebellion and subvert protest, may be obscured by too exclusive a focus on the symbolic dimension and insufficient attention to praxis. As we have seen in the case of some Lacanian feminist readings of hysteria, the result of this can be a one-sided interpretation that romanticizes the hysteric's symbolic subversion of the phallocentric order while confined to her bed. This is not to say that confinement in bed has a transparent, univocal meaning—in powerlessness, debilitation, dependency, and so forth. The "practical" body is no brute biological or material entity. It, too, is a culturally mediated form; its activities are subject to interpretation and description. The shift to the practical dimension is not a turn to biology or nature, but to another "register," as Foucault puts it, of the cultural body, the register of the "useful body" rather than the "intelligible body."[38] The distinction can prove useful, I believe, to feminist discourse.

The intelligible body includes our scientific, philosophic, and aesthetic representations of the body—our cultural *conceptions* of the body, norms of beauty, models of health, and so forth. But the same representations may also be seen as forming a set of *practical* rules and regulations through which the living body is "trained, shaped, obeys, responds," becoming, in short, a socially adapted and "useful body."[39] Consider this particularly clear and appropriate example: the nineteenth-century hourglass figure, emphasizing breasts and hips against a wasp waist, was an intelligible *symbolic* form, representing a domestic, sexualized ideal of femininity. The sharp cultural contrast between the female and the male form, made possible by the use of corsets and bustles, reflected, in symbolic terms, the dualistic division of social and economic life into clearly defined male and female spheres. At the same time, to achieve the specified look, a particular feminine *praxis* was required—straitlacing, minimal eating, reduced mobility—rendering the female body unfit to perform activities outside its designated sphere. This, in Foucauldian terms, would be the "useful body" corresponding to the aesthetic norm.

The intelligible body and the useful body are two arenas of the same discourse; they often mirror and support each other, as in the above illustration. Another example can be found in the seventeenth-century philosophic conception of the body as a machine, mirroring an increasingly more automated productive machinery of labor. But the two bodies may also contradict and mock each other. A range of contemporary representations and images, as noted earlier, have coded the transcendence of female appetite and its public display in the slenderness ideal in terms of power, will, mastery, the possibilities of success in the professional arena. These associations are carried visually by the slender superwomen of prime-time television and popular movies and promoted explicitly in advertisements and articles appearing routinely in women's fashion magazines, diet books, and weight-training publications. Yet the thousands of slender girls and women who strive to embody these images and who in that service suffer from eating disorders, exercise compulsions, and continual self-scrutiny and self-castigation are anything *but* the "masters" of their lives.

Exposure and productive cultural analysis of such contradictory and mystifying relations between image and practice are possible only if the analysis includes attention to and interpretation of the "useful" or, as I prefer to call it, the practical body. Such attention, although often in inchoate and theoretically unsophisticated form, was central to the beginnings of the contemporary feminist movement. In the late 1960s and early 1970s the objectification of the female body was a serious political issue. All the cultural paraphernalia of femininity, of learning to please visually and sexually through the practices of the body—media imagery, beauty pageants, high heels, girdles, makeup, simulated orgasm—were seen as crucial in maintaining gender domination.

Disquietingly, for the feminists of the present decade, such focus on the politics of feminine praxis, although still maintained in the work of individual feminists, is no longer a centerpiece of feminist cultural critique.[40] On the popular front, we find *Ms.* magazine presenting issues on fitness and "style," the rhetoric reconstructed for the 1980s to pitch "self-expression" and "power." Although feminist theory surely has the tools, it has not provided a critical discourse to dismantle and demystify this rhetoric. The work of French feminists has provided a powerful framework for understanding the inscription of phallocentric, dualistic culture on gendered bodies, but it has offered very little in the way of concrete analyses of the female body as a locus of practical cultural control. Among feminist theorists in this country, the study of cultural representations of the female body has flourished, and it has often been brilliantly illuminating and instrumental to a feminist rereading of culture.[41] But the study of cultural representations alone, divorced from consideration of their relation to the practical lives of bodies, can obscure and mislead.

Here, Helena Mitchie's significantly titled *The Flesh Made Word* offers a striking example. Examining nineteenth-century representations of women, appetite, and eating, Mitchie draws fascinating and astute metaphorical connections between female eating and female sexuality. Female hunger, she argues, and I agree, "figures unspeakable desires for sexuality and power."[42] The Victorian novel's "representational taboo" against depicting women eating (an activity, apparently, that only "happens offstage," as Mitchie puts it) thus functions as a "code" for the suppression of female sexuality, as does the general cultural requirement, exhibited in etiquette and sex manuals of the day, that the well-bred woman eat little and delicately. The same coding is drawn on, Mitchie argues, in contemporary feminist "inversions" of Victorian values, inversions that celebrate female sexuality and power through images exulting in female eating and female hunger, depicting it explicitly, lushly, and joyfully.

Despite the fact that Mitchie's analysis centers on issues concerning women's hunger, food, and eating practices, she makes no mention of the grave eating disorders that surfaced in the late nineteenth century and that are ravaging the lives of young women today. The practical arena of women dieting, fasting, straitlacing, and so forth is, to a certain extent, implicit in her examination of Victorian gender ideology. But when Mitchie turns, at the end of her study, to consider contemporary feminist literature celebrating female eating and female hunger, the absence of even a passing glance at how women are *actually* managing their hungers today leaves her analysis adrift, lacking any concrete social moorings. Mitchie's sole focus is on the inevitable failure of feminist literature to escape "phallic representational codes."[43] But the feminist celebration of the female body did not merely deconstruct on the written page or canvas. Largely located in the feminist counterculture of the 1970s, it has been culturally displaced by a very different contemporary reality. Its celebration of female flesh now presents itself in jarring dissonance with the fact that women, feminists included, are starving themselves to death in our culture.

This is not to deny the benefits of diet, exercise, and other forms of body management. Rather, I view our bodies as a site of struggle, where we must *work* to keep our daily practices in the service of resistance to gender domination, not in the service of docility and gender normalization. This work requires, I believe, a determinedly skeptical attitude toward the routes of seeming liberation and pleasure offered by our culture. It also demands an awareness of the often contradictory relations between image and practice, between rhetoric and reality. Popular representations, as we have seen, may forcefully employ the rhetoric and symbolism of empowerment, personal freedom, "having it all." Yet female bodies, pursuing these ideals, may find themselves as distracted, depressed, and physically ill as female bodies in the nineteenth century were made when pursuing a feminine ideal of dependency, domesticity, and delicacy. The recognition and analysis of such contradictions, and of all the other collusions, subversions, and enticements through which culture enjoins the aid of our bodies in the reproduction of gender, require that we restore a concern for female praxis to its formerly central place in feminist politics.

Notes

Early versions of this essay, under various titles, were delivered at the philosophy department of the State University of New York at Stony Brook, the University of Massachusetts conference on Histories of Sexuality, and the twenty-first annual conference for the Society of Phenomenology and Existential Philosophy. I thank all those who commented and provided encouragement on those occasions. The essay was revised and originally published in Alison Jaggar and Susan Bordo, eds., *Gender/Body/Knowledge: Feminist Reconstructions of Being and Knowing* (New Brunswick: Rutgers University Press, 1989).

1. Mary Douglas, *Natural Symbols* (New York: Pantheon, 1982), and *Purity and Danger* (London: Routledge and Kegan Paul, 1966).

2. Pierre Bourdieu, *Outline of a Theory of Practice* (Cambridge: Cambridge University Press, 1977), p. 94 (emphasis in original).

3. On docility, see Michel Foucault, *Discipline and Punish* (New York: Vintage, 1979), pp. 135–69. For a Foucauldian analysis of feminine practice, see Sandra Bartky, "Foucault, Femininity, and the Modernization of Patriarchal Power," in her *Femininity and Domination* (New York: Routledge, 1990); see also Susan Brownmiller, *Femininity* (New York: Ballantine, 1984).

4. During the late 1970s and 1980s, male concern over appearance undeniably increased. Study after study confirms, however, that there is still a large gender gap in this area. Research conducted at the University of Pennsylvania in 1985 found men to be generally satisfied with their appearance, often, in fact, "distorting their perceptions [of themselves] in a positive, self-aggrandizing way" ("Dislike of Own Bodies Found Common Among Women," *New York Times*, March 19, 1985, p. C1). Women, however, were found to exhibit extreme negative assessments and distortions of body perception. Other studies have suggested that women are judged more harshly than men when they deviate from dominant social standards of attractiveness. Thomas Cash et al., in "The Great American Shape-Up," *Psychology Today* (April 1986), p. 34, report that although the situation for men has changed, the situation for women has more than proportionally worsened. Citing results from 30,000 responses to a 1985 survey of perceptions of body image and comparing similar responses to a 1972 questionnaire, they report that the 1985 respondents were considerably more dissatisfied with their bodies than the 1972 respondents, and they note a marked intensification of concern among men. Among the 1985 group, the group most dissatisfied of all with their appearance, however, were teenage women. Women today constitute by far the largest number of consumers of diet products, attenders of spas and diet centers, and subjects of intestinal by-pass and other fat-reduction operations.

5. Michel Foucault, *The History of Sexuality.* Vol. 1: *An Introduction* (New York: Vintage, 1980), pp. 136, 94.

6. On the gendered and historical nature of these disorders: the number of female to male hysterics has been estimated at anywhere from 2:1 to 4:1, and as many as 80 percent of all agoraphobics are female (Annette Brodsky and Rachel Hare-Mustin, *Women and Psychotherapy* [New York: Guilford Press, 1980], pp. 116, 122). Although more cases of male eating disorders have been reported in the late eighties and early nineties, it is estimated that close to 90 percent of all anorectics are female (Paul Garfinkel and David Garner, *Anorexia Nervosa: A Multidimensional Perspective* [New York: Brunner/Mazel, 1982], pp. 112–13). For a sophisticated account of female psychopathology, with particular attention to nineteenth-century disorders but, unfortunately, little mention of agoraphobia or eating disorders, see Elaine Showalter, *The Female Malady: Women, Madness and English Culture, 1830–1980* (New York: Pantheon, 1985). For a discussion of social and gender issues in agoraphobia, see Robert Seidenberg and Karen DeCrow, *Women Who Marry Houses: Panic and Protest in Agoraphobia* (New York: McGraw-Hill, 1983). On the history of anorexia nervosa, see Joan Jacobs Brumberg, *Fasting Girls: The Emergence of Anorexia Nervosa as a Modern Disease* (Cambridge: Harvard University Press, 1988).

7. In constructing such a paradigm I do not pretend to do justice to any of these disorders in its individual complexity. My aim is to chart some points of intersection, to describe some similar patterns, as they emerge through a particular reading of the phenomenon—a political reading, if you will.

8. Showalter, *The Female Malady*, pp. 128–29.

9. On the epidemic of hysteria and neurasthenia, see Showalter, *The Female Malady*; Carroll Smith-Rosenberg, "The Hysterical Woman: Sex Roles and Role Conflict in Nineteenth-Century America," in her *Disorderly Conduct: Visions of Gender in Victorian America* (Oxford: Oxford University Press, 1985).

10. Martha Vicinus, "Introduction: The Perfect Victorian Lady," in Martha Vicinus, *Suffer and Be Still: Women in the Victorian Age* (Bloomington: Indiana University Press, 1972), pp. x–xi.

11. See Carol Nadelson and Malkah Notman, *The Female Patient* (New York: Plenum, 1982), p. 5; E. M. Sigsworth and T. J. Wyke, "A Study of Victorian Prostitution and Venereal Disease," in Vicinus, *Suffer and Be Still*, p. 82. For more general discussions, see Peter Gay, *The Bourgeois Experience: Victoria to Freud.* Vol. 1: *Education of the Senses* (New York: Oxford University Press, 1984), esp. pp. 109–68; Showalter, *The Female Malady*, esp. pp. 121–44. The delicate lady, an ideal that had very strong class connotations (as does slenderness today), is not the only conception of femininity to be found in Victorian cultures. But it was arguably the single most powerful ideological representation of femininity in that era, affecting women of all classes, including those without the material means to realize the ideal fully. See Helena Mitchie, *The Flesh Made Word* (New York: Oxford, 1987), for discussions of the control of female appetite and Victorian constructions of femininity.

12. Smith-Rosenberg, *Disorderly Conduct*, p. 203.

13. Showalter, *The Female Malady*, p. 129.

14. Erving Goffman, *The Presentation of the Self in Everyday Life* (Garden City, N.J.: Anchor Doubleday, 1959).

15. Betty Friedan, *The Feminine Mystique* (New York: Dell, 1962), p. 36. The theme song of one such show ran, in part, "I married Joan . . . What a girl . . . what a whirl . . . what a life! I married Joan . . . What a mind . . . love is blind . . . what a wife!"

16. See I. G. Fodor, "The Phobic Syndrome in Women," in V. Franks and V. Burtle, eds., *Women in Therapy* (New York: Brunner/Mazel, 1974), p. 119; see also Kathleen Brehony, "Women and Agoraphobia," in Violet Franks and Esther Rothblum, eds., *The Stereotyping of Women* (New York: Springer, 1983).

17. In Jonathan Culler, *Roland Barthes* (New York: Oxford University Press, 1983), p. 74.

18. For other interpretive perspectives on the slenderness ideal, see "Reading the Slender Body" in this volume; Kim Chernin, *The Obsession: Reflections on the Tyranny of Slenderness* (New York: Harper and Row, 1981); Susie Orbach, *Hunger Strike: The Anorectic's Struggle as a Metaphor for Our Age* (New York: W. W. Norton, 1985).

19. See "Hunger as Ideology," in this volume, for a discussion of how this construction of femininity is reproduced in contemporary commercials and advertisements concerning food, eating, and cooking.

20. Aimee Liu, *Solitaire* (New York: Harper and Row, 1979), p. 123.

21. Striking, in connection with this, is Catherine Steiner-Adair's 1984 study of high-school women, which reveals a dramatic association between problems with food and body image and emulation of the cool, professionally "together" and gorgeous superwoman. On the basis of a series of interviews, the high schoolers were classified into two groups: one expressed skepticism over the superwoman ideal, the other thoroughly aspired to it. Later administrations of diagnostic tests revealed that 94 percent of the pro-superwoman group fell into the eating-disordered range of the scale. Of the other group, 100 percent fell into the noneating-disordered range. Media images notwithstanding, young women today appear to sense, either consciously or through their bodies, the impossibility of simultaneously meeting the demands of two spheres whose values have been historically defined in utter opposition to each other.

22. See "Anorexia Nervosa" in this volume.

23. Dianne Hunter, "Hysteria, Psychoanalysis and Feminism," in Shirley Garner, Claire Kahane, and Madelon Sprenger, eds., *The (M)Other Tongue* (Ithaca: Cornell University Press, 1985), p. 114.

24. Catherine Clément and Hélène Cixous, *The Newly Born Woman*, trans. Betsy Wing (Minneapolis: University of Minnesota Press, 1986), p. 42.

25. Clément and Cixous, *The Newly Born Woman*, p. 95.

26. Seidenberg and DeCrow, *Women Who Marry Houses*, p. 31.

27. Smith-Rosenberg, *Disorderly Conduct*, p. 208.

28. Orbach, *Hunger Strike*, p. 102. When we look into the many autobiographies and case studies of hysterics, anorectics, and agoraphobics, we find that these are indeed the sorts of women one might expect to be frustrated by the constraints of a specified female role. Sigmund Freud and Joseph Breuer, in *Studies on Hysteria* (New York: Avon, 1966), and Freud, in the later *Dora: An Analysis of a Case of Hysteria* (New York: Macmillan, 1963), constantly remark on the ambitiousness, independence, intellectual ability, and creative strivings of their patients. We know, moreover, that many women who later became leading social activists and feminists of the nineteenth century were among those who fell ill with hysteria and neurasthenia. It has become a virtual cliché that the typical anorectic is a perfectionist, driven to excel in all areas of her life. Though less prominently, a similar theme runs throughout the literature on agoraphobia.

One must keep in mind that in drawing on case studies, one is relying on the perceptions of other acculturated individuals. One suspects, for example, that the popular portrait of the anorectic as a relentless over-achiever may be colored by the lingering or perhaps resurgent Victorianism of our culture's attitudes toward ambitious women. One does not escape this hermeneutic problem by turning to autobiography. But in autobiography one is at least dealing with social constructions and attitudes that animate the subject's own psychic reality. In this regard the autobiographical literature on anorexia, drawn on in a variety of places in this volume, is strikingly full of anxiety about the domestic world and other themes that suggest deep rebellion against traditional notions of femininity.

29. Kim Chernin, *The Hungry Self: Women, Eating, and Identity* (New York: Harper and Row, 1985), esp. pp. 41–93.

30. Mark Poster, *Foucault, Marxism, and History* (Cambridge: Polity Press, 1984), p. 28.

31. Liu, *Solitaire,* p. 99.

32. Brett Silverstein, "Possible Causes of the Thin Standard of Bodily Attractiveness for Women," *International Journal of Eating Disorders* 5 (1986): 907–16.

33. Showalter, *The Female Malady,* p. 48.

34. Smith-Rosenberg, *Disorderly Conduct,* p. 207.

35. Orbach, *Hunger Strike,* p. 103.

36. Brownmiller, *Femininity,* p. 14.

37. Toril Moi, "Representations of Patriarchy: Sex and Epistemology in Freud's Dora," in Charles Bernheimer and Claire Kahane, eds., *In Dora's Case: Freud—Hysteria—Feminism* (New York: Columbia University Press, 1985), p. 192.

38. Foucault, *Discipline and Punish,* p. 136.

39. Foucault, *Discipline and Punish,* p. 136.

40. A focus on the politics of sexualization and objectification remains central to the anti-pornography movement (e.g., in the work of Andrea Dworkin, Catherine MacKinnon). Feminists exploring the politics of appearance include Sandra Bartky, Susan Brownmiller, Wendy Chapkis, Kim Chernin, and Susie Orbach. And a developing feminist interest in the work of Michel Foucault has begun to produce a poststructuralist feminism oriented toward practice; see, for example, Irene Diamond and Lee Quinby, *Feminism and Foucault: Reflections on Resistance* (Boston: Northeastern University Press, 1988).

41. See, for example, Susan Suleiman, ed., *The Female Body in Western Culture* (Cambridge: Harvard University Press, 1986).

42. Mitchie, *The Flesh Made Word,* p. 13.

43. Mitchie, *The Flesh Made Word,* p. 149.

DON SABO

Masculinities and Men's Health: Moving Toward Post-Superman Era Prevention

My grandfather used to smile and say, "Find out where you're going to die and stay the hell away from there." Grandpa had never studied epidemiology (the study of variations in health and illness in society), but he understood that certain behaviors, attitudes, and cultural practices can put individuals at risk for accidents, illness, or death. This chapter presents an overview of men's health that proceeds from the basic assumption that aspects of traditional masculinity can be dangerous to men's health (Sabo & Gordon, 1995; Harrison, Chin, & Ficarrotto, 1992). First, I identify some gender differences in relation to morbidity (sickness) and mortality (death). Next, I examine how the risk for illness varies from one male group to another. I then discuss an array of men's health issues and a preventative strategy for enhancing men's health.

GENDER DIFFERENCES IN HEALTH AND ILLNESS

When British sociologist Ashley Montagu put forth the thesis in 1953 that women were biologically superior to men, he shook up the prevailing chauvinistic beliefs that men were stronger, smarter, and better than women. His argument was partly based on epidemiological data that show males are more vulnerable to mortality than females from before birth and throughout the life span.

Mortality

From the time of conception, men are more likely to succumb to prenatal and neonatal death than females. Men's chances of dying during the prenatal stage of development are about 12% greater than those of females and, during the neonatal (newborn) stage, 130% greater than those of females. A number of neonatal disorders are common to males but not females, such as bacterial infections, respiratory illness, digestive diseases, and some circulatory disorders of the aorta and pulmonary artery. Table 1 compares male and female infant mortality rates across historical time. Though the infant mortality rate decreases over time, the persistence of the higher rates for males than females suggests that biological factors may be operating. Data also show that males have higher mortality rates than females in every age category, from "under one year" through "over 85" (National Center for Health Statistics, 1992). In fact, men are more likely to die in 9 out of the 10 leading causes of death in the United States. (See Table 2.)

From Estelle Disch (ed.), *Reconstructing Gender: A Multicultural Anthology*, Mayfield Publishing Company, 1997, pp. 426–43. Reprinted by permission of Mayfield Publishing Company.

Table 1.

Infant Mortality Rate

Year	Both Sexes	Males	Females
1940	47.0	52.5	41.3
1950	29.2	32.8	25.5
1960	26.0	29.3	22.6
1970	20.0	22.4	17.5
1980	12.6	13.9	11.2
1989	9.8	10.8	8.8

Note: Rates are for infant (under 1 year) deaths per 1,000 live births for all races.

Source: Adapted from Monthly Vital Statistics Report, Vol. 40, No. 8. Supplement 2, January 7, 1992, p. 41.

Table 2.

Death Rates by Sex and 10 Leading Causes: 1989

Cause of Death	Age-Adjusted Death Rate per 100,000 Population			
	Total	Male	Female	Sex Differential
Diseases of the heart	155.9	210.2	112.3	1.87
Malignant neoplasms	133.0	163.4	111.7	1.45
Accidents and adverse effects	33.8	49.5	18.9	2.62
Cerebrovascular disease	28.0	30.4	26.2	1.16
Chronic liver disease, cirrhosis	8.9	12.8	5.5	2.33
Diabetes	11.5	2.0	11.0	1.09
Suicide	11.3	18.6	4.5	4.13
Homicide and legal intervention	9.4	14.7	4.1	3.59

Source: Adapted from the *U.S. Bureau of the Census: Statistical Abstracts of the United States: 1992* (112th ed., p. 84), Washington, DC.

Females have greater life expectancy than males in the United States, Canada, and postindustrial societies (Verbrugge and Wingard, 1987; Waldron, 1986). This fact suggests a female biological advantage, but a closer analysis of changing trends in the gap between women's and men's life expectancy indicates that social and cultural factors related to lifestyle, gender identity, and behavior are operating well. Life expectancy among American females is about 78.3 years but 71.3 years for males (National Center for Health Statistics, 1990). As Waldron's (1995) analysis of shifting mortality patterns between the sexes during the 20th century shows, however, women's relative advantage in life expectancy over men was rather small at the beginning of the 20th century. During the mid-20th century, female mortality declined more rapidly than male mortality, thereby increasing the gender gap in life expectancy. Whereas women benefited from decreased maternal mortality, the midcentury trend toward a lowering of men's life expectancy was slowed by increasing mortality from coronary heart disease and lung cancer that were, in turn, mainly due to higher rates of cigarette smoking among males.

The most recent trends show that differences between women's and men's mortality decreased during the 1980s; that is, female life expectancy was 7.9 years greater than that of males in 1979 and 6.9 years in 1989 (National Center for Health Statistics, 1992). Waldron explains that some changes in behavioral patterns between the sexes, such as increased smoking among women, have narrowed the gap between men's formerly higher mortality rates from lung cancer, chronic obstructive pulmonary disease, and ischemic heart disease. In summary, it appears that both biological and sociocultural factors are involved with shaping patterns of men's and women's mortality. In fact, Waldron (1976) suggests that gender-related behaviors rather than strictly biogenic factors account for about three-quarters of the variation in men's early mortality.

Morbidity

Whereas females generally outlive males, females report higher morbidity rates, even after controlling for maternity. National health surveys show that females experience acute illnesses such as respiratory conditions, infective and parasitic conditions, and digestive system disorders at higher rates than males do; however, males sustain more injuries (Givens, 1979; Cypress, 1981; Dawson & Adams, 1987). Men's higher injury rates are partly owed to gender differences in socialization and lifestyle, such as learning to prove manhood through recklessness, involvement in contact sports, and working in risky blue-collar occupations.

Females are generally more likely than males to experience chronic conditions such as anemia, chronic enteritis and colitis, migraine headaches, arthritis, diabetes, and thyroid disease. However, males are more prone to develop chronic illnesses such as coronary heart disease, emphysema, and gout. Although chronic conditions do not ordinarily cause death, they often limit activity or cause disability.

After noting gender differences in morbidity, Cockerham (1995) asks whether women really do experience more illness than men—or could it be that women are more sensitive to bodily sensations than men, or that men are not as prone as women to report symptoms and seek medical care? He concludes, "The best evidence indicates that the overall differences in morbidity are real" and, further, that they are due to a mixture of biological, psychological, and social influences (p. 42).

MASCULINITIES AND MEN'S HEALTH

There is no such thing as masculinity; there are only masculinities (Sabo & Gordon, 1995). A limitation of early gender theory was its treatment of "all men" as a single, large category in relation to "all women" (Connell, 1987). The fact is, however, that all men are not alike, nor do all male groups share the same stakes in the gender order. At any given historical moment, there are competing masculinities—some dominant, some marginalized, and some stigmatized—each with its respective structural, psychosocial, and cultural moorings. There are substantial differences between the health options of homeless men, working-class men, lower-class men, gay men, men with AIDS, prison inmates, men of color, and their comparatively advantaged middle- and upper-class, white, professional male counterparts. Similarly, a wide range of individual differences exists between the ways that men and women act out "femininity" and "masculinity" in their everyday lives. A health profile of several male groups is discussed below.

Adolescent Males

Pleck, Sonenstein, and Ku (1992) applied critical feminist perspectives to their research on problem behaviors and health among adolescent males. A national sampling of adolescent, never-married males aged 15–19 were interviewed in 1980 and 1988. Hypothesis tests were geared to assessing whether "masculine ideology" (which measured the presence of traditional male role attitudes) put boys at risk for an array of problem behaviors. The researchers found a significant, independent association with seven of ten problem behaviors. Specifically, traditionally masculine attitudes were associated with being suspended from school, drinking and use of street drugs, frequency of being picked up by the police, being sexually active, the number of heterosexual partners in the last year, and tricking or forcing someone to have sex. These kinds of behaviors, which are in part expressions of the pursuit of traditional masculinity, elevate boys' risk for sexually transmitted diseases, HIV transmission, and early death by accident or homicide. At the same time, however, these same behaviors can also encourage victimization of women through men's violence, sexual assault, unwanted teenage pregnancy, and sexually transmitted diseases.

Adolescence is a phase of accelerated physiological development, and good nutrition during this period is important to future health. Obesity puts adults at risk for a variety of diseases such as coronary heart disease, diabetes mellitus, joint disease, and certain cancers. Obese adolescents are also apt to become obese adults, thus elevating long-term risk for illness. National Health and Nutrition Examination Surveys show that obesity among adolescents increased by 6% during 1976–80 and 1988–91. During 1988–91, 22% of females of 12–18 years were overweight, and 20% of males in this age group were as well (*Morbidity and Mortality Weekly Report*, 1994a).

Males form a majority of the estimated 1.3 million teenagers who run away from home each year in the United States. For both boys and girls, living on the streets raises the risk of poor nutrition, homicide, alcoholism, drug abuse, and AIDS. Young adults in their 20s comprise about 20% of new AIDS cases and, when you calculate the lengthy latency period, it is evident that they are being infected in their teenage years. Runaways are also more likely to be victims of crime and sexual exploitation (Hull, 1994).

Clearly, adolescent males face a spectrum of potential health problems—some that threaten their present well-being, and others that could take their toll in the future.

Men of Color

Patterns of health and illness among men of color can be partly understood against the historical and social context of economic inequality. Generally, because African Americans, Hispanics, and Native Americans are disproportionately poor, they are more apt to work in low-paying and dangerous occupations, reside in polluted environments, be exposed to toxic substances, experience the threat and reality of crime, and worry about meeting basic needs. Cultural barriers can also complicate their access to available health care. Poverty is correlated with lower educational attainment, which, in turn, mitigates against adoption of preventative health behaviors.

The neglect of public health in the United States is particularly pronounced in relation to African Americans (Polych & Sabo, 1996). For example, in Harlem, where 96% of the inhabitants are African American and 41% live below the poverty line, the survival curve beyond the age of 40 for men is lower than that of men living in Bangladesh (McFord & Freeman, 1990). Even though African American men have higher rates of alcoholism, infectious diseases, and drug-related conditions, for example, they are less apt to receive health care, and when they do, they are more apt to receive inferior care (Bullard, 1992; Staples, 1995). Statistics like the following led Gibbs (1988) to describe young African American males as an "endangered species":

- The number of young African American male homicide victims in 1977 (5,734) was higher than the number killed in the Vietnam War during 1963–72 (5,640) (Gibbs, 1988:258).
- Homicide is the leading cause of death among young African American males. The probability of a black man dying from homicide is about the same as that of a white male dying from an accident (Reed, 1991).
- More than 36% of urban African American males are drug and alcohol abusers (Staples, 1995).
- In 1993 the rate of contracting AIDS for African American males aged 13 and older was almost 5 times higher than the rate for white males (*Morbidity and Mortality Weekly Report*, 1994b).

The health profile of Native Americans and Native Canadians is also poor. For example, alcohol is the number-one killer of Native Americans between the ages of 14 and 44 (May, 1986), and 42% of Native American male adolescents are problem drinkers, compared to 34% of same-age white males (Lamarine, 1988). Native Americans (10–18 years of age) comprise 34% of inpatient admissions to adolescent detoxification programs (Moore, 1988). Compared to the "all race" population, Native American youth exhibit more serious problems in the areas of depression, suicide, anxiety, substance use, and general health status (Blum et al., 1992). The rates of morbidity, mortality from injury, and contracting AIDS are also higher (Sugarman et al., 1993; Metler et al., 1991).

Like those of many other racial and ethnic groups, the health problems facing American and Canadian natives correlate with the effects of poverty and social marginalization, such as dropping out of school, a sense of hopelessness, the experience of prejudice, poor nutrition, and lack of regular health care. Those who care about men's health, therefore, need to be attuned to the potential interplay between gender, race/ethnicity, cultural differences, and economic conditions when working with racial and ethnic minorities.

Gay and Bisexual Men

Gay and bisexual men are estimated to constitute 5% to 10% of the male population. In the past, gay men have been viewed as evil, sinful, sick, emotionally immature, and socially undesirable. Many health professionals and the wider public have harbored mixed feelings and homophobic attitudes toward gay and bisexual men. Gay men's indentity, their lifestyles, and the social responses to homosexuality can impact the health of gay and bisexual men. Stigmatization and marginalization, for example, may lead to emotional confusion and suicide among gay male adolescents. For gay and bisexual men who are "in the closet," anxiety and stress can tax emotional and physical health. When seeking medical services, gay and bisexual men must often cope with the homophobia of health care workers or deal with the threat of losing health care insurance if their sexual orientation is made known.

Whether they are straight or gay, men tend to have more sexual contacts than women do, which heightens men's risk for contracting sexually transmitted diseases (STDs). Men's sexual attitudes and behaviors are closely tied to the way masculinity has been socially constructed. For example, real men are taught to suppress their emotions, which can lead to a separation of sex from feeling. Traditionally, men are also encouraged to be daring, which can lead to risky sexual decisions. In addition, contrary to common myths about gay male effeminacy, masculinity also plays a powerful role in shaping gay and bisexual men's identity and behavior. To the extent that traditional masculinity informs sexual activity of men, masculinity can be a barrier to safer sexual behavior among men. This insight leads Kimmel and Levine (1989) to assert that "to educate men about safe sex, then, means to confront the issues of masculinity" (p. 352). In addition to practicing abstinence and safer sex as preventive strategies, therefore, they argue that traditional beliefs about masculinity be challenged as a form of risk reduction.

Men who have sex with men remain the largest risk group for HIV transmission. For gay and bisexual men who are infected by the HIV virus, the personal burden of living with an AIDS diagnosis is made heavier by the stigma associated with homosexuality. The cultural meanings associated with AIDS can also filter into gender and sexual identities. Tewksbury's (1995) interviews with 45 HIV positive gay men showed how masculinity, sexuality, stigmatization, and interpersonal commitment mesh in decision making related to risky sexual behavior. Most of the men practiced celibacy in order to prevent others from contracting the disease; others practiced safe sex, and a few went on having unprotected sex.

Prison Inmates

There are 1.3 million men imprisoned in American jails and prisons (Nadelmann & Wenner, 1994). The United States has the highest rate of incarceration of any nation in the world, 426 prisoners for every 100,000 people (American College of Physicians, 1992), followed by South Africa and the former Soviet Union (Mauer, 1992). Racial and ethnic minorities are overrepresented among those behind bars. Black and Hispanic males, for example, comprise 85% of prisoners in the New York State prison system (Green, 1991).

The prison system acts as a pocket of risk, within which men already at high risk of having a preexisting AIDS infection are exposed to conditions that further heighten the risk of contracting HIV (Toepell, 1992) or other infections such as tuberculosis (Bellin, Fletcher, & Safyer, 1993) or hepatitis. The corrections system is part of an institutional chain that facilitates transmission of HIV and other infections in certain North American populations, particularly among poor, inner-city, minority males. Prisoners are burdened not only by social disadvantage but also by high rates of physical illness, mental disorder, and substance abuse that jeopardize their health (Editor, *Lancet*, 1991).

AIDS prevalence is markedly higher among state and federal inmates than in the general U.S. population, with a known aggregate rate in 1992 of 202 per 100,000 population (Brewer & Derrickson, 1992) compared to a total population prevalence of 14.65 in 100,000 (American College of Physicians, 1992). The cumulative total of American prisoners with AIDS in 1989 was estimated to be 5,411, a 72% increase over the previous year (Belbot & del Carmen, 1991). The total number of AIDS cases reported in U.S. corrections as of 1993 was 11,565 (a minimum estimate of the true cumulative incidence among U.S. inmates) (Hammett; cited in Expert Committee on AIDS and Prisons, 1994). In New York State, at least 10,000 of the state's 55,000 prisoners are believed to be infected (Prisoners with AIDS/HIV Support Action Network, 1992). In Canadian federal penitentiaries, it is believed that 1 in 20 inmates is HIV infected (Hankins; cited in Expert Committee on AIDS and Prison, 1994).

The HIV virus is primarily transmitted between adults by unprotected penetrative sex or by needle sharing, without bleaching, with an infected partner. Sexual contacts between prisoners occur mainly through consensual unions and secondarily though sexual assault and rape (Vaid; cited in Expert Committee on AIDS and Prisons, 1994). The amount of IV drug use behind prison walls is unknown, although it is known to be prevalent and the scarcity of needles often leads to sharing of needles and sharps (Prisoners with AIDS/HIV Support Action Network, 1992).

The failure to provide comprehensive health education and treatment interventions in prisons not only puts more inmates at risk for HIV infection, but also threatens the public at large. Prisons are not hermetically sealed enclaves set apart from the community but an integral part of society (Editor, *Lancet*, 1991). Prisoners regularly move in and out of the prison system. In 1989, prisons in the United States admitted 467,227 persons and discharged 386,228 (American College of Physicians, 1992). The average age of inmates admitted to prison in 1989 was 29.6, with 75% between 18 and 34 years; 94.3% were male. These former inmates return to their communities after having served an average of 18 months inside (Dubler & Sidel, 1989). Within three years, 62.5% will be rearrested and jailed. Recidivism is highest among poor black and Hispanic men. The extent to which the drug-related social practices and sexual activities of released or paroled inmates who are HIV positive are putting others at risk upon return to their communities is un-researched and unknown.

Male Athletes

Injury is everywhere in sport. It is evident in the lives and bodies of athletes who regularly experience bruises, torn ligaments, broken bones, aches, lacerations, muscle tears, and so forth. For example, about 300,000 football-related injuries per year require treatment in hospital emergency rooms (Miedzian, 1991). Critics of violent contact sports claim that athletes are paying too high a physical price for their participation. George D. Lundberg (1994), editor of the *Journal of the American Medical Association*, has called for a ban on boxing in the Olympics and in the U.S. military. His editorial entreaty, though based on clinical evidence for neurological harm from boxing, is also couched in a wider critique of the exploitative econom-ics of the sport.

Injuries are basically unavoidable in sports, but, in traditional men's sports, there has been a tendency to glorify pain and injury, to inflict injury on others, and to sacrifice one's body in order to "win at all costs." The "no pain, no gain" phi-losophy, which is rooted in traditional cultural equations between masculinity and sports, can jeopardize the health of athletes who conform to its ethos (Sabo, 1994).

The connections between sport, masculinity, and health are evidenced in Klein's (1993) study of how bodybuilders use anabolic steroids, overtrain, and en-gage in extreme dietary practices. He spent years as an ethnographic researcher in the muscled world of the bodybuilding subculture, where masculinity is equated to maximum muscularity and men's striving for bigness and physical strength hides emotional insecurity and low self-esteem.

A nationwide survey of American male high school seniors found that 6.6% used or had used anabolic steroids. About two-thirds of this group were athletes (Buckley et al., 1988). Anabolic steroid use has been linked to health risks such as liver disease, kidney problems, atrophy of the testicles, elevated risk of injury, and premature skeletal maturation.

Klein lays bare a tragic irony in American subculture—the powerful male ath-lete, a symbol of strength and health, has often sacrificed his health in pursuit of ideal masculinity (Messner & Sabo, 1994).

MEN'S HEALTH ISSUES

Advocates of men's health have identified a variety of issues that impact directly on men's lives. Some of these issues may concern you or men you care about.

Testicular Cancer

The epidemiological data on testicular cancer are sobering. Though relatively rare in the general population, it is the fourth most common cause of death among males of 15–35 years, accounting for 14% of all cancer deaths for this age group. It is the most common form of cancer affecting males of 20–34 years. The incidence of testicular cancer is increasing, and about 6,100 new U.S. cases were diagnosed in 1991 (American Cancer Society, 1991). If detected early, the cure rate is high, whereas delayed diagnosis is life threatening. Regular testicular self-examination (TSE), therefore, is a potentially effective means for ensuring early detection and successful treatment. Regrettably, however, most physicians do not teach TSE techniques (Rudolf & Quinn, 1988).

Denial may influence men's perceptions of testicular cancer and TSE (Blesch, 1986). Studies show that most males are not aware of testicular cancer, and even among those who are aware, many are reluctant to examine their testicles as a preventive measure. Even when symptoms are recognized, men sometimes postpone seeking treatment. Moreover, men who are taught TSE are often initially receptive, but their practice of TSE decreases over time. Men's resistance to TSE has been linked to awkwardness about touching themselves, associating touching genitals with homosexuality or masturbation, or the idea that TSE is not a manly behavior. And finally, men's individual reluctance to discuss testicular cancer partly derives from the widespread cultural silence that envelops it. The penis is a cultural symbol of male power, authority, and sexual domination. Its symbolic efficacy in traditional, male-dominated gender relations, therefore, would be eroded or neutralized by the realities of testicular cancer.

Disease of the Prostate

Middle-aged and elderly men are likely to develop medical problems with the prostate gland. Some men may experience benign prostatic hyperplasia, an enlargement of the prostate gland that is associated with symptoms such as dribbling after urination, frequent urination, or incontinence. Others may develop infections (prostatitis) or malignant prostatic hyperplasia (prostate cancer). Prostate cancer is the third leading cause of death from cancer in men, accounting for 15.7 deaths per 100,000 population in 1989. Prostate cancer is now more common than lung cancer (Martin, 1990). One in 10 men will develop this cancer by age 85, with African American males showing a higher prevalence rate than whites (Greco & Blank, 1993).

Treatments for prostate problems depend on the specific diagnosis and may range from medication to radiation and surgery. As is the case with testicular cancer, survival from prostate cancer is enhanced by early detection. Raising men's awareness about the health risks associated with the prostate gland, therefore, may prevent unnecessary morbidity and mortality. Unfortunately, the more invasive surgical treatments for prostate cancer can produce incontinence and impotence, and there has been no systematic research on men's psychosocial reactions and adjustment to sexual dysfunction associated with treatments for prostate cancer.

Alcohol Abuse

Although social and medical problems stemming from alcohol abuse involve both sexes, males comprise the largest segment of alcohol abusers. Some researchers have begun exploring the connections between the influence of the traditional male role on alcohol abuse. Isenhart and Silversmith (1994) show how, in a variety of occupational contexts, expectations surrounding masculinity encourage heavy drinking while working or socializing during after-work or off-duty hours. Some predominantly male occupational groups, such as longshoremen (Hitz, 1973), salesmen (Cosper, 1979), and members of the military (Pursch, 1976), are known to engage in high rates of alcohol consumption. Mass media play a role in sensationalizing links between booze and male bravado. Postman, Nystrom, Strate, and Weingartner (1987) studied the thematic content of 40 beer commercials and identified a variety of stereotypical portrayals of the male role that were used to promote been drinking: reward for a job well done; manly activities that feature strength, risk, and daring; male friendship and esprit de corps; romantic success with women. The researchers estimate that, between the ages of 2 and 18, children view about 100,000 beer commercials.

Findings from a Harvard School of Public Health (1994) survey of 17,600 students at 140 colleges found that 44% engaged in "binge drinking," defined as drinking five drinks in rapid suggestion for males and four drinks for females. Males were more apt to report binge drinking during the past two weeks than females: 50% and 39% respectively. Sixty percent of the males who binge three or more times in the past two weeks reported driving after drinking, compared to 49% of their female counterparts, thus increasing the risk for accident, injury, and death. Compared to non-binge drinkers, binge drinkers were seven times more likely to engage in unprotected sex, thus elevating the risk for unwanted pregnancy and sexually transmitted disease. Alcohol-related automobile accidents are the top cause of death among 16- to 24-year-olds, especially among males (Henderson & Anderson, 1989). For all males, the age-adjusted death rate from automobile accidents in 1991 was 26.2 per 100,000 for African American males and 24.2 per 100,000 for white males, 2.5 and 3.0 times higher than for white and African American females respectively (*Morbidity and Mortality Weekly Report*, 1994d). The number of automobile fatalities among male adolescents that results from a mixture of alcohol abuse and masculine daring is unknown.

Men and AIDS

Human immunodeficiency virus (HIV) infection became a leading cause of death among males in the 1980s. Among men aged 25–44 in 1990, HIV infection was the second leading cause of death, compared to the sixth leading cause of death among same-age women (*Morbidity and Mortality Weekly Report*, 1993a). Among reported cases of acquired immunodeficiency syndrome (AIDS) for adolescent and adult men in 1992, 60% were men who had sex with other men, 21% were intravenous drug users, 4% were exposed through heterosexual sexual contact, 6%

were men who had sex with men and injected drugs, and 1% were transfusion recipients. Among the cases of AIDS among adolescent and adult women in 1992, 45% were intravenous drug users, 39% were infected through heterosexual contact, and 4% were transfusion recipients (*Morbidity and Mortality Weekly Report,* 1993a).

Because most AIDS cases have been among men who have sex with other men, perceptions of the epidemic and its victims have been tinctured by sexual attitudes. In North American cultures, the stigma associated with AIDS is fused with the stigma linked to homosexuality. Feelings about men with AIDS can be mixed and complicated by homophobia.

Thoughts and feelings about men with AIDS are also influenced by attitudes toward race, ethnicity, drug abuse, and social marginality. Centers for Disease Control data show, for example, that men of color aged 13 and older constituted 51% (45,039) of the 89,165 AIDS cases reported in 1993. Women of color made up 71% of the cases reported among females aged 13 and older (*Morbidity and Mortality Weekly Report,* 1994b). The high rate of AIDS among racial and ethnic minorities has kindled racial prejudices in some minds, and AIDS is sometimes seen as a "minority disease." Although African American or Hispanic males may be at a greater risk of contracting HIV/AIDS, just as yellow fingers do not cause lung disease, it is not race or ethnicity that confers risk, but the behaviors they engage in and the social circumstances of their lives.

Perceptions of HIV/AIDS can also be influenced by attitudes toward poverty and poor people. HIV infection is linked to economic problems that include community disintegration, unemployment, homelessness, eroding urban tax bases, mental illness, substance abuse, and criminalization (Wallace, 1991). For example, males comprise the majority of homeless persons. Poverty and homelessness overlap with drug addiction, which, in turn, is linked to HIV infection. Of persons hospitalized with HIV in New York City, 9–18% have been found to be homeless (Torres et al, 1990). Of homeless men tested for HIV at a New York City shelter, 62% of those who took the test were seropositive (Ron & Rogers, 1989). Among runaway or homeless youth in New York City, 7% tested positive, and this rate rose to 15% among the 19- and 20-year-olds. Of homeless men in Baltimore, 85% admitted to substance use problems (Weinred & Bassuk, 1990).

Suicide

The suicide rates for both African American and white males increased between 1970 and 1989, whereas female rates decreased. Indeed, males are more likely than females to commit suicide from middle childhood until old age (Stillion, 1985, 1995). Compared to females, males typically deploy more violent means of attempting suicide (e.g., guns or hanging rather than pills) and are more likely to complete that act. Men's selection of more violent methods to kill themselves is consistent with traditionally masculine behavior (Stillion, White, McDowell, & Edwards, 1989).

Canetto (1995) interviewed male survivors of suicide attempts in order to better understand sex differences in suicidal behavior. Although she recognizes that men's psychosocial reactions and adjustments to nonfatal suicide vary by race/ethnicity, socioeconomic status, and age, she also finds that gender identity is an important factor in men's experiences. Suicide data show that men attempt suicide less often than women but are more likely to die than women. Canetto indicates that men's comparative "success" rate points toward a tragic irony that, consistent with gender stereotypes, men's failure even at suicide undercuts the cultural mandate that men are supposed to succeed at everything. A lack of embroilment in traditionally masculine expectations, she suggests, may actually increase the likelihood of surviving a suicide attempt for some men.

Elderly males in North America commit suicide significantly more often than elderly females. Whereas white women's lethal suicide rate peaks at age 50, white men age 60 and older have the highest rate of lethal suicide, even surpassing that rate for younger males (Manton et al., 1987). Canetto (1992) argues that elderly men's higher suicide mortality is chiefly owed to gender differences in coping. She writes,

> Older women may have more flexible and diverse ways of coping than older men. Compared to older men, older women may be more willing and capable of adopting different coping strategies—"passive" or "active," "connected" or "independent"—depending on the situation (p. 92).

She attributes men's limited coping abilities to gender socialization and development.

Erectile Disorders

Men often joke about their penises or tease one another about penis size and erectile potency ("not getting it up"). In contrast, they rarely discuss their concerns about impotence in a serious way. Men's silences in this regard are regrettable in that many men, both young and old, experience recurrent or periodic difficulties getting or maintaining an erection. Estimates of the number of American men with erectile disorders range from 10 million to 30 million (Krane, Goldstein, & Saenz de Tejada, 1989; National Institutes of Health, 1993). The Massachusetts Male Aging Study of the general population of noninstitutionalized, healthy American men between ages 40 and 70 years found that 52% reported minimal, moderate, or complete impotence (Feldman et al., 1994). The prevalence of erectile disorders increased with age, and 9.6% of the men were afflicted by complete impotence.

During the 1960s and 1970s, erectile disorders were largely thought to stem from psychological problems such as depression, financial worries, or work-related stress. Masculine stereotypes about male sexual prowess, phallic power, or being in charge of lovemaking were also said to put too much pressure to perform on some males (Zilbergeld, 1993). In contrast, physiological explanations of erectile disorders and medical treatments have been increasingly emphasized since the 1980s. Today diagnosis and treatment of erectile disorders should combine psychological and medical assessment (Ackerman & Carey, 1995).

Men's Violence

Men's violence is a major public health problem. The traditional masculine stereotype calls on males to be aggressive and tough. Anger is a by-product of aggression and toughness and, ultimately, part of the inner terrain of traditional masculinity (Sabo, 1993). Images of angry young men are compelling vehicles used by some males to separate themselves from women and to measure their status in respect to other males. Men's anger and violence derive, in part, from sex inequality. Men use the threat or application of violence to maintain their political and economic advantage over women and lower-status men. Male socialization reflects and reinforces these larger patterns of domination.

Homicide is the second leading cause of death among 15- to 19-year-old males. Males aged 15–34 years made up almost half (49%, or 13,122) of homicide victims in the United States in 1991. The homicide rate for this age group increased by 50% from 1985 to 1991 (*Morbidity and Mortality Weekly Report*, 1994c).

Women are especially victimized by men's anger and violence in the form of rape, date rape, wife beating, assault, sexual harassment on the job, and verbal harassment (Thorne-Finch, 1992). That the reality and potential of men's violence impact women's mental and physical health can be surely assumed. However, men's violence also exacts a toll on men themselves in the forms of fighting, gang clashes, hazing, gay-bashing, intentional infliction of injury, homicide, suicide, and organized warfare.

SUMMARY

It is ironic that two of the best-known actors who portrayed Superman have met with disaster. George Reeves, who starred in the original black-and-white television show, committed suicide, and Christopher Reeve, who portrayed the "man of steel" in recent film versions, was paralyzed by an accident during a high-risk equestrian event. Perhaps one lesson to be learned here is that, behind the cultural facade of mythic masculinity, men are vulnerable. Indeed, as we have seen in this chapter, some of the cultural messages sewn into the cloak of masculinity can put men at risk for illness and early death. A sensible preventive health strategy for the 1990s calls upon men to critically evaluate the Superman legacy, that is, to challenge the negative aspects of traditional masculinity that endanger their health, while hanging on to the positive aspects of masculinity and men's lifestyles that heighten men's physical vitality.

The promotion of men's health also requires a sharper recognition that the sources of men's risks for many diseases do not strictly reside in men's psyches, gender identities, or the roles that they enact in daily life. Men's roles, routines, and relations with others are fixed in the historical and structural relations that constitute the larger gender order. As we have seen, not all men or male groups share the same access to social resources, educational attainment, and opportunity that, in turn, can influence their health options. Yes, men need to pursue personal change in order to enhance their health, but without changing the political, economic, and ideological structures of the gender order, the subjective gains and insights forged within individuals can easily erode and fade away. If men are going to pursue self-healing, therefore, they need to create an overall preventive strategy that at once seeks to change potentially harmful aspects of traditional masculinity and meets the health needs of lower-status men.

References

Ackerman, M. D., & Carey, P. C. (1995). *Journal of Counseling & Clinical Psychology, 63*(6), 862–876.

American Cancer Society (1991). Cancer Facts and Figures—1991. Atlanta, GA: American Cancer Society.

American College of Physicians. (1992). The crisis in correctional health care: The impact of the national drug control strategy on correctional health services. *Annals of Internal Medicine, 117*(1), 71–77.

Belbot, B. A., & del Carmen, R. B. (1991). AIDS in prison: Legal issues. *Crime and Delinquency, 31*(1), 135–153.

Bellin, E. Y., Fletcher, D. D., & Safyer, S. M. (1993). Association of tuberculosis infection with increased time in or admission to the New York City jail system. *Journal of the American Medical Association. 269*(17), 2228–2231.

Blesch, K. (1986). Health beliefs about testicular cancer and self-examination among professional men. *Oncology Nursing Forum, 13*(1), 29–33.

Blum, R., Harman, B., Harris, L., Bergeissen, L., & Restrick, M. (1992). American Indian—Alaska native youth health. *Journal of American Medical Association, 267*(12), 1637–1644.

Brewer, T. F., & Derrickson, J. (1992). AIDS in prison: A review of epidemiology and preventive policy. *AIDS, 6*(7), 623–628.

Buckley, W. E., Yesalis, C. E., Friedl, K. E., Anderson, W. A., Steit, A. L., & Wright, J. E. (1988). Estimated prevalence of anabolic steroid use among male high school seniors. *Journal of the American Medical Association, 260*(23), 3441–3446.

Bullard, R. D., (1992). Urban infrastructure: Social, environmental, and health risks to African Americans. In B. J. Tidwell (Ed.), *The State of Black America* (pp. 183–196). New York: National Urban League.

Canetto, S. S. (1995). Men who survive a suicidal act: Successful coping or failed masculinity? In D. Sabo & D. Gordon (Eds.), *Men's health and illness* (pp. 292–304). Newbury Park, CA: Sage.

———. (1992). Gender and suicide in the elderly. *Suicide and Life-Threatening Behavior, 22*(1), 80–97.

Cockerham, W. C. (1995). *Medical sociology.* Englewood Cliffs, NJ: Prentice Hall.

Connell, R. W. (1987). *Gender and power.* Stanford: Stanford University Press.

Cosper, R. (1979). Drinking as conformity: A critique of sociological literature on occupational differences in drinking. *Journal of Studies on Alcoholism, 40*, 868–891.

Cypress, B. (1981). Patients' reasons for visiting physicians: National ambulatory medical care survey, U. S. 1977–78. DHHS Publication No. (PHS) 82-1717, Series 13, No. 56. Hyattsville, MD: National Center for Health Statistics, December, 1981a.

Dawson, D. A., & Adams, P. F. (1987). Current estimates from the national health interview survey: U. S. 1986. Vital Health Statistics Series, Series 10, No. 164. DHHS Publication No. (PHS) 87-1592, Public Health Service. Washington, DC: U. S. Government Printing Office.

Dubler, N. N., & Sidel, V. W. (1989). On research on HIV infection and AIDS in correctional institutions. *The Milbank Quarterly, 67*(1–2), 81–94.

Editor. (1991, March 16). Health care for prisoners: Implications of "Kalk's refusal." *Lancet, 337*, 647–648.

Expert Committee on AIDS and Prison. (1994). *HIV/AIDS in prisons: Summary report and recommendations to the Expert Committee on AIDS and Prisons* (Ministry of Supply and Services Canada Catalogue No. JS82-68/2-1994). Ottawa, Ontario, Canada: Correctional Service of Canada.

Feldman, H. A., Goldstein, I., Hatzichristou, D. G., Krane, R. J., & McKinlay, J. B. (1994). Impotence and its medical and psychosocial correlates: Results of the Massachusetts Male Aging Study. *Journal of Urology, 151*, 54–61.

Gibbs, J. T. (Ed.) (1988). *Young, black, and male in America: An endangered species.* Dover, MA: Auburn House.

Givens, J. (1979). Current estimates from the health interview survey: U. S. 1978. DHHS Publications No. (PHS) 80-1551, Series 10, No. 130. Hyattsville, MD: Office of Health Research Statistics, November 1979.

Greco, K. E., & Blank, B. (1993). Prostate-specific antigen: The new early detection test for prostate cancer. *Nurse Practitioner, 18*(5), 30–38.

Green, A. P. (1991). Blacks unheard. *Update* (Winter), New York State Coalition for Criminal Justice, 6–7.

Harrison, J., Chin, J., & Ficarrotto, T. (1992). Warning: Masculinity may be dangerous to your health. In M. S. Kimmel & M. A. Messner (Eds.), *Men's lives* (pp. 271–285). New York: Macmillian.

Harvard School of Public Health. Study reported by Wechsler, II., Davenport, A., Dowdall, G., Moeykens, B., & Castillo, S. (1994). Health and behavioral consequences of binge drinking in college: A national survery of students at 140 campuses. *Journal of the American Medical Association, 272*(21), 1672–1677.

Henderson, D. C., & Anderson, S. C., (1989). Adolescents and chemical dependency. *Social Work in Health Care, 14*(1), 87–105.

Hitz, D. (1973). Drunken sailors and others: Drinking problems in specific occupations. *Quarterly Journal of Studies on Alcohol, 34*, 496–505.

Hull, J. D. (1994, November 21). Running scared. *Time, 144*(2), 93–99.

Isenhart, C. E., & Silversmith, D. J. (1994). The influence of the traditional male role on alcohol abuse and the therapeutic process. *Journal of Men's Studies, 3*(2), 127–135.

Kimmel, M. S., and Levine, M. P. (1989). Men and AIDS. In M. S. Kimmel & M. A. Messner (Eds.), *Men's lives* (pp. 344–354). New York: Macmillian.

Klein, A. (1993). Little big men: Bodybuilding subculture and gender construction. Albany, NY: SUNY Press.

Krane, R. J., Goldstein, I., Saentz de Tejada, I. (1989). Impotence. *New England Journal of Medicine, 321*, 1648–1659.

Lamarine, R. (1988). Alcohol abuse among Native Americans. *Journal of Community Health, 13*(3), 143–153.

Lundberg, G. D. (1994, June 8). Let's stop boxing in the Olympics and the United States military. *Journal of the American Medical Association, 271*(22), 1990.

Manton, K. G., Blazer, D. G., & Woodbury, M. A. (1987). Suicide in middle age and later life: Sex and race specific life table and cohort analysis. *Journal of Gerontology, 42,* 219–227.

Martin, J. (1990). Male cancer awareness: Impact of an employee education program. *Oncology Nursing Forum, 17*(1), 59–64.

Mauer, M. (1992). Men in American prisons: Trends, causes, and issues. *Men's Studies Review, 9*(1), 10–12. A special issue on men in prison, edited by Don Sabo and Willie London.

May, P. (1986). Alcohol and drug misuse prevention programs for American Indians: Needs and opportunities. *Journal of Studies of Alcohol, 47*(3), 187–195.

McCord, C., & Freeman, H. P. (1990). Excess mortality in Harlem. *New England Journal of Medicine, 322*(22), 1606–1607.

Messner, M. A., & Sabo, D. (1994). *Sex, violence, and power in sports: Rethinking masculinity.* Freedom. CA: Crossing Press.

Metler, R., Conway, G. & Stehr-Green, J. (1991). AIDS surveillance among American Indians and Alaskan natives. *American Journal of Public Health, 81*(11), 1469–1471.

Miedzian, M. (1991). *Boys will be boys: Breaking the link between masculinity and violence.* New York: Doubleday.

Monatgu, A. (1953). *The natural superiority of women.* New York: Macmillian.

Moore, D. (1988). Reducing alcohol and other drug use among Native American youth. *Alcohol Drug Abuse and Mental Health, 15*(6), 2–3.

Morbidity and Mortality Weekly Report. (1993a). Update: Mortality attributable to HIV infection/AIDS among persons aged 25–44 years—United States, 1990–91. 42(25), 481–486.

Morbidity and Mortality Weekly Report. (1993b). Summary of notifiable diseases—United States, 1992. 41(55).

Morbidity and Mortality Weekly Report. (1994a). Prevalence of overweight among adolescents—United States, 1988–91. 43(44), 818–819.

Morbidity and Mortality Weekly Report. (1994b). AIDS among racial/ethnic minorities—United States, 1993. 43(35), 644–651.

Morbidity and Mortality Weekly Report. (1994c). Homicides among 15–19-year-old males—United States, 43(40), 725–728.

Morbidity and Mortality Weekly Report. (1994d). Deaths resulting from firearm- and motor-vehicle-related injuries—United States, 1968–1991. 43(3), 37–42.

Nadelmann, P., & Wenner, L. (1994, May 5). Toward a sane national drug policy [Editorial]. *Rolling Stone,* 24–26.

National Center for Health Statistics. (1990). *Health, United States, 1989.* Hyattsville, MD: Public Health Service.

National Center for Health Statistics. (1992). Advance report of final mortality statistics, 1989. *Monthly Vital Statistics Report, 40* (Suppl. 2) (DHHS Publication No. [PHS] 92-1120).

National Institutes of Health. (1993). Consensus development panel on impotence. *Journal of the American Medical Association, 270,* 83–90.

Pleck, J., Sonenstein, F. L., & Ku, L. C. (1992). In R. Ketterlinus, & M. E. Lamb (Eds.), *Adolescent problem behaviors.* Hillsdale, NJ: Lawrence Erlbaum Associates.

Polych, C., & Sabo, D. (1996). Gender politics, pain, and illness: The AIDS epidemic in

North American prisons. In D. Sabo & D. Gordon (Eds.), *Men's health and illness* (pp. 139–157), Newbury Park, CA: Sage.

Postman, N., Nystrom, C., Strate, L., & Weingartner, C. (1987). *Myths, men and beer: An analysis of beer commercials on broadcast television, 1987.* Falls Church, VA: Foundation for Traffic Safety.

Prisoners with AIDS/HIV Support Action Network. (1992). *HIV/AIDS in prison systems: A comprehensive strategy* (Brief to the Minister of Correctional Services and the Minister of Health). Toronto: Prisoners with AIDS/HIV Support Action Network.

Pursch, J. A. (1976). From quonset hut to naval hospital: The story of an alcoholism rehabilitation service. *Journal of Studies on Alcohol, 37,* 1655–1666.

Reed, W. L. (1991). Trends in homicide among African Americans. *Trotter Institute Review, 5,* 11–16.

Ron, A., & Rogers, D. E. (1989). AIDS in New York City: The role of intravenous drug users. *Bulletin of the New York Academy of Medicine, 65*(7), 787–800.

Rudolf, V., & Quinn, K. (1988). The practice of TSE among college men: Effectiveness of an educational program. *Oncology Nursing Forum, 15*(1), 45–48.

Sabo, D., & Gordon, D. (1995). *Men's health and illness: Gender, power, and the body.* Newbury Park, CA: Sage.

Sabo, D. (1994). The body politics of sports injury: Culture, power, and the pain principle. A paper presented at the annual meeting of the National Athletic Trainers Association, Dallas, TX, June 6, 1994.

Sabo, D. (1993). Understanding men. In Kimball G. (Ed.), *Everything you need to know to succeed after college,* (pp. 71–93), Chico, CA: Equality Press.

Staples, R. (1995). Health and illness among African-American males. In D. Sabo and D. Gordon (Eds.), *Men's health and illness,* (pp. 121–138), Newbury Park, CA: Sage.

Stillion, J. (1985). *Death and the sexes: An examination of differential longevity, attitudes, behaviors, and coping skills.* New York: Hemisphere.

———. (1995). Premature death among males: Rethinking links between masculinity and health. In D. Sabo and D. Gordon (Eds.), *Men's health and illness,* (pp. 46–67), Newbury Park, CA: Sage.

Stillion, J., White, H., McDowell, E. E., & Edwards, P. (1989). Ageism and sexism in suicide attitudes. *Death Studies, 13,* 247–261.

Sugarman, J., Soderberg, R., Gordon, J., & Rivera, F. (1993). Racial misclassifications of American Indians: Its effects on injury rates in Oregon, 1989–1990. *American Journal of Public Health, 83*(5), 681–684.

Tewksbury, R. (1995). Sexual adaptation among gay men with HIV. In D. Sabo and D. Gordon (Eds.), *Men's health and illness,* (pp. 222–245), Newbury Park, CA: Sage.

Thorne-Finch, R. (1992). *Ending the silence: The origins and treatment of male violence against women.* Toronto: University or Toronto Press.

Toepell, A. R. (1992). *Prisoners and AIDS: AIDS education needs assessment.* Toronto: John Howard Society of Metropolitan Toronto.

Torres, R. A., Mani, S., Altholz, J., & Brickner, P. W. (1990). HIV infection among homeless men in a New York City shelter. *Archives of Internal Medicine, 150,* 2030–2036.

Verbrugge, L. M., & Wingard, D. L. (1987). Sex differentials in health and mortality. *Women's Health, 12,* 103–145.

Waldron, I. (1995). Contributions of changing gender differences in mortality. In D. Sabo and D. Gordon (Eds.), *Men's health and illness,* (pp. 22–45), Newbury Park, CA: Sage.

———. (1986). What do we know about sex differences in mortality? *Population Bulletin of the U. N., No. 18-1985,* 59–76.

———. (1976). Why do women live longer than men? *Journal of Human Stress, 2,* 1–13.

Wallace, R. (1991). Traveling waves of HIV infection on a low dimensional "socio-geographic" network. *Social Science Medicine, 32*(7), 847–852.

Weinreb, L.F., & Bassuk, E. L. (1990). Substance abuse: A growing problem among homeless families. *Families and Community Health, 13*(1). 55–64.

Zilbergeld, B. (1993). *The new male sexuality.* New York: Bantam.

Portions of this reading previously appeared in *Nursing Care in the Community*, 2e, edited by J. Cookfair, St. Louis: Mosby-Year Book, 1996.

ANNE FAUSTO-STERLING

The Five Sexes: Why Male and Female Are Not Enough

In 1843 Levi Suydam, a 23-year-old resident of Salisbury, Connecticut, asked the town board of selectmen to validate his right to vote as a Whig in a hotly contested local election. The request raised a flurry of objections from the opposition party, for reasons that must be rare in the annals of American democracy: it was said that Suydam was more female than male and thus (some eighty years before suffrage was extended to women) could not be allowed to cast a ballot. To settle the dispute a physician, one William James Barry, was brought in to examine Suydam. And, presumably upon encountering a phallus, the good doctor declared the prospective voter male. With Suydam safely in their column the Whigs won the election by a majority of one.

Barry's diagnosis, however, turned out to be somewhat premature. Within a few days he discovered that, phallus notwithstanding, Suydam menstruated regularly and had a vaginal opening. Both his/her physique and his/her mental predispositions were more complex than was first suspected. S/he had narrow shoulders and broad hips and felt occasional sexual yearnings for women. Suydam's "feminine propensities, such as a fondness for gay colors, for pieces of calico, comparing and placing them together, and an aversion for bodily labor, and an inability to perform the same, were remarked by many," Barry later wrote. It is not clear whether Suydam lost or retained the vote, or whether the election results were reversed.

This article is reprinted by permission of *The Sciences* and is from the March/April 1993 issue.

Western culture is deeply committed to the idea that there are only two sexes. Even language refuses other possibilities; thus to write about Levi Suydam I have had to invent conventions—s/he and his/her—to denote someone who is clearly neither male nor female or who is perhaps both sexes at once. Legally, too, every adult is either man or woman, and the difference, of course, is not trivial. For Suydam it meant the franchise; today it means being available for, or exempt from, draft registration, as well as being subject, in various ways, to a number of laws governing marriage, the family, and human intimacy. In many parts of the United States, for instance, two people legally registered as men cannot have sexual relations without violating anti-sodomy statutes.

But if the state and the legal system have an interest in maintaining a two-party sexual system, they are in defiance of nature. For biologically speaking, there are many gradations running from female to male; and depending on how one calls the shots, one can argue that along that spectrum lie at least five sexes—and perhaps even more.

For some time medical investigators have recognized the concept of the intersexual body. But the standard medical literature uses the term *intersex* as a catch-all for three major subgroups with some mixture of male and female characteristics: the so-called true hermaphrodites, whom I call herms, who possess one testis and one ovary (the sperm- and egg-producing vessels, or gonads); the male pseudohermaphrodites (the "merms"), who have testes and some aspects of the female genitalia but no ovaries; and the female pseudohermaphrodites (the "ferms"), who have ovaries and some aspects of the male genitalia but lack testes. Each of those categories is in itself complex; the percentage of male and female characteristics, for instance, can vary enormously among members of the same subgroup. Moreover, the inner lives of the people in each subgroup—their special needs and their problems, attractions, and repulsions—have gone unexplored by science. But on the basis of what is known about them I suggest that the three intersexes, herm, merm, and ferm, deserve to be considered additional sexes each in its own right. Indeed, I would argue further that sex is a vast, infinitely malleable continuum that defies the constraints of even five categories.

Not surprisingly, it is extremely difficult to estimate the frequency of intersexuality, much less the frequency of each of the three additional sexes: it is not the sort of information one volunteers on a job application. The psychologist John Money of Johns Hopkins University, a specialist in the study of congenital sexual-organ defects, suggests intersexuals may constitute as many as 4 percent of births. As I point out to my students at Brown University, in a student body of about 6,000 that fraction, if correct, implies there may be as many as 240 intersexuals on campus—surely enough to form a minority caucus of some kind.

In reality though, few such students would make it as far as Brown in sexually diverse form. Recent advances in physiology and surgical technology now enable physicians to catch most intersexuals at the moment of birth. Almost at once such infants are entered into a program of hormonal and surgical management so that they can slip quietly into society as "normal" heterosexual males or females. I emphasize that the motive is in no way conspiratorial. The aims of the policy are genuinely humanitarian, reflecting the wish that people be able to "fit in" both physically and psychologically. In the medical community, however, the assumptions behind that wish—that there be only two sexes, that heterosexuality alone is normal, that there is one true model of psychological health—have gone virtually unexamined.

The word *hermaphrodite* comes from the Greek names Hermes, variously known as the messenger of the gods, the patron of music, the controller of dreams or the protector of livestock, and Aphrodite, the goddess of sexual love and beauty. According to Greek mythology, those two gods parented Hermaphroditus, who at age fifteen became half male and half female when his body fused with the body of a nymph he fell in love with. In some true hermaphrodites the testis and the ovary grow separately but bilaterally; in others they grow together within the same organ, forming an ovotestis. Not infrequently, at least one of the gonads functions quite well, producing either sperm cells or eggs, as well as functional levels of the sex hormones—androgens or estrogens. Although in theory it might be possible for a true hermaphrodite to become both father and mother to a child, in practice the appropriate ducts and tubes are not configured so that egg and sperm can meet.

In contrast with the true hermaphrodites, the pseudohermaphrodites possess two gonads of the same kind along with the usual male (XY) or female (XX) chromosomal makeup. But their external genitalia and secondary sex characteristics do not match their chromosomes. Thus merms have testes and XY chromosomes, yet they also have a vagina and a clitoris, and at puberty they often develop breasts. They do not menstruate, however. Ferms have ovaries, two X chromosomes and sometimes a uterus, but they also have at least partly masculine external genitalia. Without medical intervention they can develop beards, deep voices and adult-size penises. . . .

Intersexuality itself is old news. Hermaphrodites, for instance, are often featured in stories about human origins. Early biblical scholars believed Adam began life as a hermaphrodite and later divided into two people—a male and a female—after falling from grace. According to Plato there once were three sexes—male, female, and hermaphrodite—but the third sex was lost with time.

Both the Talmud and the Tosefta, the Jewish books of law, list extensive regulations for people of mixed sex. The Tosefta expressly forbids hermaphrodites to inherit their fathers' estates (like daughters), to seclude themselves with women (like sons), or to shave (like men). When hermaphrodites menstruate they must be isolated from men (like women); they are disqualified from serving as witnesses or as priests (like women), but the laws of pederasty apply to them.

In Europe a pattern emerged by the end of the Middle Ages that, in a sense, has lasted to the present day: hermaphrodites were compelled to choose an established gender role and stick with it. The penalty for transgression was often death. Thus in the 1600s a Scottish hermaphrodite living as a woman was buried alive after impregnating his/her master's daughter.

For questions of inheritance, legitimacy, paternity, succession to title, and eligibility for certain professions to be determined, modern Anglo-Saxon legal systems require that newborns be registered as either male or female. In the US today sex determination is governed by state laws. Illinois permits adults to change the sex recorded on their birth certificates should a physican attest to having performed the appropriate surgery. The New York Academy of Medicine, on the other hand, has taken an opposite view. In spite of surgical alterations of the external genitalia, the academy argued in 1966, the chromosomal sex remains the same. By that measure, a person's wish to conceal his or her original sex cannot outweigh the public interest in protection against fraud.

During this century the medical community has completed what the legal world began—the complete erasure of any form of embodied sex that does not conform to a male-female, heterosexual pattern. Ironically, a more sophisticated knowledge of the complexity of sexual systems has led to the repression of such intricacy.

In 1937 the urologist Hugh H. Young of Johns Hopkins University published a volume titled *Genital Abnormalities, Hermaphroditism and Related Adrenal Diseases.* The book is remarkable for its erudition, scientific insight, and open-mindedness. In it Young drew together a wealth of carefully documented case histories to demonstrate and study the medical treatment of such "accidents of birth." Young did not pass judgment on the people the studied, nor did he attempt to coerce into treatment those intersexuals who rejected that option. And he showed unusual even-handedness in referring to those people who had had sexual experiences as both men and women as "practicing hermaphrodites."

One of Young's more interesting cases was a hermaphrodite named Emma who had grown up as a female. Emma had both a penis-size clitoris and a vagina, which made it possible for him/her to have "normal" heterosexual sex with both men and women. As a teenager Emma had had sex with a number of girls to whom s/he was deeply attracted; but at the age of nineteen s/he had married a man. Unfortunately, he had given Emma little sexual pleasure (though he had had no complaints), and so throughout that marriage and subsequent ones Emma had kept girlfriends on the side. With some frequency s/he had pleasureable sex with them. Young describes his subject as appearing "to be quite content and even happy." In conversation Emma occasionally told him of his/her wish to be a man, a circumstance Young said would be relatively easy to bring about. But Emma's reply strikes a heroic blow for self-interest:

> Would you have to remove that vagina? I don't know about that because that's my meal ticket. If you did that, I would have to quit my husband and go to work, so I think I'll keep it and stay as I am. My husband supports me well, and even though I don't have any sexual pleasure with him, I do have lots with my girlfriends.

Yet even as Young was illuminating intersexuality with the light of scientific reason, he was beginning its suppression. For his book is also an extended treatise on the most modern surgical and hormonal methods of changing intersexuals into either males or females. Young may have differed from his successors in being less judgmental and controlling of the patients and their families, but he nonetheless supplied the foundation on which current intervention practices were built.

By 1969, when the English physicians Christopher J. Dewhurst and Ronald R.

Gordon wrote *The Intersexual Disorders,* medical and surgical approaches to intersexuality had neared a state of rigid uniformity. It is hardly surprising that such a hardening of opinion took place in the era of the feminine mystique—of the post-World War II flight to the suburbs and the strict division of family roles according to sex. That the medical consensus was not quite universal (or perhaps that it seemed poised to break apart again) can be gleaned from the near-hysterical tone of Dewhurst and Gordon's book, which contrasts markedly with the calm reason of Young's founding work. Consider their opening description of an intersexual newborn:

> One can only attempt to imagine the anguish of the parents. That a newborn should have a deformity . . . [affecting] so fundamental an issue as the very sex of the child . . . is a tragic event which immediately conjures up visions of a hopeless psychological misfit doomed to live always as a sexual freak in loneliness and frustration.

Dewhurst and Gordon warned that such a miserable fate would, indeed, be a baby's lot should the case be improperly managed; "but fortunately," they wrote, "with correct management the outlook is infinitely better than the poor parents—emotionally stunned by the event—or indeed anyone without special knowledge could ever imagine."

Scientific dogma has held fast to the assumption that without medical care hermaphrodites are doomed to a life of misery. Yet there are few empirical studies to back up that assumption, and some of the same research gathered to build a case for medical treatment contradicts it. Francies Benton, another of Young's practicing hermaphrodites, "had not worried over his condition, did not wish to be changed, and was enjoying life." The same could be said of Emma, the opportunistic hausfrau. Even Dewhurst and Gordon, adamant about the psychological importance of treating intersexuals at the infant stage, acknowledged great success in "changing the sex" of older patients. They reported on twenty cases of children reclassified into a different sex after the supposedly critical age of eighteen months. They asserted that all the reclassifications were "successful," and they wondered then whether reregistration could be "recommended more readily than [had] been suggested so far."

The treatment of intersexuality in this century provides a clear example of what the French historian Michel Foucault has called biopower. The knowledge developed in biochemistry, embryology, endocrinology, psychology, and surgery has enabled physicians to control the very sex of the human body. The multiple contradictions in that kind of power call for some scrutiny. On the one hand, the medical "management" of intersexuality certainly developed as part of an attempt to free people from perceived psychological pain (though whether the pain was the patient's, the parents', or the physician's is unclear). And if one accepts the assumption that in a sex-divided culture people can realize their greatest potential for happiness and productivity only if they are sure they belong to one of only two acknowledged sexes, modern medicine has been extremely successful.

On the other hand, the same medical accomplishments can be read not as progress but as a mode of discipline. Hermaphrodites have unruly bodies. They do not fall naturally into a binary classification; only a surgical shoehorn can put them there. But why should we care if a "woman," defined as one who has breasts, a vagina, a uterus and ovaries and who menstruates, also has a clitoris large enough to penetrate the vagina of another woman? Why should we care if there are people whose biological equipment enables them to have sex "naturally" with both men and women? The answers seem to lie in a cultural need to maintain clear distinctions between the sexes. Society mandates the control of intersexual bodies because they blur and bridge the great divide. Inasmuch as hermaphrodites literally embody both sexes, they challenge traditional beliefs about sexual difference: they possess the irritating ability to live sometimes as one sex and sometimes the other, and they raise the specter of homosexuality.

But what if things were altogether different? Imagine a world in which the same knowledge that has enabled medicine to intervene in the management of intersexual patients has been placed at the service of multiple sexualities. Imagine that the sexes have multiplied beyond currently imaginable limits. It would have to be a world of shared powers. Patient and physician, parent and child, male and female, heterosexual and homosexual—all those oppositions and others would have to be dissolved as sources of division. A new ethic of medical treatment would arise, one that would permit ambiguity in a culture that had overcome sexual division. The central mission of medical treatment would be to preserve life. Thus hermaphrodites would be concerned primarily not about whether they can conform to society but about whether they might develop potentially life-threatening conditions—hernias, gonadal tumors, salt imbalance caused by adrenal malfunction—that sometimes accompany hermaphroditic development. In my ideal world medical intervention for intersexuals would take place only rarely before the age of reason; subsequent treatment would be a cooperative venture between physician, patient, and other advisers trained in issues of gender multiplicity.

I do not pretend that the transition to my utopia would be smooth. Sex, even the supposedly "normal," heterosexual kind, continues to cause untold anxieties in Western society. And certainly a culture that has yet to come to grips— religiously and, in some states, legally—with the ancient and relatively uncomplicated reality of homosexual love will not readily embrace intersexuality. No doubt the most troublesome arena by far would be the rearing of children. Parents, at least since the Victorian era, have fretted, sometimes to the point of outright denial, over the fact that their children are sexual beings.

All that and more amply explains why intersexual children are generally squeezed into one of the two prevailing sexual categories. But what would be the psychological consequences of taking the alternative road—raising children as unabashed intersexuals? On the surface that tack seems fraught with peril. What, for example, would happen to the intersexual child amid the unrelenting cruelty of the school yard? When the time came to shower in gym class, what horrors and humiliations would await the intersexual as his/her anatomy was displayed in all its nontraditional glory? In whose gym class would s/he register to begin with? What bathroom would s/he use? And how on earth would Mom and Dad help shepherd him/her through the mine field of puberty?

In the past thirty years those questions have been ignored, as the scientific community has, with remarkable unanimity, avoided contemplating the alternative route of unimpeded intersexuality. But modern investigators tend to overlook a substantial body of case histories, most of them compiled between 1930 and 1960, before surgical intervention became rampant. Almost without exception, those reports describe children who grew up knowing they were intersexual (though they did not advertise it) and adjusted to their unusual status. Some of the studies are richly detailed—described at the level of gym-class showering (which most intersexuals avoided without incident); in any event, there is not a psychotic or a suicide in the lot.

Still, the nuances of socialization among intersexuals cry out for more sophisticated analysis. Clearly, before my vision of sexual multiplicity can be realized, the first openly intersexual children and their parents will have to be brave pioneers who will bear the brunt of society's growing pains. But in the long view—though it could take generations to achieve—the prize might be a society in which sexuality is something to be celebrated for its subtleties and not something to be feared or ridiculed.

GENDERED INTIMACIES

"Man's love is of man's life a thing apart," wrote the British Romantic poet, Lord Byron. "'Tis woman's whole existence." Nowhere are the differences between women and men more pronounced than in our intimate lives, our experiences of love, friendship, and sexuality. It is in our intimate relationships that it so often feels like men and women are truly from different planets.

The very definitions of emotional intimacy bear the mark of gender. As Francesca Cancian argues, the ideal of love has been "feminized" since the nineteenth century. No longer is love the arduous pining nor the sober shouldering of familial responsibility; today, love is expressed as the ability to sustain emotional commitment and connection—a "feminine" definition of love.

The impact of these gendered definitions of love, friendship, and intimacy ripples through our intimate lives. Ritch Savin-Williams finds that gender is often a crucial variable in understanding the different trajectories of friendships, and dating relationships among gay and lesbian and bisexual youth.

But there are signs of gender convergence. Women, it appears, find themselves more interested in pursuing explicitly sexual pleasures, despite their "Venutian" temperament that invariably links love and lust. And men's friendships are not nearly as different from women's friendships as we previously thought, suggests Scott Swain. As women and men work together outside the home, and share housework and child care inside the home, many of those intractable, inevitable, and cosmic differences between men and women will begin to evaporate into the egalitarian air of planet Earth.

FRANCESCA M. CANCIAN

The Feminization of Love

A feminized and incomplete perspective on love predominates in the United States. We identify love with emotional expression and talking about feelings, aspects of love that women prefer and in which women tend to be more skilled than men. At the same time we often ignore the instrumental and physical aspects of love that men prefer, such as providing help, sharing activities, and sex. This feminized perspective leads us to believe that women are much more capable of love than men and that the way to make relationships more loving is for men to become more like women. This paper proposes an alternative, androgynous perspective on love, one based on the premise that love is both instrumental and expressive. From this perspective, the way to make relationships more loving is for women and men to reject polarized gender roles and integrate "masculine" and "feminine" styles of love.

THE TWO PERSPECTIVES

"Love is active, doing something for your good even if it bothers me" says a fundamentalist Christian. "Love is sharing, the real sharing of feelings" says a divorced secretary who is in love again. In ancient Greece, the ideal love was the adoration of a man for a beautiful young boy who was his lover. In the thirteenth century, the exemplar of love was the chaste devotion of a knight for another man's wife. In Puritan New England, love between husband and wife was the ideal, and in Victorian times, the asexual devotion of a mother for her child seemed the essence of love. My purpose is to focus on one kind of love: long-term heterosexual love in the contemporary United States.

What is a useful definition of enduring love between a woman and a man? One guideline for a definition comes from the prototypes of enduring love—the relations between committed lovers, husband and wife, parent and child. These relationships combine care and assistance with physical and emotional closeness. Studies of attachment between infants and their mothers emphasize the importance of being protected and fed as well as touched and held. In marriage, according to most family sociologists, both practical help and affection are part of enduring love, or "the affection we feel for those with whom our lives are deeply intertwined."[1] Our own informal observations often point in the same direction: if we consider the relationships that are the prototypes of enduring love, it seems that what we really mean by love is some combination of instrumental and expressive qualities.

Historical studies provide a second guideline for defining enduring love, specifically between a woman and a man. In precapitalist America, such love was

From *Signs,* Vol. 11, no. 4 (Summer 1986), pp. 692–709. Copyright © 1986 by The University of Chicago. Reprinted by permission of University of Chicago Press. Notes have been renumbered and edited.

a complex whole that included work and feelings. Then it was split into feminine and masculine fragments by the separation of home and workplace. This historical analysis implies that affection, material help, and routine cooperation all are parts of enduring love.

Consistent with these guidelines, my working definition of enduring love between adults is a relationship wherein a small number of people are affectionate and emotionally committed to each other, define their collective well-being as a major goal, and feel obliged to provide care and practical assistance for each other. People who love each other also usually share physical contact; they communicate with each other frequently and cooperate in some routine tasks of daily life. My discussion is of enduring heterosexual love only; I will for the sake of simplicity refer to it as "love."

In contrast to this broad definition of love, the narrower, feminized definition dominates both contemporary scholarship and public opinion. Most scholars who study love, intimacy, or close friendship focus on qualities that are stereotypically feminine, such as talking about feelings. For example, Abraham Maslow defines love as "a feeling of tenderness and affection with great enjoyment, happiness, satisfaction, elation and even ecstasy." Among healthy individuals, he says, "there is a growing intimacy and honesty and self-expression."[2] Zick Rubin's "Love Scale," designed to measure the degree of passionate love as opposed to liking, includes questions about confiding in each other, longing to be together, and sexual attraction as well as caring for each other. Studies of friendship usually distinguish close friends from acquaintances on the basis of how much personal information is disclosed, and many recent studies of married couples and lovers emphasize communication and self-disclosure. A recent book on marital love by Lillian Rubin focuses on intimacy, which she defines as "reciprocal expression of feeling and thought, not out of fear or dependent need, but out of a wish to know another's inner life and to be able to share one's own."[3] She argues that intimacy is distinct from nurturance or caretaking and that men are usually unable to be intimate.

Among the general public, love is also defined primarily as expressing feelings and verbal disclosure, not as instrumental help. This is especially true among the more affluent; poorer people are more likely than they to see practical help and financial assistance as a sign of love. In a study conducted in 1980, 130 adults from a wide range of social classes and ethnic backgrounds were interviewed about the qualities that make a good love relationship. The most frequent response referred to honest and open communication. Being caring and supportive and being tolerant and understanding were the other qualities most often mentioned. Similar results were reported from Ann Swidler's study of an affluent suburb: the dominant conception of love stressed communicating feelings, working on the relationship, and self-development. Finally, a contemporary dictionary defines love as "strong affection for another arising out of kinship or personal ties" and as attraction based on sexual desire, affection, and tenderness.

These contemporary definitions of love clearly focus on qualities that are seen as feminine in our culture. A study of gender roles in 1968 found that warmth, expressiveness, and talkativeness were seen as appropriate for women and not for men. In 1978 the core features of gender stereotypes were unchanged although fewer qualities were seen as appropriate for only one sex. Expressing tender feelings, being gentle, and being aware of the feelings of others were still ideal qualities for women and not for men. The desirable qualities for men and not for women included being independent, unemotional, and interested in sex. The only component perceived as masculine in popular definitions of love is interest in sex.

The two approaches to defining love—one broad, encompassing instrumental and affective qualities, one narrow, including only the affective qualities—inform the two different perspectives on love. According to the androgynous perspective, both gender roles contain elements of love. The feminine role does not include all of the major ways of loving; some aspects of love come from the masculine role, such as sex and providing material help, and some, such as cooperating in daily tasks, are associated with neither gender role. In contrast, the feminized perspective on love implies that all of the elements of love are included in the feminine role. The capacity to love is divided by gender. Women can love and men cannot.

SOME FEMINIST INTERPRETATIONS

Feminist scholars are divided on the question of love and gender. Supporters of the feminized perspective seem most influential at present. Nancy Chodorow's psychoanalytic theory has been especially influential in promoting a feminized perspective on love among social scientists studying close relationships. Chodorow's argument—in greatly simplified form—is that as infants, both boys and girls have strong identification and intimate attachments with their mothers. Since boys grow up to be men, they must repress this early identification, and in the process they repress their capacity for intimacy. Girls retain their early identification since they will grow up to be women, and throughout their lives females see themselves as connected to others. As a result of this process, Chodorow argues, "girls come to define and experience themselves as continuous with others; . . . boys come to define themselves as more separate and distinct."[4] This theory implies that love is feminine—women are more open to love than men—and that this gender difference will remain as long as women are the primary caretakers of infants.

Scholars have used Chodorow's theory to develop the idea that love and attachment are fundamental parts of women's personalities but not of men's. Carol Gilligan's influential book on female personality development asserts that women define their identity "by a standard of responsibility and care." The predominant female image is "a network of connection, a web of relationships that is sustained by a process of communication." In contrast, males favor a "hierarchical ordering, with its imagery of winning and losing and the potential for violence which it contains." "Although the world of the self that men describe at times includes 'people' and 'deep attachments,' no particular person or relationship is mentioned. . . . Thus the male 'I' is defined in separation."[5]

A feminized conception of love can be supported by other theories as well. In past decades, for example, such a conception developed from Talcott Parsons's theory of the benefits to the nuclear family of women's specializing in expressive action and men's specializing in instrumental action. Among contemporary social scientists, the strongest support for the feminized perspective comes from such psychological theories as Chodorow's.

On the other hand, feminist historians have developed an incisive critique of the feminized perspective on love. Mary Ryan and other social historians have analyzed how the separation of home and workplace in the nineteenth century polarized gender roles and feminized love. Their argument, in simplified form, begins with the observation that in the colonial era the family household was the arena for economic production, affection, and social welfare. The integration of activities in the family produced a certain integration of expressive and instrumental traits in the personalities of men and women. Both women and men were expected to be hard working, modest, and loving toward their spouses and children, and the concept of love included instrumental cooperation as well as expression of feelings. In Ryan's words, "When early Americans spoke of love they were not withdrawing into a female byway of human experience. Domestic affection, like sex and economics, was not segregated into male and female spheres." There was a "reciprocal ideal of conjugal love" that "grew out of the day-to-day cooperation, sharing, and closeness of the diversified home economy."[6]

Economic production gradually moved out of the home and became separated from personal relationships as capitalism expanded. Husbands increasingly worked for wages in factories and shops while wives stayed at home to care for the family. This division of labor gave women more experience with close relationships and intensified women's economic dependence on men. As the daily activities of men and women grew further apart, a new worldview emerged that exaggerated the differences between the personal, loving, feminine sphere of the home and the impersonal, powerful, masculine sphere of the workplace. Work became identified with what men do for money while love became identified with women's activities at home. As a result, the conception of love shifted toward emphasizing tenderness, powerlessness, and the expression of emotion.

This partial and feminized conception of love persisted into the twentieth century as the division of labor remained stable: the workplace remained impersonal and separated from the home, and married women continued to be excluded from paid employment. According to this historical explanation, one might expect a change in the conception of love since the 1940s, as growing numbers of wives took jobs. However, women's persistent responsibility for child care and housework, and their lower wages, might explain a continued feminized conception of love.

Like the historical critiques, some psychological studies of gender also imply that our current conception of love is distorted and needs to be integrated with qualities associated with the masculine role. For example, Jean Baker Miller argues that women's ways of loving—their need to be attached to a man and to serve others—result from women's powerlessness, and that a better way of loving would integrate power with women's style of love.[7] The importance of combining activities and personality traits that have been split apart by gender is also a frequent theme in the human potential movement. These historical and psychological works emphasize the flexibility of gender roles and the inadequacy of a concept of love that includes only the feminine half of human qualities. In contrast, theories like Chodorow's emphasize the rigidity of gender differences after childhood and define love in terms of feminine qualities. The two theoretical approaches are not as inconsistent as my simplified sketches may suggest, and many scholars combine them; however, the two approaches have different implications for empirical research.

EVIDENCE ON WOMEN'S "SUPERIORITY" IN LOVE

A large number of studies show that women are more interested and more skilled in love than men. However, most of these studies use biased measures based on feminine styles of loving, such as verbal self-disclosure, emotional expression, and willingness to report that one has close relationships. When less biased measures are used, the differences between women and men are often small.

Women have a greater number of close relationships than men. At all stages of the life cycle, women see their relatives more often. Men and women report closer relations with their mothers than with their fathers and are generally closer to female kin. Thus an average Yale man in the 1970s talked about himself more with his mother than with his father and was more satisfied with his relationship with his mother. His most frequent grievance against his father was that his father gave too little of himself and was cold and uninvolved; his grievance against his mother was that she gave too much of herself and was alternately overprotective and punitive.

Throughout their lives, women are more likely to have a confidant—a person to whom one discloses personal experiences and feelings. Girls prefer to be with one friend or a small group, while boys usually play competitive games in large groups. Men usually get together with friends to play sports or do some other activity, while women get together explicitly to talk and to be together.

Men seem isolated given their weak ties with their families and friends. Among blue-collar couples interviewed in 1950, 64 percent of the husbands had no confidants other than their spouses, compared to 24 percent of the wives. The predominantly upper-middle-class men interviewed by Daniel Levinson in the 1970s were no less isolated. Levinson concludes that "close friendship with a man or a woman is rarely experienced by American men."[8] Apparently, most men have no loving relationships besides those with wife or lover; and given the estrangement that often occurs in marriages, many men may have no loving relationship at all.

Several psychologists have suggested that there is a natural reversal of these roles in middle age, as men become more concerned with relationships and women turn toward independence and achievement; but there seems to be no evidence showing that men's relationships become more numerous or more intimate after middle age, and some evidence to the contrary.

Women are also more skilled than men in talking about relationships. Whether working class or middle class, women value talking about feelings and relationships and disclose more than men about personal experiences. Men who deviate and talk a lot about their personal experiences are commonly defined as feminine and maladjusted. Working-class wives prefer to talk about themselves, their close relationships with family and friends, and their homes, while their husbands prefer to talk about cars, sports, work, and politics. The same gender-specific preferences are expressed by college students.

Men do talk more about one area of personal experience: their victories and achievements; but talking about success is associated with power, not intimacy. Women say more about their fears and disappointments, and it is disclosure of such weaknesses that usually is interpreted as a sign of intimacy. Women are also more accepting of the expression of intense feelings, including love, sadness, and fear, and they are more skilled in interpreting other people's emotions.

Finally, in their leisure time women are drawn to topics of love and human entanglements while men are drawn to competition among men. Women's preferences in television viewing run to daytime soap operas, or if they are more educated, the high-brow soap operas on educational channels, while most men like to watch competitive and often aggressive sports. Reading-tastes show the same pattern. Women read novels and magazine articles about love, while men's magazines feature stories about men's adventures and encounters with death.

However, this evidence on women's greater involvement and skill in love is not as strong as it appears. Part of the reason that men seem so much less loving than women is that their behavior is measured with a feminine ruler. Much of this research considers only the kinds of loving behavior that are associated with the feminine role and rarely compares women and men in terms of qualities associated with the masculine role. When less biased measures are used, the behavior of men and women is often quite similar. For example, in a careful study of kinship relations among young adults in a southern city, Bert Adams found that women were much more likely than men to say that their parents and relatives were very important to their lives (58 percent of women and 37 percent of men). In measures of actual contact with relatives, though, there were much smaller differences: 88 percent of women and 81 percent of men whose parents lived in the same city saw their parents weekly. Adams concluded that "differences between males and females in relations with parents are discernible primarily in the subjective sphere; contact frequencies are quite similar."[9]

The differences between the sexes can be small even when biased measures are used. For example, Marjorie Lowenthal and Clayton Haven reported the finding, later widely quoted, that elderly women were more likely than elderly men to have a friend with whom they could talk about their personal troubles—clearly a measure of a traditionally feminine behavior. The figures revealed that 81 percent of the married women and 74 percent of the married men had confidants—not a sizable difference.[10] On the other hand, whatever the measure, virtually all such studies find that women are more involved in close relationships than men, even if the difference is small.

In sum, women are only moderately superior to men in love: they have more close relationships and care more about them, and they seem to be more skilled at love, especially those aspects of love that involve expressing feelings and being vulnerable. This does not mean that men are separate and unconcerned with close relationships, however. When national surveys ask people what is most important in their lives, women tend to put family bonds first while men put family bonds first or second, along with work. For both sexes, love is clearly very important.

EVIDENCE ON THE MASCULINE STYLE OF LOVE

Men tend to have a distinctive style of love that focuses on practical help, shared physical activities, spending time together, and sex. The major elements of the masculine style of love emerged in Margaret Reedy's study of 102 married couples in the late 1970s. She showed individuals statements describing aspects of love and asked them to rate how well the statements described their marriages. On the whole, husband and wife had similar views of their marriage, but several sex differences emerged. Practical help and spending time together were more important to men. The men were more likely to give high ratings to such statements as: "When she needs help I help her," and "She would rather spend her time with me than with anyone else." Men also described themselves more often as sexually attracted and endorsed such statements as: "I get physically excited and aroused just thinking about her." In addition, emotional security was less important to men than to women, and men were less likely to describe the relationship as secure, safe, and comforting.[11] Another study in the late 1970s showed a similar pattern among young, highly educated couples. The husbands gave greater emphasis to feeling responsible for the partner's well-being and putting the spouse's needs first, as well as to spending time together. The wives gave greater importance to emotional involvement and verbal self-disclosure but also were more concerned than the men about maintaining their separate activities and their independence.

The difference between men and women in their views of the significance of practical help was demonstrated in a study in which seven couples recorded their interactions for several days. They noted how pleasant their relations were and counted how often the spouse did a helpful chore, such as cooking a good meal or repairing a faucet, and how often the spouse expressed acceptance or affection. The social scientists doing the study used a feminized definition of love. They labeled practical help as "instrumental behavior" and expressions of acceptance or affection as "affectionate behavior," thereby denying the affectionate aspect of practical help. The wives seemed to be using the same scheme; they thought their marital relations were pleasant that day if their husbands had directed a lot of affectionate behavior to them, regardless of their husbands' positive instrumental behavior. The husbands' enjoyment of their marital relations, on the other hand, depended on their wives' instrumental actions, not on their expressions of affection. The men actually saw instrumental actions as affection. One husband who was told by the researchers to increase his affectionate behavior toward his wife decided to wash her car and was surprised when neither his wife nor the researchers accepted that as an "affectionate" act.

The masculine view of instrumental help as loving behavior is clearly expressed by a husband discussing his wife's complaints about his lack of communication: "What does she want? Proof? She's got it, hasn't she? Would I be knocking myself out to get things for her—like to keep up this house—if I didn't love her? Why does a man do things like that if not because he loves his wife and kids? I swear, I can't figure what she wants." His wife, who has a feminine orientation to love, says something very different: "It is not enough that he supports us and takes care of us. I appreciate that, but I want him to share things with me. I need for him to tell me his feelings."[12] Many working-class women agree with men that a man's job is something he does out of love for his family,[13] but middle-class women and social scientists rarely recognize men's practical help as a form of love. (Indeed, among upper-middle-class men whose jobs offer a great deal of intrinsic gratification, their belief that they are "doing it for the family" may seem somewhat self-serving.)

Other differences between men's and women's styles of love involve sex. Men seem to separate sex and love while women connect them, but paradoxically, sexual intercourse seems to be the most meaningful way of giving and receiving love for many men. A twenty-nine-year-old carpenter who had been married for three years said that, after sex, "I feel so close to her and the kids. We feel like a real family then. I don't talk to her very often, I guess, but somehow I feel we have really communicated after we have made love."[14]

Because sexual intimacy is the only recognized "masculine" way of expressing love, the recent trend toward viewing sex as a way for men and women to express mutual intimacy is an important challenge to the feminization of love. However, the connection between sexuality and love is undermined both by the "sexual revolution" definition of sex as a form of casual recreation and by the view of male sexuality as a weapon—as in rape—with which men dominate and punish women.

Another paradoxical feature of men's style of love is that men have a more romantic attitude toward their partners than do women. In Reedy's study, men were more likely to select statements like "we are perfect for each other." In a survey of college students, 65 percent of the men but only 24 percent of the women said that, even if a relationship had all of the other qualities they desired, they would not marry unless they were in love. The common view of this phenomenon focuses on women. The view is that women marry for money and status and so see marriage as instrumentally, rather than emotionally, desirable. This of course is at odds with women's greater concern with self-disclosure and emotional intimacy and lesser concern with instrumental help. A better way to explain men's greater romanticism might be to focus on men. One such possible explanation is that men do not feel responsible for "working on" the emotional aspects of a relationship, and therefore see love as magically and perfectly present or absent. This is consistent with men's relative lack of concern with affective interaction and greater concern with instrumental help.

In sum, there is a masculine style of love. Except for romanticism, men's style fits the popularly conceived masculine role of being the powerful provider. From the androgynous perspective, the practical help and physical activities included in this role are as much a part of love as the expression of feelings. The feminized perspective cannot account for this masculine style of love; nor can it explain why women and men are so close in the degrees to which they are loving.

NEGATIVE CONSEQUENCES OF THE FEMINIZATION OF LOVE

The division of gender roles in our society that contributes to the two separate styles of love is reinforced by the feminized perspective and leads to political and moral problems that would be mitigated with a more androgynous approach to love. The feminized perspective works against some of the key values and goals of feminists and humanists by contributing to the devaluation and exploitation of women.

It is especially striking how the differences between men's and women's styles of love reinforce men's power over women. Men's style involves giving women important resources, such as money and protection that men control and women believe they need, and ignoring the resources that women control and men need. Thus men's dependency on women remains covert and repressed, while women's dependency on men is overt and exaggerated; and it is overt dependency that creates power, according to social exchange theory. The feminized perspective on love reinforces this power differential by leading to the belief that women need love more than do men, which is implied in the association of love with the feminine role. The effect of this belief is to intensify the asymmetrical dependency of women on men. In fact, however, evidence on the high death rates of unmarried men suggests that men need love at least as much as do women.

Sexual relations also can reinforce male dominance insofar as the man takes the initiative and intercourse is defined either as his "taking" pleasure or as his being skilled at "giving" pleasure, either way giving him control. The man's power advantage is further strengthened if the couple assumes that the man's sexual needs can be filled by any attractive woman while the woman's sexual needs can be filled only by the man she loves.

On the other hand, women's preferred ways of loving seem incompatible with control. They involve admitting dependency and sharing or losing control, and being emotionally intense. Further, the intimate talk about personal troubles that appeals to women requires of a couple a mutual vulnerability, a willingness to see oneself as weak and in need of support. It is true that a woman, like a man, can gain some power by providing her partner with services, such as understanding, sex, or cooking; but this power is largely unrecognized because the man's dependency on such services is not overt. The couple may even see these services as her duty or as her response to his requests (or demands).

The identification of love with expressing feelings also contributes to the lack of recognition of women's power by obscuring the instrumental, active component of women's love just as it obscures the loving aspect of men's work. In a culture that glorifies instrumental achievement, this identification devalues both women and love. In reality, a major way by which women are loving is in the clearly instrumental activities associated with caring for others, such as preparing meals, washing clothes, and providing care during illness; but because of our focus on the expressive side of love, this caring work of women is either ignored or redefined as expressing feelings. Thus, from the feminized perspective on love, child care is a subtle communication of attitudes, not work. A wife washing her husband's shirt is seen as expressing love, even though a husband washing his wife's car is seen as doing a job.

Gilligan, in her critique of theories of human development, shows the way in which devaluing love is linked to devaluing women. Basic to most psychological theories of development is the idea that a healthy person develops from a dependent child to an autonomous, independent adult. As Gilligan comments, "Development itself comes to be identified with separation, and attachments appear to be developmental impediments."[15] Thus women, who emphasize attachment, are judged to be developmentally retarded or insufficiently individuated.

The pervasiveness of this image was documented in a well-known study of mental health professionals who were asked to describe mental health, femininity, and masculinity. They associated both mental health and masculinity with independence, rationality, and dominance. Qualities concerning attachment, such as being tactful, gentle, or aware of the feelings of others, they associated with femininity but not with mental health.[16]

Another negative consequence of a feminized perspective on love is that it legitimates impersonal, exploitive relations in the workplace and the community. The ideology of separate spheres that developed in the nineteenth century contrasted the harsh, immoral marketplace with the warm and loving home and implied that this contrast is acceptable. Defining love as expressive, feminine, and divorced from productive activity maintains this ideology. If personal relationships and love are reserved for women and the home, then it is acceptable for a manager to underpay workers or for a community to ignore a needy family. Such behavior is not unloving; it is businesslike or shows a respect for privacy. The ideology of separate spheres also implies that men are properly judged by their instrumental and economic achievements and that poor or unsuccessful men are failures who may deserve a hard life. Levinson presents a conception of masculine development itself as centering on achieving an occupational dream.[17]

Finally, the feminization of love intensifies the conflicts over intimacy between women and men in close relationships. One of the most common conflicts is that the woman wants more closeness and verbal contact while the man withdraws and wants less pressure. Her need for more closeness is partly the result of the feminization of love, which encourages her to be more emotionally dependent on him. Because love is feminine, he in turn may feel controlled during intimate contact. Intimacy is her "turf," an area where she sets the rules and expectations. Talking about the relationship, as she wants, may well feel to him like taking a test that she made up and that he will fail. He is likely to react by withdrawing, causing her to intensify her efforts to get closer. The feminization of love thus can lead to a vicious cycle of conflict where neither partner feels in control or gets what she or he wants.

CONCLUSION

The values of improving the status of women and humanizing the public sphere are shared by many of the scholars who support a feminized conception of love; and they, too, explain the conflicts in close relationships in terms of polarized gender roles. Nancy Chodorow, Lillian Rubin, and Carol Gilligan have addressed these issues in detail and with great insight. However, by arguing that women's identity is based on attachment while men's identity is based on separation, they reinforce the distinction between feminine expressiveness and masculine instrumentality, revive the ideology of separate spheres, and legitimate the popular idea that only women know the right way to love. They also suggest that there is no way to overcome the rigidity of gender roles other than by pursuing the goal of men and women becoming equally involved in infant care. In contrast, an androgynous perspective on love challenges the identification of women and love with being expressive, powerless, and nonproductive and the identification of men with being instrumental, powerful, and productive. It rejects the ideology of separate spheres and validates masculine as well as feminine styles of love. This viewpoint suggests that progress could be made by means of a variety of social changes, including men doing child care, relations at work becoming more personal and nurturant, and cultural conceptions of love and gender becoming more androgynous. Changes that equalize power within close relationships by equalizing the economic and emotional dependency between men and women may be especially important in moving toward androgynous love.

The validity of an androgynous definition of love cannot be "proven"; the view that informs the androgynous perspective is that both the feminine style of love (characterized by emotional closeness and verbal self-disclosure) and the masculine style of love (characterized by instrumental help and sex) represent necessary parts of a good love relationship. Who is more loving: a couple who confide most of their experiences to each other but rarely cooperate or give each other practical help, or a couple who help each other through many crises and cooperate in running a household but rarely discuss their personal experiences? Both relationships are limited. Most people would probably choose a combination: a relationship that integrates feminine and masculine styles of loving, an androgynous love.

Notes

1. See John Bowlby, *Attachment and Loss* (New York: Basic Books, 1969), on mother-infant attachment. The quotation is from Elaine Walster and G. William Walster, *A New Look at*

Love (Reading, Mass.: Addison-Wesley Publishing Co., 1978), 9. Conceptions of love and adjustment used by family sociologists are reviewed in Robert Lewis and Graham Spanier, "Theorizing about the Quality and Stability of Marriage." in *Contemporary Theories about the Family*, ed. W. Burr, R. Hill, F. Nye, and I. Reiss (New York: Free Press, 1979), 268–94.

2. Abraham Maslow, *Motivation and Personality*, 2d ed. (New York: Harper & Row, 1970), 182–83.

3. Zick Rubin's scale is described in his article "Measurement of Romantic Love." *Journal of Personality and Social Psychology* 16, no. 2 (1970): 265–73; Lillian Rubin's book on marriage is *Intimate Strangers* (New York: Harper & Row, 1983), quote on 90.

4. Nancy Chodorow, *The Reproduction of Mothering* (Berkeley: University of California Press, 1978), 169. Dorothy Dinnerstein presents a similar theory in *The Mermaid and the Minotaur: Sexual Arrangements and Human Malaise* (New York: Harper & Row, 1976). Freudian and biological dispositional theories about women's nurturance are surveyed in Jean Stockard and Miriam Johnson, *Sex Roles* (Englewood Cliffs, N.J.: Prentice-Hall, Inc., 1980).

5. Carol Gilligan, *In a Different Voice* (Cambridge, Mass.: Harvard University Press, 1982), 32, 159–61; see also L. Rubin, *Intimate Strangers*.

6. I have drawn most heavily on Mary Ryan, *Womanhood in America*, 2d ed. (New York: New Viewpoints, 1978), and *The Cradle of the Middle Class: The Family in Oneida County, N.Y., 1790–1865* (New York: Cambridge University Press, 1981); Barbara Ehrenreich and Deidre English, *For Her Own Good: 150 Years of Experts Advice to Women* (New York: Anchor Books, 1978); Barbara Welter, "The Cult of True Womanhood: 1820–1860," *American Quaterly* 18, no. 2 (1966): 151–174.

7. Jean Baker Miller, *Toward a New Psychology of Women* (Boston: Beacon Press, 1976). There are, of course, many exceptions to Miller's generalization, e.g., women who need to be independent or who need an attachment with a woman.

8. Daniel Levinson, *The Seasons of a Man's Life* (New York: Alfred A. Knopf, 1978), 335.

9. Bert Adams, *Kinship in an Urban Setting* (Chicago: Markham Publishing Co., 1968), 169.

10. Marjorie Lowenthal and Clayton Haven, "Interaction and Adaptation: Intimacy as a Critical Variable." *American Sociological Review* 22, no. 4 (1968): 20–30.

11. Margaret Reedy, "Age and Sex Differences in Personal Needs and the Nature of Love." (Ph.D. diss. University of Southern California, 1977). Unlike most studies, Reedy did not find that women emphasized communication more than men. Her subjects were upper-middle-class couples who seemed to be very much in love.

12. Lillian Rubin, *Worlds of Pain* (New York: Basic Books, 1976), 147.

13. See L. Rubin, *Worlds of Pain*; also see Richard Sennett and Jonathan Cobb, *Hidden Injuries of Class* (New York: Vintage, 1973).

14. Interview by Cynthia Garlich, "Interviews of Married Couples" (University of California, Irvine, School of Social Sciences, 1982).

15. Gilligan (n. 5 above), 12–13.

16. Inge Broverman, Frank Clarkson, Paul Rosenkrantz, and Susan Vogel, "Sex-Role Stereotypes and Clinical Judgments of Mental Health," *Journal of Consulting Psychology* 34, no. 1 (1970): 1–7.

17. Levinson (n. 8 above).

SCOTT SWAIN

Covert Intimacy: Closeness in Men's Friendships

This study is an analysis of college men's intimate behavior in same-sex friendships and their standards for assessing intimacy. It documents the development, causes, and manifestation of a covert style of intimate behavior in men's friendships. Covert intimacy is a private, often nonverbal, context-specific form of communication. The concept of covert intimacy is rooted in the behaviors that men reported as indicative of closeness and intimacy in their friendships with other men.

First, I trace differences in the development of men's and women's adolescent friendships that shape and promote differing styles of intimacy. Next, such contexts are linked to the emergence of the separate worlds of men and women and how such separate worlds and microstructural contexts continue into adulthood. I analyze these separate worlds for the specific behaviors and values that shape intimacy among same-sex friends, and then clarify the distinctive cues and nuances of men's intimate behavior by comparing them to behaviors in male-female platonic friendships and friendships among women. I conclude the study with an assessment of the strengths and limitations of men's covert style of intimacy with men friends and its relationship to the inexpressive male.

THE INEXPRESSIVE MALE, OR SEX-SPECIFIC STYLES OF INTIMACY

Sex-role theorists have characterized men as instrumental, agentive, and task-oriented. Women have been characterized as expressive, communal, and empathic. Consistent with these theoretical formulations, researchers on the male role have interpreted men's interpersonal behavior as nonintimate and have stressed the restraints and limitations that cultural conceptions of masculinity impose on intimate expression. Examples of this *deficit approach* to men's intimate capabilities are Jack Balswick's "The Inexpressive Male" (1976) and Mirra Komarovsky's concept of men's "trained incapacity to share" (1964).

In recent years many of these generalizations, which were based on slight yet significant sex differences, have been reexamined. The majority of studies that measure interpersonal skills and relationship characteristics report nonsignificant sex differences. When studies report significant sex differences, the results have been mixed and sometimes conflicting. In support of the male deficit model, men are reported to be less likely than women to disclose sadness and fears, less affective and spontaneous with friends than women, and less adept than women at nonverbal decoding skills. Men are also reported to be more homophobic than women, which may inhibit the use of certain interpersonal skills in men's friendships.

However, the majority of self-disclosure studies reveal nonsignificant sex differences; and related analyses report that men score higher than women on nonverbal decoding skills, rate their friendships as more trusting and spontaneous than do women, and value intimacy in friendship as much as do women. In view of such findings and the conflicting results of other related studies, sex differences in interpersonal behavior appear to be minor or not adequately measured. However, notions of the "inexpressive male" continue to persist and guide research on men's interpersonal behavior.

Perhaps the most consistently reported difference in men's and women's friendships is men's preference for joint activities and women's preference for talking. Men's emphasis on instrumental action has been interpreted by past researchers as a less personal and less intimate form of interaction than verbal self-disclosure. This interpretation may be influenced by researchers' reliance on measuring feminine-typed styles of behavior to assess topics involving love and interpersonal behavior. This bias has been critiqued by Cancian as the "feminization of love" (1986). Researchers concerned with intimacy have assumed that verbal self-disclosure is the definitive referent for intimacy, and have thus interpreted alternative styles that involve instrumental action as a less intimate, or nonintimate, behavior. [Previous definitions of intimacy relied primarily on verbal self-disclosure as an indicator of intimacy. But, the relationship between intimacy and self-disclosure is usually only implied and not specifically defined.]

Caldwell and Peplau (1982) suggest that men and women may place the same value on intimacy in friendships, yet have different ways of assessing intimacy. Men are reported to express a wider range of intimate behaviors, including self-disclosure, while participating in gender-validating activities. Men may develop sex-specific contexts, cues, and meanings, which connote feelings and appraisals of intimacy similar to those connoted by self-disclosure for women.

Intimacy is defined in the present study as *behavior in the context of a friendship that connotes a positive and mutual sense of meaning and importance to the participants.* This definition allows respondents to determine what behaviors are meaningful and intimate, and assumes that there may be several avenues that may result in the experience of intimacy.

The results presented here are based on indepth interviews with fifteen men and five women. The college sample was young and white with a mean age of 22.5 years. This small sample was used to further explore sex-specific friendship behaviors, which have been significantly documented using larger samples of similar populations (Swain, 1984; Caldwell and Peplau, 1982).

The interview protocol was based on two empirical studies; the first was a pilot study ($N = 232$) that measured the relative value of activities in men's and women's same-sex friendships, and the second ($N = 140$) measured the relative importance and meaning that men and women attributed to those activities.

Interviews lasted an average of an hour and a half, with a female interviewer working with female subjects and a male interviewer (myself) working with the male subjects. For analysis, we then transcribed and organized the interviews by question and content. A disadvantage of such a focused sample is that the results may not generalize across age groups, or even represent this particular subgroup.

However, we selected a private and personal interview setting to collect more detailed data about sensitive information concerning intimacy in friendships than would otherwise be possible when using larger samples and less personal data-collection techniques. Because of the college setting, we expected the sample to have more friends and contact with same-sex friends than men and women from the general population. The advantages of this sample of young adults are their temporal closeness to the development of adolescent friendships and their frequent interaction with friends because of the college environment. This should promote clarity in their recollections of the development of adolescent friendship behaviors and give them a sharpened and more sensitive vantage point from which to describe their current friendships with men and women.

THE DEVELOPMENT OF SEX-SPECIFIC STYLES OF INTIMACY: THE SEPARATE WORLDS OF BOYS AND GIRLS

Men and women grow up in overlapping, yet distinctively different worlds. Sex segregation begins at an early age when boys and girls are differently rewarded for various play activities. Boys are encouraged to actively participate in the outside environment by parental acceptance of the risks of physical injury and parents' flexible attitude toward personal hygiene and appearance. Torn clothes, skinned knees, and dirty hands are signs of the normal growth of healthy boys. If girls choose these same activities, they may be tolerated; however, they may be sanctioned differently. For example, the term "tomboy" is used to distinguish a girl with "boyish" behaviors, and to designate a stage of development that deviates from normative expectations of the female child. Several men attributed the distinctive friendship behaviors of men to this early segregation while growing up. Jim said:

> Well, you do different things. Little boys, they'll play in the dirt and things, whereas a guy and a girl they might play in the house on something. The guys like . . . they don't mind getting dirty. I don't want to stereotype or anything, but it's just the way I see it. The guys are more rugged and things.

Pete responded to the question, "How do you act just around the guys?"

> You'd talk about anything, do anything. You aren't as polite. You don't care as much how you look, how you dress, what you wear, things of that nature. Even if we're just platonic friends, for some reason when you're around girls you're different. In the United States men and women don't share bathrooms together in the public restrooms. That's a good example, right there—obviously men and women are segregated then. That segregation exists in friendships, too.

Separate restrooms are a concrete manifestation of the different realms experienced by boys and girls as they grow up and of the restrictions on crossing over into the other sex's domain. The curiosity that boys and girls experience about what the bathrooms are actually like for the other sex is evidence of this separateness. A boy who is teased and pushed into the girl's bathrooms called a "girl" as he hastily exits. Thus, children internalize sex-segregated boundaries and enforce these restrictions. Evidence of the longterm influence of this segregation is the humiliation and embarrassment an adult feels when accidentally entering the "wrong" bathroom. The association between gender and specific contexts is also suggested by men referring to a woman who is included in a men's poker game as being "just like one of the guys." The separate contexts of men and women continue throughout the life cycle to shape the ways they express intimacy.

The male world is the outside environment of physical activity. Boys share and learn activities with male friends that involve an engagement with this outside world. Social encouragement is evident in such organizations as the Boy Scouts, sports and recreation programs, and a division of labor that often has boys doing home chores that are outdoors, such as mowing lawns. These outside activities have a shaping influence on their interests and values. Jack recalled his adolescence:

> I can remember only one friend that I had from years past. My friend Jim. Just kind of all the fun we had, boyhood fun. We built a fort, lit firecrackers, and all that stuff.

He refers to "boyhood" rather than "childhood" fun, implying that these experiences tended to be shared with other males. Another man recalled:

> The activities shared were a lot of outdoor-type things—fishing, hunting, Tom Sawyer type things. It's a commonality that we both shared that helped bring us together.

Men mentioned activities that ranged from dissecting lizards, riding bikes, and childhood sports to four-wheeling, lifting weights, playing practical jokes on friends, problem solving, and talking about relationships as they reached adulthood. By the time high school graduation arrives, most males have had more experiences and time with men friends than with women friends. Several men commented on this early division in their friendships. For instance, Rick replied:

> Up to the sixth or seventh grade girls are "stay away from the girls!" So during that whole time you only associate with the guys, and you have all these guy friends. And after that you kind of, you know, the first time you go out, you're kind of shy with the girls, and you don't get to know them too well. . . . I really didn't get over being shy with girls until my senior year.

His first contact with girls is in the dating context of "going out," which implies a heterosexual coupling dimension to the relationship in addition to friendship. The segregated contexts of men and women continue into adulthood, and shape the opportunities for expressing intimacy and the expectations of how that intimacy is to be expressed. As a result, men are more familiar with their men friends, and women are more familiar with their women friends.

CONSEQUENCES OF THE SEPARATE
WORLDS OF MEN AND WOMEN

Self-Disclosure: Profanity, Sameness, and Group Lingo

As boys move through adolescence surrounded and immersed in friendships with other boys, behavioral differences emerge that distinguish men's and women's friendships. Men develop language patterns that often rely on blunt, crude, and explicitly sexual terms. Bluntness, crudity, and profanity legitimize masculinity by tending to toughen the tone of any statement that a man may make. Swearing serves as a developmental credential in an adolescent boy's maturation process, much as do smoking, drinking, and getting one's drivers license. The "rugged" and "dirty" environment that boys share is translated into a coarser language during adolescence, which is also labeled as "dirty." Men felt that this language was more appropriate around other men, and they often related this sex-specific language to all-male contexts such as military service and sports. Greg responded:

> Well (laugh), not that I cuss a lot, but when I, you know, get around the baseball field and stuff like that. . . . They [women] don't like that. I try to stay away from the crude or harsh humor as much as I can (laugh).

Greg's laughing suggested a tense recognition that men's use of language in "harsh humor" does not easily translate in the company of women.

Men's harsh language and sexual explicitness in joking behavior are censored and muted when interacting with women friends. The censoring of humor to avoid offending women friends testifies to the different meaning and value men and women attribute to the same behaviors. Mike related:

> Around girls you act more of a gentleman. You don't cuss. You watch what you say. Because you don't want to say anything that will offend them.

Men felt more at ease with close men friends, partially from a perception of "sameness." Men assume that male friends will be more empathetic concerning sexual matters since they have similar bodies. Jack related:

> I find it much easier to talk about sexual things with guys, which makes sense.

A majority of the men said it was easier to talk to men about sexual matters than to women. Another man responded to the question, "What are some of the things that would be easier to talk over with a guy?"

> Anything from financial problems to problems with relationships. That's a big thing I really don't like talking to girls about. For some reason I just . . . I don't know . . . I get . . . usually because what I'm saying is from a male's point of view. And I know this is all sounding really sexist. But you know, there are certain things that I view that girls don't necessarily view the same way. And it's just easier talking to guys about that. Well, lately sex is one of those. I mean you

can talk about certain sexual things; there are certain things I had a conversation the other day, and he was talking to me about a sexual act that his girlfriend, his new girlfriend, wanted to do. And he really doesn't care to do it. There's no way I could talk to a girl about what he's talking about.

The men appeared to generalize a common world view to other men that fostered a feeling of comfort. Frank commented:

I'm more relaxed around guys. You don't have to watch what you say. Around friends like that [men] I wouldn't . . . what could you say? I wouldn't be careful I shouldn't say something like this, or I shouldn't do this. That's because with the guys, they're just like you.

Men friends used the degree of comfort and relaxation experienced with men friends as an indicator of closeness. Matt described this feeling when asked about the meaningful times he has shared with men friends.

Last week some really good friends of mine in my suite . . . one guy plays the guitar. And so he was just sitting around playing the guitar and we were making up tunes. We were making up songs to this, and that was really a lot of fun. The fun things come to mind. We rented a VCR and some movies and watched those, and just all the laughing together comes to mind as most memorable. As to the most meaningful, those also come pretty close to being the most meaningful, because there was just total relaxation, there. That I felt no need to worry. There's no need to worry about anyone making conversation. The conversation will come. And we can laugh at each other, and you can laugh at yourself, which is handy.

Men were asked to compare their friendships with men to their platonic friendships with women. Generally, men felt more at ease and relaxed when with close men friends than with women friends. John answered the question, "Are there any differences between your friendships with men and your friendships with women?"

You don't have to worry about the situation you're in. If you have to go to the bathroom, you just run up and go. You don't have to worry about "please excuse me" or anything. And it's a lot more relaxed. A lot more. Like in Jack's house we just go into the kitchen and make ourselves something to eat, you know, part of the family.

The "situation" is comfortable because the men's shared assumptions, cues, and meanings of behavior allow them "not to have to worry" whether they are acting appropriately. The formality associated with women friends is suggestive of Irving Goffman's concept of "frontstage" behavior, which is more rule-bound and distanced, while the "backstage" behavior with men friends is more intimate because of the lack of censoring and the feeling of informality associated with being "part of the family." The shared history, activities, and perception that other men are "just like you" gave a predictable familiarity to men's interactions. Women also felt that their similarity to each other produced an empathy unique between women friends. A woman responded to a question about the differences between her men and women friends:

> There are some things about a woman's feelings that I don't think a man, having never been in a woman's mind, could ever really understand. Because I think most women are a little more sensitive than men.

Men also developed unique terms with their close friends that expressed their history and connectedness. These terms acknowledged the particular experiences shared between friends and underlined their special relationship. When asked about his most meaningful experiences with his men friends, Tim related:

> The best thing, well the thing is, Rick, Mike, and me kind of have our own lingo. I haven't seen other people use them, like "Bonzo" is one of them. Like "go for Bonzo," and anybody else would just go "Well, whatever."

The "lingo" was derived from activities experienced by the group. The private meaning of the language served as a boundary separating friends from people outside the group.

Doing Versus Talking: The Intimacy of Shared Action

The men were asked, "What was the most meaningful occasion spent with a same-sex friend, and why was it meaningful?" The men mentioned a total of 26 meaningful occasions with men friends, and several men mentioned more than one meaningful experience. We analyzed the responses to clarify the link between sharing an activity and feeling close to a friend. Of those occasions, 20 meaningful times were spent in an activity other than talking. Men related a wide variety of meaningful experiences from "flirting with disaster" in an out-of-control car and winning a court case to being with a close friend the night that the friend found out his sister had committed suicide. Activities such as fishing, playing guitars, diving, backpacking, drinking, and weightlifting were central to men's meaningful experiences.

Nine meaningful experiences directly referenced the sharing of skills and accomplishments. These meaningful times involved the shared enjoyment of learning and mastering skills and accomplishing goals ranging from a sexual experience with a woman to staying up all night on a weeknight. The essential ingredients in these experiences seemed to be comfort with a competitive challenge and a sense of shared accomplishment. A man responded to the question of what was the most meaningful experience he had shared with a male friend, and later a group of male friends:

> I've always been extremely shy with women, and one of my friends in between, after high school . . . women were always chasing after him like crazy— and I'm defensive and stuff with women when one time we went to the river. And a couple of girls picked us up and we got laid and everything. And it was

kind of, this is going to sound like the standard male thing, but we all kind of went, after, we went and had a few beers and compared notes. You know, and I felt totally accepted because I had just as many good things to say as they did, and I could relate. I knew what they were talking about, because most of my life I've never known what these guys were talking about sexually.

Although this quote might imply sexual exploitation, several aspects should be considered. First, this man admits he is shy with women, and furthermore he indicates that the women initiated the interaction. He was able to discuss with his men friends a new experience that had been alien to him until this occasion. The argument here is not that the sexual experience was exploitive or intimate; it appears to have been a purely physical encounter between strangers. However, the commonality gained from a shared life experience did provide meaningful interaction among the men.

We further examined the influence of men's active emphasis and women's verbal emphasis on intimate friendship behavior by asking men to compare their friendships with men to their friendships with women. Tim responded to the questions, "What part of you do you share with your men friends and what part of you do you share with your women friends? How would you characterize those two different parts of you?"

I think that the men characteristics would be the whole thing, would be just the whole thing about being a man. You know, you go out and play sports with your brothers, and have a good time with them. You just . . . you're doing that. And there are some things that you can experience, as far as emotional, [with] your best friends that are men . . . you experience both. And that's what makes it so good is that. With most of the girls you're not going to go out and drink beer and have fun with them. Well, you can, but it's different. I mean it's like a different kind of emotion. It's like with the guys you can have all of it. . . .

Tim says that you can have "the whole thing" with men, suggesting that he can do things and talk about things with his close men friends. With women friends doing things is "different." Tim refers to a "different kind of emotion" and speaks of a "good time" when he is with his men friends. This good feeling may result from the ease and comfort of interacting with close friends who have developed a familiar style of communication from sharing activities.

The value of doing things is apparent in Matt's response, which described his most meaningful times with men friends:

It was like we were doing a lot of things together. It just seemed like we just grew on each other. Can't think of just one thing that stood out in my mind. It was more like a push-pull type thing. Like I'd pull him through things and he'd pull me through things. It wasn't like there was just one thing I can just think of right now, just a lot of things he did, whatever. Just the things we like to do, we just did them together, and just had a good time.

The closeness is in the "doing"—the sharing of interests and activities. When Matt was asked about his meaningful times with his women friends, he responded:

> It's like the things that you'd talk—it's really just like "talk" with them. It's not so much like you'd go out and do something with them, or go out and maybe be with them.

Several men said that with women friends it's "just talking" and referred to inter-action with women as "the lighter side of things." For men, it appears that actions speak louder than words and carry greater interpersonal value.

Women were also aware of a difference in men's style of expressing caring. A women commented on the differences in how her men and women friends let her know that they like her:

> Women talk more about feelings than men do. A man might let me know that he likes me because when he was in New York, he saw a book I'd been looking for and he brought it to me. And so I know that he likes me because he did that. Where a woman might say, twelve days in a row, "I've been looking all over for that book, but I can't find it."

Her male friend expressed his caring through a direct action, while her female friend expressed her caring verbally.

The emphasis on activities in men's friendship shapes their communication of closeness and caring. The significance of the doing/talking emphases in men's and women's styles of intimacy is apparent in the following response of a man to the question, "Why do you think they'd [women friends] be more verbal than your guy friends [in showing that they like you]?"

> I don't know why. I think there's just more ways to . . . I think there's more ways for the males to show me their appreciation that's nonverbal. I don't know why. I just think that if, in the way that they respond to things we do to-gether and stuff like that. There's more ways to show it. Like if we're, I make a good shot in a game or something, just give me a high-five or something like that. You don't have to say anything with the guys. That's just an example, it doesn't have to be just sports. But the same type of things, off the field or what-ever, just a thumbs-up type thing from a guy or whatever. There's just more ways to show being around [each other]. Where with the girls, you know, what can they do? You know, run up and just give you a kiss or something, I know girls who would do that in high school. So it—I think their options are just less—so they opt for the verbal type of thing.

He views talking as one option or style of expressing caring. From his activity-oriented perspective, he actually views women as restricted by a lack of alterna-tives to verbal expressiveness. These expressive alternatives are available to men through cues developed by sharing and understanding common activities. Non-verbal cues, expressed in active settings, contribute to private, covert, and in gen-eral, sex-specific styles of intimacy. This suggests that each sex tends to overlook, devalue, and not fully comprehend the other sex's style of expressing care.

Men and women have different styles of intimacy that reflect the often-separate realms in which they express it. The activities and contexts that men share provide a common general experience from which emerge certain values, gestures, and ways of talking about things that show intimacy. Both men and women are restricted in crossing over into each other's realm by early sex segregation, which results in a lack of experience with the meanings and contexts of the other sex. Researchers often underestimate this segregation because of an emphasis on the loosening of sex-related boundaries in the past several decades. Despite such changes, sex segregation still influences men and women, especially during the development of friendships in adolescence.

Covert Intimacy in Sports and Competition

Sports are the primary format for rewarding the attainment and demonstration of physical and emotional skills among adolescent boys. A man stated:

> I would have rather taken my basketball out than I would a girl . . . you know how young men are in the seventh, eighth, and ninth grade . . . if I had the choice I'd play basketball with the guys instead of going out that night.

Researchers have documented detrimental interpersonal consequences that may result from sports participation. However, the productive aspects of the sports context have received less attention from researchers. For men, the giving and receiving of help and assistance in a challenge context demonstrates trust and caring in a friendship. Engaging in the risk and drama of performing in a competitive activity provides the glue that secures the men in an intimate process of accomplishing shared goals. Jim responded to the question, "What situations or activities would you choose or would you feel most comfortable in with your close men friends?"

> I'm very comfortable, like playing racquetball. A lot of one-on-one things where you're actually doing something. Playing backgammon. Now being competitive makes it a little easier, because it's like a small battle going on. Not that you're out to show who's best, but it gives you something more that you two have in common in the situation.

The competition provides a structured context where friends can use their skills to create "something more" than they previously had in common. Each friend brings his own experiences and talents to join the other friend in the common arena of a competitive activity. The competition provides an overt and practical meaning; the covert goal, however, is not to "show who's best" but to give "something more that you two have in common."

The sports context provides a common experience whereby men can implicitly demonstrate closeness without directly verbalizing the relationship. Nonverbal communication skills, which are essential for achieving goals in the fast-moving sports context, also provide avenues for communicating intimacy. Greg responded to the question, "What were the most meaningful times that you spent with your men friends?"

In athletics, the majority of these friends that are close to me were on teams of mine. We played together. We were on the same team, me playing first and him catcher, or at times he played third. You know, first and third looking across the infield at each other. Knowing that we were close friends, and winning the CIF championship. I could just see that it meant a lot to me in terms of friendship too. As soon as that last pitch was made, we just clinched the title, to see the first person that he looked for to give, you know, to hug or congratulate, or whatever, was me. And the same for me to him. That was a big, another emotional thing for the two of us. Because I could just . . . it's just . . . you could just see how close your friends really are, or something like that. When there's twenty-five guys on the team and they're all going crazy, you're just trying to rejoice together, or whatever, for the victory. And the first, the main thing you wanted to do was run across the diamond and get to each other, and just congratulate each other first. And that meant a lot to me emotionally as well as far as friendship is concerned. It was only a split second, because after it was just a mob.

The two friends had grown up playing baseball together. Sharing the accomplishment of winning the championship provided a context where a close friendship could be affirmed and acknowledged nonverbally in "only a split second." Other members of the team, and perhaps even family members, may not have been aware of the intimacy that took place. The nonverbal nature of the glance and the context of excitement in the team's rejoicing after the victory allowed the intimacy to be expressed privately in a covert fashion. Both the intimate style and the context in which the intimacy was expressed contributed to an environment that was relatively safe from ridicule.

How Do I Know You Like Me: Intimacy and Affection in Men's Friendships

When asked, "How do you know that your men friends like you?" only one man responded that his friend tells him directly that he likes him. If men do not tend to self-disclose to each other the closeness of their friendship, how do they evaluate closeness and intimacy with a man friend? In men's friendships with other men, doing something together and choosing a friend and asking him if he wants to participate in an activity demonstrate that they like one another and enjoy being together. These acts have a meaning similar to a boy who asks a girl to a dance; it's assumed that he likes her by the nature of the action. Mike responded to the question, "How do you know or get the idea that they [men friends] like you?"

When I suggest that we do something I can tell in their voice or the way their actions are that they want to do it. Like hey! they really want to do it. Like, "Anyone want to go to the baseball game?" "Yeah, great! That's exactly what I want to do." That's a good feeling to know that you can make some sort of a suggestion that fits. Laughter, the joking, the noise. Knowing that they like to do the things that I like to do and that I like to do the things that they like to do. And it's the same in reverse, and basically I want to do it as well, me agreeing with them. As far as that goes, you'd say, I like it when they show me by asking me, if they want to do it with me.

Men mentioned physical gestures, laughing at jokes, doing one another favors, keeping in touch, "doing stuff," teasing, and just being around friends as ways they know that men friends like each other. The most common responses to the question of how their men friends let them know that they liked them were "doing things together" and "initiating contact." John responded:

> I think it's just something you can sense, that you feel by . . . obviously if you continue to go out and do things with them.

Mike responded:

> Well, they'll call me up and ask me to do stuff, if they have nothing to do, or if they do have something to do and they want me to be a part of it.

Men feel liked by other men as a result of being asked to spend time in activities of common interest. Within such active contexts, reciprocated assistance, physical gestures, language patterns, and joking behaviors all had distinctive meanings that indicated intimacy between male friends.

Reciprocity of Assistance. Men mentioned doing favors, which included mailing a letter, fixing a car, loaning money, and talking about problems relating to heterosexual relationships. The men emphasized a reciprocity of assistance and a goal-orientation to both problem solving and situations that involved self-disclosure. This reciprocity demonstrated mutual interest and also was a means to achieve a balanced dependency. Pete responded to the question, "How do your friends let you know that they like you?"

> We help each other out, just like doing favors for someone. Like right now, me and my roommate were going to class, and he was asking me questions because he slept in and didn't study. So I go "what's this—ok, here, just have my notes." Even though I'm going to need them for my thing at three. You know, just little stuff like that.

Matt referred to the assistance given between his closest male friend and himself as a "barter" arrangement.

> Jack and I had a good relationship about this. He's a very good mechanic, and I would ask him. And I would develop something that I do that was rewarding for him. Like I could pull strings and get free boat trips and stuff like that when I was an [diving] instructor. And he would work on my car and I would turn him on to the Islands and dives and stuff. It was sort of a barter situation.

The sharing of their skills and access to opportunities fostered interdependency, yet also maintained their independence through a mutual give-and-take.

Physical Gestures. Men also reported physically demonstrating affection to each other. However, the physical gestures had a distinctively masculine style that protected them from the fear of an interpretation of a homosexual preference. Men mentioned handshakes, bear hugs, slaps on the back, and an arm on the shoulder as ways that friends demonstrated affection.

Handshakes were the most frequently mentioned. Handshakes offer controlled physical contact between men and are often considered an indicator of strength and manliness. A strong, crisp, and forthright grip is a sign of "respectable" masculinity while a limp and less robust handshake may be associated with femininity and a homosexual orientation. A bear hug also offers a demonstration of strength, often with one friend lifting another off the ground. Gary described an occasion in his response to the question, "How do your men friends let you know that they like you?"

> I came back from a swim meet in Arkansas last week, and I hadn't seen Mike for two weeks. When I came back he came right at me and gave me a big old bear hug, you know, stuff like that. And my mom and dad were in the room, and they're going, "Hey, put my son down!" and we were all laughing.

Men give the affectionate hug a "rugged," nonfeminine veneer by feigning playful aggression through the demonstration of physical strength. The garb and trappings of roughness allow a man to express affection while reducing the risks of making his friend uncomfortable or having his sexual identity ridiculed. A slap on the back is much less risky for a man than a caress on the cheek, although they may have a similar message in the communication of closeness.

Joking Behavior. Men developed joking behaviors that communicate closeness and similar ways of viewing the world. Ken responded to the question, "How do you get the idea that they [men friends] are close friends?"

> Laughter is one of them. I'll admit, when I'm around anybody really, not just them, I try to be the world's best comic. Like I said, humor is just important and I love it. I'd rather . . . I just like to laugh. And when they laugh, and they get along with me, and we joke with each other, and not get personal, they don't take it too harshly.

Although Ken says he attempts to be a comic "when I'm around anybody," he goes on to elaborate about the differences in joking when around men or around women:

> For the girls, not so much the laughter because you can't, with the comedian atmosphere, or whatever, you can't tell with the women. . . . Because, you know, if you get together with some girl or someone that likes you a little bit, or whatever—you can tell them that your dog just died, and they'll laugh. You know what I mean, you know how it goes. It's just, they'll laugh at anything, just to . . . I don't know why it is. But you get together with certain girls and they'll just laugh no matter what you say. So it's kind of hard to base it on that. Because the guys, you know, you can judge that with the guys. Because they'll say it's a crappy joke or something like that, or say that was a terrible thing.

Women friends did not respond to his humor in as straightforward and rigorous a manner as did his men friends. This appears to be a result of a covert sexual agenda between the cross-sex friends and a misunderstanding of the cues and nuances of male joking behavior by his women friends. Joking behaviors often are rooted in the contexts of men's shared experience, an experience that women may have little access to. Joking relationships are used by men to show caring and to establish trust in the midst of competitive activities. The following response to the question, "What are the most meaningful occasions that you spent with a male friend?" demonstrated a context where joking behavior expressed intimacy in the midst of competitive action. First, Greg describes the context in which the joking took place.

> The first time I'd been waterskiing was last summer. And among these guys I was really athletic, maybe more so than them even. And he knew how to waterski and I didn't. And we got there, and I tried maybe six or eight times, and couldn't do it, just couldn't do it. I don't know what the deal was because I'm really an athletic person and I figure it wouldn't be that tough, and it was tough. As far as the friendship goes, for Mark, for him to sit there and have the patience to teach me what to do, what was going on, it must have taken an hour or so or more of just intense teaching. Like he was the coach and I was the player, and we got done with that and I did it. And the next time we went I was on one ski, thanks to him. It was that much of an improvement. And to know that we could communicate that well around something that I love, sports, and to know that we could communicate that well in something that we both like a lot, athletics, that meant a lot to our friendship.

Mark provided assistance that altered a potential traumatic experience into a positive success. Specifically, Mark used a joking relationship to reduce the pressure on Greg and allowed him to perform while in a vulnerable position. Mark did not exploit his superior capabilities, but shared them and empowered his friends. Greg explains:

> We were just able to make jokes about it, and we laughed at each other all day. And it finally worked out. I mean it was great for me to be that frustrated and that up-tight about it and know the only thing he was going to do was laugh at me. That may seem bad to some people. They'd have gotten more upset. But for me that was good. . . . It really put things in perspective.

The joking cues expressed acceptance and communicated to Greg that it was okay to fail, and that failing would not jeopardize continuing the lesson. Mark's acceptance of a friend's failures reduced the performance pressure on Greg, and thus released him to concentrate on learning to water-ski.

Joking behavior is important to men because it offers a style of communication that consists of implicit meanings not readily accessible to people outside the group. "In" jokes between friends demand attentiveness to an individual's thinking, emotional states and reactions, and nuances of behavior. They provide a format where a man can be meticulously attentive to the feelings and tastes of another man. An elaborate reciprocation of jokes can be a proxy for more overt forms of caring. Yet, because joking behavior is often used as a distancing gesture and hostile act, joking behavior is not interpreted as an expression of attachment. This adds to the covert nature of the act and further protects men from possible ridicule. The tenuous line between aggression and affection is demonstrated by Tim's response to the question, "Can you think of any other qualities that would be important to a close friendship?"

> Basically that they'll understand you. Like if you do something wrong and they go, "Oh, what a jerk." I mean they can say it, but they'll say it in a different way than some guy who shoots his mouth off, "What a jerk, you fell off your bicycle."

Tim was questioned further, "How would it be different—I know what you mean—but can you describe it?"

> You know, they'll poke fun at you but they'll say it in a friendly way. Where someone else will just laugh, "What an idiot," and they'll mean it. Where your friend will say . . . you know, just make fun of you and stuff. I don't know if I explained it too well.

The same words used by two different men are interpreted and reacted to in very different ways. The tone of voice and social distance between the two men are essential factors in the determination of an understanding friend as opposed to an aggressive enemy. Tim's reactions to both cues reveal the different meanings. The question was asked, "Okay, maybe if I ask another question to get at it, say you fell off your bike, how would you feel when your friend joked about you as opposed to . . .?"

> I would just start laughing, you know. I mean he'd start laughing at me and I'd just look and he'd go, "You jerk," and I'll start laughing. We know each other and stuff. Some guy off the street—I'll just cuss at him and flip him off, you know. So it's a little different.

Such discriminations are difficult for men to explain and describe. This would suggest that the discriminating task may be even more difficult for women, who have not had the experience in the contexts from which men's friendships have developed. Matt explained how he lets his closest male friend know that he likes him.

> I'll have a tendency to say, "Well, why don't you write?" in a teasing way, and "Okay, when are we going to get together? . . . and this bullshit of you being up there in Stockton."

Coarse language is injected into the teasing to legitimize the implicit meaning that he misses his friend and wishes that they were together. Joking relationships provide men with an implicit form of expressing affection, which is an alternative to explicit forms such as hugging and telling people that they care about them. Joking also may be more personal, since it often relies on a knowledge and sensitivity to a friend's attitudes and tastes, thus recognizing and affirming a unique part of him. The following portion of an interview demonstrates this masculine style. Jim responds to the question, "Why do you think [women are more likely than men to come out and tell you that they like you] that is?"

> Oh, it's just the way you were raised. It's society. You might hug a girl and say, "See you later and good luck on your test tomorrow." Whereas you'll joke around with a guy about it.

"Why would you joke around with a guy?"

> It's just a . . . it's just a different relationship, you know. I think society would accept two girls hugging each other and a guy hugging a girl, but it's a little different when you're two guys. I don't know if you saw the movie *Grease* where there, like Danny and that other guy who's driving the car, they do it, well like they hug each other right? After they pull the car out of the shop, it's kind of like that, they stop, they realize what they did. You might even want to, you might wanna say, "Hey, thanks a lot." You do stuff like that. But you don't act silly. You might shake their hand.

Jim was asked if he hugged his closest male friend, to which he responded, "No, I don't do that." He was then asked, "How would it feel if you went up to hug Fred [closest male friend]? How do you think he would react?"

> Well, I can remember a couple of times that we had . . . after a football game when you're real excited and things. It all depends on the situation. If I just did it, you know, out of the clear blue sky, he'd probably look at me and, you know. I could do it jokingly. It might even be pretty funny. I might try that. But I don't think he'd like it. He'd probably think it was a little strange.

Jim was able to hug his friend after a football game, when emotions ran high, and the men's masculinity had just been validated by participating in, and presumably winning, the game. The football context insulated the hugging from being interpreted as unmanly or gay. Jim says, "It depends on the situation." At one point when Jim was asked what it would be like to hug his friend, he interpreted it as a challenge or a dare. "I could do that." However, he translates the act into a joking behavior, "I could do it jokingly," in an effort to stylize the hug as masculine. Men's styles of intimacy attempt to minimize the risks taken when overtly expressing affection. These risks are summed up best by Jim when asked why he would feel strange if he hugged his best male friend. Jim said:

> The guys are more rugged and things, and it wouldn't be rugged to hug another man. That's not a masculine act, where it could be, you know, there's noth-

ing unmasculine about it. But somebody might not see it as masculine and you don't want somebody else to think that you're not, you know—masculine or . . . but you still don't want to be outcast. Nobody I think wants to be outcast.

Thus Jim could not hug his friend "out of the clear blue sky," overtly and without a gender-validating context. The styles of male intimacy attempt to limit these risks. Joking behavior camouflages the hidden agenda of closeness by combining elements of a private awareness of a friend's history and personal nuances with a public tone of aggression and humiliation. A man describes his most meaningful times with men friends.

The conversation will come and we can kind of laugh at each other. And you can laugh at yourself, which is really handy.

Much as the slap on the back covers an affectionate greeting with an aggressive movement, joking behavior provides a covert avenue in which to express caring and intimacy.

CONCLUSIONS

These findings suggest that microstructural variables, particularly interactional expectations, are powerful explanations for male intimacy styles. Intimacy between men is influenced by their awareness of the restrictive sanctions that are often imposed on men who express certain emotions, such as sadness or fear. Men's intimate verbal style is partially shaped by the fear of sanctions that may be imposed on emotional behaviors deemed culturally unacceptable. Homophobia and the difficulty men have disclosing weaknesses testify to the limitations they experience when attempting to explore certain aspects of their selves. These limitations of male intimacy may distance men from all but their closest men friends, and may also create a premium on privacy and trust in close friendships. Such limitations may be more detrimental later in life where structural settings are less conducive and supportive to maintaining active friendships. A college environment fosters casual access to friendships and friendships may also be integral and functional for the successful completion of a degree. Thus, the sample in the present study may be experiencing an intimacy that is more difficult for men to maintain in job and career settings.

The interview data show that although constraints in the masculine role limit men in certain situations and in verbal intimacy, men do develop intimate friendship behavior that is based on shared action. Men's intimacy often depends on nonverbal cues that are developed in contexts of active engagement. Men expressed intimacy with close friends by exchanging favors, engaging in competitive action, joking, touching, sharing accomplishments, and including one another in activities. The strengths of men's active style of intimacy involve sharing and empowering each other with the skills necessary for problem solving, and gaining a sense of engagement and control of their lives by sharing resources and accomplishments. Nonverbal cues offered an intimacy based on a private affirmation and exchange of the special history that two men share. This unique form of intimacy cannot be replicated solely by self-disclosure.

In addition to the men's active style of intimacy, they also reported self-disclosure to friends. Contrary to previous research, most men reported that they were more comfortable expressing themselves to a close male friend than to female friends. These men assumed that close male friends would be more understanding because of their shared experiences. Men said that self-disclosure and hugging "depended on the situation," and were more likely to self-disclose in a gender-validating context. Thus, men overcome cultural prohibitions against intimacy with this gender-validating strategy.

There are advantages and disadvantages to both feminine and masculine styles of intimacy. Feminine intimacy is productive for acknowledging fears and weaknesses that comprise a person's vulnerability. Admitting and expressing an emotional problem are enhanced by verbal self-disclosure skills. Masculine styles of intimacy are productive for confronting a fear or weakness with alternative strategies that empower them to creatively deal with a difficulty. Both styles appear necessary for a balanced approach to self-realization and the challenge of integrating that realization into a healthy and productive life.

Although this study focused on generalized sex differences to document a previously unrecognized active style of intimacy, women also demonstrated active styles of intimacy, and men demonstrated verbal styles of intimacy. Thus, although the results are based on generalized tendencies, the data also support the flexibility of gender-based behavior and the ability of men and women to cross over and use both active and verbal styles of intimacy.

The documentation of active styles of intimacy sharpens the understanding of intimate male behavior, and it provides a more accurate and useful interpretation of the "inexpressive male." The deficit model of male expressiveness does not recognize men's active style of intimacy, and stresses men's need to be taught feminine-typed skills to foster intimacy in their relationships. This negation or denial of men's active style of intimacy may alienate and threaten men who then assume that intimacy is a challenge they will fail. An awareness of the strengths in men's covert style of intimacy provides a substantive basis from which to address and augment changes in restrictive and debilitating aspects of masculinity. The finding that gender-validating activities foster male self-disclosure suggests that strategies for developing more intimate capabilities in men would be most successful when accompanied by a gender-validating setting that acknowledges, enhances, and expands the use of the intimate skills that men have previously acquired.

The data suggest the influence that sex-segregated worlds exert on the ways women and men choose, and are most comfortable in expressing, intimacy. The separate adult social worlds that women and men often experience shape the opportunities and forms of intimacy shared between friends. These structural opportunities and the styles of intimacy that become integral to specific opportunities become familiar, expected, and assumed between friends of the same sex, and often are bewildering, inaccessible, and misinterpreted by cross-sex friends or partners.

The implications are clear: men and women will have to be integrated in similar microstructural realms in the private and public spheres if we are to expect men and women to develop fluency in what are now termed "male" and "female" styles of intimacy. If such integration does indeed take place, the reduction of misunderstanding, frustration, and abuse in cross-sex relationships could be profound.

References

Balswick, J. "The Inexpressive Male: A Tragedy of American Society." In D. David and R. Brannon (eds.), *The Forty-Nine Percent Majority*. Reading, MA: Addison-Wesley, 1976: 55–67.

Caldwell, R., and Peplau, L. "Sex Differences in Same-Sex Friendship." *Sex Roles* 8 (1982):721–732.

Cancian, F. M. "The Feminization of Love." *Signs* 11 (1986):629–709.

Goffman, Irving. *Presentation of Self*. Garden City, NY: Doubleday, 1959.

Komarovsky, M. *Blue-Collar Marriage*. New York: Vintage, 1964.

Swain, S. "Male Intimacy in Same-Sex Friendships: The Influence of Gender-Validating Activities." Conference paper presented at the American Sociological Association Annual Meetings, San Antonio, 1984.

RITCH C. SAVIN-WILLIAMS

Dating and Romantic Relationships Among Gay, Lesbian, and Bisexual Youths

THE IMPORTANCE OF DATING AND ROMANCE

According to Scarf (1987), the developmental significance of an intimate relationship is to help us "contact archaic, dimly perceived and yet powerfully meaningful aspects of our inner selves" (p. 79). We desire closeness within the context of a trusting, intimate relationship. Attachment theory posits that humans are prewired for loving and developing strongly felt emotional attachments (Bowlby, 1973). When established, we experience safety, security, and nurturance. Early attachments, including those in infancy, are thought to circumscribe an internal blueprint that profoundly affects future relationships, such as the establishment of intimate friendships and romances in adolescence and adulthood (Hazan & Shaver, 1987).

Developmentally, dating is a means by which romantic relationships are practiced, pursued, and established. It serves a number of important functions, such as entertainment, recreation, and socialization, that assist participants in developing appropriate means of interacting. It also enhances peer group status and facilitates the selection of a mate (Skipper & Nass, 1966). Adolescents who are most confident in their dating abilities begin dating during early adolescence, date frequently, are satisfied with their dating, and are most likely to become involved in a "committed" dating relationship (Herold, 1979).

The establishment of romantic relationships is important for youths regardless of sexual orientation. Isay (1989) noted that falling in love was a critical factor in helping his gay clients feel comfortable with their gay identity and that "the self-affirming value of a mutual relationship over time cannot be overemphasized" (p. 50). Browning (1987) regarded lesbian love relationships as an opportunity to enhance:

> ... the development of the individual's adult identity by validating her personhood, reinforcing that she deserves to receive and give love. A relationship can also be a source of tremendous emotional support as the woman explores her goals, values, and relationship to the world. (p. 51)

Because dating experience increases the likelihood that an intimate romantic relationship will evolve, the absence of this opportunity may have long-term repercussions. Malyon (1981) noted some of the reverberations:

> Their most charged sexual desires are usually seen as perverted, and their deepest feelings of psychological attachment are regarded as unacceptable. This social disapproval interferes with the preintimacy involvement that fosters the evolution of maturity and self-respect in the domain of object relations. (p. 326)

CULTURE'S DEVALUATION OF SAME-SEX RELATIONSHIPS

Relatively speaking, our culture is far more willing to turn a blind eye to sexual than to romantic relationships among same-sex adolescent partners. Same-sex activity may appear "temporary," an experiment, a phase, or a perverted source of fun. But falling in love with someone of the same gender and maintaining a sustained emotional involvement with that person implies an irreversible deviancy at worst and a bad decision at best. In our homes, schools, religious institutions, and media, we teach that intense relationships after early adolescence among members of the same sex "should" raise the concern of good parents, good friends, and good teachers. One result is that youths of all sexual orientations may become frightened of developing close friendships with same-sex peers. They fear that these friendships will be viewed as sexually intimate.

It is hardly surprising that a sexual-minority adolescent can easily become "the loneliest person . . . in the typical high school of today" (Norton, 1976:376):

> For the homosexual-identified student, high school is often a lonely place where, from every vantage point, there are couples: couples holding hands as they enter school; couples dissolving into an endless wet kiss between school bells; couples exchanging rings with ephemeral vows of devotion and love. (Sears, 1991:326–327)

The separation of a youth's homoerotic passion from the socially sanctioned act of heterosexual dating can generate self-doubt, anger, and resentment, and can ultimately retard or distort the development of interpersonal intimacy during the adolescent years. Thus, many youths never consider same-sex dating to be a reasonable option, except in their fantasies. Scientific and clinical writings that ignore same-sex romance and dating among youth contribute to this conspiracy of silence. Sexual-minority youth struggle with issues of identity and intimacy because important impediments rooted in our cultural values and attitudes deter them from dating those they love and instead mandate that they date those they cannot love.

EMPIRICAL STUDIES OF SAME-SEX ROMANTIC RELATIONSHIPS AMONG YOUTH

Until the last several years same-sex relationships among sexual-minority youths were seldom recognized in the empirical, scientific literature. With the recent visibility of gay, bisexual, and lesbian youths in the culture at large, social and behavioral scientists are beginning to conduct research focusing on various developmental processes of such youths, including their sexuality and intimacy.

Bisexual, lesbian, and gay youths, whether in Detroit, Minneapolis, Pennsylvania, New York, or the Netherlands, report that they desire to have long-lasting, committed same-sex romantic relationships in their future (D'Augelli, 1991; Sanders, 1980; Savin-Williams, 1990). According to Silverstein (1981), establishing a romantic relationship with a same-sex partner helps one to feel "chosen," to resolve issues of sexual identity, and to feel more complete. Indeed, those who are in a long-term love relationship generally have high levels of self-esteem and self-acceptance.[1]

Although there are few published studies of teens that focus primarily on their same-sex dating or romantic relationships, there are suggestive data that debunk the myth in our culture that gays, lesbians, and bisexuals neither want nor maintain steady, loving same-sex relationships. In two studies of gay and bisexual male youths, same-sex relationships are regarded as highly desirable. Among 29 Minnesota youths, 10 had a steady male partner at the time of the interview, 11 had been in a same-sex relationship, and, most tellingly, all but 2 hoped for a steady male partner in their future (Remafedi, 1987). For these youths, many of whom were living independently with friends or on the street, being in a long-term relationship was considered to be an ideal state. With a college-age sample of 61 males, D'Augelli (1991) reported similar results. One half of his sample was "partnered," and their most troubling mental health concern was termination of a close relationship, ranking just ahead of telling parents about their homosexuality.

The difficulty, however, is to maintain a visible same-sex romance in high school. Sears (1991) interviewed 36 Southern late adolescent and young adult lesbians, gays, and bisexuals. He discovered that although nearly everyone had heterosexually dated in high school, very few dated a member of the same sex during that time. Because of concerns about secrecy and the lack of social support, most same-sex romances involved little emotional commitment and were of short duration. None were overt.

Research with over 300 gay, bisexual, and lesbian youths between the ages of 14 and 23 years (Savin-Williams, 1990) supports the finding that sexual-minority youths have romantic relationships during adolescence and young adulthood. Almost 90 percent of the females and two thirds of the males reported that they have had a romantic relationship. Of the total number of romances listed, 60 percent were with same-sex partners. The male youths were slightly more likely than lesbian and bisexual female youths to begin their romantic career with a same-sex, rather than an opposite-sex partner.

In the same study, the lesbians and bisexual females who had a high proportion of same-sex romances were most likely to be "out" to others. However, their self-esteem level was essentially the same as those who had a high percentage of heterosexual relationships. If she began same-sex dating early, during adolescence, then a lesbian or bisexual female also tended to be in a current relationship and to experience long-lasting romances. Gay and bisexual male youths who had a large percentage of adolescent romantic relationships with boys had high self-esteem. They were more likely to be publicly "out" to friends and family if they had had a large number of romances. Boys who initiated same-sex romances at an early age were more likely to report that they have had long-term and multiple same-sex relationships.

The findings from these studies are admittedly sparse and do not provide the depth and insight that are needed to help us better understand the experience of being in a same-sex romantic relationship. They do illustrate that youths have same-sex romances while in high school. Where there is desire, some youths will find a way. Sexually active same-sex friendships may evolve into romantic relationships (Savin-Williams, 1995), and those most publicly out are most likely to have had adolescent same-sex romances. Certainly, most lesbian, gay, and bisexual youths value the importance of a same-sex, lifelong, committed relationship in their adult years.

Perhaps the primary issue is not the absence of same-sex romances during adolescence, but the hidden nature of the romances. They are seldom recognized and rarely supported or celebrated. The research data offer little information regarding the psychological impact of not being involved in a same-sex romantic relationship or of having to hide such a relationship when it exists. For this, one must turn to stories of the personal struggles of adolescents.

PERSONAL STRUGGLES

Youths who have same-sex romances during their adolescence face a severe struggle to have these relationships acknowledged and supported. Gibson (1989) noted the troubling contradictions:

> The first romantic involvements of lesbian and gay male youth are a source of great joy to them in affirming their sexual identity, providing them with support, and assuring them that they too can experience love. However, society places extreme hardships on these relationships that make them difficult to establish and maintain. (p. 130)

A significant number of youths, perhaps those feeling most insecure regarding their sexual identity, may fantasize about being sexually intimate with a same-sex partner but have little hope that it could in fact become a reality. One youth, Lawrence, reported this feeling in his coming-out story:

> While growing up, love was something I watched other people experience and enjoy. . . . The countless men I secretly loved and fantasized about were only in private, empty dreams in which love was never returned. I seemed to be the only person in the world with no need for love and companionship. . . . Throughout high school and college I had no way to meet people of the same sex and sexual orientation. These were more years of isolation and secrecy. I saw what other guys my age did, listened to what they said and how they felt. I was expected to be part of a world with which I had nothing in common. (Curtis, 1988:109–110)

A young lesbian, Diane, recalled that "love of women was never a possibility that I even realized could be. You loved your mother and your aunts, and you had girlfriends for a while. Someday, though, you would always meet a man" (Stanley & Wolfe, 1980:47). Girls dated boys and not other girls. Because she did not want to date boys, she did not date.

Another youth knew he had homoerotic attractions, but he never fathomed that they could be expressed to the boy that he most admired, his high school soccer teammate. It took alcohol and the right situation:

> I knew I was checking out the guys in the shower after soccer practice. I thought of myself as hetero who had the urge for males. I fought it, said it was a phase. And then it happened.
>
> Derek was my best friend. After soccer practice the fall of our junior year we celebrated both making the "A" team by getting really drunk. We were just fooling around and suddenly our pants were off. I was so scared I stayed out of school for three days but we kept being friends and nothing was said until a

year later when I came out to everyone and he came up to me with these tears and asked if he made me homosexual. (Savin-Williams, 1995)

It is never easy for youths to directly confront the mores of peers whose values and attitudes are routinely supported by the culture. Nearly all youths know implicitly the rules of socially appropriate behavior and the consequences of nonconformity. This single, most influential barrier to same-sex dating, the threat posed by peers, can have severe repercussions. The penalty for crossing the line of "normalcy" can result in emotional and physical pain.

PEER HARASSMENT AS A BARRIER TO DATING

Price (1982) concluded, "Adolescents can be very cruel to others who are different, who do not conform to the expectations of the peer group" (p. 472). Very little has changed in the last decade. For example, 17-year-old actor Ryan Phillippe worried about the consequences on his family and friends if he played a gay teen on ABC's soap opera *One Life to Live* (Gable, 1992:3D). David Ruffin, 19, of Ferndale, Michigan, explained why he boycotted his high school senior prom: "The kids could tell I was different from them, and I think I was different because I was gay. And when you're dealing with young people, different means not cool" (Bruni, 1992:10A).

Unlike heterosexual dating, little social advantage, such as peer popularity or acceptance, is gained by holding hands and kissing a same-sex peer in school hallways, shopping malls, or synagogues. Lies are spun to protect secrets and to avoid peer harassment. One lesbian youth, Kim, felt that she had to be an actress around her friends. She lied to friends by creating "Andrew" when she was dating "Andrea" over the weekend (Bruni, 1992).

To avoid harassment, sexual minority adolescents may monitor their interpersonal interactions. They may wonder, "Am I standing too close?" or "Do I appear too happy to see him(her)?" (Anderson, 1987). Hetrick and Martin (1987) found that youths are often apprehensive to show "friendship for a friend of the same sex for fear of being misunderstood or giving away their secretly held sexual orientation" (p. 31). If erotic desires become aroused and threaten expression, youths may seek to terminate same-sex friendships rather than risk revealing their secret. For many adolescents, especially bisexual youths, relationships with the other sex may be easier to develop. The appeal of such relationships is that the youths will be viewed by peers as heterosexual, thus peer acceptance will be enhanced and the threat of harassment and rejection will be reduced. The result is that some sexual-minority youths feel inherently "fake" and they therefore retreat from becoming intimate with others. Although they may meet the implicit and explicit demands of their culture, it is at a cost—their sense of authenticity.

FAKING IT: HETEROSEXUAL SEX AND DATING

Retrospective data from gay, bisexual, and lesbian adults reveal the extent to which heterosexual dating and sex are commonplace during the adolescent and young adult years (Bell & Weinberg, 1978; Schafer, 1976; Troiden & Goode, 1980). These might be one-night stands, brief romances, or long-term relationships. Across various studies, nearly two-thirds of gay men and three-quarters of lesbians report having had heterosexual sex in their past. Motivations include fun, curiosity, denial of homoerotic feelings, and pressure to conform to society's insistence on heterosexual norms and behaviors. Even though heterosexual sex often results in a low level of sexual gratification, it is deemed a necessary sacrifice to meet the expectations of peers and, by extension, receive their approval. Only later, as adults, when they have the opportunity to compare these heterosexual relationships with same-sex ones do they fully realize that which they had missed during their younger years.

Several studies with lesbian, bisexual, and gay adolescents document the extent to which they are sexually involved with opposite-sex partners. Few gay and bisexual [male] youth had *extensive* sexual contact with females, even among those who began heterosexual sex at an early age. Sex with one or two girls was usually considered "quite enough." Not infrequently these girls were best friends who expressed a romantic or sexual interest in the gay boys. The male youths liked the girls, but they preferred friendships rather than sexual relations. One youth expressed this dilemma:

> She was a year older and we had been friends for a long time before beginning dating. It was a date with the full thing: dinner, theater, alcohol, making out, sex. At her house and I think we both came during intercourse. I was disappointed because it was such hard work—not physically I mean but emotionally. Later on in my masturbation my fantasies were never of her. We did it once more in high school and then once more when we were in college. I labeled it love but not sexual love. I really wanted them to occur together. It all ended when I labeled myself gay. (Savin-Williams, 1995)

An even greater percentage of lesbian and bisexual female adolescents engaged in heterosexual sexual experiences—2 of every 3 (Herdt & Boxer, 1993), 3 of every 4 (Sears, 1991), and 8 of 10 (Savin-Williams, 1990). Heterosexual activity began as early as second grade and as late as senior year in high school. Few of these girls, however, had extensive sex with boys—usually with two or three boys within the context of dating. Eighteen-year-old Kimba noted that she went through a heterosexual stage:

> ... trying to figure out what was so great about guys sexually. I still don't understand. I guess that, for straights, it is like it is for me when I am with a woman. . . . I experimented in whatever ways I thought would make a difference, but it was no go. My closest friends are guys; there is caring and closeness between us. (Heron, 1983:82)

Georgina also tried to follow a heterosexual script:

> In sixth and seventh grades you start wearing makeup, you start getting your hair cut, you start liking boys—you start thinking about letting them "French

> kiss" you. I did all those major things. But, I still didn't feel very satisfied with myself. I remember I never really wanted to be intimate with any guy. I always wanted to be their best friend. (Sears, 1991:327)

One young lesbian, Lisa, found herself "having sex with boys to prove I wasn't gay. Maybe I was even trying to prove it to myself! I didn't enjoy having sex with boys" (Heron, 1983:76). These three lesbian youths forfeited a sense of authenticity, intimacy, and love because they were taught that emotional intimacy can only be achieved with members of the other sex.

The reasons sexual-minority adolescents gave as to why they engaged in heterosexual sex were similar to those reported in retrospective studies by adults. The youths needed to test whether their heterosexual attractions were as strong as their homoerotic ones—thus attempting to disconfirm their homosexuality—and to mask their homosexuality so as to win peer- and self-acceptance and to avoid peer rejection. Many youths believed that they could not really know whether they were lesbian, gay, bisexual, or heterosexual without first experiencing heterosexual sex. For many, however, heterosexual activities consisted of sex without feelings that they tried to enjoy without much success (Herdt & Boxer, 1993). Heterosexual sex felt unnatural because it lacked the desired emotional intensity. One young gay youth reported:

> We'd been dating for three months. I was 15 and she, a year or so older. We had petted previously and so she planned this event. We attempted intercourse in her barn, but I was too nervous. I didn't feel good afterwards because it was not successful. We did it every week for a month or so. It was fun but it wasn't a big deal. But then I did not have a great lust or drive. This was just normal I guess. It gave me something to do to tell the other guys who were always bragging. (Savin-Williams, 1995)

Similarly, Kimberly always had a steady heterosexual relationship: "It was like I was just going through the motions. It was expected of me, so I did it. I'd kiss him or embrace him but it was like I was just there. He was probably enjoying it, but I wasn't" (Sears, 1991:327).

Jacob, an African American adolescent, dated the prettiest girls in his school in order to maintain his image: "It was more like President Reagan entertaining heads of state. It's expected of you when you're in a certain position" (Sears, 1991:126–127). Another Southern male youth, Grant, used "group dates" to reinforce his heterosexual image. Rumors that he was gay were squelched because his jock friends came to his defense: "He's not a fag. He has a girlfriend" (Sears, 1991:328).

These and other personal stories of youths vividly recount the use of heterosexual sex and dating as a cover for an emerging same-sex or bisexual identity. Dating provides opportunities to temporarily "pass" as straight until the meaning of homoerotic feelings are resolved or youths find a safe haven to be lesbian or gay. Heterosexual sex and dating may be less pleasurable than same-sex encounters, but many sexual-minority youths feel that the former are the only safe, acceptable options.

IMPEDIMENTS AND CONSEQUENCES

The difficulties inherent in dating same-sex partners during adolescence are monumental. First is the fundamental difficulty of finding a suitable partner. The vast majority of lesbian, bisexual, and gay youths are closeted, not out to themselves, let alone to others. A second barrier is the consequences of same-sex dating, such as verbal and physical harassment from peers. A third impediment is the lack of public recognition or "celebration" of those who are romantically involved with a member of the same gender. Thus, same-sex dating remains hidden and mysterious, something that is either ridiculed, condemned, or ignored.

The consequences of an exclusively heterosexually oriented atmosphere in the peer social world can be severe and enduring. An adolescent may feel isolated and socially excluded from the world of peers. Sex with others of the same gender may be associated exclusively with anonymous, guilt-ridden encounters, handicapping the ability to develop healthy intimate relationships in adulthood. Denied the opportunity for romantic involvement with someone of the same sex, a youth may suffer impaired self-esteem that reinforces the belief that one is unworthy of love, affection, and intimacy. One youth, Rick, even doubted his ability to love:

> When I started my senior year, I was still unclear about my sexuality. I had dated women with increasing frequency, but never felt love for any of them. I discovered that I could perform sexually with a woman, but heterosexual experiences were not satisfying emotionally. I felt neither love nor emotional oneness with women. Indeed, I had concluded that I was incapable of human love. (Heron, 1983:95–96)

If youths are to take advantage of opportunities to explore their erotic sexuality, it is sometimes, at least for males, confined to clandestine sexual encounters, void of romance, affection, and intimacy but replete with misgivings, anonymity, and guilt.

> Ted was 21 and me, 16. It was New Year's Eve and it was a swimming pool party at my rich friend's house. Not sure why Ted was there but he really came on to me, even putting his arm around me in front of everyone. I wasn't ready for that but I liked it. New Year's Day, every time Ted looked at me I looked away because I thought it was obvious that we had had sex. It did clarify things for me. It didn't feel like I was cheating on [my girlfriend] Beth because the sex felt so different, so right. (Savin-Williams, 1995)

A gay youth may have genital contact with another boy without ever kissing him because to do so would be too meaningful. Remafedi (1990) found this escape from intimacy to be very damaging: "Without appropriate opportunities for peer dating and socialization, gay youth frequently eschew intimacy altogether and resort to transient and anonymous sexual encounters with adults" (p. 1173). One consequence is the increased risk for contracting sexually transmitted diseases, including HIV. This is particularly risky for youths who turn to prostitution to meet their intimacy needs (Coleman, 1989).

When youths eventually match their erotic and intimacy needs, they may be surprised with the results. This was Jacob's experience (Sears, 1991) when he fell in love with Warren, an African American senior who also sang in the choir. Sex quickly evolved into "an emotional thing." Jacob explained: "He got to the point of telling me he loved me. That was the first time anybody ever said any thing like that. It was kind of hard to believe that even after sex there are really feelings" (p. 127).

Equally common, however, especially among closeted youths, is that lesbian, bisexual, and gay teens may experience a poverty of intimacy in their lives and considerable social and emotional isolation. One youth, Grant, enjoyed occasional sex with a star football player, but he was devastated by the subsequent exclusion the athlete meted out to him: "We would see each other and barely speak but after school we'd see each other a lot. He had his image that he had to keep up and, since it was rumored that I was gay, he didn't want to get a close identity with me" (Sears, 1991:330).

Largely because of negative peer prohibitions and the lack of social support and recognition, same-sex romances that are initiated have difficulty flourishing. Irwin met Benji in the eighth grade and was immediately attracted to him (Sears, 1991). They shared interests in music and academics and enjoyed long conversations, playing music, and riding in the country-side. Eventually, their attractions for each other were expressed and a romantic, sexual relationship began. Although Irwin was in love with Benji, their relationship soon ended because it was no match for the social pressures and personal goals that conflicted with Irwin being in a same-sex relationship.

Georgina's relationship with Kay began dramatically with intense feelings that were at times ambivalent for both of them. At one point she overheard Kay praying, "Dear Lord, forgive me for the way I am" (Sears, 1991:333). Georgina's parents demanded that she end her "friendship" with Kay. Georgina told classmates they were just "good friends" and began dating boys as a cover. Despite her love for Kay, the relationship ended when Georgina's boyfriend told her that no one liked her because she hung around "that dyke, Kay." In retrospect, Georgina wished: "If everybody would have accepted everybody, I would have stayed with Kay" (p. 334).

Given this situation, lesbian, bisexual, and gay youths in same-sex relationships may place unreasonable and ultimately destructive demands on each other. For example, they may expect that the relationship will resolve all fears of loneliness and isolation and validate all aspects of their personal identity (Browning, 1987).

A SUCCESS STORY

A vivid account of how a same-sex romantic relationship can empower a youth is depicted in the seminal autobiography of Aaron Fricke (1981), *Reflections of a Rock Lobster*. He fell in love with a classmate, Paul:

With Paul's help, I started to challenge all the prejudice I had encountered during 16 1/2 years of life. Sure, it was scary to think that half my classmates might hate me if they knew my secret, but from Paul's example I knew it was possible to one day be strong and face them without apprehension. (Fricke, 1981:44)

Through Paul, Aaron became more resilient and self-confident:

His strengths were my strengths. . . . I realized that my feelings for him were unlike anything I had felt before. The sense of camaraderie was familiar from other friendships; the deep spiritual love I felt for Paul was new. So was the openness, the sense of communication with another. (Fricke, 1981:45)

Life gained significance. He wrote poems. He planned a future. He learned to express both kindness and strength. Aaron was in love, with another boy. But no guidelines or models existed on how best to express these feelings:

Heterosexuals learn early in life what behavior is expected of them. They get practice in their early teens having crushes, talking to their friends about their feelings, going on first dates and to chaperoned parties, and figuring out their feelings. Paul and I hadn't gotten all that practice; our relationship was formed without much of a model to base it on. It was the first time either of us had been in love like this and we spent much of our time just figuring out what that meant for us. (Fricke, 1981:46)

Eventually, after a court case that received national attention, Aaron won the right to take Paul to the senior prom as his date. This victory was relatively minor compared to the self-respect, authenticity, and pride in being gay that their relationship won for each of them.

FINAL REFLECTIONS

As a clinical and developmental psychologist, I find it disheartening to observe our culture ignoring and condemning sexual-minority youth. One consequence is that myths and stereotypes are perpetuated that interfere with or prevent youths from developing intimate same-sex relationships with those to whom they are erotically and emotionally attracted. Separating passion from affection, engaging in sex with strangers in impersonal and sometimes unsafe places, and finding alienation rather than intimacy in those relationships are not conducive to psychological health. In one study the most common reason given for initial suicide attempts by lesbians and gay men was relationship problems (Bell & Weinberg, 1978).

A youth's limited ability to meet other bisexual, lesbian, and gay adolescents compounds a sense of isolation and alienation. Crushes may develop on "unknowing friends, teachers, and peers. These are often cases of unrequited love with the youth never revealing their true feelings" (Gibson, 1989:131).

Sexual-minority youths need the validation of those around them as they attempt to develop a personal integrity and to discover those similar to themselves.

How long can gay, bisexual, and lesbian adolescents maintain their charades before they encounter difficulty separating the pretensions from the realities? Many "use" heterosexual dating to blind themselves and others. By so doing they attempt to disconfirm to themselves the growing encroachment of their homoerotic attractions while escaping derogatory name calling and gaining peer status and prestige. The incidence of heterosexual sex and relationships in the adolescence of gay men and lesbians attests to these desires.

Future generations of adolescents will no doubt find it easier to establish same-sex relationships. This is due in part to the dramatic increase in the visibility that adult same-sex relationships have received during the last few years. Domestic partnership ordinances in several cities and counties, victories for spousal equivalency rights in businesses, court cases addressing adoption by lesbian couples and challenges to marriage laws by several male couples, the dramatic story of the life partnership of Karen Thompson and Sharon Kowalski, and the "marriage" of former Mr. Universe Bob Paris to male Supermodel Rod Jackson raise public awareness of same-sex romantic relationships. Even Ann Landers (1992) is spreading the word. In a column, an 18-year-old gay teen from Santa Barbara requested that girls quit hitting on him because, as he explained, "I have a very special friend who is a student at the local university . . . and [we] are very happy with each other" (Landers, 1992: 2B).

A decade after Aaron Fricke fought for and won the right to take his boyfriend to the prom, a dozen lesbian, gay, and bisexual youths in the Detroit-Ann Arbor area arranged to have their own prom. Most felt excluded from the traditional high school prom, which they considered "a final, bitter postscript to painful years of feeling left out" (Bruni, 1992:10A). Seventeen-year-old Brenda said, "I want to feel rich for one moment. I want to feel all glamorous, just for one night" (Bruni, 1992:10A). Going to the "Fantasy" prom was a celebration that created a sense of pride, a connection with other sexual-minority teens, and a chance to dance—"two girls together, unguarded and unashamed, in the middle of a room filled with teenagers just like them" (Bruni, 1992:10A). One year later, I attended this prom with my life partner and the number of youths in attendance had increased sixfold.

We need to listen to youths such as Aaron, Diane, and Georgina, to hear their concerns, insights, and solutions. Most of all, we need to end the invisibility of same-sex romantic relationships. It is easily within our power to enhance the well-being of millions of youths, including "Billy Joe," a character in a famous Bobbie Gentry song. If Billy Joe had seen an option to a heterosexual life style, he might have considered an alternative to ending his life by jumping off the Tallahatchie Bridge.

Note

1. The causal pathway, however, is unclear (Savin-Williams, 1990). That is, being in a same-sex romance may build positive self-regard, but it may also be true that those with high self-esteem are more likely to form love relationships and to stay in them.

References

Anderson, D. (1987). Family and peer relations of gay adolescents. In S. C. Geinstein (Ed.), *Adolescent psychiatry: Developmental and clinical* studies: Vol. 14 (pp. 162–178). Chicago: The University of Chicago Press.

Bell, A. P., & Weinberg, M. S. (1978). *Homosexualities: A study of diversity among men and women.* New York: Simon & Schuster.

Bowlby, J. (1973). *Attachment and loss: Vol. 2. Separation.* New York: Basic Books.

Browning, C. (1987). Therapeutic issues and intervention strategies with young adult lesbian clients: A developmental approach. *Journal of Homosexuality, 14,* 45–52.

Bruni, F. (1992, May 22). A prom night of their own to dance, laugh, reminisce. *Detroit Free Press,* pp. 1A, 10A.

Coleman, E. (1989). The development of male prostitution activity among gay and bisexual adolescents. *Journal of Homosexuality, 17,* 131–149.

Curtis, W. (Ed.). (1988). *Revelations: A collection of gay male coming out stories.* Boston: Alyson.

D'Augelli, A. R. (1991). Gay men in college: Identity processes and adaptations. *Journal of College Student Development, 32,* 140–146.

Fricke, A. (1981). *Reflections of a rock lobster: A story about growing up gay.* Boston: Alyson.

Gable, D. (1992, June 2). "Life" story looks at roots of homophobia. *USA Today,* p. 3D.

Gibson, P. (1989). Gay male and lesbian youth suicide. In M. R. Feinleib (Ed.), *Report of the secretary's task force on youth suicide, Vol. 3: Prevention and interventions in youth suicide (3-110-3-142).* Rockville, MD: U.S. Department of Health and Human Services.

Hazan, C., & Shaver, P. (1987). Romantic love conceptualized as an attachment process. *Journal of Personality and Social Psychology, 52,* 511–524.

Herdt, G., & Boxer, A. (1993). *Children of horizons: How gay and lesbian teens are leading a new way out of the closet.* Boston: Beacon.

Herold, E. S. (1979). Variables influencing the dating adjustment of university students. *Journal of Youth and Adolescence, 8,* 73–79.

Heron, A. (Ed.). (1983). *One teenager in ten.* Boston: Alyson.

Hetrick, E. S., & Martin, A. D. (1987). Developmental issues and their resolution for gay and lesbian adolescents. *Journal of Homosexuality, 14,* 25–44.

Isay, R. A. (1989). *Being homosexual: Gay men and their development.* New York: Avon.

Landers, A. (1992, May 26). Gay teen tired of advances from sexually aggressive girls. *Detroit Free Press,* p. 2B.

Malyon, A. K. (1981). The homosexual adolescent: Developmental issues and social bias. *Child Welfare, 60,* 321–330.

Norton, J. L. (1976). The homosexual and counseling. *Personnel and Guidance Journal, 54,* 374–377.

Price, J. H. (1982). High school students' attitudes toward homosexuality. *Journal of School Health, 52,* 469–474.

Remafedi, G. (1987). Male homosexuality: The adolescent's perspective. *Pediatrics, 79,* 326–330.

Remafedi, G. (1990). Fundamental issues in the care of homosexual youth. *Adolescent Medicine, 74,* 1169–1179.

Sanders, G. (1980). Homosexualities in the Netherlands. *Alternative Lifestyles, 3,* 278–311.

Savin-Williams, R. C. (1990). *Gay and lesbian youth: Expressions of identity.* New York: Hemisphere.

———. (1994). Dating those you can't love and loving those you can't date. In R. Montemayor, G. R. Adams, & T. P. Gullotta (Eds.), *Personal relationships during adolescence: Vol 6. Advances in adolescent development* (pp. 196–215). Newbury Park, CA: Sage.

———. (1995). *Sex and sexual identity among gay and bisexual males.* Manuscript in preparation, Cornell University, Ithaca, NY.

Scarf, M. (1987). *Intimate partners: Patterns in love and marriage.* New York: Random House.

Schafer, S. (1976). Sexual and social problems of lesbians. *Journal of Sex Research, 12,* 50–69.

Sears, J. T. (1991). *Growing up gay in the South: Race, gender, and journeys of the spirit.* New York: Harrington Park Press.

Silverstein, C. (1981). *Man to man: Gay couples in America.* New York: William Morrow.

Skipper, J. K., Jr., & Nass, G. (1966). Dating behavior: A framework for analysis and an illustration. *Journal of Marriage and the Family, 27,* 412–420.

Stanley, J. P., & Wolfe, S. J. (Eds.). (1980). *The coming out stories.* New York: Persephone.

Troiden, R. R., & Goode, E. (1980). Variables related to the acquisition of a gay identity. *Journal of Homosexuality, 5,* 383–392.

PART 10 ~ THE GENDER OF VIOLENCE

As a nation, we fret about "teen violence," complain about "inner city crime" or fear "urban gangs." We express shock at the violence in our nation's public schools, where metal detectors crowd the doorways, and knives and guns compete with pencils and erasers in students' backpacks. Those public school shootings left us speechless and sick at heart. Yet when we think about these wrenching events, do we ever consider that, whether white or black, inner city or suburban, these bands of marauding "youths" or these troubled teenagers are virtually all young men?

Men constitute 99 percent of all persons arrested for rape; 88 percent of those arrested for murder; 92 percent of those arrested for robbery; 87 percent for aggravated assault; 85 percent of other assaults; 83 percent of all family violence; 82 percent of disorderly conduct. Men are overwhelmingly more violent than women. Nearly 90 percent of all murder victims are murdered by other men, according to the United States Department of Justice (Uniform Crime Reports 1991, 17).

From early childhood to old age, violence is perhaps the most obdurate, intractable gender difference we have observed. The National Academy of Sciences puts the case most starkly: "The most consistent pattern with respect to gender is the extent to which male criminal participation in serious crimes at any age greatly exceeds that of females, regardless of source of data, crime type, level of involvement, or measure of participation." "Men are always and everywhere more likely than women to commit criminal acts," write the criminologists Michael Gottfredson and Travis Hirschi (both 1990, 145). Yet how do we understand this obvious association between masculinity and violence? Is it a biological fact of nature, caused by something inherent in male anatomy? Is it culturally universal? And in the United States, what has been the association between gender and violence? Has that association become stronger or weaker over time? What can we, as a culture, do to prevent or at least ameliorate the problem of male violence?

My concern throughout this book has been to observe the construction of gender difference and gender inequality at both the individual level of identity and at the institutional level. The readings here reflect these concerns. Carol Cohn's insightful essay penetrates the gendered language of masculine "war-talk," in which the human tragedy of nuclear war preparation is masked behind discussions of kill ratios, body counts, and megaton delivery.

And Russell and R. Emerson Dobash and their colleagues use a gendered power analysis to explain why it is that men batter women they say they love in far greater numbers than women hit men. They bring a sensible sobriety to current discussions that suggest that women are just as likely to commit acts of violence against their husbands as men are against their wives.

In his insightful work on violence, James Gilligan locates the source of this dramatic gender disparity in men's fears of shame and humiliation, a desire, he argues, to make the other feel the pain that you, yourself, are trying to avoid feeling.

Of course, to argue that men are more prone to violence than women are does not resolve the political question of what to do about it. It would be foolish to resignedly throw up our hands in despair that "boys will be boys." Whether you believe this gender difference in violence derives from different biological predispositions (which I regard as dubious because these biological impulses do not seem to be culturally universal) or because male violence is socially sanctioned and legitimated as an expression of masculine control and domination (a far more convincing explanation), the policy question remains open. Do we organize society so as to maximize this male propensity toward violence, or do we organize society so as to minimize and constrain it? The answers to this question, like the answer to the questions about alleviating gender inequality in the family, in our educational institutions, and in the workplace are more likely to come from the voting booth than from the laboratories of scientists. As a society, we decide how much weight to give what few gender differences there are, and how best to alleviate the pain of those who are the victims of gendered violence.

CAROL COHN

Wars, Wimps, and Women: Talking Gender and Thinking War

I start with a true story, told to me by a white male physicist:

> Several colleagues and I were working on modeling counterforce attacks, trying to get realistic estimates of the number of immediate fatalities that would result from different deployments. At one point, we remodeled a particular attack, using slightly different assumptions, and found that instead of there being thirty-six million immediate fatalities, there would only be thirty million. And everybody was sitting around nodding, saying, "Oh yeah, that's great, only thirty million," when all of a sudden, I heard what we were saying. And I

From *Gendering War Talk,* edited by Miriam Cooke and Angela Woollacott. Copyright © 1993 by Princeton University Press. Reprinted by permission of Princeton University Press. Notes have been renumbered and edited.

blurted out, "Wait, I've just heard how we're talking—Only thirty million! Only thirty million human beings killed instantly?" Silence fell upon the room. Nobody said a word. They didn't even look at me. It was awful. I felt like a woman.

The physicist added that henceforth he was careful to never blurt out anything like that again.

During the early years of the Reagan presidency, in the era of the Evil Empire, the cold war, and loose talk in Washington about the possibility of fighting and "prevailing" in a nuclear war, I went off to do participant observation in a community of North American nuclear defense intellectuals and security affairs analysts—a community virtually entirely composed of white men. They work in universities, think tanks, and as advisers to government. They theorize about nuclear deterrence and arms control, and nuclear and conventional war fighting, about how to best translate military might into political power; in short, they create the discourse that underwrites American national security policy. The exact relation of their theories to American political and military practice is a complex and thorny one; the argument can be made, for example, that their ideas do not so much shape policy decisions as legitimate them after the fact. But one thing that is clear is that the body of language and thinking they have generated filters out to the military, politicians, and the public, and increasingly shapes how we talk and think about war. This was amply evident during the Gulf War: Gulf War "news," as generated by the military briefers, reported by newscasters, and analyzed by the television networks' resident security experts, was marked by its use of the professional language of defense analysis, nearly to the exclusion of other ways of speaking.

My goal has been to understand something about how defense intellectuals think, and why they think that way. Despite the parsimonious appeal of ascribing the nuclear arms race to "missile envy," I felt certain that masculinity was not a sufficient explanation of why men think about war in the ways that they do. Indeed, I found many ways to understand what these men were doing that had little or nothing to do with gender. But ultimately, the physicist's story and others like it made confronting the role of gender unavoidable. Thus, in this paper I will explore gender discourse, and its role in shaping nuclear and national security discourse.

I want to stress, this is not a paper about men and women, and what they are or are not like. I will not be claiming that men are aggressive and women peace loving. I will not even address the question of how men's and women's relations to war may differ, nor of the different propensities they may have to committing acts of violence. Neither will I pay more than passing attention to the question which so often crops up in discussions of war and gender, that is, would it be a more peaceful world if our national leaders were women? These questions are valid and important, and recent feminist discussion of them has been complex, interesting, and contentious. But my focus is elsewhere. I wish to direct attention away from gendered individuals and toward gendered discourses. My question is about the way that civilian defense analysts think about war, and the ways in which that thinking is shaped not by their maleness (or, in extremely rare instances, femaleness), but by the ways in which gender discourse intertwines with and permeates that thinking.

Let me be more specific about my terms. I use the term *gender* to refer to the constellation of meanings that a given culture assigns to biological sex differences. But more than that, I use gender to refer to a symbolic system, a central organizing discourse of culture, one that not only shapes how we experience and understand ourselves as men and women, but that also interweaves with other discourses and shapes *them*—and therefore shapes other aspects of our world—such as how nuclear weapons are thought about and deployed.

So when I talk about "gender discourse," I am talking not only about words or language but about a system of meanings, of ways of thinking, images and words that first shape how we experience, understand, and represent ourselves as men and women, but that also do more than that; they shape many other aspects of our lives and culture. In this symbolic system, human characteristics are dichotomized, divided into pairs of polar opposites that are supposedly mutually exclusive: mind is opposed to body; culture to nature; thought to feeling; logic to intuition; objectivity to subjectivity; aggression to passivity; confrontation to accommodation; abstraction to particularity; public to private; political to personal, ad nauseam. In each case, the first term of the "opposites" is associated with male, the second with female. And in each case, our society values the first over the second.

I break it into steps like this—analytically separating the *existence* of these groupings of binary oppositions, from the association of each group with a gender, from the valuing of one over the other, the so-called male over the so-called female, for two reasons: first, to try to make visible the fact that this system of dichotomies is encoding many meanings that may be quite unrelated to male and female bodies. Yet once that first step is made—the association of each side of those lists with a gender—gender now becomes tied to many other kinds of cultural representations. If a human activity, such as engineering, fits some of the characteristics, it becomes gendered.

My second reason for breaking it into those steps is to try to help make it clear that the meanings can flow in different directions; that is, in gender discourse, men and women are supposed to exemplify the characteristics on the lists. It also works in reverse, however; to evidence any of these characteristics—to be abstract, logical or dispassionate, for example—is not simply to be those things, but also to be manly. And to be manly is not simply to be manly, but also to be in the more highly valued position in the discourse. In other words, to exhibit a trait on that list is not neutral—it is not simply displaying some basic human characteristic. It also positions you in a discourse of gender. It associates you with a particular gender, and also with a higher or lower valuation.

In stressing that this is a *symbolic* system, I want first to emphasize that while real women and men do not really fit these gender "ideals," the existence of this system of meaning affects all of us, nonetheless. Whether we want to or not, we see ourselves and others against its templates, we interpret our own and others' actions against it. A man who cries easily cannot avoid in some way confronting that he is likely to be seen as less than fully manly. A woman who is very aggressive and incisive may enjoy that quality in herself, but the fact of her aggressiveness does not exist by itself; she cannot avoid having her own and others' perceptions of that quality of hers, the meaning it has for people, being in some way mediated by the discourse of gender. Or, a different kind of example: Why does it mean one thing when George Bush gets teary-eyed in public, and something entirely different when Patricia Shroeder does? The same act is viewed through the lens of gender and is seen to mean two very different things.

Second, as gender discourse assigns gender to human characteristics, we can think of the discourse as something we are positioned *by*. If I say, for example, that a corporation should stop dumping toxic waste because it is damaging the creations of mother earth, (i.e., articulating a valuing and sentimental vision of nature), I am speaking in a manner associated with women, and our cultural discourse of gender positions me as female. As such I am then associated with the whole constellation of traits—irrational, emotional, subjective, and so forth—and I am in the devalued position. If, on the other hand, I say the corporation should stop dumping toxic wastes because I have calculated that it is causing $8.215 billion of damage to eight nonrenewable resources, which should be seen as equivalent to lowering the GDP by 0.15 percent per annum, (i.e., using a rational, calculative mode of thought), the discourse positions me as masculine—rational, objective, logical, and so forth—the dominant, valued position.

But if we are positioned *by* discourses, we can also take different positions *within* them. Although I am female, and this would "naturally" fall into the devalued term, I can choose to "speak like a man"—to be hard-nosed, realistic, unsentimental, dispassionate. Jeanne Kirkpatrick is a formidable example. While we can choose a position in a discourse, however, it means something different for a woman to "speak like a man" than for a man to do so. It is heard differently.

One other note about my use of the term *gender discourse:* I am using it in the general sense to refer to the phenomenon of symbolically organizing the world in these gender-associated opposites. I do not mean to suggest that there is a single discourse defining a single set of gender ideals. In fact, there are many specific discourses of gender, which vary by race, class, ethnicity, locale, sexuality, nationality, and other factors. The masculinity idealized in the gender discourse of new Haitian immigrants is in some ways different from that of sixth-generation white Anglo-Saxon Protestant business executives, and both differ somewhat from that of white-male defense intellectuals and security analysts. One version of masculinity is mobilized and enforced in the armed forces in order to enable men to fight wars, while a somewhat different version of masculinity is drawn upon and expressed by abstract theoreticians of war.

Let us now return to the physicist who felt like a woman: what happened when he "blurted out" his sudden awareness of the "only thirty million" dead people? First, he was transgressing a code of professional conduct. In the civilian defense intellectuals' world, when you are in professional settings you do not discuss the bloody reality behind the calculations. It is not required that you be completely unaware of them in your outside life, or that you have no feelings about them, but it is required that you do not bring them to the foreground in the context of professional activities. There is a general awareness that you *could not* do your work if you did; in addition, most defense intellectuals believe that emotion and description of human reality distort the process required to think well about nuclear weapons and warfare.

So the physicist violated a behavioral norm, in and of itself a difficult thing to do because it threatens your relationships to and your standing with your colleagues.

But even worse than that, he demonstrated some of the characteristics on the "female" side of the dichotomies—in his "blurting" he was impulsive, uncontrolled, emotional, concrete, and attentive to human bodies, at the very least. Thus, he marked himself not only as unprofessional but as feminine, and this, in turn, was doubly threatening. It was not only a threat to his own sense of self as masculine, his gender identity, it also identified him with a devalued status—of a woman—or put him in the devalued or subordinate position in the discourse.

Thus, both his statement, "I felt like a woman," and his subsequent silence in that and other settings are completely understandable. To have the strength of character and courage to transgress the strictures of both professional and gender codes *and* to associate yourself with a lower status is very difficult.

This story is not simply about one individual, his feelings and actions; it is about the role of gender discourse. The impact of gender discourse in that room (and countless others like it) is that some things get left out. Certain ideas, concerns, interests, information, feelings, and meanings are marked in national security discourse as feminine, and are devalued. They are therefore, first, very difficult to *speak,* as exemplified by the physicist who felt like a woman. And second, they are very difficult to *hear,* to take in and work with seriously, even if they *are* said. For the others in the room, the way in which the physicist's comments were marked as female and devalued served to delegitimate them. It is almost as though they had become an accidental excrescence in the middle of the room. Embarrassed politeness demanded that they be ignored.

I must stress that this is not simply the product of the idiosyncratic personal composition of that particular room. In other professional settings, I have experienced the feeling that something terribly important is being left out and must be spoken; and yet, it has felt almost physically impossible to utter the words, almost as though they could not be pushed out into the smooth, cool, opaque air of the room.

What is it that cannot be spoken? First, any words that express an emotional awareness of the desperate human reality behind the sanitized abstractions of death and destruction—as in the physicist's sudden vision of thirty million rotting corpses. Similarly, weapons' effects may be spoken of only in the most clinical and abstract terms, leaving no room to imagine a seven-year-old boy with his flesh melting away from his bones or a toddler with her skin hanging down in strips. Voicing concern about the number of casualties in the enemy's armed forces, imagining the suffering of the killed and wounded young men, is out of bounds. (Within the military itself, it is permissible, even desirable, to attempt to minimize immediate civilian casualties if it is possible to do so without compromising military objectives, but as we learned in the Persian Gulf War, this is only an extremely limited enterprise; the planning and precision of military targeting does not admit of consideration of the cost in human lives of such actions as destroying power systems, or water and sewer systems, or highways and food distribution systems.) Psychological effects—on the soldiers fighting the war or on the citizens injured, or fearing for their own safety, or living through tremendous deprivation, or helplessly watching their babies die from diarrhea due to the lack of clean water—all of these are not to be talked about.

But it is not only particular subjects that are out of bounds. It is also tone of voice that counts. A speaking style that is identified as cool, dispassionate, and distanced is required. One that vibrates with the intensity of emotion almost always disqualifies the speaker, who is heard to sound like "a hysterical housewife."

What gets left out, then, is the emotional, the concrete, the particular, the human bodies and their vulnerability, human lives and their subjectivity—all of which are marked as feminine in the binary dichotomies of gender discourse. In other words, gender discourse informs and shapes nuclear and national security discourse, and in so doing creates silences and absences. It keeps things out of the room, unsaid, and keeps them ignored if they manage to get in. As such, it degrades our ability to think *well* and *fully* about nuclear weapons and national security, and shapes and limits the possible outcomes of our deliberations.

What becomes clear, then, is that defense intellectuals' standards of what constitutes "good thinking" about weapons and security have not simply evolved out of trial and error; it is not that the history of nuclear discourse has been filled with exploration of other ideas, concerns, interests, information, questions, feelings, meanings and stances which were then found to create distorted or poor thought. It is that these options have been *preempted* by gender discourse, and by the feelings evoked by living up to or transgressing gender codes.

To borrow a term from defense intellectuals, you might say that gender discourse becomes a "preemptive deterrent" to certain kinds of thought.

Let me give you another example of what I mean—another story, this one my own experience:

One Saturday morning I, two other women, and about fifty-five men gathered to play a war game designed by the RAND Corporation. Our "controllers" (the people running the game) first divided us up into three sets of teams; there would be three simultaneous games being played, each pitting a Red Team against a Blue Team (I leave the reader to figure out which color represents which country). All three women were put onto the same team, a Red Team.

The teams were then placed in different rooms so that we had no way of communicating with each other, except through our military actions (or lack of them) or by sending demands and responses to those demands via the controllers. There was no way to negotiate or to take actions other than military ones. (This was supposed to simulate reality.) The controllers then presented us with maps and pages covered with numbers representing each side's forces. We were also given a "scenario," a situation of escalating tensions and military conflicts, starting in the Middle East and spreading to Central Europe. We were to decide what to do, the controllers would go back and forth between the two teams to relate the other team's actions, and periodically the controllers themselves would add something that would ratchet up the conflict—an announcement of an "intercepted intelligence report" from the other side, the authenticity of which we had no way of judging.

Our Red Team was heavily into strategizing, attacking ground forces, and generally playing war. We also, at one point, decided that we were going to pull our troops out of Afghanistan, reasoning it was bad for us to have them there and that the Afghanis had the right to self-determination. At another point we removed some troops from Eastern Europe. I must add that later on my team was accused of being wildly "unrealistic," that this group of experts found the idea that the Soviet Union might voluntarily choose to pull troops out of Afghanistan and Eastern Europe so utterly absurd. (It was about six months before Gorbachev actually did the same thing.)

Gradually our game escalated to nuclear war. The Blue Team used tactical nuclear weapons against our troops, but our Red Team decided, initially at least, against nuclear retaliation. When the game ended (at the end of the allotted time) our Red Team had "lost the war" (meaning that we had political control over less territory than we had started with, although our homeland had remained completely unviolated and our civilian population safe).

In the debriefing afterwards, all six teams returned to one room and reported on their games. Since we had had absolutely no way to know why the other team had taken any of its actions, we now had the opportunity to find out what they had been thinking. A member of the team that had played against us said, "Well, when he took his troops out of Afghanistan, I knew he was weak and I could push him around. And then, when we nuked him and he didn't nuke us back, I knew he was just such a wimp, I could take him for everything he's got and I nuked him again. He just wimped out."

There are many different possible comments to make at this point. I will restrict myself to a couple. First, when the man from the Blue Team called me a wimp (which is what it felt like for each of us on the Red Team—a personal accusation), I felt silenced. My reality, the careful reasoning that had gone into my strategic and tactical choices, the intelligence, the politics, the morality—all of it just disappeared, completely invalidated. I could not explain the reasons for my actions, could not protest, "Wait, you idiot, I didn't do it because I was weak, I did it because it made sense to do it that way, given my understandings of strategy and tactics, history and politics, my goals and my values." The protestation would be met with knowing sneers. In this discourse, the coding of an act as wimpish is hegemonic. Its emotional heat and resonance is like a bath of sulfuric acid: it erases everything else.

"Acting like a wimp" is an *interpretation* of a person's acts (or, in national security discourse, a country's acts, an important distinction I will return to later). As with any other interpretation, it is a selection of one among many possible different ways to understand something—once the selection is made, the other possibilities recede into invisibility. In national security discourse, "acting like a wimp," being insufficiently masculine, is one of the most readily available interpretive codes. (You do not need to do participant observation in a community of defense intellectuals to know this—just look at the "geopolitical analyses" in the media and on Capitol Hill of the way in which George Bush's military intervention in Panama and the Persian Gulf War finally allowed him to beat the "wimp factor.") You learn that someone is being a wimp if he perceives an international crisis as very dangerous and urges caution; if he thinks it might not be important to have just as many weapons that are just as big as the other guy's; if he suggests that an attack should not necessarily be answered by an even more destructive counterattack; or, until recently, if he suggested that making unilateral arms reductions might be useful for our own security. All of these are "wimping out."

The prevalence of this particular interpretive code is another example of how gender discourse affects the quality of thinking within the national security community, first, because, as in the case of the physicist who "felt like a woman," it is internalized to become a self-censor; there are things professionals simply will not *say* in groups, options they simply will not argue nor write about, because they know that to do so is to brand themselves as wimps. Thus, a whole range of inputs is left out, a whole series of options is foreclosed from their deliberations.

Equally, if not more damagingly, is the way in which this interpretive coding not only limits what is *said,* but even limits what is *thought.* "He's a wimp" is a phrase that *stops* thought. When we were playing the game, once my opponent on the Blue Team "recognized the fact that I was a wimp," that is, once he interpreted my team's actions through the lens of this common interpretive code in national security discourse, he *stopped thinking;* he stopped looking for ways to understand what we were doing. He did not ask, "Why on earth would the Red Team do that? What does it tell me about them, about their motives and purposes and goals and capabilities? What does it tell me about their possible understandings of *my* actions, or of the situation they're in?" or any other of the many questions that might have enabled him to revise his own conception of the situation or perhaps achieve his goals at a far lower level of violence and destruction. Here, again, gender discourse acts as a preemptive deterrent to thought.

"Wimp" is, of course, not the only gendered pejorative used in the national security community; "pussy" is another popular epithet, conjoining the imagery of harmless domesticated (read demasculinized) pets with contemptuous reference to women's genitals. In an informal setting, an analyst worrying about the other side's casualties, for example, might be asked, "What kind of pussy are you, anyway?" It need not happen more than once or twice before everyone gets the message; they quickly learn not to raise the issue in their discussions. Attention to and care for the living, suffering, and dying of human beings (in this case, soldiers and their families and friends) is again banished from the discourse through the expedient means of gender-bashing.

Other words are also used to impugn someone's masculinity and, in the process, to delegitimate his position and avoid thinking seriously about it. "Those Krauts are a bunch of limp-dicked wimps" was the way one U.S. defense intellectual dismissed the West German politicians who were concerned about popular opposition to Euromissile deployments. I have heard our NATO allies referred to as "the Euro-fags" when they disagreed with American policy on such issues as the Contra War or the bombing of Libya. Labeling them "fags" is an effective strategy; it immediately dismisses and trivializes their opposition to U.S. policy by coding it as due to inadequate masculinity. In other words, the American analyst need not seriously confront the Europeans' arguments, since the Europeans' doubts about U.S. policy obviously stem not from their reasoning but from the "fact" that they "just don't have the stones for war." Here, again, gender discourse deters thought.

"Fag" imagery is not, of course, confined to the professional community of security analysts; it also appears in popular "political" discourse. The Gulf War was replete with examples. American derision of Saddam Hussein included bumper stickers that read "Saddam, Bend Over." American soldiers reported that the "U.S.A." stenciled on their uniforms stood for "Up Saddam's Ass." A widely reprinted cartoon, surely one of the most multiply offensive that came out of the war, depicted Saddam bowing down in the Islamic posture of prayer, with a huge U.S. missile, approximately five times the size of the prostrate figure, about to penetrate his upraised bottom. Over and over, defeat for the Iraqis was portrayed as humiliating anal penetration by the more powerful and manly United States.

Within the defense community discourse, manliness is equated not only with the ability to win a war (or to "prevail," as some like to say when talking about nuclear war); it is also equated with the willingness (which they would call courage) to threaten and use force. During the Carter administration, for example, a well-known academic security affairs specialist was quoted as saying that "under Jimmy Carter the United States is spreading its legs for the Soviet Union." Once this image is evoked, how does rational discourse about the value of U.S. policy proceed?

In 1989 and 1990, as Gorbachev presided over the withdrawal of Soviet forces from Eastern Europe, I heard some defense analysts sneeringly say things like, "They're a bunch of pussies for pulling out of Eastern Europe." This is extraordinary. Here they were, men who for years railed against Soviet domination of Eastern Europe. You would assume that if they were politically and ideologically consistent, if they were rational, they would be applauding the Soviet actions. Yet in their informal conversations, it was not their rational analyses that dominated their response, but the fact that for them, the decision for war, the willingness to use force, is cast as a question of masculinity—not prudence, thoughtfulness, efficacy, "rational" cost-benefit calculation, or morality, but masculinity.

In the face of this equation, genuine political discourse disappears. One more example: After Iraq invaded Kuwait and President Bush hastily sent U.S. forces to Saudi Arabia, there was a period in which the Bush administration struggled to find a convincing political justification for U.S. military involvement and the security affairs community debated the political merit of U.S. intervention. Then Bush set the deadline, January 16, high noon at the OK Corral, and as the day approached conversations changed. More of these centered on the question compellingly articulated by one defense intellectual as "Does George Bush have the stones for war?" This, too, is utterly extraordinary. This was a time when crucial political questions abounded: Can the sanctions work if given more time? Just what vital interests does the United States actually have at stake? What would be the goals of military intervention? Could they be accomplished by other means? Is the difference between what sanctions might accomplish and what military violence might accomplish worth the greater cost in human suffering, human lives, even dollars? What will the long-term effects on the people of the region be? On the ecology? Given the apparent successes of Gorbachev's last-minute diplomacy and Hussein's series of nearly daily small concessions, can and should Bush put off the deadline? Does he have the strength to let another leader play a major role in solving the problem? Does he have the political flexibility to not fight, or is he hellbent on war at all costs? And so on, ad infinitum. All of these disappear in the sulfuric acid test of the size of Mr. Bush's private parts.

I want to return to the RAND war simulation story to make one other observation. First, it requires a true confession: *I was stung by being called a wimp.* Yes, I thought the remark was deeply inane, and it infuriated me. But even so, I was also stung. Let me hasten to add, this was not because my identity is very wrapped up with not being wimpish—it actually is not a term that normally figures very heavily in my self-image one way or the other. But it was impossible to be in that room, hear his comment and the snickering laughter with which it was met, and not to feel stung, and humiliated.

Why? There I was, a woman and a feminist, not only contemptuous of the mentality that measures human beings by their degree of so-called wimpishness, but also someone for whom the term *wimp* does not have a deeply resonant personal meaning. How could it have affected me so much?

The answer lies in the role of the context within which I was experiencing myself—the discursive framework. For in that room I was not "simply me," but I was a participant in a discourse, a shared set of words, concepts, symbols that constituted not only the linguistic possibilities available to us but also constituted *me* in that situation. This is not entirely true, of course. How I experienced myself was at least partly shaped by other experiences and other discursive frameworks—certainly those of feminist politics and antimilitarist politics; in fact, I would say my reactions were predominantly shaped by those frameworks. But that is quite different from saying "I am a feminist, and that individual, psychological self simply moves encapsulated through the world being itself"—and therefore assuming that I am unaffected. No matter who else I was at that moment, I was unavoidably a participant in a discourse in which being a wimp has a meaning, and a deeply pejorative one at that. By calling me a wimp, my accuser on the Blue Team *positioned* me in that discourse, and I could not but feel the sting.

In other words, I am suggesting that national security discourse can be seen as having different positions within it—ones that are starkly gender coded; indeed, the enormous strength of their evocative power comes from gender. Thus, when you participate in conversation in that community, you do not simply choose what to say and how to say it; you advertently or inadvertently choose a position in the discourse. As a woman, I can choose the "masculine" (thoughtful, rational, logical) position. If I do, I am seen as legitimate, but I limit what I can say. Or, I can say things that place me in the "feminine" position—in which case no one will listen to me.

Finally, I would like to briefly explore a phenomenon I call the "unitary masculine actor problem" in national security discourse. During the Persian Gulf War, many feminists probably noticed that both the military briefers and George Bush himself frequently used the singular masculine pronoun "he" when referring to Iraq and Iraq's army. Someone not listening carefully could simply assume that "he" referred to Saddam Hussein. Sometimes it did; much of the time it simply reflected the defense community's characteristic habit of calling opponents "he" or "the other guy." A battalion commander, for example, was quoted as saying "Saddam knows where we are and we know where he is. We will move a lot now to keep him off guard."[1] In these sentences, "he" and "him" appear to refer to Saddam Hussein. But, of course, the American forces had *no idea* where Saddam Hussein himself was; the singular masculine pronouns are actually being used to refer to the Iraqi military.

This linguistic move, frequently heard in discussions within the security affairs and defense communities, turns a complex state and set of forces into a singular male opponents. In fact, discussions that purport to be serious explorations of the strategy and tactics of war can have a tone which sounds more like the story of a sporting match, a fistfight, or a personal vendetta.

> I would want to suck him out into the desert as far as I could, and then pound him to death.[2]

> Once we had taken out his eyes, we did what could be best described as the "Hail Mary play" in football.[3]

> [I]f the adversary decides to embark on a very high roll, because he's frightened that something even worse is in the works, does grabbing him by the scruff of the neck and slapping him up the side of the head, does that make him behave better or is it plausible that it makes him behave even worse?[4]

Most defense intellectuals would claim that using "he" is just a convenient shorthand, without significant import or effects. I believe, however, that the effects of this usage are many and the implications far-reaching. Here I will sketch just a few, starting first with the usage throughout defense discourse generally, and then coming back to the Gulf War in particular.

The use of "he" distorts the analyst's understanding of the opposing state and the conflict in which they are engaged. When the analyst refers to the opposing state as "he" or "the other guy," the image evoked is that of a person, a unitary actor; yet states are not people. Nor are they unitary and unified. They comprise complex, multifaceted governmental and military apparatuses, each with opposing forces within it, each, in turn, with its own internal institutional dynamics, its own varied needs in relation to domestic politics, and so on. In other words, if the state is referred to and pictured as a unitary actor, what becomes unavailable to the analyst and policy-maker is a series of much more complex truths that might enable him to imagine many more policy options, many more ways to interact with that state.

If one kind of distortion of the state results from the image of the state as a person, a unitary actor, another can be seen to stem from the image of the state as a specifically *male* actor. Although states are almost uniformly run by men, states are not men; they are complex social institutions, and they act and react as such. Yet, when "he" and "the other guy" are used to refer to states, the words do not simply function as shorthand codes; instead, they have their own entailments, including assumptions about how men act, which just might be different from how states act, but which invisibly become assumed to be isomorphic with how states act.

It also entails emotional responses on the part of the speaker. The reference to the opposing state as "he" evokes male competitive identity issues, as in, "I'm not going to let him push me around," or, "I'm not going to let him get the best of me." While these responses may or may not be adaptive for a barroom brawl, it is probably safe to say that they are less functional when trying to determine the best way for one state to respond to another state. Defense analysts and foreign policy experts can usually agree upon the supreme desirability of dispassionate, logical analysis and its ensuing rationally calculated action. Yet the emotions evoked by the portrayal of global conflict in the personalized terms of male competition must, at the very least, exert a strong pull in exactly the opposite direction.

A third problem is that even while the use of "he" acts to personalize the conflict, it simultaneously abstracts both the opponent and the war itself. That is, the use of "he" functions in very much the same way that discussions about "Red" and "Blue" do. It facilitates treating war within a kind of game-playing model, A against B, Red against Blue, he against me. For even while "he" is evocative of male identity issues, it is also just an abstract piece to moved around on a game board, or, more appropriately, a computer screen.

That tension between personalization and abstraction was striking in Gulf War discourse. In the Gulf War, not only was "he" frequently used to refer to the Iraqi military, but so was "Saddam," as in "Saddam really took a pounding today," or "Our goal remains the same: to liberate Kuwait by forcing Saddam Hussein out."[5] The personalization is obvious: in this locution, the U.S. armed forces are not destroying a nation, killing people; instead, they (or George) are giving Saddam a good pounding, or bodily removing him from where he does not belong. Our emotional response is to get fired up about a bully getting his comeuppance.

Yet this personalization, this conflation of Iraq and Iraqi forces with Saddam himself, also abstracts: it functions to substitute in the mind's eye the abstraction of an implacably, impeccably evil enemy for the particular human beings, the men, women, and children being pounded, burned, torn, and eviscerated. A cartoon image of Saddam being ejected from Kuwait preempts the image of the blackened, charred, decomposing bodies of nineteen-year-old boys tossed in ditches by the side of the road, and the other concrete images of the acts of violence that constitute "forcing Hussein [sic] out of Kuwait."[6] Paradoxical as it may seem, in personalizing the Iraqi army as Saddam, the individual human beings in Iraq were abstracted out of existence.

In summary, I have been exploring the way in which defense intellectuals talk to each other—the comments they make to each other, the particular usages that appear in their informal conversations or their lectures. In addition, I have occasionally left the professional community to draw upon public talk about the Gulf War. My analysis does *not* lead me to conclude that "national security thinking is masculine"—that is, a separate, and different, discussion. Instead, I have tried to show that national security discourse is gendered, and that it matters. Gender discourse is interwoven through national security discourse. It sets fixed boundaries, and in so doing, it skews what is discussed and how it is thought about. It shapes expectations of other nations' actions, and in so doing it affects both our interpretations of international events and conceptions of how the United States should respond.

In a world where professionals pride themselves on their ability to engage in cool, rational, objective calculation while others around them are letting their thinking be sullied by emotion, the unacknowledged interweaving of gender discourse in security discourse allows men to not acknowledge that their pristine rational thought is in fact riddled with emotional response. In an "objective" "universal" discourse that valorizes the "masculine" and deauthorizes the "feminine," it is only the "feminine" emotions that are noticed and labeled as emotions, and thus in need of banning from the analytic process. "Masculine" emotions—such as feelings of aggression, competition, macho pride and swagger, or the sense of identity resting on carefully defended borders—are not so easily noticed and identified as emotions, and are instead invisibly folded into "self-evident," so-called realist paradigms and analyses. It is both the interweaving of gender discourse in national security thinking *and* the blindness to its presence and impact that have deleterious effects. Finally, the impact is to distort, degrade, and deter roundly rational, fully complex thought within the community of defense intellectuals and national security elites and, by extension, to cripple democratic deliberation about crucial matters of war and peace.

Notes

1. Chris Hedges, "War Is Vivid in the Gun Sights of the Sniper," *New York Times,* February 3, 1991, A1.

2. General Norman Schwarzkopf, National Public Radio broadcast, February 8, 1991.

3. General Norman Schwarzkopf, CENTCOM News Briefing, Riyadh, Saudi Arabia, February 27, 1991, p. 2.

4. Transcript of a strategic studies specialist's lecture on NATO and the Warsaw Pact (summer institute on Regional Conflict and Global Security: The Nuclear Dimension, Madison, Wisconsin, June 29, 1987).

5. Defense Secretary Dick Cheney, "Excerpts from Briefing at Pentagon by Cheney and Powell," *New York Times,* January 24, 1991, A 11.

6. Scarry explains that when an army is described as a single "embodied combatant," injury, (as in Saddam's "pounding"), may be referred to but is "no longer recognizable or interpretable." It is not only that Americans might be happy to imagine Saddam being pounded; we also on some level know that it is not really happening, and thus need not feel the pain of the wounded. We "respond to the injury . . . as an imaginary wound to an imaginary body, despite the fact that that imaginary body is itself made up of thousands of real human bodies" (Elaine Scarry, *Body in Pain: The Making and Unmaking of the World* [New York: Oxford, 1984], p. 72).

RUSSELL P. DOBASH, R. EMERSON DOBASH, MARGO WILSON,
AND MARTIN DALY

The Myth of Sexual Symmetry in Marital Violence

Long denied, legitimized, and made light of, wife-beating is at last the object of widespread public concern and condemnation. Extensive survey research and intensive interpretive investigations tell a common story. Violence against wives (by which term we encompass *de facto* as well as registered unions) is often persistent and severe, occurs in the context of continuous intimidation and coercion, and is inextricably linked to attempts to dominate and control women. Historical and contemporary investigations further reveal that this violence has been explicitly decriminalized, ignored, or treated in an ineffectual manner by criminal justice systems, by medical and social service institutions, and by communities. Increased attention to these failures has inspired increased efforts to redress them, and in many places legislative amendments have mandated arrest and made assault a crime whether the offender is married to the victim or not.

A number of researchers and commentators have suggested that assaults upon men by their wives constitute a social problem comparable in nature and magnitude to that of wife-beating. Two main bodies of evidence have been offered in support of these authors' claims that husbands and wives are similarly victimized: (1) self-reports of violent acts perpetrated and suffered by survey respondents, especially those in two U.S. national probability samples; and (2) U.S. homicide data. Unlike the case of violence against wives, however, the victimization of husbands allegedly continues to be denied and trivialized. "Violence by wives has not been an object of public concern," note Straus and Gelles (1986:472). "There has been no publicity, and no funds have been invested in ameliorating this problem because it has not been defined as a problem."

We shall argue that claims of sexual symmetry in marital violence are exaggerated, and that wives' and husbands' uses of violence differ greatly, both quantitatively and qualitatively. We shall further argue that there is no reason to expect the sexes to be alike in this domain, and that efforts to avoid sexism by lumping male and female data and by the use of gender-neutral terms such as "spouse-beating" are misguided. If violence is gendered, as it assuredly is, explicit characterization of gender's relevance to violence is essential. The alleged similarity of women and men in their use of violence in intimate relationships stands in marked contrast to men's virtual monopoly on the use of violence in other social contexts, and we challenge the proponents of the sexual symmetry thesis to develop coherent theoretical models that would account for a sexual monomorphism of violence in one social context and not in others.

From *Social Problems,* Vol. 39, no. 1 (February 1992), pp. 71–91. Copyright © 1992 by The Society for the Study of Social Problems. Reprinted by permission of University of California Press. References have been edited.

A final thesis of this paper is that resolution of controversies about the "facts" of family violence requires critical examination of theories, methods, and data, with explicit attention to the development of coherent conceptual frameworks, valid and meaningful forms of measurement, and appropriate inferential procedures. Such problems are not peculiar to this research domain, but analysis of the claims regarding violence against husbands provides an excellent example of how a particular approach to construct formation and measurement has led to misrepresentation of the phenomena under investigation.

THE CLAIM OF SEXUALLY SYMMETRICAL MARITAL VIOLENCE

Authoritative claims about the prevalence and sexual symmetry of spousal violence in America began with a 1975 U.S. national survey in which 2,143 married or cohabiting persons were interviewed in person about their actions in the preceding year. Straus (1977/78) announced that the survey results showed that the "marriage license is a hitting license," and moreover that the rates of perpetrating spousal violence, including severe violence, were higher for wives than for husbands. He concluded:

> Violence between husband and wife is far from a one way street. The old cartoons of the wife chasing the husband with a rolling pin or throwing pots and pans are closer to reality than most (and especially those with feminist sympathies) realize (Straus 1977/78:447–448).

In 1985, the survey was repeated by telephone with a new national probability sample including 3,520 husband-wife households, and with similar results. In each survey, the researchers interviewed either the wife or the husband (but not both) in each contacted household about how the couple settled their differences when they had a disagreement. The individual who was interviewed was presented with a list of eighteen "acts" ranging from "discussed an issue calmly" and "cried" to "threw something at him/her/you" and "beat him/her/you up," with the addition of "choked him/her/you" in 1985 (Straus 1990a:33). These acts constituted the Conflict Tactics Scales (CTS) and were intended to measure three constructs: "Reasoning," "Verbal Aggression," and "Physical Aggression" or "Violence," which was further subdivided into "Minor Violence" and "Severe Violence" according to a presumed potential for injury (Straus 1979, Straus and Gelles 1990a). Respondents were asked how frequently they had perpetrated each act in the course of "conflicts or disagreements" with their spouses (and with one randomly selected child) within the past year, and how frequently they had been on the receiving end. Each respondent's self-reports of victimization and perpetration contributed to estimates of rates of violence by both husbands and wives.

According to both surveys, rates of violence by husbands and wives were strikingly similar. The authors estimated that in the year prior to the 1975 survey 11.6 percent of U.S. husbands were victims of physical violence perpetrated by their wives, while 12.1 percent of wives were victims of their husbands' violence. In 1985, these percentages had scarcely changed, but husbands seemed more vulnerable: 12.1 percent of husbands and 11.3 percent of wives were victims. In both surveys, husbands were more likely to be victims of acts of "severe violence": in 1975, 4.6 percent of husbands were such victims versus 3.8 percent of wives, and in 1985, 4.4 percent of husbands versus 3.0 percent of wives were victims. In reporting their results, the surveys' authors stressed the surprising assaultiveness of wives:

> The repeated finding that the rate of assault by women is similar to the rate by their male partners is an important and distressing aspect of violence in American families. It contrasts markedly to the behavior of women outside the family. It shows that within the family or in dating and cohabiting relationships, women are about as violent as men (Straus and Gelles 1990b:104).

Others have endorsed and publicized these conclusions. For example, a recent review of marital violence concludes, with heavy reliance on Straus and Gelles's survey results, that "(a) women are more prone than men to engage in severely violent acts; (b) each year more men than women are victimized by their intimates" (McNeely and Mann 1990:130). One of Straus and Gelles's collaborators in the 1975 survey, Steinmetz (1977/78), used the same survey evidence to proclaim the existence of "battered husbands" and a "battered husband syndrome." She has remained one of the leading defenders of the claim that violence between men and women in the family is symmetrical. Steinmetz and her collaborators maintain that the problem is not wife-beating perpetrated by violent men, but "violent couples" and "violent people". Men may be stronger on average, argues Steinmetz, but weaponry equalizes matters, as is allegedly shown by the nearly equivalent numbers of U.S. husbands and wives who are killed by their partners. The reason why battered husbands are inconspicuous and seemingly rare is supposedly that shame prevents them from seeking help.

Straus and his collaborators have sometimes qualified their claims that their surveys demonstrate sexual symmetry in marital violence, noting, for example, that men are usually larger and stronger than women and thus able to inflict more damage and that women are more likely to use violence in self-defense or retaliation. However, the survey results indicate a symmetry not just in the perpetration of violence but in its initiation as well, and from this further symmetry, Stets and Straus (1990:154–155) conclude that the equal assaultiveness of husbands and wives cannot be attributed to the wives acting in self-defense, after all.

Other surveys using the CTS in the United States and in other countries have replicated the finding that wives are about as violent as husbands. The CTS has also been used to study violence in dating relationships, with the same sexually symmetrical results.

Some authors maintain not only that wives initiate violence at rates comparable to husbands, but that they rival them in the damage they inflict as well. McNeely and Robinson-Simpson (1987), for example, argue that research shows that the "truth about domestic violence" is that "women are as violent, if not more violent than men," in their inclinations, in their actions, and in the damage they inflict. The most dramatic evidence invoked in this context is again the fact that wives kill: spousal homicides—for which detection should be minimally or not at all biased because homicides are nearly always discovered and recorded— produce much more nearly equivalent numbers of male and female victims in the United States than do sublethal assault data, which are subject to sampling biases when obtained from police, shelters and hospitals. According to McNeely and Mann (1990:130), "the average man's size and strength are neutralized by guns and knives, boiling water, bricks, fireplace pokers, and baseball bats."

A corollary of the notion that the sexes are alike in their use of violence is that satisfactory causal accounts of violence will be gender-blind. Discussion thus focuses, for example, on the role of one's prior experiences with violence as a child, social stresses, frustration, inability to control anger, impoverished social skills, and so forth, without reference to gender. This presumption that the sexes are alike not merely in action but in the reasons for that action is occasionally explicit, such as when Shupe et al. (1987:56) write: "Everything we have found points to parallel processes that lead women and men to become violent. . . . Women may be more likely than men to use kitchen utensils or sewing scissors when they commit assault, but their frustrations, motives and lack of control over these feelings predictably resemble men's."

In sum, the existence of an invisibles legion of assaulted husbands is an inference which strikes many family violence researchers as reasonable. Two lines of evidence—homicide data and the CTS survey results—suggest to those supporting the sexual-symmetry-of-violence thesis that large numbers of men are trapped in violent relationships. These men are allegedly being denied medical, social welfare, and criminal justice services because of an unwillingness to accept the evidence from homicide statistics and the CTS surveys.

VIOLENCE AGAINST WIVES

Any argument that marital violence is sexually symmetrical must either dismiss or ignore a large body of contradictory evidence indicating that wives greatly outnumber husbands as victims. While CTS researchers were discovering and publicizing the mutual violence of wives and husbands, other researchers—using evidence from courts, police, and women's shelters—were finding that wives were much more likely than husbands to be victims. After an extensive review of extant research, Lystad (1975) expressed the consensus: "The occurrence of adult violence in the home usually involves males as aggressors towards females." This conclusion was subsequently supported by numerous further studies of divorce records, emergency room patients treated for non-accidental injuries, police assault records, and spouses seeking assistance and refuge. Analyses of police and court records in North America and Europe have persistently indicated that women constitute ninety to ninety-five percent of the victims of those assaults in the home reported to the criminal justice system.

Defenders of the sexual-symmetry-of-violence thesis do not deny these results, but they question their representativeness: these studies could be biased be-

cause samples of victims were self-selected. However, criminal victimization surveys using national probability samples similarly indicate that wives are much
more often victimized than husbands. Such surveys in the United States, Canada
and Great Britain have been replicated in various years, with essentially the same
results. Beginning in 1972 and using a panel survey method involving up to seven
consecutive interviews at six-month intervals, the U.S. National Crime Survey has
generated nearly a million interviews. Gaquin's (1977/78) analysis of U.S. National Crime Survey data for 1973–1975 led her to conclude that men "have almost no
risk of being assaulted by their wives" (634–635); only 3 percent of the violence reported from these surveys involved attacks on men by their female partners. Another analysis of the National Crime Survey data from 1973 to 1980 found that 6
percent of spousal assault incidents were directed at men (McLeod 1984).
Schwartz (1987) re-analyzed the same victimization surveys with the addition of
the 1981 and 1982 data, and found 102 men who claimed to have been victims of
assaults by their wives (4 percent of domestic assault incidents) in contrast to 1,641
women who said they were assaulted by husbands. The 1981 Canadian Urban
Victimization Survey and the 1987 General Social Survey produced analogous
findings, from which Johnson (1989) concluded that "women account for 80–90
percent of victims in assaults or sexual assaults between spouses or former spouses. In fact, the number of domestic assaults involving males was too low in both
surveys to provide reliable estimates" (1–2). The 1982 and 1984 British Crime Surveys found that women accounted for all the victims of marital assaults. Self-
reports of criminal victimization based on national probability surveys, while not
without methodological weaknesses, are not subject to the same reporting biases
as divorce, police and hospital records.

The national crime surveys also indicate that women are much more likely
than men to suffer injury as a result of assaults in the home. After analyzing the results of the U.S. National Crime Surveys, Schwartz (1987:67) concludes, "there are
still more than 13 times as many women seeking medical care from a private
physician for injuries received in a spousal assault." This result again replicates
the typical findings of studies of police or hospital records. For example, women
constituted 94 percent of the injury victims in an analysis of the spousal assault
cases among 262 domestic disturbance calls to police in Santa Barbara County,
California; moreover, the women's injuries were more serious than the men's.
Berk et al. (1983:207) conclude that "when injuries are used as the outcome of interest, a marriage license is a hitting license but for men only." Brush (1990) reports that a U.S. national probability sample survey of over 13,000 respondents in
1987–1988 replicated the evident symmetry of marital violence when CTS-like
questions about acts were posed, but also revealed that women were much more
often injured than men (and that men down-played women's injuries).

In response, defenders of the sexual-symmetry-of-violence thesis contend that
data from police, courts, hospitals, and social service agencies are suspect because
men are reluctant to report physical violence by their wives. For example, Steinmetz (1977/78) asserts that husband-beating is a camouflaged social problem because men must overcome extraordinary stigma in order to report that their wives
have beaten them. Similarly, Shupe et al. (1987) maintain that men are unwilling to

report their wives because "it would be unmanly or unchivalrous to go to the police for protection from a woman" (52). However, the limited available evidence does not support these authors' presumption that men are less likely to report assaults by their spouses than are women. Schwartz's (1987) analysis of the 1973–1982 U.S. National Crime Survey data found that 67.2 percent of men and 56.8 percent of women called the police after being assaulted by their spouses. One may protest that these high percentages imply that only a tiny proportion of the most severe spousal assaults were acknowledged as assaults by respondents to these crime surveys, but the results are nonetheless contrary to the notion that assaulted men are especially reticent. Moreover, Rouse et al. (1988), using "act" definitions of assaults which inspired much higher proportions to acknowledge victimization, similarly report that men were likelier than women to call the police after assaults by intimate partners, both among married couples and among those dating. In addition, a sample of 337 cases of domestic violence drawn from family court cases in Ontario showed that men were more likely than women to press charges against their spouses: there were 17 times as many female victims as male victims, but only 22 percent of women laid charges in contrast to 40 percent of the men, and men were less likely to drop the charges, too. What those who argue that men are reluctant or ashamed to report their wives' assaults over look is that women have their own reasons to be reticent, fearing both the loss of a jailed or alienated husband's economic support and his vengeance. Whereas the claim that husbands underreport because of shame or chivalry is largely speculative, there is considerable evidence that women report very little of the violence perpetrated by their male partners.

The CTS survey data indicating equivalent violence by wives and husbands thus stand in contradiction to injury data, to police incident reports, to help-seeking statistics, and even to other, larger, national probability sample surveys of self-reported victimization. The CTS researchers insist that their results alone are accurate because husbands' victimizations are unlikely to be detected or reported by any other method. It is therefore important to consider in detail the CTS and the data it generates.

DO CTS DATA REFLECT THE REALITY
OF MARITAL VIOLENCE?

The CTS instrument has been much used and much criticized. Critics have complained that its exclusive focus on "acts" ignores the actors' interpretations, motivations, and intentions; that physical violence is arbitrarily delimited, excluding, for example, sexual assault and rape; that retrospective reports of the past year's events are unlikely to be accurate; that researchers' attributions of "violence" (with resultant claims about its statistical prevalence) are based on respondents' admitting to acts described in such an impoverished manner as to conflate severe assaults with trivial gestures; that the formulaic distinction between "minor" and "severe violence" (whereby, for example, "tried to hit with something" is definitionally "severe" and "slapped" is definitionally "minor") constitutes a poor operationalization of severity; that the responses of aggressors and victims have been given identical evidentiary status in deriving incidence estimates, while their inconsistencies have been ignored; that the CTS omits the contexts of violence, the events precipitating it, and the sequences of events by which it progresses; and that it fails to connect outcomes, especially injury, with the acts producing them.

Straus (1990b) has defended the CTS against its critics, maintaining that the CTS addresses context with its "verbal aggression" scale (although the assessment of "verbal aggression" is not incident-linked with the assessment of "violence"); that the minor-severe categorization "is roughly parallel to the legal distinction between 'simple assault' and 'aggravated assault'" (58); that other measurement instruments have problems, too; and that you cannot measure everything. Above all, the defense rests on the widespread use of the instrument, on its reliability, and on its validity. That the CTS is widely used cannot be gainsaid, but whether it is reliable or valid is questionable.

Problems with the Reliability and Validity of CTS Responses

Straus (1990b:64) claims that six studies have assessed "the internal consistency reliability" of the CTS. One of the six (Barling and Rosenbaum 1986) contains no such assessment, a second is unreferenced, and a third unpublished. However, a moderate degree of "internal consistency reliability" of the CTS can probably be conceded. For example, those who admit to having "beat up" their spouses are also likely to admit to having "hit" them.

The crucial matter of interobserver reliability is much more problematic. The degree of concordance in couples' responses is an assay of "interspousal reliability" (Jouriles and O'Leary 1985), and such reliability must be high if CTS scores are to be taken at face value. For example, incidence estimates of husband-to-wife and wife-to-husband violence have been generated from national surveys in which the CTS was administered to only one adult per family, with claims of victimization and perpetration by male and female respondents all granted equal evidentiary status and summated. The validity of these widely cited incidence estimates is predicated upon interspousal reliability.

Straus (1990b:66) considers the assessment of spousal concordance to constitute an assay of "concurrent validity" rather than "interspousal reliability," in effect treating each partner's report as the violence criterion that validates the other. But spousal concordance is analogous to interobserver reliability: it is a necessary but by no means sufficient condition for concluding that the self-reports accurately reflect reality. If couples generally produce consistent reports—Mr. and Mrs. Jones both indicate that he struck her, while Mr. and Mrs. Smith both indicate that neither has struck the other—then it is possible though by no means certain that their CTS self-reports constitute valid (veridical) information about the blows actually struck. However, if couples routinely provide discrepant CTS responses, data derived from the CTS simply cannot be valid.

In this light, studies of husband/wife concordance in CTS responses should be devastating to those who imagine that the CTS provides a valid account of the respondents' acts. In what Straus correctly calls "the most detailed and thorough analysis of agreement between spouses in response to the CTS," Szinovacz (1983) found that 103 couples' accounts of the violence in their interactions matched to a degree little greater than chance. On several CTS items, mainly the most severe ones, agreement was actually below chance. On the item "beat up," concordance was nil: although there were respondents of both sexes who claimed to have administered beatings and respondents of both sexes who claimed to have been on the receiving end, there was not a single couple in which one party claimed to have administered and the other to have received such a beating. In a similar study, Jouriles and O'Leary (1985) administered the CTS to 65 couples attending a marital therapy clinic, and 37 control couples from the local community. For many of the acts, the frequency and percentage data reported are impossible to reconcile; for others, Jouriles and O'Leary reported a concordance statistic (Cohen's Kappa) as equalling zero when the correct values were negative. Straus (1990b) cites this study as conferring validity on the CTS, but in fact, its results replicated Szinovacz's (1983): husband/wife agreement scarcely exceeded chance expectation and actually fell below chance on some items.

Straus (1990b) acknowledges that these and the other studies he reviews "found large discrepancies between the reports of violence given by husbands and by wives" (69). He concludes, however, that "validity measures of agreement between family members are within the range of validity coefficients typically reported" (71), and that "the weakest aspect of the CTS are [sic] the scales that have received the least criticism: Reasoning and Verbal aggression" (71), by which he implies that the assessment of violence is relatively strong.

Ultimately, Straus's defense of the CTS is that the proof of the pudding is in the eating: "The strongest evidence concerns the construct validity of the CTS. It has been used in a large number of studies producing findings that tend to be consistent with previous research (when available), consistent regardless of gender of respondent, and theoretically meaningful." And indeed, with respect to marital violence, the CTS is capable of making certain gross discriminations. Various studies have found CTS responses to vary as a function of age, race, poverty, duration of relationship, and registered versus de facto marital unions, and these effects have generally been directionally similar to those found with less problematic measures of violence such as homicides. However, the CTS has also failed to detect certain massive differences, and we do not refer only to sex differences.

Consider the case of child abuse by stepparents versus birth parents. In various countries, including the United States, a stepparent is more likely to fatally assault a small child than is a birth parent, by a factor on the order of 100-fold; sublethal violence also exhibits huge differences in the same direction. Using the CTS, however, Gelles and Harrop (1991) were unable to detect any difference in self-reports of violence by step- versus birth parents. Users of the CTS have sometimes conceded that the results of their self-report surveys cannot provide an accurate picture of the prevalence of violence, but they have made this concession only to infer that the estimates must be gross underestimates of the true prevalence. However, the CTS's failure to differentiate the behavior of step- versus birth parents indicates that CTS-based estimates are not just underestimates but may misrepresent between-group differences in systematically biased ways. One must be concerned, then, whether this sort of bias also arises in CTS-based comparisons between husbands and wives.

Problems with the Interpretation of CTS Responses

With the specific intention of circumventing imprecision and subjectivity in asking about such abstractions as "violence," the CTS is confined to questions about "acts": Respondents are asked whether they have "pushed" their partners, have "slapped" them, and so forth, rather than whether they have "assaulted" them or behaved "violently." This focus on "acts" is intended to reduce problems of self-serving and biased definitional criteria on the part of the respondents. However, any gain in objectivity has been undermined by the way that CTS survey data have then been analyzed and interpreted. Any respondent who acknowledges a single instance of having "pushed," "grabbed," "shoved," "slapped" or "hit or tried to hit" another person is deemed a perpetrator of "violence" by the researchers, regardless of the act's context, consequences, or meaning to the parties involved. Similarly, a single instance of having "kicked," "bit," "hit or tried to hit with an object," "beat up," "choked," "threatened with a knife or gun," or "used a knife or fired a gun" makes one a perpetrator of "severe violence."

Affirmation of any one of the "violence" items provides the basis for estimates such as Straus and Gelles's (1990b:97) claim that 6.8 million U.S. husbands and 6.25 million U.S. wives were spousal assault victims in 1985. Similarly, estimates of large numbers of "beaten" or "battered" wives and husbands have been based on affirmation of any one of the "severe violence" items. For example, Steinmetz (1986:734) and Straus and Gelles (1987:638) claim on this basis that 1.8 million U.S. women are "beaten" by their husbands annually. But note that any man who once threw an "object" at his wife, regardless of its nature and regardless of whether the throw missed, qualifies as having "beaten" her; some unknown proportion of the women and men who are alleged to have been "beaten," on the basis of their survey responses, never claimed to have been struck at all. Thus, the "objective" scoring of the CTS not only fails to explore the meanings and intentions associated with the acts but has in practice entailed interpretive transformations that guarantee exaggeration, misinterpretation, and ultimately trivialization of the genuine problems of violence.

Consider a "slap." The word encompasses anything from a slap on the hand chastising a dinner companion for reaching for a bite of one's dessert to a tooth-loosening assault intended to punish, humiliate, and terrorize. These are not trivial distinctions; indeed, they constitute the essence of definitional issues concerning violence. Almost all definitions of violence and violent acts refer to intentions. Malevolent intent is crucial, for example, to legal definitions of "assault" (to which supporters of the CTS have often mistakenly claimed that their "acts" correspond; e.g., Straus 1990b:58). However, no one has systematically investigated how respondents vary in their subjective definitions of the "acts" listed on the CTS. If, for example, some respondents interpret phrases such as "tried to hit with an object" literally, then a good deal of relatively harmless behavior surely taints the estimates of "severe violence." Although this problem has not been investigated systematically, one author has shown that it is potentially serious. In a study of 103 couples, Margolin (1987) found that wives surpassed husbands in their use of "severe violence" according to the CTS, but unlike others who have obtained this result, Margolin troubled to check its meaningfulness with more intensive interviews. She concluded:

> While CTS items appear behaviorally specific, their meanings still are open to interpretation. In one couple who endorsed the item "kicking," for example, we discovered that the kicking took place in bed in a more kidding, than serious, fashion. Although this behavior meets the criterion for severe abuse on the CTS, neither spouse viewed it as aggressive, let alone violent. In another couple, the wife scored on severe physical aggression while the husband scored on low-level aggression only. The inquiry revealed that, after years of passively accepting the husband's repeated abuse, this wife finally decided, on one occasion, to retaliate by hitting him over the head with a wine decanter (1987:82).

By the criteria of Steinmetz (1977/78:501), this incident would qualify as a "battered husband" case. But however dangerous this retaliatory blow may have been and however reprehensible or justified one may consider it, it is not "battering," whose most basic definitional criterion is its repetitiveness. A failure to consider intentions, interpretations, and the history of the individuals' relationship is a significant shortcoming of CTS research. Only through a consideration of behaviors, intentions and intersubjective understandings associated with specific violent events will we come to a fuller understanding of violence between men and women. Studies employing more intensive interviews and detailed case reports addressing the contexts and motivations of marital violence help unravel the assertions of those who claim the widespread existence of beaten and battered husbands. Research focusing on specific violent events shows that women almost always employ violence in defense of self and children in response to cues of imminent assault in the past and in retaliation for previous physical abuse. Proponents of the sexual-symmetry-of-violence thesis have made much of the fact that CTS surveys indicate that women "initiate" the violence about as often as men, but a case in which a woman struck the first blow is unlikely to be the mirror image of one in which her husband "initiated." A noteworthy feature of the literature proclaiming the existence of battered husbands and battering wives is how little the meager case descriptions resemble those of battered wives and battering husbands. Especially lacking in the alleged male victim cases is any indication of the sort of chronic intimidation characteristic of prototypical woman battering cases.

Any self-report method must constitute an imperfect reflection of behavior, and the CTS is no exception. That in itself is hardly a fatal flaw. But for such an instrument to retain utility for the investigation of a particular domain such as family violence, an essential point is that its inaccuracies and misrepresentations must not be systematically related to the distinctions under investigation. The CTS's inability to detect the immense differences in violence between stepparents and birth parents, as noted above, provides strong reason to suspect that the test's shortcomings produce not just noise but systematic bias. In the case of marital violence, the other sorts of evidence reviewed in this paper indicate that there are massive differences in the use of confrontational violence against spouses by husbands versus wives, and yet the CTS has consistently failed to detect them. CTS users have taken this failure as evidence for the null hypothesis, apparently assuming that their questionnaire data have a validity that battered women's injuries and deaths lack.

HOMICIDES

The second line of evidence that has been invoked in support of the claim that marital violence is more or less sexually symmetrical is the number of lethal outcomes:

> Data on homicide between spouses suggest that an almost equal number of wives kill their husbands as husbands kill their wives (Wolfgang 1958). Thus it appears that men and women might have equal potential for violent marital interaction; initiate similar acts of violence; and when differences of physical strength are equalized by weapons, commit similar amounts of spousal homicide (Steinmetz and Lucca 1988:241).

McNeely and Robinson-Simpson (1987:485) elevated the latter hypothesis about the relevance of weapons to the status of a fact: "Steinmetz observed that when weapons neutralize differences in physical strength, about as many men as women are victims of homicide."

Steinmetz and Lucca's citation of Wolfgang refers to his finding that 53 Philadelphia men killed their wives between 1948 and 1952, while, 47 women killed their husbands. This is a slender basis for such generalization, but fuller information does indeed bear Steinmetz out as regards the near equivalence of body counts in the United States: Maxfield (1989) reported that there were 10,529 wives and 7,888 husbands killed by their mates in the entire country between 1976 and 1985, a 1.3:1 ratio of female to male victims.

Husbands are indeed almost as often slain as are wives in the United States, then. However, there remain several problems with Steinmetz and Lucca's (as well as McNeely and Robinson-Simpson's) interpretation of this fact. Studies of actual cases lend no support to the facile claim that homicidal husbands and wives "initiate similar acts of violence." Men often kill wives after lengthy periods of prolonged physical violence accompanied by other forms of abuse and coercion; the roles in such cases are seldom if ever reversed. Men perpetrate familicidal massacres, killing spouse and children together; women do not. Men commonly hunt down and kill wives who have left them; women hardly ever behave similarly. Men kill wives as part of planned murder-suicides; analogous acts by women are almost unheard of. Men kill in response to revelations of wifely infidelity; women almost never respond similarly, though their mates are more often adulterous. The evidence is overwhelming that a large proportion of the spousekillings perpetrated by wives, but almost none of those perpetrated by husbands, are acts of self-defense. Unlike men, women kill male partners after years of suffering physical violence, after they have exhausted all available sources of assistance, when they feel trapped, and because they fear for their own lives.

A further problem with the invocation of spousal homicide data as evidence against sex differences in marital violence is that this numerical equivalence is peculiar to the United States. Whereas the ratio of wives to husbands as homicide victims in the United States was 1.3:1, corresponding ratios from other countries are much higher: 3.3:1 for a 10-year period in Canada, for example, 4.3:1 for Great Britain, and 6:1 for Denmark. The reason why this is problematic is that U.S. homicide data and CTS data from several countries have been invoked as complementary pieces of evidence for women's and men's equivalent uses of violence. One cannot have it both ways. If the lack of sex differences in CTS results is considered proof of sexually symmetrical violence, then homicide data must somehow be dismissed as irrelevant, since homicides generally fail to exhibit this supposedly more basic symmetry. Conversely, if U.S. homicide counts constitute relevant evidence, the large sex differences found elsewhere surely indicate that violence is peculiarly symmetrical only in the United States, and the fact that the CTS fails to detect sex differences in other countries must then be taken to mean that the CTS is insensitive to genuine differences.

A possible way out of this dilemma is hinted at in Steinmetz and Lucca's (1988) allusion to the effect of weapons: perhaps it is the availability of guns that has neutralized men's advantage in lethal marital conflict in the United States. Gun use is indeed relatively prevalent in the U.S., accounting for 51 percent of a sample of 1706 spousal homicides in Chicago, for example, as compared to 40 percent of 1060 Canadian cases, 42 percent of 395 Australian cases, and just 8 percent of 1204 cases in England and Wales (Wilson and Daly forthcoming). Nevertheless, the plausible hypothesis that gun use can account for the different sex ratios among victims fails. When shootings and other spousal homicides are analyzed separately, national differences in the sex ratios of spousal homicide remain dramatic. For example, the ratio of wives to husbands as gunshot homicide victims in Chicago was 1.2:1, compared to 4:1 in Canada and 3.5:1 in Britain; the ratio of wives to husbands as victims of non-gun homicides was 0.8:1 in Chicago, compared to 2.9:1 in Canada and 4.5:1 in Britain (Wilson and Daly forthcoming). Moreover, the near equivalence of husband and wife victims in the U.S. antedates the contemporary prevalence of gun killings. In Wolfgang's (1958) classic study, only 34 of the 100 spousal homicide victims were shot (15 husbands and 19 wives), while 30 husbands were stabbed and 31 wives were beaten or stabbed. Whatever may explain the exceptionally similar death rates of U.S. husbands and wives, it is not simply that guns "equalize."

Nor is the unusual U.S. pattern to be explained in terms of a peculiar convergence in the United States of the sexes in their violent inclinations or capabilities across all domains and relationships. Although U.S. data depart radically from other industrialized countries in the sex ratio of spousal homicide victimization, they do not depart similarly in the sex ratios of other sorts of homicides (Wilson and Daly forthcoming). For example, in the United States as elsewhere men kill unrelated men about 40 times as often as women kill unrelated women.

Even among lethal acts, it is essential to discriminate among different victim-killer relationships, because motives, risk factors, and conflict typologies are relationship-specific. Steinmetz (1977/78, Steinmetz and Lucca 1998) has invoked the occurrence of maternally perpetrated infanticides as evidence of women's violence, imagining that the fact that some women commit infanticide somehow bolsters the claim that they batter their husbands, too. But maternal infanticides are more often motivated by desperation than by hostile aggression and are often effected by acts of neglect or abandonment rather than by assault. To conflate such acts with aggressive attacks is to misunderstand their utterly distinct motives, forms, and perpetrator profiles, and the distinct social and material circumstances in which they occur.

HOW TO GAIN A VALID ACCOUNT
OF MARITAL VIOLENCE?

How ought researchers to conceive of "violence"? People differ in their views about whether a particular act was a violent one and about who was responsible. Assessments of intention and justifiability are no less relevant to the labelling of an event as "violent" than are more directly observable considerations like the force exerted or the damage inflicted. Presumably, it is this problem of subjectivity that has inspired efforts to objectify the study of family violence by the counting of "acts," as in the Conflict Tactics Scales.

Unfortunately, the presumed gain in objectivity achieved by asking research subjects to report only "acts," while refraining from elaborating upon their meanings and consequences, is illusory. As noted above, couples exhibit little agreement in reporting the occurrence of acts in which both were allegedly involved, and self-reported acts sometimes fail to differentiate the behavior of groups known to exhibit huge differences in the perpetration of violence. The implication must be that concerns about the validity of self-report data cannot be allayed merely by confining self-reports to a checklist of named acts. We have no more reason to suppose that people will consensually and objectively label events as instances of someone having "grabbed" or "hit or tried to hit" or "used a knife" (items from the CTS) than to suppose that people will consensually and objectively label events as instances of "violence."

If these "acts" were scored by trained observers examining the entire event, there might be grounds for such behavioristic austerity in measurement: whatever the virtues and limitations of behavioristic methodology, a case can at least be made that observational data are more objective than the actors' accounts. However, when researchers have access only to self-reports, the cognitions of the actors are neither more nor less accessible to research than their actions. Failures of candor and memory threaten the validity of both sorts of self-report data, and researchers' chances of detecting such failures can only be improved by the collection of richer detail about the violent event. The behavioristic rigor of observational research cannot be simulated by leaving data collection to the subjects, nor by active inattention to "subjective" matters like people's perceptions of their own and others' intentions, attributions of loss of control, perceived provocations and justifications, intimidatory consequences, and so forth. Moreover, even a purely behavioristic account could be enriched by attending to sequences of events and subsequent behavior rather than merely counting acts.

Enormous differences in meaning and consequence exist between a woman pummelling her laughing husband in an attempt to convey strong feelings and a man pummelling his weeping wife in an attempt to punish her for coming home late. It is not enough to acknowledge such contrasts (as CTS researchers have sometimes done), if such acknowledgments neither inform further research nor alter such conclusions as "within the family or in dating and cohabiting relationships, women are about as violent as men" (Straus and Gelles 1990b:104). What is needed are forms of analysis that will lead to a comprehensive description of the violence itself as well as an explanation of it. In order to do this, it is, at the very least, necessary to analyze the violent event in a holistic manner, with attention to the entire sequences of distinct acts as well as associated motives, intentions, and consequences, all of which must in turn be situated within the wider context of the relationship.

THE NEED FOR THEORY

If the arguments and evidence that we have presented are correct, then currently fashionable claims about the symmetry of marital violence are unfounded. How is it that so many experts have been persuaded of a notion that is at once counterintuitive and counterfactual? Part of the answer, we believe, is that researchers too often operate without sound (or indeed any) theoretical visions of marital relationships, of interpersonal conflicts, or of violence.

Straus (1990a:30), for example, introduces the task of investigating family violence by characterizing families as instances of "social groups" and by noting that conflicts of interest are endemic to groups of individuals, "each seeking to live out their lives in accordance with personal agendas that inevitably differ." This is a good start, but the analysis proceeds no further. The characteristic features of families as distinct from other groups are not explored, and the particular domains within which the "agendas" of wives and husbands conflict are not elucidated. Instead, Straus illustrates family conflicts with the hypothetical example of "Which TV show will be watched at eight?" and discusses negotiated and coerced resolutions in terms that would be equally applicable to a conflict among male acquaintances in a bar. Such analysis obscures all that is distinctive about violence against wives which occurs in a particular context of perceived entitlement and institutionalized power asymmetry. Moreover, marital violence occurs around recurring themes, especially male sexual jealousy and proprietariness, expectations of obedience and domestic service, and women's attempts to leave the marital relationship. In the self-consciously gender-blind literature on "violent couples," these themes are invisible.

Those who claim that wives and husbands are equally violent have offered no conceptual framework for understanding why women and men should think and act alike. Indeed, the claim that violence is gender-neutral cannot easily be reconciled with other coincident claims. For example, many family violence researchers who propose sexual symmetry in violence attribute the inculcation and legitimation of violence to socializing processes and cultural institutions, but then overlook the fact that these processes and institutions define and treat females and males differently. If sexually differentiated socialization and entitlements play a causal role in violence, how can we understand the alleged equivalence of women's and men's violent inclinations and actions?

Another theoretical problem confronting anyone who claims that violent inclinations are sexually monomorphic concerns the oft-noted fact that men are larger than women and likelier to inflict damage by similar acts. Human passions have their own "rationality," and it would be curious if women and men were identically motivated to initiate assaults in contexts where the expectable results were far more damaging for women. Insofar as both parties to a potentially violent transaction are aware of such differences, it is inappropriate to treat a slap (or other "act") by one party as equivalent to a slap by the other, not only because there is an asymmetry in the damage the two slaps might inflict, but because the parties differ in the responses available to them and hence in their control over the dénouement. Women's motives may be expected to differ systematically from those of men wherever the predictable consequences of their actions differ systematically. Those who contend that women and men are equally inclined to violence need to articulate why this should be so, given the sex differences in physical traits, such as size and muscularity, affecting the probable consequences of violence.

In fact, there is a great deal of evidence that men's and women's psychologies are not at all alike in this domain. Men's violent reactions to challenges to their authority, honor, and self-esteem are well-known; comparable behavior by a woman is a curiosity. A variety of convergent evidence supports the conclusion that men (especially young men) are more specialized for and more motivated to engage in dangerous risk-taking, confrontational competition, and interpersonal violence than are women. When comparisons are confined to interactions with members of one's own sex so that size and power asymmetries are largely irrelevant, the differences between men and women in these behavioral domains are universally large.

We cannot hope to understand violence in marital, cohabiting, and dating relationships without explicit attention to the qualities that make them different from other relationships. It is a cross-culturally and historically ubiquitous aspect of human affairs that women and men form individualized unions, recognized by themselves and by others as conferring certain obligations and entitlements, such that the partners' productive and reproductive careers become intertwined. Family violence research might usefully begin by examining the consonant and discordant desires, expectations, grievances, perceived entitlements, and preoccupations of husbands and wives, and by investigating theoretically derived hypotheses about circumstantial, ecological, contextual, and demographic correlates of such conflict. Having described the conflict of interest that characterize marital relationships with explicit reference to the distinct agendas of women and men, violence researchers must proceed to an analysis that acknowledges and accounts for those gender differences. It is crucial to establish differences in the patterns of male and female violence, to thoroughly describe and explain the overall process of violent events within their immediate and wider contexts, and to analyze the reasons why conflict results in differentially violent action by women and men.

References

Barling, Julian, and Alan Rosenbaum. 1986. "Work stressors and wife abuse." Journal of Applied Psychology 71:346–348.

Berk, Richard A., Sarah F. Berk, Donileen R. Loseke, and D. Rauma. 1983. "Mutual combat and other family violence myths." In The Dark Side of Families, ed. David Finkelhor, Richard J. Gelles, Gerald T. Hotaling, and Murray A. Straus, 197–212. Beverly Hills, Calif.: Sage.

Brush, Lisa D. 1990. "Violent acts and injurious outcomes in married couples: Methodological issues in the National Survey of Families and Households." Gender and Society 4:56–67.

Gaquin, Deirdre A. 1977/78. "Spouse abuse: Data from the National Crime Survey." Victimology 2:632–643.

Gelles, Richard J., and John W. Harrop. 1991. "The risk of abusive violence among children with nongenetic caretakers." Family Relations 40:78–83.

Johnson, Holly. 1989. "Wife assault in Canada." Paper presented at the Annual Meeting of the American Society of Criminology, November, Reno, Nevada.

Jouriles, Ernest N., and K. Daniel O'Leary. 1985. "Interspousal reliability of reports of marital violence." Journal of Consulting and Clinical Psychology 53:419–421.

Lystad, Mary H. 1975. "Violence at home: A review of literature." American Journal of Orthopsychiatry 45:328–345.

Margolin, Gayla. 1987. "The multiple forms of aggressiveness between marital partners: How do we identify them?" Journal of Marital and Family Therapy 13:77–84.

Maxfield, Michael G. 1989. "Circumstances in Supplementary Homicide Reports: Variety and validity." Criminology 27:671–695.

McLeod, Maureen. 1984. "Women against men: An examination of domestic violence based on an analysis of official data and national victimization data." Justice Quarterly 1:171–193.

McNeely, R.L., and CoraMae Richey Mann. 1990. "Domestic violence is a human issue." Journal of Interpersonal Violence 5:129–132.

McNeely, R.L., and Gloria Robinson-Simpson. 1987. "The truth about domestic violence: A falsely framed issue." Social Work 32:485–490.

Rouse, Linda P., Richard Ereen, and Marilyn Howell. 1988. "Abuse in intimate relationships. A comparison of married and dating college students." Journal of Interpersonal Violence 3:414–429.

Schwartz, Martin D. 1987. "Gender and injury in spousal assault." Sociological Focus 20:61–75.

Shupe, Anson, William A. Stacey, and Lonnie R. Hazelwood. 1987. Violent Men, Violent Couples: The Dynamics of Domestic Violence. Lexington Mass.: Lexington Books.

Steinmetz, Suzanne K. 1977/78. "The battered husband syndrome." Victimology 2:499–509.

———. 1986. "Family violence. Past, present, and future." In Handbook of Marriage and the Family, ed. Marvin B. Sussman and Suzanne K. Steinmetz, 725–765. New York: Plenum.

Steinmetz, Suzanne K., and Joseph S. Lucca. 1988. "Husband battering." In Handbook of Family Violence ed. Vincent B. Van Hasselt, R.L. Morrison, A.S. Bellack and M. Hersen, 233–246. New York: Plenum Press.

Stets, Jan E., and Murray A. Straus 1990. "Gender differences in reporting marital violence and its medical and psychological consequences." In Physical Violence in American Families, ed. Murray A. Straus and Richard J. Gelles, 151–165. New Brunswick, N.J.: Transaction Publishers.

Straus, Murray A. 1977/78. "Wife-beating: How common, and why?" Victimology 2:443–458.

———. 1990a. "Measuring intrafamily conflict and violence: The Conflict Tactics (CT) Scales." In Physical Violence in American Families, ed. Murray A. Straus and Richard J. Gelles, 29–47. New Brunswick, N.J.: Transaction Publishers.

———. 1990b. "The Conflict Tactics Scales and its critics: An evaluation and new data on validity and reliability." In Physical Violence in American Families, ed. Murray A. Straus and Richard J. Gelles, 49–73. New Brunswick, N.J.: Transaction Publishers.

Straus, Murray A., and Richard J. Gelles, eds. 1990a. Physical Violence in American Families. New Brunswick, N.J.: Transaction Publishers.

Straus, Murray A., and Richard J. Gelles. 1986. "Societal change and change in family violence from 1975 to 1985 as revealed by two national surveys." Journal of Marriage and the Family 48:465–480.

1987. "The costs of family violence." Public Health Reports 102:638–641.

———. 1990b "How violent are American families? Estimates from the National Family Violence Resurvey and other studies." In Physical Violence in American Families ed. Murray A. Straus and Richard J. Gelles, 95–112. New Brunswick, N.J.: Transaction Publishers.

Szinovacz, Maximiliane E. 1983. "Using couple data as a methodological tool: The case of marital violence." Journal of Marriage and the Family 45:633–644.

Wilson, Margo, and Martin Daly. Forthcoming. "Who kills whom in spouse-killings? On the exceptional sex ratio of spousal homicides in the United States." Criminology.

Wolfgang, Marvin E. 1958. Patterns in Criminal Homicide. Philadelphia: University of Pennsylvania Press.

JAMES GILLIGAN

Culture, Gender, and Violence: "We Are Not Women"

Even those biological factors that do correlate with increased rates of murder, such as age and sex, are not primary determinants or independent causes of violent behavior. They do not spontaneously, in and of themselves, create violent impulses; they act only to increase the predisposition to engage in violence, when the individual is exposed to the social and psychological stimuli that do stimulate violent impulses. In the absence of those stimuli, these biological factors acting alone do not seem to stimulate or cause violence spontaneously or independently.

That is good news; for while we cannot alter or eliminate the biological realities of age and sex, which are made by God, we can bring about fundamental changes in the social and cultural conditions that expose people to increased rates and intensities of shame and humiliation, since culture and society are made by us. In this chapter I will analyze some of the cultural patterns, values, and practices that stimulate violence, and how they might be altered to prevent violence.

When these conditions are altered the exposure of human populations to shame is dramatically reduced—and so is violence. Those economically developed democracies all over the world that have evolved into "welfare states" since the end of the Second World War, including all of Western Europe, Japan, Canada, Australia, and New Zealand, offer universal and free health care, generous public housing, unemployment and family leave policies, and so on. Every one of those countries has a more equitable (and hence less shame-inducing) socioeconomic system than the United States does. There is a much greater sharing of the collective wealth of the society as measured, for example, by the smaller gap between the income and wealth of the most and least affluent segments of their populations. Our rate of violent crime (murder, rape) is from two to twenty times as high as it is in any of the other economically developed democracies. This is precisely what the theory presented in this book would predict.

Other cultures have also altered their social conditions so as to protect their members from exposure to overwhelming degrees of shame and humiliation, and have experienced the dramatic diminution in rates of violence that the theory espoused in this book would lead us to expect. They demonstrate the degree to which rates of violence are determined by social, cultural, and economic conditions. One example would be those societies that practice what has been called "primitive Christian communism," and are truly classless societies whose economic systems are based on communal sharing—Anabaptist sects such as the Hutterities, Mennonites, and Amish. One remarkable feature of these societies is that the incidence of violence in them is virtually zero. The Hutterites, for example, do not appear to have had a single confirmed case of murder, rape, aggravated assault, or armed robbery since they arrived in America more than a hundred years ago. They also practice a strict and absolute pacifism, which is why they had to emigrate to America from Europe in the last century—to escape becoming victims of genocide at the hands of governments there which were persecuting them. While that aspect of their experience is one reason why I do not propose them as a model for our own society to emulate in any concrete, literal way, they do demonstrate that violence does not have to be universal; and that altering social, cultural, and economic conditions can dramatically reduce, and for all practical purposes eliminate, human violence from the face of the earth.

One apparent exception to the generalizations I am making here is Japan, which has often been cited as a "shame culture." If frequent exposure and intense sensitivity to shame (in the absence of a correspondingly powerful exposure to guilt) stimulates violence toward others, then why does Japan have a relatively low homicide and high suicide rate—the same pattern that characterizes those societies that have sometimes been called "guilt cultures," namely, the European and other economically developed "welfare state" democracies? There are two answers to that question, one that refers to the period before World War II, and the other, the time since then.

During both periods, Japan has been described by those who know it best as an intensely homogeneous and conformist society, with strong pressures against individual deviations from group norms and behaviors. That social pattern had, and still has, a powerful influence on the patterns of Japanese violence. Until the end of the Second World War, Japan was an extremely violent society—indeed, one of the most violent in the history of the world; they have been described, both by themselves and by their neighbors, as "a nation of warriors" since they first emerged as an independent nation two to three thousand years ago. However, that violence was directed almost entirely toward non-Japanese. Some cultures, such as Japan's, have been more successful than others in channeling the homicidal behavior of their members toward members of other cultures, so that it is labeled warfare or genocide, rather than toward members of their own culture, which is called murder. Thus, the Japanese engaged in a degree of violence toward their Asian neighbors from 1930 to 1945 that was just as genocidal as what the Germans perpetrated in Europe. When compared to the number of suicides that Japanese citizens committed during the first half of this century, the number of homicides that they committed (in the form of warfare) during that same period was astronomical—exactly as the theory proposed in this book would predict.

However, since 1945 the social and economic conditions in Japan have changed remarkably. Japan today has the lowest degree of economic inequity among its citizens in the world (as judged by the World Bank's measures of relative income and wealth). So it is not surprising that Japan also has a remarkably low frequency both of violent crime and of structural violence. For if socioeconomic inequities expose those at the bottom of the ladder to intense feelings of inferiority; if relative equality protects people from those feelings; and if inferiority feelings stimulate violent impulses, then it is not surprising that Japan's current socioeconomic structure would be marked by a low level of violence toward others, as indeed it is—even if the Japanese are unusually sensitive to feelings and experiences of shame, and even if (as some observers have claimed) they are not especially sensitive to or likely to experience guilt feelings. For their socioeconomic system, even if it does revolve primarily around sensitivity to shame rather than guilt, actively protects most individuals from being exposed to overwhelming degrees of shame, and also provides them with nonviolent (e.g., economic) means by which to prevent or undo any "loss of face" that is experienced.

If the main causes of violence are these social and psychological variables (shame versus honor), an apparent anomaly lies in the fact that men are and always have been more violent than women, throughout history and throughout the world. If shame stimulates violence; if being treated as inferior stimulates shame; and if women have been treated throughout history as inferior to men, then why are women less violent than men? (And they are indeed vastly less likely than men are to commit homicide, suicide, warfare, and assault, in every culture and every period of history.)

THE MAKING OF "MANHOOD" AND THE VIOLENCE OF MEN

To understand this apparent anomaly, we must examine the cultural construction of masculinity and femininity, and the contrasting conditions under which the two sexes, once they have been cast into patriarchally defined "gender roles," are exposed to feelings of private shame or public dishonor. To understand physical violence we must understand male violence, since most violence is committed by males, and on other males. And we can only understand male violence if we understand the sex roles, or gender roles, into which males are socialized by the gender codes of their particular cultures. Moreover, we can only understand male gender roles if we understand how those are reciprocally related to the contrasting but complementary sex or gender roles into which females are socialized in that same culture, so that the male and female roles require and reinforce each other.

Gender codes reinforce the socialization of girls and women, socializing them to acquiesce in, support, defend, and cling to the traditional set of social roles, and to enforce conformity on other females as well. Restrictions on their freedom to engage in sexual as well as aggressive behavior is the price women pay for their relative freedom from the risk of lethal and life-threatening violence to which men and boys are much more frequently exposed (a dubious bribe, at best, and one which shortchanges women, as more and more women realize).

The outpouring of scholarship across disciplines on the asymmetrical social roles assigned to males and females by the various cultures and civilizations of the world, including our own, has included works in history, economics, literary theory, philosophy, sociology, anthropology, psychology, science, law, religious studies, ethnic studies, and women's studies. One thing all this work has made clear to me (and to many others) is that listening to women (for the first time), and opening up a dialogue between men and women, rather than merely continuing what has throughout most of the history of civilization been primarily a male monologue, is a necessary prerequisite for learning how to transform our civilization into a culture that is compatible with life. And to do that requires that men and women both learn to interact in ways that have simply not been permitted by the gender codes of the past.

My work has focused on the ways in which male gender codes reinforce the socialization of boys and men, teaching them to acquiesce in (and support, defend, and cling to) their own set of social roles, and a code of honor that defines and obligates these roles. Boys and men are exposed thereby to substantially greater frequencies of physical injury, pain, mutilation, disability, and premature death. This code of honor requires men to inflict these same violent injuries on others of both sexes, but most frequently and severely on themselves and other males, whether or not they want to be violent toward anyone of either sex.

Among the most interesting findings reported by social scientists is the fact that men and women stand in a markedly different relationship to the whole system of allotting honor in "cultures of honor." For example, one observation that has been made recurrently is that men are the only possible sources, or active generators (agents), of honor. The only active effect that women can have on honor, in those cultures in which this is a central value, is to destroy it. But women do have that power: They can destroy the honor of the males in their household. The culturally defined symbol system through which women in patriarchies bring honor or dishonor to men is the world of sex—that is, female sexual behavior. In this value system, which is both absurd from any rational standpoint and highly dangerous to the continued survival of our species given its effect of stimulating male violence, men delegate to women the power to bring dishonor on men. That is, men put their honor in the hands of "their" women. The most emotionally powerful means by which women can dishonor men (in this male construction) is by engaging in nonmarital sex, i.e., by being too sexually active or aggressive ("unchaste" or "unfaithful") before, during, or even after marriage.

These themes are prominent in one well-known "culture of honor," for example, the American South. Bertram Wyatt-Brown illustrated this by quoting from a letter Lucius Quintus Cincinnatus Lamar wrote to Mary Chesnut in 1861, in which he compares the men of the South to Homer's heroes, who "fought like brave men, long and well," and then went on to say "We are men, not women." The real tragedy for Lamar, as Wyatt-Brown saw, was that "for him, as for many, the Civil War was reduced to a simple test of manhood."

And women can adopt those same views of manhood, as Mary Chesnut recounts in her diary: "'Are you like Aunt Mary? Would you be happier if all the men in the family were killed?' To our amazement, quiet Miss C. took up the cudgels—nobly: 'Yes, if their life disgraced them. There are worse things than death.'"[1] These attitudes are exactly the same as those of the men I have known in maximum-security prisons.

That the same relative differences between the two gender roles can be found in many civilizations throughout history and throughout the world emphasizes the importance of understanding that it is men who are expected to be violent, and who are honored for doing so and dishonored for being unwilling to be violent. A woman's worthiness to be honored or shamed is judged by how well she fills her roles in sexually related activities, especially the roles of actual or potential wife and mother. Men are honored for activity (ultimately, violent activity); and they are dishonored for passivity (or pacifism), which renders them vulnerable to the charge of being a non-man ("a wimp, a punk, and a pussy," to quote the phrase that was so central to the identity of the murderer I analyzed in Chapter Three). Women are honored for inactivity or passivity, for not engaging in forbidden activities. They are shamed or dishonored if they are active where they should not be—sexually or in realms that are forbidden (professional ambition, aggressiveness, competitiveness and success; or violent activity, such as warfare or other forms of murder). Lady Macbeth, for example, realized that to commit murder she would have to be "unsex'd," i.e., freed from the restraints on violence that were imposed on her by virtue of her belonging to the female sex; and even then, she was unable to commit murder herself, but had to shame her husband into committing murder for her, so that she could only participate in violent behavior vicariously (just as she could only gain honor vicariously, through the honor she would obtain through being his queen when he became king).

Further evidence that men are violence objects and women, sex objects, can be found by examining the kinds of crimes that are committed against each sex. Men constitute, on the average, 75 percent or more of the victims of lethal physical violence in the United States—homicide, suicide, so-called unintentional injuries (from working in hazardous occupations, engaging in violent athletic contests, and participating in other high-risk activities), deaths in military combat, and so on. And throughout the world, men die from all these same forms of violence from two to five times as often as women do, as the World Health Organization documents each year. Women, on the other hand, according to the best available evidence, seem to be the victims of sex crimes (such as rape and incest) more often than men are. Both men and women seem to feel that men are more acceptable as objects of physical violence than women are, for both sexes kill men several times more often than they kill women. Even in experimental studies conducted by psychologists, both men and women exhibit greater readiness and willingness to inflict pain on men than on women, under otherwise identical conditions. Studies of child abuse in those countries in which reasonably accurate statistics are available find that boys are more often victims of lethal or life-threatening violent child abuse (being treated as violence objects), whereas girls are more often victims of sexual abuse (being treated as sex objects)—with few exceptions. Virtually every nation that has had a military draft has decided either that only men should be drafted, or that only men should be sent into combat. Again, none of this should surprise us, given the competition between men for status, valor, bravery, heroism—and honor—in patriarchal societies.

We cannot think about preventing violence without a radical change in the gender roles to which men and women are subjected. The male gender role generates violence by exposing men to shame if they are not violent, and rewarding them with honor when they are. The female gender role also stimulates male violence at the same time that it inhibits female violence. It does this by restricting women to the role of highly unfree sex objects, and honoring them to the degree that they submit to those roles or shaming them when they rebel. This encourages men to treat women as sex objects, and encourages women to conform to that sex role; but it also encourages women (and men) to treat men as violence objects. It also encourages a man to become violent if the woman to whom he is related or married "dishonors" him by acting in ways that transgress her prescribed sexual role.

Since culture is itself constructed, by all of us, if we want to take steps to diminish the amount of violence in our society, both physical and sexual, we can take those steps. To speak of eliminating the sexual asymmetry that casts men and women into opposing sex roles is to speak of liberating both men and women from arbitrary and destructive stereotypes, and to begin treating both women and men as individuals, responding to their individual goals and abilities, rather than to the group (male or female) to which they belong.

There is a deep and tragic paradox about civilization. On the one hand, it has been, up to now, the most life-enhancing innovation the human species has created. The sciences have made it possible for more people to live, and to live longer lives, and to live better lives, freer of pain and illness, cold and hunger, than was ever possible before civilization was invented; and the many forms of art that could not and did not exist except under conditions of civilization are among the main things that make life worth living. But the paradox is that civilization has also increased both the level of human violence, and the scale of the human potential for violence, far beyond anything that any precivilized human culture had done. In the past, the primary threat to human survival was nature, now it is culture. Human suffering before civilization was mainly pathos; since the creation of civilization, it has become, increasingly, tragedy. In fact, it would not be going too far to say that violence is the tragic flaw of civilization. The task confronting us now is to see whether we can end the tragic (violent) element of civilization while maintaining its life-enhancing aspects.

Why has civilization resulted in the most enormous augmentation of human violence since the human species first evolved from its primate forebears? I believe that that question can only be answered by taking into account the psychology of shame. Shame not only motivates destructive behavior, it also motivates constructive behavior. It is the emotion that motivates the ambition and the need for achievement that in turn motivates the invention of civilization.

But—and this is the crux of the matter—this same emotion, shame, that motivates the ambition, activity, and need for achievement that is necessary for the creation of civilization also motivates violence. And when the enormous increase in technological power that civilization brings with it is joined to the enormous increase in violent impulses that shame brings with it, the stage is set for exactly the drama that the history (that is, the civilization) of the world shows us—namely, human social life as an almost uninterrupted, and almost uninterruptedly escalating, series of mass slaughters, "total" and increasingly genocidal wars, and an unprecedented threat to the very continuation not only of civilization itself (which brought this situation about, it cannot be emphasized too strongly) but much more importantly, of the human species for the sake of whose survival civilization was invented in the first place.

Through my clinical work with violent men and my analysis of the psychodynamics of shame and guilt, I have come to view the relationship between civilization and violence in a way that is the diametrical opposite of Freud's. Freud saw violence as an inevitable, spontaneously occurring, natural, innate, instinctual impulse, and civilization and morality as attempts at "taming," neutralizing, inhibiting or controlling that violent impulse. I see violence, in contrast, as defensive, caused, interpretable, and therefore preventable; and I see civilization, as it has existed up to now (because of class, caste and age stratification, and sexual asymmetry), as among the most potent causes of violence.

One of the puzzles of this century is the phenomenon of Nazism: how could one of the most civilized nations on earth have been capable of such uncivilized, barbaric behavior? (One could ask the same question about Japan's record in World War II.) But from the perspective being elaborated here, genocide is not a regression or an aberration from civilization, or a repudiation of it. It is the inner destiny of civilization, its core tendency—its tragic flaw. Genocide has characterized the behavior of most of the great world civilizations, from ancient Mesopotamia to Rome, to medieval Europe, to the African slave trade and the conquest of the Americas, to the Holocaust and atomic weapons.

How to deal with violence, then? The moral value system (which I will call "shame-ethics") that underlies the code of honor of those patriarchal cultures and subcultures in which behavioral norms are enforced primarily by the sanctions of shame versus honor, such as the Mafia, urban street gangs, and much of the rest of American culture, rationalizes, legitimates, encourages, and even commands violence: it does not prohibit or inhibit it.

The kind of morality that I am calling guilt-ethics (that says "Thou shalt not kill") is an attempt at a kind of therapy, an attempt to cure the human propensity to engage in violence, which is stimulated by shame-ethics. And that was a noble attempt, which one can only wish had been successful. Why has it not worked? I think that the analysis of violence presented in this book can enable us to see the answer to that question. The reason that guilt-ethics has not solved and cannot solve the problem of violence is because it does not dismantle the motivational structure that causes violence in the first place (namely, shame, and the shame-ethics that it motivates). Guilt, and guilt-ethics, merely changes the direction of the violence that shame has generated, it does not prevent the violence in the first place. It primarily redirects, onto the self, the violent impulses that shame generates toward other people. But it does not prevent violence, or even inhibit it. Suicide is no solution to the problem of homicide; both forms of violence are equally lethal. Masochism is no solution to the problem of sadism; both forms of pathology are equally destructive and painful.

Neither shame nor guilt, then, can solve the problem of violence; shame causes hate, which becomes violence (usually toward other people), and guilt merely redirects it (usually onto the self). But to say simply that we need more love, and less shame and guilt, is vacuous. What we really need is to be able to specify the conditions that can enable love to grow without being inhibited by either shame or guilt. And it is clear that shame and guilt do inhibit love. Shame inhibits people from loving others, because shame consists of a deficiency of self-love, and thus it motivates people to withdraw love from others and ration it for the self. Guilt, on the other hand, inhibits self-love, or pride, which the Christian guilt-ethic calls the deadliest of the seven deadly sins. Guilt motivates people to hate themselves, not love themselves, because the feeling of guilt is the feeling that one is guilty and therefore deserves punishment (pain, hate), not reward (pleasure, love).

If we approach violence as a problem in public health and preventive medicine then we need to ask: What are the conditions that stimulate shame and guilt on a socially and epidemiologically significant scale? The conditions that are most important are relative poverty, race and age discrimination, and sexual asymmetry. If we wish to prevent violence, then, our agenda is political and economic reform.

The social policies that would be most effective in preventing violence are those that would reduce the amount of shame. To reduce the amount of shame, we need to reduce the intensity of the passive, dependent regressive wishes that stimulate shame. And to reduce the intensity of those wishes, we must gratify those wishes, by taking better care of each other, especially the neediest among us—particularly beginning in childhood, when the needs for love and care are most intense and peremptory. To quote again the phrase that Dostoevsky put in the mouth of Father Zossima, we then would recognize that "all are responsible for all."

We have a horror of dependency in this country—particularly dependency on the part of men. No wonder we have so much violence—especially male violence. For the horror of dependency is what causes violence. The emotion that causes the horror of dependency is shame. Men, much more than women, are taught that to want love or care from others is to be passive, dependent, unaggressive and unambitious or, in short, unmanly; and that they will be subjected to shaming, ridicule, and disrespect if they appear unmanly in the eyes of others. Women, by contrast, have traditionally been taught that they will be honored if, and only if, they accept a role that restricts them to the relatively passive aim of arranging to be loved by men and to depend on men for their social and economic status, foregoing or severely limiting or disguising activity, ambition, independence, and initiative of their own. This set of injunctions decreases women's vulnerability to behaving violently, but it also inhibits women from participating actively or directly in the building of civilization, in part by reducing them to the role of men's sex objects.

We Americans, as a society, appear to be horrified by the thought that a man could be dependent on anyone (other than himself), and that a woman could be dependent on anyone (other than "her man," that is, her father or husband). The extent of our horror of dependency can be seen in our horror of what is somewhat misleadingly called "welfare dependency"—whether it is the "dependency" on society of an unemployed or disabled man, of an unmarried mother, or of a child without a father. This conceals, or rather reveals, that we as a nation do less for our own citizens than does any other democracy on earth; less health care, child care, housing, support to families, and so on. So that we end up shaming and blaming those whose needs are exposed. Therefore it is not surprising that we also have more violence than does any other democracy on earth, as well as more imprisonment—since we shame some people for having needs that all people have.

For needs that are repressed do not get met, nor do they just disappear. The return of repressed needs, in unconscious, disguised form, is what the various symptoms of psychopathology consist of. One form in which repressed needs for care return is chronic institutionalization—that is, long-term imprisonment or mental hospitalization—which allows us as a society to punish massively, while we gratify grudgingly, those needs of which we are so intolerant.

In fact, the violence of our society reveals our shame at being less "independent" than we "declared" ourselves to be two centuries ago. In contemporary America, to want love, to depend on others, to be less than completely self-sufficient, is to be shamed by all the institutions of our society, from welfare offices to mental hospitals to prisons. One can pretend that one is in an institution only because one is so tough and dangerous and scary, so active and aggressive, and so independent of the community's standards, that the courts insisted on locking one up against one's own wishes. But nevertheless, it is true that for many men in our society it is only in prison that one is given three meals a day, a warm bed to sleep in at night, a roof over one's head, and people who care enough about one to make sure that one is there every night.

Those are among the reasons why the most effective way to increase the amount of violence and crime is to do exactly what we have been doing increasingly over the past decades, namely, to permit—or rather, to force—more and more of our children and adults to be poor, neglected, hungry, homeless, uneducated, and sick. What is particularly effective in increasing the amount of violence in the world is to widen the gap between the rich and the poor. We have not restricted that strategy to this country, but are practicing it on a worldwide scale, among the increasingly impoverished nations of the third world; and we can well expect it to culminate in increasing levels of violence, all over the world.

Relative poverty—poverty for some groups coexisting with wealth for others—is much more effective in stimulating shame, and hence violence, than is a level of poverty that is higher in absolute terms but is universally shared. Shame exists in the eye of the beholder—though it is more likely to exist there if the beheld is perceived as richer and more powerful than oneself. In that archaic, prescientific language called morality, this gap is called injustice; but most people throughout the world still think in moral terms, and the perception that one is a victim of injustice is what causes shame, which in turn causes violence.

From the standpoint of public health, then, the social psychology of shame, discrimination, and violence becomes central to any preventive psychiatry. The causes and consequences of the feelings of shame as well as their psychodynamic parameters have become more urgently compelling as a focus of investigation, given the potential ultimacy of violence in a nuclear age, as well as the continuing high rate of violence in American society. In my analysis of the psychological consequences of the feelings of shame, I have set out to show how such seemingly trivial events as personal experiences of chagrin or embarrassment can explode into epidemics of violence, just as the physical consequences of organisms as insignificant as microbes can have the gravest implications for public health. As Rudolph Virchow, who helped to lay the foundations of preventive medicine and public health more than a century ago, put it, "Medicine is a social science, and politics is simply medicine on a larger scale."

If cleaning up sewer systems could prevent more deaths than all the physicians in the world, then perhaps reforming the social, economic, and legal institutions that systematically humiliate people can do more to prevent violence than all the preaching and punishing in the world. The task before us now is to integrate the psychodynamic understanding of shame and guilt with the broader social and economic factors that intensify those feelings to murderous and suicidal extremes on a mass scale.